OXFORD

ALEXA

ALEXANDER POPE was bo........... ....s elderly parents moved to Binfield in W......... Forest around 1700 because of anti-Catholic laws. From early boyhood Pope suffered from a tubercular disease which retarded his growth and left him a lifelong invalid. A precocious poet, his first published work was the set of four pastorals published in 1709. A succession of brilliant poems followed, including *An Essay on Criticism* (1711), *Windsor Forest* (1713), and the five-canto version of *The Rape of the Lock*. Pope then embarked on a translation of the *Iliad* (1715–20), which together with the *Odyssey* (1725–6) left him financially secure. His position as the major living English poet was confirmed by the appearance of his *Works* in 1717. There followed a break in creative activity, during which Pope edited Shakespeare (1725). However, the appearance of the first *Dunciad* (1728) marked the beginning of a brilliant new phase, including the imitations of Horace, the *Essay on Man*, and the epistles to various friends. In 1742 Pope added a new fourth book to *The Dunciad*, and the complete work was published in 1743. Pope spent the last twenty-five years of his life at his villa in Twickenham, devoting much of his time to his celebrated garden and grotto. He died in 1744.

PAT ROGERS, DeBartolo Professor in the Liberal Arts at the University of South Florida, has written many books on Augustan satire including *Grub Street* (1972), *Literature and Popular Culture in Eighteenth-Century England* (1985), *The Alexander Pope Encyclopedia* (2004), and *Pope and the Destiny of the Stuarts* (2005).

OXFORD WORLD'S CLASSICS

*For over 100 years Oxford World's Classics have brought
readers closer to the world's great literature. Now with over 700
titles—from the 4,000-year-old myths of Mesopotamia to the
twentieth century's greatest novels—the series makes available
lesser-known as well as celebrated writing.*

*The pocket-sized hardbacks of the early years contained
introductions by Virginia Woolf, T. S. Eliot, Graham Greene,
and other literary figures which enriched the experience of reading.
Today the series is recognized for its fine scholarship and
reliability in texts that span world literature, drama and poetry,
religion, philosophy and politics. Each edition includes perceptive
commentary and essential background information to meet the
changing needs of readers.*

OXFORD WORLD'S CLASSICS

ALEXANDER POPE
The Major Works

Edited with an Introduction and Notes by
PAT ROGERS

OXFORD
UNIVERSITY PRESS

Great Clarendon Street, Oxford OX2 6DP

Oxford University Press is a department of the University of Oxford.
It furthers the University's objective of excellence in research, scholarship,
and education by publishing worldwide in

Oxford New York

Auckland Cape Town Dar es Salaam Hong Kong Karachi
Kuala Lumpur Madrid Melbourne Mexico City Nairobi
New Delhi Shanghai Taipei Toronto

With offices in

Argentina Austria Brazil Chile Czech Republic France Greece
Guatemala Hungary Italy Japan Poland Portugal Singapore
South Korea Switzerland Thailand Turkey Ukraine Vietnam

Oxford is a registered trade mark of Oxford University Press
in the UK and in certain other countries

Published in the United States
by Oxford University Press Inc., New York

Introduction and editorial matter © Pat Rogers 1993

First published with revisions as an
Oxford World's Classics paperback 2006
Reissued 2008

British Library Cataloguing in Publication Data

Data available

Library of Congress Cataloging in Publication Data

Data available

ISBN 978–0–19–953761–7

3

Typeset in Ehrhardt
Printed in Great Britain by
Clays Ltd, St Ives plc

CONTENTS

INTRODUCTION

THE aim of this volume is to give a representative selection of Pope's most important work. His chief lifelong vocation was that of the poet, and this is reflected by the inclusion of all his major poems, omitting only the translations of Homer. In addition, a characteristic sample of his prose is provided, including satires, pamphlets, and periodical writing. His criticism is represented by the influential preface to his edition of Shakespeare. Finally, the personal side of his work is illustrated by short passages from his conversations with Joseph Spence, and by examples of his wide-ranging correspondence. In all categories there are inevitably omissions, caused by the demands of space. Pope is a highly allusive poet, and even with a number of self-denying ordinances I have been obliged to annotate the text quite fully in order to enable a reader to follow its sense.

Among the poems there are several casualties which are particularly to be regretted. It has not been possible to find room for some of the early translations (although *Sappho to Phaon* is included); for *Messiah* and the *Ode on St Cecilia's Day*; for the original version of *The Rape of the Lock* and *The Dunciad*; and for many shorter items which demonstrate Pope's skill in occasional verse, especially in ballads, epigrams, and epitaphs. The largest gap, as already indicated, surrounds the translations of Homer, but a single book of the *Iliad* is included to give some sense of Pope's attempt to bring 'primitive' epic within Augustan norms. The drama, which is nearly all collaborative, has had to be excluded. However, *Peri Bathous* is present in full to illustrate the Scriblerian carping against solemn folly, as well as the prose squibs which emerged from Pope's prolonged struggle with the rascally bookseller Curll. As for the correspondence, ten typical letters are given in full, and whilst they cannot speak adequately for the entire body of over two thousand letters they do show some of his best effects in the familiar epistle. The items are printed in chronological order, regardless of their literary category (except for the extracts from Spence), to enable a reader to follow the shape of Pope's career. Brief rationale behind these editorial decisions will be found in the Note on the Text, p. xxvii below.

Pope has often been termed the first truly professional poet in English. This is a fair judgement, even though (as Pope realized sooner than anyone) his poetic father John Dryden had led the way. In the review of Pope's life and writings which follows, I shall try to give a more detailed justification for this description; at this point it is enough to observe that Pope had a peculiarly acute awareness of the traditions he inherited, as well as a clear-sighted vision of where he stood in literary history. His dealings with the book trade mark a significant moment in the development of the literary profession. This can be seen in the care with which Pope prepared his texts and supervised their appearance in print; his choice of outlets and occasions for publication; and his battles with the redoubtable Curll in print and in the lawcourts. Curll was a key figure in the evolution of print culture, a never-failing irritant to Pope but also an essential combatant in the battle of the books which helped to produce the literary market-place of the nineteenth and twentieth centuries. Apart from the ruse by which Pope tricked Curll into producing the first collection of a writer's private letters in 1735, we might consider the ideas at stake in the pamphlets against Curll printed below, pp. 124–34.

The great Popian scholar Maynard Mack has used an epigraph from Thomas Mann: 'Who is the poet? He whose life is symbolic.' The application can be made in several ways: Mack probably had in mind the way in which Pope inhabited both the garden and the city, actively engaged in the political fisticuffs of his turbulent times and yet holding part of himself in reserve. The emblem of this divided life is the grotto he created at Twickenham. This was a shrine to family life and to retirement, garnished with a dense array of historical and mythological references, but it was also a repository of geological discoveries. It was set in a secluded garden, but this Eden was itself planted in an almost suburban location, only a matter of miles upstream from London. Pope's villa offers itself as a miniature of the grand country house owned by his aristocratic friends like Burlington and Bathurst. But his 'estate' ran not to thousands of acres of protected parkland, but to 'five rented acres' on a busy road, directly abutting on to the Thames. In the same way, Pope's situation as a Catholic meant that he was not quite a full citizen of the realm, someone almost in the situation of a naturalized alien. His invalid condition ensured that he could participate in the business of life only through writing. It is no accident that this successful careerist, with his grand acquaintance and his pampered visits to the stateliest homes of England, should have been personally dispossessed, disinherited, and deprived; hence, among other things, the ability of his poetry to enter into the feelings of women, whose social and physical position his own mimicked. Hence, too, the symbolic marginality of his role as a poet: famous, widely respected, and even feared, Pope still had at his command only the illusory weapons of the imagination.

'The life of a wit is a warfare upon earth', he wrote in the preface to his first collection in 1717. He duly took part in the contest of ancients and moderns, originality and imitation, Tory and Whig, city and court, which eddied around him as Stuart gave way to Hanoverian. No great work in English literature, with the possible exception of Shakespearian comedy, is so explicitly a battle of the sexes as *The Rape of the Lock*. No work enacts more directly the political takeover of a nation than does the *Dunciad*, with its *coup d'état* by the all-conquering forces of dulness. But these are mythical battles. Pope imagined them the more keenly because he had so little power to affect the real course of events, whether the great issues of state or the domestic dramas of sexual politics—where he was forced to remain on the sidelines as a maimed non-combatant. Pope thus prefigures the willed self-positioning of the Romantic and modern poet, asserting the spiritual primacy of the fictive in the face of the primacy of raw life in the everyday world. For Pope this was not a pose, but a genuine existential destiny.

Moreover, Pope is a professional poet in a more obvious and direct sense than the discussion so far reveals. It is noteworthy that the early masters of English fiction—Defoe, Richardson, Fielding, Sterne, Smollett—had all been otherwise employed before they found the novel, or the novel found them. Pope is the great exception to this rule. Where the age often cultivated a pose of genteel amateurism, he stood out as a serious player in the literary market-place. From an early age he was dedicated, purposeful, single-minded; he brought the intensity of a specialist to his vocation. He dabbled in drama, dipped his toe a tentative inch into scholarship, and threw off the occasional essay in criticism or satiric squib in prose. (He also wrote some remarkable letters but they were—or affected to be—at the informal end of the writer's craft.) All his deepest energies were monopolized by poetry. The two translations of Homer are considerable works, but in so far as they are Pope, rather than as true renderings of the original. We need not root about to find and assemble from *disjecta membra* 'the essential Pope'. In his works we find his very self and voice.

His life is in many ways an interesting one; and his literary career is splendid and historic. But from childhood on, his biography is only a background to the art. Alexander Pope was born on 21 May 1688 in the heart of the City of London, at his parents' home on the south side of Lombard Street. It was a prosperous area, still associated with money-lenders, but with bustling markets around to give it a less bleak and institutional air than it has today. Across the street were two churches destroyed in the Great Fire, just a generation back, and Sir Christopher Wren was then restoring them. Pope's father and mother were both well into their forties: indeed, his father was on the point of retiring from business. He had done well enough out of the linen trade to amass a respectable stock of capital, perhaps £10,000, comparable to thirty times as much today.

This sounds like a stable enough family; but there were cracks in the placid bourgeois front. Alexander Pope senior, born an Anglican, had become a Roman Catholic; his second wife Editha (the poet's mother) belonged to the same faith. Apart, possibly, from 1558, when Queen Elizabeth succeeded Mary, the year 1688 was the least propitious moment in English history for a Catholic to enter the world. James II was forced from the throne within months of Pope's birth, and his religion was to be from now on an officially proscribed un-English activity. As Pope grew up under William and Mary, he found himself a member of a beleaguered and unpopular minority. One reason for his father's early retirement, in fact, was the need to comply with anti-Catholic legislation which sought to drive papists from the capital. The Pope family moved first to Hammersmith, at this time an outer suburb, and then to the country in Berkshire, where the second Mrs Pope had connections. When young Alexander was about 10 he came with his parents to Binfield, deep in the forest between Windsor and Reading. It was the first settled home he had known, and his rural surroundings were to furnish a classic ground from which his imagination would develop. He immersed himself in the pastoral, as perhaps only a sensitive boy would do when plucked from the noise of the town and the effigies of prejudice. Robert Hooke's primly doric Monument stood

> pointing at the skies,
> Like a tall bully
>
> (*Epistle to Bathurst*)

just two hundred yards from Pope's birthplace, with its true-blue Protestant message reinscribed in the 1690s.

In Windsor Forest Pope was to some extent protected from the discriminations suffered by the Catholic community. If the active life was hemmed in by restrictions on public participation, at least a contemplative existence was possible. But there was no defence against the second great handicap which fell to Pope's lot. At the age of about 12, he contracted a form of tuberculosis of the bone, probably as a result of drinking infected milk. This produced severe curvature of the spine, and progressively affected his mobility. The first onset of the illness (which was soon to be identified by Dr Percival Pott, hence its later name 'Pott's disease') lasted until Pope was around 16. After that he seems to have found a way of living with his disorder, and it was only in middle age that he submitted to the state of an outright invalid. But he remained dwarfish in build (perhaps four feet six inches tall), and underwent a variety of humiliations throughout life. He needed help to perform ordinary functions like dressing and undressing; he suffered excruciating torments every time he travelled along the bumpy roads of eighteenth-century England; and a normal sex life was debarred him. In his later years he had asthma, recurrent migraine, heart trouble, and an eye condition, as well as a urethral stricture which involved a painful operation in 1740. Most people know that Pope was a hunchback and some awareness of the fact hovers behind our reading of his poems. But we generally make too little allowance for it. We are conscious of his physique as it makes for *oddity* (and hence, perhaps, his prickly nature and satiric leanings); we too rarely comprehend the sheer pain, inconvenience, and embarrassment to which his 'crazy carcass' put him. A medical case-history cannot explain away Pope's flaws, as a man or a writer; nor, for that matter, can his 'long Disease' be identified with his creativity. But it is critically prudent, as well as humane, to remind ourselves of the obstacles he had to face. There is a hint of compensatory over-achievement in Pope's career, but we ought to be clear just what was involved—not a freakish father or a bad prep school, but the condition (doubly so) of a total outsider.

Excluded by his physical condition from normal education, Pope had to rely on his own resources. His bookish tastes led him to the great literature of Greece and Rome, and in his youth it seems to have been the epic and pastoral writers who meant more than moral or satiric poets. In English his masters were, as they remained, Spenser, Shakespeare, Milton, and Dryden (who died just as Pope approached his twelfth birthday). But his interests were eclectic enough to prompt imitations of such different models as Chaucer and the influential seventeenth-century lyricists Cowley and Waller. Nobody at this date fully understood Chaucer's metric, and 'imitating' his poetry involved greater liberties than we readily countenance today. The lines 'Women ben full of Ragerie', written *c.*1702, have a callow mocking air, which combines pseudo-medieval inflexions like *stoppen* and *callen* with pure

Augustan attitudes ('Miss star'd'). But even a century later Wordsworth thought it worth retaining in his versions of Chaucer 'sprinklings of antiquity' to supply a historical local colour. At all events, Pope's long tutelage did him no harm in the end. He acquired a patron in Berkshire —Sir William Trumbull, a lawyer, ambassador, and government minister who had retired to a life of dignified idleness a few miles from Binfield. At the age of about 17, Pope was strong enough to face the hurly-burly of the capital, and there he gained the notice of littérateurs in the coffee-houses, notably the playwright Wycherley and the physician-poet Garth, author of *The Dispensary*. The youthful Pope had a talent for charming old people, which suggests that a certain consciously winsome quality may have formed part of his make-up.

These men, along with other established literary figures, helped to usher him into print in 1709. The leading publisher Jacob Tonson included various items, including the four *Pastorals*, in a volume of miscellanies which took its place in a highly regarded series. The virtuosity of the *Pastorals* would have been apparent in any mode of publication, but here they were set off to the maximum advantage. Within a year or two Pope had reached the fringe of the *Spectator* circle, then at the pinnacle of all literary affairs. He soon afterwards made the acquaintance of Jonathan Swift and John Gay: one consequence was the formation of the Scriblerus Club, to which Thomas Parnell and Dr John Arbuthnot were also admitted. The club perfected a kind of high-spirited spoofing, involving parody, intellectual practical jokes, and an onslaught upon all things pedantic. The roots of *The Dunciad*, as indeed of *Gulliver's Travels*, may well lie in this convivial association. At the same time Pope was coming to know some of the greatest figures in the land, including the two Tory statesmen, Oxford and Bolingbroke, who dominated political life. Every year brought a fresh triumph for Pope: in 1711, *An Essay on Criticism*, both elegant and incisive; in 1712, the original *Rape of the Locke* in its two-canto form; in 1713, *Windsor Forest*, celebrating the end of the long-drawn Marlborough wars and also evoking the scenes of Pope's boyhood; then in 1714 the revised *Rape of the Lock*, wonderfully enriched by its expansion to five cantos. All these poems, together with *Eloisa to Abelard*, appeared in a handsome folio collection in 1717, which provided a conspectus of his career to date.

This pattern of unbroken success might well have been disturbed by the events of 1714, when Queen Anne died and the Tory ministry fell. Certainly the Hanoverian regime promised a different set of values, and it was one seen by many creative people as hostile to their purposes.

Swift was exiled to Dublin, landlocked in a safely remote deanery when he had envisaged himself as Bishop of Bath and Wells (later, no doubt, of London or Winchester). Gay, too, went through many years of neglect and self-pity. Even the robust Dr Arbuthnot had to endure the loss of his court post and his lodgings in St James's Palace. But Pope had no official encumbrances. He was already plotting his own road to independence: a verse translation of the *Iliad*, begun during the Tory ascendancy. The first instalment appeared in June 1715, and thereafter the poem came out in segments until its completion in 1720. The *Iliad* confirmed Pope's now unchallengeable standing as the leading poet of his day. It also laid the foundations of a secure and even comfortable way of life.

Up to this time Pope had not made very much money. For most of his work he had been paid between £15 and £30, and the original copyright of *The Rape of the Locke* earned him no more than £7. But the *Iliad* was published by private subscription, and Pope organized a massive campaign to attract names for his list. He also obtained particularly good terms from his bookseller, Lintot, which meant that he took a higher proportion of the profits than was customary (Lintot hoped to get his own returns from a separate trade edition, and in the end he did so). The *Iliad* carries a list of 575 subscribers, who ordered just over 650 sets at 6 guineas per head. Dr Johnson in the *Lives of the Poets* estimated Pope's receipts at £5,320; this may be a little on the high side, as Pope had to pay Lintot for distribution expenses of later volumes. However, he certainly cleared a very considerable sum and had gone far to set himself up for life. He started painting in a genteel way and then became an expert on landscape gardening. The family had moved from Berkshire to Chiswick in 1716; after the death of Pope's father he took up residence with his mother in Twickenham. From 1718 this would be his home for the rest of his life.

The South Sea Bubble in 1720 was to mark a turning-point in national affairs, preparing the way for the long dominance of Robert Walpole. Pope and the Prime Minister have been described as 'mighty opposites', and it is true that the rise of Walpole coincided with a dip in Pope's fortunes. After completing the *Iliad* in 1720, he embarked on a similar project for translating the *Odyssey*. Although the subscription list was even larger (over 600 names, taking 850 copies) and he made something like £4,500, his energies seem to have flagged. He was responsible for only half of the text, twelve books of Homer having been allotted to discreet assistants in William Broome and Elijah Fenton. The facts eventually trickled out, as they always will, and Pope lost something in reputation as a consequence. At the same period he was engaged in an edition of Shakespeare, mounted for the benefit of the publisher Tonson. It was not particularly successful commercially, and it suffered critically at the hands of Lewis Theobald, whose *Shakespeare Restored* (1726) exposed the poet's limitations as a historical scholar. There are good things in the edition, notably an impressive defence of Shakespeare in the preface; but Pope's handling of textual matters was perfunctory even by the far from rigorous standards of the age. Theobald's own edition (1733) was to mark an improvement in this respect, and later in the century Malone was to continue the process.

Another of Pope's undertakings was an edition of the works of an aristocratic poetaster, the Duke of Buckingham (1723), which the ministry seized in the belief that it might contain some coded Jacobite message. A few months later he was summoned to appear before the House of Lords as a character witness for his friend Francis Atterbury, Bishop of Rochester, who was accused of plotting on behalf of the Pretender. As a matter of fact Pope had survived the first Jacobite rising in 1715, and subsequent minor attempts in favour of this cause, without a great deal of trouble; whether he would have found it possible to come to terms with a restored Stuart monarchy, had one of these *coups* succeeded, is a matter of guesswork. But it was again uncomfortable to be a Catholic in 1723, and when Pope's own brother-in-law and nephew were pursued by the authorities that year (ostensibly for deer-stealing in Windsor Forest, though there were political overtones) he was understandably disturbed—indeed, he came closer to the writer's notorious 'block' than he ever did again.

As he approached the age of 40, he made an astounding recovery from his creative lethargy. He was, for one thing, rid of Homer and Shakespeare for the first time for over a decade. He also experienced the invigorating company of Swift once more, during two visits the Dean paid to England in 1726 and 1727. Curiously there may even have been some stimulus in the death of George I, in the first of those years, and the accession of George II. *The Dunciad* made it pretty clear what Pope felt about that event:

> Still *Dunce the second reigns like Dunce the first!*

But somehow this confirmation of Hanoverian rule, with Walpole against all the odds entrenched even more firmly in power, provided Pope with a fresh burst of imaginative energy. The first version of *The Dunciad* appeared in May 1728, twenty months after *Gulliver* and four

months after *The Beggar's Opera*. There were as yet no notes, and most
of the names were not spelt out in full. But there was already enough
damaging particularity to arouse the whole of Grub Street against Pope.
The poem deals with the transference of sovereignty from one King
Dunce (in the fiction Elkanah Settle, a deceased compiler of funeral
tributes and stage-manager of official pageantry) to another (Lewis
Theobald, here styled 'Tibbald', a hack dramatist and critic who had
irked Pope with *Shakespeare Restored*). The pretended occasion for this
handover of power is the Lord Mayor's Day procession, held each year
in November when the new civic dignitaries took up office. In reality
Pope is making covert allusion to the royal succession; Queen Dulness
has a marked tincture of Queen Caroline about her, whilst the cer-
emonial of enthronement and anointing (e.g. i. 231–46) directly recalls
the coronation of George and Caroline in October 1727. Pope was, of
course, very well advanced in composing his poem by that date; but he
was too skilful a reviser and adaptor not to make use of this gift from
fortune.

Three volumes of miscellanies by the Scriblerian wits appeared in
1727 and 1728. The most important single item was *Peri Bathous*, or
The Art of Sinking in Poetry, an ironic course of instruction in achieving
literary depths. Pope was mainly responsible, and his assiduous collec-
tion of inflated or anti-climactic writing served his purposes well. In
1729 he published *The Dunciad Variorum*, still in three books, but with
many gaps filled in and extensive preliminaries attached. The general
effect was to emphasize the burlesque of pedantry; but the broader
political and cultural message ran no risk of occlusion in the process.
Much of the action concerns the scribblers of Grub Street, and Pope
takes the opportunity to pay off some personal scores. (He had a spy
among the garrets in the shape of Richard Savage, best known to history
as the hero of Samuel Johnson's remarkable biography.) However,
patrons and sponsors are equally in the line of fire: the malign organism
of Dulness has corrupted the fashionable West End in addition to the
seamier quarters of town. The metaphoric life of the poetry asserts a
connection between the miasmic squalor of Grub Street and the sordid
lucre of the court. And the mock-heroic framework—a parody of the
removal of Troy to Latium in the *Aeneid*—supplies a constant reminder
of alien dignity and vanished significance.

The 1730s represent the decade of Pope's most diverse achievement.
He embarked on a massive new project, first mentioned in November
1729, which was to treat a vast range of social and ethical concerns.
This philosophical *opus magnum* was never to attain a finished state,

and indeed recent research has shown that its scope and content veered about in Pope's mind for the remaining fifteen years of his life. However, most of his important poetry in the 1730s bears a definite relation to the scheme; and many individual poems were composed at this time with a particular slot in the scheme marked out for them.

Among the eight finished epistles intended as component parts of the scheme, the first to appear was the verse letter to the Earl of Burlington, published in 1731. Later this became the fourth and last of the *Epistles to Several Persons*, which Pope's literary executor Warburton rechristened 'Moral Essays' when editing the works in 1751. It was followed by the *Epistle to Bathurst* (1733), the *Epistle to Cobham* (1734), and the *Epistle to a Lady* (1735). Each of these poems is addressed to an individual well known to Pope, though the degree of intimacy varies. The lady in question, Martha Blount, was Pope's closest woman friend for more than thirty years. Each epistle has a theme, broadly social in nature, and the method of the poem allows for direct apostrophe together with discursive argument, character sketches, parables, and satiric asides. Meanwhile Pope was busy about another portion of the planned 'ethic epistles', namely the four instalments of a poem now known as the *Essay on Man*, published at intervals in 1733 and 1734. Their concerns interlock closely with those of the *Epistles to Several Persons*, but the tone is generally more elevated and the scale of imaginative operation more cosmic. Pope himself wrote to Swift of a choice which lay before him, of proceeding 'in the same grave march like Lucretius' or of descending 'to the gaieties of Horace'. Modern critics on the whole have found it more congenial to detect the affinities with Horace, but Pope would probably have laid the emphasis rather on its Lucretian (and anti-Lucretian) vein of metaphysical enquiry, enacted in the exclamatory, interrogatory, and hortatory gestures of its language.

But it is impossible ever to banish Horace from the Augustan poetic scene. At the very same juncture Pope was engaged in a series of *Imitations of Horace*, the first of which dates from 1733. It has been suggested by Miriam Leranbaum that Pope began the imitations 'as a kind of *jeu d'esprit* to provide relaxation from the greater moral seriousness demanded by the *opus magnum* project', but that in time they came to possess their own 'moral earnestness and intensity'. This may well be true, and it is a relevant consideration that the Horatian poems cluster in time around the period of maximum absorption in the *opus magnum*. For an eighteenth-century audience, an 'imitation' meant an adaptation of some earlier text, modernizing references and inserting topical material, but not departing too widely from the original. An imitator twined his parasitic poem closely around the host; if the new growth totally obliterated the old, then he had failed in his task. Pope's most substantial attempt in this direction is his version of the first epistle of the second book. Horace had inscribed his poem to the Emperor Augustus: Pope retains this formula, though it is understood by everyone that he means the King, George Augustus. The imitation, published in 1737, brilliantly reverses Horace's drift to convert a Roman celebration into an English lament. When these Horatian poems were collected by Warburton in 1751 the famous *Epistle to Dr Arbuthnot* was set at their head, and a subtitle 'Prologue to the Satires' appended. We cannot be sure that this would have had Pope's blessing, but all in all it makes reasonable sense. On the other hand, the two *Epilogues* published in 1738 were certainly intended as a tailpiece to the series of imitations—and a splendidly trenchant conclusion they form, too.

The last period of a writer's life is often the best documented: recipients are more likely to keep letters, and anecdotalists to report conversations. So it is with Pope. We know a good deal about both his doings and his opinions towards the end. A young protégé called Joseph Spence began to collect his *obiter dicta*, whilst a large body of correspondence survives to record his activity as a writer (and by this time, effectively, publisher of his own works). We also learn much of his beloved 'rambles' around the country, which enabled him to keep in touch with a wide circle of friends and to put into practice some of his theories on landscape design. At home in Twickenham he was obsessively occupied with his garden and especially its centre-piece, the famous grotto. As Maynard Mack has shown, the grotto became an emblem of retirement and the poetic imagination. As for his far-flung friends, they included the Bath entrepreneur Ralph Allen, the ageing politician Bolingbroke (once disgraced for his Jacobite activity, but permitted a limited reinstatement during the 1730s), the mercurial ex-soldier Peterborough, and the rather withdrawn architect-earl, Burlington. Although his health was declining, Pope seems to have attained a wide measure of fulfilment as he reached his fiftieth birthday.

But politics were never far off. He had been enlisted as a fringe member of the so-called 'Patriot' Opposition to Walpole, a high-minded and ideologically intense campaign to oust the Prime Minister which was led by men of distinction including William Pulteney, the Earl of Chesterfield, and William Pitt, later to be celebrated as the Great Commoner and then as the Earl of Chatham. It is a matter of contention how much active support Pope gave to this movement, which had many writers (James Thomson, Henry Fielding for a time, the young Samuel Johnson) on its side. We know at least that he was willing to attend the first night of nakedly partisan plays mounted by the Opposition, even if there is a possibility that interest in drama had something to do with his presence. But it is undeniable that his Horatian poems contain many thrusts at the ministry. He was planning an epic called *Brutus* (never completed) which would have celebrated liberty in terms close to those of Opposition polemic. And at the very end of his life, a new fourth book for *The Dunciad* (1742) implicated in its satire not just Walpole, then finally poised for the fall, but also the King—who would outlast Pope and half the Opposition. A revised version of the full *Dunciad* in four books (1743) recast the main role, with Theobald's place as King Dunce now taken by the Poet Laureate Colley Cibber, an eccentric and seemingly easy-going man who had acquired a large measure of influence in the world of the arts. Cibber's fitness for the part derived both from his court appointment and from his history as an actor-manager. At the same time Pope widened the scope of his poem to include a whole range of current issues, from deism to education, and from opera to antiquarianism. The resonant last paragraph of Book III was transferred to the new last book, where it still forms a conclusion of startling pungency.

Pope died on 30 May 1744, just after his fifty-sixth birthday. His health had been deteriorating steadily, with his asthma little alleviated by a quack who treated him for dropsy. Most of his old literary allies were dead: Swift alone survived, bereft of almost all his faculties, for another year. There began a process of reassessment such as eminent authors are bound to undergo. Biographies, pamphlets, and critical essays followed one another. Warburton's edition of the works in 1751 provoked fresh controversy; new poems and new biographical facts continued to emerge. In this extensive debate the two most important figures were the poet and literary historian Joseph Warton and the redoubtable Samuel Johnson. Warton's *Essay on the Genius and Writings of Pope* (1756–82) contains a searching review of the poetry: with a few exceptions, he finds Pope deficient in originality and in imaginative power. Johnson's study in *The Lives of the Poets* (1781) constituted in some respects an answer to the first volume of Warton's *Essay*. It is more sympathetic to what might be termed the central Augustan virtues in Pope (harmony, chastity of language, architectural skill), but it acknowledges faults in both the man and the poet. Johnson's Life remains the single most distinguished item in the long critical debate that has raged around Pope.

In the nineteenth century, Pope was especially fortunate in his admirers. Byron was a resolute defender of Pope's reputation, adducing his example in opposition to what he saw as the provincialism and self-indulgence of much Romantic poetry. On a famous occasion Charles Lamb singled out Pope's compliments, by which he must have meant the tributes to eminent contemporaries which are so skilfully worked into the fabric of the satire. Hazlitt reports Lamb as saying, 'Each of them is worth an estate for life—nay, is an immortality.' A generation later, Ruskin was to see Pope as a case-study in the effects of the 'classical spirit'; though this 'spoiled half his work, he broke through it continually into true enthusiasm and tender thought'. Elsewhere Ruskin linked Pope with Virgil as 'two great masters of the absolute art of language'. Better known is Matthew Arnold's critique in 'The Study of Poetry' (1880), where he concludes that 'Dryden and Pope are not classics of our poetry, they are classics of our prose'. This attitude remained dominant in the English-speaking world until the 1930s, when poets like W. H. Auden and Edith Sitwell offered a higher estimate of Pope's imaginative powers, and academic studies made a significant advance. The edition of the *Works* (1871–89) by Elwin and Courthope has gradually been supplanted. The poems, including the Homer translations, were splendidly edited by a team of distinguished scholars headed by John Butt and Maynard Mack. A second volume of the prose works has been prepared by Rosemary Cowler to supplant the earlier edition by Norman Ault. The correspondence has been edited by George Sherburn. Stimulating monographs have illuminated various areas of Pope's work, for example R. A. Brower's consideration of his habits of allusion, Ian Jack's exploration of the mock-heroic device, Geoffrey Tillotson's analysis of stylistic features, and Howard Weinbrot's review of the relation to formal verse satire from earlier periods. Maynard Mack has produced the deepest study of Pope's life and a host of important essays on the poet's imagery, his physical being, and his relations with Walpole. A further generation of critics including Emrys Jones and Howard Erskine-Hill have drawn attention to a vein of fantasy, surrealism, and the comic 'absurd' in Pope. Most recently, feminist scholarship has opened up new vistas on all of Pope's writing, as exemplified by the contributions of Carole Fabricant, Ellen Pollak, and Valerie Rumbold.

Pope is primarily a comic writer. By this I mean not simply that he is often very funny, as in the pose of self-pity at the start of his *Epistle to Dr Arbuthnot*. I refer equally to the domain of his best work: its visible *dramatis personae* are those of a living, breathing society, its settings are beguilingly familiar, and its emotional range reflects our own daily moods. It is important to add 'visible', for Pope's imagination may at any time take off to stranger and more grotesque countries of the mind. *The Rape of the Lock* is in the first place a poem concerning beaux and belles, prompted by a scandalous story of a peer who snipped off some curls from the head of a giddy young socialite. Its milieu seems to be domestic (dressing-tables, coffee-tables, card-tables). Yet the plot gets mixed up with Rosicrucian mysteries, and we visit a nightmare world of psycho-sexual disorders in the Cave of Spleen. Similarly, *The Dunciad* is formally constructed around the doings of a squalid array of recognizable hack writers. But the imagery, the allusions, and the dense poetic texture all encourage us to see these *louche* and farcical doings within the wider sweep of history.

Pope was lucky in that the seventeenth-century 'reform of our numbers' no longer needed to be argued about as in Dryden's day:

> Late, very late, correctness grew our care,
> When the tired nation breathed from civil war.
>
> (*Epistle to Augustus*)

The ingredients that made for correctness (pure diction, clean syntax, smooth versification) could be largely taken for granted, and Pope could harness these to express thought, feeling, and observation. In civic terms, in bodily constitution, he was a pariah, an outsider. But he understood his age—both the larger workings of society and the psychology of individuals—as fully as anyone then alive. His dedication to the art of poetry enables us to share that insight, dispensed to us in the richest possible way through pleasures of the imagination.

ACKNOWLEDGEMENTS

THE major debt accrued by an editor is to former generations of scholars who have built up our knowledge of the life and works of Pope. My deepest gratitude goes to those who have produced the two great editions of the poet: the unduly maligned Elwin and Courthope in the nineteenth century, and the group headed by John Butt who were responsible for the Twickenham edition in the twentieth century. As a modern spelling edition, my own has different textual priorities, and the series policy calls for a different style of explanatory gloss. Nevertheless, the work of these predecessors has left a solid groundwork on which we continue to rely. Among one-volume editions, I have found some useful material in the selection of poetry and prose edited by Aubrey Williams (Riverside Editions, 1969).

The text of Pope's letters is based on *The Correspondence of Alexander Pope*, ed. George Sherburn (Oxford University Press, 1956). The excerpts from Pope's conversations with Spence are taken from *Observations, Anecdotes, and Characters of Books and Men* by Joseph Spence, ed. James M. Osborn (Oxford University Press, 1966). Permission to use this material is gratefully acknowledged.

A wider indebtedness is to the biographical, critical, and bibliographical work of Maynard Mack, which it would be impossible to conceal even if I desired to hide the fact. Such acknowledgement may perhaps stand in the place of a formal dedication.

CHRONOLOGY

1688   21 May, P born in London.

1688–9   Protestant Revolution: James II forced to abdicate in favour of William and Mary.

c.1700   P's family moves from London to Binfield, in Windsor Forest.

1702   Queen Anne succeeds to throne.

1704   Swift, *A Tale of a Tub*.

1709   P's first published works, including his *Pastorals*, appear in a London miscellany.

1710   Formation of Tory Government led by Harley and St John (Bolingbroke), later close friend of P.

1711   P's *Essay on Criticism* brings him fame; Addison and Steele launch the *Spectator* (P and Swift occasional contributions).

1712   20 May, first appearance of *Rape of the Lock* (two-canto version).

1713   7 March, *Windsor Forest* published; P writes essays for Steele's journal the *Guardian*. Scriblerus Club becomes active, with P, Swift, Gay, Arbuthnot, Parnell, and Harley (now Lord Oxford) members.

1714   4 March, five-canto version of *Rape of the Lock* published. 1 August, death of Queen Anne and accession of first Hanoverian king, George I. Tories out of office for the remainder of P's life. Swift settled in Dublin as Dean of St Patrick's.

1715   1 February, *The Temple of Fame*; 6 June, first instalment of P's *Iliad* translation. Jacobite rising in Scotland in support of the Old Pretender, put down with relative ease. Anti-Catholic legislation limits P's personal liberties.

1716   P's family moves to Chiswick on outskirts of London. P attacks the bookseller Curll in prose pamphlets.

1716–20   Remaining volumes of *Iliad* translation published.

1717   P, Gay, and Arbuthnot collaborate in farce *Three Hours after Marriage*. P's father dies. 3 June, P's first major collection of *Works* published, including new poems such as *Eloisa to Abelard*.

1718   Death of Parnell. P moves to Twickenham.

1719   Death of Addison. Defoe, *Robinson Crusoe*, admired by P.

1720   South Sea Bubble.

1721   Walpole comes to power.

1722   P edits Parnell's poems. P's friend Atterbury implicated in Jacobite plot (exiled 1723).

1723   P edits works of Duke of Buckingham. P's brother-in-law arrested for deer-stealing in the 'Windsor Blacks' affair, involving a series of anti-Jacobite measures.

1724   Swift, *Drapier's Letters*, attacking English Government's treatment of Ireland.

1725   March, P's subscription edition of Shakespeare published. April, first instalment of P's translation of *Odyssey* published.

1726   Remaining volumes of *Odyssey* published. Swift visits England for publication of *Gulliver's Travels*.

1727   First two volumes of Pope–Swift *Miscellanies* published. Swift visits England for last time.

1728   7 March, third volume of *Miscellanies* including *Peri Bathous*. May, first version of *The Dunciad* in three books. Gay, *Beggar's Opera*, premiered with great success.

1729   April, *Dunciad Variorum* adds extensive apparatus and notes. Swift, *A Modest Proposal*.

1730   Fielding, *The Author's Farce*.

1731   14 December, *Epistle to Burlington*. Death of Defoe.

1732   Further volume of *Miscellanies*. Death of Gay.

1733   15 January, *Epistle to Bathurst*; 20 February, *Essay on Man*, i–iii. First in the series of *Imitations of Horace* appear. Death of P's mother.

1734   2 January, *Epistle to Cobham*; 24 January, *Essay on Man*, iv. Further Horatian imitations published.

1735   2 January, *Epistle to Arbuthnot*; 8 February, *Epistle to a Lady*. Second volume of P's *Works*. Death of Arbuthnot. P engineers publication of his letters.

NOTE ON THE TEXT

THIS volume is designed in part as a successor to the edition of Pope's *Poetical Works*, which was prepared for the Oxford Standard Authors by Herbert Davis in 1966. As well as adding many extracts from the prose and the correspondence, I have made a different selection from Pope's poetry. However, the modernized text is based for the most part on the same original printings as those Davis used to establish his text. That is, the text of the *Essay on Criticism*, the *Essay on Man*, and what have usually been known as the *Moral Essays* is based on the quarto editions of 1744 printed by William Bowyer under the close supervision of Pope. *The Dunciad* is based on the first printing of the full work in 1743. These are already clean and rather 'modern' printings, with less elaborate typographical signalling than had generally been the custom up to this time. Otherwise the text is based on the posthumous edition put out by Pope's executor William Warburton in 1751, largely following the same principles. An important study by David Foxon, *Pope and the Early Eighteenth-Century Book Trade* (Oxford, 1991), has shown that Pope consciously adopted the simpler and less cluttered style, even in his own manuscripts, as his career progressed.

In a few respects I have departed from Davis's editorial methods. Most crucially, I have abandoned a practice which has been adopted by every editor since Pope's death. In this volume the imitations of Horace and the so-called *Moral Essays* are printed not as a group but separately, as they first appeared at intervals over a period of years. It is undeniably the case that Pope did not envisage the full series when he wrote the first items in each category, and indeed it was only over a very slow process that the familiar headings came into being. The *Moral Essays* were at one stage intended to form part of Pope's *opus magnum*, built around the *Essay on Man*, but this scheme too was abandoned. In my view we get a much clearer sense of Pope's actual working procedures if we read the poems in the order that they appeared, with a recognition that the series developed out of what were at first occasional and disparate poems. (This view is strengthened by Foxon's book, which shows how opportunistic Pope was in shaping his poetic career *post facto* by rearranging items in his collected *Works*.) The same reasoning does not apply to the *Essay on Man*, which was all along devised as a work in four parts; moreover, printing its four epistles in sequence leads to only one minor break in strict chronology, since the fourth epistle appeared eight months after the third in January 1734, that is, eight days after the *Epistle to Cobham*. The arrangement here involves the tiniest displacement of chronological order, whereas the normal layout of Pope's collected poetry conceals the fact that the imitations of Horace began not long after the first version of *The Dunciad* and ended not long before the final version. It should be added that *The Rape of the Lock* and *The Dunciad*, since they are present here in their expanded form, are printed in the chronological position appropriate to this state. There are some drawbacks in this procedure, since ideally one should have the felt presence of *The Dunciad* when reading all the poems of the 1730s, but the alternative—that of inserting the 1743 version, complete with the new fourth book, at the point appropriate to the 1728 version—is obviously unacceptable: it would make nonsense of the new material and the enthronement of Cibber, who only became Poet Laureate in 1730.

The extracts from conversations with Joseph Spence, which are all brief, have been collected together at the end, rather than scattered piecemeal through the volume. Letters are placed according to date of writing; printed works are normally placed according to date of publication, except in one or two cases where there was an abnormal delay before the item reached the press. In this latter instance, the date of composition is used. The Spence materials are quoted from the edition by J. M. Osborn (1966) and the correspondence is based on the text edited by George Sherburn (1956).

Modernization has been carried through in a systematic manner, affecting spelling, capitalization, typography, and punctuation (although the last is altered more sparingly, in cases where obscurity might arise). Spelling is left unaltered where there is a real difference in sound or meaning. But *Terras* is just *terrace*, and so it becomes: as with *blest*, which becomes *blessed*. On the other hand, *learned* indicates the modern pronunciation with one syllable, and an accent is marked to indicate the pronunciation *learnèd*. I have eliminated the mark of elision in words such as *confess'd*, *pow'r*, *sev'ral*, *nat'ral*, *ev'ry*, *av'rice*, *degen'rate*, and many others, since the full spelling indicates normal modern pronunciation, and this is what Pope's metre requires. The apostrophe is retained only in cases such as *th' oppressor*, where a reader may add an unwanted syllable if the article is spelt out in full. Proper names are subject to the same treatment, since *Aegypt* is no more or less than *Egypt*, precisely on a par with *aethereal/ethereal*. This leads to some delicate decisions, as where *Heideggre* is and is not quite *Heidegger*, and I have perhaps inconsistently left *Twitnam* for *Twickenham*, on the basis that the middle consonant does seem to make a substantial difference to the feel of the word. Where Pope vacillates (as in *Curl/Curll*) I have always adopted the familiar modern form *Curll*. Deliberate distortions such as *Tibbald* for *Theobald* are naturally retained. Names originally printed as blanks are, where possible, filled in (thus *P-p-le* becomes *Popple*): there may be some loss of suggestiveness here, but the main reason for Pope's reticence was fear of reprisal (a fate his modern editor need not dread), and he was in any case much bolder in setting out the full name than were most writers of the age.

One change regularly made in the punctuation is to observe modern rules with regard to cues for direct speech. Thus, a line from the *Iliad* runs in the original:

> Return? (said *Hector*, fir'd with stern Disdain)

This is modernized as follows:

> 'Return?', said Hector, fired with stern disdain,

The reason is that as soon as we adopt modern conventions with regard to quotation marks, the need for brackets disappears; their inclusion suggests a parenthetic note which is not truly a part of the original. I have also suppressed question marks of a rhetorical order where they do not indicate a true query, and have eliminated a few exclamation marks which would not be used in a similar context today.

Notes at the end are signalled by a degree sign (°) in the text. It should be noted that individuals mentioned in *The Dunciad* are routinely entered in the Biographical Index and no textual sign is given. All footnotes are those of Pope himself or, in a very few cases, those supplied by Warburton in the name of the poet.

PASTORALS

Rura mihi et rigui placeant in vallibus amnes,
Flumina amem, sylvasque, inglorius!
VIRGIL.°

SPRING

THE

FIRST PASTORAL

OR

DAMON

To Sir WILLIAM TRUMBULL

First in these fields I try the sylvan strains,   1
Nor blush to sport on Windsor's blissful plains:

These Pastorals were written at the age of sixteen, and then passed through the
hands of Mr Walsh, Mr Wycherley, G. Granville afterwards Lord Lansdowne, Sir
William Trumbull, Dr Garth, Lord Halifax, Lord Somers, Mr Mainwaring, and
others. All these gave our author the greatest encouragement, and particularly Mr
Walsh (whom Mr Dryden, in his Postscript to Virgil, calls the best critic of his age.)
'The author (says he) seems to have a particular genius for this kind of Poetry, and
a judgment that much exceeds his years. He has taken very freely from the Ancients.
But what he has mixed of his own with theirs is no way inferior to what he has taken
from them. It is not flattery at all to say that Virgil had written nothing so good at
his age. His Preface is very judicious and learned'. *Letter to Mr Wycherley*, Ap. 1705.
The Lord Lansdowne about the same time, mentioning the youth of our poet, says
(in a printed Letter of the Character of Mr Wycherley) 'that if he goes on as he has
begun in the pastoral way, as Virgil first tried his strength, we may hope to see
English poetry vie with the Roman,' etc. Notwithstanding the early time of their
production, the author esteemed these as the most correct in the versification, and
musical in the numbers, of all his works. The reason for his labouring them into so
much softness, was, doubtless, that this sort of poetry derives almost its whole beauty
from a natural ease of thought and smoothness of verse; whereas that of most other
kinds consists in the strength and fullness of both. In a letter of his to Mr Walsh
about this time we find an enumeration of several niceties in versification, which
perhaps have never been strictly observed in any English poem, except in these
Pastorals. They were not printed till 1709.
 Sir William Trumbull.] Our author's friendship with this gentleman commenced
at very unequal years; he was under sixteen, but Sir William above sixty, and had
lately resigned his employment of Secretary of State to King William.°

 1. *Prima Syracosio dignata est ludere versu,*
    Nostra nec erubuit sylvas habitare Thalia.

Fair Thames, flow gently from thy sacred spring,
While on thy banks Sicilian° Muses sing;
Let vernal airs through trembling osiers° play,
And Albion's cliffs resound the rural lay.
   You, that too wise for pride, too good for power,
Enjoy the glory to be great no more,
And carrying with you all the world can boast,
To all the world illustriously° are lost!   10
O let my Muse her slender reed inspire,°
Till in your native shades you tune the lyre:
So when the nightingale to rest removes,
The thrush may chant to the forsaken groves,
But, charmed to silence, listens while she sings,
And all th' aërial audience clap their wings.
   Soon as the flocks shook off the nightly dews,
Two swains, whom love kept wakeful, and the Muse,
Poured o'er the whitening vale their fleecy care,
Fresh as the morn, and as the season fair: 20

   This is the general exordium and opening of the Pastorals, in imitation of the
sixth of Virgil, which some have therefore not improbably thought to have been the
first originally. In the beginnings of the other three Pastorals, he imitates expressly
those which now stand first of the three chief poets in this kind, Spenser, Virgil,
Theocritus.

> A shepherd's boy (he seeks no better name),—
> Beneath the shade a spreading beech displays,—
> Thyrsis, the music of that murm'ring spring.—

are manifestly imitations of

> A Shepherd's Boy (no better do him call)—
> Tityre, tu patulae recubans sub tegmine fagi.—
> Ἀδύ τι τὸ ψιθύρισμα καὶ ἁ πίτυς, αἰπόλε, τήνα.—

12. Sir W. Trumbull was born in Windsor Forest, to which he retreated after he
had resigned the post of Secretary of State to King William III.

17. The scene of this Pastoral a valley, the time the morning. It stood originally
thus,

> Daphnis and Strephon to the shades retired
> Both warmed by love, and by the Muse inspired,
> Fresh as the morn, and as the season fair,
> In flowery vales they fed their fleecy care;
> And while Aurora gilds the mountain's side,
> Thus Daphnis spoke and Strephon thus replied.

The dawn now blushing on the mountain's side,
Thus Daphnis spoke, and Strephon thus replied.

Daphnis

Hear how the birds, on every bloomy spray,
With joyous music wake the dawning day!
Why sit we mute when early linnets sing,
When warbling Philomel° salutes the spring?
Why sit we sad when Phosphor° shines so clear,
And lavish Nature paints the purple° year?

Strephon

Sing then, and Damon shall attend the strain,
While yon slow oxen turn the furrowed plain.   30
Here the bright crocus and blue violet glow;
Here western winds on breathing° roses blow.
I'll stake yon lamb, that near the fountain plays,
And from the brink his dancing shade surveys.

Daphnis

And I this bowl, where wanton ivy twines,
And swelling clusters bend the curling vines:
Four figures rising° from the work appear,
The various seasons of the rolling year;
And what is that, which binds the radiant sky,
Where twelve fair signs° in beauteous order lie?   40

34. The first reading was,
    And his own image from the bank surveys.

35, 36. *Lenta quibus torno facili superaddita vitis,*
         Diffusos edera vestit pallente corymbos.
                                        Virgil.

36. *And clusters lurk beneath the curling vines.*

38. The subject of these Pastorals engraven on the bowl is not without its pro-
priety. The shepherd's hesitation at the name of the zodiac, imitates that in Virgil,

              Et quis fuit alter,
    Descripsit radio totum qui gentibus orbem?

Damon

Then sing by turns, by turns the Muses sing.
Now hawthorns blossom, now the daisies spring,
Now leaves the trees, and flowers adorn the
        ground;
Begin, the vales shall every note rebound.

Strephon

Inspire me, Phoebus, in my Delia's praise,
With Waller's strains, or Granville's° moving lays!
A milk-white bull shall at your altars stand,
That threats a fight, and spurns° the rising sand.

Daphnis

O Love! for Sylvia let me gain the prize,
And make my tongue victorious as her eyes;   50
No lambs or sheep for victims I'll impart,
Thy victim, Love, shall be the shepherd's heart.

Strephon

Me gentle Delia beckons from the plain,
Then hid in shades, eludes her eager swain;
But feigns a laugh, to see me search around,
And by that laugh the willing fair is found.

Daphnis

The sprightly Sylvia trips along the green,
She runs, but hopes she does not run unseen;
While a kind glance at her pursuer flies,
How much at variance are her feet and eyes!   60

41. Literally from Virgil,

> Alternis dicetis, amant alterna Camoenae;
> Et nunc omnis ager, nunc omnis parturit arbos,
> Nunc frondent sylvae, nunc formosissimus annus.

46. George Granville, afterwards Lord Lansdowne, known for his poems, most
of which he composed very young, and proposed Waller as his model.

47. Virgil—*Pascite taurum, Qui cornu petat, et pedibus jam spargat arenam.*

58. Imitation of Virgil,

> Malo me Galatea petit, lasciva puella,
> Et fugit ad salices, sed se cupit ante videri.

Strephon

O'er golden sands let rich Pactolus° flow
And trees weep amber on the banks of Po;°
Blessed Thames's shores the brightest beauties yield,
Feed here my lambs, I'll seek no distant field.

Daphnis

Celestial Venus haunts Idalia's° groves;
Diana Cynthus,° Ceres Hybla° loves:
If Windsor-shades delight the matchless maid,
Cynthus and Hybla yield to Windsor-shade.

Strephon

All nature mourns, the skies relent in showers,
Hushed are the birds, and closed the drooping flowers;   70
If Delia smile, the flowers begin to spring,
The skies to brighten, and the birds to sing.

Daphnis

All nature laughs, the groves are fresh and fair,
The sun's mild lustre warms the vital air;
If Sylvia smiles, new glories gild the shore,
And vanquished nature seems to charm no more.

Strephon

In spring the fields, in autumn hills I love,
At morn the plains, at noon the shady grove,

61. It stood thus at first,

> Let rich Iberia golden fleeces boast,
> Her purple wool the proud Assyrian coast,
> Blessed Thames's shores, etc.

69. *All nature mourns,*]

> Virgil *Aret ager, vitio moriens sitit aëris herba,* etc.
> *Phyllidis adventu nostrae nemus omne virebit.*

69. These verses were thus at first:

> All nature mourns, the birds their songs deny,
> Nor wasted brooks the thirsty flowers supply;
> If Delia smile, the flowers begin to spring,
> The brooks to murmur, and the birds to sing.

But Delia always; absent from her sight,
Nor plains at morn, nor groves at noon delight.   80

Daphnis

Sylvia's like autumn ripe, yet mild as May,
More bright than noon, yet fresh as early day;
Ev'n spring displeases, when she shines not here;
But blessed with her, 'tis spring throughout the year.

Strephon

Say, Daphnis, say, in what glad soil appears,
A wondrous tree that sacred monarchs bears?
Tell me but this, and I'll disclaim the prize,
And give the conquest to thy Sylvia's eyes.

Daphnis

Nay tell me first, in what more happy fields
The thistle springs, to which the lily yields?   90
And then a nobler prize I will resign;
For Sylvia, charming Sylvia shall be thine.

Damon

Cease to contend, for, Daphnis, I decree,
The bowl to Strephon, and the lamb to thee:
Blessed swains, whose nymphs in every grace excel;
Blessed nymphs, whose swains those graces sing so well!
Now rise, and haste to yonder woodbine bowers,
A soft retreat from sudden vernal showers;
The turf with rural dainties shall be crowned,
While opening blooms diffuse their sweets around.   100

---

86. An allusion to the Royal Oak, in which Charles II had been hid from the
pursuit after the battle of Worcester.°

90. Alludes to the device of the Scots monarchs, the thistle, worn by Queen
Anne; and to the arms of France, the fleur de lys. The two riddles are in imitation
of those in Virgil *Ecl.* iii.

Dic quibus in terris inscripti nomina Regum
Nascantur Flores, *& Phyllida solus habebis.*°

99. was originally,

The turf with country dainties shall be spread,
And trees with twining branches shade your head.

For see! the gathering flocks to shelter tend,
And from the Pleiades° fruitful showers descend.

SUMMER

THE

SECOND PASTORAL

OR

ALEXIS

To Dr Garth

A shepherd's boy (he seeks no better name)   1
Led forth his flocks along the silver Thame,
Where dancing sun-beams on the waters played,
And verdant alders formed a quivering shade.
Soft as he mourned, the streams forgot to flow,
The flocks around a dumb compassion show,
The Naiads wept in every watery bower,
And Jove consented in a silent shower.
  Accept, O Garth, the Muse's early lays,
That adds this wreath of ivy to thy bays;   10
Hear what from Love unpractised hearts endure,
From Love, the sole disease thou canst not cure.
  'Ye shady beeches, and ye cooling streams,
Defence from Phoebus', not from Cupid's beams,
To you I mourn, nor to the deaf I sing,

1, 2, 3, 4. were thus printed in the first edition:

> *A faithful swain, whom Love had taught to sing,*
> *Bewailed his fate beside a silver spring;*
> *Where gentle Thames his winding waters leads*
> *Through verdant forests, and through flowery meads.*

3. The scene of this Pastoral by the river's side; suitable to the heat of the season; the time noon.

8. *Jupiter et laeto descendet plurimus imbri.* Virgil.

9. Dr Samuel Garth, author of the *Dispensary*, was one of the first friends of the author, whose acquaintance with him began at fourteen or fifteen. Their friendship continued from the year 1703 to 1718, which was that of his death.°

15. *Non canimus surdis, respondent omnia sylvae.* Virgil.

The woods shall answer, and their echo ring.
The hills and rocks attend my doleful lay,
Why art thou prouder and more hard than they?
The bleating sheep with my complaints agree,
They parched with heat, and I inflamed by thee.   20
The sultry Sirius° burns the thirsty plains,
While in thy heart eternal winter reigns.

   Where stray ye Muses, in what lawn or grove,
While your Alexis pines in hopeless love?
In those fair fields where sacred Isis° glides,
Or else where Cam his winding vales divides?
As in the crystal spring I view my face,
Fresh rising blushes paint the watery glass;
But since those graces please thy eyes no more,
I shun the fountains which I sought before.   30
Once I was skilled in every herb that grew,
And every plant that drinks the morning dew;
Ah wretched shepherd, what avails thy art,
To cure thy lambs, but not to heal thy heart!

   Let other swains attend the rural care,
Feed fairer flocks, or richer fleeces share:°
But nigh yon mountain let me tune my lays,
Embrace my love, and bind my brows with bays.
That flute is mine which Colin's tuneful breath

16. *The woods shall answer and their echo ring*, is a line out of Spenser's *Epitha-lamion*.

23.   *Quae nemora, aut qui vos saltus habuere, puellae*
                       Naiades, indigno cum Gallus amore periret?
                       Nam neque Parnassi vobis juga, nam neque Pindi
                       Ulla moram fecere, neque Aonia Aganippe.
                                        Virgil out of Theocritus.

27.   *Oft in the crystal spring I cast a view,*
                       And equalled Hylas, if the glass be true;
                       But since those graces meet my eyes no more,
                       I shun, etc.
Virgil again from the Cyclops of Theocritus,
                            nuper me in littore vidi
                       Cum placidum ventis staret mare, non ego Daphnim,
                       Judice te, metuam, si nunquam fallit imago.

39. *Colin*] The name taken by Spenser in his Eclogues, where his mistress is celebrated under that of Rosalinda.

Inspired when living, and bequeathed in death; 40
He said, "Alexis,° take this pipe, the same
That taught the groves my Rosalinda's name":
But now the reeds shall hang on yonder tree,
For ever silent, since despised by thee.
Oh! were I made by some transforming power
The captive bird that sings within thy bower!
Then might my voice thy listening ears employ,
And I those kisses he receives, enjoy.

And yet my numbers please the rural throng,
Rough satyrs dance, and Pan applauds the song: 50
The nymphs, forsaking every cave and spring,
Their early fruit, and milk-white turtles° bring;
Each amorous nymph prefers her gifts in vain,
On you their gifts are all bestowed again.
For you the swains the fairest flowers design,
And in one garland all their beauties join;°
Accept the wreath which you deserve alone,
In whom all beauties are comprised in one.

See what delights in sylvan scenes appear!
Descending Gods have found Elysium here. 60
In woods bright Venus with Adonis strayed,
And chaste Diana haunts the forest-shade.
Come, lovely nymph, and bless the silent hours,
When swains from shearing seek their nightly
    bowers;
When weary reapers quit the sultry field,
And crowned with corn, their thanks to Ceres yield,
This harmless grove no lurking viper hides,
But in my breast the serpent Love abides.
Here bees from blossoms sip the rosy dew,
But your Alexis knows no sweets but you. 70
Oh deign to visit our forsaken seats,
The mossy fountains, and the green retreats!

40. Virgil *Ecl.* ii.

> *Est mihi disparibus septem compacta cicutis*
> *Fistula, Damaetas dono mihi quam dedit olim,*
> *Et dixit moriens, Te nunc habet ista secundum.*

60.   *Habitarunt Di quoque sylvas*—Virgil.
> *Et formosus oves ad flumina pavit Adonis.* Idem.

Where'er you walk, cool gales shall fan the glade,
Trees, where you sit, shall crowd into a shade:
Where'er you tread, the blushing flowers shall rise,
And all things flourish where you turn your eyes.°
Oh! how I long with you to pass my days,
Invoke the Muses, and resound your praise!
Your praise the birds shall chant in every grove,
And winds shall waft it to the powers above.   80
But would you sing, and rival Orpheus' strain,
The wondering forests soon should dance again,
The moving mountains hear the powerful call,
And headlong streams hang listening in their fall!

But see, the shepherds shun the noon-day heat,
The lowing herds to murmuring brooks retreat,
To closer shades the panting flocks remove;
Ye Gods! and is there no relief for Love?
But soon the sun with milder rays descends
To the cool ocean, where his journey ends: 90
On me love's fiercer flames for ever prey,
By night he scorches, as he burns by day.'

AUTUMN
THE
THIRD PASTORAL
OR
HYLAS and AEGON
To Mr WYCHERLEY

Beneath the shade a spreading beech displays,°   1

79, 80. *Your praise the tuneful birds to heaven shall bear,*
And listening wolves grow milder as they hear.

So the verses were originally written. But the author, young as he was, soon found the
absurdity which Spenser himself overlooked, of introducing wolves into England.°

80. *Partèm aliquam, venti, divùm referatis ad aures!*   Virgil.

88. *Me tamen urit amor, quis enim modus adsit amori?*   Idem.

91. *Me love inflames, nor will his fires allay.*

This Pastoral consists of two parts, like the viiith of Virgil: the scene, a hill; the
time at sunset.

Hylas and Aegon sung their rural lays;
This mourned a faithless, that an absent love,
And Delia's name and Doris filled the Grove.°
Ye Mantuan° nymphs, your sacred succour bring;
Hylas and Aegon's rural lays I sing.

Thou, whom the Nine with Plautus' wit inspire,
The art of Terence, and Menander's fire;°
Whose sense instructs us, and whose humour charms,
Whose judgment sways us, and whose spirit warms!   10
Oh, skilled in nature! see the hearts of swains,
Their artless passions, and their tender pains.
Now setting Phoebus shone serenely bright,
And fleecy clouds were streaked with purple light;
When tuneful Hylas with melodious moan,
Taught rocks to weep and made the mountains groan.

'Go, gentle gales, and bear my sighs away!
To Delia's ear the tender notes convey.
As some sad turtle° his lost love deplores,
And with deep murmurs fills the sounding shores;   20
Thus, far from Delia, to the winds I mourn
Alike unheard, unpitied, and forlorn.

Go, gentle gales, and bear my sighs along!
For her, the feathered choirs neglect their song;
For her, the limes their pleasing shades deny;
For her, the lilies hang their heads and die.
Ye flowers that droop, forsaken by the spring,
Ye birds that, left by summer, cease to sing,
Ye trees that fade when autumn-heats remove,
Say, is not absence death to those who love?   30

Go, gentle gales, and bear my sighs away!
Cursed be the fields that cause my Delia's stay;
Fade every blossom, wither every tree,
Die every flower, and perish all, but she.
What have I said? where'er my Delia flies,
Let spring attend, and sudden flowers arise:

7. Mr Wycherley, a famous author of comedies; of which the most celebrated
were the *Plain Dealer* and *Country Wife*. He was a writer of infinite spirit, satire, and
wit. The only objection made to him was that he had too much. However he was
followed in the same way by Mr Congreve; though with a little more correctness.°

Let opening roses knotted oaks adorn,
And liquid amber drop from every thorn.
   Go, gentle gales, and bear my sighs along!
The birds shall cease to tune their evening song,   40
The winds to breathe, the waving woods to move,
And streams to murmur, e'er I cease to love.
Not bubbling fountains to the thirsty swain,
Not balmy sleep to labourers faint with pain,°
Not showers to larks, or sunshine to the bee,
Are half so charming as thy sight to me.
   Go, gentle gales, and bear my sighs away!
Come, Delia, come; ah why this long delay?
Through rocks and caves the name of Delia sounds,
Delia, each cave and echoing rock rebounds.   50
Ye powers, what pleasing frenzy soothes my mind!
Do lovers dream, or is my Delia kind?
She comes, my Delia comes!—Now cease my lay,
And cease, ye gales, to bear my sighs away!'
   Next Aegon sung, while Windsor groves admired;
Rehearse, ye Muses, what yourselves inspired.
   'Resound, ye hills, resound my mournful strain!
Of perjured Doris, dying I complain:
Here where the mountains lessening as they rise
Lose the low vales, and steal into the skies: 60
While labouring oxen, spent with toil and heat,
In their loose traces from the field retreat:
While curling smokes from village-tops are seen,
And the fleet shades glide o'er the dusky green.
   Resound, ye hills, resound my mournful lay!
Beneath yon poplar oft we passed the day:
Oft on the rind I carved her amorous vows,

37.   *Aurea durae*
   Mala ferant quercus: narcisso floreat alnus,
   Pinguia corticibus sudent electra myricae.
                          Virgil *Ecl.* viii.

43 f.]   *Quale sopor fessis in gramine, quale per aestum*
         Dulcis aquae saliente sitim restinguere rivo.
                          Ecl. v.

52. *An qui amant, ipsi sibi somnia fingunt?* Id. viii.
64. *And the fleet shades fly gliding o'er the green.*

While she with garlands hung the bending boughs:
The garlands fade, the vows are worn away;
So dies her love, and so my hopes decay.   70
   Resound, ye hills, resound my mournful strain!
Now bright Arcturus° glads the teeming grain,
Now golden fruits on loaded branches shine,
And grateful clusters° swell with floods of wine;
Now blushing berries paint the yellow grove;
Just Gods! shall all things yield returns but love?
   Resound, ye hills, resound my mournful lay!
The shepherds cry, "Thy flocks are left a prey—"
Ah! what avails it me, the flocks to keep,
Who lost my heart while I preserved my sheep.   80
Pan came, and asked, what magic caused my smart,
Or what ill eyes malignant glances dart?
What eyes but hers, alas, have power to move!
And is there magic but what dwells in love?
   Resound, ye hills, resound my mournful strains!
I'll fly from shepherds, flocks, and flowery plains.
From shepherds, flocks, and plains, I may remove,
Forsake mankind, and all the world—but love!
I know thee, Love! on foreign mountains bred,
Wolves gave thee suck, and savage tigers fed.   90
Thou wert from Etna's burning entrails torn,
Got by fierce whirlwinds, and in thunder born!
   Resound, ye hills, resound my mournful lay!
Farewell, ye woods, adieu the light of day!
One leap from yonder cliff shall end my pains,
No more, ye hills, no more resound my strains!'
   Thus sung the shepherds till th'approach of night,
The skies yet blushing with departing light,
When falling dews with spangles decked the glade,
And the low sun had lengthened every shade.   100

---

82. *Nescio quis teneros oculus mihi fascinat agnos.*

83. *What eyes but hers, alas, have power on me!*
   Oh mighty Love! What magic is like thee!

89. *Nunc scio quid sit Amor: duris in cotibus illum*, etc.

WINTER
THE
FOURTH PASTORAL
OR
DAPHNE

To the Memory of Mrs TEMPEST

Lycidas

Thyrsis, the music of that murmuring spring   I
Is not so mournful as the strains you sing.
Nor rivers winding through the vales below,
So sweetly warble, or so smoothly flow.
Now sleeping flocks on their soft fleeces lie,
The moon, serene in glory, mounts the sky,
While silent birds forget their tuneful lays,
Oh sing of Daphne's fate, and Daphne's praise!

Thyrsis

Behold the groves that shine with silver frost,
Their beauty withered, and their verdure lost.   10
Here shall I try the sweet Alexis' strain,
That called the listening dryads° to the plain?
Thames heard the numbers as he flowed along,
And bade his willows° learn the moving song.

Lycidas

So may kind rains their vital moisture yield,
And swell the future harvest of the field.
Begin; this charge the dying Daphne gave,
And said, 'Ye shepherds, sing around my grave!'

Mrs Tempest.] This lady was of an ancient family in Yorkshire, and particularly admired by the author's friend Mr Walsh, who, having celebrated her in a Pastoral Elegy, desired his friend to do the same, as appears from one of his letters, dated Sept. 9, 1706. 'Your last Eclogue being on the same subject with mine on Mrs Tempest's death, I should take it very kindly in you to give it a little turn as if it were to the memory of the same lady.' Her death having happened on the night of the great storm in 1703, gave a propriety to this eclogue, which in its general turn alludes to it. The scene of the Pastoral lies in a grove, the time at midnight.

13. *Audiit Eurotas, jussitque ediscere lauros.*   Virgil.

Sing, while beside the shaded tomb I mourn,
And with fresh bays her rural shrine adorn.   20

Thyrsis

  Ye gentle Muses, leave your crystal spring,
Let nymphs and sylvans° cypress garlands bring;
Ye weeping Loves, the stream with myrtles° hide,
And break your bows, as when Adonis died;
And with your golden darts, now useless grown,
Inscribe a verse on this relenting° stone:
'Let nature change, let heaven and earth deplore,
Fair Daphne's dead, and love is now no more!'
  'Tis done, and nature's various charms decay,
See gloomy clouds obscure the cheerful day!   30
Now hung with pearls the dropping trees appear,
Their faded honours scattered on her bier.
See, where on earth the flowery glories lie,
With her they flourished, and with her they die.
Ah what avail the beauties nature wore?
Fair Daphne's dead, and beauty is no more!°
  For her the flocks refuse their verdant food,
The thirsty heifers shun the gliding flood.
The silver swans her hapless fate bemoan,
In notes more sad than when they sing their own.   40
In hollow caves sweet Echo° silent lies,
Silent, or only to her name replies;
Her name with pleasure once she taught the shore,
Now Daphne's dead, and pleasure is no more!
  No grateful dews descend from evening skies,
Nor morning odours from the flowers arise;
No rich perfumes refresh the fruitful field,
Nor fragrant herbs their native incense yield.
The balmy zephyrs, silent since her death,
Lament the ceasing of a sweeter breath.   50
Th' industrious bees neglect their golden store;
Fair Daphne's dead, and sweetness is no more!°

---

23 f. *Inducite fontibus umbras—*
    Et tumulum facite, et tumulo superaddite carmen.
38. *For her the flocks the dewy herb disdain,*
    Nor hungry heifers graze the tender plain.

No more the mounting larks, while Daphne sings,
Shall listening in mid air suspend their wings;
No more the birds shall imitate her lays,
Or hushed with wonder, hearken from the sprays:
No more the streams their murmurs shall forbear,
A sweeter music than their own to hear,
But tell the reeds, and tell the vocal shore,
Fair Daphne's dead, and music is no more!   60

   Her fate is whispered by the gentle breeze,
And told in sighs to all the trembling trees;
The trembling trees, in every plain and wood,
Her fate remurmur to the silver flood;
The silver flood, so lately calm, appears
Swelled with new passion, and o'erflows with tears;
The winds and trees and floods her death deplore,
Daphne, our grief! our glory now no more!

   But see! where Daphne wondering mounts on high,
Above the clouds, above the starry sky!   70
Eternal beauties grace the shining scene,
Fields ever fresh, and groves for ever green!
There while you rest in amaranthine° bowers,
Or from those meads select unfading flowers,
Behold us kindly, who your name implore,
Daphne, our Goddess, and our grief no more!

Lycidas

   How all things listen, while thy Muse complains!
Such silence waits on Philomela's strains,
In some still evening, when the whispering breeze
Pants on the leaves, and dies upon the trees.   80
To thee, bright goddess, oft a lamb shall bleed,
If teeming ewes increase my fleecy breed.
While plants their shade, or flowers their odours give,
Thy name, thy honour, and thy praise shall live!

69, 70. *miratur limen Olympi,*
    Sub pedibusque vidit nubes et sydera Daphnis.
                           Virgil.

81.   *illius aram*
Saepe tener nostris ab ovilibus imbuet agnus.
                           Virgil.

Thyrsis

But see, Orion° sheds unwholesome dews,
Arise, the pines a noxious shade diffuse;
Sharp Boreas blows, and nature feels decay,
Time conquers all, and we must Time obey.°
Adieu, ye vales, ye mountains, streams and groves,
Adieu, ye shepherd's rural lays and loves;   90
Adieu, my flocks, farewell ye sylvan crew,
Daphne farewell, and all the world adieu!

AN
ESSAY
ON
CRITICISM
Written in the Year MDCCIX

CONTENTS
PART I

86. *solet esse gravis cantantibus umbra,*
    Juniperi gravis umbra.
                        Virgil.

89 f. These four last lines allude to the several subjects of the four *Pastorals*, and
to the several scenes of them, particularized before in each.°

That therefore the Ancients *are necessary to be studied by a critic, particularly*
   Homer *and* Virgil, v. 120 *to* 138.
Of licenses, *and the use of them by the Ancients,* v. 140 *to* 180.
Reverence due to the Ancients, *and praise of them,* v. 181, *etc.*

PART II. Ver. 203, etc.

Causes hindering a true judgment. 1. Pride, v. 208. 2. Imperfect learning,
v. 215. 3. *Judging by* parts, *and not by the* whole, v. 233 *to* 288. *Critics
in* wit, language, versification, *only,* v. 288. 305. 339, *etc.* 4. *Being too
hard to please, or too apt to admire,* v. 384. 5. Partiality—*too much love to
a* sect,—*to the* Ancients *or* Moderns, v. 394. 6. Prejudice *or* Prevention,
v. 408. 7. Singularity, v. 424. 8. Inconstancy, v. 430. 9. Party spirit,
v. 452, *etc.* 10. Envy, v. 466. *Against envy, and in praise of good nature,*
v. 508, *etc. When severity is chiefly to be used by critics,* v. 526, *etc.*

PART III. Ver. 560, etc.

Rules for the conduct *of* manners *in a critic,* 1. Candour, v. 563. Modesty,
v. 566. Good breeding, v. 572. Sincerity, *and* freedom *of advice,* v. 578.
2. *When one's counsel is to be restrained,* v. 584. *Character of an* incorrigible
poet, v. 600. *And of an* impertinent critic, v. 610, *etc. Character of a* good
critic, v. 629. *The* history *of* criticism, *and characters of the best critics,*
Aristotle, v. 645. Horace, v. 653. Dionysius, v. 665. Petronius, v. 667.
Quintilian, v. 670. Longinus, v. 675. *Of the decay of criticism, and its
revival.* Erasmus, v. 693. Vida, v. 705. Boileau, v. 714. Lord Roscom-
mon, *etc.* v. 725. *Conclusion.*

—Si quid novisti rectius istis,
Candidus imperti; si non, his utere mecum.

HORACE.°

'Tis hard to say, if greater want of skill   1
Appear in writing or in judging ill;
But, of the two, less dangerous is th' offence
To tire our patience, than mislead our sense.
Some few in that, but numbers err in this,
Ten censure wrong for one who writes amiss;
A fool might once himself alone expose,

Now one in verse makes many more in prose.°
'Tis with our judgments as our watches, none
Go just alike, yet each believes his own.   10
In poets as true genius is but rare,
True taste as seldom is the critic's share;
Both must alike from Heaven derive their light,
These born to judge, as well as those to write.°
Let such teach others who themselves excel,
And censure freely who have written well.
Authors are partial to their wit, 'tis true,
But are not critics to their judgment too?

   Yet if we look more closely, we shall find
Most have the seeds of judgment in their mind: 20
Nature affords at least a glimmering light;
The lines, though touched but faintly, are drawn right.
But as the slightest sketch, if justly traced,
Is by ill-colouring but the more disgraced,
So by false learning is good sense defaced:
Some are bewildered in the maze of schools,°
And some made coxcombs Nature meant but fools.
In search of wit these lose their common sense,°
And then turn critics in their own defence:
Each burns alike, who can, or cannot write,   30
Or with a rival's, or an eunuch's spite.
All fools have still an itching to deride,
And fain would be upon the laughing side.
If Maevius° scribble in Apollo's spite,°
There are, who judge still worse than he can write.

   Some have at first for wits, then poets passed,

15. *Qui scribit artificiose, ab aliis commode scripta facile intelligere poterit.* Cicero *ad Herenn.* lib. 4. *De pictore, sculptore, fictore, nisi artifex, judicare non potest.* Pliny.

20. *Omnes tacito quodam sensu, sine ulla arte, aut ratione, quae sint in artibus ac rationibus recta et prava dijudicant.* Cicero *de Orat.* lib. iii.°

25. *Plus sine doctrina prudentia, quam sine prudentia valet doctrina.* Quintilian.

Between v. 25 and 26 were these lines:
        Many are spoiled by that pedantic throng,
        Who with great pains teach youth to reason wrong.
        Tutors, like virtuosos, oft inclined
        By strange transfusion to improve the mind,
        Draw off the sense we have, to pour in new;
        Which yet, with all their skill, they ne'er could do.

Turned critics next, and proved plain fools at last.
Some neither can for wits nor critics pass,
As heavy mules are neither horse nor ass.
Those half-learned witlings, numerous in our isle,   40
As half-formed insects on the banks of Nile;
Unfinished things, one knows not what to call,
Their generation's so equivocal:°
To tell° 'em, would a hundred tongues require,
Or one vain wit's, that might a hundred tire.
    But you who seek to give and merit fame,
And justly bear a critic's noble name,
Be sure yourself and your own reach to know,
How far your genius, taste, and learning go;
Launch not beyond your depth, but be discreet,   50
And mark that point where sense and dullness meet.
    Nature to all things fixed the limits fit,
And wisely curbed proud man's pretending wit.
As on the land while here the ocean gains,
In other parts it leaves wide sandy plains;
Thus in the soul while memory prevails,
The solid power of understanding fails;
Where beams of warm imagination play,
The memory's soft figures melt away.
One science only will one genius fit;   60
So vast is art,° so narrow human wit:
Not only bounded to peculiar arts,
But oft in those confined to single parts.
Like kings we lose the conquests gained before,
By vain ambition still to make them more;
Each might his several province well command,
Would all but stoop° to what they understand.
    First follow *Nature*, and your judgment frame
By her just standard, which is still° the same:
Unerring NATURE, still divinely bright,   70
One clear, unchanged, and universal light,
Life, force, and beauty, must to all impart,
At once the source, and end, and test of art.
Art from that fund each just supply provides,
Works without show, and without pomp presides:
In some fair body thus th' informing° soul
With spirits° feeds, with vigour fills the whole,

Each motion guides, and every nerve sustains;
Itself unseen, but in th' effects, remains.
Some, to whom Heaven in wit has been profuse,   80
Want as much more, to turn it to its use;
For wit and judgment often are at strife,
Though meant each other's aid, like man and wife.
'Tis more to guide, than spur the Muse's steed;°
Restrain his fury, than provoke his speed;
The winged courser, like a generous° horse,
Shows most true mettle when you check his course.
  Those RULES of old discovered, not devised,
Are Nature still, but Nature methodized;
Nature, like liberty, is but restrained   90
By the same laws which first herself ordained.
  Hear how learned Greece her useful rules indites,
When to repress, and when indulge our flights:
High on Parnassus' top her sons she showed,
And pointed out those arduous paths they trod;
Held from afar, aloft, th' immortal prize,
And urged the rest by equal steps to rise.
Just precepts thus from great examples given,
She drew from them what they derived from Heaven.
The generous critic fanned the poet's fire,   100
And taught the world with reason to admire.
Then criticism the Muse's handmaid proved,
To dress her charms, and make her more beloved:
But following wits from that intention strayed,
Who could not win the mistress, wooed the maid;
Against the poets their own arms they turned,
Sure to hate most the men from whom they learned.
So modern 'pothecaries, taught the art
By doctor's bills° to play the doctor's part,
Bold in the practice of mistaken rules,   110
Prescribe, apply, and call their masters fools.°
Some on the leaves of ancient authors prey,
Nor time nor moths e'er spoiled so much as they.
Some drily plain, without invention's aid,
Write dull receipts° how poems may be made.

---

98. *Nec enim artibus editis factum est ut argumenta inveniremus, sed dicta sunt omnia antequam praeciperentur: mox ea scriptores observata et collecta ediderunt.* Quintilian.

These leave the sense, their learning to display,
And those explain the meaning quite away.
  You then whose judgment the right course would steer,
Know well each ANCIENT's proper character;
His fable,° subject, scope in every page;   120
Religion, country, genius of his age:
Without all these at once before your eyes,
Cavil you may, but never criticize.
Be Homer's works your study, and delight,
Read them by day, and meditate by night;
Thence form your judgment, thence your maxims bring,
And trace the Muses upward to their spring.
Still with itself compared, his text peruse;
And let your comment° be the Mantuan Muse.°
  When first young Maro° in his boundless mind   130
A work t'outlast immortal Rome designed,
Perhaps he seemed above the critic's law,
And but from Nature's fountains scorned to draw:
But when t'examine every part he came,
Nature and Homer were, he found, the same.
Convinced, amazed, he checks the bold design; ⎫
And rules as strict his laboured work confine, ⎬
As if the Stagyrite° o'erlooked each line.   ⎭
Learn hence for ancient rules a just esteem;
To copy nature is to copy them.   140
  Some beauties yet no precepts can declare,°
For there's a happiness° as well as care.

Between 123 and 124 were these lines:
  Zoilus, had these been known, without a name
  Had died, and Perrault ne'er been damned to fame;
  The sense of sound Antiquity had reigned,
  And sacred Homer yet been unprophaned.
  None e'er had thought his comprehensive mind ⎫
  To modern-customs, modern rules confined;   ⎬
  Who for all ages writ, and all mankind.°   ⎭

130. Virgil *Ecl.* vi. *Cum canerem reges et proelia, Cynthius aurem*
                              Vellit.

It is a tradition preserved by Servius, that Virgil began with writing a poem of the
Alban and Roman affairs; which he found above his years, and descended first to
imitate Theocritus on rural subjects, and afterwards to copy Homer in heroic poetry.

Music resembles poetry, in each
Are nameless graces which no methods teach,)
And which a master-hand alone can reach.)
If, where the rules not far enough extend,
(Since rules were made but to promote their end)
Some lucky licence answers to the full
Th'intent proposed, that licence is a rule.
Thus Pegasus, a nearer way to take,   150
May boldly deviate from the common track.
Great wits sometimes may gloriously offend,
And rise to faults true critics dare not mend;
From vulgar bounds with brave disorder part,
And snatch a grace beyond the reach of art,°
Which without passing through the judgment, gains
The heart, and all its end at once attains.
In prospects thus, some objects please our eyes,)
Which out of nature's common order rise,)
The shapeless rock, or hanging precipice.)   160
But though the Ancients thus their rules invade,
(As kings dispense with laws themselves have made)
Moderns, beware! or if you must offend
Against the precept, ne'er transgress its end;
Let it be seldom, and compelled by need;
And have, at least, their precedent to plead.
The critic else proceeds without remorse,
Seizes° your fame, and puts his laws in force.
   I know there are, to whose presumptuous thoughts
Those freer beauties, ev'n in them, seem faults.°   170
Some figures monstrous and mis-shaped appear,
Considered singly, or beheld too near,
Which, but proportioned to their light, or place,
Due distance reconciles to form and grace.
A prudent chief not always must display
His powers in equal ranks, and fair array,
But with th'occasion and the place comply,
Conceal his force, nay seem sometimes to fly.
Those oft are stratagems which errors seem,
Nor is it Homer nods,° but we that dream.   180

180. *Modeste, et circumspecto judicio de tantis viris pronunciandum est, ne (quod plerisque accidit) damnent quod non intelligunt. Ac si necesse est in alteram errare partem, omnia eorum legentibus placere, quam multa displicere maluerim.* Quintilian.

Still green with bays each ancient altar stands,
Above the reach of sacrilegious hands;
Secure from flames, from envy's fiercer rage,
Destructive war, and all-involving age.°
See, from each clime the learned their incense bring!
Hear, in all tongues consenting° paeans ring!
In praise so just let every voice be joined,°
And fill the general chorus of mankind.
Hail, bards triumphant! born in happier days;
Immortal heirs of universal praise!   190
Whose honours with increase of ages grow,
As streams roll down, enlarging as they flow;
Nations unborn your mighty names shall sound,
And worlds applaud that must not yet be found!
Oh may some spark of your celestial fire,
The last, the meanest of your sons inspire,
(That on weak wings, from far, pursues your flights;
Glows while he reads, but trembles as he writes)
To teach vain wits a science little known,
T'admire superior sense, and doubt their own!   200

   Of all the causes which conspire to blind
Man's erring judgment, and misguide the mind
What the weak head with strongest bias rules,
Is *pride*, the never-failing vice of fools.
Whatever Nature has in worth deny'd,
She gives in large recruits° of needful pride;
For as in bodies, thus in souls, we find
What wants° in blood and spirits, swelled with wind:
Pride, where wit fails, steps in to our defence,
And fills up all the mighty void of sense.   210
If once right reason drives that cloud away,
Truth breaks upon us with resistless day.
Trust not yourself; but your defects to know,
Make use of every friend—and every foe.
   A *little learning* is a dangerous thing;
Drink deep, or taste not the Pierian spring:°
There shallow draughts intoxicate the brain,
And drinking largely sobers us again.
Fired at first sight with what the Muse imparts,
In fearless youth we tempt° the heights of arts,   220

While from the bounded level of our mind,
Short views we take, nor see the lengths behind;
But, more advanced, behold with strange surprise
New distant scenes of endless science° rise!
So pleased at first the towering Alps we try,
Mount o'er the vales, and seem to tread the sky,
Th' eternal snows appear already past,
And the first clouds and mountains seem the last:
But, those attained, we tremble to survey
The growing labours of the lengthened way,   230
Th' increasing prospect tires our wandering eyes,
Hills peep o'er hills, and Alps on Alps arise!
   A perfect judge will read each work of wit
With the same spirit that its author writ:
Survey the WHOLE, nor seek slight faults to find
Where nature moves, and rapture warms the mind;
Nor lose, for that malignant dull delight,
The generous pleasure to be charmed with wit.
But in such lays as neither ebb, nor flow,
Correctly cold, and regularly low,   240
That shunning faults, one quiet tenor keep;
We cannot blame indeed—but we may sleep.
In wit, as nature, what affects our hearts
Is not th' exactness of peculiar parts;
'Tis not a lip, or eye, we beauty call,
But the joint force and full result of all.
Thus when we view some well-proportioned dome,
(The world's just wonder, and ev'n thine, O Rome!)°
No single parts unequally surprise,
All comes united to th' admiring eyes;   250
No monstrous height, or breadth, or length appear;
The whole at once is bold, and regular.
    Whoever thinks a faultless piece to see,
Thinks what ne'er was, nor is, nor e'er shall be.

225.   *So pleased at first the towering Alps to try,*
        Filled with ideas of fair Italy,
        The traveller beholds with cheerful eyes
        The lessening vales, and seems to tread the skies.

233. *Diligenter legendum est, ac poene ad scribendi sollicitudinem: Nec per partes modo scrutanda sunt omnia, sed perlectus liber utique ex integro resumendus.* Quintilian.

In every work regard the writer's end,
Since none can compass more than they intend;
And if the means be just, the conduct true,
Applause, in spite of trivial faults, is due.
As men of breeding, sometimes men of wit,
T' avoid great errors, must the less commit: 260
Neglect the rules each verbal critic° lays,
For not to know some trifles, is a praise.
Most critics, fond of some subservient art,
Still make the whole depend upon a part:
They talk of principles, but notions prize,
And all to one loved folly sacrifice.

    Once on a time, La Mancha's knight, they say,
A certain bard encountering on the way,
Discoursed in terms as just, with looks as sage,
As e'er could Dennis,° of the Grecian stage;   270
Concluding all were desperate sots and fools,
Who durst depart from Aristotle's rules.
Our author, happy in a judge so nice,°
Produced his play, and begged the knight's advice;
Made him observe the subject, and the plot,
The manners, passions, unities;° what not?
All which, exact to rule, were brought about,
Were but a combat in the lists left out.
'What! leave the combat out?' exclaims the knight;
Yes, or we must renounce the Stagyrite.   280
'Not so by Heaven' (he answers in a rage)
'Knights, squires, and steeds, must enter on the stage.'
So vast a throng the stage can ne'er contain.
'Then build a new, or act it in a plain.'°

    Thus critics, of less judgment than caprice,
Curious not knowing, not exact but nice,
Form short ideas; and offend in arts
(As most in manners) by a love to parts.

    Some to *conceit* alone their taste confine,
And glittering thoughts struck out at every line;   290
Pleased with a work where nothing's just or fit;
One glaring chaos and wild heap of wit.
Poets like painters, thus, unskilled to trace
The naked nature and the living grace,
With gold and jewels cover every part,

And hide with ornaments their want of art.°
True wit is nature to advantage dressed,
What oft was thought, but ne'er so well expressed;
Something, whose truth convinced at sight we find,
That gives us back the image of our mind.   300
As shades more sweetly recommend the light,
So modest plainness sets off sprightly wit.
For works may have more wit than does 'em good,
As bodies perish through excess of blood.

    Others for *language* all their care express,
And value books, as women men, for dress:
Their praise is still,—the style is excellent:
The sense, they humbly take upon content.°
Words are like leaves; and where they most abound,
Much fruit of sense beneath is rarely found.   310
False eloquence, like the prismatic glass,
Its gaudy colours spreads on every place;
The face of nature we no more survey,
All glares alike, without distinction gay:
But true expression, like th' unchanging sun,   ⎞
Clears, and improves whate'er it shines upon,   ⎬
It gilds all objects, but it alters none.   ⎠
Expression is the dress of thought, and still
Appears more decent, as more suitable;
A vile conceit in pompous words expressed,   320
Is like a clown° in regal purple dressed:
For different styles with different subjects sort,
As several garbs with country, town, and court.°
Some by old words to fame have made pretence,
Ancients in phrase, mere moderns in their sense:
Such laboured nothings, in so strange a style,
Amaze th' unlearned, and make the learned smile.

---

297. *Naturam intueamur, hanc sequamur: id facillime accipiunt animi quod agnoscunt.* Quintilian lib. viii. c. 3.

324. *Abolita et abrogata retinere, insolentiae cujusdam est, et frivolae in parvis jactantiae.* Quintilian lib. i. c. 6.

Opus est ut verba a vetustate repetita neque crebra sint, neque manifesta, quia nil est odiosius affectatione, nec utique ab ultimis repetita temporibus. Oratio cujus summa virtus est perspicuitas, quam sit vitiosa, si egeat interprete? Ergo ut novorum optima erunt maxime vetera, ita veterum maxime nova. Idem.

Unlucky, as Fungoso° in the play,
These sparks with awkward vanity display
What the fine gentleman wore yesterday;   330
And but so mimic ancient wits at best,
As apes our grandsires, in their doublets dressed.
In words, as fashions, the same rule will hold;
Alike fantastic, if too new, or old;
Be not the first by whom the new are tried,
Nor yet the last to lay the old aside.

  But most by numbers° judge a poet's song,
And smooth or rough, with them, is right or wrong;
In the bright Muse though thousand charms conspire,
Her voice is all these tuneful fools admire;   340
Who haunt Parnassus but to please their ear,
Not mend their minds; as some to church repair,
Not for the doctrine, but the music there.
These equal syllables alone require,
Though oft the ear the open vowels° tire;
While expletives their feeble aid do join;
And ten low words oft creep in one dull line;
While they ring round the same unvaried chimes,
With sure returns of still expected rhymes.
Where-e'er you find 'the cooling western breeze,'   350
In the next line, it 'whispers through the trees;'
If crystal streams 'with pleasing murmurs creep,'
The reader's threatened (not in vain) with 'sleep.'
Then, at the last and only couplet fraught
With some unmeaning thing they call a thought,
A needless Alexandrine ends the song,
That, like a wounded snake, drags its slow length along.°
Leave such to tune their own dull rhymes, and know
What's roundly smooth, or languishingly slow;

---

328. *See* Ben Jonson's *Every Man in* [rather, *out of*] *his Humour.*

337.   *Quis populi sermo est? quis enim? nisi carmine molli*
              Nunc demum numero fluere, ut per laeve severos
              Effundat junctura ungues: scit tendere versum
              Non secus ac si oculo rubricam dirigat uno.

                                          Persius *Sat.* i.

345. *Fugiemus crebras vocalium concursiones, quae vastam atque hiantem orationem reddunt.* Cicero *ad Herenn.* lib. iv. Vide etiam Quintilian lib. ix. c. 4.

And praise the easy vigour of a line,   360
Where Denham's strength,° and Waller's sweetness° join.
True ease in writing comes from art, not chance,
As those move easiest who have learned to dance.
'Tis not enough no harshness gives offence,
The sound must seem an echo to the sense:
Soft is the strain when Zephyr gently blows,
And the smooth stream in smoother numbers flows;
But when loud surges lash the sounding shore,
The hoarse, rough verse should like the torrent roar.
When Ajax strives, some rock's vast weight to throw,   370
The line too labours, and the words move slow;
Not so, when swift Camilla° scours the plain,
Flies o'er th' unbending corn, and skims along the main.
Hear how Timotheus'° varied lays surprise,
And bid alternate passions fall and rise!
While, at each change, the son of Libyan Jove°
Now burns with glory, and then melts with love;
Now his fierce eyes with sparkling fury glow,
Now sighs steal out, and tears begin to flow:
Persians and Greeks like turns of nature found,   380
And the world's victor stood subdued by sound!
The power of music all our hearts allow,
And what Timotheus was, is DRYDEN now.

Avoid *extremes*; and shun the fault of such,
Who still are pleased too little or too much.
At every trifle scorn to take offence,
That always shows great pride, or little sense;
Those heads, as stomachs, are not sure the best,
Which nauseate all, and nothing can digest.
Yet let not each gay turn° thy rapture move,   390
For fools admire, but men of sense approve:
As things seem large which we through mists descry,
Dulness is ever apt to magnify.

Some foreign writers, some our own despise;
The Ancients only, or the Moderns prize.
Thus wit, like faith, by each man is applied
To one small sect, and all are damned beside.
Meanly they seek the blessing° to confine,

374. *See* Alexander's Feast, *or* the Power of Music; *an ode by Mr Dryden.*

And force that sun but on a part to shine,
Which not alone the southern wit sublimes,°   400
But ripens spirits in cold northern climes;
Which from the first has shone on ages past,
Enlights the present, and shall warm the last:
Though each may feel increases and decays,
And see now clearer and now darker days.
Regard not then if wit be old or new,
But blame the false, and value still the true.

    Some ne'er advance a judgment of their own,
But catch the spreading notion of the town;
They reason and conclude by precedent,   410
And own stale nonsense which they ne'er invent.
Some judge of authors' names, not works, and then
Nor praise nor blame the writings, but the men.
Of all this servile herd, the worst is he
That in proud dulness joins with quality.°
A constant critic at the great man's board,
To fetch and carry nonsense for my Lord.
What woeful stuff this madrigal would be,
In some starved hackney sonneteer,° or me?
But let a lord once own the happy lines,   420
How the wit brightens! how the style refines!
Before his sacred name flies every fault,
And each exalted stanza teems with thought!

    The vulgar thus through imitation err;
As oft the learned by being singular;
So much they scorn the crowd, that if the throng
By chance go right, they purposely go wrong:
So schismatics° the plain believers quit,
And are but damned for having too much wit.

    Some praise at morning what they blame at night;   430
But always think the last opinion right.
A Muse by these is like a mistress used,
This hour she's idolized, the next abused;
While their weak heads, like towns unfortified,
'Twixt sense and nonsense daily change their side.
Ask them the cause; they're wiser still, they say;
And still tomorrow's wiser than today.
We think our fathers fools, so wise we grow;
Our wiser sons, no doubt, will think us so.

Once school-divines° this zealous isle o'er-spread;   440
Who knew most sentences,° was deepest read;
Faith, gospel, all, seemed made to be disputed,
And none had sense enough to be confuted:
Scotists and Thomists,° now, in peace remain,
Amidst their kindred cobwebs in Duck Lane.
If faith itself has different dresses worn,
What wonder modes in wit should take their turn?
Oft, leaving what is natural and fit,
The current folly proves the ready wit;
And authors think their reputation safe,   450
Which lives as long as fools are pleased to laugh.
    Some valuing those of their own side or mind,
Still make themselves the measure of mankind:
Fondly° we think we honour merit then,
When we but praise ourselves in other men.
Parties in wit attend on those of state,
And public faction doubles private hate.
Pride, Malice, Folly, against Dryden rose,
In various shapes of parsons, critics, beaux;°
But sense survived, when merry jests were past;   460
For rising merit will buoy up at last.
Might he return, and bless once more our eyes,
New Blackmores and new Milbournes° must arise:
Nay should great Homer lift his awful head,
Zoilus° again would start up from the dead.
Envy will merit, as its shade, pursue;
But like a shadow, proves the substance true;

445. A place where old and second-hand books were sold formerly, near Smithfield.°

447. Between this and 448:

> The rhyming clowns that gladded Shakespeare's age,
> No more with crambo entertain the stage.
> Who now in anagrams their patron praise,
> Or sing their mistress in acrostic lays?
> Ev'n pulpits pleased with merry puns of yore;
> Now all are banished to the Hibernian shore!
> Thus leaving what was natural and fit,
> The current folly proved their ready wit;
> And authors thought their reputation safe,
> Which lived as long as fools were pleased to laugh.

For envied wit, like Sol eclipsed, makes known
Th' opposing body's grossness, not its own.
When first that sun too powerful beams displays,   470
It draws up vapours which obscure its rays;
But ev'n those clouds at last adorn its way,
Reflect new glories, and augment the day.

  Be thou the first true merit to befriend;
His praise is lost, who stays till all commend.
Short is the date, alas, of modern rhymes,
And 'tis but just to let them live betimes.
No longer now that golden age appears,
When patriarch-wits survived a thousand years:
Now length of fame (our second life) is lost,   480
And bare threescore is all ev'n that can boast;
Our sons their fathers failing language see,
And such as Chaucer is, shall Dryden be.
So when the faithful pencil has designed
Some bright idea of the master's mind,
Where a new world leaps out at his command,
And ready Nature waits upon his hand;
When the ripe colours soften and unite,
And sweetly melt into just shade and light,
When mellowing years their full perfection give,   490
And each bold figure just begins to live;
The treacherous colours the fair art betray,
And all the bright creation fades away!

  Unhappy wit, like most mistaken things,
Atones not for that envy which it brings.
In youth alone its empty praise we boast,
But soon the short-lived vanity is lost:
Like some fair flower the early spring supplies,
That gaily blooms, but ev'n in blooming dies.
What is this wit, which must our cares employ?   500
The owner's wife, that other men enjoy;
Then most our trouble still when most admired,
And still the more we give, the more required;
Whose fame with pains we guard, but lose with ease,
Sure some to vex, but never all to please;
'Tis what the vicious fear, the virtuous shun,
By fools 'tis hated, and by knaves undone!

  If wit so much from ignorance undergo,

Ah let not learning too commence its foe!
Of old, those met rewards who could excel,   510
And such were praised who but endeavoured well:
Though triumphs were to generals only due,
Crowns were reserved to grace the soldiers too.
Now, they who reach Parnassus' lofty crown,
Employ their pains to spurn some others down;
And while self-love each jealous writer rules,
Contending wits become the sport of fools:
But still the worst with most regret commend,
For each ill author is as bad a friend.
To what base ends, and by what abject ways,   520
Are mortals urged through sacred° lust of praise!
Ah ne'er so dire a thirst of glory boast,
Nor in the critic let the man be lost.
Good nature and good sense must ever join;
To err is human, to forgive, divine.°
    But if in noble minds some dregs remain
Not yet purged off, of spleen and sour disdain;
Discharge that rage on more provoking crimes,
Nor fear a dearth in these flagitious times.
No pardon vile obscenity should find,   530
Though wit and art conspire to move your mind;
But dulness with obscenity must prove
As shameful sure as impotence in love.
In the fat age of pleasure, wealth, and ease,
Sprung the rank weed, and thrived with large increase;
When love was all an easy monarch's° care;
Seldom at council, never in a war:
Jilts ruled the state, and statesmen farces writ;
Nay wits had pensions, and young lords had wit:
The fair sate panting at a courtier's play,   540
And not a mask° went unimproved away:
The modest fan was lifted up no more,
And virgins smiled at what they blushed before.
The following licence of a foreign reign°
Did all the dregs of bold Socinus° drain;
Then unbelieving priests reformed the nation,

546. The author has omitted two lines which stood here, as containing a *national reflection*, which in his stricter judgment he could not but disapprove on any people whatever.

And taught more pleasant methods of salvation;
Where Heaven's free subjects might their rights dispute,
Lest God himself should seem too absolute:
Pulpits their sacred satire learned to spare,
And vice admired to find a flatterer there!°   550
Encouraged thus, wit's Titans° braved the skies,
And the press groaned with licensed blasphemies.°
These monsters, critics! with your darts engage,
Here point your thunder, and exhaust your rage!
Yet shun their fault, who, scandalously nice,
Will needs mistake an author into vice;
All seems infected that th' infected spy,
As all looks yellow to the jaundiced eye.

    LEARN then what MORALS critics ought to show,   560
For 'tis but half a judge's task, to know.
'Tis not enough, taste, judgment, learning, join;
In all you speak, let truth and candour° shine:
That not alone what to your sense is due
All may allow; but seek your friendship too.

    Be silent always when you doubt your sense;
And speak, though sure, with seeming diffidence:
Some positive, persisting fops we know,
Who, if once wrong, will needs be always so;
But you, with pleasure own your errors past,   570
And make each day a critic on the last.

    'Tis not enough, your counsel still be true;
Blunt truths more mischief than nice falsehoods do;
Men must be taught as if you taught them not,
And things unknown proposed as things forgot.
Without good breeding, truth is disapproved;
That only makes superior sense beloved.

    Be niggards of advice on no pretence;
For the worst avarice is that of sense.
With mean complacence° ne'er betray your trust,   580
Nor be so civil as to prove unjust.
Fear not the anger of the wise to raise;
Those best can bear reproof, who merit praise.

    'Twere well might critics still this freedom take;
But Appius° reddens at each word you speak,
And stares, tremendous, with a threatening eye,

586. This picture was taken to himself by John Dennis, a furious old critic by

Like some fierce tyrant in old tapestry.
Fear most to tax an honourable fool,
Whose right it is, uncensured to be dull;
Such, without wit, are poets when they please,   590
As without learning they can take degrees.°
Leave dangerous truths to unsuccessful satires,°
And flattery to fulsome dedicators,
Whom, when they praise, the world believes no more,
Than when they promise to give scribbling o'er.
'Tis best sometimes your censure to restrain,
And charitably let the dull be vain:
Your silence there is better than your spite,
For who can rail so long as they can write?
Still humming on, their drowsy course they keep,   600
And lashed so long, like tops,° are lashed asleep.
False steps but help them to renew the race,
As, after stumbling, jades will mend their pace.
What crowds of these, impenitently bold,
In sounds and jingling syllables grown old,
Still run on poets, in a raging vein,
Ev'n to the dregs and squeezings of the brain,
Strain out the last dull droppings of their sense,
And rhyme with all the rage of impotence.

    Such shameless bards we have, and yet 'tis true,   610
There are as mad, abandoned critics too.
The bookful blockhead, ignorantly read,
With loads of learnèd lumber in his head,
With his own tongue still edifies his ears,
And always listening to himself appears.
All books he reads, and all he reads assails,
From Dryden's fables down to Durfey's° tales.
With him, most authors steal their works, or buy;
Garth did not write his own *Dispensary*.
Name a new play, and he's the poet's friend,   620

profession, who, upon no other provocation, wrote against this *Essay* and its author,
in a manner perfectly lunatic: for, as to the mention made of him in v. 270. he took
it as a compliment, and said it was treacherously meant to cause him to overlook
this *abuse* of his *person*.

   619. A common slander at that time in prejudice of that deserving author. Our
poet did him this justice, when that slander most prevailed; and it is now (perhaps
the sooner for this very verse) dead and forgotten.

Nay showed his faults—but when would poets mend?
No place so sacred from such fops is barred,
Nor is Paul's church more safe than Paul's church
    yard:°
Nay, fly to altars; there they'll talk you dead:
For fools rush in where angels fear to tread.
Distrustful sense with modest caution speaks,   ⎫
It still looks home, and short excursions makes; ⎬
But rattling nonsense in full volleys breaks,   ⎭
And never shocked, and never turned aside,
Bursts out, resistless, with a thundering tide.   630

    But where's the man, who counsel can bestow,
Still pleased to teach, and yet not proud to know?
Unbiassed, or by favour, or by spite:
Not dully prepossessed, nor blindly right;
Though learned, well-bred; and though well-bred,
    sincere;
Modestly bold, and humanly severe:
Who to a friend his faults can freely show,
And gladly praise the merit of a foe?
Blessed with a taste exact, yet unconfined;
A knowledge both of books and human kind;   640
Generous converse; a soul exempt from pride;
And love to praise, with reason on his side?

    Such once were critics; such the happy few,
Athens and Rome in better ages knew.
The mighty Stagyrite first left the shore,
Spread all his sails, and durst the deeps explore;
He steered securely, and discovered far,
Led by the light of the Maeonian star.°

623. Between this and 624:

> In vain you shrug, and sweat, and strive to fly;
> These know no manners but in poetry.
> They'll stop a hungry chaplain in his grace,
> To treat of unities of time and place.

Between 648 and 649:

> He, when all Nature was subdued before,
> Like his great pupil, sighed, and longed for more:
> Fancy's wild regions yet unvanquished lay,
> A boundless empire, and that owned no sway.
> Poets, etc.

Poets, a race long unconfined, and free,
Still fond and proud of savage liberty,   650
Received his laws; and stood convinced 'twas fit,
Who conquered nature, should preside o'er wit.

Horace still charms with graceful negligence,
And without method talks us into sense,
Will, like a friend, familiarly convey
The truest notions in the easiest way.
He, who supreme in judgment, as in wit,
Might boldly censure, as he boldly writ,
Yet judged with coolness, though he sung with fire,
His precepts teach but what his works inspire.   660
Our critics take a contrary extreme,
They judge with fury, but they write with phlegm.
Nor suffers Horace more in wrong translations
By wits, than critics in as wrong quotations.

See Dionysius° Homer's thoughts refine,
And call new beauties forth from every line!

Fancy and art in gay Petronius° please,
The scholar's learning, with the courtier's ease.

In grave Quintilian's° copious work, we find
The justest rules, and clearest method joined: 670
Thus useful arms in magazines we place,
All ranged in order, and disposed with grace,
But less to please the eye, than arm the hand,
Still fit for use, and ready at command.

Thee, bold Longinus!° all the Nine inspire,
And bless their critic with a poet's fire.
An ardent judge, who zealous in his trust,
With warmth gives sentence, yet is always just;
Whose own example strengthens all his laws,
And is himself that great sublime he draws.   680

Thus long succeeding critics justly reigned,
Licence repressed, and useful laws ordained.
Learning and Rome alike in empire grew;
And arts still followed where her eagles° flew:
From the same foes, at last, both felt their doom,
And the same age saw learning fall, and Rome.°
With tyranny, then superstition joined,

---

665. *Dionysius*] Of Halicarnassus.

As that the body, this enslaved the mind;
Much was believed, but little understood,
And to be dull was construed to be good;
A second deluge learning thus o'er-run,   690
And the monks finished what the Goths begun.

    At length Erasmus, that great, injured name,°
(The glory of the priesthood, and the shame!)
Stemmed the wild torrent of a barbarous age,
And drove those holy vandals off the stage.

    But see! each Muse, in LEO's golden days,°
Starts from her trance, and trims her withered bays!
Rome's ancient Genius, o'er its ruins spread,
Shakes off the dust, and rears his reverend head.   700
Then sculpture and her sister-arts revive;
Stones leaped to form, and rocks began to live;
With sweeter notes each rising temple rung;
A Raphael painted, and a Vida sung.
Immortal Vida: on whose honoured brow
The poet's bays and critics ivy grow:
Cremona now shall ever boast thy name,
As next in place to Mantua, next in fame!

    But soon by impious arms from Latium chased,
Their ancient bounds the banished Muses passed;   710
Thence arts o'er all the northern world advance,
But critic-learning flourished most in France:
The rules a nation, born to serve, obeys;
And Boileau still in right of Horace sways.
But we, brave Britons, foreign laws despised,
And kept unconquered, and uncivilized;
Fierce for the liberties of wit, and bold,
We still defied the Romans, as of old.
Yet some there were, among the sounder few
Of those who less presumed, and better knew,   720
Who durst assert the juster ancient cause,
And here restored wit's fundamental laws.

Between 690 and 691:
    Vain wits and critics were no more allowed,
    When none but saints had licence to be proud.
705. M. Hieronymus Vida, an excellent Latin poet, who wrote an *Art of Poetry* in
verse. He flourished in the time of Leo the Tenth.°

Such was the Muse, whose rules and practice tell,
'Nature's chief masterpiece is writing well.'
Such was Roscommon, not more learned than good,
With manners generous as his noble blood;
To him the wit of Greece and Rome was known,
And every author's merit, but his own.
Such late was Walsh—the Muse's judge and friend,
Who justly knew to blame or to commend;   730
To failings mild, but zealous for desert;
The clearest head, and the sincerest heart.
This humble praise, lamented shade! receive,
This praise at least a grateful Muse may give:
The Muse, whose early voice you taught to sing,
Prescribed her heights, and pruned her tender wing,
(Her guide now lost) no more attempts to rise,
But in low numbers short excursions tries:
Content, if hence th' unlearned their wants may view,
The learned reflect on what before they knew: 740
Careless of censure, nor too fond of fame;
Still pleased to praise, yet not afraid to blame;
Averse alike to flatter, or offend;
Not free from faults, nor yet too vain to mend.

---

723. *Essay on Poetry* by the Duke of Buckingham. Our poet is not the only one of his time who complimented this *Essay*, and its noble author. Mr Dryden had done it very largely in the Dedication to his translation of the *Aeneid*; and Dr Garth in the first edition of his *Dispensary* says,

> The Tiber now no courtly Gallus sees,
> But smiling Thames enjoys his Normanbys.

Though afterwards omitted, when parties were carried so high in the reign of Queen Anne, as to allow no commendation to an opposite in politics. The Duke was all his life a steady adherent to the Church of England party, yet an enemy to the extravagant measures of the court in the reign of Charles II. On which account after having strongly patronized Mr Dryden, a coolness succeeded between them on that poet's absolute attachment to the court, which carried him some lengths beyond what the Duke could approve of. This nobleman's true character had been very well marked by Mr Dryden before,

> the Muse's friend,
> Himself a Muse. In Sanadrin's debate
> True to his prince, but not a slave of state.

> *Absalom and Achitophel.*

Our author was more happy, he was honoured very young with his friendship, and it continued till his death in all the circumstances of a familiar esteem.

SAPPHO
TO
PHAON

Say, lovely youth, that dost my heart command,°   1
Can Phaon's eyes forget his Sappho's hand?
Must then her name the wretched writer prove,
To thy remembrance lost, as to thy love?
Ask not the cause that I new numbers° choose,
The lute neglected, and the lyric muse;
Love taught my tears in sadder notes to flow,
And tuned my heart to elegies of woe.
I burn, I burn, as when through ripened corn
By driving winds the spreading flames are borne!   10
Phaon to Etna's scorching fields retires,°
While I consume with more than Etna's fires!
No more my soul a charm in music finds,
Music has charms alone for peaceful minds.°
Soft scenes of solitude no more can please,
Love enters there, and I'm my own disease.
No more the Lesbian dames° my passion move,
Once the dear objects of my guilty love;
All other loves are lost in only thine,
Ah youth ungrateful to a flame like mine!   20
Whom would not all those blooming charms surprise,
Those heavenly looks, and dear deluding eyes?
The harp and bow would you like Phoebus bear,
A brighter Phoebus Phaon might appear;
Would you with ivy wreath your flowing hair,
Not Bacchus' self with Phaon could compare:
Yet Phoebus loved, and Bacchus felt the flame,
One Daphne warmed, and one the Cretan dame;°
Nymphs° that in verse no more could rival me,
Than even those gods contend in charms with thee.   30
The Muses teach me all their softest lays,

And the wide world resounds with Sappho's praise.
Though great Alcaeus° more sublimely sings,
And strikes with bolder rage the sounding strings,
No less renown attends the moving lyre,
Which Venus tunes, and all her loves inspire.
To me what nature has in charms denied,
Is well by wit's° more lasting flames supplied.
Though short my stature,° yet my name extends
To heaven itself, and earth's remotest ends.   40
Brown as I am, an Ethiopian dame°
Inspired young Perseus with a generous flame;
Turtles and doves of differing hues unite,
And glossy jet is paired with shining white.
If to no charms thou wilt thy heart resign,
But such as merit, such as equal thine,
By none, alas! by none thou canst be moved,
Phaon alone by Phaon must be loved!
Yet once thy Sappho could thy cares employ,
Once in her arms you centered all your joy: 50
No time the dear remembrance can remove,
For oh! how vast a memory has love?
My music, then, you could for ever hear,
And all my words were music to your ear.
You stopped with kisses my enchanting tongue,
And found my kisses sweeter than my song.
In all I pleased, but most in what was best;
And the last joy was dearer than the rest.
Then with each word, each glance, each motion fired,   60
You still enjoyed, and yet you still desired,
Till all dissolving in the trance we lay,
And in tumultuous raptures died away.
The fair Sicilians now thy soul inflame;
Why was I born, ye gods, a Lesbian dame?
But ah beware, Sicilian nymphs! nor boast
That wandering heart which I so lately lost;
Nor be with all those tempting words abused,
Those tempting words were all to Sappho used.
And you that rule Sicilia's happy plains,
Have pity, Venus,° on your poet's pains!   70
Shall fortune still in one sad tenor run,
And still increase the woes so soon begun?

Inured to sorrow from my tender years,
My parent's ashes drank my early tears:
My brother° next, neglecting wealth and fame,
Ignobly burned in a destructive flame:
An infant daughter late my griefs increased,
And all a mother's cares distract my breast.
Alas, what more could fate itself impose,
But thee, the last and greatest of my woes?   80
No more my robes in waving purple flow,
Nor on my hand the sparkling diamonds glow;
No more my locks in ringlets curled diffuse
The costly sweetness of Arabian dews,°
Nor braids of gold the varied tresses bind,
That fly disordered with the wanton wind:
For whom should Sappho use such arts as these?
He's gone, whom only° she desired to please!
Cupid's light darts my tender bosom move,
Still is there cause for Sappho still to love:°   90
So from my birth the sisters° fixed my doom,
And gave to Venus all my life to come;
Or while my Muse in melting notes complains,
My yielding heart keeps measure to my strains.
By charms like thine which all my soul have won,
Who might not—ah! who would not be undone?
For those Aurora Cephalus° might scorn,
And with fresh blushes paint the conscious° morn.
For those might Cynthia° lengthen Phaon's sleep,
And bid Endymion nightly tend his sheep.   100
Venus for those had rapt thee to the skies,
But Mars on thee might look with Venus' eyes.
O scarce a youth, yet scarce a tender boy!
O useful time for lovers to employ!
Pride of thy age, and glory of thy race,
Come to these arms, and melt in this embrace!
The vows you never will return, receive;
And take at least the love you will not give.
See, while I write, my words are lost in tears;
The less my sense, the more my love appears.   110
Sure 'twas not much to bid one kind adieu,
(At least to feign was never hard to you)
'Farewell, my Lesbian love', you might have said,

Or coldly thus, 'Farewell, oh Lesbian maid!'
No tear did you, no parting kiss receive,
Nor knew I then how much I was to grieve.
No lover's gift your Sappho could confer,
And wrongs and woes were all you left with her.
No charge I gave you, and no charge could give,
But this: 'Be mindful of our loves, and live.'   120
Now by the Nine,° those powers adored by me,
And Love, the god that ever waits on thee,
When first I heard (from whom I hardly knew)
That you were fled, and all my joys with you,
Like some sad statue, speechless, pale, I stood,
Grief chilled my breast, and stopped my freezing blood;
No sigh to rise, no tear had power to flow,
Fixed in a stupid lethargy of woe:
But when its way th'impetuous passion found,
I rend my tresses, and my breast I wound,   130
I rave, then weep, I curse, and then complain,
Now swell to rage, now melt in tears again.
Not fiercer pangs° distract the mournful dame,
Whose first-born infant feeds the funeral flame.
My scornful brother with a smile appears,
Insults my woes, and triumphs in my tears,
His hated image ever haunts my eyes,
'And why this grief? thy daughter lives', he cries.
Stung with my love, and furious with despair,
All torn my garments, and my bosom bare,   140
My woes, thy crimes, I to the world proclaim;
Such inconsistent things are love and shame!
'Tis thou art all my care and my delight,
My daily longing, and my dream by night:
Oh night more pleasing than the brightest day,
When fancy gives what absence takes away,
And, dressed in all its visionary charms,
Restores my fair deserter to my arms!
Then round your neck in wanton wreaths I twine,
Then you, methinks, as fondly circle mine: 150
A thousand tender words, I hear and speak;
A thousand melting kisses, give, and take:
Then fiercer joys, I blush to mention these,
Yet while I blush, confess how much they please.

But when, with day, the sweet delusions fly,
And all things wake to life and joy, but I,
As if once more forsaken, I complain,
And close my eyes, to dream of you again:
Then frantic rise, and like some Fury° rove
Through lonely plains, and through the silent grove,   160
As if the silent grove, and lonely plains,
That knew my pleasures, could relieve my pains.
I view the grotto, once the scene of love,
The rocks around, the hanging roofs above,
That charmed me more, with native moss o'ergrown,
Than Phrygian marble, or the Parian stone.°
I find the shades that veiled our joys before;
But, Phaon gone, those shades delight no more.
Here the pressed herbs with bending tops betray
Where oft entwined in amorous folds we lay;   170
I kiss that earth which once was pressed by you,
And all with tears the withering herbs bedew.
For thee the fading trees appear to mourn,
And birds defer their songs till thy return:
Night shades the groves, and all in silence lie,
All, but the mournful Philomel and I:
With mournful Philomel I join my strain,
Of Tereus° she, of Phaon I complain.
     A spring there is, whose silver waters show,
Clear as a glass, the shining sands below: 180
A flowery lotus° spreads its arms above,
Shades all the banks, and seems itself a grove;
Eternal greens the mossy margin grace,
Watched by the sylvan genius of the place.°
Here as I lay, and swelled with tears the flood,
Before my sight a watery virgin stood:
She stood and cried, 'O you that love in vain!
Fly hence, and seek the fair Leucadian main;°
There stands a rock, from whose impending° steep
Apollo's fane° surveys the rolling deep;   190
There injured lovers, leaping from above,
Their flames extinguish, and forget to love.
Deucalion once with hopeless fury burned,°
In vain he loved, relentless Pyrrha scorned;
But when from hence he plunged into the main,

Deucalion scorned, and Pyrrha loved in vain.
Haste, Sappho, haste, from high Leucadia throw
The wretched weight, nor dread the deeps below!'
She spoke, and vanished with the voice—I rise,
And silent tears fall trickling from my eyes. 200
I go, ye nymphs! those rocks and seas to prove;°
How much I fear, but ah, how much I love!
I go, ye nymphs! where furious love inspires;
Let female fears submit to female fires.
To rocks and seas I fly from Phaon's hate,
And hope from seas and rocks a milder fate.
Ye gentle gales, beneath my body blow,
And softly lay me on the waves below!
And thou, kind Love, my sinking limbs sustain,
Spread thy soft wings, and waft me o'er the main, 210
Nor let a lover's death the guiltless flood profane!
On Phoebus' shrine my harp I'll then bestow,
And this inscription shall be placed below.
'Here she who sung, to him that did inspire,
Sappho to Phoebus consecrates her lyre:
What suits with Sappho, Phoebus, suits with thee;
The gift, the giver, and the god agree.'
   But why, alas, relentless youth, ah why
To distant seas must tender Sappho fly?
Thy charms than those may far more powerful be, 220
And Phoebus' self is less a god to me.
Ah! canst thou doom me to the rocks and sea,
O far more faithless and more hard than they?
Ah! canst thou rather see this tender breast
Dashed on these rocks than to thy bosom pressed?
This breast which once, in vain! you liked so well;
Where the loves° played, and where the muses dwell.
Alas! the Muses now no more inspire,
Untuned my lute, and silent is my lyre,
My languid numbers have forgot to flow, 230
And fancy sinks beneath a weight of woe.
Ye Lesbian virgins, and ye Lesbian dames,
Themes of my verse, and objects of my flames,
No more your groves with my glad songs shall ring,
No more these hands shall touch the trembling string:
My Phaon's fled, and I those arts resign

(Wretch that I am, to call that Phaon mine!)
Return, fair youth, return, and bring along
Joy to my soul, and vigour to my song:
Absent from thee, the poet's flame expires;   240
But ah! how fiercely burn the lover's fires?
Gods! can no prayers, no sighs, no numbers move
One savage heart, or teach it how to love?
The winds my prayers, my sighs, my numbers° bear,
The flying winds have lost them all in air!
Oh when, alas! shall more auspicious gales
To these fond eyes restore thy welcome sails?
If you return—ah why these long delays?
Poor Sappho dies while careless Phaon stays.
O launch thy bark, nor fear the watery plain;   250
Venus for thee shall smooth her native main.
O launch thy bark, secure of prosperous gales;
Cupid for thee shall spread the swelling sails.
If you will fly—(yet ah! what cause can be,
Too cruel youth, that you should fly from me?)
If not from Phaon I must hope for ease,
Ah let me seek it from the raging seas:
To raging seas unpitied I'll remove,
And either cease to live, or cease to love!

EPISTLE
To Miss BLOUNT
With the WORKS of VOITURE

In these gay thoughts the Loves° and Graces shine,   1
And all the writer lives in every line;
His easy art may happy nature seem,
Trifles themselves are elegant in him.
Sure to charm all was his peculiar fate,
Who without flattery pleased the fair and great;
Still with esteem no less conversed than read;
With wit well-natured, and with books well-bred:

His heart, his mistress, and his friend did share,
His time, the Muse, the witty, and the fair. 10
Thus wisely careless, innocently gay,
Cheerful he played the trifle, life, away;
Till fate scarce felt his gentle breath suppressed,
As smiling infants sport themselves to rest.
Ev'n rival wits did Voiture's death deplore,
And the gay mourned who never mourned before;
The truest hearts for Voiture heaved with sighs,
Voiture was wept by all the brightest eyes:
The smiles and loves had died in Voiture's death,
But that for ever in his lines they breathe. 20

Let the strict life of graver mortals be
A long, exact, and serious comedy;
In every scene some moral let it teach,
And, if it can, at once both please and preach.
Let mine, an innocent gay farce appear,
And more diverting still than regular,°
Have humour, wit, a native ease and grace,
Though not too strictly bound to time and place:°
Critics in wit, or life, are hard to please,
Few write to those, and none can live to these. 30

Too much your sex is by their forms° confined,
Severe to all, but most to womankind;
Custom, grown blind with age, must be your guide;
Your pleasure is a vice, but not your pride;
By nature yielding, stubborn but for fame;°
Made slaves by honour, and made fools by shame.
Marriage may all those petty tyrants chase,
But sets up one, a greater in their place;
Well might you wish for change by those accursed,
But the last tyrant ever proves the worst. 40
Still in constraint your suffering sex remains,
Or bound in formal, or in real chains:
Whole years neglected, for some months adored,
The fawning servant turns a haughty lord.
Ah quit not the free innocence of life,
For the dull glory of a virtuous wife;
Nor let false shows, or empty titles please:
Aim not at joy, but rest content with ease.

The gods, to curse Pamela° with her prayers,

Gave the gilt coach and dappled Flanders mares,   50
The shining robes, rich jewels, beds of state,
And, to complete her bliss, a fool for mate.
She glares in balls, front boxes, and the Ring,°
A vain, unquiet, glittering, wretched thing!
Pride, pomp, and state but reach her outward part;
She sighs, and is no Duchess at her heart.

    But, Madam, if the fates withstand, and you
Are destined Hymen's willing victim too;
Trust not too much your now resistless charms,
Those, age or sickness, soon or late, disarms: 60
Good humour only teaches charms to last,
Still° makes new conquests, and maintains the past;
Love, raised on beauty, will like that decay,
Our hearts may bear its slender chain a day;
As flowery bands in wantonness are worn,
A morning's pleasure, and at evening torn;
This° binds in ties more easy, yet more strong,
The willing heart, and only holds it long.

    Thus *Voiture's early care still shone the same,
And Monthausier° was only changed in name: 70
By this, ev'n now they live, ev'n now they charm,
Their wit still sparkling, and their flames still warm.

    Now crowned with myrtle,° on th' Elysian coast,
Amid these lovers, joys his gentle ghost:
Pleased, while with smiles his happy lines you view,
And finds a fairer Rambouillet in you.
The brightest eyes of France inspired his Muse;
The brightest eyes of Britain now peruse;
And dead, as living, 'tis our author's pride
Still to charm those who charm the world beside.   80

* Mademoiselle Paulet.°

WINDSOR FOREST
To the Right Honourable
GEORGE Lord LANSDOWNE°

Non injussa cano: Te nostrae, *Vare*, myricae,
Te *Nemus* omne canet; nec Phoebo gratior ulla est
Quam sibi quae *Vari* praescripsit pagina nomen.

VIRGIL.°

Thy forests, Windsor!° and thy green retreats,   1
At once the monarch's and the muse's seats,
Invite my lays. Be present, sylvan maids!
Unlock your springs, and open all your shades.
GRANVILLE° commands; your aid, O muses, bring!
What muse for GRANVILLE can refuse to sing?
  The groves of Eden, vanished now so long,
Live in description, and look green in song:
These, were my breast inspired with equal flame,
Like them in beauty, should be like in fame.°   10
Here hills and vales, the woodland and the plain,
Here earth and water seem to strive again,
Not chaos-like together crushed and bruised,
But, as the world, harmoniously confused:°
Where order in variety we see,
And where, though all things differ, all agree.
Here waving groves a chequered scene display,
And part admit, and part exclude the day;
As some coy nymph her lover's warm address

This poem was written at two different times: the first part of it, which relates to
the country, in the year 1704, at the same time with the *Pastorals*: the latter part was
not added till the year 1713, in which it was published.

  3 f. originally thus,

Chaste Goddess of the woods,
Nymphs of the vales, and naiads of the floods,
Lead me through arching bowers, and glimmering glades.
Unlock your springs—

Nor quite indulges, nor can quite repress.   20
There, interspersed in lawns° and opening glades,
Thin trees arise that shun each other's shades.
Here in full light the russet plains extend:
There wrapped in clouds the blueish hills ascend.
Ev'n the wild heath displays her purple dyes,
And 'midst the desert° fruitful fields arise,
That crowned with tufted trees° and springing corn,
Like verdant isles the sable waste adorn.
Let India boast her plants, nor envy we
The weeping amber or the balmy tree,
While by our oaks the precious loads are borne,°   30
And realms commanded which those trees adorn.
Not proud Olympus yields a nobler sight,
Though Gods assembled grace his towering height,
Than what more humble mountains offer here,
Where, in their blessings, all those Gods appear.
See Pan with flocks, with fruits Pomona° crowned,
Here blushing Flora paints th'enamelled ground,°
Here Ceres' gifts in waving prospect stand,
And nodding tempt the joyful reaper's hand;   40
Rich Industry sits smiling on the plains,
And peace and plenty tell, a STUART° reigns.

     Not thus the land appeared in ages past,
A dreary desert, and a gloomy waste,
To savage beasts and savage laws a prey,
And kings more furious and severe than they;
Who claimed the skies, dispeopled air and floods,
The lonely lords of empty wilds and woods:
Cities laid waste, they stormed the dens and caves,
(For wiser brutes were backward to be slaves.)   50
What could be free, when lawless beasts obeyed,
And ev'n the elements a tyrant swayed?
In vain kind seasons swelled the teeming grain,

25. Originally thus,

> *Why should I sing our better suns or air,*
> *Whose vital draughts prevent the leech's care,*
> *While through fresh fields th' enlivening odours breathe,*
> *Or spread with vernal blooms the purple heath?*

45. *savage laws*] The forest laws.°

Soft showers distilled, and suns grew warm in vain;
The swain with tears his frustrate labour yields,
And famished dies amidst his ripened fields.
What wonder then, a beast or subject slain
Were equal crimes in a despotic reign?
Both doomed alike, for sportive tyrants bled,
But while the subject starved, the beast was fed.   60
Proud Nimrod° first the bloody chase began,
A mighty hunter, and his prey was man:
Our haughty Norman boasts that barbarous name,
And makes his trembling slaves the royal game.
The fields are ravished from th'industrious swains,
From men their cities, and from Gods their fanes:°
The levelled towns with weeds lie covered o'er;
The hollow winds through naked temples roar;
Round broken columns clasping ivy twined;
O'er heaps of ruin stalked the stately hind;   70
The fox obscene° to gaping tombs retires,
And savage howlings fill the sacred quires.
Awed by his nobles, by his commons cursed,
Th'oppressor ruled tyrannic where he durst,
Stretched o'er the poor and church his iron rod,
And served alike his vassals and his God.
Whom ev'n the Saxon spared and bloody Dane,
The wanton victims of his sport remain.
But see, the man who spacious regions gave
A waste for beasts, himself denied a grave!°   80

57 f. *No wonder savages or subjects slain—*
          But subjects starved while savages were fed.

It was originally thus, but the word savages is not properly applied to beasts but to
men; which occasioned the alteration.

65. Alluding to the destruction made in the New Forest, and the tyrannies exer-
cised there by William I.

65, 66. Translated from

          Templa adimit divis, fora civibus, arva colonis,

by an old monkish writer, I forget who.°

72. *And wolves with howling fill,* etc.

The author thought this an error, wolves not being common in England at the time
of the Conqueror.

Stretched on the lawn his second hope survey,
At once the chaser, and at once the prey:
Lo Rufus, tugging at the deadly dart,
Bleeds in the forest, like a wounded hart.°
Succeeding monarchs heard the subjects' cries,
Nor saw displeased the peaceful cottage rise.
Then gathering flocks on unknown mountains fed,
O'er sandy wilds were yellow harvests spread,
The forests wondered at th' unusual grain,
And secret transport touched the conscious° swain.   90
Fair Liberty, Britannia's Goddess, rears
Her cheerful head, and leads the golden years.°

    Ye vigorous swains! while youth ferments your blood,
And purer spirits swell the sprightly flood,°
Now range the hills, the gameful woods beset,
Wind the shrill horn, or spread the waving net.
When milder autumn summer's heat succeeds,
And in the new-shorn field the partridge feeds,
Before his lord the ready spaniel bounds,
Panting with hope, he tries the furrowed grounds;   100
But when the tainted° gales the game betray,
Couched close he lies, and meditates the prey:
Secure they trust th' unfaithful field, beset,
Till hovering o'er 'em sweeps the swelling net.
Thus (if small things we may with great compare)
When Albion sends her eager sons to war,
Some thoughtless town, with ease and plenty blessed,
Near, and more near, the closing lines invest;
Sudden they seize th' amazed, defenceless prize,
And high in air Britannia's standard flies.°   110

81. *second hope*] Richard, second son of William the Conqueror.°

91.   *Oh may no more a foreign master's rage,*
         With wrongs yet legal, curse a future age!
        Still spread, fair Liberty! thy heavenly wings,
        Breathe plenty on the fields, and fragrance on the springs.

97.   *When yellow autumn summer's heat succeeds,*
        And into wine the purple harvest bleeds,[a]
        The partridge feeding in the new-shorn fields,
        Both morning sports and evening pleasures yields.

  [a] Perhaps the author thought it not allowable to describe the season by a circumstance not proper to our climate, the vintage.

See! from the brake the whirring pheasant springs,
And mounts exulting on triumphant wings:
Short is his joy; he feels the fiery wound,
Flutters in blood, and panting beats the ground.
Ah! what avail his glossy, varying dyes,
His purple crest, and scarlet-circled eyes,
The vivid green his shining plumes unfold,
His painted wings, and breast that flames with gold?
   Nor yet, when moist Arcturus° clouds the sky,
The woods and fields their pleasing toils deny. 120
To plains with well-breathed beagles we repair,
And trace the mazes of the circling hare:
(Beasts, urged by us, their fellow-beasts pursue,
And learn of man each other to undo.)
With slaughtering guns th' unwearied fowler roves,
When frosts have whitened all the naked groves;
Where doves in flocks the leafless trees o'ershade,
And lonely woodcocks haunt the watery glade.
He lifts the tube, and levels with his eye;
Straight a short thunder breaks the frozen sky. 130
Oft, as in airy rings they skim the heath,
The clamorous lapwings feel the leaden death:
Oft, as the mounting larks their notes prepare,
They fall, and leave their little lives in air.
   In genial° spring, beneath the quivering shade,
Where cooling vapours breathe along the mead,
The patient fisher takes his silent stand,
Intent, his angle trembling in his hand;
With looks unmoved, he hopes the scaly breed,
And eyes the dancing cork, and bending reed. 140
Our plenteous streams a various race supply,
The bright-eyed perch with fins of Tyrian dye,°
The silver eel, in shining volumes° rolled,
The yellow carp, in scales bedropped with gold,
Swift trouts, diversified with crimson stains,

119. *When hoary winter clothes the year in white,*
    The woods and fields to pleasing toils invite.
129. *The fowler lifts his levelled tube on high.*

And pikes, the tyrants of the watery plains.
   Now Cancer glows with Phoebus' fiery car:°
The youth rush eager to the sylvan war,
Swarm o'er the lawns, the forest walks surround,
Rouse the fleet hart, and cheer the opening° hound.   150
Th' impatient courser pants in every vein,
And pawing, seems to beat the distant plain:
Hills, vales, and floods appear already crossed,
And e'er he starts, a thousand steps are lost.
See the bold youth strain up the threatening steep,
Rush through the thickets, down the valleys sweep,
Hang o'er their coursers heads with eager speed,
And earth rolls back beneath the flying steed.
Let old Arcadia boast her ample plain,
Th' immortal huntress, and her virgin-train;   160
Nor envy, Windsor! since thy shades have seen
As bright a Goddess, and as chaste a QUEEN;°
Whose care, like hers, protects the sylvan reign,
The earth's fair light, and empress of the main.
   Here too, 'tis sung, of old Diana strayed,
And Cynthus'° top forsook for Windsor shade;
Here was she seen o'er airy wastes to rove,
Seek the clear spring, or haunt the pathless grove;
Here armed with silver bows, in early dawn,
Her buskined virgins traced the dewy lawn.   170
   Above the rest a rural nymph was famed,
Thy offspring, Thames! the fair Lodona named;
(Lodona's fate, in long oblivion cast,
The Muse shall sing, and what she sings shall last.)
Scarce could the Goddess from her nymph be known,
But by the crescent° and the golden zone:°
She scorned the praise of beauty, and the care;
A belt her waist, a fillet° binds her hair;
A painted quiver on her shoulder sounds,
And with her dart the flying deer she wounds.   180
It chanced, as eager of the chase the maid
Beyond the forest's verdant limits strayed,
Pan saw and loved, and burning with desire
Pursued her flight, her flight increased his fire.
Not half so swift the trembling doves can fly,
When the fierce eagle cleaves the liquid° sky;

Not half so swiftly the fierce eagle moves,
When through the clouds he drives the trembling doves;
As from the God she flew with furious pace,
Or as the God, more furious, urged the chase.   190
Now fainting, sinking, pale, the nymph appears;
Now close behind his sounding steps she hears;
And now his shadow reached her as she run,
(His shadow lengthened by the setting sun)
And now his shorter breath, with sultry air,
Pants on her neck, and fans her parting hair.
In vain on Father Thames she calls for aid,
Nor could Diana help her injured maid.
Faint, breathless, thus she prayed, nor prayed in vain;
'Ah Cynthia! ah—though banished from thy train,   200
Let me, O let me, to the shades repair,
My native shades—there weep, and murmur there.'
She said, and melting as in tears she lay,
In a soft, silver stream dissolved away.
The silver stream her virgin coldness keeps,
For ever murmurs, and for ever weeps;
Still bears the name the hapless virgin bore,
And bathes the forest where she ranged before.
In her chaste current oft the Goddess laves,
And with celestial tears augments the waves.   210
Oft in her glass the musing shepherd spies
The headlong mountains and the downward skies.
The watery landskip of the pendant woods,
And absent trees that tremble in the floods;
In the clear azure gleam the flocks are seen,
And floating forests paint the waves with green.
Through the fair scene roll slow the lingering streams,
Then foaming pour along, and rush into the Thames.
    Thou too, great father of the British floods!
With joyful pride surveyst our lofty woods;   220
Where towering oaks their growing honours° rear,
And future navies on thy shores appear.
Not Neptune's self from all her streams receives
A wealthier tribute, than to thine he gives.

207. The River Loddon.°
211–16. These six lines were added after the first writing of this poem.

No seas so rich, so gay no banks appear,
No lake so gentle, and no spring so clear.
Nor Po so swells the fabling poet's lays,
While led along the skies his current strays,°
As thine, which visits Windsor's famed abodes,
To grace the mansion of our earthly Gods: 230
Nor all his stars above a lustre show,
Like the bright beauties on thy banks below;
Where Jove, subdued by mortal passion still,
Might change Olympus for a nobler hill.

    Happy the man whom this bright court approves,
His sovereign favours, and his country loves:
Happy next him, who to these shades retires,
Whom nature charms, and whom the Muse inspires:
Whom humbler joys of home-felt quiet please,
Successive study, exercise, and ease.   240
He gathers health from herbs the forest yields,
And of their fragrant physic spoils the fields:
With chymic art exalts° the mineral powers,
And draws° the aromatic souls of flowers:
Now marks the course of rolling orbs on high;
O'er figured worlds° now travels with his eye;
Of ancient writ unlocks the learned store,
Consults the dead, and lives past ages o'er:
Or wandering thoughtful in the silent wood,
Attends the duties of the wise and good,   250
T'observe a mean, be to himself a friend,
To follow nature, and regard his end;
Or looks on heaven with more than mortal eyes,
Bids his free soul expatiate in the skies,
Amid her kindred° stars familiar roam,
Survey the region, and confess her home!
Such was the life great Scipio° once admired,
Thus Atticus,° and TRUMBULL thus retired.

    Ye sacred Nine! that all my soul possess,
Whose raptures fire me, and whole visions bless,   260

235:       *Happy the man, who to the shades retires,*
        But doubly happy, if the Muse inspires!
        Blessed whom the sweets of home-felt quiet please;
        But far more blessed, who study joins with ease.

Bear me, oh bear me to sequestered scenes,
The bowery mazes, and surrounding greens:
To Thames's banks which fragrant breezes fill,
Or where ye Muses sport on COOPER's HILL.°
(On COOPER's HILL eternal wreaths shall grow,
While lasts the mountain, or while Thames shall flow)
I seem through consecrated walks to rove,
I hear soft music die along the grove:
Led by the sound, I roam from shade to shade,
By god-like poets venerable made: 270
Here his first lays majestic DENHAM sung;
There the last numbers flowed from COWLEY's tongue.
O early lost! what tears the river shed,
When the sad pomp along his banks was led?°
His drooping swans on every note expire,°
And on his willows hung each Muse's lyre.

    Since fate relentless stopped their heavenly voice,
No more the forests ring, or groves rejoice;
Who now shall charm the shades, where COWLEY strung
His living harp, and lofty DENHAM sung?   280
But hark! the groves rejoice, the forest rings!
Are these revived? or is it GRANVILLE sings?
'Tis yours, my lord, to bless our soft retreats,
And call the Muses to their ancient seats;
To paint anew the flowery sylvan scenes,
To crown the forests with immortal greens,
Make Windsor hills in lofty numbers rise,
And lift her turrets nearer to the skies;
To sing those honours you deserve to wear,
And add new lustre to her silver star.°   290

272. Mr Cowley died at Chertsey, on the borders of the Forest, and was from thence conveyed to Westminster.°

275. *What sighs, what murmurs filled the vocal shore!*
His tuneful swans were heard to sing no more.

290. All the lines that follow were not added to the poem till the year 1710.°
What immediately followed this, and made the conclusion, were these,

        My humble Muse in unambitious strains
        Paints the green forests and the flowery plains;
        Where I obscurely pass my careless days,
        Pleased in the silent shade with empty praise,
        Enough for me that to the listening swains
        First in these fields I sung the sylvan strains.

Here noble SURREY felt the sacred rage,
SURREY, the GRANVILLE of a former age:
Matchless his pen, victorious was his lance,
Bold in the lists, and graceful in the dance:
In the same shades the Cupids tuned his lyre,
To the same notes, of love, and soft desire:
Fair Geraldine,° bright object of his vow,
Then filled the groves, as heavenly Myra° now.

Oh wouldst thou sing what heroes Windsor bore,
What kings first breathed upon her winding shore,°   300
Or raise old warriors, whose adored remains
In weeping vaults her hallowed earth contains!
With Edward's acts adorn the shining page,
Stretch his long triumphs down through every age,
Draw monarchs chained,° and Cressi's° glorious field,
The lilies blazing on the regal shield:°
Then, from her roofs when Verrio's colours° fall,
And leave inanimate the naked wall,
Still in thy song should vanquished France appear,
And bleed for ever under Britain's spear.   310
Let softer strains ill-fated Henry° mourn,
And palms eternal flourish round his urn.
Here o'er the Martyr-King the marble weeps,
And fast beside him, once-feared Edward sleeps:
Whom not th' extended Albion could contain,
From old Belerium° to the northern main,
The grave unites; where ev'n the great find rest,
And blended lie th' oppressor and th' oppressed!
Make sacred Charles's tomb for ever known,
(Obscure the place, and un-inscribed the stone)°   320
Oh fact° accursed! what tears has Albion shed,
Heavens, what new wounds! and how her old have bled?
She saw her sons with purple deaths expire,
Her sacred domes involved in rolling fire,
A dreadful series of intestine wars,

291. Henry Howard, Earl of Surrey, one of the first refiners of the English poetry who flourished in the time of Henry VIII.°

303. Edward III born here.°

311. Henry VI.

314. Edward IV.

Inglorious triumphs and dishonest° scars,°
At length great ANNA said—'Let Discord cease!'°
She said, the world obeyed, and all was peace!
　　In that blessed moment from his oozy bed
Old Father Thames advanced his reverend head.　　　　　330
His tresses dropped with dews, and o'er the stream
His shining horns° diffused a golden gleam:
Graved on his urn appeared the moon, that guides
His swelling waters, and alternate tides;
The figured streams in waves of silver rolled,
And on their banks Augusta° rose in gold.
Around his throne the sea-born brothers stood,
Who swell with tributary urns his flood;
First the famed authors of his ancient name,
The winding Isis and the fruitful Thame:°　　　　　　340
The Kennet swift, for silver eels renowned;
The Loddon slow, with verdant alders crowned;
Cole,° whose dark streams his flowery islands lave;
And chalky Wey, that rolls a milky wave:
The blue, transparent Vandalis° appears;
The gulphy° Lea his sedgy tresses rears;
And sullen Mole, that hides his diving flood;°
And silent Darent, stained with Danish blood.°
　　High in the midst, upon his urn reclined,
(His sea-green mantle waving with the wind)　　　　　350
The God appeared: he turned his azure eyes
Where Windsor domes and pompous turrets rise;
Then bowed and spoke; the winds forget to roar,
And the hushed waves glide softly to the shore.°
　　Hail, sacred Peace! hail long-expected days,
That Thames's glory to the stars shall raise!
Though Tiber's streams immortal Rome behold,

Between verse 330 and 331 originally stood these lines,
　　　　From shore to shore exulting shouts he heard,
　　　　O'er all his banks a lambent light appeared,
　　　　With sparkling flames heaven's glowing concave shone,
　　　　Fictitious stars, and glories not her own.
　　　　He saw, and gently rose above the stream;
　　　　His shining horns diffuse a golden gleam:
　　　　With pearl and gold his towery front was dressed,
　　　　The tributes of the distant East and West.

Though foaming Hermus° swells with tides of gold,
From heaven itself though seven-fold Nilus flows,°
And harvests on a hundred realms bestows;   360
These now no more shall be the Muse's themes,
Lost in my fame, as in the sea their streams.
Let Volga's banks° with iron squadrons shine,
And groves of lances glitter on the Rhine,
Let barbarous Ganges° arm a servile train;
Be mine the blessings of a peaceful reign.
No more my sons shall dye with British blood
Red Iber's sands,° or Ister's° foaming flood:
Safe on my shore each unmolested swain
Shall tend the flocks, or reap the bearded grain;   370
The shady empire shall retain no trace
Of war or blood, but in the sylvan chase;
The trumpets sleep, while cheerful horns are blown,
And arms employed on birds and beasts alone.
Behold! th' ascending villas on my side,
Project long shadows o'er the crystal tide.
Behold! Augusta's glittering spires increase,
And temples rise, the beauteous works of peace.
I see, I see where two fair cities° bend
Their ample bow, a new Whitehall° ascend!   380
There mighty nations shall enquire their doom,
The world's great oracle in times to come;
There kings shall sue, and suppliant states be seen
Once more° to bend before a BRITISH QUEEN.
    Thy trees, fair Windsor! now shall leave their woods,
And half thy forests rush into my floods,
Bear Britain's thunder, and her cross° display,
To the bright regions of the rising day;
Tempt° icy seas, where scarce the waters roll,
Where clearer flames glow round the frozen pole;   390

---

378. The fifty new churches.°
385 f. were originally thus,

> Now shall our fleets the bloody cross display
> To the rich regions of the rising day,
> Or those green isles, where headlong Titan steeps
> His hissing axle in th' Atlantic deeps;
> Tempt icy seas, etc.

Or under southern skies exalt their sails,
Led by new stars, and borne by spicy gales!
For me the balm shall bleed, and amber flow,
The coral redden, and the ruby glow,
The pearly shell its lucid globe infold,
And Phoebus warm the ripening ore to gold.°
The time shall come, when free as seas or wind
Unbounded Thames shall flow for all mankind,
Whole nations enter with each swelling tide,
And seas but join the regions they divide;   400
Earth's distant ends our glory shall behold,
And the new world launch forth to seek the old.
Then ships of uncouth form shall stem the tide,
And feathered people crowd my wealthy side,°
And naked youths and painted chiefs admire
Our speech, our colour, and our strange attire!
Oh stretch thy reign, fair Peace! from shore to shore,
Till conquest cease, and slavery be no more;
Till the freed Indians° in their native groves
Reap their own fruits, and woo their sable loves,   410
Peru once more a race of kings° behold,
And other Mexicos be roofed with gold.
Exiled by thee from earth to deepest hell,
In brazen bonds shall barbarous Discord dwell;
Gigantic Pride, pale Terror, gloomy Care,
And mad Ambition shall attend her there:
There purple Vengeance bathed in gore retires,
Her weapons blunted, and extinct her fires:
There hateful Envy her own snakes shall feel,
And Persecution mourn her broken wheel:°   420
There Faction roar, Rebellion bite her chain,
And gasping Furies thirst for blood in vain.°
    Here cease thy flight, nor with unhallowed lays
Touch the fair fame of Albion's golden days:
The thoughts of Gods let GRANVILLE's verse recite,
And bring the scenes of opening fate to light.
My humble Muse, in unambitious strains,
Paints the green forests and the flowery plains,
Where Peace descending bids her olives spring,

398. A wish that London may be made a free port.

And scatters blessings from her dove-like wing. 430
Ev'n I more sweetly pass my careless days,
Pleased in the silent shade with empty praise;
Enough for me, that to the listening swains
First in these fields I sung the sylvan strains.°

THE GUARDIAN, no. 173
TUESDAY, 29 SEPTEMBER 1713

—Nec sera comantem
Narcissum, aut flexi tacuissem Vimen Acanthi,
Pallentesque Haederas, & amantes littora myrtos.

VIRGIL.°

ON GARDENS

I lately took a particular friend of mine to my house in the country, not without some apprehension that it could afford little entertainment to a man of his polite taste, particularly in architecture and gardening, who had so long been conversant with all that is beautiful and great in either. But it was a pleasant surprise to me, to hear him often declare, he had found in my little retirement that beauty which he always thought wanting in the most celebrated seats, or if you will villas, of the nation. This he described to me in those verses with which Martial° begins one of his epigrams:

> *Baiana nostri Villa, Basse, Faustini,*
> *Non otiosis ordinata myrtetis,*
> *Viduaque platano, tonsilique buxeto,*
> *Ingrata lati spatia detinet campi,*
> *Sed rure vero, barbaroque laetatur.*

There is certainly something in the amiable simplicity of unadorned nature, that spreads over the mind a more noble sort of tranquillity, and a loftier sensation of pleasure, than can be raised from the nicer° scenes of art.

This was the taste of the ancients in their gardens, as we may discover from the descriptions that are extant of them. The two most celebrated wits of the world have each of them left us a particular picture of a garden; wherein those great masters, being wholly unconfined, and painting at pleasure, may be thought to have given a full idea of what they esteemed most excellent in this way. These (one may observe) consist entirely of the useful part of horticulture, fruit trees, herbs, water, etc. The pieces I am speaking of are Virgil's account° of the garden of the old Corycian, and Homer's° of that of Alcinous. The first of these is already known to the English reader, by the excellent versions of Mr Dryden and Mr Addison. The other having never been attempted in our language with any elegance, and being the most beautiful plan of this sort that can be imagined, I shall here present the reader with a translation of it.

The Gardens of Alcinous, from Homer's *Odyss. 7.*

Close to the gates a spacious garden lies,
From storms defended and inclement skies:
Four acres was th' allotted space of ground,
Fenced with a green enclosure all around.
Tall thriving trees confessed the fruitful mold;
The reddening apple ripens here to gold,
Here the blue fig with luscious juice o'erflows,
With deeper red the full pomegranate glows,
The branch here bends beneath the weighty pear,
And verdant olives flourish round the year.
The balmy spirit of the western gale
Eternal breathes on fruits untaught to fail:
Each dropping pear a following pear supplies,
On apples apples, figs on figs arise:
The same mild season gives the blooms to blow,
The buds to harden, and the fruits to grow.

Here ordered vines in equal ranks appear
With all th' united labours of the year,
Some to unload the fertile branches run,
Some dry the blackening clusters in the sun,
Others to tread the liquid harvest join,
The groaning presses foam with floods of wine.
Here are the vines in early flower descried, ⎞
Here grapes discoloured on the sunny side, ⎟
And there in Autumn's richest purple dyed. ⎠
Beds of all various herbs, forever green,
In beauteous order terminate the scene.

Two plenteous fountains the whole prospect crowned;)
This through the gardens leads its streams around, |
Visits each plant, and waters all the ground:)
While that in pipes beneath the palace flows,
And thence its current on the town bestows;
To various use their various streams they bring,
The people one, and one supplies the king.

Sir William Temple° has remarked, that this description contains all the justest rules and provisions which can go toward composing the best gardens. Its extent was four acres, which, in those times of simplicity, was looked upon as a large one, even for a prince. It was enclosed all round for defence; and for conveniency joined close to the gates of the palace.

He mentions next the trees, which were standards, and suffered to grow to their full height. The fine description of the fruits that never failed, and the eternal zephyrs, is only a more noble and poetical way of expressing the continual succession of one fruit after another throughout the year.

The *vineyard* seems to have been a plantation distinct from the *garden*; as also the *beds of greens* mentioned afterwards at the extremity of the enclosure, in the nature and usual place of our *kitchen gardens*.

The two fountains are disposed very remarkably. They rose within the enclosure, and were brought by conduits or ducts, one of them to water all parts of the gardens, and the other underneath the palace into the town, for the service of the public.

How contrary to this simplicity is the modern practice of gardening; we seem to make it our study to recede from nature, not only in the various tonsure of greens into the most regular and formal shapes, but even in monstrous attempts beyond the reach of the art itself. We run into sculpture, and are yet better pleased to have our trees in the most awkward figures of men and animals, than in the most regular of their own.

Hinc & nexilibus videas e frondibus hortos,
Implexos late muros, & Moenia circum
Porrigere, & latas e ramis surgere turres;
Deflexam & Myrtum in Puppes, atque aerea rostra:
In buxisque undare fretum, atque e rore rudentes.
Parte alià frondere suis tentoria Castris;
Scutaque spiculaque & jaculantia citria Vallos.°

I believe it is no wrong observation that persons of genius, and those who are most capable of art, are always most fond of nature, as such are chiefly sensible, that all art consists in the imitation and study of nature. On the contrary, people of the common level of understanding are principally delighted with the little niceties and fantastical operations of art, and constantly think that *finest* which is least natural. A citizen is no sooner proprietor of a couple of yews, but he entertains thoughts of erecting them into giants,° like those of Guildhall. I know an eminent cook, who beautified his country seat with a coronation dinner in greens, where you see the Champion flourishing on horseback at one end of the table, and the Queen in perpetual youth at the other.

For the benefit of all my loving countrymen of this curious taste, I shall here publish a catalogue of greens to be disposed of by an eminent town-gardener, who has lately applied to me upon this head. He represents, that for the advancement of a politer sort of ornament in the villas and gardens adjacent to this great city, and in order to distinguish those places from the mere barbarous countries of gross nature, the world stands much in need of a virtuoso gardener who has a turn to sculpture, and is thereby capable of improving upon the ancients of his profession in the imagery of evergreens. My correspondent is arrived to such perfection, that he cuts family pieces of men, women or children. Any ladies that please may have their own effigies in myrtle, or their husbands in hornbeam. He is a puritan wag, and never fails, when he shows his garden, to repeat that passage in the Psalms, *Thy wife shall be as the fruitful vine, and thy children as olive branches round thy table.*° I shall proceed to his catalogue, as he sent it for my recommendation.

Adam and Eve in yew; Adam a little shattered by the fall of the tree of knowledge in the Great Storm;° Eve and the serpent very flourishing.

The Tower of Babel, not yet finished.

St George in box; his arm scarce long enough, but will be in a condition to stick the dragon by next April.

A green dragon of the same, with a tail of ground ivy for the present. N.B. *These two not to be sold separately.*

Edward the Black Prince in cypress.

A Laurustine bear in blossom, with a juniper hunter in berries.

A pair of giants, *stunted*, to be sold cheap.

A Queen Elizabeth in phylyraea, a little inclining to the green sickness, but of full growth.

Another Queen Elizabeth in myrtle, which was very forward, but miscarried by being too near a savin.

An old maid of honour in wormwood.

A topping Ben Jonson in laurel.

Divers eminent modern poets in bays, somewhat blighted, to be disposed of a pennyworth.

A quick-set hog shot up into a porcupine, by its being forgot a week in rainy weather.

A lavender pig with sage growing in his belly.

Noah's Ark in holly, standing on the mount; the ribs a little damaged for want of water.

A pair of Maidenheads in fir, in great forwardness.

THE
WIFE of BATH
FROM
CHAUCER

Behold the woes of matrimonial life,　　　　　　　1
And hear with reverence an experienced wife!
To dear-bought wisdom give the credit due,
And think, for once, a woman tells you true.
In all these trials I have borne a part,
I was myself the scourge that caused the smart;
For, since fifteen,° in triumph have I led
Five captive husbands from the church to bed.

　Christ saw a wedding once, the scripture° says,
And saw but one, 'tis thought, in all his days;　　10
Whence some infer, whose conscience is too nice,
No pious Christian ought to marry twice.

　But let them read, and solve me, if they can,
The words addressed to the Samaritan:°
Five times in lawful wedlock she was joined;
And sure the certain stint was ne'er defined.

　'Increase and multiply,'° was heaven's command,
And that's a text I clearly understand.
This too, 'Let men their sires and mothers leave,
And to their dearer wives for ever cleave.'°　　20
More wives than one by Solomon were tried,°

Or else the wisest of mankind's belied.°
I've had myself full many a merry fit,°
And trust in heaven I may have many yet.
For when my transitory spouse, unkind,   ⎤
Shall die, and leave his woeful wife behind, ⎬
I'll take the next good Christian I can find. ⎦

   Paul, knowing one could never serve our turn,
Declared 'twas better far to wed than burn.°
There's danger in assembling fire and tow;   30
I grant 'em that, and what it means you know.
The same apostle too has elsewhere owned,
No precept for virginity he found:
'Tis but a counsel—and we women still
Take which we like, the counsel, or our will.

   I envy not their bliss, if he or she
Think fit to live in perfect chastity;
Pure let them be, and free from taint of vice;
I, for a few slight spots, am not so nice.
Heaven calls us different ways, on these bestows   40
One proper gift, another grants to those:
Not every man's obliged to sell his store,
And give up all his substance to the poor;°
Such as are perfect, may, I can't deny;
But, by your leave, divines, so am not I.

   Full many a saint, since first the world began,
Lived an unspotted maid, in spite of man:
Let such (a-God's name) with fine wheat be fed,
And let us honest wives eat barley bread.
For me, I'll keep the post assigned by heaven,   50
And use the copious talent it has given:°
Let my good spouse pay tribute, do me right,
And keep an equal reckoning every night:
His proper body is not his, but mine;°
For so said Paul, and Paul's a sound divine.

   Know then, of those five husbands I have had,
Three were just tolerable, two were bad.
The three were old, but rich and fond beside,
And toiled most piteously to please their bride:
But since their wealth (the best they had) was mine,   60
The rest, without much loss, I could resign.
Sure to be loved, I took no pains to please,

Yet had more pleasure far than they had ease.
    Presents flowed in apace: with showers of gold,°
They made their court, like Jupiter of old.
If I but smiled, a sudden youth they found,
And a new palsy seized them when I frowned.
    Ye sovereign wives! give ear, and understand;
Thus shall ye speak, and exercise command.
For never was it given to mortal man,   70
To lie so boldly as we women can:
Forswear the fact, though seen with both his eyes,
And call your maids to witness how he lies.
    'Hark, old Sir Paul' ('twas thus I used to say)
'Whence is our neighbour's wife so rich and gay?
Treated, caressed, where'er she's pleased to roam—
I sit in tatters, and immured at home.
Why to her house dost thou so oft repair?
Art thou so amorous? and is she so fair?
If I but see a cousin or a friend,   80
Lord! how you swell, and rage like any fiend!
But you reel home, a drunken beastly bear,
Then preach till midnight in your easy chair;
Cry, wives are false, and every woman evil,
And give up all that's female to the devil.
    If poor (you say) she drains her husband's purse;
If rich, she keeps her priest, or something worse;
If highly born, intolerably vain;
Vapours° and pride by turns possess her brain:
Now gaily mad, now sourly splenetic,   90
Freakish when well, and fretful when she's sick.
If fair, then chaste she cannot long abide,
By pressing youth attacked on every side.
If foul, her wealth the lusty lover lures,
Or else her wit some fool-gallant procures,
Or else she dances with becoming grace,
Or shape excuses the defects of face.
There swims no goose so grey, but soon or late,
She finds some honest gander for her mate.°
    Horses (thou sayst) and asses, men may try,   100
And ring° suspected vessels ere they buy:
But wives, a random choice, untried they take,
They dream in courtship, but in wedlock wake;

Then, nor till then, the veil's removed away,
And all the woman glares in open day.
    You tell me, to preserve your wife's good grace,
Your eyes must always languish on my face,
Your tongue with constant flatteries feed my ear,
And tag each sentence with, 'My life! my dear!'
If by strange chance, a modest blush be raised,   110
Be sure my fine complexion must be praised:
My garments always must be new and gay,
And feasts still kept upon my wedding-day:
Then must my nurse be pleased, and favourite maid;
And endless treats, and endless visits paid,
To a long train of kindred, friends, allies;
All this thou sayst, and all thou sayst are lies.
    On Jenkin too you cast a squinting eye:
What! can your prentice raise your jealousy?
Fresh are his ruddy cheeks, his forehead fair,   120
And like the burnished gold his curling hair.
But clear thy wrinkled brow, and quit thy sorrow,
I'd scorn your prentice, should you die tomorrow.
    Why are thy chests all locked? on what design?
Are not thy worldly goods and treasure mine?°
Sir, I'm no fool: nor shall you, by St John,
Have goods and body to yourself alone.
One you shall quit, in spite of both your eyes—°
I heed not, I, the bolts, the locks, the spies.
If you had wit, you'd say, 'Go where you will,   130
Dear spouse, I credit not the tales they tell:
Take all the freedoms of a married life;
I know thee for a virtuous, faithful wife.'
    Lord! when you have enough, what need you care
How merrily soever others fare?
Though all the day I give and take delight,
Doubt not, sufficient will be left at night.
'Tis but a just and rational desire,
To light a taper at a neighbour's fire.
    There's danger too, you think, in rich array,   140
And none can long be modest that are gay.
The cat, if you but singe her tabby skin,
The chimney keeps, and sits content within;
But once grown sleek, will from her corner run,

Sport with her tail, and wanton in the sun;
She licks her fair round face, and frisks abroad,
To show her fur, and to be catterwawed.'
    Lo thus, my friends, I wrought to my desires
These three right ancient venerable sires.
I told 'em, 'Thus you say, and thus you do'—   150
And told 'em false, but Jenkin swore 'twas true.
I, like a dog, could bite as well as whine,
And first complained, whene'er the guilt was mine.
I taxed them oft with wenching and amours,
When their weak legs scarce dragged 'em out of doors;
And swore the rambles that I took by night,
Were all to spy what damsels they bedight.°
That colour brought me many hours of mirth;
For all this wit is given us from our birth.
Heaven gave to woman the peculiar grace   160
To spin, to weep, and cully° human race.
By this nice conduct, and this prudent course,
By murmuring, wheedling, stratagem, and force,
I still° prevailed, and would be in the right,
Or curtain-lectures° made a restless night.
If once my husband's arm was o'er my side,
'What! so familiar with your spouse?' I cried:
I levied first a tax upon his need,
Then let him—'twas a nicety indeed!
Let all mankind this certain maxim hold,   170
Marry who will, our sex is to be sold!
With empty hands no tassels° you can lure,
But fulsome love for gain we can endure;
For gold we love the impotent and old,
And heave, and pant, and kiss, and cling, for gold.
Yet with embraces, curses oft I mixed,
Then kissed again, and chid and railed betwixt.
Well, I may make my will in peace, and die,
For not one word in man's arrears am I.
To drop a dear dispute I was unable,   180
Ev'n though the Pope himself had sat at table.
But when my point was gained, then thus I spoke,
'Billy, my dear, how sheepishly you look!
Approach, my spouse, and let me kiss thy cheek!
Thou shouldst be always thus, resigned and meek!'

Of Job's great patience since so oft you preach,°
Well should you practise, who so well can teach,
'Tis difficult to do, I must allow,
But I, my dearest, will instruct you how.
Great is the blessing of a prudent wife,   190
Who puts a period to domestic strife.
One of us two must rule, and one obey;   ⎫
And since in man right reason bears the sway,   ⎬
Let that frail thing, weak woman, have her way.   ⎭
The wives of all my family have ruled
Their tender husbands, and their passions cooled.
Fie, 'tis unmanly thus to sigh and groan;
What! would you have me to yourself alone?
Why take me, love! take all and every part!
Here's your revenge! you love it at your heart,   200
Would I vouchsafe to sell what nature gave,
You little think what custom I could have.
But see! I'm all your own—nay hold—for shame!
What means my dear—indeed—you are to blame.'

     Thus with my first three lords I passed my life;
A very woman, and a very wife.
What sums from these old spouses I could raise,
Procured young husbands in my riper days.
Though past my bloom, not yet decayed was I,
Wanton and wild, and chattered like a pye.°   210
In country dances still I bore the bell,
And sung as sweet as evening Philomel.°
To clear my quail-pipe, and refresh my soul,
Full oft I drained the spicy nut-brown bowl;°
Rich luscious wines, that youthful blood improve,
And warm the swelling veins to feats of love:
For 'tis as sure as cold engenders hail,
A liquorish mouth must have a lecherous tail;
Wine lets no lover unrewarded go,
As all true gamesters by experience know.   220

     But oh, good Gods! whene'er a thought I cast
On all the joys of youth and beauty past,
To find in pleasures I have had my part,
Still warms me to the bottom of my heart.
This wicked world was once my dear delight;
Now all my conquests, all my charms good night!

The flour consumed, the best that now I can,
Is e'en to make my market of the bran.
    My fourth dear spouse was not exceeding true;
He kept, 'twas thought, a private miss or two: 230
But all that score I paid—as how? you'll say,
Not with my body, in a filthy way:
But I so dressed, and danced, and drank, and dined;
And viewed a friend, with eyes so very kind,
As stung his heart, and made his marrow fry,
With burning rage, and frantic jealousy.
His soul, I hope, enjoys eternal glory,
For here on earth I was his purgatory.
Oft, when his shoe the most severely wrung,
He put on careless airs, and sat and sung.   240
How sore I galled him, only heaven could know,
And he that felt, and I that caused the woe.
He died, when last from pilgrimage I came,
With other gossips,° from Jerusalem;
And now lies buried underneath a rood,°
Fair to be seen, and reared of honest wood.
A tomb, indeed, with fewer sculptures graced,
Than that Mausolus' pious widow placed,
Or where enshrined the great Darius lay;°
But cost on graves is merely thrown away.   250
The pit filled up, with turf we covered o'er;
So bless the good man's soul, I say no more.
    Now for my fifth loved lord, the last and best;
(Kind heaven afford him everlasting rest)
Full hearty° was his love, and I can show
The tokens on my ribs, in black and blue;
Yet, with a knack, my heart he could have won,
While yet the smart was shooting in the bone.
How quaint an appetite in women reigns!
Free gifts we scorn, and love what costs us pains: 260
Let men avoid us, and on them we leap;
A glutted market makes provision cheap.
    In pure good will I took this jovial spark,
Of Oxford he, a most egregious clerk.
He boarded with a widow in the town,
A trusty gossip, one dame Alison.
Full well the secrets of my soul she knew,

Better than e'er our parish priest could do.
To her I told whatever could befall:
Had but my husband pissed against a wall,　　　　270
Or done a thing that might have cost his life,
She—and my niece—and one more worthy wife,
Had known it all: what most he would conceal,
To these I made no scruple to reveal.
Oft has he blushed from ear to ear for shame,
That e'er he told a secret to his dame.

It so befell, in holy time of Lent,
That oft a day I to this gossip went;
(My husband, thank my stars, was out of town)
From house to house we rambled up and down,　　280
This clerk, myself, and my good neighbour Alice,
To see, be seen, to tell, and gather tales.
Visits to every church we daily paid,
And marched in every holy masquerade,
The stations° duly, and the vigils kept;
Not much we fasted, but scarce ever slept.
At sermons too I shone in scarlet gay,
The wasting moth ne'er spoiled my best array;°
The cause was this, I wore it every day.

'Twas when fresh May her early blossoms yields,　　290
This clerk and I were walking in the fields.
We grew so intimate, I can't tell how,
I pawned my honour, and engaged my vow,
If e'er I laid my husband in his urn,
That he, and only he, should serve my turn.
We straight struck hands; the bargain was agreed;
I still have shifts against a time of need:
The mouse that always trusts to one poor hole,°
Can never be a mouse of any soul.

I vowed, I scarce could sleep since first I knew him,　　300
And durst be sworn he had bewitched me to him;
If e'er I slept, I dreamed of him alone,
And dreams foretell, as learned men have shown:
All this I said; but dream, sirs, I had none:
I followed but my crafty crony's lore,
Who bid me tell this lie—and twenty more.

Thus day by day, and month by month we passed;
It pleased the Lord to take my spouse at last.

I tore my gown, I soiled my locks with dust,
And beat my breasts, as wretched widows—must.   310
Before my face my handkerchief I spread,
To hide the flood of tears I did—not shed.
The good man's coffin to the church was borne;
Around, the neighbours, and my clerk, too, mourn.
But as he marched, good Gods! he showed a pair
Of legs and feet, so clean, so strong, so fair!
Of twenty winters' age he seemed to be;
I (to say truth) was twenty more than he;
But vigorous still, a lively buxom dame;
And had a wondrous gift to quench a flame.   320
A conjurer once, that deeply could divine,
Assured me, Mars in Taurus was my sign.
As the stars ordered, such my life has been:
Alas, alas, that ever love was sin!
Fair Venus gave me fire, and sprightly grace,
And Mars assurance, and a dauntless face.
By virtue of this powerful constellation,
I followed always my own inclination.

But to my tale: a month scarce passed away,
With dance and song we kept the nuptial day.   330
All I possessed I gave to his command,
My goods and chattels, money, house, and land:
But oft repented, and repent it still;
He proved a rebel to my sovereign will:
Nay once by heaven he struck me on the face;
Hear but the fact, and judge yourselves the case.

Stubborn as any lioness was I;
And knew full well to raise my voice on high;
As true a rambler as I was before,
And would be so, in spite of all he swore.   340
He, against this, right sagely would advise,
And old examples set before my eyes;
Tell how the Roman matrons led their life,
Of Gracchus' mother,° and Duilius' wife;°
And close the sermon, as beseemed his wit,
With some grave sentence out of holy writ.
Oft would he say, who builds his house on sands,°
Pricks his blind horse across the fallow lands,
Or lets his wife abroad with pilgrims roam,

Deserves a fool's cap and long ears at home.　350
All this availed not; for whoe'er he be
That tells my faults, I hate him mortally:
And so do numbers more, I'll boldly say,
Men, women, clergy, regular and lay.

My spouse (who was, you know, to learning bred)
A certain treatise oft at evening read,
Where divers authors (whom the devil confound
For all their lies) were in one volume bound.
Valerius, whole; and of St Jerome, part;
Chrysippus and Tertullian, Ovid's Art,　360
Solomon's proverbs, Eloïsa's loves;°
And many more than sure the church approves.
More legends were there here, of wicked wives,
Than good, in all the Bible and saints' lives.
Who drew the lion vanquished? 'Twas a man.°
But could we women write as scholars can,
Men should stand marked with far more wickedness,
Than all the sons of Adam could redress.
Love seldom haunts the breast where learning lies,
And Venus sets ere Mercury can rise.　370
Those play the scholars who can't play the men,
And use that weapon which they have, their pen;
When old, and past the relish of delight,
Then down they sit, and in their dotage write,
That not one woman keeps her marriage-vow.
(This by the way, but to my purpose now.)

It chanced my husband, on a winter's night,
Read in this book, aloud, with strange delight,
How the first female (as the scriptures show)
Brought her own spouse and all his race to woe.　380
How Samson fell; and he whom Dejanire
Wrapped in th' envenomed shirt, and set on fire.°
How cursed Eryphile her lord betrayed,
And the dire ambush Clytaemnestra laid.°
But what most pleased him was the Cretan dame,°
And husband-bull—oh monstrous! fie for shame!

He had by heart, the whole detail of woe
Xantippe° made her good man undergo;
How oft she scolded in a day, he knew,
How many piss-pots on the sage she threw;　390

Who took it patiently, and wiped his head;
Rain follows thunder,° that was all he said.
　　He read, how Arius° to his friend complained,
A fatal tree was growing in his land.
On which three wives successively had twined
A sliding noose, and wavered in the wind.
'Where grows this plant,' replied the friend, 'oh where?
For better fruit did never orchard bear.
Give me some slip of this most blissful tree,
And in my garden planted shall it be.'   400
　　Then how two wives their lord's destruction prove
Through hatred one, and one through too much love;
That for her husband mixed a poisonous draught,
And this for lust an amorous philtre bought:
The nimble juice soon seized his giddy head,
Frantic at night, and in the morning dead.
　　How some with swords their sleeping lords have slain,
And some have hammered nails into their brain,
And some have drenched them with a deadly potion;
All this he read, and read with great devotion.   410
　　Long time I heard, and swelled, and blushed, and
　　　　frowned;
But when no end of these vile tales I found,
When still he read, and laughed, and read again,
And half the night was thus consumed in vain;
Provoked to vengeance, three large leaves I tore
And with one buffet felled him on the floor.
With that my husband in a fury rose,
And down he settled me with hearty blows.
I groaned, and lay extended on my side;
'Oh! thou hast slain me for my wealth,' I cried,   420
'Yet I forgive thee—take my last embrace—'
He wept, kind soul! and stooped to kiss my face;
I took him such a box as turned him blue,
Then sighed and cried, 'Adieu, my dear, adieu!'
　　But after many a hearty struggle past,
I condescended to be pleased at last.
Soon as he said, 'My mistress and my wife,
Do what you list, the term of all your life':
I took to heart the merits of the cause,
And stood content to rule by wholesome laws;   430

Received the reins of absolute command,
With all the government of house and land; ⎫
And empire o'er his tongue, and o'er his hand. ⎭
As for the volume that reviled the dames,
'Twas torn to fragments, and condemned to flames.
  Now heaven on all my husbands gone, bestow
Pleasures above, for tortures felt below:
That rest they wished for, grant them in the grave,
And bless those souls my conduct helped to save!

THE
RAPE of the LOCK
AN
HEROI-COMICAL
POEM
Written in the Year MDCCXII

TO
Mrs ARABELLA FERMOR°

MADAM,
It will be in vain to deny that I have some regard for this piece, since
I dedicate it to you. Yet you may bear me witness, it was intended only
to divert a few young ladies, who have good sense and good humour
enough to laugh not only at their sex's little unguarded follies, but at
their own. But as it was communicated with the air of a secret, it soon
found its way into the world. An imperfect copy having been offered
to a bookseller, you had the good nature for my sake to consent to the
publication of one more correct: this I was forced to, before I had
executed half my design, for the machinery was entirely wanting to
complete it.
  The machinery,° Madam, is a term invented by the critics, to signify
that part which the deities, angels, or daemons are made to act in a
poem: for the ancient poets are in one respect like many modern ladies;
let an action be never so trivial in itself, they always make it appear of

the utmost importance. These machines I determined to raise on a very new and odd foundation, the Rosicrucian doctrine of spirits.

I know how disagreeable it is to make use of hard words before a lady; but 'tis so much the concern of a poet to have his works understood, and particularly by your sex, that you must give me leave to explain two or three difficult terms.

The Rosicrucians° are a people I must bring you acquainted with. The best account I know of them is in a French book called *Le Comte de Gabalis*, which both in its title and size is so like a novel, that many of the fair sex have read it for one by mistake. According to these gentlemen, the four elements° are inhabited by spirits, which they call sylphs, gnomes, nymphs, and salamanders. The gnomes or daemons of earth delight in mischief; but the sylphs, whose habitation is in the air, are the best conditioned creatures imaginable. For they say, any mortals may enjoy the most intimate familiarities with these gentle spirits, upon a condition very easy to all true adepts, an inviolate preservation of chastity.

As to the following cantos, all the passages of them are as fabulous, as the vision at the beginning, or the transformation at the end (except the loss of your hair, which I always mention with reverence.) The human persons are as fictitious as the airy ones; and the character of Belinda, as it is now managed, resembles you in nothing but in beauty.

If this poem had as many graces as there are in your person, or in your mind, yet I could never hope it should pass through the word half so uncensured as you have done. But let its fortune be what it will, mine is happy enough, to have given me this occasion of assuring you that I am, with the truest esteem,

MADAM,
Your most obedient, humble servant,

A. POPE.

Nolueram, Belinda, tuos violare capillos;
Sed juvat, hoc precibus me tribuisse tuis.

MARTIAL.°

CANTO I

What dire offence from amorous causes springs,   1
What mighty contests rise from trivial things,
I sing°—This verse to CARYLL, Muse! is due:
This, ev'n Belinda may vouchsafe to view:
Slight is the subject, but not so the praise,
If She inspire, and He approve my lays.

   Say what strange motive, Goddess! could compel
A well-bred lord t'assault a gentle belle?
Oh say what stranger cause, yet unexplored,°
Could make a gentle belle° reject a lord?   10
In tasks so bold, can little men° engage,
And in soft bosoms dwells such mighty rage?

   Sol through white curtains shot a timorous ray,
And oped those eyes that must eclipse the day:
Now lapdogs give themselves the rousing shake,
And sleepless lovers, just at twelve, awake:
Thrice rung the bell, the slipper knocked the ground,
And the pressed watch returned a silver sound.°
Belinda still her downy pillow pressed,
Her guardian SYLPH prolonged the balmy rest: 20
'Twas he had summoned to her silent bed
The morning-dream that hovered o'er her head.
A youth more glittering than a birth-night beau,°
(That ev'n in slumber caused her cheek to glow)
Seemed to her ear his winning lips to lay,
And thus in whispers said, or seemed to say:°

   'Fairest of mortals, thou distinguished care
Of thousand bright inhabitants of air!
If e'er one vision touched thy infant thought,
Of all the nurse and all the priest have taught;   30
Of airy elves by moonlight shadows seen,
The silver token, and the circled green,
Or virgins visited by angel-powers,
With golden crowns and wreaths of heavenly flowers;
Hear and believe! thy own importance know,°

The first sketch of this poem was written in less than a fortnight's time, in 1711, in two cantos, and so printed in a miscellany, without the name of the author. The machines were not inserted till a year after, when he published it, and annexed the foregoing dedication.

Nor bound thy narrow views to things below.
Some secret truths, from learned pride concealed,
To maids alone and children are revealed:°
What though no credit doubting wits may give?
The fair and innocent shall still believe.   40
Know then, unnumbered spirits round thee fly,
The light militia of the lower sky;
These, though unseen, are ever on the wing,
Hang o'er the box, and hover round the ring:°
Think what an equipage° thou hast in air,
And view with scorn two pages and a chair.°
As now your own, our beings were of old,
And once enclosed in woman's beauteous mould;
Thence, by a soft transition, we repair
From earthly vehicles to these of air.   50
Think not, when woman's transient breath is fled,
That all her vanities at once are dead;
Succeeding vanities she still regards,
And though she plays no more, o'erlooks the cards.
Her joy in gilded chariots,° when alive,
And love of ombre,° after death survive.
For when the fair in all their pride expire,
To their first elements° their souls retire:
The sprites of fiery termagants° in flame
Mount up, and take a salamander's° name.   60
Soft yielding minds to water glide away,
And sip, with nymphs, their elemental tea.°
The graver prude sinks downward to a gnome,
In search of mischief still on earth to roam.
The light coquettes in sylphs aloft repair,
And sport and flutter in the fields of air.
Know farther yet; whoever fair and chaste
Rejects mankind, is by some sylph embraced:
For spirits, freed from mortal laws, with ease
Assume what sexes and what shapes they please.°   70
What guards the purity of melting maids,

54-55.   *Quae gratia currùm*
            Armorumque fuit vivis, quae cura nitentes
            Pascere equos, eadem sequitur tellure repostos.
                                        Virgil *Aen.* vi.

In courtly balls, and midnight masquerades,
Safe from the treacherous friend, the daring spark,°
The glance by day, the whisper in the dark,
When kind occasion prompts their warm desires,
When music softens, and when dancing fires?
'Tis but their sylph, the wise celestials know,
Though honour is the word with men below.

Some nymphs there are, too conscious of their face,
For life predestined to the gnomes' embrace.   80
These swell their prospects and exalt their pride,
When offers are disdained, and love denied.
Then gay ideas crowd the vacant brain,
While peers and dukes, and all their sweeping train,
And garters, stars, and coronets appear,
And in soft sounds, 'Your Grace' salutes their ear.
'Tis these that early taint the female soul,
Instruct the eyes of young coquettes to roll,
Teach infant-cheeks a bidden blush° to know,
And little hearts to flutter at a beau.   90

Oft, when the world imagine women stray,
The sylphs through mystic mazes guide their way,
Through all the giddy circle they pursue,
And old impertinence° expel by new.
What tender maid but must a victim fall
To one man's treat, but for another's ball?
When Florio speaks, what virgin could withstand,
If gentle Damon did not squeeze her hand?
With varying vanities, from every part,
They shift the moving toyshop° of their heart;   100
Where wigs with wigs, with sword-knots° sword-knots
     strive,
Beaux banish beaux, and coaches coaches drive.
This erring mortals levity may call,
Oh blind to truth! the sylphs contrive it all.

Of these am I, who thy protection claim,
A watchful sprite, and Ariel is my name.
Late, as I ranged the crystal wilds of air,
In the clear mirror of thy ruling star

108. The language of the Platonists, the writers of the intelligible world of spirits, etc.

I saw, alas! some dread event impend,
Ere to the main this morning sun descend,   110
But heaven reveals not what, or how, or where:
Warned by the sylph, oh pious maid, beware!
This to disclose is all thy guardian can:
Beware of all, but most beware of man!'
     He said; when Shock,° who thought she slept too long,°
Leaped up, and waked his mistress with his tongue.
'Twas then Belinda, if report say true,
Thy eyes first opened on a billet-doux;
Wounds, charms, and ardours, were no sooner read,
But all the vision vanished from thy head.   120
     And now, unveiled, the toilet° stands displayed,
Each silver vase in mystic order laid.
First, robed in white, the nymph intent adores,
With head uncovered, the cosmetic powers.
A heavenly image in the glass appears,
To that she bends, to that her eyes she rears;
Th' inferior priestess, at her altar's side,
Trembling, begins the sacred rites of pride.
Unnumbered treasures ope at once, and here
The various offerings of the world appear;°   130
From each she nicely culls with curious toil,
And decks the goddess with the glittering spoil.
This casket India's glowing gems unlocks,
And all Arabia breathes from yonder box.
The tortoise here and elephant unite,
Transformed to combs, the speckled, and the white.
Here files of pins extend their shining rows,
Puffs, powders, patches, bibles,° billet-doux.
Now awful beauty puts on all its arms;
The fair each moment rises in her charms,   140
Repairs her smiles, awakens every grace,
And calls forth all the wonders of her face;
Sees by degrees a purer blush arise,
And keener lightnings quicken in her eyes.°
The busy sylphs surround their darling care,

145. Ancient traditions of the Rabbis relate, that several of the fallen angels became amorous of women, and particularize some; among the rest Asael, who lay with Naamah, the wife of Noah, or of Ham; and who continuing impenitent, still presides over the women's toilets. Bereshi Rabbi in Genes. vi. 2.

These set the head, and those divide the hair,
Some fold the sleeve, whilst others plait the gown;
And Betty's° praised for labours not her own.

CANTO II

Not with more glories, in th' ethereal plain,   1
The sun first rises o'er the purpled main,
Than, issuing forth, the rival of his beams
Launched on the bosom of the silver Thames.°
Fair nymphs, and well-dressed youths around her shone,
But every eye was fixed on her alone.
On her white breast a sparkling cross° she wore,
Which Jews might kiss, and infidels adore.
Her lively looks a sprightly mind disclose,
Quick as her eyes, and as unfixed as those: 10
Favours to none, to all she smiles extends;
Oft she rejects, but never once offends.
Bright as the sun, her eyes the gazers strike,
And, like the sun, they shine on all alike.
Yet graceful ease, and sweetness void of pride
Might hide her faults, if belles had faults to hide:
If to her share some female errors fall,
Look on her face, and you'll forget 'em all.
    This nymph, to the destruction of mankind,
Nourished two locks,° which graceful hung behind   20
In equal curls, and well conspired to deck
With shining ringlets her smooth ivory neck.
Love in these labyrinths his slaves detains,
And mighty hearts are held in slender chains.
With hairy springes we the birds betray,
Slight lines of hair surprise the finny prey,
Fair tresses man's imperial race ensnare,
And beauty draws us with a single hair.
    Th' adventurous Baron the bright locks admired;
He saw, he wished, and to the prize aspired.   30
Resolved to win, he meditates the way,
By force to ravish, or by fraud betray;
For when success a lover's toil attends,
Few ask, if fraud or force attained his ends.

For this, ere Phoebus rose, he had implored
Propitious heaven, and every power adored,
But chiefly love—to love an altar built,
Of twelve vast French romances, neatly gilt.
There lay three garters, half a pair of gloves;
And all the trophies of his former loves;
With tender billet-doux he lights the pyre,   40
And breathes three amorous sighs to raise the fire.
Then prostrate falls, and begs with ardent eyes
Soon to obtain, and long possess the prize:
The powers gave ear, and granted half his prayer,°
The rest, the winds dispersed in empty air.
    But now secure the painted vessel glides,
The sunbeams trembling on the floating tides;
While melting music steals upon the sky,
And softened sounds along the waters die;
Smooth flow the waves, the zephyrs gently play,   50
Belinda smiled, and all the world was gay.
All but the sylph—with careful thoughts oppressed,
Th' impending woe sat heavy on his breast.
He summons straight his denizens of air;
The lucid squadrons round the sails repair:
Soft o'er the shrouds aërial whispers breathe,
That seemed but zephyrs to the train beneath.
Some to the sun their insect-wings unfold,
Waft on the breeze, or sink in clouds of gold;   60
Transparent forms, too fine for mortal sight,
Their fluid bodies half dissolved in light.
Loose to the wind their airy garments flew,
Thin glittering textures of the filmy dew,°
Dipped in the richest tincture of the skies,
Where light disports in ever-mingling dyes,
While every beam new transient colours flings,
Colours that change whene'er they wave their wings.
Amid the circle, on the gilded mast,
Superior by the head, was Ariel placed;   70
His purple pinions opening to the sun,

<hr>

45. *Audiit et voti Phoebus succedere partem*
    Mente dedit, partem volucris dispersit in auras.
                                        Virgil *Aen.* xi.

He raised his azure wand, and thus begun:
  'Ye sylphs and sylphids, to your chief give ear,
Fays, fairies, genii, elves, and daemons hear!
Ye know the spheres and various talks assigned
By laws eternal to th' aërial kind.
Some in the fields of purest ether play,
And bask and whiten in the blaze of day.
Some guide the course of wandering orbs on high,
Or roll the planets through the boundless sky.   80
Some less refined, beneath the moon's pale light
Pursue the stars that shoot athwart the night,
Or suck the mists in grosser air below,
Or dip their pinions in the painted bow,
Or brew fierce tempests on the wintry main,
Or o'er the glebe distil the kindly rain.
Others on earth o'er human race preside,
Watch all their ways, and all their actions guide:
Of these the chief the care of nations own,
And guard with arms divine the British throne.   90
  Our humbler province is to tend the fair,
Not a less pleasing, though less glorious care;
To save the powder from too rude a gale,
Nor let th' imprisoned essences exhale;
To draw fresh colours from the vernal flowers;
To steal from rainbows e'er they drop in showers
A brighter wash; to curl their waving hairs,
Assist their blushes, and inspire their airs;
Nay oft, in dreams, invention° we bestow,
To change a flounce, or add a furbelow.°   100
  This day, black omens threat the brightest fair
That e'er deserved a watchful spirit's care;
Some dire disaster, or by force, or slight;
But what, or where, the fates have wrapped in night.
Whether the nymph shall break Diana's law,°
Or some frail china jar receive a flaw;
Or stain her honour, or her new brocade;
Forget her prayers, or miss a masquerade;
Or lose her heart, or necklace, at a ball;
Or whether Heaven has doomed that Shock must fall.   110
Haste then, ye spirits! to your charge repair:
The fluttering fan be Zephyretta's care;

The drops° to thee, Brillante, we consign;
And, Momentilla, let the watch be thine;
Do thou, Crispissa, tend her favourite lock;
Ariel himself shall be the guard of Shock.

    To fifty chosen sylphs, of special note,
We trust th' important charge, the petticoat:°
Oft have we known that seven-fold fence to fail,
Though stiff with hoops, and armed with ribs of whale;   120
Form a strong line about the silver bound,
And guard the wide circumference around.

    Whatever spirit, careless of his charge,
His post neglects, or leaves the fair at large,
Shall feel sharp vengeance soon o'ertake his sins,
Be stopped in vials, or transfixed with pins;
Or plunged in lakes of bitter washes lie,
Or wedged whole ages in a bodkin's eye:
Gums and pomatums shall his flight restrain,
While clogged he beats his silken wings in vain;   130
Or alum styptics° with contracting power
Shrink his thin essence like a rivelled° flower:
Or, as Ixion° fixed, the wretch shall feel
The giddy motion of the whirling mill,°
In fumes of burning chocolate shall glow,
And tremble at the sea that froths below!'

    He spoke; the spirits from the sails descend;
Some, orb in orb, around the nymph extend,
Some thread the mazy ringlets of her hair,
Some hang upon the pendants of her ear;   140
With beating hearts the dire event they wait,
Anxious, and trembling for the birth of fate.

CANTO III

Close by those meads, for ever crowned with flowers,   1
Where Thames with pride surveys his rising towers,
There stands a structure of majestic frame,
Which from the neighbouring Hampton° takes its name.
Here Britain's statesmen oft the fall foredoom
Of foreign tyrants, and of nymphs at home;
Here thou, great ANNA! whom three realms° obey,

Dost sometimes counsel take—and sometimes tea.
   Hither the heroes and the nymphs resort,
To taste awhile the pleasures of a court;   10
In various talk th' instructive hours they passed,
Who gave the ball, or paid the visit last:
One speaks the glory of the British Queen,
And one describes a charming Indian screen;°
A third interprets motions, looks, and eyes;
At every word a reputation dies.
Snuff,° or the fan, supply each pause of chat,
With singing, laughing, ogling, and all that.
   Meanwhile, declining from the noon of day,
The sun obliquely shoots his burning ray;   20
The hungry judges soon the sentence sign,
And wretches hang that jurymen may dine;
The merchant from th'Exchange° returns in peace,
And the long labours of the toilet cease.
Belinda now, whom thirst of fame invites,
Burns to encounter two adventurous knights,
At ombre° singly to decide their doom;
And swells her breast with conquests yet to come.
Straight the three bands prepare in arms to join,
Each band the number of the sacred nine.°   30
Soon as she spreads her hand, th' aërial guard
Descend, and sit on each important° card:
First Ariel perched upon a matadore,°
Then each, according to the rank they bore;
For sylphs, yet mindful of their ancient race,
Are, as when women, wondrous fond of place.
   Behold, four kings in majesty revered,
With hoary whiskers and a forky beard;
And four fair queens whose hands sustain a flower,
Th' expressive emblem of their softer power;   40
Four knaves in garbs succinct,° a trusty band,
Caps on their heads, and halberts in their hand;
And particoloured troops, a shining train,
Draw forth to combat on the velvet plain.
   The skilful nymph reviews her force with care:
'Let spades be trumps!' she said, and trumps they were.°
   Now move to war her sable matadores,
In show like leaders of the swarthy Moors.

Spadillio° first, unconquerable lord!
Led off two captive trumps, and swept the board.   50
As many more Manillio° forced to yield,
And marched a victor from the verdant field.°
Him Basto° followed, but his fate more hard
Gained but one trump and one plebeian card.
With his broad sabre next, a chief in years,
The hoary majesty of spades appears,
Puts forth one manly leg, to sight revealed,
The rest, his many-coloured robe concealed.
The rebel knave, who dares his prince engage,
Proves the just victim of his royal rage.   60
Ev'n mighty Pam,° that kings and queens o'erthrew
And mowed down armies in the fights of lu,
Sad chance of war! now destitute of aid,
Falls undistinguished by the victor spade!
    Thus far both armies to Belinda yield;
Now to the Baron fate inclines the field.
His warlike Amazon her host invades,
Th' imperial consort of the crown of spades.
The club's black tyrant first her victim died,
Spite of his haughty mien, and barbarous pride: 70
What boots the regal circle on his head,
His giant limbs, in state unwieldy spread;
That long behind he trails his pompous robe,
And, of all monarchs, only grasps the globe?°
    The Baron now his diamonds pours apace;
Th' embroidered king who shows but half his face,
And his refulgent queen, with powers combined,
Of broken troops an easy conquest find.
Clubs, diamonds, hearts, in wild disorder seen,
With throngs promiscuous strow the level green.   80
Thus when dispersed a routed army runs,
Of Asia's troops, and Afric's sable sons,
With like confusion different nations fly,
Of various habit, and of various dye,
The pierced battalions disunited fall,
In heaps on heaps; one fate o'erwhelms them all.
    The knave of diamonds tries his wily arts,
And wins (oh shameful chance!) the queen of hearts.
At this, the blood the virgin's cheek forsook,

A livid paleness spreads o'er all her look;
She sees, and trembles at th' approaching ill,
Just in the jaws of ruin, and codille.°
And now, (as oft in some distempered state)
On one nice trick° depends the general fate.
An ace of hearts steps forth: the king unseen
Lurked in her hand, and mourned his captive queen:
He springs to vengeance with an eager pace,
And falls like thunder on the prostrate ace.
The nymph exulting fills with shouts the sky;
The walls, the woods, and long canals reply.   100

   Oh thoughtless mortals! ever blind to fate,
Too soon dejected, and too soon elate.
Sudden, these honours shall be snatched away,
And cursed for ever this victorious day.

   For lo! the board with cups and spoons is crowned,
The berries crackle, and the mill turns round;°
On shining altars of Japan° they raise
The silver lamp; the fiery spirits blaze:
From silver spouts the grateful liquors glide,
While China's earth receives the smoking tide: 110
At once they gratify their scent and taste,
And frequent cups prolong the rich repast.
Straight hover round the fair her airy band;
Some, as she sipped, the fuming liquor fanned,
Some o'er her lap their careful plumes displayed,
Trembling, and conscious of the rich brocade.
Coffee° (which makes the politician wise,
And see through all things with his half-shut eyes)
Sent up in vapours to the Baron's brain
New stratagems, the radiant lock to gain.   120
Ah cease, rash youth! desist ere 'tis too late,
Fear the just gods, and think of Scylla's fate!
Changed to a bird, and sent to flit in air,
She dearly pays for Nisus' injured hair!°

   But when to mischief mortals bend their will,
How soon they find fit instruments of ill?
Just then, Clarissa drew with tempting grace
A two-edged° weapon from her shining case:

122. Vide Ovid, *Metam.* viii.

So ladies in romance assist their knight,
Present the spear, and arm him for the fight.   130
He takes the gift with reverence, and extends
The little engine on his finger's ends;
This just behind Belinda's neck he spread,
As o'er the fragrant steams she bends her head.
Swift to the lock a thousand sprites repair,
A thousand wings, by turns, blow back the hair;
And thrice they twitched the diamond in her ear;
Thrice she looked back, and thrice the foe drew near.
Just in that instant, anxious Ariel sought
The close recesses of the virgin's thought;   140
As on the nosegay in her breast reclined,
He watched th' ideas rising in her mind,
Sudden he viewed, in spite of all her art,
An earthly lover lurking at her heart.
Amazed, confused, he found his power expired,
Resigned to fate, and with a sigh retired.
　　The peer now spreads the glittering forfex wide,
T' enclose the lock; now joins it, to divide.
Ev'n then, before the fatal engine closed,
A wretched sylph too fondly interposed;   150
Fate urged the shears, and cut the sylph in twain,
(But airy substance soon unites again)°
The meeting points the sacred hair dissever
From the fair head, for ever, and for ever!
　　Then flashed the living lightning from her eyes,
And screams of horror rend th' affrighted skies.
Not louder shrieks to pitying heaven are cast,
When husbands, or when lapdogs breathe their last,
Or when rich china vessels, fallen from high,
In glittering dust, and painted fragments lie!   160
　　'Let wreaths of triumph now my temples twine,'
The victor cried, 'the glorious prize is mine!
While fish in streams, or birds delight in air,
Or in a coach and six° the British fair,
As long as *Atalantis*° shall be read,
Or the small pillow grace a lady's bed,
While visits shall be paid on solemn days,

152. See Milton, lib. vi. of Satan cut asunder by the angel Michael.

When numerous wax-lights in bright order blaze,
While nymphs take treats, or assignations give,
So long my honour, name, and praise shall live! 170
What time would spare, from steel receives its date,
And monuments, like men, submit to fate!
Steel could the labour of the Gods destroy,
And strike to dust th' imperial towers of Troy;°
Steel could the works of mortal pride confound,
And hew triumphal arches to the ground.
What wonder then, fair nymph! thy hairs should feel
The conquering force of unresisted steel?'

CANTO IV

But anxious cares the pensive nymph oppressed, 1
And secret passions laboured in her breast.
Not youthful kings in battle seized alive,
Not scornful virgins who their charms survive,
Not ardent lovers robbed of all their bliss,
Not ancient ladies when refused a kiss,
Not tyrants fierce than unrepenting die,
Not Cynthia when her manteau's° pinned awry,
E'er felt such rage, resentment, and despair,
As thou, sad virgin! for thy ravished hair. 10

For, that sad moment, when the sylphs withdrew,
And Ariel weeping from Belinda flew,
Umbriel, a dusky, melancholy sprite,
As ever sullied the fair face of light,
Down to the central earth, his proper scene,
Repaired to search the gloomy Cave of Spleen.°
Swift on his sooty pinions flits the gnome,
And in a vapour° reached the dismal dome.
No cheerful breeze this sullen region knows,
The dreaded east° is all the wind that blows. 20
Here in a grotto, sheltered close from air,
And screened in shades from day's detested glare,
She sighs for ever on her pensive bed,
Pain at her side,° and megrim° at her head.

1. Virgil *Aen.* iv. *At regina gravi*, etc.

Two handmaids wait° the throne: alike in place,
But differing far in figure and in face.
Here stood Ill-nature like an ancient maid,
Her wrinkled form in black and white arrayed;
With store of prayers, for mornings, nights, and noons,
Her hand is filled; her bosom with lampoons.   30
    There Affectation, with a sickly mien,
Shows in her cheek the roses of eighteen,
Practised to lisp, and hang the head aside,°
Faints into airs, and languishes with pride,°
On the rich quilt sinks with becoming woe,
Wrapped in a gown, for sickness, and for show.
The fair ones feel such maladies as these,
When each new nightdress gives a new disease.
    A constant vapour o'er the palace flies;
Strange phantoms rising as the mists arise;   40
Dreadful, as hermit's dreams in haunted shades,°
Or bright, as visions of expiring maids.
Now glaring fiends, and snakes on rolling spires,°
Pale spectres, gaping tombs, and purple fires:
Now lakes of liquid gold, Elysian scenes,
And crystal domes, and angels in machines.°
    Unnumbered throngs on every side are seen,
Of bodies changed to various forms by spleen.
Here living teapots stand, one arm held out,
One bent; the handle this, and that the spout: 50
A pipkin° there like Homer's tripod walks;
Here sighs a jar, and there a goose-pie talks;
Men prove with child, as powerful fancy works,
And maids turned bottles, call aloud for corks.
    Safe passed the gnome through this fantastic band,
A branch of healing spleenwort in his hand.°
Then thus addressed the power: 'Hail wayward Queen!
Who rule the sex to fifty from fifteen:°
Parent of vapours and of female wit,
Who give th' hysteric, or poetic fit,   60
On various tempers act by various ways,

51. See Homer, *Iliad* xviii, of Vulcan's walking tripods.
    52. *and there a goose-pie talks*] Alludes to a real fact, a lady of distinction imagined herself in this condition.

Make some take physic, others scribble plays;
Who cause the proud their visits to delay,
And send the godly in a pet to pray.
A nymph there is, that all thy power disdains,
And thousands more in equal mirth maintains.
But oh! if e'er thy gnome could spoil a grace,
Or raise a pimple on a beauteous face,
Like citron-waters° matrons cheeks inflame,
Or change complexions at a losing game;   70
If e'er with airy horns° I planted heads,
Or rumpled petticoats, or tumbled beds,
Or caused suspicion when no soul was rude,
Or discomposed the head-dress of a prude,
Or e'er to costive lap-dog gave disease,
Which not the tears of brightest eyes could ease:
Hear me, and touch Belinda with chagrin;°
That single act gives half the world° the spleen.'
    The goddess with a discontented air
Seems to reject him, though she grants his prayer.   80
A wondrous bag with both her hands she binds,
Like that where once Ulysses° held the winds;
There she collects the force of female lungs,
Sighs, sobs, and passions, and the war of tongues.
A vial next she fills with fainting fears,
Soft sorrows, melting griefs, and flowing tears.
The gnome rejoicing bears her gifts away,
Spreads his black wings, and slowly mounts to day.°
    Sunk in Thalestris'° arms the nymph he found,
Her eyes dejected and her hair unbound.   90
Full o'er their heads the swelling bag he rent,
And all the furies issued at the vent.
Belinda burns with more than mortal ire,
And fierce Thalestris fans the rising fire.
'O wretched maid!' she spread her hands, and cried,
(While Hampton's echoes, 'wretched maid!' replied)
'Was it for this° you took such constant care
The bodkin, comb, and essence to prepare?
For this your locks in paper durance° bound,
For this with torturing irons wreathed around?   100
For this with fillets strained your tender head,
And bravely bore the double loads of lead?

Gods! shall the ravisher display your hair,
While the fops envy, and the ladies stare!
Honour forbid! at whose unrivalled shrine
Ease, pleasure, virtue, all, our sex resign.
Methinks already I your tears survey,
Already hear the horrid things they say,
Already see you a degraded toast,°
And all your honour in a whisper lost!   110
How shall I, then, your helpless fame defend?
'Twill then be infamy to seem your friend!
And shall this prize, th' inestimable prize,
Exposed through crystal to the gazing eyes,
And heightened by the diamond's circling rays,
On that rapacious hand for ever blaze?
Sooner shall grass in Hyde Park Circus° grow,
And wits take lodgings in the sound of Bow;°
Sooner let earth, air, sea, to chaos fall,
Men, monkeys, lapdogs, parrots, perish all!'   120
    She said; then raging to Sir Plume° repairs,
And bids her beau demand the precious hairs:
(Sir Plume of amber snuff-box justly vain,
And the nice conduct of a clouded cane)°
With earnest eyes, and round unthinking face,
He first the snuff-box opened, then the case,
And thus broke out—'My Lord, why, what the devil?
Z—ds! damn the lock! 'fore Gad, you must be civil!
Plague on't! 'tis past a jest—nay prithee, pox!
Give her the hair'—he spoke, and rapped his box.°   130
    'It grieves me much,' replied the peer again,
'Who speaks so well should ever speak in vain.
But by this lock, this sacred lock I swear,
(Which never more shall join its parted hair;
Which never more its honours shall renew,
Clipped from the lovely head where late it grew)
That while my nostrils draw the vital air,
This hand, which won it, shall for ever wear.'
He spoke, and speaking, in proud triumph spread
The long-contended honours of her head.   140

133. In allusion to Achilles's oath in Homer, *Il.* i.

But Umbriel, hateful gnome! forbears not so;
He breaks the vial whence the sorrows flow.
Then see! the nymph in beauteous grief appears,
Her eyes half-languishing, half-drowned in tears;
On her heaved bosom hung her drooping head,
Which, with a sigh, she raised, and thus she said:
  'For ever cursed be this detested day,
Which snatched my best, my favourite curl away!
Happy! ah ten times happy had I been,
If Hampton Court these eyes had never seen!   150
Yet am not I the first mistaken maid,
By love of courts to numerous ills betrayed.
Oh had I rather un-admired remained
In some lone isle, or distant northern land;
Where the gilt chariot never marks the way,
Where none learn ombre, none e'er taste bohea!°
There kept my charms concealed from mortal eye,
Like roses that in deserts bloom and die.
What moved my mind with youthful lords to roam?
O had I stayed, and said my prayers at home!   160
'Twas this, the morning omens° seemed to tell;
Thrice from my trembling hand the patch-box° fell;
The tottering china shook without a wind,
Nay Poll sat mute, and Shock was most unkind!
A sylph too warned me of the threats of fate,
In mystic visions, now believed too late!
See the poor remnants of these slighted hairs!
My hands shall rend what ev'n thy rapine spares:
These in two sable ringlets taught to break
Once gave new beauties to the snowy neck;   170
The sister-lock now sits uncouth, alone,
And in its fellow's fate foresees its own;
Uncurled it hangs, the fatal shears demands,
And tempts once more thy sacrilegious hands.
Oh hadst thou, cruel! been content to seize
Hairs less in sight, or any hairs but these!'°

141–142. These two lines are additional; and assign the cause of the different operation on the passions of the two ladies. The poem went on before without that distinction, as without any machinery to the end of the canto.

CANTO V

She said: the pitying audience melt in tears.   1
But Fate and Jove had stopped the Baron's ears.
In vain Thalestris with reproach assails,
For who can move when fair Belinda fails?
Not half so fixed the Trojan could remain,
While Anna begged and Dido raged in vain.°
Then grave Clarissa° graceful waved her fan;
Silence ensued, and thus the nymph began:
    'Say why are beauties praised and honoured most,
The wise man's passion, and the vain man's toast?   10
Why decked with all that land and sea afford,
Why angels called, and angel-like adored?
Why round our coaches crowd the white-gloved beaux,
Why bows the side-box from its inmost rows?
How vain are all these glories, all our pains,
Unless good sense preserve what beauty gains:
That men may say, when we the front-box grace,
Behold the first in virtue as in face!
Oh! if to dance all night, and dress all day,
Charmed the smallpox,° or chased old age away;   20
Who would not scorn what housewife's cares produce,
Or who would learn one earthly thing of use?
To patch, nay ogle, might become a saint,
Nor could it sure be such a sin to paint.
But since, alas! frail beauty must decay,
Curled or uncurled, since locks will turn to grey;
Since painted, or not painted, all shall fade,
And she who scorns a man, must die a maid;
What then remains but well our power to use,
And keep good-humour still whate'er we lose?   30
And trust me, dear! good-humour can prevail,
When airs, and flights, and screams, and scolding fail.
Beauties in vain their pretty eyes may roll;
Charms strike the sight, but merit wins the soul.'

7. *Clarissa*] A new character introduced in the subsequent editions, to open more clearly the MORAL of the poem, in a parody of the speech of Sarpedon to Glaucus in Homer.

So spoke the dame, but no applause ensued;
Belinda frowned, Thalestris called her prude.
'To arms, to arms!' the fierce virago° cries,
And swift as lightning to the combat flies.
All side in parties and begin th' attack;
Fans clap, silks rustle and tough whalebones crack;   40
Heroes' and heroines' shouts confusedly rise,
And bass and treble voices strike the skies.
No common weapons in their hands are found,
Like gods they fight, nor dread a mortal wound.
    So when bold Homer makes the gods engage,
And heavenly breasts with human passions rage;
'Gainst Pallas, Mars; Latona,° Hermes arms;
And all Olympus rings with loud alarms:
Jove's thunder roars, heaven trembles all around,
Blue Neptune storms, the bellowing deeps resound: 50
Earth shakes her nodding towers, the ground gives way,
And the pale ghosts start at the flash of day!
    Triumphant Umbriel on a sconce's° height
Clapped his glad wings, and sate to view the fight:
Propped on their bodkin spears, the sprites survey
The growing combat, or assist the fray.
    While through the press enraged Thalestris flies,
And scatters deaths around from both her eyes,
A beau and witling perished in the throng,
One died in metaphor, and one in song.   60
'O cruel nymph! a living death I bear,'
Cried Dapperwit,° and sunk beside his chair.
A mournful glance Sir Fopling° upwards cast,
'Those eyes are made so killing'—was his last.

35. It is a verse frequently repeated in Homer after any speech,
    So spoke—and all the heroes applauded.

37. From hence the first edition goes on to the conclusion, except a very few
short insertions added, to keep the machinery in view to the end of the poem.

45. Homer *Il.* xx.

53-6. These four lines added, for the reason before mentioned.°

53. Minerva in like manner, during the battle of Ulysses with the suitors in *Odyss.*
perches on a beam of the roof to behold it.°

64. *Those eyes are made so killing*] The words of a song in the opera of *Camilla.*°

Thus on Maeander's flowery margin lies
Th' expiring swan, and as he sings he dies.

When bold Sir Plume had drawn Clarissa down,
Chloe stepped in, and killed him with a frown;
She smiled to see the doughty hero slain,
But, at her smile, the beau revived again.   70

Now Jove suspends his golden scales in air,
Weighs the men's wits against the lady's hair;
The doubtful beam long nods from side to side;
At length the wits mount up, the hairs subside.

See fierce Belinda on the Baron flies,
With more than usual lightning in her eyes:
Nor feared the chief th' unequal fight to try,
Who sought no more than on his foe to die.°
But this bold lord with manly strength endued,
She with one finger and a thumb subdued: 80
Just where the breath of life his nostrils drew,
A charge of snuff the wily virgin threw;
The gnomes direct, to every atom just,
The pungent grains of titillating dust.
Sudden, with starting tears each eye o'erflows,
And the high dome re-echoes to his nose.

'Now meet thy fate,' incensed Belinda cried,
And drew a deadly bodkin° from her side.
(The same, his ancient personage to deck,
Her great great grandsire wore about his neck   90
In three seal-rings; which after, melted down,
Formed a vast buckle for his widow's gown:
Her infant grandame's whistle next it grew,
The bells she jingled, and the whistle blew;
Then in a bodkin graced her mother's hairs,
Which long she wore, and now Belinda wears.)

'Boast not my fall,' he cried, 'insulting foe!
Thou by some other shalt be laid as low.

---

65. *Sic ubi fata vocant, udis abjectus in herbis,*
     Ad vada Maeandri concinit albus olor.
                                          Ovid *Ep.*°
71. Vid. Homer *Il.* viii. and Virgil *Aen.* xii.
83–84. These two lines added for the above reason.
89. In imitation of the progress of Agamemnon's sceptre in Homer, *Il.* ii.

Nor think, to die dejects my lofty mind:
All that I dread is leaving you behind!   100
Rather than so, ah let me still survive,
And burn in Cupid's flames,—but burn alive.'
    'Restore the lock!' she cries; and all around
'Restore the lock!' the vaulted roofs rebound.
Not fierce Othello in so loud a strain
Roared for the handkerchief that caused his pain.
But see how oft ambitious aims are crossed,
And chiefs contend till all the prize is lost!
The lock, obtained with guilt, and kept with pain,
In every place is sought, but sought in vain: 110
With such a prize no mortal must be blest,
So heaven decrees! with heaven who can contest?
    Some thought it mounted to the lunar sphere,
Since all things lost on earth are treasured there.
There heroes' wits are kept in ponderous vases,
And beaux' in snuff-boxes and tweezer-cases.
There broken vows, and death-bed alms are found,
And lovers' hearts with ends of ribband bound,
The courtier's promises, and sick man's prayers,
The smiles of harlots, and the tears of heirs,   120
Cages for gnats, and chains to yoke a flea,
Dried butterflies, and tomes of casuistry.
    But trust the Muse—she saw it upward rise,
Though marked by none but quick, poetic eyes:
(So Rome's great founder to the heavens withdrew,
To Proculus° alone confessed in view)
A sudden star, it shot through liquid° air,
And drew behind a radiant trail of hair.
Not Berenice's° locks first rose so bright,
The heavens bespangling with dishevelled light.   130
The sylphs behold it kindling as it flies,
And pleased pursue its progress through the skies.
    This the beau monde shall from the Mall° survey,
And hail with music its propitious ray.
This the blessed lover shall for Venus take,

114. *Vid.* Ariosto, Canto xxxiv.°

131 f. These two lines added for the same reason to keep in view the machinery
of the poem.

And send up vows from Rosamonda's lake.°
This Partridge soon shall view in cloudless skies,
When next he looks through Galileo's eyes;°
And hence th' egregious wizard shall foredoom
The fate of Louis,° and the fall of Rome.   140
    Then cease, bright nymph! to mourn thy ravished hair,
Which adds new glory to the shining sphere!°
Not all the tresses that fair head can boast,
Shall draw such envy as the lock you lost.
For, after all the murders of your eye,
When, after millions slain, yourself shall die;
When those fair suns shall set, as set they must,
And all those tresses shall be laid in dust;
This lock, the Muse shall consecrate to fame,
And 'midst the stars inscribe Belinda's name.   150

To Belinda *on the* Rape of the Lock

Pleased in these lines, Belinda, you may view   1
How things are prized, which once belonged to you:
If on some meaner head this lock had grown,
The nymph despised, the rape had been unknown.
But what concerns the valiant and the fair,
The Muse asserts as her peculiar care.
Thus Helen's rape and Menelaus' wrong
Became the subject of great Homer's song;°
And, lost in ancient times, the golden fleece°
Was raised to fame by all the wits of Greece.   10
    Had fate decreed, propitious to your prayers,
To give their utmost date to all your hairs;
This lock, of which late ages now shall tell,
Had dropped like fruit, neglected, when it fell.
    Nature to your undoing arms mankind
With strength of body, artifice of mind;

---

137. John Partridge was a ridiculous stargazer, who in his almanacs every year
never failed to predict the downfall of the Pope, and the King of France, then at
war with the English.

But gives your feeble sex, made up of fears,
No guard but virtue, no redress but tears.
Yet custom (seldom to your favour gained)
Absolves the virgin when by force constrained.   20
Thus Lucrece lives unblemished in her fame,
A bright example° of young Tarquin's shame.
Such praise is yours—and such shall you possess,
Your virtue equal, though your loss be less.
Then smile Belinda at reproachful tongues,
Still warm our hearts, and still inspire our songs.
But would your charms to distant times extend,
Let Jervas° paint them, and let Pope commend.
Who censure most, more precious hairs would lose,
To have the *Rape* recorded by his Muse.°   30

POPE TO MARTHA BLOUNT
November 1714

Most Divine!—'Tis some proof of my sincerity towards you that I write
when I am prepared by drinking to speak truth, and sure a letter after
twelve at night must abound with that noble ingredient. That heart
must have abundance of flames which is at once warmed by wine and
you; wine awakens and refreshes the lurking passions of the mind, as
varnish does the colours that are sunk in a picture, and brings them
out in all their natural glowings. My good qualities have been so frozen
and locked up in a dull constitution at all my former sober hours,
that it is very astonishing to me, now I am drunk, to find so much
virtue in me.

In these overflowings of my heart I pay you my thanks for those two
obliging letters you favoured me with of the 18th and 24th instant.
That which begins with 'Dear Creature', and 'my charming Mr Pope',
was a delight to me beyond all expression. You have at last entirely
gained the conquest over your fair sister; 'tis true you are not handsome,
for you are a woman and think you are not; but this good humour and
tenderness for me has a charm that cannot be resisted. That face must
needs be irresistible which was adorned with smiles even when it could
not see the Coronation.°

I must own I have long been shocked at your sister° on several accounts, but above all things at her prudery: I am resolved to break with her for ever; and therefore tell her I shall take the first opportunity of sending back all her letters.

I do suppose you will not show this epistle out of vanity, as I doubt not your said sister does all I writ to her. Indeed to correspond with Mr Pope may make anyone proud who lives under a dejection of heart in the country. Every one values Mr Pope, but every one for a different reason. One for his firm adherence to the Catholic faith, another for his neglect of Popish superstition, one for his grave behaviour, another for his whimsicalness. Mr Tidcombe for his pretty atheistical jests, Mr Caryll° for his moral and Christian sentences, Mrs Teresa for his reflections on Mrs Patty,° and Mrs Patty for his reflections on Mrs Teresa.

My acquaintance runs so much in an anti-Catholic channel, that it was but t'other day I heard of Mrs Fermor's° being actually, directly, and consummatively, married. I wonder how the guilty couple and their accessories at Whiteknights look, stare, or simper, since that grand secret came out which they so well concealed before. They concealed it as well as a barber does his utensils when he goes to trim upon a Sunday and his towels hang out all the way: or as well as a friar concealed a little wench, whom he was carrying under his habit to Mr Colingwood's convent; 'Pray, Father', said one in the street to him, 'what's that under your arm?' 'A saddle for one of the brothers to ride with', quoth the friar. 'Then Father', cried he, 'take care and shorten the stirrups'—For the girl's legs hung out—

You know your doctor is gone the way of all his patients, and was hard put to it how to dispose of an estate miserably unwieldy, and splendidly unuseful to him. Sir Sam. Garth says, that for Radcliffe° to leave a library was as if an eunuch should found a seraglio. Dr Shadwell lately told a lady he wondered she could be alive after him; she made answer she wondered at it too, both because Dr Radcliffe was dead, and because Dr Shadwell was alive.

Poor Parnell° is now on the briny ocean which he increases with his briny tears for the loss of you etc. Pray for him, if you please, but not for me. Don't so much as hope I may go to Heaven: 'tis a place I am not very fond of, I hear no great good of it. All the descriptions I ever heard of it amount to no more than just this: it is eternal singing, and piping, and sitting in sunshine. Much good may it do the saints; and those who intend to be saints. For my part I am better than a saint, for I am, Madam, Your most faithful admirer, friend, servant, anything.

I send you Gay's poem° on the Princess. She is very fat. God keep her husband.

THE
TEMPLE
OF
FAME

Advertisement

The hint of the following piece was taken from Chaucer's *House of Fame*. The design is in a manner entirely altered, the descriptions and most of the particular thoughts my own: yet I could not suffer it to be printed without this acknowledgment. The reader who would compare this with Chaucer, may begin with his third book of *Fame*, there being nothing in the two first books that answers to their title: wherever any hint is taken from him, the passage itself is set down in the marginal notes.

In that soft season, when descending showers°   1
Call forth the greens, and wake the rising flowers;
When opening buds salute the welcome day,
And earth relenting° feels the genial ray;
As balmy sleep had charmed my cares to rest,
And love itself was banished from my breast,
(What time the morn mysterious visions brings,
While purer slumbers spread their golden wings)
A train of phantoms in wild order rose,
And, joined, this intellectual° scene compose.   10

1. This poem is introduced in the manner of the Provençal poets, whose works were for the most part visions, or pieces of imagination and constantly descriptive. From these, Petrarch and Chaucer frequently borrow the idea of their poems. See the *Trionfi* of the former and the *Dream, Flower and the Leaf*, etc. of the latter. The author of this therefore chose the same sort of exordium.°

I stood, methought, betwixt earth, seas, and skies;
The whole creation open to my eyes:
In air self-balanced hung the globe below,
Where mountains rise, and circling oceans flow;
Here naked rocks, and empty wastes were seen;
There towery cities, and the forests green:
Here sailing ships delight the wandering eyes:
There trees, and intermingled temples rise;
Now a clear sun the shining scene displays,
The transient landscape now in clouds decays.   20
    O'er the wide prospect as I gazed around,
Sudden I heard a wild promiscuous sound,
Like broken thunders that at distance roar,
Or billows murmuring on the hollow shore:
Then gazing up, a glorious pile beheld,
Whose towering summit ambient clouds concealed.
High on a rock of ice the structure lay,
Steep its ascent, and slippery was the way;
The wondrous rock like Parian° marble shone,
And seemed, to distant sight, of solid stone.   30
Inscriptions here of various names I viewed,
The greater part by hostile time subdued;
Yet wide was spread their fame in ages past,
And poets once had promised they should last.
Some fresh engraved appeared of wits renowned;
I looked again, nor could their trace be found.
Critics I saw, that other names deface,
And fix their own, with labour, in their place:
Their own, like others, soon their place resigned,
Or disappeared, and left the first behind.   40
Nor was the work impaired by storms alone,
But felt th'approaches of too warm a sun;
For Fame, impatient of extremes, decays
Not more by envy than excess of praise.
Yet part no injuries of heaven could feel,
Like crystal faithful to the graving steel:
The rock's high summit, in the temple's shade,
Nor heat cold melt, nor beating storm invade.
There names inscribed unnumbered ages past
From time's first birth, with time itself shall last;   50
These ever new, nor subject to decays,

Spread, and grow brighter with the length of days.
  So Zembla's rocks (the beauteous work of frost)
Rise white in air, and glitter o'er the coast;
Pale suns, unfelt, at distance roll away,
And on th'impassive ice the lightnings play;
Eternal snows the growing mass supply,
Till the bright mountains prop th'incumbent sky:
As Atlas fixed, each hoary pile appears,
The gathered winter of a thousand years.   60
  On this foundation Fame's high temple stands;
Stupendous pile! not reared by mortal hands.°
Whate'er proud Rome or artful Greece beheld,
Or elder Babylon, its frame excelled.
Four faces had the dome,° and every face
Of various structure, but of equal grace:
Four brazen gates, on columns lifted high,
Salute the different quarters of the sky.
Here fabled chiefs in darker ages born,
Or worthies old, whom arms or arts adorn,   70
Who cities raised, or tamed a monstrous race;
The walls in venerable order grace:
Heroes in animated marble frown,
And legislators seem to think in stone.
  Westward, a sumptuous frontispiece° appeared,
On Doric pillars of white marble reared,
Crowned with an architrave of antique mold,
And sculpture rising on the roughened gold.
In shaggy spoils here Theseus was beheld,
And Perseus dreadful with Minerva's shield: 80
There great Alcides° stooping with his toil,
Rests on his club, and holds th' Hesperian spoil.°
Here Orpheus sings; trees moving to the sound
Start from their roots, and form a shade around:

65. The temple is described to be square, the four fronts with open gates facing
the different quarters of the world, as an intimation that all nations of the earth may
alike be received into it. The western front is of Grecian architecture: the Doric
order was peculiarly sacred to heroes and worthies. Those whose statues are after
mentioned, were the first names of old Greece in arms and arts.

81. This figure of Hercules is drawn with an eye to the position of the famous
statue of Farnese.

Amphion there the loud creating lyre
Strikes, and behold a sudden Thebes aspire!
Cythaeron's° echoes answer to his call,
And half the mountain rolls into a wall:
There might you see the lengthening spires ascend,
The domes swell up, the widening arches bend,   90
The growing towers like exhalations rise,
And the huge columns heave into the skies.

   The eastern front was glorious to behold,
With diamond flaming, and barbaric gold.
There Ninus shone, who spread th'Assyrian fame,
And the great founder of the Persian name:
There in long robes the royal Magi stand,
Grave Zoroaster waves the circling wand:
The sage Chaldaeans robed in white appeared,
And Brachmans, deep in desert woods revered.   100
These stopped the moon, and called th'unbodied shades
To midnight banquets in the glimmering glades;
Made visionary fabrics round them rise,
And airy spectres skim before their eyes;
Of talismans and sigils° knew the power,
And careful watched the planetary hour.°
Superior, and alone, Confucius stood,
Who taught that useful science, to be good.

   But on the south, a long majestic race
Of Egypt's priests the gilded niches grace,   110
Who measured earth, described the starry spheres,
And traced the long records of lunar years.
High on his car Sesostris struck my view,

---

96. Cyrus was the beginning of the Persian, as Ninus was of the Assyrian monarchy. The Magi and Chaldeans (the chief of whom was Zoroaster) employed their studies upon magic and astrology, which was in a manner almost all the learning of the ancient Asian people. We have scarce any account of a moral philosopher except Confucius, the great law-giver of the Chinese, who lived about two thousand years ago.

110. The learning of the old Egyptian priests consisted for the most part in geometry and astronomy; they also preserved the history of their nation. Their greatest hero upon record is Sesostris, whose actions and conquests may be seen at large in Diodorus, etc. He is said to have caused the kings he vanquished to draw him in his chariot. The posture of his statue, in these verses, is correspondent to the description which Herodotus gives of one of them remaining in his own time.

Whom sceptered slaves in golden harness drew:
His hands a bow and pointed javelin hold;
His giant limbs are armed in scales of gold.
Between the statues obelisks were placed,
And the learned walls with hieroglyphics graced.

    Of Gothic structure was the northern side,
O'erwrought with ornaments of barbarous pride.   120
There huge colosses rose, with trophies crowned,
And runic characters were graved around.
There sate Zamolxis with erected eyes,
And Odin here in mimic trances dies.
There on rude iron columns, smeared with blood,
The horrid forms of Scythian heroes stood,
Druids and bards (their once loud harps unstrung)
And youths that died to be by poets sung.
These and a thousand more of doubtful fame,
To whom old fables gave a lasting name,   130
In ranks adorned the Temple's outward face;
The wall in lustre and effect like glass,
Which o'er each object casting various dyes,
Enlarges some, and others multiplies:
Nor void of emblem was the mystic wall,
For thus romantic° Fame increases all.°

    The temple shakes, the sounding gates unfold,
Wide vaults appear, and roofs of fretted gold:
Raised on a thousand pillars, wreathed around
With laurel-foliage, and with eagles crowned: 140
Of bright, transparent beryl were the walls,
The friezes gold, and gold the capitals:
As heaven with stars, the roof with jewels glows,

---

119. The architecture is agreeable to that part of the world. The learning of the northern nations lay more obscure than that of the rest; Zamolxis was the disciple of Pythagoras, who taught the immortality of the soul to the Scythians. Odin, or Woden, was the great legislator and hero of the Goths. They tell us of him, that being subject to fits, he persuaded his followers, that during those trances he received inspirations, from whence he dictated his laws: he is said to have been the inventor of the runic characters.

127. These were the priests and poets of those people, so celebrated for their savage virtue. Those heroic barbarians accounted it a dishonour to die in their beds, and rushed on to certain death in the prospect of an afterlife, and for the glory of a song from their bards in praise of their actions.

And ever-living lamps depend in rows.
Full in the passage of each spacious gate,
The sage historians in white garments wait;
Graved o'er their seats the form of Time was found,
His scythe reversed,° and both his pinions bound.
Within stood heroes, who through loud alarms
In bloody fields pursued renown in arms.   150
High on a throne with trophies charged, I viewed
The youth that all things but himself subdued;
His feet on sceptres and tiaras trod,
And his horned head belied° the Libyan god.
There Caesar, graced with both Minervas, shone;
Caesar, the world's great master, and his own;
Unmoved, superior still in every state,
And scarce detested in his country's fate.
But chief were those, who not for empire fought,
But with their toils their people's safety bought: 160
High o'er the rest Epaminondas stood;
Timoleon, glorious in his brother's blood;
Bold Scipio, saviour of the Roman state;
Great in his triumphs, in retirement great;
And wise Aurelius, in whose well-taught mind ⎫
With boundless power unbounded virtue joined, ⎬
His own strict judge, and patron of mankind. ⎭
    Much-suffering heroes next their honours claim,
Those of less noisy, and less guilty fame,
Fair Virtue's silent train: supreme of these   170
Here ever shines the godlike Socrates:
He whom ungrateful Athens could expel,

152. Alexander the Great: the tiara was the crown peculiar to the Asian princes:
his desire to be thought the son of Jupiter Ammon, caused him to wear the horns
of that God, and to represent the same upon his coins; which was continued by
several of his successors.

162. Timoleon had saved the life of his brother Timophanes in the battle between
the Argives and Corinthians; but afterwards killed him when he affected the tyranny,
preferring his duty to his country to all the obligations of blood.

172. Aristides, who for his great integrity was distinguished by the appellation of
the Just. When his countrymen would have banished him by the ostracism, where it
was the custom for every man to sign the name of the person he voted to exile in
an oyster-shell; a peasant, who could not write, came to Aristides to do it for him,
who readily signed his own name.

At all times just, but when he signed the shell:
Here his abode the martyred Phocion claims,
With Agis, not the last of Spartan names:
Unconquered Cato shows the wound he tore,
And Brutus his ill genius meets no more.
     But in the centre of the hallowed choir,
Six pompous columns° o'er the rest aspire;
Around the shrine itself of Fame they stand;   180
Hold the chief honours, and the fane command.
High on the first, the mighty Homer shone;
Eternal adamant composed his throne;
Father of verse! in holy fillets dressed,
His silver beard waved gently o'er his breast;
Though blind, a boldness in his looks appears;
In years he seemed, but not impaired by years.
The wars of Troy were round the pillar seen:
Here fierce Tydides wounds the Cyprian Queen;
Here Hector glorious from Patroclus' fall,   190
Here dragged in triumph round the Trojan wall.
Motion and life did every part inspire,
Bold was the work, and proved the master's fire;
A strong expression most he seemed t'affect,
And here and there disclosed a brave neglect.
     A golden column next in rank appeared,
On which a shrine of purest gold was reared;
Finished the whole, and laboured every part,
With patient touches of unwearied art:
The Mantuan there in sober triumph sate,   200
Composed his posture, and his look sedate;
On Homer still he fixed a reverend eye,
Great without pride, in modest majesty.
In living sculpture on the sides were spread
The Latian wars, and haughty Turnus dead;
Eliza stretched upon the funeral pyre,

178. In the midst of the temple, nearest the throne of Fame, are placed the greatest names in learning of all antiquity. These are described in such attitudes as express their different characters: the columns on which they are raised are adorned with sculptures, taken from the most striking subjects of their works; which sculpture bears a resemblance, in its manner and character, to the manner and character of their writings.

Aeneas bending with his aged sire:
Troy flamed in burning gold, and o'er the throne
ARMS AND THE MAN in golden cyphers shone.

Four swans sustain a car of silver bright,   210
With heads advanced, and pinions stretched for flight:
Here, like some furious prophet, Pindar rode,
And seemed to labour with th'inspiring god.
Across the harp a careless hand he flings,
And boldly sinks into the sounding strings.
The figured games of Greece the column grace,
Neptune and Jove survey the rapid race:
The youths hang o'er their chariots as they run;
The fiery steeds seem starting from the stone;
The champions in distorted postures threat;   220
And all appeared irregularly great.

Here happy Horace tuned th'Ausonian° lyre
To sweeter sounds, and tempered Pindar's fire:
Pleased with Alcaeus' manly rage t'infuse
The softer spirit of the Sapphic Muse.
The polished pillar different sculptures grace;
A work outlasting monumental brass.°
Here smiling Loves and Bacchanals appear,
The Julian star, and great Augustus here.
The doves that round the infant poet spread   230
Myrtles and bays, hung hovering o'er his head.

Here in a shrine that cast a dazzling light,
Sate fixed in thought the mighty Stagyrite;°
His sacred head a radiant Zodiac crowned,
And various animals his sides surround;
His piercing eyes, erect, appear to view
Superior worlds, and look all Nature through.

With equal rays immortal Tully° shone,
The Roman rostra decked the consul's throne:
Gathering his flowing robe, he seemed to stand   240
In act to speak, and graceful stretched his hand.
Behind, Rome's genius waits with civic crowns,

---

210. Pindar being seated in a chariot, alludes to the chariot-races he celebrated
in the Grecian games. The swans are emblems of poetry, their soaring posture
intimates the sublimity and activity of his genius. Neptune presided over the Isthmian,
and Jupiter over the Olympian games.

And the great father of his country owns.

   These massy columns in a circle rise,
O'er which a pompous dome invades the skies:
Scarce to the top I stretched my aching sight,
So large it spread, and swelled to such a height.
Full in the midst proud Fame's imperial seat
With jewels blazed, magnificently great;
The vivid emeralds there revive the eye,   250
The flaming rubies show their sanguine dye,
Bright azure rays from lively sapphires stream,
And lucid amber casts a golden gleam.
With various-coloured light the pavement shone,
And all on fire appeared the glowing throne;
The dome's high arch reflects the mingled blaze,
And forms a rainbow of alternate rays.
When on the Goddess first I cast my sight,
Scarce seemed her stature of a cubit's° height,
But swelled to larger size, the more I gazed,   260
Till to the roof her towering front she raised.
With her, the temple every moment grew,
And ampler vistas opened to my view:
Upward the columns shoot, the roofs ascend,
And arches widen, and long aisles extend.
Such was her form as ancient bards have told,
Wings raise her arms, and wings her feet enfold;
A thousand busy tongues the Goddess bears,
And thousand open eyes, and thousand listening ears.
Beneath, in order ranged, the tuneful Nine°   270
(Her virgin handmaids) still attend the shrine:
With eyes on Fame for ever fixed, they sing;
For Fame they raise the voice, and tune the string.
With time's first birth began the heavenly lays,
And last, eternal, through the length of days.
   Around these wonders° as I cast a look,
The trumpet sounded, and the temple shook,
And all the nations, summoned at the call,
From different quarters fill the crowded hall:
Of various tongues the mingled sounds were heard;   280
In various garbs promiscuous throngs appeared;
Thick as the bees, that with the spring renew
Their flowery toils, and sip the fragrant dew,

When the winged colonies first tempt° the sky,
O'er dusky fields and shaded waters fly,
Or settling, seize the sweets the blossoms yield,
And a low murmur runs along the field.
Millions of suppliant crowds the shrine attend,
And all degrees before the Goddess bend;
The poor, the rich, the valiant, and the sage,
And boasting youth, and narrative° old-age.   290
Their pleas were different, their request the same:
For good and bad alike are fond of Fame.
Some she disgraced, and some with honours crowned;
Unlike successes equal merits found.
Thus her blind sister, fickle Fortune, reigns,
And, undiscerning, scatters crowns and chains.

   First at the shrine the learnéd world appear,
And to the Goddess thus prefer their prayer:
'Long have we sought t'instruct and please mankind,   300
With studies pale, with midnight vigils blind;
But thanked by few, rewarded yet by none,
We here appeal to thy superior throne:
On wit and learning the just prize bestow,
For fame is all we must expect below.'

   The Goddess heard, and bade the Muses raise
The golden trumpet of eternal praise:
From pole to pole the winds diffuse the sound,
That fills the circuit of the world around;
Not all at once, as thunder breaks the cloud;   310
The notes at first were rather sweet than loud:
By just degrees they every moment rise,
Fill the wide earth, and gain upon the skies.
At every breath were balmy odours shed,
Which still grew sweeter as they wider spread;
Less fragrant scents th'unfolding rose exhales,
Or spices breathing in Arabian gales.

   Next these the good and just, an awful train,
Thus on their knees address the sacred fane.
'Since living virtue is with envy cursed,   320
And the best men are treated like the worst,
Do thou, just Goddess, call our merits forth,
And give each deed th'exact intrinsic worth.'
'Not with bare justice shall your act be crowned'

Said Fame, 'but high above desert renowned:
Let fuller notes th'applauding world amaze,
And the loud clarion labour in your praise.'
  This band dismissed, behold another crowd
Preferred the same request, and lowly bowed;
The constant tenor of whose well-spent days   330
No less deserved a just return of praise.
But straight the direful trump of slander sounds;
Through the big dome the doubling thunder bounds;
Loud as the burst of cannon rends the skies,
The dire report through every region flies:
In every ear incessant rumours rung,
And gathering scandals grew on every tongue.
From the black trumpet's rusty concave broke
Sulphureous flames, and clouds of rolling smoke:
The poisonous vapour blots the purple° skies,   340
And withers all before it as it flies.
  A troop came next, who crowns and armour wore,
And proud defiance in their looks they bore:
'For thee' (they cried) 'amidst alarms and strife,
We sailed in tempests down the stream of life;
For thee whole nations filled with flames and blood,
And swam to empire through the purple flood.
Those ills we dared, thy inspiration own,
What virtue seemed, was done for thee alone.'
'Ambitious fools!' (the Queen replied, and frowned)   350
'Be all your acts in dark oblivion drowned;
There sleep forgot, with mighty tyrants gone,
Your statues mouldered, and your names unknown!'
A sudden cloud straight snatched them from my sight,
And each majestic phantom sunk in night.
  Then came the smallest tribe I yet had seen;
Plain was their dress, and modest was their mien.
'Great idol of mankind! we neither claim
The praise of merit, nor aspire to fame!
But safe in deserts from th'applause of men,   360
Would die unheard of, as we lived unseen.
'Tis all we beg thee, to conceal from sight
Those acts of goodness, which themselves requite.
O let us still the secret joy partake,
To follow virtue ev'n for virtue's sake.'

'And live there men who slight immortal fame?
Who then with incense shall adore our name?
But mortals! know, 'tis still our greatest pride
To blaze those virtues which the good would hide.
Rise! Muses, rise, add all your tuneful breath,   370
These must not sleep in darkness and in death.'
She said: in air the trembling music floats,
And on the winds triumphant swell the notes;
So soft, though high, so loud, and yet so clear,
Ev'n listening angels leaned from heaven to hear:
To farthest shores th'ambrosial spirit° flies,
Sweet to the world, and grateful to the skies.
    Next these a youthful train their vows expressed,
With feathers crowned, with gay embroidery dressed:
'Hither', they cried, 'direct your eyes, and see   380
The men of pleasure, dress, and gallantry;
Ours is the place at banquets, balls, and plays;
Sprightly our nights, polite are all our days;
Courts we frequent, where 'tis our pleasing care
To pay due visits, and address the fair:
In fact, 'tis true, no nymph we could persuade,
But still in fancy vanquished every maid;
Of unknown duchesses lewd tales we tell,
Yet, would the world believe us, all were well.
The joy let others have, and we the name,   390
And what we want in pleasure, grant in fame.'
    The Queen assents, the trumpet rends the skies,
And at each blast a lady's honour dies.
    Pleased with the strange success, vast numbers pressed
Around the shrine, and made the same request:
'What you' (she cried) 'unlearned in arts to please,
Slaves to yourselves, and ev'n fatigued with ease,
Who lose a length of undeserving days,
Would you usurp the lover's dear-bought praise?
To just contempt, ye vain pretenders, fall,   400
The people's fable,° and the scorn of all.'
Straight the black clarion sends a horrid sound,
Loud laughs burst out, and bitter scoffs fly round,
Whispers are heard, with taunts reviling loud,
And scornful hisses run through all the crowd.
    Last, those who boast of mighty mischiefs done,

Enslave their country, or usurp a throne;
Or who their glory's dire foundation laid
On sovereigns ruined, or on friends betrayed;
Calm, thinking villains, whom no faith could fix,   410
Of crooked counsels and dark politics;
Of these a gloomy tribe surround the throne,
And beg to make th'immortal treasons known.
The trumpet roars, long flaky flames expire,
With sparks, that seemed to set the world on fire.
At the dread sound, pale mortals stood aghast,
And startled nature trembled with the blast.

   This having heard and seen, some power unknown
Straight changed the scene, and snatched me from the
      throne.
Before my view appeared a structure fair,   420
Its site uncertain, if in earth or air;
With rapid motion turned the mansion round;
With ceaseless noise the ringing walls resound:
Not less in number were the spacious doors,
Than leaves on trees, or sands upon the shores;
Which still unfolded stand, by night, by day,
Pervious to winds, and open every way.
As flames by nature to the skies ascend,
As weighty bodies to the centre tend,
As to the sea returning rivers roll,   430
And the touched needle trembles to the pole:
Hither, as to their proper place, arise
All various sounds from earth, and seas, and skies,
Or spoke aloud, or whispered in the ear;
Nor ever silence, rest, or peace in here.
As on the smooth expanse of crystal lakes
The sinking stone at first a circle makes;
The trembling surface, by the motion stirred,
Spreads in a second circle, then a third;
Wide, and more wide, the floating rings advance,   440
Fill all the watery plain, and to the margin dance:
Thus every voice and sound, when first they break,
On neighbouring air a soft impression make;
Another ambient circle then they move;
That, in its turn, impels the next above;
Through undulating air the sounds are sent,

And spread o'er all the fluid element.
   There various news I heard, of love and strife,
Of peace and war, health, sickness, death, and life,
Of loss and gain, of famine and of store,   450
Of storms at sea, and travels on the shore,
Of prodigies, and portents seen in air,
Of fires and plagues, and stars with blazing hair,°
Of turns of fortune, changes in the state,
The falls of favourites, projects of the great,
Of old mismanagements, taxations new:
All neither wholly false, nor wholly true.
   Above, below, without, within, around,
Confused, unnumbered multitudes are found,
Who pass, repass, advance, and glide away;   460
Hosts raised by fear, and phantoms of a day:
Astrologers, that future fates foreshow,
Projectors,° quacks, and lawyers not a few;
And priests, and party-zealots, numerous bands
With home-born lies, or tales from foreign lands;
Each talked aloud, or in some secret place,
And wild impatience stared in every face.
The flying rumours gathered as they rolled.
Scarce any tale was sooner heard than told;
And all who told it added something new,   )
And all who heard it, made enlargements too, } 470
In every ear it spread, on every tongue it grew.)
Thus flying east and west, and north and south,
News travelled with increase from mouth to mouth.
So from a spark, that kindled first by chance,
With gathering force the quickening flames advance;
Till to the clouds their curling heads aspire,
And towers and temples sink in floods of fire.
   When thus ripe lies are to perfection sprung,
Full grown, and fit to grace a mortal tongue,   480
Through thousand vents, impatient forth they flow,
And rush in millions on the world below.
Fame sits aloft, and points them out their course,
Their date determines, and prescribes their force:
Some to remain, and some to perish soon;
Or wane and wax alternate like the moon.
Around, a thousand wingèd wonders fly,

Borne by the trumpet's blast, and scattered through the
  sky.
There, at one passage, oft you might survey
A lie and truth contending for the way;   490
And long 'twas doubtful, both so closely pent,
Which first should issue through the narrow vent:
At last agreed, together out they fly,
Inseparable now, the truth and lie;
The strict companions are for ever joined,
And this or that unmixed, no mortal e'er shall find.

While thus I stood, intent to see and hear,
One came, methought, and whispered in my ear:
'What could thus high thy rash ambition raise?
Art thou, fond youth, a candidate for praise?'   500
  ''Tis true', said I, 'not void of hopes I came,
For who so fond as youthful bards of Fame?
But few, alas! the casual blessing boast,
So hard to gain, so easy to be lost.
How vain that second life in others' breath,
Th'estate which wits inherit after death!
Ease, health, and life, for this they must resign,
(Unsure the tenure, but how vast the fine!)°
The great man's curse, without the gains, endure,
Be envied, wretched, and be flattered, poor;   510
All luckless wits their enemies professed,
And all successful, jealous friends at best.
Nor Fame I slight, nor for her favours call;
She comes unlooked for, if she comes at all.°
But if the purchase costs so dear a price,
As soothing Folly, or exalting Vice:
Oh! if the Muse must flatter lawless sway,
And follow still where fortune leads the way;
Or if no basis bear my rising name,
But the fallen ruins of another's fame;   520
Then teach me, heaven! to scorn the guilty bays,

---

497. The hint is taken from a passage in another part of the third book, but here
more naturally made the conclusion, with the addition of a *moral* to the whole. In
Chaucer he only answers 'he came to see the place'; and the book ends abruptly,
with his being surprised at the sight of a *man of great authority*, and awakening in a
fright.

Drive from my breast that wretched lust of praise,
Unblemished let me live, or die unknown;
Oh grant an honest fame, or grant me none!'

A FAREWELL TO LONDON
in the Year 1715

Dear, damned, distracting town, farewell!   1
    Thy fools no more I'll tease:
This year in peace, ye critics, dwell,
    Ye harlots, sleep at ease!°

Soft Bethel and rough Craggs,° adieu!
    Earl Warwick make your moan,
The lively Hinchinbrook and you
    May knock up whores alone.

To drink and droll be Rowe allowed
    Till the third watchman's toll;   10
Let Jervas gratis paint, and Frowde
    Save threepence and his soul.

Farewell Arbuthnot's raillery
    On every learned sot;
And Garth, the best good Christian he,
    Although he knows it not.

Lintot, farewell! thy bard must go;
    Farewell, unhappy Tonson!
Heaven gives thee for thy loss of Rowe,
    Lean Philips, and fat Johnson.   20

Why should I stay? Both parties rage;
    My vixen mistress squalls;
The wits in envious feuds engage:
    And Homer (damn him) calls.

The love of arts lies cold and dead
  In Halifax's urn;°
And not one muse of all he fed,
  Has yet the grace to mourn.

My friends, by turns, my friends confound,
  Betray, and are betrayed: 30
Poor Younger's sold for fifty pound,
  And Bicknell is a jade.

Why make I friendships with the great,
  When I no favour seek?°
Or follow girls seven hours in eight?
  I need but once a week.

Still idle, with a busy air,
  Deep whimsies to contrive;
The gayest valetudinaire,
  Most thinking rake alive.   40

Solicitous for others ends,
  Though fond of dear repose;
Careless or drowsy with my friends,
  And frolic with my foes.

Luxurious lobster-nights, farewell,
  For sober, studious days;
And Burlington's delicious meal,
  For salads, tarts, and pease.°

Adieu to all but Gay alone,
  Whose soul, sincere and free,   50
Loves all mankind, but flatters none,
  And so may starve with me.

EPISTLE
To Mr JERVAS

With DRYDEN's Translation of FRESNOY's Art of Painting

This verse be thine, my friend, nor thou refuse   1
This, from no venal or ungrateful Muse.
Whether thy hand strike out some free design,
Where life awakes, and dawns at every line;
Or blend in beauteous tints the coloured mass,
And from the canvas call the mimic face:
Read these instructive leaves, in which conspire
Fresnoy's close art, and Dryden's native fire:
And reading wish, like theirs, our fate and fame,
So mixed our studies, and so joined our name;   10
Like them to shine through long succeeding age,
So just thy skill, so regular my rage.°
    Smit with the love of sister-arts° we came,
And met congenial,° mingling flame with flame;
Like friendly colours found them both unite,
And each from each contract new strength and light.
How oft in pleasing tasks we wear the day,
While summer-suns roll unperceived away?
How oft our slowly-growing works impart,
While images reflect from art to art?   20
How oft review; each finding like a friend
Something to blame, and something to commend?
    What flattering scenes our wandering fancy wrought,
Rome's pompous glories rising to our thought!
Together o'er the Alps methinks we fly,
Fired with ideas of fair Italy.
With thee, on Raphael's monument I mourn,
Or wait inspiring dreams at Maro's° urn:
With thee repose, where Tully° once was laid,

Or seek some ruin's formidable shade: 30
While fancy brings the vanished piles to view,
And builds imaginary Rome anew,
Here thy well-studied marbles fix our eye;
A fading fresco here demands a sigh:
Each heavenly piece unwearied we compare,
Match Raphael's grace with thy loved Guido's air,
Carracci's strength, Correggio's softer line,
Paulo's free stroke, and Titian's warmth° divine.
    How finished with illustrious toil appears
This small, well-polished gem, the *work of years!   40
Yet still how faint by precept is expressed
The living image in the painter's breast?
Thence endless streams of fair ideas flow,
Strike in the sketch, or in the picture glow;
Thence beauty, waking all her forms, supplies
An angel's sweetness, or Bridgewater's° eyes.
    Muse! at that name thy sacred sorrows shed,
Those tears eternal, that embalm the dead:
Call round her tomb each object of desire,
Each purer frame informed with purer fire: 50
Bid her be all that cheers or softens life,
The tender sister, daughter, friend, and wife:
Bid her be all that makes mankind adore;
Then view this marble, and be vain no more!
    Yet still her charms in breathing paint engage;
Her modest cheek shall warm a future age.
Beauty, frail flower that every season fears,
Blooms in thy colours for a thousand years.
Thus Churchill's race° shall other hearts surprise,
And other beauties envy Worsley's° eyes;   60
Each pleasing Blount° shall endless smiles bestow,
And soft Belinda's° blush for ever glow.
    Oh lasting as those colours may they shine,
Free as thy stroke, yet faultless as thy line;
New graces yearly like thy works display,
Soft without weakness, without glaring gay;°
Led by some rule, that guides, but not constrains;
And finished more through happiness than pains.

* Fresnoy employed above twenty years in finishing his poem.

The kindred arts shall in their praise conspire,
One dip the pencil, and one string the lyre.   70
Yet should the Graces all thy figures place,
And breathe an air divine on every face;
Yet should the Muses bid my numbers roll
Strong as their charms, and gentle as their soul;
With Zeuxis'° Helen thy Bridgewater vie,
And these be sung till Granville's Myra° die:
Alas, how little from the grave we claim!
Thou but preserv'st a face, and I a name.

EPISTLE
To Miss BLOUNT
On her leaving the Town after the CORONATION

As some fond° virgin, whom her mother's care   1
Drags from the town to wholesome country air,
Just when she learns to roll a melting eye,°
And hear a spark,° yet think no danger nigh;
From the dear man unwilling she must sever,
Yet takes one kiss before she parts for ever:
Thus from the world fair Zephalinda° flew,
Saw others happy, and with sighs withdrew;
Not that their pleasures caused her discontent,
She sighed not that They stayed, but that She went.   10
    She went, to plain-work,° and to purling brooks,
Old-fashioned halls, dull aunts, and croaking rooks:
She went from opera, park, assembly, play,
To morning-walks, and prayers three hours a day;
To part her time 'twixt reading and bohea,°
To muse, and spill her solitary tea,
Or o'er cold coffee trifle with the spoon,°
Count the slow clock, and dine exact at noon;°
Divert her eyes with pictures in the fire,

Coronation.] Of King George the first, [1714].

Hum half a tune, tell stories to the squire;   20
Up to her godly garret after seven,
There starve and pray, for that's the way to heaven.

    Some squire, perhaps, you take delight to rack;°
Whose game is whisk,° whose treat a toast in sack;°
Who visits with a gun, presents you birds,
Then gives a smacking buss,° and cries,—'No words!'
Or with his hound comes hallowing from the stable,
Makes love with nods, and knees beneath a table;
Whose laughs are hearty, though his jests are coarse,
And loves you best of all things—but his horse.   30

    In some fair evening, on your elbow laid,
You dream of triumphs° in the rural shade;
In pensive thought recall the fancied scene,
See coronations rise on every green;
Before you pass th' imaginary sights
Of lords, and earls, and dukes, and gartered knights,
While the spread fan o'ershades your closing eyes;
Then give one flirt,° and all the vision flies.
Thus vanish sceptres, coronets, and balls,
And leave you in lone woods, or empty walls!   40

    So when your slave, at some dear idle time,
(Not plagued with head-aches, or the want of rhyme)
Stands in the streets, abstracted from the crew,
And while he seems to study, thinks of you;
Just when his fancy points your sprightly eyes,
Or sees the blush of soft Parthenia° rise,
Gay° pats my shoulder, and you vanish quite,
Streets, chairs,° and coxcombs rush upon my sight;
Vexed to be still in town, I knit my brow,
Look sour, and hum a tune, as you may now.°   50

A FULL AND TRUE ACCOUNT OF
A HORRID AND BARBAROUS REVENGE
BY POISON,
ON THE BODY OF
MR EDMUND CURLL,
BOOKSELLER;
WITH A FAITHFUL COPY OF
HIS LAST WILL AND TESTAMENT
PUBLISHED BY AN EYE-WITNESS

> So when Curll's stomach the strong drench o'ercame,
> (Infused in vengeance of insulted fame)
> Th' avenger sees, with a delighted eye,
> His long jaws open, and his colour fly;
> And while his guts the keen emetics urge,
> Smiles on the vomit, and enjoys the purge.

History furnishes us with examples of many satirical authors who have fallen sacrifices to revenge, but not of any booksellers that I know of, except the unfortunate subject of the following papers. I mean Mr Edmund Curll, at the Bible and Dial in Fleet Street, who was yesterday poisoned by Mr Pope, after having lived many years an instance of the mild temper of the British nation.

Everybody knows that the said Mr Edmund Curll, on Monday the 26th instant, published a satirical piece, entitled *Court Poems*, in the preface whereof they were attributed to a Lady of Quality,° Mr Pope, or Mr Gay; by which indiscreet method, though he had escaped one revenge, there were still two behind in reserve.

Now on the Wednesday ensuing, between the hours of 10 and 11, Mr Lintot, a neighbouring bookseller, desired a conference with Mr Curll about settling the title page of *Wiquefort's Ambassador*,° inviting him at the same time to take a whet together. Mr Pope, (who is not the only instance how persons of bright parts may be carried away by the instigations of the devil) found means to convey himself into the same room, under pretence of business with Mr Lintot, who it seems is the printer of his *Homer*. This gentleman with a seeming coolness, reprimanded Mr Curll for wrongfully ascribing to him the aforesaid poems. He excused himself, by declaring that one of his authors (Mr Oldmixon by name) gave the copies to the press, and wrote the Preface.° Upon this Mr Pope (being to all appearance reconciled) very civilly drank a glass of sack to Mr Curll, which he as civilly pledged; and though the liquor in colour and taste differed not from common sack, yet was it plain by the pangs this unhappy stationer felt soon after, that some poisonous drug had been secretly infused therein.

About eleven o'clock he went home, where his wife observing his colour changed, said, 'Are you not sick, my dear?' He replied, 'Bloody sick', and incontinently fell a vomiting and straining in an uncommon and unnatural manner, the contents of his vomiting being as green as grass. His wife had been just reading a book of her husband's printing, concerning Jane Wenham,° the famous witch of Hertford, and her mind misgave her that he was bewitched; but he soon let her know that he suspected *poison*, and recounted to her, between the intervals of his yawnings and reachings, every circumstance of his interview with Mr Pope.

Mr Lintot in the meantime coming in, was extremely affrighted at the sudden alteration he observed in him: 'Brother Curll,' says he, 'I fear you have got the vomiting distemper, which (I have heard) kills in half an hour. This comes from your not following my advice, to drink old hock as I do, and abstain from sack.' Mr Curll replied, in a moving tone, 'Your author's sack I fear has done my business.' 'Z—ds,' says Mr Lintot, 'My author!—Why did not you drink old hock?' Notwithstanding which rough remonstrance, he did in the most friendly manner press him to take warm water; but Mr Curll did with great obstinacy refuse it; which made Mr Lintot infer, that he chose to die, as thinking to recover greater damages.

All this time the symptoms increased violently, with acute pains in the lower belly. 'Brother Lintot,' says he, 'I perceive my last hour approaching, do me the friendly office to call my partner, Mr Pemberton,° that we may settle our worldly affairs.' Mr Lintot, like a kind neighbour, was hastening out of the room, while Mr Curll raved aloud in this manner, 'If I survive this, I will be revenged on Tonson,° it was he first detected me as the printer of these poems, and I will reprint these very poems in his name.' His wife admonished him not to think of revenge, but to take care of his stock and his soul: and in the same instant, Mr Lintot (whose goodness can never be enough applauded) returned with Mr Pemberton. After some tears jointly shed by these humane booksellers, Mr Curll, being (as he said) in his perfect senses though in great bodily pain, immediately proceeded to make a verbal will (Mrs Curll having first put on his nightcap) in the following manner.

'Gentlemen, in the first place, I do sincerely pray forgiveness for those indirect methods I have pursued in inventing new titles to old books, putting authors' names to things they never saw, publishing private quarrels for public entertainment; all which, I hope will be pardoned, as being done to get an honest livelihood.

I do also heartily beg pardon of all persons of honour, lords spiritual and temporal, gentry, burgesses, and commonalty, to whose abuse I have any, or every way, contributed by my publications. Particularly, I hope it will be considered, that if I have vilified his Grace the Duke of Marlborough, I have likewise aspersed the late Duke of Ormond;° if I have abused the honourable Mr Walpole, I have also libelled the late Lord Bolingbroke; so that I have preserved that equality and impartiality which becomes an honest man in times of faction and division.

I call my conscience to witness, that many of these things which may seem malicious, were done out of charity; I having made it wholly my business to print for poor disconsolate authors, whom all other booksellers refuse. Only God bless Sir Richard Blackmore, you know he takes no copy money.°

The book of the *Conduct of the Earl of Nottingham*,° is yet unpublished; as you are to have the profit of it, Mr Pemberton, you are to run the risk of the resentments of all that noble family. Indeed I caused the author to assert several things in it as facts, which are only idle stories of the town; because I thought it would make the book sell. Do you pay the author for copy money, and the printer and publisher. I heartily beg God's, and my Lord Nottingham's pardon; but all trades must live.

The second Collection of Poems, which I groundlessly called Mr Prior's,° will sell for nothing, and hath not yet paid the charge of the advertisements, which I was obliged to publish against him. Therefore you may as well suppress the edition, and beg that gentleman's pardon in the name of a dying Christian.

The French *Cato*,° with the criticism, showing how superior it is to Mr Addison's, (which I wickedly inscribed to Madam Dacier) may be suppressed at a reasonable rate, being damnably translated.

I protest I have no animosity to Mr Rowe,° having printed part of his *Callipaedia*, and an incorrect edition of his poems without his leave, in quarto. Mr Gildon's *Rehearsal;*° or *Bays the Younger,* did more harm to me than to Mr Rowe; though upon the faith of an honest man, I paid him double for abusing both him and Mr Pope.

Heaven pardon me for publishing the *Trials of Sodomy*° in an Elzevir letter; but I humbly hope, my printing Sir Richard Blackmore's *Essays*° will atone for them. I beg that you will take what remains of these last, which is near the whole impression, (presents excepted) and let my poor widow have in exchange the sole propriety of the copy of Madam Mascranny.°

Here Mr Pemberton interrupted, and would by no means consent to this article, about which some dispute might have arisen, unbecoming a dying person, if Mr Lintot had not interposed, and Mr Curll vomited.

What this poor unfortunate man spoke afterwards, was so indistinct, and in such broken accents, (being perpetually interrupted by vomitings) that the reader is entreated to excuse the confusion and imperfection of this account.

Dear Mr Pemberton, I beg you to beware of the indictment at Hicks's Hall, for publishing Rochester's bawdy poems;° that copy will otherwise be my best legacy to my dear wife, and helpless child.

The Case of Impotence° was my best support all the last long vacation.

In this last paragraph Mr Curll's voice grew more free, for his vomitings abated upon his dejections, and he spoke what follows from his close-stool.

For the copies of noblemen's and bishops' *Last Wills and Testaments,* I solemnly declare I printed them not with any purpose of defamation; but merely as I thought those copies lawfully purchased from Doctors' Commons, at one shilling a piece. Our trade in wills turning to small account, we may divide them blindfold.

For Mr Maynwaring's *Life,*° I ask Mrs Oldfield's pardon. Neither *His,* nor my Lord Halifax's° *Lives,* though they were of great service to their country, were of any to me: but I was resolved, since I could not print their works while they lived, to print their lives after they were dead.'

While he was speaking these words, Mr Oldmixon° entered. 'Ah! Mr Oldmixon' (said poor Mr Curll) 'to what a condition have your works reduced me! I die a martyr to that unlucky preface. However, in these my last moments, I will be just to all men; you shall have your third share of the *Court Poems,* as was stipulated. When I am dead, where will you find another bookseller? Your *Protestant Packet* might have supported you, had you writ a little less scurrilously, There is a mean in all things.'

Then turning to Mr Pemberton, he told him, he had several *taking title-pages*° that only wanted treatises to be wrote to them, and earnestly entreated, that when they were writ, his heirs might have some share of the profit of them.

After he had said this he fell into horrible gripings, upon which Mr Lintot advised him to repeat the Lord's Prayer. He desired his wife to step into the shop for a Common Prayer-Book, and read it by the help of a candle, without hesitation. He closed the book, fetched a groan, and recommended to Mrs Curll to give forty shillings to the poor of the parish of St Dunstan's, and a week's wages advance to each of his gentlemen authors, with some small gratuity in particular to Mrs Centlivre.°

The poor man continued for some hours with all his disconsolate family about him in tears, expecting his final dissolution; when of a sudden he was surprisingly relieved by a plentiful fetid stool, which obliged them all to retire out of the room. Notwithstanding, it is judged by Sir Richard Blackmore, that the poison is still latent in his body, and will infallibly destroy him by slow degrees, in less than a month. It is to be hoped the other enemies of this wretched stationer, will not further pursue their revenge, or shorten this small period of his miserable life.

A FURTHER
ACCOUNT
OF THE MOST
DEPLORABLE CONDITION
OF
MR *EDMUND CURLL*,
BOOKSELLER

Since his being POISONED on the
28th of *March*

The public is already acquainted with the manner of Mr Curll's impoisonment, by a faithful, though unpolite, historian of Grub Street. I am but the continuer of his history; yet I hope a due distinction will be made, between an undignified scribbler of a sheet and half, and the author of a threepenny stitched book, like myself.

'Wit' (saith Sir Richard Blackmore°) 'proceeds from a concurrence of regular and exalted ferments, and an affluence of animal spirits rectified and refined to a degree of purity.' On the contrary, when the igneous particles rise with the vital liquor, they produce an abstraction of the rational part of the soul, which we commonly call *madness*. The verity of this hypothesis, is justified by the symptoms with which the unfortunate Mr Edmund Curll, bookseller, hath been afflicted ever since his swallowing the poison at the Swan Tavern in Fleet Street. For though the neck of his retort, which carries up the animal spirits to the head, is of an extraordinary length, yet the said animal spirits rise muddy, being contaminated with the inflammable particles of this uncommon poison.

The symptoms of his departure from his usual temper of mind, were at first only *speaking civilly to his customers*, taking a fancy to *say his prayers, singeing a pig with a new purchased libel*, and *refusing two and ninepence for Sir Richard Blackmore's Essays*.

As the poor man's frenzy increased, he began to *void his excrements in his bed, read Rochester's bawdy poems to his wife*, gave *Oldmixon a slap on the chops*, and *would have kissed Mr Pemberton's a— by violence*.

But at last he came to such a pass, that he would *dine upon nothing but copperplates, took a clyster for a whipped syllabub, and ate a suppository* for a *raddish with bread and butter*.

We leave it to every tender wife to imagine how sorely all this afflicted poor Mrs Curll. At first she privately put a bill into several churches, desiring the prayers of the congregation for a *wretched stationer* distempered in mind. But when she was sadly convinced that his misfortune was public to all the world, writ the following letter to her good neighbour Mr Lintot.

A true copy of Mrs Curll's Letter to Mr Lintot.

Worthy Mr Lintot,
You, and all the neighbours know too well, the frenzy with which my poor man is visited. I never perceived he was out of himself, till that melancholy day that he thought he was poisoned in a glass of sack; upon this, he took a strange fancy to run a vomiting all over the house, and in the new washed dining-room. Alas! this is the greatest adversity that ever befell my poor man since he lost *one testicle* at school by the bite of a black boar. Good Lord! if he should die, where should I dispose of the stock? unless Mr Pemberton or you would help a distressed widow; for God knows he never published any books that lasted

above a week, so that if we wanted *daily books*, we wanted *daily bread*. I can write no more, for I hear the rap of Mr Curll's ivory-headed cane upon the counter.—Pray recommend me to your pastry cook, who furnishes you yearly with tarts in exchange for your papers, for Mr Curll has disobliged ours since his fits came upon him;—before that, we generally lived upon baked meats.— He is coming in, and I have but just time to put his son out of the way for fear of mischief: so wishing you a merry Easter, I remain your

most humble Servant,
C. Curll.

P.S. As to the report of my poor husband's stealing a *calf*, it is really ground-less, for he always binds in *sheep*.

But return we to Mr Curll, who all Wednesday continued outrage-ously mad. On Thursday he had a *lucid interval*, that enabled him to send a general summons to all his authors. There was but one porter who could perform this office, to whom he gave the following bill of directions where to find 'em. This bill, together with Mrs Curll's origi-nal letter, lie at Mr Lintot's shop to be perused by the curious.

Instructions° to a Porter how to find Mr Curll's Authors.

'At a tallow-chandler's in Petty France, half way under the blind arch: Ask for the *historian*.

'At the Bedstead and Bolster, a music house in Moorfields, two translators in a bed together.

'At the Hercules and Still in Vinegar Yard, a schoolmaster with carbuncles on his nose.

'At a blacksmith's shop in the Friars, a Pindaric writer in red stockings.

'In the calendar mill room at Exeter Change, a composer of medi-tations.

'At the Three Tobacco Pipes in Dog and Bitch Yard, one that has been a parson, he wears a blue camblet coat trimmed with black: my best writer against *revealed religion*.

'At Mr Summers° a thiefcatcher's in Lewkners Lane, the man that wrote against the impiety of Mr Rowe's plays.

'At the Farthing Pie House in Tooting° Fields, the young man who is writing my new *Pastorals*.

'At the laundresses, at the Hole in the Wall in Cursitors Alley, up three pairs of stairs, the author of my *Church History*—if his flux be over—you may also speak to the gentleman who lies by him in the flock bed, my *index-maker*.

'The cook's wife° in Buckingham Court; bid her bring along with her the *similes* that were lent her for her next new play.

'Call at Budge Row for the gentleman you use to go to in the cockloft; I have taken away the ladder, but his landlady has it in keeping.

'I don't much care if you ask at the Mint for the old beetle-browed critic, and the purblind poet at the Alley over against St Andrew's Holborn. But this as you have time.'

All these gentlemen appeared at the hour appointed, in Mr Curll's dining-room, two excepted; one of whom was the gentleman in the cockloft, his landlady being out of the way, and the *Gradus ad Parnassum*° taken down; the other happened to be too closely watched by the bailiffs.

They no sooner entered the room, but all of them showed in their behaviour some suspicion of each other; some turning away their heads with an air of contempt; others squinting with a leer that showed at once fear and indignation, each with a haggard abstracted mien, the lively picture of *scorn*, *solitude*, and *short commons*. So when a keeper feeds his hungry charge, of vultures, panthers, and of Lybian leopards, each eyes his fellow with a fiery glare: high hung, the bloody liver tempts their maw. Or as a housewife stands before her pales, surrounded by her geese; they fight, they hiss, they gaggle, beat their wings, and down is scattered as the winter's snow, for a poor grain of oat, or tare, or barley. Such looks shot through the room transverse, oblique, direct; such was the stir and din, till Curll thus spoke, (but without rising from his close-stool.)

'*Whores* and *authors* must be paid beforehand to put them in good humour; therefore here is half a crown a piece for you to drink your own healths, and confusion to Mr Addison, and all other successful writers.

'Ah gentlemen! What have I not done, what have I not suffered, rather than the world should be deprived of your lucubrations? I have taken involuntary purges, I have been vomited, three times have I been caned, once was I hunted, twice was my head broke by a grenadier, twice was I tossed in a blanket; I have had boxes on the ear, slaps on the chops; I have been frighted, pumped, kicked, slandered and beshitten.—I hope, gentlemen, you are all convinced that this author of Mr Lintot's could mean nothing else but starving you by poisoning me. It remains for us to consult the best and speediest methods of revenge.'

He had scarce done speaking, but the historian proposed a history of his life. The Exeter Exchange gentleman was for penning articles of his faith. Some pretty smart Pindaric (says the red-stocking gentleman) would effectually do his business. But the index-maker said there was nothing like an index to his *Homer*.

After several debates they came to the following resolutions.

'*Resolved*, That every member of this society, according to his several abilities, shall contribute some way or other to the defamation of Mr Pope.

'*Resolved*, That towards the libelling of the said Mr Pope, there be a sum employed not exceeding six pounds sixteen shillings and ninepence (not including advertisements.)

'*Resolved*, That Mr Dennis make an affidavit before Mr Justice Tully, that in Mr Pope's *Homer*, there are several passages contrary to the established rules of OUR Sublime.

'*Resolved*, That he has on purpose in several passages perverted the true ancient heathen sense of *Homer*, for the more effectual propagation of the Popish religion.

'*Resolved*, That the printing of *Homer*'s battles at this juncture, has been the occasion of all the disturbances of this kingdom.°

'*Ordered*, That Mr Barnivelt° be invited to be a member of this society, in order to make further discoveries.

'*Resolved*, That a number of effective Erratas be raised out of Mr Pope's *Homer* (not exceeding 1746) and that every gentleman, who shall send in one error, for his encouragement shall have the whole works of this society *gratis*.

'*Resolved*, That a sum not exceeding ten shillings and sixpence be distributed among the members of this society for *coffee* and *tobacco*, in order to enable them the more effectually to defame him in *coffee-houses*.

'*Resolved*, That towards the further lessening the character of the said Mr Pope, some persons be deputed to abuse him at ladies' *tea tables*, and that in consideration our authors are not *well dressed* enough, Mr C—y° be deputed for that service.

'*Resolved*, That a *ballad* be made against Mr Pope, and that Mr Old-mixon, Mr Gildon and Mrs Centlivre do prepare and bring in the same.

'*Resolved*, That above all, some effectual ways and means be found to increase the joint stock of the reputation of this society, which at present is exceedingly low, and to give their works the greater currency; whether by raising the denomination of the said works by counterfeit title-pages, or mixing a greater quantity of the fine metal of other authors, with the alloy of this society.

'*Resolved*, That no member of this society for the future mix *stout* in his *ale* in a morning, and that Mr *B*. remove from the Hercules and Still.

'*Resolved*, That all our members, (except the cook's wife) be provided with a sufficient quantity of the *vivifying drops*, or *Byfield*'s *Sal Volatile*.

'*Resolved*, That Sir Richard Blackmore be appointed to endue this society with a large quantity of *regular and exalted ferments*, in order to *enliven their cold sentiments* (being his true receipt to make wits.)

These resolutions being taken, the assembly was ready to break up, but they took so near a part in Mr Curll's afflictions, that none of them could leave him without giving some advice to reinstate him in his health.

Mr Gildon was of opinion, that in order to drive a Pope out of his belly, he should get the mummy of some deceased Moderator of the General Assembly in Scotland, to be taken inwardly as an effectual antidote against Antichrist; but Mr Oldmixon did conceive, that the *liver* of the person who administered the poison, boiled in broth, would be a more certain cure.

While the company were expecting the thanks of Mr Curll, for these demonstrations of their zeal, a whole pile of *Essays* on a sudden fell on his head; the shock of which in an instant brought back his delirium. He immediately rose up, over-turned the close-stool, and beshit the *Essays* (which may probably occasion a second edition), then without putting up his breeches, in a most furious tone, he thus broke out to his books, which his distempered imagination represented to him as alive, coming down from their shelves, fluttering their leaves, and flapping their covers at him.

'Now G—d damn all *folios, quartos, octavos* and *duodecimos!* ungrateful varlets that you are, who have so long taken up my house without paying for your lodging?—Are you not the beggarly brood of fumbling *journeymen*; born in *garrets*, among *lice* and *cobwebs*, nursed upon *grey peas*, *bullock's liver*, and *porter's ale*?—Was not the first light you saw, the farthing candle I paid for? Did you not come before your time into *dirty sheets* of brown paper?—And have not I clothed you in double *Royal*, lodged you handsomely on *decent shelves*, laced your *backs* with *gold*, equipped you with splendid *titles*, and sent you into the world with the names of *persons of quality*? Must I be *always* plagued with you?— Why flutter ye your leaves, and flap your covers at me? Damn ye all, ye *wolves in sheep's clothing*; *rags ye were*,° *and to rags ye shall return*. Why hold you forth your *texts* to me, ye paltry *sermons*? Why cry ye—at every word to me, ye *bawdy poems*?—To my shop at Tunbridge ye shall go, by G— and thence be drawn like the rest of your predecessors, bit by bit, to the *passage-house*:° for in this present emotion of my bowels, how do I compassionate those who have great need, and nothing to wipe their breech with?'

Having said this, and at the same time recollecting that his own was yet unwiped, he abated of his fury, and with great gravity, applied to that function the unfinished sheets of the *Conduct of the Earl of Nottingham*.

POPE TO LORD BURLINGTON
November 1716

My Lord,—If your mare could speak, she would give you an account of the extraordinary company she had on the road; which since she cannot do, I will.

It was the enterprising Mr Lintot,° the redoubtable rival of Mr Tonson, who mounted on a stonehorse, (no disagreeable companion to your Lordship's mare) overtook me in Windsor Forest. He said, he heard I designed for Oxford, the seat of the muses, and would, as my bookseller, by all means, accompany me thither.

I asked him where he got his horse? He answered, he got it of his publisher:° 'For that rogue, my printer', said he, 'disappointed me: I hoped to put him in a good humour by a treat at the tavern, of a brown fricassee of rabbits which cost two shillings, with two quarts of wine, besides my conversation. I thought my self cocksure of his horse, which he readily promised me, but said, that Mr Tonson had just such another design of going to Cambridge, expecting there the copy of a *Comment upon the Revelations*; and if Mr Tonson went, he was preingaged to attend him, being to have the printing of the said copy.'

'So in short, I borrowed this stonehorse of my publisher, which he had of Mr Oldmixon° for a debt; he lent me too the pretty boy you see after me; he was a smutty dog yesterday, and cost me near two hours to wash the ink off his face: but the devil is a fair-conditioned devil, and very forward in his catechise: if you have any more bags, he shall carry them.'

I thought Mr Lintot's civility not to be neglected, so gave the boy a small bag, containing three shirts and an Elzevir Virgil; and mounting in an instant proceeded on the road, with my man before, my courteous stationer beside, and the aforesaid devil behind.

Mr Lintot began in this manner. 'Now damn them! what if they should put it into the newspaper, how you and I went together to Oxford? why what would I care? If I should go down into Sussex, they would say I was gone to the Speaker.° But what of that? if my son were but big enough to go on with the business, by G—d I would keep as good company as old Jacob.'

Hereupon I enquired of his son. 'The lad', says he, 'has fine parts, but is somewhat sickly, *much as you are*—I spare for nothing in his education at Westminster. Pray don't you think Westminster to be the best school in England? most of the late *ministry* came out of it, so did many of *this ministry*; I hope the boy will make his fortune.'

Don't you design to let him pass a year at Oxford? 'To what purpose?' said he, 'the universities do but make pedants, and I intend to breed him a man of business.'

As Mr Lintot was talking, I observed he sate uneasy on his saddle, for which I expressed some solicitude. 'Nothing', says he, 'I can bear it well enough; but since we have the day before us, methinks it would be very pleasant for you to rest awhile under the woods.' When we were alighted, 'See here, what a mighty pretty *Horace* I have in my pocket? what if you amused yourself in turning an ode, till we mount again? Lord! if you pleased, what a clever *Miscellany* might you make at leisure hours.' Perhaps I may, said I, if we ride on; the motion is an aid to my fancy; a round trot very much awakens my spirits. Then jog on apace, and I'll think as hard as I can.

Silence ensued for a full hour; after which Mr Lintot lugged the reins, stopped short, and broke out, 'Well, Sir, how far have you gone?' I answered seven miles. 'Z—ds, Sir,' said Lintot, 'I thought you had done seven stanzas. Oldisworth° in a ramble round Wimbledon Hill, would translate a whole ode in half this time. I'll say that for Oldisworth, (though I lost by his *Timothy*'s) he translates an ode of Horace the *quickest* of any man in England. I remember Dr King° would write verses in a tavern three hours after he couldn't speak: and there's Sir Richard° in that rumbling old chariot of his, between Fleet Ditch and St Giles's pound shall make you half a *Job*.'

'Pray Mr Lintot', said I, 'now you talk of translators, what is your method of managing them?' 'Sir,' replied he, 'those are the saddest pack of rogues in the world. In a hungry fit, they'll swear they understand all the languages in the universe: I have known one of them take down a Greek book upon my counter and cry, Ay this is Hebrew, I must read it from the latter end. By G——d I can never be sure in these fellows, for I neither understand Greek, Latin, French, nor Italian myself. But this is my way: I agree with them for ten shillings per sheet, with a proviso, that I will have their doings corrected by whom I please; so by one or other they are led at last to the true sense of an author; my judgment giving the negative to all my translators.' But how are you secure that those correctors may not impose upon you? 'Why, I get any civil gentleman, (especially any Scotchman) that comes into my shop, to read the original to me in English; by this I know whether my first translator be deficient, and whether my corrector merits his money or no.

'I'll tell you what happened to me last month: I bargained with Sewell° for a new version of *Lucretius* to publish against Tonson's; agreeing to pay the author so many shillings at his producing so many lines. He made a great progress in a very short time, and I gave it to the corrector to compare with the Latin; but he went directly to Creech's translation, and found it the same word for word, all but the first page. Now, what d'ye think I did? I arrested the *translator* for a cheat; nay, and I stopped the *corrector's pay* too, upon this proof that he had made use of Creech instead of the original.'

Pray, tell me next how you deal with the critics? 'Sir,' said he, 'nothing more easy. I can silence the most formidable of them; the rich ones for a sheet apiece of the blotted manuscript, which costs me nothing. They'll go about with it to their acquaintance, and pretend they had it from the author, who submitted to their correction: this has given some of them such an air, that in time they come to be consulted with, and dedicated to, as the top critics of the town.—As for the poor critics, I'll give you one instance of my management, by which you may guess at the rest. A lean man that looked like a very good scholar came to me t'other day; he turned over *Homer*, shook his head, shrugged up his shoulders, and pished at every line of it; '*One would wonder*,' says he, '*at the strange presumption of men; Homer is no such easy task, that* every *stripling,* every *versifier*'—he was going on when my wife called to dinner: 'Sir,' said I, 'will you please to eat a *piece of beef* with me?' '*Mr Lintot,*' said he, '*I am sorry you should be at the expense of this great book, I am really concerned on your account*'—'Sir, I am obliged to you: if you can dine upon a piece of beef, together with a slice of pudding'—'*Mr Lintot, I do not say but Mr Pope, if he would condescend to advise with men of learning*'—'Sir, the *pudding* is upon the table, if you please to go in'—My critic complies, he comes to a taste of your poetry, and tells me in the same breath, that the *book* is commendable, and the *pudding* excellent.'

'Now, Sir,' concluded Mr Lintot, 'in return to the frankness I have shown, pray tell me, Is it the opinion of your friends at court that my Lord Lansdown will be brought to the bar or not?' I told him I heard *not*, and I hoped it, my Lord being one I had particular obligations to. 'That may be,' replied Mr Lintot, 'but by G—d if he is not, I shall lose the printing of a very good trial.'

These, my Lord are a few traits by which you may discern the genius of my friend Mr Lintot, which I have chosen for the subject of a letter. I dropped him as soon as I got to Oxford, and paid a visit to my Lord Carlton° at Middleton.

The conversations I enjoy here are not to be prejudiced by my pen, and the pleasures from them only to be equalled when I meet your Lordship. I hope in a few days to cast myself from your horse at your feet.

I am, etc.

ELOISA
TO
ABELARD

ARGUMENT

Abelard and Eloisa flourished in the twelfth century;° they were two of the most distinguished persons of their age in learning and beauty, but for nothing more famous than for their unfortunate passion. After a long course of calamities, they retired each to a several convent, and

consecrated the remainder of their days to religion. It was many years
after this separation, that a letter of Abelard's to a friend, which con-
tained the history of his misfortune, fell into the hands of Eloisa. This
awakening all her tenderness, occasioned those celebrated letters (out
of which the following is partly extracted) which give so lively a picture
of the struggles of grace and nature, virtue and passion.

In these deep solitudes and awful cells,   1
Where heavenly-pensive contemplation dwells,
And ever-musing melancholy reigns;
What means this tumult in a vestal's veins?
Why rove my thoughts beyond this last retreat?
Why feels my heart its long-forgotten heat?
Yet, yet I love!—From Abelard it came,
And Eloïsa yet must kiss the name.
Dear fatal name! rest ever unrevealed,
Nor pass these lips in holy silence sealed: 10
Hide it, my heart, within that close disguise,
Where, mixed with God's, his loved idea lies:
O write it not, my hand—the name appears
Already written—wash it out, my tears!
In vain lost Eloïsa weeps and prays,
Her heart still dictates,° and her hand obeys.
Relentless walls! whose darksome round contains
Repentant sighs, and voluntary pains:
Ye rugged rocks! which holy knees have worn;
Ye grots and caverns shagged with horrid thorn!°   20
Shrines! where their vigils pale-eyed virgins keep,
And pitying saints, whose statues learn to weep!
Though cold like you, unmoved and silent grown,
I have not yet forgot myself to stone.
All is not heaven's while Abelard has part,
Still rebel nature holds out half my heart;
Nor prayers nor fasts its stubborn pulse restrain,
Nor tears, for ages, taught to flow in vain.
Soon as thy letters trembling I unclose,
That well-known name awakens all my woes.   30
Oh name for ever sad! for ever dear!
Still breathed in sighs, still ushered with a tear.
I tremble too where'er my own I find,
Some dire misfortune follows close behind.

Line after line my gushing eyes o'erflow,
Led through a sad variety of woe:
Now warm in love, now withering in my bloom,
Lost in a convent's solitary gloom!
There stern religion quenched th'unwilling flame,
There died the best of passions, love and fame.   40

    Yet write, oh write me all, that I may join
Griefs to thy griefs, and echo sighs to thine.
Nor foes nor fortune take this power away;
And is my Abelard less kind than they?
Tears still are mine, and those I need not spare,
Love but demands what else were shed in prayer;
No happier task these faded eyes pursue;
To read and weep is all they now can do.

    Then share thy pain, allow that sad relief;
Ah, more than share it! give me all thy grief.   50
Heaven first taught letters for some wretch's aid,
Some banished lover, or some captive maid;
They live, they speak, they breathe what love inspires,
Warm from the soul, and faithful to its fires,
The virgin's wish without her fears impart,
Excuse° the blush, and pour out all the heart,
Speed the soft intercourse from soul to soul,
And waft a sigh from Indus to the Pole.

    Thou knowst how guiltless first I met thy flame,
When love approached me under friendship's name;   60
My fancy formed thee of angelic kind,
Some emanation of th'all-beauteous mind.
Those smiling eyes, attempering° every ray,
Shone sweetly lambent with celestial day:
Guiltless I gazed; heaven listened while you sung;
And truths divine came mended from that tongue.
From lips like those what precept failed to move?
Too soon they taught me 'twas no sin to love:
Back through the paths of pleasing sense I ran,
Nor wished an angel whom I loved a man.   70
Dim and remote the joys of saints I see,
Nor envy them that heaven I lose for thee.

    How oft, when pressed to marriage, have I said,

66. He was her preceptor in philosophy and divinity.

Curse on all laws but those which love has made?
Love, free as air, at sight of human ties,
Spreads his light wings, and in a moment flies.
Let wealth, let honour, wait the wedded dame,
August her deed, and sacred be her fame;
Before true passion all those views remove,
Fame, wealth, and honour! what are you to love?   80
The jealous god, when we profane his fires,
Those restless passions in revenge inspires,
And bids them make mistaken mortals groan,
Who seek in love for aught but love alone.
Should at my feet the world's great master fall,
Himself, his throne, his world, I'd scorn 'em all:
Not Caesar's empress would I deign to prove;
No, make me mistress to the man I love;
If there be yet another name more free,
More fond than mistress, make me that to thee!   90
Oh happy state! when souls each other draw,
When love is liberty, and nature, law:
All then is full, possessing, and possessed,
No craving void left aching in the breast:
Ev'n thought meets thought, ere from the lips it part,
And each warm wish springs mutual from the heart.
This sure is bliss (if bliss on earth there be)
And once the lot of Abelard and me.

    Alas how changed! what sudden horrors rise!
A naked lover bound and bleeding lies!   100
Where, where was Eloïse? her voice, her hand,
Her poniard, had opposed the dire command.
Barbarian, stay! that bloody stroke restrain;
The crime was common, common° be the pain.
I can no more; by shame, by rage suppressed,
Let tears, and burning blushes speak the rest.

    Canst thou forget that sad, that solemn day,
When victims at yon altar's foot we lay?
Canst thou forget what tears that moment fell,

75.   *Love will not be confined by maisterie:*
              When maisterie comes, the lord of love anon
              Flutters his wings, and forthwith is he gone.
                           Chaucer.

When, warm in youth, I bade the world farewell?   110
As with cold lips I kissed the sacred veil,
The shrines all trembled, and the lamps grew pale:
Heaven scarce believed the conquest it surveyed,
And saints with wonder heard the vows I made.
Yet then, to those dread altars as I drew,
Not on the cross my eyes were fixed, but you:
Not grace, or zeal, love only was my call,
And if I lose thy love, I lose my all.
Come! with thy looks, thy words, relieve my woe;
Those still at least are left thee to bestow.   120
Still on that breast enamoured let me lie,
Still drink delicious poison from thy eye,
Pant on thy lip, and to thy heart be pressed;
Give all thou canst—and let me dream the rest.
Ah no! instruct me other joys to prize,
With other beauties charm my partial° eyes,
Full in my view set all the bright abode,
And make my soul quit Abelard for God.

    Ah think at least thy flock deserve thy care,
Plants of thy hand, and children of thy prayer.   130
From the false world in early youth they fled,
By thee to mountains, wilds, and deserts led.
You raised these hallowed walls;° the desert smiled,
And paradise was opened in the wild.
No weeping orphan saw his father's stores
Our shrines irradiate, or emblaze the floors;
No silver saints, by dying misers given,
Here bribed the rage of ill-requited heaven:
But such plain roofs as piety could raise,
And only vocal with the Maker's praise.   140
In these lone walls (their days eternal bound)
These moss-grown domes° with spiry turrets crowned,
Where awful arches make a noon-day night,
And the dim windows shed a solemn light;
Thy eyes diffused a reconciling ray,
And gleams of glory brightened all the day.
But now no face divine contentment wears,
'Tis all blank sadness, or continual tears.

133. He founded the monastery.

See how the force of others prayers I try,
(O pious fraud of amorous charity!)   150
But why should I on others prayers depend?
Come thou, my father, brother, husband, friend!
Ah let thy handmaid, sister, daughter move,
And all those tender names in one, thy love!
The darksome pines that o'er yon rocks reclined
Wave high, and murmur to the hollow wind,
The wandering streams that shine between the hills,
The grots that echo to the tinkling rills,
The dying gales that pant upon the trees,
The lakes that quiver to the curling breeze;   160
No more these scenes my meditation aid,
Or lull to rest the visionary maid.
But o'er the twilight groves and dusky caves,
Long-sounding isles, and intermingled graves,
Black Melancholy sits, and round her throws
A death-like silence, and a dread repose:
Her gloomy presence saddens all the scene,
Shades every flower, and darkens every green,
Deepens the murmur of the falling floods,
And breathes a browner horror on the woods.   170

    Yet here for ever, ever must I stay;
Sad proof how well a lover can obey!
Death, only death, can break the lasting chain;
And here, ev'n then, shall my cold dust remain,
Here all its frailties, all its flames resign,
And wait, till 'tis no sin to mix with thine.

    Ah wretch! believed the spouse of God in vain,
Confessed within the slave of love and man.
Assist me, heaven! but whence arose that prayer?
Sprung it from piety, or from despair?   180
Ev'n here, where frozen chastity retires,
Love finds an altar for forbidden fires.
I ought to grieve, but cannot what I ought;
I mourn the lover, not lament the fault;
I view my crime, but kindle at the view,
Repent old pleasures, and solicit new;
Now turned to heaven, I weep my past offence,
Now think of thee, and curse my innocence.
Of all affliction taught a lover yet,

'Tis sure the hardest science to forget!   190
How shall I lose the sin, yet keep the sense,
And love th'offender, yet detest th'offence?°
How the dear object from the crime remove,
Or how distinguish penitence from love?
Unequal task! a passion to resign,
For hearts so touched, so pierced, so lost as mine.
Ere such a soul regains its peaceful state,
How often must it love, how often hate!
How often hope, despair, resent, regret,
Conceal, disdain—do all things but forget.   200
But let heaven seize it, all at once 'tis fired;
Not touched, but rapt; not wakened, but inspired!
Oh come! oh teach me nature to subdue,
Renounce my love, my life, my self—and you.
Fill my fond heart with God alone, for he
Alone can rival, can succeed to thee.
    How happy is the blameless vestal's lot?
The world forgetting, by the world forgot:
Eternal sunshine of the spotless mind!
Each prayer accepted, and each wish resigned;   210
Labour and rest, that equal periods keep;
'Obedient slumbers that can wake and weep;'°
Desires composed, affections ever even;
Tears that delight, and sighs that waft to heaven.
Grace shines around her with serenest beams,
And whispering angels prompt her golden dreams.
For her th'unfading rose of Eden blooms,
And wings of seraphs shed divine perfumes,
For her the spouse prepares the bridal ring,°
For her white virgins hymeneals sing;   220
To sounds of heavenly harps she dies away,
And melts in visions of eternal day.
    Far other dreams my erring soul employ,
Far other raptures, of unholy joy:
When at the close of each sad, sorrowing day,
Fancy restores what vengeance snatched away,
Then conscience sleeps, and leaving nature free,
All my loose soul unbounded springs to thee.

212. Taken from Crashaw.

O cursed, dear horrors of all-conscious night!°
How glowing guilt exalts the keen delight!　　　　　　230
Provoking daemons all restraint remove,
And stir within me every source of love.
I hear thee, view thee, gaze o'er all thy charms,
And round thy phantom glue my clasping arms.
I wake—no more I hear, no more I view,
The phantom flies me, as unkind as you.
I call aloud; it hears not what I say:
I stretch my empty arms; it glides away.
To dream once more I close my willing eyes;
Ye soft illusions, dear deceits, arise!　　　　　　240
Alas, no more! methinks we wandering go
Through dreary wastes, and weep each other's woe,
Where round some mouldering tower pale ivy creeps,
And low-browed rocks hang nodding o'er the deeps.
Sudden you mount! you beckon from the skies;
Clouds interpose, waves roar, and winds arise.
I shriek, start up, the same sad prospect find,
And wake to all the griefs I left behind.
　　For thee the fates, severely kind, ordain
A cool suspense from pleasure and from pain;　　　　　　250
Thy life a long, dead calm of fixed repose;
No pulse that riots, and no blood that glows.
Still as the sea, ere winds were taught to blow,
Or moving spirit bade the waters flow;
Soft as the slumbers of a saint forgiven,
And mild as opening gleams of promised heaven.
　　Come, Abelard! for what hast thou to dread?
The torch of Venus burns not for the dead.
Nature stands checked; religion disapproves;
Ev'n thou art cold—yet Eloïsa loves.　　　　　　260
Ah hopeless, lasting flames! like those that burn
To light the dead, and warm th'unfruitful urn.
　　What scenes appear where'er I turn my view?
The dear ideas, where I fly, pursue,
Rise in the grove, before the altar rise,
Stain all my soul, and wanton in my eyes.
I waste the matin lamp in sighs for thee,
Thy image steals between my God and me,
Thy voice I seem in every hymn to hear,

With every bead I drop too soft a tear. 270
When from the censer clouds of fragrance roll,
And swelling organs lift the rising soul,
One thought of thee puts all the pomp to flight,
Priests, tapers, temples, swim before my sight:
In seas of flame my plunging soul is drowned,
While altars blaze, and angels tremble round.

 While prostrate here in humble grief I lie,
Kind, virtuous drops just gathering in my eye,
While praying, trembling, in the dust I roll,
And dawning grace is opening on my soul: 280
Come, if thou darest, all charming as thou art!
Oppose thyself to heaven; dispute° my heart;
Come, with one glance of those deluding eyes
Blot out each bright idea of the skies;°
Take back that grace, those sorrows, and those tears,
Take back my fruitless penitence and prayers,
Snatch me, just mounting, from the blest abode,
Assist the fiends,° and tear me from my God!

 No, fly me, fly me, far as pole from pole;
Rise Alps between us! and whole oceans roll! 290
Ah, come not, write not, think not once of me,
Nor share one pang of all I felt for thee.
Thy oaths I quit, thy memory resign;
Forget, renounce me, hate whate'er was mine.
Fair eyes, and tempting looks (which yet I view!)
Long loved, adored ideas, all adieu!
O grace serene! oh virtue heavenly fair!
Divine oblivion of low-thoughted care!
Fresh blooming hope, gay daughter of the sky!
And faith, our early immortality! 300
Enter, each mild, each amicable guest;
Receive, and wrap me in eternal rest!

 See in her cell sad Eloïsa spread,
Propped on some tomb, a neighbour of the dead.
In each low wind methinks a spirit calls,
And more than echoes talk along the walls.
Here, as I watched the dying lamps around,
From yonder shrine I heard a hollow sound.
'Come, sister, come!' (it said, or seemed to say)
'Thy place is here, sad sister, come away! 310

Once like thyself, I trembled, wept, and prayed,
Love's victim then, though now a sainted maid:
But all is calm in this eternal sleep;
Here grief forgets to groan, and love to weep,
Ev'n superstition loses every fear:
For God, not man, absolves our frailties here.'

    I come, I come! prepare your roseate bowers,
Celestial palms, and ever-blooming flowers.
Thither, where sinners may have rest, I go,
Where flames refined in breasts seraphic glow.   320
Thou, Abelard! the last sad office pay,
And smooth my passage to the realms of day;
See my lips tremble, and my eye-balls roll,
Suck my last breath, and catch my flying soul!
Ah no—in sacred vestments mayst thou stand,
The hallowed taper trembling in thy hand,
Present the cross before my lifted eye,
Teach me at once, and learn of me to die.
Ah then, thy once-loved Eloïsa see!
It will be then no crime to gaze on me.   330
See from my cheek the transient roses fly!
See the last sparkle languish in my eye!
Till every motion, pulse, and breath be o'er;
And ev'n my Abelard beloved no more.
O Death all-eloquent! you only prove
What dust we dote on, when 'tis man we love.

    Then too, when fate shall thy fair frame destroy,
(That cause of all my guilt, and all my joy)
In trance ecstatic may thy pangs be drowned,
Bright clouds descend, and angels watch thee round,   340
From opening skies may streaming glories shine,
And saints embrace thee with a love like mine.

    May one kind grave unite each hapless name,
And graft my love immortal on thy fame!
Then, ages hence, when all my woes are o'er,
When this rebellious heart shall beat no more;
If ever chance two wandering lovers brings
To Paraclete's white walls and silver springs,

---

343. Abelard and Eloïsa were interred in the same grave, or in monuments adjoining, in the monastery of the Paraclete: he died in the year 1142, she in 1163.°

O'er the pale marble shall they join their heads,
And drink the falling tears each other sheds;   350
Then sadly say, with mutual pity° moved,
'Oh may we never love as these have loved!'
From the full choir when loud hosannas rise,
And swell the pomp of dreadful sacrifice,°
Amid that scene, if some relenting° eye
Glance on the stone where our cold relics lie,
Devotion's self shall steal a thought from heaven,
One human tear shall drop, and be forgiven.
And sure if fate some future bard shall join
In sad similitude of griefs to mine,   360
Condemned whole years in absence to deplore,
And image charms he must behold no more;°
Such if there be, who loves so long, so well;
Let him our sad, our tender story tell;
The well-sung woes will soothe my pensive ghost;
He best can paint 'em, who shall feel 'em most.

ELEGY
To the MEMORY of an
UNFORTUNATE LADY*

What beckoning ghost, along the moonlight shade   1
Invites my step, and points to yonder glade?
'Tis she!—but why that bleeding bosom gored,
Why dimly gleams the visionary sword?
Oh ever beauteous, ever friendly! tell,
Is it, in heaven, a crime to love too well?
To bear too tender, or too firm a heart,
To act a lover's or a Roman's part?°
Is there no bright reversion° in the sky,
For those who greatly think, or bravely die?   10

* See the Duke of Buckingham's verses to a lady designing to retire into a
monastery compared with Mr Pope's Letters to several ladies, p. 206. She seems to
be the same person whose unfortunate death is the subject of this poem.°

Why bade ye else, ye powers! her soul aspire
Above the vulgar flight of low desire?
Ambition first sprung from your blessed abodes;
The glorious fault° of angels and of gods:
Thence to their images on earth it flows,
And in the breasts of kings and heroes glows.
Most souls, 'tis true, but peep out once an age,
Dull sullen prisoners in the body's cage:
Dim lights of life, that burn a length of years
Useless, unseen, as lamps in sepulchres;   20
Like eastern kings a lazy state they keep,
And close confined in their own palace sleep.

   From these perhaps (ere nature bade her die)
Fate snatched her early to the pitying sky.
As into air the purer spirits flow,
And separate from their kindred dregs below;
So flew the soul to its congenial place,
Nor left one virtue to redeem her race.

   But thou, false guardian of a charge too good,
Thou, mean deserter of thy brother's blood!   30
See on these ruby lips the trembling breath,
These cheeks, now fading at the blast of death;
Cold is that breast which warmed the world before,
And those love-darting eyes must roll no more.
Thus, if eternal justice rules the ball,°
Thus shall your wives, and thus your children fall:
On all the line a sudden vengeance waits,
And frequent hearses shall besiege your gates.
There passengers shall stand, and pointing say,
(While the long funerals blacken all the way)   40
Lo these were they, whose souls the Furies° steeled,
And cursed with hearts unknowing how to yield.
Thus unlamented pass the proud away,
The gaze of fools, and pageant of a day!
So perish all, whose breast ne'er learned to glow
For others good, or melt at others woe.

   What can atone (oh ever-injured shade!)
Thy fate unpitied, and thy rites unpaid?
No friend's complaint, no kind domestic tear
Pleased thy pale ghost, or graced thy mournful bier;   50
By foreign hands thy dying eyes were closed,

By foreign hands thy decent limbs composed,
By foreign hands thy humble grave adorned,
By strangers honoured, and by strangers mourned!
What though no friends in sable weeds appear,
Grieve for an hour, perhaps, then mourn a year,
And bear about the mockery of woe
To midnight dances, and the public show?
What though no weeping loves thy ashes grace,   60
Nor polished marble emulate thy face?
What though no sacred earth allow thee room,
Nor hallowed dirge be muttered o'er thy tomb?
Yet shall thy grave with rising flowers be dressed,
And the green turf lie lightly on thy breast:°
There shall the morn her earliest tears bestow,
There the first roses of the year shall blow;
While angels with their silver wings o'ershade
The ground, now sacred by thy relics made.°
   So peaceful rests, without a stone, a name,
What once had beauty, titles, wealth, and fame.   70
How loved, how honoured once, avails thee not,
To whom related, or by whom begot;
A heap of dust alone remains of thee;
'Tis all thou art, and all the proud shall be!
   Poets themselves must fall, like those they sung;
Deaf the praised ear, and mute the tuneful tongue.
Ev'n he, whose soul now melts in mournful lays,
Shall shortly want the generous tear he pays;
Then from his closing eyes thy form shall part,
And the last pang shall tear thee from his heart,   80
Life's idle business at one gasp be o'er,
The Muse forgot, and thou beloved no more!

POPE TO TERESA AND MARTHA BLOUNT
September 1717

Ladies,—I came from Stonor (its master not being at home) to Oxford the same night. Nothing could have more of that melancholy which once used to please me, than that day's journey: for after having passed through my favourite woods in the forest, with a thousand reveries of past pleasures; I rid over hanging hills, whose tops were edged with groves, and whose feet watered with winding rivers, listening to the falls of cataracts below, and the murmuring of winds above. The gloomy verdure of Stonor succeeded to these, and then the shades of the evening overtook me, the moon rose in the clearest sky I ever saw, by whose solemn light I paced on slowly, without company, or any interruption to the range of my thoughts. About a mile before I reached Oxford, all the night bells tolled, in different notes; the clocks of every college answered one another; and told me, some in a deeper, some in a softer voice, that it was eleven o'clock.

All this was no ill preparation to the life I have led since; among those old walls, venerable galleries, stone porticos, studious walks and solitary scenes of the University. I wanted nothing but a black gown and a salary, to be as mere a bookworm as any there. I conformed myself to the college hours, was rolled up in books and wrapped in meditation, lay in one of the most ancient, dusky parts of the University, and was as dead to the world as any hermit of the desert. If anything was awake or alive in me, it was a little vanity, such as even those good men used to entertain when the monks of their own order extolled their piety and abstractedness. For I found myself received with a sort of respect, which this idle part of mankind, the learned, pay to their own species; who are as considerable here, as the busy, the gay and the ambitious are in your world. Indeed I was so treated, that I could not but sometimes ask myself in my mind, what college I was founder of, or what library I had built? Methinks I do very ill, to return to the world again, to leave the only place where I make a good figure, and from seeing myself seated with dignity on the most conspicuous shelves

of a library, go to contemplate this wretched person in the abject con-
dition of lying at a lady's feet in Bolton Street.°

I will not deny, but that like Alexander, in the midst of my glory, I
am wounded, and find myself a mere man. To tell you from whence
the dart comes, is to no purpose, since neither of you will take the
tender care to draw it out of my heart, and suck the poison with your
lips; or are in any disposition to take in a part of the venom yourselves,
to ease me. Here, at my Lord Harcourt's,° I see a creature nearer an
angel than a woman, (though a woman be very near as good as an
angel). I think you have formerly heard me mention Mrs Jennings as
a credit to the maker of angels. She is a relation of his lordship's, and
he gravely proposed her to me for a wife, being tender of her interests
and knowing (what is a shame to Providence) that she is less indebted
to fortune than I. I told him his Lordship could never have thought of
such a thing but for his misfortune of being blind, and that I never
could till I was so: but that, as matters now were, I did not care to force
so fine a woman to give the finishing stroke to all my deformities, by
the last mark of a beast, horns.

Now I am talking of beauty, I shall see my Lady Jane Hyde°
tomorrow, at Cornbury. I shall pass a day and night at Blenheim Park,
and will then hasten home, (taking Reading in my way). I have every-
where made enquiry if it be possible to get any annuities on sound
security: it would really be an inexpressible joy to me if I could serve
you, and I will always do my utmost to give myself pleasure.

I beg you both to think as well of me, that is to think me as much yours,
as any one else. What degree of friendship and tenderness I feel for you,
I must be content with being sure of myself; but I shall be glad if you
believe it in any degree. Allow me as much as you can: and think as well
as you are able of one whose imperfections are so manifest, and who
thinks so little of himself, as to think ten times more of either of you.

POPE TO LADY MARY WORTLEY
MONTAGU
1718

Dear Madam,—'Tis not possible to express the least part of the joy,
your return gives me. Time only, and experience, will convince you
how very sincere it is—I excessively long to meet you; to say so much,

so very much to you, that I believe I shall say nothing—I have given orders to be sent for the first minute of your arrival, (which I beg you'll let them know at Mr Jervas's.) I am fourscore miles from London, a short journey, compared to that I so often thought at least of under-taking, rather than die without seeing you again. Though the place I am in is such as I would not quit for the town, if I did not value you more than any, nay every, body else, there. And you'll be convinced, how little the town has engaged my affection in your absence from it, when you know what a place this is, which I prefer to it. I shall therefore describe it to you at large, as the true picture of a genuine ancient country seat.°

You must expect nothing regular in my description of a house that seems to be built before rules were in fashion. The whole is so dis-jointed, and the parts so detached from each other, and yet so joining again one can't tell how; that in a poetical fit you'd imagine it had been a village in Amphion's time,° where twenty cottages had taken a dance together, were all out, and stood still in amazement ever since. A stranger would be grievously disappointed, who should ever think to get into this house the right way. One would expect, after entering through the porch, to be let into the hall: alas nothing less—you find yourself in a brewhouse. From the parlour you think to step into the drawing room, but upon opening the iron-nailed door, you are con-vinced by a flight of birds about your ears and a cloud of dust in your eyes, that 'tis the pigeon-house. One each side our porch are two chimneys, that wear their greens on the outside, which would do as well within, for whenever we make a fire we let the smoke out of the windows. Over the parlour window hangs a sloping balcony, which time has turned to a very convenient penthouse. The top is crowned with a very venerable tower, so like that of the church just by, that the jackdaws build in it as if it were the true steeple.

The great hall is high and spacious, flanked with long tables (images of ancient hospitality) ornamented with monstrous horns, about twenty broken pikes, and a matchlock musket or two, which they say were used in the Civil Wars. Here is one vast arched window, beautifully darkened with divers scutcheons of painted glass. There seems to be great propriety in this old manner of blazoning upon glass, ancient families being like ancient windows, in the course of generations seldom free from cracks. One shining pane bears date 1286. There the face of Dame Elinor owes more to this single piece, than to all the glasses she ever consulted in her life. Who can say after this, that glass is frail, when it is not half so perishable as human beauty, or glory? For in another pane you see the memory of a knight preserved, whose marble nose is mouldered from his monument in the church adjoining. And yet, must not one sigh to reflect, that the most authentic record of so ancient a family should lie at the mercy of every boy that throws a stone? In this hall, in former days have dined gartered knights and courtly dames, with ushers, sewers, and seneschals; and yet it was but t'other night that an owl flew in hither, and mistook it for a barn.

This hall lets you up, (and down) over a very high threshold into the parlour. It is furnished with historical tapestry, whose marginal fringes do confess the moisture of the air. The other contents of this room are a broken-bellied virginal, a couple of crippled velvet chairs, with two or three mildewed pictures of mouldy ancestors who look as dismally as if they came fresh from hell with all their brimstone about 'em. These are carefully set at the further corner; for the windows being everywhere broken, make it so convenient a place to dry poppies and mustard seed in, that the room is appropriated to that use.

Next this parlour lies (as I said before) the pigeon-house: by the side of which runs an entry that leads on one hand and t'other, into a bedchamber, a buttery, and small hole called the chaplain's study. Then follow a brewhouse, a little green-and-gilt parlour, and the great stairs, under which is the dairy. A little further on the right, the servants' hall, and by the side of it up six steps, the old lady's closet, which has a lattice into the side hall, that while she said her prayers, she might cast an eye on the men and maids. There are upon this ground-floor in all twenty-four apartments, hard to be distinguished by particular names, among which I must not forget a chamber, that has in it a large antiquity of timber, which seems to have been either a bedstead or a ciderpress.

Our best room above, is very long and low; of the exact proportion of a bandbox. It has hangings of the finest work in the world, those I mean which Arachne° spins out of her own bowels. Indeed the roof is so decayed, that after a favourable shower of rain we may (with God's blessing) expect a crop of mushrooms between the chinks of the floors.

All this upper storey has for many years had no other inhabitants than certain rats, whose very age renders them worthy of this venerable mansion, for the very rats of this ancient seat are gray. Since these have not yet quitted it, we hope at least this house may stand during the small remainder of days these poor animals have to live, who are now too infirm to remove to another. They have still a small subsistence left them, in the few remaining books of the library.

I had never seen half what I have described, but for an old starched grey-headed steward, who is as much an antiquity as any in the place, and looks like an old family picture walked out of its frame. He failed not as we passed from room to room to relate several memoirs of the family, but his observations were particularly curious in the cellar. He showed where stood the triple rows of butts of sack, and where were ranged the bottles of tent for toasts in the morning. He pointed to the stands that supported the iron-hooped hogsheads of strong beer. Then stepping to a corner, he lugged out the tattered fragment of an unframed picture— 'This', says he, with tears in his eyes, 'was poor Sir Thomas! once master of all the drink I told you of! He had two sons, (poor young masters) that never arrived to the age of his beer! They both fell ill in this very cellar, and never went out upon their own legs.' He could not pass by a broken bottle, without taking it up to show us the arms of the family on it. He then led me up the tower, by dark winding stone steps, which landed us into several little rooms one above another. One of these was nailed up, and my guide whispered to me the occasion of it. It seems, the course of this noble blood was interrupted about two centuries ago, by a freak of the Lady Frances, who was here taken with a neighbouring prior: ever since which, the room has been made up, and branded with the name of the adultery-chamber. The ghost of Lady Frances° is supposed to walk here; some prying maids of the family formerly reported that they saw a lady in a farthingale through the keyhole; but this matter was hushed up, and the servants forbid to talk of it.

I must needs have tired you with this long letter: but what engaged me in the description was a generous principle to preserve the memory of a thing that must itself soon fall to ruin, nay perhaps, some part of it before this reaches your hands. Indeed I owe this old house the same sort of gratitude that we do to an old friend, that harbours us in his declining condition, nay even in his last extremities. I have found this an excellent place for retirement and study, where no one who passes by can dream there is an inhabitant, and even anybody that would visit me, dares not venture under my roof. You will not wonder I have translated a great deal of Homer in this retreat; any one that sees it will own, I could not have chosen a fitter or more likely place to converse with the dead. As soon as I return to the living, it shall be to converse with the best of them. I hope therefore very speedily to tell you in person how sincerely and unalterably I am

Madam

Your most faithfull, obliged
& obedient servant,

A. Pope

I beg Mr Wortley° to believe me his most humble Servant.

THE
EIGHTEENTH BOOK
OF THE
ILIAD

The ARGUMENT
The Grief of Achilles, and new Armour
made him by Vulcan

*The news of the death of Patroclus, is brought to Achilles by Antilochus. Thetis
hearing his lamentations comes with all her sea-nymphs to comfort him. The
speeches of the mother and son on this occasion. Iris appears to Achilles by the
command of Juno, and orders him to show himself at the head of the entrench-
ments. The sight of him turns the fortune of the day, and the body of Patroclus
is carried off by the Greeks. The Trojans call a council, where Hector and
Polydamas disagree in their opinions; but the advice of the former prevails,
to remain encamped in the field. The grief of Achilles over the body of Patroclus.*

*Thetis goes to the palace of Vulcan to obtain new arms for her son. The
description of the wonderful works of Vulcan, and lastly, that noble shield of
Achilles.*

*The latter part of the nine and twentieth day, and the night ensuing, take
up this book. The scene is at Achilles's tent on the seashore, from whence it
changes to the palace of Vulcan.*

Thus like the rage of fire the combat burns,   1
And now it rises, now it sinks by turns.
Meanwhile, where Hellespont's broad waters flow
Stood Nestor's son,° the messenger of woe:
There sate Achilles, shaded by his sails,
On hoisted yards extended to the gales;
Pensive he sate; for all that fate designed,

Rose in sad prospect to his boding mind.
Thus to his soul he said: 'Ah! what constrains
The Greeks, late victors, now to quit the plains?   10
Is this the day, which heaven so long ago
Ordained, to sink me with the weight of woe?
(So Thetis warned) when by a Trojan hand,
The bravest of the Myrmidonian band°
Should lose the light? Fulfilled is that decree;
Fallen is the warrior, and Patroclus° he!
In vain I charged him soon to quit the plain,
. And warned to shun Hectorean force in vain!'
    Thus while he thinks, Antilochus appears,
And tells the melancholy tale with tears.   20
'Sad tidings, son of Peleus! thou must hear;
And wretched I, th' unwilling messenger!
Dead is Patroclus! For his corpse they fight;
His naked corpse: his arms are Hector's right.'
    A sudden horror shot through all the chief,
And wrapped his senses in the cloud of grief;
Cast on the ground, with furious hands he spread
The scorching ashes o'er his graceful head;
His purple° garments, and his golden hairs,
Those he deforms with dust, and these he tears: 30
On the hard soil his groaning breast he threw,
And rolled and grovelled, as to earth he grew.
The virgin captives, with disordered charms,
(Won by his own, or by Patroclus' arms)
Rushed from the tents with cries; and gathering round
Beat their white breasts, and fainted on the ground:
While Nestor's son sustains a manlier part,
And mourns the warrior with a warrior's heart;
Hangs on his arms, amidst his frantic woe,
And oft prevents the meditated blow.   40
    Far in the deep abysses of the main,
With hoary Nereus, and the watery train,
The mother goddess from her crystal throne
Heard his loud cries, and answered groan for groan.
The circling Nereids° with their mistress weep,
And all the sea-green sisters of the deep.
Thalia, Glauce, (every watery name)
Nesaea mild, and silver Spio came.

Cymothoe and Cymodoce were nigh,
And the blue languish of soft Alia's eye.   50
Their locks Actaea and Limnoria rear,
Then Proto, Doris, Panope appear;
Thoa, Pherusa, Doto, Melita;
Agave gentle, and Amphithoe gay:
Next Callianira, Callianassa show
Their sister looks; Dexamene the slow,
And swift Dynamene, now cut the tides:
Iaera now the verdant wave divides;
Nemertes with Apseudes lifts the head:
Bright Galatea quits her pearly bed: 60
These Orythia, Clymene, attend,
Maera, Amphinome, the train extend,
And black Janira, and Janassa fair,
And Amatheia with her amber hair.
All these, and all that deep in ocean held
Their sacred seats, the glimmering grotto filled;
Each beat her ivory breast with silent woe,
Till Thetis' sorrows thus began to flow.
    'Hear me, and judge, ye sisters of the main!
How just a cause has Thetis to complain?   70
How wretched, were I mortal, were my fate!
How more than wretched in th' immortal state!
Sprung from my bed a godlike hero came,
The bravest far that ever bore the name;
Like some fair olive, by my careful hand
He grew, he flourished, and adorned the land:
To Troy I sent him; but the fates ordain
He never, never must return again.
So short a space the light of heaven to view,
So short alas! and filled with anguish too.   80
Hear how his sorrows echo through the shore!
I cannot ease them, but I must deplore;
I go at least to bear a tender part,
And mourn my loved one with a mother's heart.'
    She said, and left the caverns of the main.
All bathed in tears, the melancholy train
Attend her way. Wide-opening part the tides,
While the long pomp the silver wave divides.
Approaching now, they touched the Trojan land;

Then, two by two, ascended up the strand.   90
Th' immortal mother, standing close beside
Her mournful offspring, to his sighs replied;
Along the coast their mingled clamours ran,
And thus the silver-footed dame began.

    'Why mourns my son? thy late-preferred request
The god has granted, and the Greeks distressed:
Why mourns my son? thy anguish let me share,
Reveal the cause, and trust a parent's care.'

    He, deeply groaning—'To this cureless grief
Not even the Thunderer's° favour brings relief.   100
Patroclus—Ah!—Say, Goddess, can I boast
A pleasure now? Revenge itself is lost:
Patroclus, loved of all my martial train,
Beyond mankind, beyond my self, is slain!
Lost are those arms the gods themselves bestowed
On Peleus; Hector bears the glorious load.
Cursed be that day, when all the powers above
Thy charms submitted to a mortal love:
Oh hadst thou still, a sister of the main,
Pursued the pleasures of the watery reign;   110
And happier Peleus, less ambitious, led
A mortal beauty to his equal bed!°
E'er the sad fruit of thy unhappy womb
Had caused such sorrows past, and woes to come.
For soon alas! that wretched offspring slain,
New woes, new sorrows shall create again:
'Tis not in fate th' alternate now to give;
Patroclus dead, Achilles hates to live.
Let me revenge it on proud Hector's heart,
Let his last spirit smoke upon my dart;   120
On these conditions will I breathe: till then,
I blush to walk among the race of men.'

    A flood of tears, at this, the Goddess shed;
'Ah then, I see thee dying, see thee dead!
When Hector falls, thou diest.'—'Let Hector die,
And let me fall!', Achilles made reply,
'Far lies Patroclus from his native plain!
He fell, and falling wished my aid in vain.
Ah then, since from this miserable day
I cast all hope of my return away,   130

Since unrevenged, a hundred ghosts demand
The fate of Hector from Achilles' hand;
Since here, for brutal courage far renowned,
I live an idle burden to the ground,
(Others in council famed for nobler skill,
More useful to preserve, than I to kill)
Let me—But oh! ye gracious powers above!
Wrath and revenge from men and gods remove:
Far, far too dear to every mortal breast,
Sweet to the soul, as honey to the taste;   140
Gathering like vapours of a noxious kind
From fiery blood, and darkening all the mind.
Me Agamemnon urged to deadly hate;
'Tis past—I quell it; I resign to fate.
Yes—I will meet the murderer of my friend,
Or (if the gods ordain it) meet my end.
The stroke of fate the bravest cannot shun:
The great Alcides,° Jove's unequalled son,
To Juno's hate at length resigned his breath,
And sunk the victim of all-conquering death.   150
So shall Achilles fall! stretched pale and dead,
No more the Grecian hope, or Trojan dread!
Let me, this instant, rush into the fields,
And reap what glory life's short harvest yields.
Shall I not force some widowed dame to tear
With frantic hands, her long dishevelled hair?
Shall I not force her breast to heave with sighs,
And the soft tears to trickle from her eyes?
Yes, I shall give the fair those mournful charms—
In vain you hold me—Hence! my arms, my arms!   160
Soon shall the sanguine torrent spread so wide,
That all shall know, Achilles swells the tide.'
   'My son', Caerulean° Thetis made reply,
To fate submitting with a secret sigh,
'The host to succour, and thy friends to save,
Is worthy thee; the duty of the brave.
But canst thou, naked, issue to the plains?
Thy radiant arms the Trojan foe detains,
Insulting Hector bears the spoils on high,
But vainly glories, for his fate is nigh.   170
Yet, yet awhile, thy generous ardour stay;

Assured, I meet thee at the dawn of day,
Charged with refulgent arms (a glorious load)
Vulcanian arms, the labour of a god.'
    Then turning to the daughters of the main,
The goddess thus dismissed her azure train.
    'Ye sister Nereids! to your deeps descend,
Haste, and our father's sacred seat attend,
I go to find the architect divine,
Where vast Olympus' starry summits shine: 180
So tell our hoary sire'—This charge she gave:
The sea-green sisters plunge beneath the wave:
Thetis once more ascends the blessed abodes,
And treads the brazen threshold of the Gods.
    And now the Greeks, from furious Hector's force,
Urge to broad Hellespont their headlong course:
Nor yet their chiefs Patroclus' body bore
Safe through the tempest, to the tented shore.
The horse, the foot, with equal fury joined,
Poured on the rear, and thundered close behind;   190
And like a flame through fields of ripened corn,
The rage of Hector o'er the ranks was borne:
Thrice the slain hero by the foot he drew;
Thrice to the skies the Trojan clamours flew.
As oft th' Ajaces his assault sustain;
But checked, he turns; repulsed, attacks again.
With fiercer shouts his lingering troops he fires,
Nor yields a step, nor from his post retires:
So watchful shepherds strive to force, in vain,
The hungry lion from a carcass slain.   200
Ev'n yet, Patroclus had he borne away,
And all the glories of th' extended day;
Had not high Juno, from the realms of air,
Secret, dispatched her trusty messenger.°
The various goddess of the showery bow,
Shot in a whirlwind to the shore below;
To great Achilles at his ships she came,
And thus began the many-coloured dame.
    'Rise, son of Peleus! rise divinely brave!
Assist the combat, and Patroclus save: 210
For him the slaughter to the fleet they spread,
And fall by mutual wounds around the dead.

To drag him back to Troy the foe contends;
Nor with his death the rage of Hector ends:
A prey to dogs he dooms the corse to lie,
And marks the place to fix his head on high.
Rise, and prevent (if yet thou think of fame)
Thy friend's disgrace, thy own eternal shame!'
    'Who sends thee, Goddess! from th' ethereal skies?'
Achilles thus. And Iris thus replies,   220
'I come, Pelides! from the Queen of Jove,
Th' immortal empress of the realms above;
Unknown to him who sits remote on high,
Unknown to all the synod of the sky.'
'Thou comest in vain,' he cries (with fury warmed)
'Arms I have none, and can I fight unarmed?
Unwilling as I am, of force I stay,
Till Thetis bring me at the dawn of day
Vulcanian arms: what other should I wield?
Except the mighty Telamonian° shield?   230
That, in my friend's defence, has Ajax spread,
While his strong lance around him heaps the dead:
The gallant chief defends Menoetius' son,°
And does, what his Achilles should have done.'
    'Thy want of arms,' said Iris, 'well we know,
But though unarmed, yet clad in terrors, go!
Let but Achilles o'er yon trench appear,
Proud Troy shall tremble, and consent to fear;
Greece from one glance of that tremendous eye
Shall take new courage, and disdain to fly.'   240
    She spoke, and passed in air. The hero rose;
Her Aegis, Pallas o'er his shoulders throws;
Around his brows a golden cloud she spread;
A stream of glory flamed above his head.
As when from some beleaguered town arise
The smokes high-curling to the shaded skies;
(Seen from some island, o'er the main afar,
When men distressed hang out the sign of war)
Soon as the sun in ocean hides his rays,
Thick on the hills the flaming beacons blaze;   250
With long-projected beams the seas are bright,
And heaven's high arch reflects the ruddy light;
So from Achilles' head the splendours rise,

Reflecting blaze on blaze, against the skies.
Forth marched the chief, and distant from the crowd,
High on the rampart raised his voice aloud;
With her own shout Minerva swells the sound;
Troy starts astonished, and the shores rebound.
As the loud trumpet's brazen mouth from far
With shrilling clangour sounds th' alarm of war;   260
Struck from the walls, the echoes float on high,
And the round bulwarks, and thick towers reply:
So high his brazen voice the hero reared:
Hosts dropped their arms, and trembled as they heard;
And back the chariots roll, and coursers bound,
And steeds and men lie mingled on the ground.
Aghast they see the living lightnings play,
And turn their eye-balls from the flashing ray.
Thrice from the trench his dreadful voice he raised;
And thrice they fled, confounded and amazed.   270
Twelve in the tumult wedged, untimely rushed
On their own spears, by their own chariots crushed:
While shielded from the darts, the Greeks obtain
The long-contended carcass of the slain.

A lofty bier the breathless warrior bears;
Around, his sad companions melt in tears:
But chief Achilles, bending down his head,
Pours unavailing sorrows o'er the dead.
Whom late, triumphant with his steeds and car,
He sent refulgent to the field of war,   280
(Unhappy change!) now senseless, pale, he found,
Stretched forth, and gashed with many a gaping wound.

Meantime, unwearied with his heavenly way,
In ocean's waves th' unwilling light of day
Quenched his red orb, at Juno's high command,
And from their labours eased th' Achaean band.°
The frighted Trojans (panting from the war,
Their steeds unharnessed from the weary car)
A sudden° council called: each chief appeared
In haste, and standing; for to sit they feared.   290
'Twas now no season for prolonged debate;
They saw Achilles, and in him their fate.
Silent they stood: Polydamas at last,
Skilled to discern the future by the past,

The son of Panthus, thus expressed his fears;
(The friend of Hector, and of equal years:
The self-same night to both a being gave,
One wise in council, one in action brave.)
'In free debate, my friends, your sentence speak:
For me, I move, before the morning break   300
To raise our camp: too dangerous here our post,
Far from Troy walls, and on a naked coast.
I deemed not Greece so dreadful, while engaged
In mutual feuds, her king and hero raged;
Then, while we hoped our armies might prevail,
We boldly camped beside a thousand sail.
I dread Pelides now: his rage of mind
Not long continues to the shores confined,
Nor to the fields, where long in equal fray
Contending nations won and lost the day;   310
For Troy, for Troy, shall henceforth be the strife,
And the hard contest not for fame, but life.
Haste then to Ilion,° while the favouring night
Detains those terrors, keeps that arm from fight;
If but the morrow's sun behold us here,
That arm, those terrors, we shall feel, not fear;
And hearts that now disdain, shall leap with joy,
If heaven permits them then to enter Troy.
Let not my fatal prophecy be true,
Nor what I tremble but to think, ensue.   320
Whatever be our fate, yet let us try
What force of thought and reason can supply;
Let us on counsel for our guard depend:
The town, her gates and bulwarks shall defend:
When morning dawns, our well-appointed powers
Arrayed in arms, shall line the lofty towers.
Let the fierce hero then, when fury calls,
Vent his mad vengeance on our rocky walls,
Or fetch a thousand circles round the plain,
Till his spent coursers seek the fleet again: 330
So may his rage be tired, and laboured down;
And dogs shall tear him, e'er he sack the town.'
    'Return?', said Hector, fired with stern disdain,
'What, coop whole armies in our walls again?
Was't not enough, ye valiant warriors say,

Nine years imprisoned in those towers ye lay?
Wide o'er the world was Ilion famed of old
For brass exhaustless, and for mines of gold:
But while inglorious in her walls we stayed,
Sunk were her treasures, and her stores decayed;   340
The Phrygians now her scattered spoils enjoy,
And proud Maeonia° wastes the fruits of Troy.
Great Jove at length my arms to conquest calls,
And shuts the Grecians in their wooden walls:
Darest thou dispirit whom the gods incite?
Flies any Trojan? I shall stop his flight.
To better counsel then attention lend,
Take due refreshment, and the watch attend.
If there be one whose riches cost him care,
Forth let him bring them, for the troops to share;   350
'Tis better generously bestowed on those,
Than left the plunder of our country's foes.
Soon as the morn the rosy welkin warms
Fierce on yon navy will we pour our arms.
If great Achilles rise in all his might,
His be the danger: I shall stand the fight.
Honour, ye gods! or let me gain, or give;
And live he glorious, whosoe'er shall live!
Mars is our common lord, alike to all;
And oft the victor triumphs, but to fall.'   360
    The shouting host in loud applauses joined;
So Pallas robbed the many of their mind,
To their own sense condemned! and left to choose
The worst advice, the better to refuse.
    While the long night extends her sable reign,
Around Patroclus mourned the Grecian train.
Stern in superior grief Pelides stood;
Those slaughtering arms, so used to bathe in blood,
Now clasp his clay-cold limbs: then gushing start
The tears, and sighs burst from his swelling heart.   370
The lion thus, with dreadful anguish stung,
Roars through the desert, and demands his young;
When the grim savage to his rifled den
Too late returning, snuffs the track of men,
And o'er the vales, and o'er the forest bounds;
His clamorous grief the bellowing wood resounds.

So grieves Achilles; and impetuous, vents
To all his Myrmidons, his loud laments.
   'In what vain promise, gods! did I engage?
When to console Menaetius' feeble age,   380
I vowed his much-loved offspring to restore,
Charged with rich spoils, to fair Opuntia's shore!
But mighty Jove cuts short, with just disdain,
The long, long views of poor, designing man!
One fate the warrior and the friend shall strike,
And Troy's black sands must drink our blood alike:
Me too, a wretched mother shall deplore,
An aged father never see me more!
Yet, my Patroclus! yet a space I stay,
Then swift pursue thee on the darksome way.   390
E'er thy dear relics in the grave are laid,
Shall Hector's head be offered to thy shade;
That, with his arms, shall hang before thy shrine,
And twelve, the noblest of the Trojan line,
Sacred to vengeance, by this hand expire;
Their lives effused around thy flaming pyre.
Thus let me lie till then! thus, closely pressed,
Bathe thy cold face, and sob upon thy breast!
While Trojan captives here thy mourners stay,
Weep all the night, and murmur all the day: 400
Spoils of my arms, and thine; when, wasting wide,
Our swords kept time, and conquered side by side.'
   He spoke, and bid the sad attendants round
Cleanse the pale corse, and wash each honoured wound.
A massy cauldron of stupendous frame
They brought, and placed it o'er the rising flame:
Then heap the lighted wood; the flame divides
Beneath the vase, and climbs around the sides:
In its wide womb they pour the rushing stream;
The boiling water bubbles to the brim: 410
The body then they bathe with pious toil,
Embalm the wounds, anoint the limbs with oil;
High on a bed of state extended laid,
And decent covered with a linen shade;
Last o'er the dead the milkwhite mantle threw;
That done, their sorrows and their sighs renew.
   Meanwhile to Juno, in the realms above,

(His wife and sister) spoke almighty Jove.
'At last thy will prevails: great Peleus' son
Rises in arms: such grace thy Greeks have won.   420
Say (for I know not) is their race divine,
And thou the mother of that martial line?'

    'What words are these,' th' imperial dame replies,
While anger flashed from her majestic eyes,
'Succour like this a mortal arm might lend,
And such success mere human wit attend:
And shall not I, the second power above,
Heaven's queen, and consort of the thundering Jove,
Say, shall not I one nation's fate command,
Not wreak my vengeance on one guilty land?'   430
    So they. Meanwhile the silver-footed dame
Reached the Vulcanian dome, eternal frame!
High eminent amid the works divine,
Where heaven's far-beaming, brazen mansions shine.
There the lame architect° the goddess found,
Obscure in smoke, his forges flaming round,
While bathed in sweat from fire to fire he flew,
And puffing loud, the roaring bellows blew.
That day, no common task his labour claimed;
Full twenty tripods for his hall he framed,   440
That placed on living wheels of massy gold,
(Wondrous to tell) instinct with spirit rolled
From place to place, around the blessed abodes,
Self-moved, obedient to the beck of gods:
For their fair handles now, o'erwrought with flowers,
In moulds prepared, the glowing ore he pours.
Just as responsive to his thought, the frame
Stood prompt to move, the azure goddess came:
Charis,° his spouse, a grace divinely fair,
(With purple fillets round her braided hair)   450
Observed her entering; her soft hand she pressed,
And smiling, thus the watery queen addressed.
    'What, goddess! this unusual favour draws?
All hail, and welcome! whatsoe'er the cause:
Till now a stranger, in a happy hour
Approach, and taste the dainties of the bower.'
    High on a throne, with stars of silver graced
And various artifice, the queen she placed;

A footstool at her feet: then calling, said,
'Vulcan draw near, 'tis Thetis asks your aid.'   460
   'Thetis,' replied the god, 'our powers may claim,
An ever dear, and ever honoured name!
When my proud mother° hurled me from the sky,
(My awkward form, it seems, displeased her eye)
She, and Eurynome, my griefs redressed,
And soft received me on their silver breast.
Ev'n then, these arts employed my infant thought;
Chains, bracelets, pendants, all their toys I wrought.
Nine years kept secret in the dark abode,
Secure I lay, concealed from man and god: 470
Deep in a caverned rock my days were led;
The rushing ocean murmured o'er my head.
Now since her presence glads our mansion, say,
For such desert what service can I pay?
Vouchsafe, O Thetis! at our board to share
The genial rites, and hospitable fare;
While I my labours of the forge forego,
And bid the roaring bellows cease to blow.'
   Then from his anvil the lame artist rose;
Wide with distorted legs, oblique he goes,   480
And stills the bellows, and (in order laid)
Locks in their chest his instruments of trade.
Then with a sponge the sooty workman dressed
His brawny arms imbrowned, and hairy breast.
With his huge sceptre graced, and red attire,
Came halting forth the sovereign of the fire:
The monarch's steps two female forms uphold,
That moved, and breathed, in animated gold;
To whom was voice, and sense, and science given
Of works divine (such wonders are in heaven!)   490
On these supported, with unequal gait,
He reached the throne where pensive Thetis sate;
There placed beside her on the shining frame,
He thus addressed the silver-footed dame.
   'Thee, welcome goddess! what occasion calls,
(So long a stranger) to these honoured walls?
'Tis thine, fair Thetis, the command to lay,
And Vulcan's joy, and duty, to obey.'
   To whom the mournful mother thus replies,

(The crystal drops stood trembling in her eyes)   500
'Oh Vulcan! say, was ever breast divine
So pierced with sorrows, so o'erwhelmed as mine?
Of all the goddesses, did Jove prepare
For Thetis only such a weight of care?
I, only I, of all the watery race,
By force subjected to a man's embrace,
Who, sinking now with age, and sorrow, pays
The mighty fine imposed on length of days.
Sprung from my bed a godlike hero came,
The bravest sure that ever bore the name;   510
Like some fair plant beneath my careful hand
He grew, he flourished, and he graced the land:
To Troy I sent him! but his native shore
Never, ah never, shall receive him more;
(Ev'n while he lives, he wastes with secret woe)
Nor I, a goddess, can retard the blow!
Robbed of the prize the Grecian suffrage gave,
The king of nations forced his royal slave:
For this he grieved; and till the Greeks oppressed
Required his arm, he sorrowed unredressed.   520
Large gifts they promise, and their elders send;
In vain—he arms not, but permits his friend°
His arms, his steeds, his forces to employ;
He marches, combats, almost conquers Troy:
Then slain by Phoebus (Hector had the name)
At once resigns his armour, life, and fame.
But thou, in pity, by my prayer be won;
Grace with immortal arms this short-lived son,
And to the field in martial pomp restore,
To shine with glory, till he shines no more!'   530
     To her the artist-god: 'Thy griefs resign,
Secure, what Vulcan can, is ever thine.
O could I hide him from the fates as well,
Or with these hands the cruel stroke repel,
As I shall forge most envied arms, the gaze
Of wondering ages, and the world's amaze!'
     Thus having said, the father of the fires
To the black labours of his forge retires.
Soon as he bade them blow, the bellows turned
Their iron mouths; and where the furnace burned,   540

Resounding breathed: at once the blast expires,
And twenty forges catch at once the fires;
Just as the god directs, now loud, now low,
They raise a tempest, or they gently blow.
In hissing flames huge silver bars are rolled,
And stubborn brass, and tin, and solid gold:
Before, deep fixed, th' eternal anvils stand;
The ponderous hammer loads his better hand,
His left with tongs turns the vexed metal round;
And thick, strong strokes, the doubling vaults rebound.   550

   Then first he formed th' immense and solid shield;
Rich, various artifice emblazed the field;
Its utmost verge a threefold circle bound;
A silver chain suspends the massy round,
Five ample plates the broad expanse compose,
And godlike labours on the surface rose.
There shone the image of the master mind:
There earth, there heaven, there ocean he designed;
Th' unwearied sun, the moon completely round;
The starry lights that heaven's high convex crowned;   560
The Pleiads, Hyades,° with the northern team;
And great Orion's more refulgent beam;
To which, around the axle of the sky,
The bear revolving, points his golden eye,
Still shines exalted on th' ethereal plain,
Nor bends his blazing forehead to the main.

   Two cities radiant on the shield appear,
The image one of peace, and one of war.
Here sacred pomp, and genial feast delight,
And solemn dance, and Hymeneal rite;   570
Along the street the new-made brides are led,
With torches flaming, to the nuptial bed;
The youthful dancers in a circle bound
To the soft flute, and cittern's silver sound:
Through the fair streets, the matrons in a row,
Stand in their porches, and enjoy the show.

    There, in the forum swarm a numerous train;
The subject of debate, a townsman slain:
One pleads the fine discharged, which one denied,
And bade the public and the laws decide: 580
The witness is produced on either hand;

For this, or that, the partial people stand:
Th' appointed heralds still the noisy bands,
And form a ring, with sceptres in their hands;
On seats of stone, within the sacred place,
The reverend elders nodded o'er the case;
Alternate, each th' attesting sceptre took,
And rising solemn, each his sentence spoke.
Two golden talents lay amidst, in sight,
The prize of him who best adjudged the right.   590
    Another part (a prospect differing far)
Glowed with refulgent arms, and horrid war.
Two mighty hosts a leaguered town embrace,
And one would pillage, one would burn the place.
Meantime the townsmen, armed with silent care,
A secret ambush on the foe prepare:
Their wives, their children, and the watchful band,
Of trembling parents on the turrets stand.
They march; by Pallas and by Mars made bold;
Gold were the gods, their radiant garments gold,   600
And gold their armour: these the squadron led,
August, divine, superior by the head!
A place for ambush fit, they found, and stood
Covered with shields, beside a silver flood.
Two spies at distance lurk, and watchful seem
If sheep or oxen seek the winding stream.
Soon the white flocks proceeded o'er the plains,
And steers slow-moving, and two shepherd swains;
Behind them, piping on their reeds, they go,
Nor fear an ambush, nor suspect a foe.   610
In arms the glittering squadron rising round
Rush sudden; hills of slaughter heap the ground,
Whole flocks and herds lie bleeding on the plains,
And, all amidst them, dead, the shepherd swains!
The bellowing oxen the besiegers hear;
They rise, take horse, approach, and meet the war;
They fight, they fall, beside the silver flood;
The waving silver seemed to blush with blood.
There tumult, there contention stood confessed;°
One reared a dagger at a captive's breast,   620
One held a living foe, that freshly bled
With new-made wounds; another dragged a dead;

Now here, now there, the carcasses they tore:
Fate stalked amidst them, grim with human gore.
And the whole war came out, and met the eye;
And each bold figure seemed to live, or die.
    A field deep-furrowed, next the god designed,
The third time laboured by the sweating hind;
The shining shares full many ploughmen guide,
And turn their crooked yokes on every side. 630
Still as at either end they wheel around,
The master meets 'em with his goblet crowned;
The hearty draught rewards, renews their toil;
Then back the turning plough-shares cleave the soil:
Behind, the rising earth in ridges rolled;
And sable looked, though formed of molten gold.
    Another field rose high with waving grain;
With bended sickles stand the reaper-train:
Here stretched in ranks the levelled swarths are found,
Sheaves heaped on sheaves, here thicken up the ground. 640
With sweeping stroke the mowers strow the lands;
The gatherers follow, and collect in bands;
And last the children, in whose arms are borne
(Too short to gripe them) the brown sheaves of corn.
The rustic monarch of the field descries
With silent glee, the heaps around him rise.
A ready banquet on the turf is laid,
Beneath an ample oak's expanded shade.
The victim-ox the sturdy youth prepare;
The reaper's due repast, the women's care. 650
    Next, ripe in yellow gold, a vineyard shines,
Bent with the ponderous harvest of its vines;
A deeper dye the dangling clusters show,
And curled on silver props, in order glow:
A darker metal mixed, entrenched the place,
And pales of glittering tin th' enclosure grace.
To this, one pathway gently winding leads,
Where march a train with baskets on their heads,
(Fair maids, and blooming youths) that smiling bear
The purple product of th' autumnal year. 660
To these a youth awakes the warbling strings,
Whose tender lay the fate of Linus° sings;
In measured dance behind him move the train,

Tune soft the voice, and answer to the strain.
 Here, herds of oxen march, erect and bold,
Rear high their horns, and seem to low in gold,
And speed to meadows on whose sounding shores
A rapid torrent through the rushes roars:
Four golden herdsmen as their guardians stand,
And nine sour dogs complete the rustic band.   670
Two lions rushing from the wood appeared;
And seized a bull, the master of the herd:
He roared: in vain the dogs, the men withstood,
They tore his flesh, and drank the sable blood.
The dogs (oft cheered in vain) desert the prey,
Dread the grim terrors, and at distance bay.
 Next this, the eye the art of Vulcan leads
Deep through fair forests, and a length of meads;
And stalls, and folds, and scattered cots between;
And fleecy flocks, that whiten all the scene.   680
 A figured dance succeeds: such once was seen
In lofty Gnossus, for the Cretan queen,
Formed by Daedalean art.° A comely band
Of youths and maidens, bounding hand in hand:
The maids in soft cymars of linen dressed;
The youths all graceful in the glossy vest;
Of those the locks with flowery wreaths enrolled,
Of these the sides adorned with swords of gold,
That glittering gay, from silver belts depend.
Now all at once they rise, at once descend,   690
With well-taught feet: now shape, in oblique ways,
Confusedly regular, the moving maze:
Now forth at once, too swift for sight, they spring,
And undistinguished blend the flying ring:
So whirls a wheel, in giddy circle tossed,
And rapid as it runs, the single spokes are lost.
The gazing multitudes admire around;
Two active tumblers in the centre bound;
Now high, now low, their pliant limbs they bend,
And general songs the sprightly revel end.   700
 Thus the broad shield complete the artist crowned
With his last hand, and poured the ocean round:
In living silver seemed the waves to roll,
And beat the buckler's verge, and bound the whole.

This done, whate'er a warrior's use requires
He forged; the cuirass that outshone the fires;
The greaves of ductile tin, the helm impressed
With various sculpture, and the golden crest.
At Thetis' feet the finished labour lay;
She, as a falcon cuts th' aerial way,   710
Swift from Olympus' snowy summit flies,
And bears the blazing present through the skies.

To Mr Gay

Congratulating Pope on finishing his house and gardens

Ah, friend! 'tis true—this truth you lovers know—
In vain my structures rise, my gardens grow,
In vain fair Thames reflects the double scenes
Of hanging mountains, and of sloping greens:
Joy lives not here, to happier seats it flies,
And only dwells where WORTLEY casts her eyes.
What are the gay parterre, the chequered shade,
The morning bower, the evening colonnade,
But soft recesses of uneasy minds,
To sigh unheard in, to the passing winds?   10
So the struck deer° in some sequestered part
Lies down to die, the arrow at his heart,
There, stretched unseen in coverts hid from day,
Bleeds drop by drop, and pants his life away.

TO

Mr *Addison*

Occasioned by his Dialogues on MEDALS°

See the wild waste of all-devouring years!   1
How Rome her own sad sepulchre appears,
With nodding arches, broken temples spread!
The very tombs now vanished like their dead!
Imperial wonders raised on nations spoiled,
Where mixed with slaves the groaning martyr toiled:
Huge theatres, that now unpeopled woods,
Now drained a distant country of her floods:°
Fanes,° which admiring gods with pride survey,
Statues of men, scarce less alive than they!   10
Some felt the silent stroke of mouldering age,
Some hostile fury, some religious rage.
Barbarian blindness, Christian zeal conspire,
And Papal piety, and Gothic fire.
Perhaps, by its own ruins saved from flame,
Some buried marble half preserves a name;
That name the learned with fierce disputes pursue,
And give to Titus old Vespasian's due.°
   Ambition sighed: she found it vain to trust
The faithless column and the crumbling bust: 20
Huge moles,° whose shadow stretched from shore to
      shore,
Their ruins ruined, and their place no more!
Convinced, she now contracts her vast design,
And all her triumphs° shrink into a coin:
A narrow orb each crowded conquest keeps,
Beneath her palm here sad Judea weeps,

This was originally written in the year 1715 when Mr Addison intended to publish
his book of medals; it was sometime before he was secretary of state; but not
published till Mr Tickell's edition of his works; at which time the verses on Mr
Craggs, which conclude the poem, were added, viz. in 1720.

Here scantier limits the proud arch confine,
And scarce are seen the prostrate Nile or Rhine;
A small Euphrates through the piece is rolled,
And little eagles wave their wings in gold.°   30
    The medal, faithful to its charge of fame,
Through climes and ages bears each form and name:
In one short view subjected to your eye
Gods, emperors, heroes, sages, beauties, lie.
With sharpened° sight pale antiquaries pore,
Th' inscription value, but the rust adore;
This the blue varnish,° that the green endears,
The sacred rust of twice ten hundred years!
To gain Pescennius° one employs his schemes,
One grasps a Cecrops° in ecstatic dreams,   40
Poor Vadius,° long with learned spleen devoured,
Can taste no pleasure since his shield was scoured;
And Curio, restless by the fair one's side,
Sighs for an Otho,° and neglects his bride.
    Theirs is the vanity, the learning thine:
Touched by thy hand, again Rome's glories shine;
Her gods, and godlike heroes rise to view,
And all her faded garlands bloom anew.
Nor blush, these studies thy regard engage;
These pleased the fathers of poetic rage;°   50
The verse and sculpture bore an equal part,
And art reflected images to art.
    Oh when shall Britain, conscious of her claim,
Stand emulous of Greek and Roman fame?
In living° medals see her wars enrolled,
And vanquished realms supply recording gold?
Here, rising bold,° the patriot's honest face;
There warriors frowning in historic brass:
Then future ages with delight shall see
How Plato's, Bacon's, Newton's looks° agree;   60
Or in fair series laurelled bards be shown,
A Virgil there, and here an Addison.
Then shall thy CRAGGS (and let me call him mine)
On the cast ore, another Pollio,° shine;
With aspect open, shall erect his head,
And round the orb in lasting notes be read,
'Statesman, yet friend to truth! of soul sincere,

In action faithful, and in honour clear;
Who broke no promise, served no private end,
Who gained no title, and who lost no friend;
Ennobled by himself, by all approved,
And praised, unenvied, by the Muse he loved.'°

70

EPISTLE
TO
ROBERT Earl of OXFORD
and Earl MORTIMER

Such were the notes thy once-loved poet° sung,
Till Death untimely stopped his tuneful tongue.
Oh just beheld, and lost! admired and mourned!
With softest manners, gentlest arts adorned!
Blessed in each science,° blessed in every strain!
Dear to the Muse! to HARLEY dear—in vain!
   For him, thou oft hast bid the world attend,
Fond to forget the statesman in the friend;
For SWIFT and him, despised the farce of state,
The sober follies of the wise and great;
Dexterous,° the craving, fawning crowd to quit,
And pleased to 'scape from Flattery to Wit.
   Absent or dead,° still let a friend be dear,
(A sigh the absent claims, the dead a tear)
Recall those nights that closed thy toilsome days,
Still hear thy Parnell in his living lays,
Who, careless now of interest, fame, or fate,
Perhaps forgets that OXFORD e'er was great;
Or deeming meanest what we greatest call,
Beholds thee glorious only in thy fall.
   And sure, if aught below the seats divine

1

10

20

This Epistle was sent to the Earl of Oxford with Dr Parnell's *Poems* published by
our author, after the said Earl's imprisonment in the Tower, and retreat into the
country, in the year 1721.

Can touch immortals, 'tis a soul like thine:
A soul supreme, in each hard instance tried,
Above all pain, all passion, and all pride,
The rage of power, the blast of public breath,
The lust of lucre, and the dread of death.
   In vain to deserts thy retreat is made;
The Muse attends thee to thy silent shade:°
'Tis hers, the brave man's latest steps to trace,
Rejudge his acts, and dignify disgrace.   30
When interest calls off all her sneaking train,
And all th' obliged desert, and all the vain;
She waits, or to the scaffold,° or the cell,
When the last lingering friend has bid farewell.
Ev'n now, she shades thy evening-walk with bays,
(No hireling she, no prostitute to praise)
Ev'n now, observant of the parting ray,
Eyes the calm sunset of thy various day,
Through Fortune's cloud one truly great can see,
Nor fears to tell, that MORTIMER° is he.

POPE TO SWIFT
August 1723

I find a rebuke in a late letter of yours that both stings and pleases
me extremely. Your saying that I ought to have writ a postscript to my
friend Gay's, makes me not content to write less than a whole letter,
and your seeming to receive his kindly gives me hopes you'll look upon
this as a sincere effect of friendship. Indeed as I cannot but own, the
laziness with which you tax me, and with which I may equally charge
you (for both of us I believe have had and one of us has both had and
given a surfeit of writing) so I really thought you would know yourself
to be so certainly entitled to my friendship, that 'twas a possession, you
could not imagine needed any further deeds or writings to assure you
of it. It is an honest truth, there's no one living or dead of whom I
think oftener, or better than yourself. I look upon you to be, (as to me)
in a state between both: you have from me all the passions, and good
wishes, that can attend the living; and all that respect and tender sense

of loss, that we feel for the dead. Whatever you seem to think of your withdrawn and separate state, at this distance, and in this absence, Dr Swift lives still in England, in every place and company where he would choose to live; and I find him in all the conversations I keep, and in all the hearts in which I would have any share. We have never met these many years without mention of you. Besides my old acquaintances I have found that all my friends of a later date, were such as were yours before. Lord Oxford,° Lord Harcourt, and Lord Harley, may look upon me as one immediately entailed upon them by you. Lord Bolingbroke° is now returned (as I hope) to take me, with all his other hereditary rights; and indeed he seems grown so much a philosopher as to set his heart upon some of 'em as little as upon the poet you gave him. 'Tis sure my particular ill fate, that all those I have most loved and with whom I have most lived, must be banished. After both of you left England, my constant host was the Bishop of Rochester.° Sure this is a nation that is cursedly afraid of being overrun with too much politeness, and cannot regain one great genius but at the expense of another. I tremble for my Lord Peterborough° (whom I now lodge with) he has too much wit, as well as courage to make a solid General, and if he escapes being banished by others, I fear he will banish himself. This leads me to give you some account of my manner of life and conversation which has been infinitely more various and dissipated than when you knew me, among all sexes, parties and professions. A glut of study and retirement in the first part of my life cast me into this, and this I begin to see will throw me again into study and retirement. The civilities I have met with from opposite sets of people have hindered me from being either violent or sour to any party: but at the same time the observations and experiences I cannot but have collected, have made me less fond of, and less surprised at any. I am therefore the more afflicted and the more angry, at the violences and hardships I see practised by either. The merry vein you knew me in, is sunk into a turn of reflexion, that has made the world pretty indifferent to me, and yet I have acquired a quietness of mind which by fits improves into a certain degree of cheerfulness, enough to make me just so good humoured as to wish that world well. My friendships are increased by new ones, yet no part of the warmth I felt for the old is diminished. Aversions I have none but to knaves, (for fools I have learned to bear with) and those I cannot be commonly civil to: for I think those are next of knaves who converse with them. The greatest man in power of this sort, shall hardly make me bow to him, unless I had a personal obligation to him and that I will take care not to have. The top-pleasure of my life is one I learned from you both how to gain, and how to use the freedoms of friendship with men much my superiors. To have pleased great men according to Horace° is a praise; but not to have flattered them and yet not to have displeased them is a greater. I have carefully avoided all intercourse with poets and scribblers, unless where by great chance I find a modest one. By these means I have had no quarrels with any personally, and none have been enemies, but who were also strangers to me. And as there is no great need of eclaircissements with such, whatever they writ or said I never retaliated; not only never seeming to know, but often really never knowing anything of the matter. There are very few things that give me the anxiety of a wish: the strongest I have would be to pass my days with you, and a few such as you. But Fate has dispersed them all about the world. And I find to wish it is as vain as to wish to live to see the millennium, and the Kingdom of the Just upon earth.

If I have sinned in my long silence consider there is one, to whom you yourself have been as great a sinner. As soon as you see his hand° you'll learn to do me justice, and feel in your own heart how long a man may be silent to those he truly loves and respects.

I am Dear Sir
Your ever faithful servant
A. Pope

POPE TO MARTHA BLOUNT
22 June 1724

June 22nd

Madam,—I promised you an account of Sherborne, before I had seen it, or knew what I undertook. I imagined it to be one of those fine old seats of which there are numbers scattered over England. But this is so peculiar and its situation of so uncommon a kind, that it merits a more particular description.

The house is in the form of an H. The body of it, which was built by Sir Walter Ralegh,° consists of four storeys, with four six-angled towers at the ends. These have since been joined to four wings, with a regular stone balustrade at the top and four towers more that finish the building. The windows and gates are of a yellow stone throughout, and one of the flat sides toward the garden has the wings of a newer architecture with beautiful Italian window-frames done by the first Earl of Bristol,° which, if they were joined in the middle by a portico covering the old building, would be a noble front. The design of such an one I have been amusing myself with drawing, but 'tis a question whether my Lord Digby will not be better amused than to execute it. The finest room is a salon fifty feet long, and a parlour hung with very excellent tapestry of Rubens, which was a present from the King of Spain to the Earl of Bristol in his embassy there.

This stands in a park, finely crowned with very high woods, on all the tops of the hills, which form a great amphitheatre sloping down to the house. On the garden sides the woods approach close, so that it appears there with a thick line and depth of groves on each hand, and so it shows from most parts of the park. The gardens are so irregular, that 'tis very hard to give an exact idea of 'em but by a plan. Their beauty rises from this irregularity, for not only the several parts of the garden itself make the better contrast° by these sudden rises, falls, and turns of ground; but the views about it are let in, and hang over the walls, in very different figures and aspects. You come first out of the house into a green walk of standard limes with a hedge behind them that makes a colonnade, thence into a little triangular wilderness, from whose centre you see the town of Sherborne in a valley, interspersed with trees. From the corner of this you issue at once upon a high green terrace the whole breadth of the garden, which has five more green terraces hanging under each other, without hedges, only a few pyramid yews and large round honeysuckles between them. The honeysuckles hereabouts are the largest and finest I ever saw. You'll be pleased when I tell you the quarters of the above mentioned little wilderness are filled with these and with cherry trees of the best kinds all within reach of the hand. At the ends of these terraces run two long walks under the side walls of the garden which communicate with the other terraces that front these opposite. Between, the valley is laid level and divided into two regular groves of horse chestnuts, and a bowling-green in the middle of about 180 foot. This is bounded behind with a canal, that runs quite across the groves and also along one side, in the form of a T. Behind this, is a semicircular berceau, and a thicket of mixed trees that completes the crown of the amphitheatre which is of equal extent with the bowling-green. Beyond that runs a natural river through green banks of turf, over which rises another row of terraces, the first supported by a slope wall planted with vines (so is also the wall that bounds the channel of the river.) A second and third appeared above this, but they are to be turned into a line of wilderness with wild winding walks for the convenience of passing from one side to the other in shade, the heads of whose trees will lie below the uppermost terrace of all, which completes the garden and overlooks both that and the country. Even above the wall of this the natural ground rises, and is crowned with several venerable ruins of an old castle, with arches and broken views, of which I must say more hereafter.

When you are at the left corner of the canal and the chestnut groves in the bottom, you turn of a sudden under very old trees into the deepest shade. One walk winds you up a hill of venerable wood overarched by nature, and of a vast height, into a circular grove, on one side of which is a close high arbour, on the other a sudden open seat that overlooks the meadows and river with a large distant prospect. Another walk under this hill winds by the riverside quite covered with high trees on both banks, overhung with ivy, where falls a natural cascade with never-ceasing murmurs. On the opposite hanging of the bank (which is a steep of fifty feet) is placed, with a very fine fancy, a rustic seat of stone, flagged and rough, with two urns in the same rude taste upon pedestals, on each side: from whence you lose your eyes upon the glimmering of the waters under the wood, and your ears in the constant dashing of the waves. In view of this, is a bridge that crosses this stream, built in the same ruinous taste: the wall of the garden hanging over it, is humoured so as to appear the ruin of another arch or two above the bridge. Hence you mount the hill over the hermit's seat (as they call it) described before, and so to the highest terrace, again.

On the left, full behind these old trees, which make this whole part inexpressibly awful and solemn, runs a little, old, low wall, beside a trench, covered with elder trees and ivies; which being crossed by another bridge, brings you to the ruins, to complete the solemnity of the scene. You first see an old tower penetrated by a large arch, and others above it through which the whole country appears in prospect, even when you are at the top of the other ruins, for they stand very high, and the ground slopes down on all sides. These venerable broken walls, some arches almost entire of 30 or 40 feet deep, some open like porticos with fragments of pillars, some circular or enclosed on three sides, but exposed at top, with steps which time has made of disjointed stones to climb to the highest points of the ruin. These I say might have a prodigious beauty, mixed with greens and parterres from part to part, and the whole heap standing as it does on a round hill, kept smooth in green turf, which makes a bold basement to show it. The open courts from building to building might be thrown into circles or octagons of grass or flowers, and even in the gaming rooms you have fine trees grown, that might be made a natural tapestry to the walls, and arch you overhead where time has uncovered them to the sky. Little paths of earth, or sand, might be made, up the half-tumbled walls; to guide from one view to another on the higher parts; and seats placed here and there, to enjoy those views, which are more romantic than imagination can form them. I could very much wish this were done, as well as a little temple built on a neighbouring round hill that is seen from all points of the garden and is extremely pretty. It would finish some walks, and particularly be a fine termination to the river to be seen from the entrance into that deep scene I have described by the cascade where it would appear as in the clouds, between the tops of some very lofty trees that form an arch before it, with a great slope downward to the end of the said river.

What should induce my Lord D. the rather to cultivate these ruins and do honour to them, is that they do no small honour to his family; that castle, which was very ancient, being demolished in the Civil Wars after it was nobly defended by one of his ancestors in the cause of the King. I would set up at the entrance of 'em an obelisk, with an inscription of the fact: which would be a monument erected to the very ruins; as the adorning and beautifying them in the manner I have been imagining, would not be unlike the Egyptian finery of bestowing ornament and curiosity on dead bodies. The present master of this place (and I verily believe I can engage the same for the next successors) needs not to fear the record, or shun the remembrance of the actions of his forefathers. He will not disgrace them, as most modern progeny do, by an unworthy degeneracy, of principle, or of practice. When I have been describing his agreeable seat, I cannot make the reflection I've often done upon contemplating the beautiful villas of other noblemen, raised upon the spoils of plundered nations, or aggrandized by the wealth of the public. I cannot ask myself the question, 'What else has this man to be liked? what else has he cultivated or improved? What good, or what desirable thing appears of him, without these walls?' I dare say his goodness and benevolence extend as far as his territories; that his tenants live almost as happy and contented as himself; and that not one of his children wishes to see this seat his own. I have not looked much about, since I was here. All I can tell you of my own knowledge is, that going to see the cathedral in the town hard by, I took notice as the finest things, of a noble monument and a beautiful altar-piece of architecture; but if I had not inquired in particular, he nor his, had ever told me that both the one and the other was erected by himself. The next pretty thing that catched my eye was a neat chapel for the use of the townspeople, (who are too numerous for the cathedral). My Lord modestly told me, he was glad I liked it, because it was of his own architecture.

I hope this long letter will be some entertainment to you, I was pleased not a little in writing it; but don't let any lady° from hence imagine that my head is so full of any gardens as to forget hers. The greatest proof I could give her to the contrary is, that I have spent many hours here in studying for hers, and in drawing new plans for her. I shall soon come home, and have nothing to say when we meet, having here told you all that has pleased me. But Wilton° is in my way, and I depend upon that for new matter. Believe me ever yours, with a sincerity as old-fashioned, and as different from modern sincerity, as this house, this family, and these ruins, are from the court, and all its neighbourhood.

Dear Madam, Adieu.

PREFACE TO
THE WORKS OF SHAKESPEARE

It is not my design to enter into a criticism upon this author; though to do it effectually and not superficially, would be the best occasion that any just writer could take, to form the judgment and taste of our nation. For of all English poets Shakespeare must be confessed to be the fairest and fullest subject for criticism, and to afford the most numerous, as well as most conspicuous instances, both of beauties and faults of all sorts. But this far exceeds the bounds of a preface, the business of which is only to give an account of the fate of his works, and the disadvantages under which they have been transmitted to us. We shall hereby extenuate many faults which are his, and clear him from the imputation of many which are not: a design, which though it can be no guide to future critics to do him justice in one way, will at least be sufficient to prevent their doing him an injustice in the other.

I cannot however but mention some of his principal and characteristic excellencies, for which (notwithstanding his defects) he is justly and universally elevated above all other dramatic writers. Not that this is the proper place of praising him, but because I would not omit any occasion of doing it.

If ever any author deserved the name of an *original*, it was Shakespeare. Homer himself drew not his art so immediately from the fountains of nature, it proceeded through Egyptian strainers and channels,° and came to him not without some tincture of the learning, or some cast of the models, of those before him. The poetry of Shakespeare was inspiration indeed: he is not so much an imitator, as an instrument, of nature; and 'tis not so just to say that he speaks from her, as that she speaks through him.

His *characters* are so much nature herself, that 'tis a sort of injury to call them by so distant a name as copies of her. Those of other poets have a constant resemblance, which shows that they received them from one another, and were but multipliers of the same image: each picture like a mock-rainbow is but the reflection of a reflection. But every single character in Shakespeare is as much an individual, as those in life itself; it is as impossible to find any two alike; and such as from their relation or affinity in any respect appear most to be twins, will upon comparison be found remarkably distinct. To this life and variety of character, we must add the wonderful preservation of it; which is such throughout his plays, that had all the speeches been printed without the very names of the persons, I believe one might have applied them with certainty to every speaker.

The *power* over our *passions* was never possessed in a more eminent degree, or displayed in so different instances. Yet all along, there is seen no labour, no pains to raise them; no preparation to guide our guess to the effect, or be perceived to lead toward it: but the heart swells, and the tears burst out, just at the proper places. We are surprised, the moment we weep; and yet upon reflection find the passion so just, that we should be surprised if we had not wept, and wept at that very moment.

How astonishing is it again, that the passions directly opposite to these, laughter and spleen, are no less at his command! that he is not more a master of the *great*, than of the *ridiculous* in human nature; of our noblest tendernesses, than of our vainest foibles; of our strongest emotions, than of our idlest sensations!

Nor does he only excel in the passions: in the coolness of reflection and reasoning he is full as admirable. His *sentiments* are not only in general the most pertinent and judicious upon every subject; but by a talent very peculiar, something between penetration and felicity, he hits upon that particular point on which the bent of each argument turns, or the force of each motive depends. This is perfectly amazing, from a man of no education or experience in those great and public scenes of life which are usually the subject of his thoughts: so that he seems to have known the world by intuition, to have looked through human nature at one glance, and to be the only author that gives ground for a very new opinion, that the philosopher and even the man of the world, may be *born*,° as well as the poet.

It must be owned that with all these great excellencies, he has almost as great defects; and that as he has certainly written better, so he has perhaps written worse, than any other. But I think I can in some measure account for these defects, from several causes and accidents; without which it is hard to imagine that so large and so enlightened a mind could ever have been susceptible of them. That all these contingencies should unite to his disadvantage seems to me almost as singularly unlucky, as that so many various (nay contrary) talents should meet in one man, was happy and extraordinary.

It must be allowed that stage-poetry of all other, is more particularly levelled to please the *populace*, and its success more immediately depending upon the *common suffrage*. One cannot therefore wonder, if Shakespeare, having at his first appearance no other aim in his writings than to procure a subsistence, directed his endeavours solely to hit the taste and humour that then prevailed. The audience was generally composed of the meaner sort of people; and therefore the images of life were to be drawn from those of their own rank. Accordingly we find, that not our author's only but almost all the old comedies have their scene among *tradesmen* and *mechanics*:° and even their historical plays strictly follow the common *old stories* or *vulgar traditions* of that kind of people. In tragedy, nothing was so sure to *surprise* and cause *admiration*, as the most strange, unexpected, and consequently most unnatural, events and incidents; the most exaggerated thoughts; the most verbose and bombast expression; the most pompous rhymes, and thundering versification. In comedy, nothing was so sure to *please*, as mean buffoonery, vile ribaldry, and unmannerly jests of fools and clowns.° Yet even in these, our author's wit buoys up, and is borne above his subject. His genius in those low parts is like some prince of a romance in the disguise of a shepherd or peasant; a certain greatness and spirit now and then break out, which manifest his higher extraction and qualities.

It may be added, that not only the common audience had no notion of the rules of writing, but few even of the better sort piqued themselves upon any great degree of knowledge or nicety that way; till Ben Jonson getting possession of the stage, brought critical learning into vogue. And that this was not done without difficulty, may appear from those frequent lessons (and indeed almost declamations) which he was forced to prefix to his first plays, and put into the mouth of his actors, the *Grex*,° *Chorus*, etc. to remove the prejudices, and inform the judgment of his hearers. Till then, our authors had no thoughts of writing on the model of the ancients: their tragedies were only histories in dialogue; and their comedies followed the thread of any novel° as they found it, no less implicitly than if it had been true history.

To judge therefore of Shakespeare by Aristotle's rules, is like trying a man by the laws of one country, who acted under those of another. He writ to the *people*; and writ at first without patronage from the better sort, and therefore without aims of pleasing them; without assistance or advice from the learned, as without the advantage of education or acquaintance among them; without that knowledge of the best models, the ancients, to inspire him with an emulation of them; in a word, without any views of reputation, and of what poets are pleased to call immortality: some or all of which have encouraged the vanity, or animated the ambition, of other writers.

Yet it must be observed, that when his performances had merited the protection of his prince, and when the encouragement of the court had succeeded to that of the town; the works of his riper years are manifestly raised above those of his former. The dates of his plays sufficiently evidence that his productions improved, in proportion to the respect he had for his auditors. And I make no doubt this observation would be found true in every instance, were but editions extant from which we might learn the exact time when every piece was composed, and whether writ for the town, or the court.

Another cause (and no less strong than the former) may be deduced from our author's being a *player*, and forming himself first upon the judgments of that body of men whereof he was a member. They have ever had a standard to themselves, upon other principles than those of Aristotle. As they live by the majority, they know no rule but that of pleasing the present humour, and complying with the wit in fashion; a consideration which brings all their judgment to a short point. Players are just such judges of what is *right*, as tailors are of what is *graceful*. And in this view it will be but fair to allow, that most of our author's faults are less to be ascribed to his wrong judgment as a poet, than to his right judgment as a player.

By these men it was thought a praise to Shakespeare, that he scarce ever *blotted a line*. This they industriously propagated, as appears from what we are told by Ben Jonson° in his *Discoveries*, and from the preface of Hemings and Condell to the first folio edition. But in reality (however it has prevailed) there never was a more groundless report, or to the contrary of which there are more undeniable evidences. As, the comedy of the *Merry Wives of Windsor*, which he entirely new writ; the *History of Henry the 6th*, which was first published under the title of the *Contention of York and Lancaster*, and that of *Henry the 5th*, extremely improved; that of *Hamlet* enlarged to almost as much again as at first, and many others. I believe the common opinion of his want of learning° proceeded from no better ground. This too might be thought a praise by some, and to this his errors have as injudiciously been ascribed by others. For 'tis certain, were it true, it could concern but a small part of them; the most are such as are not properly defects, but superfetations:° and arise not from want of learning or reading, but from want of thinking or judging: or rather (to be more just to our author) from a compliance to those wants in others. As to a wrong choice of the subject, a wrong conduct of the incidents, false thoughts, forced expressions, etc. if these are not to be ascribed to the foresaid accidental reasons, they must be charged upon the poet himself, and there is no help for it. But I think the two disadvantages which I have mentioned (to be obliged to please the lowest of people, and to keep the worst of company) if the consideration be extended as far as it reasonably may, will appear sufficient to mislead and depress the greatest genius upon earth. Nay the more modesty with which such a one is endued, the more he is in danger of submitting and conforming to others, against his own better judgment.

But as to his *want of learning*, it may be necessary to say something more: there is certainly a vast difference between *learning* and *languages*. How far he was ignorant of the latter, I cannot determine; but 'tis plain he had much reading at least, if they will not call it learning. Nor is it any great matter, if a man has knowledge, whether he has it from one language or from another. Nothing is more evident than that he had a taste of natural philosophy, mechanics, ancient and modern history, poetical learning and mythology. We find him very knowing in the customs, rites, and manners of antiquity. In *Coriolanus* and *Julius Caesar*, not only the spirit, but manners, of the Romans are exactly drawn; and still a nicer distinction is shown, between the manners of the Romans in the time of the former, and of the latter. His reading in the ancient historians is no less conspicuous, in many references to particular passages: and the speeches copied from Plutarch in *Coriolanus* may, I think, as well be made an instance of his learning, as those copied from Cicero in *Catiline*, of Ben Jonson's. The manners of other nations in general, the Egyptians, Venetians, French, etc. are drawn with equal propriety. Whatever object of nature, or branch of science, he either speaks of or describes; it is always with competent, if not extensive knowledge: his descriptions are still exact; all his metaphors appropriated, and remarkably drawn from the true nature and inherent qualities of each subject. When he treats of ethic or politic, we may constantly observe a wonderful justness of distinction, as well as extent of comprehension. No one is more a master of the poetical story, or has more frequent allusions to the various parts of it: Mr Waller (who has been celebrated for this last particular) has not shown more learning this way than Shakespeare. We have translations from Ovid° published in his name, among those poems which pass for his, and for some of which we have undoubted authority (being published by himself, and dedicated to his noble patron the Earl of Southampton): he appears also to have been conversant in Plautus, from whom he has taken the plot of one of his plays:° he follows the Greek authors, and particularly Dares Phrygius, in another° (although I will not pretend to say in what language he read them). The modern Italian writers of novels° he was manifestly acquainted with; and we may conclude him to be no less conversant with the ancients of his own country, from the use he has made of Chaucer in *Troilus and Cressida*, and in the *Two Noble Kinsmen*, if that play be his, as there goes a tradition it was (and indeed it has little resemblance of Fletcher, and more of our author than some of those which have been received as genuine).

I am inclined to think, this opinion proceeded originally from the zeal of the partisans of our author and Ben Jonson; as they endeavoured to exalt the one at the expense of the other. It is ever the nature of parties to be in extremes; and nothing is so probable, as that because Ben Jonson had much the most learning, it was said on the one hand that Shakespeare had none at all; and because Shakespeare had much the most wit and fancy, it was retorted on the other, that Jonson wanted both. Because Shakespeare borrowed nothing, it was said that Ben Jonson borrowed everything. Because Jonson did not write extempore, he was reproached with being a year about every piece; and because Shakespeare wrote with ease and rapidity, they cried, he never once made a blot. Nay the spirit of opposition ran so high, that whatever those of the one side objected to the other, was taken at the rebound, and turned into praises; as injudiciously as their antagonists before had made them objections.

Poets are always afraid of envy; but sure they have as much reason to be afraid of admiration. They are the Scylla and Charybdis of authors; those who escape one, often fall by the other. *Pessimum genus inimicorum Laudantes*, says Tacitus:° and Virgil° desires to wear a charm against those who praise a poet without rule or reason.

> —*Si ultra placitum laudarit, baccare frontem*
> *Cingito, ne Vati noceat—*

But however this contention might be carried on by the partisans on either side, I cannot help thinking these two great poets were good friends, and lived on amicable terms and in offices of society with each other. It is an acknowledged fact, that Ben Jonson was introduced upon the stage, and his first works encouraged, by Shakespeare. And after his death, that author writes *To the memory of his beloved Mr William Shakespeare*, which shows as if the friendship had continued through life. I cannot for my own part find anything *invidious* or *sparing* in those verses, but wonder Mr Dryden° was of that opinion. He exalts him not only above all his contemporaries, but above Chaucer and Spenser, whom he will not allow to be great enough to be ranked with him; and challenges the names of Sophocles, Euripides, and Aeschylus, nay all Greece and Rome at once, to equal him. And (which is very particular) expressly vindicates him from the imputation of wanting *art*, not enduring that all his excellencies should be attributed to *nature*. It is remarkable too, that the praise he gives him in his *Discoveries* seems to proceed from a *personal kindness*; he tells us that he loved the man, as well as honoured his memory; celebrates the honesty, openness, and frankness of his temper; and only distinguishes, as he reasonably ought, between the real merit of the author, and the silly and derogatory applauses of the players. Ben Jonson might indeed be sparing in his commendations (though certainly he is not so in this instance) partly from his own nature, and partly from judgment. For men of judgment think they do any man more service in praising him justly, than lavishly. I say, I would fain believe they were friends, though the violence and ill-breeding of their followers and flatterers were enough to give rise to the contrary report. I would hope that it may be with *parties*, both in wit and state, as with those monsters described by the poets; and that their *heads* at least may have something humane, though their *bodies* and *tails* are wild beasts and serpents.

As I believe that what I have mentioned gave rise to the opinion of Shakespeare's want of learning; so what has continued it down to us may have been the many blunders and illiteracies of the first publishers of his works. In these editions their ignorance shines almost in every page; nothing is more common than *Actus tertia. Exit Omnes. Enter three Witches solus.*° Their French is as bad as their Latin, both in construction and spelling; their very Welsh is false. Nothing is more likely than that those palpable blunders of Hector's quoting Aristotle, with others of that gross kind, sprung from the same root. It not being at all credible that these could be the errors of any man who had the least tincture of a school, or the least conversation with such as had. Ben Jonson (whom they will not think partial to him) allows him at least to have had *some Latin*; which is utterly inconsistent with mistakes like these. Nay the constant blunders in proper names of persons and places, are such as must have proceeded from a man, who had not so much as read any history, in any language: so could not be Shakespeare's.

I shall now lay before the reader some of those almost innumerable errors, which have risen from one source, the ignorance of the players, both as his actors, and as his editors. When the nature and kinds of these are enumerated and considered, I dare to say that not Shakespeare only but Aristotle or Cicero, had their works undergone the same fate, might have appeared to want sense as well as learning.

It is not certain that any one of his plays was published by himself. During the time of his employment in the theatre, several of his pieces were printed separately in quarto. What makes me think that most of these were not published by him, is the excessive carelessness of the press: every page is so scandalously false spelled, and almost all the learned or unusual words so intolerably mangled, that it's plain there either was no corrector to the press at all, or one totally illiterate. If any were supervised by himself, I should fancy the two parts of *Henry the 4th*, and *Midsummer Night's Dream* might have been so: because I find no other printed with any exactness; and (contrary to the rest) there is very little variation in all the subsequent editions of them. There are extant two prefaces, to the first quarto edition of *Troilus and Cressida* in 1609, and to that of *Othello*; by which it appears, that the first was published without his knowledge or consent, and even before it was acted, so late as seven or eight years before he died: and that the latter was not printed till after his death. The whole number of genuine plays which we have been able to find printed in his life-time, amounts but to eleven.° And of some of these, we meet with two or more editions by different printers, each of which has whole heaps of trash different from the other: which I should fancy was occasioned, by their being taken from different copies, belonging to different play-houses.

The folio edition (in which all the plays we now receive as his, were first collected) was published by two players, Hemings and Condell, in 1623, seven years after his decease. They declare, that all the other editions were stolen and surreptitious, and affirm theirs to be purged from the errors of the former. This is true as to the literal errors, and no other; for in all respects else it is far worse than the quartos.

First, because the additions of trifling and bombast passages are in this edition far more numerous. For whatever had been added, since those quartos, by the actors, or had stolen from their mouths into the written parts, were from thence conveyed into the printed text, and all stand charged upon the author. He himself complained of this usage in *Hamlet*,° where he wishes that *Those who play the clowns would speak no more than is set down for them* (Act. 3. Sc. 4). But as a proof that he could not escape it, in the old editions of *Romeo and Juliet* there is no hint of a great number of the mean conceits and ribaldries now to be found there. In others, the low scenes of mobs, plebeians and clowns, are vastly shorter than at present. And I have seen one in particular (which seems to have belonged to the playhouse, by having the parts divided with lines, and the actors names in the margin) where several of those very passages were added in a written hand, which are since to be found in the folio.

In the next place, a number of beautiful passages which are extant in the first single editions, are omitted in this: as it seems, without any other reason, than their willingness to shorten some scenes: these men (as it was said of Procrustes) either lopping, or stretching an author, to make him just fit for their stage.

This edition is said to be printed from the *original copies*; I believe they meant those which had lain ever since the author's days in the playhouse, and had from time to time been cut, or added to, arbitrarily. It appears that this edition, as well as the quartos, was printed (at least partly) from no better copies than the *prompter's book*, or *piecemeal parts* written out for the use of the actors: for in some places their very names° are through carelessness set down instead of the *Personae Dramatis*: and in others the notes of direction to the *property-men* for their *moveables*, and to the *players* for their *entries*, are inserted into the text, through the ignorance of the transcribers.

The plays not having been before so much as distinguished by *acts* and *scenes*, they are in this edition divided according as they played them; often where there is no pause in the action, or where they thought fit to make a breach in it, for the sake of music, masques, or monsters.

Sometimes the scenes are transposed and shuffled backward and forward; a thing which could no otherwise happen, but by their being taken from separate and piecemeal-written parts.

Many verses are omitted entirely, and others transposed; from whence invincible obscurities have arisen, past the guess of any commentator to clear up, but just where the accidental glimpse of an old edition enlightens us.

Some characters were confounded and mixed, or two put into one, for want of a competent number of actors. Thus in the quarto edition of *Midsummer Night's Dream*, Act 5, Shakespeare introduces a kind of Master of the Revels called Philostratus: all whose part is given to another character (that of Aegeus) in the subsequent editions: so also in *Hamlet* and *King Lear*. This too makes it probable that the prompter's books were what they called the original copies.

From liberties of this kind, many speeches also were put into the mouths of wrong persons, where the author now seems chargeable with making them speak out of character; or sometimes perhaps for no better reason, than that a governing player, to have the mouthing of some favourite speech himself, would snatch it from the unworthy lips of an underling.

Prose from verse they did not know, and they accordingly printed one for the other throughout the volume.

Having been forced to say so much of the players, I think I ought in justice to remark, that the judgment, as well as condition, of that class of people was then far inferior to what it is in our days. As then the best playhouses were inns and taverns (the *Globe*, the *Hope*, the *Red Bull*, the *Fortune*, etc.) so the top of the profession were then mere players, not gentlemen of the stage. They were led into the buttery by the steward, not placed at the lord's table, or lady's toilette: and consequently were entirely deprived of those advantages they now enjoy, in the familiar conversation of our nobility, and an intimacy (not to say dearness) with people of the first condition.

From what has been said, there can be no question but had Shakespeare published his works himself (especially in his latter time, and after his retreat from the stage) we should not only be certain which are genuine; but should find in those that are, the errors lessened by some thousands. If I may judge from all the distinguishing marks of his style, and his manner of thinking and writing, I make no doubt to declare that those wretched plays, *Pericles*,° *Locrine*, *Sir John Oldcastle*, *Yorkshire Tragedy*, *Lord Cromwell*, *The Puritan*, and *London Prodigal*, cannot be admitted as his. And I should conjecture of some of the others (particularly *Love's Labour Lost*, *The Winter's Tale*, and *Titus*

Andronicus) that only some characters, single scenes, or perhaps a few particular passages, were of his hand. It is very probable what occasioned some plays to be supposed Shakespeare's was only this; that they were pieces produced by unknown authors, or fitted up for the theatre while it was under his administration; and no owner claiming them, they were adjudged to him, as they give strays to the lord of the manor. A mistake, which (one may also observe) it was not for the interest of the house to remove. Yet the players themselves, Hemings and Condell, afterwards did Shakespeare the justice to reject those eight plays in their edition; though they were then printed in his name, in everybody's hands, and acted with some applause (as we learn from what Ben Jonson° says of *Pericles* in his ode on the *New Inn*). That *Titus Andronicus* is one of this class I am the rather induced to believe, by finding the same author openly express his contempt of it in the Induction to *Bartholomew Fair*, in the year 1614, when Shakespeare was yet living. And there is no better authority for these latter sort, than for the former, which were equally published in his lifetime.

If we give in to this opinion, how many low and vicious parts and passages might no longer reflect upon this great genius, but appear unworthily charged upon him? And even in those which are really his, how many faults may have been unjustly laid to his account from arbitrary additions, expunctions, transpositions of scenes and lines, confusion of characters and persons, wrong application of speeches, corruptions of innumerable passages by the ignorance, and wrong corrections of 'em again by the impertinence, of his first editors? From one or other of these considerations, I am verily persuaded, that the greatest and the grossest part of what are thought his errors would vanish, and leave his character in a light very different from that disadvantageous one, in which it now appears to us.

This is the state in which Shakespeare's writings lie at present; for since the above-mentioned folio edition, all the rest have implicitly followed it, without having recourse to any of the former, or ever making the comparison between them. It is impossible to repair the injuries already done him; too much time has elapsed, and the materials are too few. In what I have done I have rather given a proof of my willingness and desire, than of my ability to do him justice. I have discharged the dull duty of an editor, to my best judgment, with more labour than I expect thanks, with a religious abhorrence of all innovation, and without any indulgence to my private sense or conjecture. The method taken in this edition will show itself. The various readings are fairly put in the margin, so that every one may compare 'em; and those I have preferred into the text are constantly *ex fide Codicum*, upon authority. The alterations or additions which Shakespeare himself made, are taken notice of as they occur. Some suspected passages which are excessively bad (and which seem interpolations by being so inserted that one can entirely omit them without any chasm, or deficience in the context), are degraded to the bottom of the page; with an asterisk referring to the places of their insertion. The scenes are marked so distinctly that every removal of place is specified; which is more necessary in this author than any other, since he shifts them more frequently: and sometimes without attending to this particular, the reader would have met with obscurities. The more obsolete or unusual words are explained. Some of the most shining passages are distinguished by commas in the margin; and where the beauty lay not in particulars but in the whole, a star is prefixed to the scene. This seems to me a shorter and less ostentatious method of performing the better half of criticism (namely the pointing out an author's excellencies) than to fill a whole paper with citations of fine passages, with *general applauses*, or *empty exclamations* at the tail of them. There is also subjoined a catalogue of those first editions by which the greater part of the various readings and of the corrected passages are authorised (most of which are such as carry their own evidence along with them). These editions now hold the place of originals, and are the only materials left to repair the deficiencies or restore the corrupted sense of the author: I can only wish that a greater number of them (if a greater were ever published) may yet be found, by a search more successful than mine, for the better accomplishment of this end.

I will conclude by saying of Shakespeare, that with all his faults, and with all the irregularity of his *drama*, one may look upon his works, in comparison of those that are more finished and regular, as upon an ancient majestic piece of Gothic architecture, compared with a neat modern building: the latter is more elegant and glaring,° but the former is more strong and more solemn. It must be allowed, that in one of these there are materials enough to make many of the other. It has much the greater variety, and much the nobler apartments; though we are often conducted to them by dark, odd, and uncouth passages. Nor does the whole fail to strike us with greater reverence, though many of the parts are childish, ill-placed, and unequal to its grandeur.

ΠΕΡΙ ΒΑΘΟΥΣ:

OR,

MARTINUS SCRIBLERUS°

HIS

TREATISE

OF THE

ART OF SINKING

IN

POETRY

CONTENTS
TO THE
BATHOS

Chap. I

It hath been long (my dear countrymen) the subject of my concern and surprise, that whereas numberless poets, critics and orators have compiled and digested the art of *ancient poesy*, there hath not arisen among us one person so public-spirited, as to perform the like for the *modern*. Although it is universally known, that our every-way-industrious moderns, both in the weight of their *writings*, and in the velocity of their *judgments*, do so infinitely excel the said ancients.

NEVERTHELESS, too true it is, that while a plain and direct road is paved to their ὕψος, or *sublime*; no track has been yet chalked out, to arrive at our βάθος, or *profound*. The Latins, as they came between the Greeks and us, make use of the word *Altitudo*, which implies equally *height* and *depth*. Wherefore considering with no small grief, how many promising geniuses of this age are wandering (as I may say) in the dark without a guide, I have undertaken this arduous but necessary task, to lead them as it were by the hand, and step by step, the gentle downhill way to the *Bathos*; the bottom, the end, the central point, the *non plus ultra* of true modern poesy!

WHEN I consider (my dear countrymen) the extent, fertility, and populousness of our *lowlands* of *Parnassus*, the flourishing state of our trade, and the plenty of our manufacture; there are two reflections which administer great occasion of surprise; the one, that all dignities and honours should be bestowed upon the exceeding few meagre inhabitants of the top of the mountain; the other, that our own nation should have arrived to that pitch of greatness it now possesses, without any regular *system of laws*. As to the first, it is with great pleasure I have observed of late the gradual decay of delicacy and refinement among mankind, who are become too reasonable to require that we should labour with infinite pains to come up to the taste of those mountaineers, when they without any, may condescend to ours. But as we have now an *unquestionable majority* on our side, I doubt not but we shall shortly be able to level the Highlanders, and procure a farther vent for our own product, which is already so much relished, encouraged, and rewarded, by the nobility and gentry of Great Britain.

THEREFORE to supply our former defect, I purpose to collect the scattered rules of our art into regular institutes, from the example and practice of the deep geniuses of our nation; imitating herein my predecessors, the Master of Alexander,° and the secretary of the renowned Zenobia.° And in this my undertaking I am the more animated, as I expect more success than has attended even those great critics, since their laws (though they might be good) have ever been slackly executed, and their precepts (however strict) obeyed only by fits, and by a very small number.

AT the same time I intend to do justice upon our neighbours, inhabitants of the *upper Parnassus*; who taking advantage of the rising ground, are perpetually throwing down rubbish, dirt, and stones upon us, never suffering us to live in peace. These men, while they enjoy the crystal stream of Helicon, envy us our common water, which (thank our stars) though it is somewhat muddy, flows in much greater abundance. Nor is this the greatest injustice we have to complain of; for though it is evident that we never made the least *attempt* or *inroad* into *their* territories, but lived contented in our native fens; they have often, not only committed *petty larcenies* upon our borders, but driven the country, and carried off at once *whole cartloads* of our *manufacture*; to reclaim some of which stolen goods is part of the design of this treatise.

FOR we shall see in the course of this work, that our greatest adversaries have sometimes descended towards us; and doubtless might now and then have arrived at the *Bathos* itself, had it not been for that mistaken opinion they all entertained, that the *rules* of the *ancients* were *equally necessary* to the *moderns*, than which there cannot be a more grievous error, as will be amply proved in the following discourse.

AND indeed when any of these have gone so far, as by the light of their own genius to attempt upon *new models*, it is wonderful to observe, how nearly they have approached us in those particular pieces; though in all their others they differed *toto coelo* from us.

CHAP. II

That the Bathos, *or* Profound, *is the natural Taste of Man,*
and in particular, of the present Age

The taste of the *Bathos* is implanted by Nature itself in the soul of man; till perverted by custom or example he is taught, or rather compelled, to relish the *Sublime*. Accordingly, we see the unprejudiced minds of children delight only in such productions, and in such images, as our true modern writers set before them. I have observed how fast the general taste is returning to this first simplicity and innocence; and if the intent of all poetry be to divert and instruct, certainly that kind which diverts and instructs the greatest number, is to be preferred. Let us look round among the admirers of poetry, we shall find those who have a taste of the *Sublime* to be very few, but the *Profound* strikes universally, and is adapted to every capacity. 'Tis a fruitless undertaking to write for men of a nice and foppish *gusto*,° whom, after all, it is almost impossible to please; and 'tis still more chimerical to write for *posterity*, of whose taste we cannot make any judgment, and whose applause we can never enjoy. It must be confessed, our wiser authors have a present end,

Et prodesse volunt, & delectare Poetae.°

Their true design is *profit* or *gain*; in order to acquire which, 'tis necessary to procure applause, by administering *pleasure* to the reader. From whence it follows demonstrably, that their productions must be suited to the *present taste*; and I cannot but congratulate our age on this peculiar felicity, that though we have made indeed great progress in all other branches of luxury, we are not yet debauched with any *high relish* in poetry, but are in this one taste, less *nice* than our ancestors. If an art is to be estimated by its success, I appeal to experience, whether there have not been, in proportion to their number, as many starving good poets, as bad ones?

NEVERTHELESS, in making *gain* the principal end of our art, far be it from me to exclude any great *geniuses* of *rank* or *fortune* from diverting themselves this way. They ought to be praised no less than those princes, who pass their vacant hours in some ingenious mechanical or manual art: and to such as these, it would be ingratitude not to own, that our art has been often infinitely indebted.

CHAP. III

The Necessity of the Bathos, *Physically considered*

Farthermore, it were great cruelty and injustice, if all such authors as cannot write in the other way, were prohibited from writing at all. Against this, I draw an argument from what seems to me an undoubted physical maxim, that poetry is a *natural* or *morbid secretion from the brain*. As I would not suddenly stop a cold in the head, or dry up my neighbour's issue, I would as little hinder him from necessary writing. It may be affirmed with great truth, that there is hardly any human creature past childhood, but at one time or other has had some poetical evacuation, and no question was much the better for it in his health; so true is the saying, *Nascimur poetae:*° therefore is the desire of writing properly termed *Pruritus*,° the *titillation of the generative faculty of the brain*; and the person is said to *conceive*; now such as conceive must *bring forth*. I have known a man thoughtful, melancholy, and raving for divers days, but forthwith grow wonderfully easy, lightsome and cheerful, upon a discharge of the peccant humour, in exceeding purulent metre. Nor can I question, but abundance of untimely deaths are occasioned by want of this laudable vent of unruly passions; yea, perhaps, in poor wretches, (which is very lamentable) for mere want of pen, ink, and paper! From hence it follows, that a suppression of the very worst poetry is of dangerous consequence to the state: we find by experience, that the same humours which vent themselves in summer in *ballads* and *sonnets*, are condensed by the winter's cold into *pamphlets* and *speeches* for and against the *ministry*: nay I know not, but many times a piece of poetry may be the most innocent composition of a *minister himself*.

It is therefore manifest that *mediocrity* ought to be allowed, yea indulged, to the good subjects of England. Nor can I conceive how the world has swallowed the contrary as a maxim, upon the single authority of that Horace?° Why should the *golden mean*,° and quintessence of all virtues, be deemed so offensive only in this art? Or *coolness* or *mediocrity* be so amiable a quality in a man, and so detestable in a poet?

HOWEVER, far be it from me to compare these writers with those *great spirits*, who are born with a *vivacité de pesanteur*, or (as an English author° calls it) an *alacrity of sinking*, and who by *strength of nature* alone can excel. All I mean is to evince the *necessity* of rules to these lesser geniuses, as well as the *usefulness* of them to the greater.

CHAP. IV

That there is an Art of the Bathos, *or* Profound

We come now to prove, that there is an *Art of Sinking* in poetry. Is there not an architecture of vaults and cellars, as well as of lofty domes and pyramids? Is there not as much skill and labour in making of *dykes*, as in raising of *mounts*? Is there not an art of *diving* as well as of *flying*? And will any sober practitioner affirm, that a diving engine is not of singular use in making him long-winded, assisting his sight, and furnishing him with other ingenious means of keeping under water?

IF we search the authors of antiquity, we shall find as few to have been distinguished in the *true Profound*, as in the *true Sublime*. And the very same thing (as it appears from Longinus) had been imagined of that, as now of this; namely, that it was entirely the gift of nature. I grant, that to excel in the *Bathos* a genius is requisite; yet the rules of art must be allowed so far useful, as to add weight, or as I may say, hang on lead, to facilitate and enforce our descent, to guide us to the most advantageous declivities, and habituate our imagination to a depth of thinking. Many there are that can fall, but few can arrive at the felicity of falling gracefully; much more for a man who is amongst the lowest of the creation at the very bottom of the atmosphere, to descend *beneath himself*, is not so easy a task unless he calls in art to his assistance. It is with the *Bathos* as with small beer,° which is indeed vapid and insipid, if left at large and let abroad; but being by our rules confined, and well stopped, nothing grows so frothy, pert and bouncing.

THE *Sublime* of nature is the sky, the sun, moon, stars, etc. The *Profound* of nature is gold, pearls, precious stones, and the treasures of the deep, which are inestimable as unknown. But all that lies between these, as corn, flowers, fruits, animals, and things for the mere use of man, are of mean price, and so common as not to be greatly esteemed by the curious: it being certain, that any thing, of which we know the true use, cannot be invaluable: which affords a solution, why *common sense* hath either been totally despised, or held in small repute, by the greatest modern critics and authors.

CHAP. V

Of the true Genius for the Profound, *and by what it is constituted*

And I will venture to lay it down, as the first maxim and cornerstone of this our art, that whoever would excel therein must studiously avoid, detest, and turn his head from all the ideas, ways, and workings of that pestilent foe to wit and destroyer of fine figures, which is known by the name of *common sense*. His business must be to contract the true *goût de travers*;° and to acquire a most *happy, uncommon, unaccountable way of thinking*.

HE is to consider himself as a *grotesque* painter, whose works would be spoiled by an imitation of nature, or uniformity of design. He is to mingle bits of the most various, or discordant kinds, landscape, history, portraits, animals, and connect them with a great deal of *flourishing*, by *heads* or *tails*, as it shall please his imagination, and contribute to his principal end, which is to glare by strong oppositions of colours, and surprise by contrariety of images.

Serpentes avibus geminentur, tigribus agni.°   *Horace.*

His design ought to be like a labyrinth, out of which nobody can get you clear but himself. And since the great art of all poetry is to mix truth and fiction, in order to join the credible with the surprising; our author shall produce the *credible*, by painting nature in her *lowest simplicity*; and the *surprising*, by contradicting *common opinion*. In the very *manners* he will affect the marvellous; he will draw Achilles with the patience of Job; a prince talking like a jack-pudding;° a maid of honour selling bargains;° a footman speaking like a philosopher; and a fine gentleman like a scholar. Whoever is conversant in *modern plays*, may make a most noble collection of this kind, and at the same time, form a complete body of *modern ethics and morality*.

NOTHING seemed more plain to our great authors, than that the world had long been weary of natural things. How much the contrary is formed to please, is evident from the universal applause daily given to the admirable entertainments of harlequins and magicians on our stage. When an audience behold a coach turned into a wheelbarrow, a conjurer into an old woman, or a man's head where his heels should be; how are they struck with transport and delight? Which can only be imputed to this cause, that each object is changed into that which hath been suggested to them by their own low ideas before.

HE ought therefore to render himself master of this happy and anti-natural way of thinking to such a degree, as to be able, on the appearance of any object, to furnish his imagination with ideas infinitely below it. And his eyes should be like unto the wrong end of a perspective glass,° by which all the objects of nature are lessened.

FOR example, when a true genius looks upon the *sky*, he immediately catches the idea of a piece of *blue lutestring*,° or a *child's mantle*.

The skies, whose spreading volumes scarce have room,
Spun thin, and wove in nature's finest loom,
The new-born *world in* their soft lap *embraced,*
And all around their starry mantle *cast.*

Pr. Arthur, p. 41, 42.

IF he looks upon a *tempest,* he shall have the image of a tumbled bed, and describe a succeeding calm in this manner,

The ocean joyed to see the tempest fled,
New lays *his waves and* smooths his ruffled bed.

p. 14.

THE *triumphs* and *acclamations* of the *angels,* at the creation of the universe, present to his imagination the *rejoicings of the Lord Mayor's Day*; and he beholds those glorious beings celebrating the creator, by huzzaing, making illuminations, and flinging squibs, crackers and sky-rockets.

Glorious illuminations, *made on high*
By all the stars and planets of the sky,
In just degrees, *and* shining order *placed,*
Spectators charmed, and the blessed dwelling *graced.*
Through all th' enlightened air swift fireworks *flew,*
Which with repeated shouts *glad cherubs* threw.
Comets ascended with their sweeping train,
Then fell in starry showers *and* glittering rain.
In air ten thousand meteors blazing hung,
Which from th' eternal battlements *were* flung.

page 50.

IF a man who is violently fond of *wit,* will sacrifice to that passion his friend or his god; would it not be a shame, if he who is smit with the love of the *Bathos* should not sacrifice to it all other transitory regards? You shall hear a zealous protestant deacon invoke a saint, and modestly beseech her only to change the course of providence and destiny, for the sake of three or four weighty lines.

Look down, blessed saint, with pity then look down,
Shed on this land thy kinder influence,
And guide us through the mists of Providence,
In which we stray.—

A. Philips. On the *Death of Queen Mary.*

Neither will he, if a goodly simile come in his way, scruple to affirm himself an eye-witness of things never yet beheld by man, or never in existence; as thus,

> *Thus have I seen, in* Araby *the blessed,*
> *A* Phoenix *couched upon her funeral nest.*
>
> *Anon.*

BUT to convince you, that nothing is so great which a marvellous genius, prompted by this laudable zeal, is not able to lessen; hear how the most sublime of all beings is represented in the following images.

First he is a PAINTER.

> *Sometimes the Lord of Nature in the air,*
> *Spreads forth his clouds, his* sable canvas, *where*
> *His pencil, dipped in heavenly* colour *bright,*
> *Paints his fair rainbow, charming to the sight.*
>
> Blackmore, *Job*, opt. edit. *duod.* 1716, pag. 172.

Now he is a CHEMIST.

> *Th'* Almighty Chemist *does his work prepare,*
> *Pours down his* waters *on the thirsty plain,*
> *Digests his lightning, and* distils *his rain.*
>
> Blackmore, Ps. 104, p. 263.

Now he is a WRESTLER.

> *Me in his* griping arms *th' Eternal took,*
> *And with such mighty force my* body shook,
> *That the* strong grasp *my members* sorely bruised,
> *Broke all my* bones, *and all my* sinews loosed.
>
> Pag. 75.

Now a RECRUITING OFFICER.

> *For clouds the sunbeams* levy fresh supplies,
> *And raise* recruits *of vapours, which arise,*
> *Drawn from the seas, to* muster *in the skies.*
>
> Pag. 170.

Now a peaceable GUARANTEE.

In leagues *of* peace *the* neighbours *did agree,*
And to maintain them, God was guarantee.

Pag. 70.

Then he is an ATTORNEY.

Job, *as a vile offender,* God indicts,
And terrible decrees against me writes.—
God *will not be my* advocate,
My cause *to* manage, *or* debate.

Pag. 61.

In the following lines he is a GOLDBEATER.

Who the rich metal beats, *and then, with care,*
Unfolds *the* golden leaves, *to* gild *the fields of air.*

Pag. 181.

Then a FULLER.°

—th' exhaling reeks that secret rise,
Borne on rebounding sunbeams thro' the skies;
Are thickened, wrought, *and* whitened, *till they grow*
A heavenly fleece.—

Pag. 180.

A MERCER, or PACKER.

Didst thou one end *of air's wide* curtain *hold,*
And help the bales *of* ether *to* unfold;
Say, which cerulean° pile was by thy hand unrolled?

Pag. 174.

A BUTLER.

He measures all the drops *with* wondrous skill,
Which the black clouds, his floating bottles, fill.

page 131.

And a Baker.

God in the wilderness his table spread,
And in his airy ovens baked their bread.
                              Blackmore, Song of *Moses*, p. 218.

Chap. VI

Of the several Kinds of Geniuses in the Profound, *and the*
Marks and Characters of each

I DOUBT not but the reader, by this *cloud* of examples, begins to be convinced of the truth of our assertion, that the *Bathos* is an *art*; and that the genius of no mortal whatever, following the mere ideas of nature, and unassisted with an habitual, nay laborious peculiarity of thinking, could arrive at images so wonderfully low and unaccountable. The great author,° from whose treasury we have drawn all these instances (the father of the *Bathos*, and indeed the Homer of it) has like that immortal Greek, confined his labours to the greater poetry, and thereby left room for others to acquire a due share of praise in inferior kinds. Many painters who could never hit a nose or an eye, have with felicity copied a smallpox, or been admirable at a toad or a red herring. And seldom are we without *geniuses* for *still life*, which they can work up and stiffen with incredible accuracy.

AN universal genius rises not in an age; but when he rises, armies rise in him! he pours forth five or six epic poems with greater facility, than five or six pages can be produced by an elaborate and servile copier after nature or the ancients. It is affirmed by Quintilian, that the same genius which made Germanicus° so great a general, would with equal application have made him an excellent heroic poet. In like manner, reasoning from the affinity there appears between arts and sciences, I doubt not but an active catcher of butterflies, a careful and fanciful pattern-drawer, an industrious collector of shells, a laborious and tuneful bagpiper, or a diligent breeder of tame rabbits, might severally excel in their respective parts of the *Bathos*.

I SHALL range these confined and less copious geniuses under proper classes, and (the better to give their pictures to the reader) under the names of animals of some sort or other; whereby he will be enabled, at the first sight of such as shall daily come forth, to know to what *kind* to refer, and with what *authors*° to compare them.

1. THE *Flying Fishes*; these are writers who now and then *rise* upon their *fins*, and fly out of the *profound*; but their wings are soon *dry*, and they drop down to the *bottom*. G. S.   A. H.   C. G.

2. THE *Swallows* are authors that are eternally *skimming* and *fluttering* up and down, but all their agility is employed to *catch flies*. L. T.   W. P. Lord *R*.

3. THE *Ostriches* are such whose heaviness rarely permits them to raise themselves from the ground; their wings are of no use to lift them up, and their motion is between *flying* and *walking*; but then they *run* very fast. D. F.   L. E.   The Hon. *E. H.*

4. THE *Parrots* are they that repeat *another's words*, in such a *hoarse, odd* voice, that makes them seem *their own*. W. B.   W. H.   C. C.   The Reverend *D. D.*

5. THE *Didappers*° are authors that keep themselves long *out of sight*, under water, and *come up* now and then where you *least expected* them. L. W.   — D. Esq;   The Hon. Sir *W. Y.*

6. THE *Porpoises* are unwieldly and big; they put all their numbers into a great *turmoil* and *tempest*, but whenever they appear in *plain light*, (which is seldom) they are only *shapeless* and *ugly monsters*. J. D.   C. G. J. O.

7. THE *Frogs* are such as can neither *walk* nor *fly*, but can *leap* and *bound* to admiration: they live generally in the *bottom of a ditch*, and make a *great noise* whenever they thrust their *heads above water*. E. W. J. M. Esq;   T. D.   Gent.

8. THE *Eels* are obscure authors, that wrap themselves up in their *own mud*, but are mighty *nimble* and *pert*. L. W.   L. T.   P. M. General *C*.

9. THE *Tortoises* are *slow* and *chill*, and like *pastoral writers* delight much in *gardens*: they have for the most part a *fine embroidered shell*, and underneath it, a *heavy lump*. A. P.   W. B.   L. E.   The Rt. Hon. *E*. of *S*.

THESE are the chief characteristics of the *Bathos*, and in each of these kinds we have the comfort to be blessed with sundry and manifold choice spirits in this our island.

CHAP. VII

Of the Profound, *when it consists in the Thought*

We have already laid down the principles upon which our author is to proceed, and the manner of forming his thoughts by familiarizing his mind to the lowest objects; to which it may be added, that *vulgar conversation* will greatly contribute. There is no question but the *garret* or the *printer's boy* may often be discerned in the compositions made in such scenes, and company; and much of Mr Curll himself has been insensibly infused into the works of his learned writers.

THE physician, by the study and inspection of urine and ordure, approves° himself in the science; and in like sort should our author accustom and exercise his imagination upon the dregs of nature.

THIS will render his thoughts truly and fundamentally low, and carry him many fathoms beyond mediocrity. For, certain it is, (though some lukewarm heads imagine they may be safe by temporizing between the extremes) that where there is a triticalness° or mediocrity in the *thought*, it can never be sunk into the genuine and perfect *Bathos*, by the most elaborate low *expression*. It can, at most, be only carefully obscured, or metaphorically debased. But 'tis the *thought* alone that strikes, and gives the whole that spirit, which we admire and stare at. For instance, in that ingenious piece on a lady's drinking the Bath waters.

> *She drinks! She drinks! Behold the matchless dame!*
> *To her 'tis water, but to us 'tis flame:*
> *Thus fire is water, water fire, by turns,*
> *And the same stream at once both cools and burns.*

Anon.

WHAT can be more easy and unaffected than the *diction* of these verses? 'Tis the turn of *thought* alone, and the variety of imagination, that charm and surprise us. And when the same lady goes into the bath, the thought (as in justness it ought) goes still deeper.

> Venus *beheld her*, 'midst her crowd of slaves,
> And thought herself *just risen from the waves.*

Idem.

How much out of the way of common sense is this reflection of Venus, not knowing herself from the lady?

OF the same nature is that noble mistake of a frighted stag in full chase, of which the poet,

> *Hears his own feet, and thinks they sound like more;*
> *And fears the hind feet will o'ertake the fore.*

So astonishing as these are, they yield to the following, which is *profundity* itself,

> *None but* himself *can be his* parallel.
>
> Theobald, *Double Distress.*

unless it may seem borrowed from the thought of that *master of a show* in Smithfield,° who writ in large letters, over the picture of his elephant,

This is the greatest elephant in the world, except himself.

However our next instance is certainly an original: speaking of a beautiful infant,

> *So fair thou art, that if great* Cupid *be*
> *A* child, *as poets say, sure* thou art He.
> *Fair* Venus *would mistake thee for her own,*
> *Did not thy eyes proclaim thee* not her son.
> *There all the lightnings of thy* mother*'s shine,*
> *And with a fatal brightness* kill *in* thine.

First he is Cupid, then he is not Cupid; first Venus would mistake him, then she would not mistake him; next his eyes are his mother's; and lastly they are not his mother's, but his own.

Another author, describing a poet that shines forth amidst a circle of critics,

> *Thus* Phoebus *through the zodiac takes his way,*
> *And amid* monsters *rises into day.*

What a peculiarity is here of invention? The author's pencil, like the wand of Circe, turns all into *monsters* at a stroke. A great genius takes things in the lump, without stopping at minute considerations. In vain might the Ram, the Bull, the Goat, the Lion, the Crab, the Scorpion, the Fishes, all stand in his way, as mere natural animals: much more might it be pleaded that a pair of Scales, an old man, and two innocent children, were no monsters: there were only the Centaur and the Maid that could be esteemed out of nature. But what of that? with a boldness peculiar to these daring geniuses, what he found not monsters, he made so.

CHAP. VIII

Of the Profound *consisting in the Circumstances, and of Amplification and Periphrase in general*

What in a great measure distinguishes other writers from ours, is their choosing and separating such circumstances in a description as illustrate or elevate the subject.

THE circumstances which are most natural are obvious, therefore not astonishing or peculiar. But those that are far-fetched, or unexpected, or hardly compatible, will surprise prodigiously. These therefore we must principally hunt out; but above all, preserve a laudable *prolixity*; presenting the whole and every side at once of the image to view. For choice and distinction are not only a curb to the spirit, and limit the descriptive faculty, but also lessen the book, which is frequently of the worst consequence of all to our author.

WHEN Job° says in short, *He washed his feet in butter*, (a circumstance some poets would have softened, or passed over) hear how it is spread out by the great genius.

> *With teats distended with their milky store,*
> *Such numerous lowing herds, before my door,*
> *Their painful burden to unload did meet,*
> *That we with butter might have washed our feet.*
> *Blackmore, Job*, p. 133.

How cautious! and particular! He had (says our author) so many herds, which herds thrived so well, and thriving so well, gave so much milk, and that milk produced so much butter, that if he *did not*, he *might* have washed his feet in it.

THE ensuing description of Hell is no less remarkable in the circumstances.

> *In flaming heaps the raging ocean rolls,*
> *Whose livid waves involve despairing souls;*
> *The liquid burnings dreadful colours show,*
> *Some deeply red, and others faintly blue.*
> *Pr. Arth.*, p. 89.

COULD the most minute Dutch painter have been more exact? How inimitably circumstantial is this also of a war-horse!

His eye-balls burn, he wounds the smoking plain,
And knots of scarlet ribbon *deck* his *mane.*

Anon.

Of certain cudgel-players:

They brandish high in air their threatening staves,
Their hands *a woven guard of osier* saves,
In which, they fix their hazel *weapon's* end.

Pr. Arth., p. 197.

Who would not think the poet had passed his whole life at wakes in such laudable diversions? He even teaches us how to hold, and to make, a cudgel!

Periphrase is another great aid to *prolixity*; being a diffused circumlocutory manner of expressing a known idea, which should be so mysteriously couched, as to give the reader the pleasure of guessing what it is that the author can possibly mean; and a surprise when he finds it.

The poet I last mentioned is incomparable in this figure.

A waving sea of heads was round me spread,
And still fresh streams the gazing deluge fed.

Job, p. 78.

Here is a waving sea of heads, which by a fresh stream of heads, grows to be a gazing deluge of heads. You come at last to find it means a *great crowd.*

How pretty and how genteel is the following.

Nature's confectioner,—
Whose suckets are moist alchemy:
The still of his refining mould,
Minting the garden into gold.

Cleveland.

What is this, but a *bee* gathering honey?

Little siren of the stage
Empty warbler, breathing lyre,
Wanton gale of fond desire,
Tuneful mischief, vocal spell—

Ph. to C—.

Who would think this was only a poor gentlewoman that sung finely?

WE may define *amplification* to be making the most of a *thought*; it is the spinning wheel of the *Bathos*, which draws out and spreads it in the finest thread. There are amplifiers who can extend half a dozen thin thoughts over a whole folio; but for which, the tale of many a vast romance, and the substance of many a fair volume might be reduced into the size of a *primer*.

IN the Book of *Job*, are these words, '*Hast thou commanded the morning, and caused the day spring to know his place?*' How is this extended by the most celebrated amplifier of our age?

> *Canst thou set forth th' ethereal* mines on high,
> *Which the refulgent* ore *of light supply?*
> *Is the celestial* furnace *to thee known,*
> *In which I* melt *the golden* metal *down?*
> *Treasures, as from whence I* deal *out light as fast,*
> *As all my stars and* lavish *suns can* waste.
>
> *Job*, p. 180.

THE same author has amplified a passage in the 104th Psalm: '*He looks on the earth, and it trembles. He touches the hills, and they smoke.*'

> *The hills* forget they're fixed, *and in their fright,*
> Cast off their weight, *and* ease *themselves for flight:*
> *The woods, with terror* winged, outfly *the wind,*
> *And leave the* heavy, panting *hills behind.*
>
> p. 267.

YOU here see the hills not only trembling, but shaking off their woods from their backs, to run the faster. After this you are presented with a foot-race of mountains and woods, where the woods distance the mountains, that like corpulent pursy° fellows, come puffing and panting a vast way behind them.

CHAP. IX

Of Imitation, and the manner of Imitating

That the true authors of the *Profound* are to imitate diligently the examples in their own way, is not to be questioned, and that divers have by this means attained to a depth whereunto their own weight could not have carried them, is evident by sundry instances. Who sees not that Defoe was the poetical son of Withers,° T[a]te of Ogilby, E. Ward of John Taylor, and Eusden of Blackmore? Therefore when we sit down to write, let us bring some great author to our mind, and ask ourselves this question; how would Sir Richard have said this? Do I express myself as simply as A. Philips? or flow my numbers with the quiet thoughtlessness of Mr Welsted?

BUT it may seem somewhat strange to assert, that our proficient should also read the works of those famous poets who have excelled in the sublime: yet is not this a paradox? As Virgil is said to have read Ennius,° out of his dunghill to draw gold; so may our author read Shakespeare, Milton, and Dryden, for the contrary end, to bury their gold in his own dunghill. A true genius, when he finds anything lofty or shining in them, will have the skill to bring it down, take off the gloss, or quite discharge the colour, by some ingenious circumstance, or periphrase, some addition, or diminution, or by some of those figures the use of which we shall show in our next chapter.

THE Book of *Job* is acknowledged to be infinitely sublime, and yet has not our father of the *Bathos* reduced it in every page? Is there a passage in all Virgil more painted up and laboured than the description of Etna in the third *Aeneid*.

> —*Horrificis juxta tonat* Aetna *ruinis,*
> *Interdumque atram prorumpit ad aethera nubem,*
> *Turbine fumantem piceo, & candente favilla,*
> *Attollitque globos flammarum, & sidera lambit.*
> *Interdum scopulos avulsaque viscera montis*
> *Erigit eructans, liquefactaque saxa sub auras*
> *Cum gemitu glomerat, fundoque exaestuat imo.*°

(I beg pardon of the gentle English reader, and such of our writers as understand not Latin) But lo! how this is taken down by our British poet, by the single happy thought of throwing the mountain into a fit of the *cholic*.

> Etna, *and all the burning mountains, find*
> *Their kindled stores with* inbred *storms of* wind
> Blown up *to rage, and* roaring out, *complain,*
> *As* torn *with* inward gripes, *and* torturing pain:
> *Labouring, they cast their dreadful* vomit *round,*
> *And with their* melted bowels, *spread the ground.*

Pr. Arth., Pag. 75.

HORACE,° in search of the *Sublime*, struck his head against the stars; but Empedocles, to fathom the *Profound*, threw himself into Etna: and who but would imagine our excellent Modern had also been there, from this description?

IMITATION is of two sorts; the first is when we force to our own purposes the thoughts of others; the second consists in copying the imperfections, or blemishes of celebrated authors. I have seen a play° professedly writ in the style of Shakespeare, wherein the greatest resemblance lay in one single line,

And so good morrow t'ye, good Master Lieutenant.

And sundry poems in imitation of Milton, where with the utmost exactness, and not so much as one exception, nevertheless was constantly *nathless*, embroidered was *broidered*, hermits were *eremites*, disdained was *'sdeigned*, shady *umbrageous*, enterprise *emprize*, pagan *paynim*, pinions *pennons*, sweet *dulcet*, orchards *orchats*, bridge-work *pontifical*; nay, her was *hir*, and their was *thir* through the whole poem. And in very deed, there is no other way by which the true modern poet could read to any purpose the works of such men as Milton and Shakespeare.

IT may be expected, that like other critics, I should next speak of the PASSIONS: but as the main end and principal effect of the *Bathos* is to produce *tranquillity of mind* (and sure it is a better design to promote sleep than madness) we have little to say on this subject. Nor will the short bounds of this discourse allow us to treat at large of the *emollients* and *opiates* of *poesy*, of the *cool*, and the manner of producing it, or of the *methods* used by our authors in *managing* the *passions*. I shall but transiently remark, that nothing contributes so much to the *cool*, as the use of *wit* in expressing passion. The true genius rarely fails of *points*,° *conceits*, and proper *similes* on such occasions: this we may term the *pathetic epigrammatical*, in which even puns are made use of with good success. Hereby our best authors have avoided throwing themselves or their readers into any indecent transports.

BUT forasmuch as it is sometimes needful to excite the passions of our antagonist in the polemic way, the true students in the *low* have constantly taken their methods from *low*-life, where they observed, that to move *anger*, use is made of *scolding* and *railing*; to move *love*, of *bawdry*; to beget *favour* and friendship, of gross *flattery*; and to produce *fear*, by calumniating an adversary with *crimes* obnoxious to the *state*. As for *shame*, it is a silly passion, of which as our authors are incapable themselves, so they would not produce it in others.

Chap. X

Of Tropes *and* Figures: *and first of the variegating, confusing, and reversing* Figures

But we proceed to the *figures*. We cannot too earnestly recommend to our authors the study of the *abuse of speech*. They ought to lay it down as a principle, to say nothing in the usual way, but (if possible) in the direct contrary. Therefore the figures must be so turned, as to manifest that intricate and wonderful *cast* of *head*, which distinguishes all writers of this genius; or (as I may say) to refer° exactly the *mould* in which they were formed, in all its *inequalities*, *cavities*, *obliquities*, odd *crannies*, and *distortions*.

It would be endless, nay impossible to enumerate all *such figures*; but we shall content ourselves to range the principal which most powerfully contribute to the *Bathos*, under three classes.

I. The Variegating, Confusing, or Reversing *tropes* and *figures*.

II. The Magnifying, and

III. The Diminishing.

We cannot avoid giving to these the Greek or Roman names; but in tenderness to our countrymen and fellow writers, many of whom, however exquisite,° are wholly ignorant of those languages, we have also explained them in our mother tongue.

Of the first sort, nothing so much conduces to the *abuse* of *speech*, as the

Catachresis.

A master of this will say,
  Mow the beard,
  Shave the grass,
  Pin the plank,
  Nail my sleeve.

From whence results the same kind of pleasure to the mind, as doth to the eye when we behold Harlequin trimming himself with a hatchet, hewing down a tree with a razor, making his tea in a cauldron, and brewing his ale in a teapot, to the incredible satisfaction of the British spectator.° Another source of the *Bathos* is

The METONYMY,

the inversion of causes for effects, of inventors for inventions, etc.

> *Laced in her *Cosins new appeared the bride,*
> *A *bubble-boy and *Tompion at her side,*
> *And with an air divine her *Colmar plied.*
> *And 'oh!' she cries, 'what slaves I round me see?*
> *Here a bright redcoat, there a smart *toupee.'°*

The SYNECHDOCHE.

Which consists, in the use of a *part* for the *whole*; you may call a young woman sometimes pretty-*face* and pig's-*eyes*, and sometimes snotty-*nose* and draggle-*tail*. Or of *accidents* for *persons*; as a lawyer is called *Split-cause*, a tailor *Prick-louse*, etc. Or of things belonging to a man, for the man himself; as a *Sword*-man, a *Gown*-man, a *Tom-Turd-man*;° a *White Staff*,° a *Turnkey*, etc.

The APOSIOPESIS.

An excellent figure for the ignorant, as, '*What shall I say?*' when one has nothing to say; or '*I can no more*', when one really can no more: expressions which the gentle reader is so good, as never to take in earnest.

The METAPHOR.

The first rule is to draw it from the lowest things, which is a certain way to sink the highest; as when you speak of the thunder of Heaven, say,

> *The* lords above *are* angry *and* talk big.   Lee, Alex.

IF you would describe a rich man refunding his treasures, express it thus,

> *Though he (as said) may riches gorge, the spoil*
> *Painful in massy vomit shall recoil.*
> *Soon shall he perish with a swift decay,*
> *Like his own ordure, cast with scorn away.*

Blackmore, Job, p. 91, 93.

The second, that whenever you *start* a metaphor, you must be sure to *run it down*, and pursue it as far as it can go. If you get the scent of a state negotiation, follow it in this manner.

> *The stones and all the elements with thee*
> *Shall ratify a strict confederacy;*
> *Wild beasts their savage temper shall forget,*
> *And for a firm alliance with thee treat;*
> *The finny tyrant of the spacious seas*
> *Shall send a scaly embassy for peace:*
> *His plighted faith the crocodile shall keep,*
> *And seeing thee, for joy sincerely weep.*

Job, p. 22.

Or if you represent the Creator denouncing war against the wicked, be sure not to omit one circumstance usual in proclaiming and levying war.

> *Envoys and agents, who by my command*
> *Reside in Palestina's land,*
> *To whom commissions I have given,*
> *To manage there the interests of Heaven.*
> *Ye holy heralds who proclaim*
> *Or war or peace, in mine your master's name.*
> *Ye pioneers of Heaven, prepare a road,*
> *Make it plain, direct and broad;—*
> *For I in person will my people head;*
> *—For the divine deliverer*
> *Will on his march in majesty appear,*
> *And needs the aid of no confederate power.*

Blackmore, Isaiah, chap. 40.

Under the article of the *confusing*, we rank

The Mixture of Figures,

which raises so many images, as to give you no image at all. But its principal beauty is when it gives an idea just opposite to what it seemed meant to describe. Thus an ingenious artist painting the *spring*, talks of a *snow* of blossoms, and thereby raises an unexpected picture of *winter*. Of this sort is the following:

> *The gaping clouds pour lakes of sulphur down,*
> *Whose livid flashes sickening sunbeams drown.*
>
> > *Pr. Arthur*, p. 73.

WHAT a noble confusion? Clouds, lakes, brimstone, flames, sunbeams, gaping, pouring, sickening, drowning! all in two lines.

The JARGON,

> *Thy head shall rise, though buried in the dust,*
> *And 'midst the clouds his glittering turrets thrust.*
>
> > *Job*, p. 107.

Quaere, what are the glittering turrets of a man's head?

> *Upon the shore, as frequent as the sand,*
> *To meet the prince, the glad Dimetians stand.*
>
> > *Pr. Arthur*, p. 157.

Quaere, where these Dimetians stood? and of what size they were?

> *Destruction's empire shall no longer last,*
> *And desolation lie for ever waste.*
>
> > *Job*, p. 89.

BUT for variegation and confusion of objects, nothing is more useful than

The ANTITHESIS, or SEE-SAW,

Whereby contraries and oppositions are balanced in such a way, as to cause a reader to remain suspended between them, to his exceeding delight and recreation. Such are these, on a lady who made herself appear out of size, by hiding a young princess under her clothes.

> *While the kind nymph changing her faultless shape*
> *Becomes unhandsome, handsomely to 'scape.*
>
> > *Waller.*

On the maids of honour in mourning:

> *Sadly they charm, and dismally they please.*
>
> St-. on *Q. Mary*.°

> ——*His eyes so bright*
> Let in *the object; and* let out *the light.*   *Quarles.*

> *The gods look* pale *to see us look so* red.   *Lee*, Alex.

> ——*The fairies and their queen*
> In mantles blue *came tripping o'er the* green.   Phil. Past.

> *All nature felt a reverential shock,*
> *The sea* stood still *to see the mountains* rock.
>
> Blackmore, Job, p. 176.

Chap. XI

The Figures continued: Of the Magnifying and Diminishing Figures

A genuine writer of the *Profound* will take care never to *magnify* any object without *clouding* it at the same time; his thought will appear in a true *mist*, and very unlike what it is in nature. It must always be remembered that *darkness* is an essential quality of the *Profound*, or if there chance to be a glimmering, it must be as Milton expresses it,

> *No light, but rather darkness visible.*

The chief figure of this sort is,

The Hyperbole, or *Impossible*,

For instance, of a lion;

> *He roared so loud, and looked so wondrous grim,*
> *His very shadow durst not follow him.*
>
> Vet. Aut.°

Of a lady at dinner.

> *The silver whiteness that adorns thy neck,*
> *Sullies the plate, and makes the napkin black.*

Of the same.

—*Th' obscureness of her birth*
Cannot eclipse the lustre of her eyes,
Which make her all one light.

Theobald, *Double Distress.*

Of a bull-baiting.

Up to the stars the sprawling mastiffs fly,
And add new monsters to the frighted sky.

Blackmore.

Of a scene of misery.

Behold a scene of misery and woe!
Here Argus *soon might weep himself quite blind,*
Ev'n though he had Briareus' *hundred hands*
To wipe those hundred eyes—

Anon.

And that modest request of two absent lovers,

Ye gods! annihilate but space *and* time,
And make two lovers happy.—

The PERIPHRASIS, which the moderns call the *Circumbendibus,* whereof we have given examples in the ninth Chapter, and shall again in the twelfth.

To the same class of the *Magnifying* may be referred the following, which are so excellently modern, that we have yet no name for them. In describing a country prospect

I'd call them mountains, but can't call them so,
For fear to wrong them with a name too low;
While the fair vales beneath so humbly lie,
That even humble seems a term too high.

Anon.

III. THE third class remains, of the *Diminishing* figures: And first, The ANTICLIMAX, where the second line drops quite short of the first, than which nothing creates greater surprise.

On the extent of the British arms.

Under the tropics is our language spoke,
And part of Flanders hath received our yoke.

Waller.

On a warrior.

And thou *Dalhoussy* the great god of war,
Lieutenant Colonel to the Earl of Mar.

                                            Anon.

On the valour of the English.

Nor death, nor hell itself can keep them out,
—*Nor* fortified redoubt.

                                    Dennis *on* Namur.

AT other times this figure operates in a larger extent; and when the
gentle reader is in expectation of some great image, he either finds it
surprisingly *imperfect*, or is presented with something very *low*, or quite
ridiculous. A surprise resembling that of a curious person in a cabinet°
of antique statues, who beholds on the pedestal the names of Homer,
or Cato; but looking up, finds Homer without a head, and nothing to
be seen of Cato but his privy member. Such are these lines on a
leviathan at sea.

> *His motion works, and beats the oozy mud,*
> *And with its slime incorporates the flood,*
> *Till all th' encumbered, thick, fermenting stream*
> *Does* one vast pot of boiling ointment seem.
> *Where'er he swims, he leaves along the lake*
> *Such frothy furrows, such a foamy track,*
> *That all the waters of the deep appear*
> Hoary—*with* age, *or grey with sudden fear.*

                                    Blackmore, Job, p. 197.

BUT perhaps even these are excelled by the ensuing.

> *Now the resisted flames and fiery store,* ⎞
> *By winds assaulted, in wide forges roar,* ⎟
> *And raging seas flow down of melted ore.* ⎠
> *Sometimes they hear* long iron bars removed,
> *And* to *and* fro *huge* heaps of cinders shoved.

                                    Pr. Arthur, p. 157.

The VULGAR

Is also a species of the *Diminishing*; by this a spear flying in the air is
compared to a boy whistling as he goes on an errand.

> *The mighty* Stuffa *threw a massy spear,*
> *Which, with its* errand pleased, sung *through the air.*
>
> > *Pr. Arthur.*

A man raging with grief to a mastiff dog.

> *I cannot stifle this gigantic woe,*
> *Nor on my raging grief a* muzzle *throw.*
>
> > *Job*, p. 41.

And clouds big with water to a woman in great necessity.

> Distended *with the* waters *in 'em pent,*
> *The clouds* hang deep *in air, but* hang unrent.

The INFANTILE.

THIS is when a poet grows so very simple, as to think and talk like a child. I shall take my examples from the greatest master in this way. Hear how he fondles, like a mere stammerer.

> Little charm *of placid mien,*
> Miniature *of beauty's queen,*
> *Hither* British *muse* of mine,
> *Hither, all ye* Graecian nine,
> *With the lovely Graces* three,
> *And your* pretty nurseling *see.*
> *When the meadows next are seen,*
> *Sweet enamel, white and green.*
> *When again the lambkins play,*
> Pretty sportlings *full of* May,
> *Then the neck so white and round,*
> (*Little neck with brilliants bound.*)
> *And thy* gentleness *of mind,*
> (*Gentle from a* gentle *kind*) etc.
> Happy *thrice, and* thrice again,
> Happiest *he of* happy *men,* etc.
>
> > *A. Philips* on Miss C—.

With the rest of those excellent *lullabies* of his composition.
How prettily he asks the sheep to teach him to bleat?

> *Teach me to grieve with bleating moan, my sheep.*   *Philips*, Past.

Hear how a babe would reason on his nurse's death:

> *That ever she could die! Oh most unkind!*
> *To die, and leave poor Colinet behind?*
> *And yet,—Why blame I her?—*

Philips, Past.

His shepherd reasons as much like an innocent, in love:

> *I love in secret all a beauteous maid,*
> *And have my love in secret all repaid:*
> *This coming night she does reserve for me.*

Ibid.

THE love of this maiden to him appears by her allowing him the reserve of one night from her other lovers; which you see he takes extremely kindly.

WITH no less simplicity does he suppose that shepherdesses tear their hair and beat their breasts, at their own deaths:

> *Ye brighter maids, faint emblems of my fair,*
> *With looks cast down, and with dishevelled hair,*
> *In bitter anguish beat your breasts, and moan*
> *Her death untimely, as it were your own.*

Ibid.

The INANITY, or NOTHINGNESS.

OF this the same author furnishes us with most beautiful instances:

> *Ah silly I, more silly than my sheep,*
> *(Which on the flowery plain I once did keep.)*

Philips, Past.

> *To the grave senate she could counsel give,*
> *(Which with astonishment they did receive.)*

Philips on Q. Mary.

> *He whom loud cannon could not terrify,*
> *Falls (from the grandeur of his majesty.)*

Ibid.

> *The noise returning with returning light,*

What did it?

> —*Dispersed the silence, and dispelled the night.*
>
> *Anon.*

> *The glories of proud London to survey,*
> *The sun himself shall rise—by break of day.*
>
> *Autor Vet.*

The Expletive,

admirably exemplified in the epithets of many authors.

> *Th' umbrageous shadow, and the verdant green,*
> *The running current, and odorous fragrance,*
> *Cheer my lone solitude with joyous gladness.*

The Macrology and Pleonasm,

are as generally coupled, as a lean rabbit with a fat one; nor is it a wonder, the superfluity of words and vacuity of sense, being just the same thing. I am pleased to see one of our greatest adversaries employ this figure.

> *The growth of meadows, and the pride of fields;*
> *The food of armies and support of wars.*
> *Refuse of swords, and gleanings of a fight;*
> *Lessen his numbers, and contract his host.*
> *Where'er his friends retire, or foes succeed.*
> *Covered with tempests, and in oceans drowned,*
>
> *Camp.*°

Of all which the perfection is

The Tautology.

> *Break through the billows, and—divide the main.*
> *In smoother numbers, and—in softer verse.*
> Tonson, Misc. *duod.*, vol. 4, p. 291, fourth edition.

> *Divide—and part—the severed world—in two.*
> *Ibid.*, vol. 6, p. 121.

Wɪᴛʜ ten thousand others equally musical, and plentifully flowing through most of our celebrated modern poems.

Cʜᴀᴘ. XII

Of Expression, *and the several Sorts of* Style *of the present Age*

The *Expression* is adequate, when it is proportionably low to the profundity of the thought. It must not be always *grammatical*, lest it appear pedantic and ungentlemanly; nor too *clear*, for fear it become vulgar; for obscurity bestows a cast of the wonderful, and throws an oracular dignity upon a piece which hath no meaning.

Fᴏʀ example, sometimes use the wrong number; *The sword and pestilence at once* devours, instead of *devour*. Sometimes the wrong case; *And who more fit to soothe the god than* thee, instead of *thou*: And rather than say, *Thetis°* saw *Achilles* weep, she *heard* him weep.

Tickell, Hom. Il. 1.

Wᴇ must be exceeding careful in two things; first, in the *choice* of *low words*; secondly, in the *sober* and *orderly* way of *ranging* them. Many of our poets are naturally blessed with this talent, insomuch that they are in the circumstance of that honest citizen,° who had made *prose* all his life without knowing it. Let verses run in this manner, just to be a vehicle to the words. (I take them from my last cited author, who though otherwise by no means of our rank, seemed once in his life to have a mind to be simple.)

> *If not, a prize I will my self decree,*
> *From him, or him, or else perhaps from thee.*

Tickell, Hom. Il. 1, p. 11.

> *——full of days was he;*
> *Two ages past, he lived the third to see.*

Idem. p. 17.

> *The king of forty kings, and honoured more*
> *By mighty* Jove *than e'er was king before.*

p. 19.

> *That I may know, if thou my prayer deny,*
> *The most despised of all the gods am I.*

p. 34.

Then let my mother once be ruled by me,
Though much more wise than I pretend to be.

p. 38.

Or these of the same hand.°

I leave the arts of poetry and verse
To them that practise them with more success:
Of greater truths I now prepare to tell,
And so at once, dear friend and muse, farewell.

Tonson, Misc. 12ves, vol. 4, p. 292, fourth edition.

Sometimes a single *word* will familiarize a poetical idea; as where a ship set on fire owes all the spirit of the *Bathos* to one choice word that ends the line.

And his scorched ribs the hot contagion fried.

Pr. Arthur, p. 151.

And in that description of a world in ruins.

Should the whole frame of nature round him break,
He unconcerned would hear the mighty crack.

Tonson, Misc. vol. 6, 119.

So also in these:

Beasts tame and savage to the river's brink
Come from the fields and wild abodes—to drink.

Job, p. 263.

FREQUENTLY two or three words will do it effectually.

He from the clouds does the sweet liquor squeeze,
That cheers the forest and the garden trees.

Id. Job, p. 264.

IT is also useful to employ *technical terms*, which estrange your style from the great and general ideas of nature. And the higher your subject is, the lower should you search into mechanics for your expression. If you describe the garment of an angel, say that his *linen* was *finely spun*, and *bleached on the happy plains*. Call an army of angels, *angelic cuirassiers*, and if you have occasion to mention a number of misfortunes, style them   Pr. Arth., p. 19.
                                                                    Ibid., p. 139.

Fresh troops *of pains, and* regimented *woes.*

Job, p. 86.

STYLE is divided by the rhetoricians into the proper and the figured. Of the figured we have already treated, and the proper is what our authors have nothing to do with. Of styles we shall mention only the principal, which owe to the *moderns* either their *chief improvement*, or entire *invention*.

1. The FLORID,

Than which none is more proper to the *Bathos*, as flowers which are the *lowest* of vegetables are the most *gaudy*, and do many times grow in great plenty at the bottom of *ponds* and *ditches*.

A fine writer in this kind presents you with the following posy:

> *The groves appear all dressed with wreaths of flowers,*
> *And from their leaves drop aromatic showers,*
> *Whose fragrant heads in mystic twines above,*
> *Exchanged their sweets, and mixed with thousand kisses,*
> *As if the willing branches strove*
> *To beautify and shade the grove.—*

Behn's Poems, p. 2.

(Which indeed most branches do). But this is still excelled by our laureate.

> *Branches in branches twined compose the grove,*
> *And shoot and spread, and blossom into love.*
> *The trembling palms their mutual vows repeat,*
> *And bending poplars bending poplars meet.*
> *The distant platanes seems to press more nigh,*
> *And to the sighing alders, alders sigh.*

Guardian, 12ves, 127.

Hear also our Homer.

> *His robe of state is formed of light refined,*
> *An endless train of lustre spreads behind.*
> *His thrones of bright compacted glory made,*
> *With pearl celestial, and with gems inlaid:*
> *Whence floods of joy, and seas of splendour flow,*
> *On all th' angelic gazing throng below.*

Blackmore, Ps. 104.

2. The PERT *Style.*

This does in as peculiar a manner become the low in wit, as a pert air does the low in stature. Mr Thomas Brown, the author of the *London Spy*, and all the *Spies* and *Trips*° in general, are herein to be diligently studied: in verse, Mr Cibber's *Prologues.*

BUT the beauty and energy of it is never so conspicuous, as when it is employed in *modernizing* and *adapting* to the *taste of the times* the works of the ancients. This we rightly phrase *doing* them *into English*, and *making* them *English*; two expressions of great propriety, the one denoting our *neglect* of the *manner how*, the other the *force* and *compulsion* with which, it is brought about. It is by virtue of this style that Tacitus talks like a coffee-house politician, Josephus° like the *British Gazetteer*, Tully is as short and smart as Seneca or Mr Asgill,° Marcus Aurelius is excellent at *snipsnap*,° and honest Thomas a Kempis as *prim* and *polite* as any preacher at court.

3. The ALAMODE Style,

Which is fine by being *new*, and has this happiness attending it, that it is as durable and extensive as the poem itself. Take some examples of it, in the description of the sun in a mourning coach upon the death of Queen Mary.

> *See* Phoebus *now, as once for* Phaeton,
> *Has* masked *his face; and put* deep mourning *on*;
> *Dark clouds his* sable chariot *do surround*,
> *And the* dull steeds stalk o'er *the* melancholy round.

> *A. Philips.*

Of Prince Arthur's Soldiers drinking.

> *While rich* Burgundian *wine, and bright* champagne,
> *Chase from their minds the terrors of the main.*

> *Pr. Ar.*, p. 16.

(Whence we also learn, that *burgundy* and *champagne* make a man on shore despise a storm at sea.)

Of the Almighty encamping his Regiments.

> *—He sunk a vast capacious deep,*
> *Where he his* liquid regiments *does keep.*

Thither the waves file off, *and make their way,*
To form the mighty body *of the sea;*
Where they encamp, and in their station stand,
Entrenched *in* works *of rock, and* lines *of sand.*

Blackmore, Ps. 104, p. 261.

Of two Armies on the Point of engaging.

Yon armies are the cards *which both must play;*
At least come off a saver *if you may:*
Throw boldly *at the* sum *the gods have* set;
These on your side will all their fortunes bet.

Lee, *Sophon.*

All perfectly agreeable to the present customs and best fashions of this our metropolis.

BUT the principal branch of the *Alamode* is the PRURIENT, a style greatly advanced and honoured of late by the practice of persons of the *first quality*, and by the encouragement of the *ladies* not unsuccessfully introduced even into the *drawing-room*. Indeed its *incredible progress* and *conquests* may be compared to those of the great Sesostris,° and are everywhere known by the *same marks*, the images of the genital parts of men or women. It consists wholly of metaphors drawn from two most fruitful sources or springs, the very *Bathos* of the human body, that is to say *** and ************** *Hiatus Magnus lachrymabilis.* ********************************. And *selling of bargains*, and *double entendre*, and Κιββερισμος and Ολφιελδισμος,° all derived from the said sources.

4. THE FINICAL, which consists of the most curious, affected, mincing metaphors, and partakes of the last mentioned.

As this, of a brook dried by the sun.

Won *by the summer's* importuning *ray.*
Th' eloping stream did from her channel stray.
And with enticing *sunbeams* stole away.

Blackmore, Job, p. 26.

Of an easy Death.

When watchful death shall on his harvest look,
And see thee ripe with age, invite *the hook;*
He'll gently cut *thy* bending stalk, *and thee*
Lay kindly *in the* grave, *his* granary.

Ibid., p. 23.

Of Trees in a Storm.

Oaks with extended arms the winds defy,
The tempest sees their strength, and sighs, and passes by.

Dennis.

Of Water simmering over the Fire.

The sparkling flames raise water to a smile,
Yet the pleased *liquor* pines, *and lessens all the while.*

Anon. in *Tonson's* Misc., Part 6, p. 234.

5. LASTLY, I shall place the CUMBROUS, which moves heavily under a load of metaphors, and draws after it a long train of words.

AND the BUSKIN, or *stately*, frequently and with great felicity mixed with the former. For as the first is the proper engine to depress what is high, so is the second to raise what is base and low to a ridiculous visibility: when both these can be done at once, then is the *Bathos* in perfection; as when a man is set with his head downward, and his breech upright, his degradation is complete: one end of him is as high as ever, only that end is the wrong one. Will not every true lover of the *Profound* be delighted to behold the most vulgar and low actions of life exalted in this manner?

Who knocks at the Door?

For whom thus rudely pleads my loud-tongued gate,
That he may enter?—

See who is there?

Advance the fringed curtains of thy eyes,
And tell me who comes yonder.—

Temp.

Shut the Door.

The wooden guardian of our privacy
Quick on its axle turn.—

Bring my Clothes.

Bring me what nature, tailor to the bear,
To man *himself denied: She gave me cold,*
But would not give me clothes.—

Light the Fire.

Bring forth some remnant of Promethean *theft,*
Quick to expand th' inclement air congealed
By Boreas's *rude breath.—*

Snuff the Candle.

Yon luminary amputation needs,
Thus shall you save its half-extinguished life.

Open the Letter.

Wax! render up thy trust.—

Theobald, Double Distress.

Uncork the Bottle, and chip the Bread.

Apply thine engine to the spongy door,
Set Bacchus *from his glassy prison free,*
And strip white Ceres *of her nut-brown coat.*

APPENDIX

Chap. XIII

A Project for the Advancement of the Bathos

Thus have I (my dear countrymen) with incredible pains and diligence, discovered the hidden sources of the *Bathos*, or as I may say broke open the abysses of this *Great Deep*. And having now established the good and wholesome *laws*, what remains but that all true moderns with their utmost might do proceed to put the same in execution? In order whereto, I think I shall in the second place highly deserve of my country, by proposing such a *scheme*, as may facilitate this great end.

As our number is confessedly far superior to that of the enemy, there seems nothing wanting but unanimity among ourselves. It is therefore humbly offered, that all and every individual of the *Bathos* do enter into a firm *association*, and incorporate into *one regular body*, whereof every member, even the meanest, will some way contribute to the support of the whole; in like manner as the weakest reeds when joined in one bundle, become infrangible. To which end our art ought to be put upon the same foot with other arts of this age. The vast improvement of modern manufactures ariseth from their being divided into several branches, and parcelled out to several *trades*. For instance, in *clockmaking*, one artist makes the balance, another the spring, another the crown-wheels, a fourth

the case, and the principal workman puts all together; to this economy°
we owe the perfection of our modern watches; and doubtless we also
might that of our modern poetry and rhetoric, were the several parts
branched out in the like manner.

NOTHING is more evident than that divers persons, no other way
remarkable, have each a strong disposition to the formation of some
particular trope or figure. Aristotle° saith, that the *Hyperbole* is an orna-
ment of speech fit for *young men of quality*; accordingly we find in those
gentlemen a wonderful propensity toward it, which is marvellously
improved by *travelling*. Soldiers also and seamen are very happy in the
same figure. The *Periphrasis* or *Circumlocution* is the peculiar talent of
country farmers, the Proverb and Apologue of *old men* at their clubs, the
Ellipsis or Speech by half-words of *ministers* and *politicians*, the *Aposio-
pesis* of *courtiers*, the *Litotes* or Diminution of *ladies*, *whisperers* and *back-
biters*; and the *Anadyplosis* of common *criers* and *hawkers*, who by
redoubling the same words, persuade people to buy their oysters, green
hastings,° or new ballads. *Epithets* may be found in great plenty at
Billingsgate, *Sarcasm* and *Irony* learned upon the *water*, and the *Epi-
phonema* or *Exclamation* frequently from the Bear-Garden, and as fre-
quently from the '*Hear him*' of the House of Commons.

Now each man applying his whole time and genius upon his particu-
lar figure, would doubtless attain to perfection; and when each became
incorporated and sworn into the society, (as hath been proposed;) a
poet or orator would have no more to do, but to send to the particular
traders in each kind; to the Metaphorist for his *Allegories*, to the Simile-
maker for his *Comparisons*, to the Ironist for his *Sarcasms*, to the Apo-
thegmatist for his *Sentences*,° etc. whereby a dedication or speech would
be composed in a moment, the superior artist having nothing to do but
to put together all the materials.

I THEREFORE propose that there be contrived with all convenient
dispatch, at the public expense, a *Rhetorical Chest of Drawers*, consisting
of three storeys, the highest for the *Deliberative*, the middle for the
Demonstrative, and the lowest for the *Judicial*. These shall be divided
into *loci* or *places*,° being repositories for matter and argument in the
several kinds of oration or writing; and every drawer shall again be
subdivided into cells, resembling those of cabinets for rarities. The
apartment for *peace* or *war*, and that of the *liberty* of the *press*, may in a
very few days be filled with several arguments *perfectly new*; and the
vituperative partition will as easily be replenished with a most choice
collection, entirely of the growth and manufacture of the present age.
Every composer will soon be taught the use of this cabinet, and how

to manage all the registers of it, which will be drawn out much in the manner of those of an organ.

THE keys of it must be kept in honest hands, by some *reverend prelate*, or *valiant officer*, of unquestioned loyalty and affection to every present establishment in Church and State; which will sufficiently guard against any mischief which might otherwise be apprehended from it.

AND being lodged in such hands, it may be at discretion *let out* by the *day*, to several great orators in both Houses; from whence it is to be hoped much *profit* or *gain* will also accrue to our society.

CHAP. XIV

How to make Dedications, Panegyrics *or* Satires, *and of* the Colours *of Honourable and Dishonourable*

Now of what necessity the foregoing project may prove, will appear from this single consideration, that nothing is of equal consequence to the success of our works, as *speed* and *dispatch*. Great pity it is, that solid brains are not, like other solid bodies, constantly endowed with a *velocity* in sinking, proportioned to their *heaviness*: for it is with the *flowers* of the *Bathos* as with those of nature, which if the careful gardener brings not hastily to the market in the *morning*, must unprofitably perish and wither before *night*. And of all our productions none is so short-lived as the *dedication* and *panegyric*, which are often but the *praise of a day*, and become by the next, utterly useless, improper, indecent and false. This is the more to be lamented, inasmuch as they are the very two sorts whereon in a manner depends that *gain* or *profit*, which must still be remembered to be the whole end of *our writers* and *speakers*.

WE shall therefore .employ this chapter in showing the *quickest* method of composing them; after which we will teach a *short way* to *epic poetry*. And these being confessedly the works of most importance and difficulty, it is presumed we may leave the rest to each author's own learning or practice.

FIRST of *panegyric*: every man is *honourable*, who is so by *law*, *custom* or *title*; the public are better judges of what is honourable, than private men. The virtues of great men, like those of plants, are *inherent* in them whether they are *exerted* or not; and the more strongly inherent the less they are exerted; as a man is the more rich the less he spends.

ALL great ministers, without either private or economical° virtue, are virtuous by their *posts*; liberal and generous upon the *public money*, provident upon *parliamentary supplies*, just by paying *public interest*, courageous and magnanimous by the *fleets* and *armies*, magnificent upon the *public expenses*, and prudent by *public success*. They have by their *office*, a right to a share of the *public stock* of virtues; besides they are by *prescription immemorial* invested in all the celebrated virtues of their *predecessors* in the same *stations*, especially those of their own *ancestors*.

As to what are commonly called the *colours* of *honourable* and *dishonourable*, they are various in different countries: in this they are *blue*, *green* and *red*.° But forasmuch as the duty we owe to the public doth often require that we should put some things in a strong light, and throw a shade over others, I shall explain the method of turning a vicious man into a hero.

THE first and chief rule is *the Golden Rule of Transformation*, which consists in converting vices into their *bordering* virtues. A man who is a spendthrift and will not pay a just debt, may have his injustice *transformed* into liberality; cowardice may be metamorphosed into prudence; intemperance into good nature and good fellowship, corruption into patriotism, and lewdness into tenderness and facility.°

THE second is the *Rule of Contraries*: it is certain the less a man is endued with any virtue, the more need he has to have it plentifully bestowed, especially those good qualities of which the world generally believes he hath none at all: for who will thank a man for giving him that which he *has*?

THE reverse of these precepts will serve for *satire*, wherein we are ever to remark, that whoso loseth his place, or becomes out of favour with the government, hath forfeited his share of *public praise* and *honour*. Therefore the truly public-spirited writer ought in duty to strip him whom the government has stripped: which is the real *poetical justice* of this age. For a full collection of topics and epithets to be used in the praise and dispraise of ministerial and unministerial persons, I refer to our *rhetorical cabinet*; concluding with an earnest exhortation to all my brethren, to observe the precepts here laid down; the neglect of which hath cost some of them their *ears* in a *pillory*.

CHAP. XV°

A Receipt° *to make an* Epic Poem

An epic poem, the critics agree, is the greatest work human nature is capable of. They have already laid down many mechanical rules for compositions of this sort, but at the same time they cut off almost all undertakers from the possibility of ever performing them; for the first qualification they unanimously require in a poet, is a *genius*. I shall here endeavour (for the benefit of my countrymen) to make it manifest, that epic poems may be made *without a genius*, nay without learning or much reading. This must necessarily be of great use to all those who confess they never *read*, and of whom the world is convinced they never *learn*. What Molière° observes of making a dinner, that any man can do it *with money*, and if a professed cook cannot do it *without* he has his art for nothing; the same may be said of making a poem, 'tis easily brought about by him that *has* a genius, but the skill lies in doing it without one. In pursuance of this end, I shall present the reader with a plain and certain *recipe*, by which any author in the *Bathos* may be qualified for this grand performance.

For the Fable.

TAKE out of any old poem, history book, romance, or legend, (for instance, Geoffrey of Monmouth or *Don Belianis° of Greece*) those parts of story which afford most scope for *long descriptions*. Put these pieces together, and throw all the adventures you fancy into *one tale*. Then take a hero, whom you may choose for the sound of his name, and put him into the midst of these adventures. There let him *work*, for twelve books; at the end of which you may take him out, ready prepared to *conquer* or to *marry*; it being necessary that the conclusion of an epic poem be *fortunate*.

To make an Episode.

TAKE any remaining adventure of your former collection, in which you could no way involve your hero; or any unfortunate accident that was too good to be thrown away; and it will be of use, applied to any other person; who may be lost and *evaporate* in the course of the work, without the least damage to the composition.

For the Moral and Allegory.

THESE you may extract out of the fable afterwards, at your leisure: be sure you *strain* them sufficiently.

For the Manners.

FOR those of the *hero*, take all the best qualities you can find in the most celebrated heroes of antiquity; if they will not be reduced to a *consistency*, lay 'em *all on a heap* upon him. But be sure they are qualities which your *patron* would be thought to have; and to prevent any mistake which the world may be subject to select from the alphabet those capital letters that compose his name, and set them at the head of a dedication before your poem. However, do not absolutely observe the exact quantity of these virtues, it not being determined whether or no it be necessary for the hero of a poem to be an *honest man*. For the *under-characters*, gather them from Homer and Virgil, and change the names as occasion serves.

For the Machines.

TAKE of *deities*, male and female, as many as you can use. Separate them into two equal parts, and keep Jupiter in the middle. Let Juno put him in a ferment, and Venus mollify him. Remember on all occasions to make use of volatile Mercury. If you have need of devils, draw them out of Milton's Paradise, and extract your *spirits* from Tasso. The use of these machines is evident; for since no epic poem can possibly subsist without them, the wisest way is to reserve them for your greatest necessities. When you cannot extricate your hero by any human means, or yourself by your own wit, seek relief from heaven, and the gods will do your business very readily. This is according to the direct prescription of Horace° in his *Art of Poetry*.

Nec Deus intersit, nisi dignus vindice Nodus *Inciderit.—*

That is to say, '*A poet should never call upon the gods for their assistance, but when he is in great perplexity.*'

For the Descriptions.

FOR a *tempest*. Take Eurus, Zephyr, Auster and Boreas, and cast them together in one verse. Add to these of rain, lightning and of thunder (the loudest you can) *quantum sufficit*. Mix your clouds and billows well together till they foam, and thicken your description here and there with a quicksand. Brew your tempest well in your head, before you set it a blowing.

For a *battle*. Pick a large quantity of images and descriptions from Homer's *Iliads*, with a spice or two of Virgil, and if there remain any overplus, you may lay them by for a *skirmish*. Season it well with *similes*, and it will make an *excellent battle*.

For a *burning town*. If such a description be necessary (because it is certain there is one in Virgil) old Troy is ready burnt to your hands. But if you fear that would be thought borrowed, a chapter or two of the theory of the *Conflagration*, well circumstanced, and done into verse, will be a good *succedaneum*.

As for *similes* and *metaphors*, they may be found all over the creation; the most ignorant may *gather* them, but the danger is in *applying* them. For this advise with your *bookseller*.°

Chap. XVI

A Project for the Advancement of the Stage

It may be thought that we should not wholly omit the *drama*, which makes so great and so lucrative a part of poetry. But this province is so well taken care of, by the present *managers* of the theatre, that it is perfectly needless to suggest to them any other methods than they have already practised for the advancement of the *Bathos*.

Here therefore, in the name of all our brethren, let me return our sincere and humble thanks to the Most August Mr Barton Booth, the Most Serene Mr Wilks,° and the Most Undaunted Mr Colley Cibber; of whom, let it be known *when the people of this age shall be ancestors*, and to all *the succession of our successors*, that to this present day they continue to *out-do* even their *own out-doings*.° And when the inevitable hand of sweeping *Time* shall have brushed off all the works of *Today*, may this testimony of a *contemporary critic* to their fame, be extended as far as *tomorrow*!

Yet, if to so wise an administration it be possible anything can be added, it is that more ample and comprehensive scheme which Mr Dennis and Mr Gildon, (the two greatest critics and reformers then living) made public in the year 1720 in a project signed with their names, and dated the 2nd of February. I cannot better conclude than by presenting the reader with the substance of it.

1. It is proposed that the two *theatres* be incorporated into one company; that the Royal Academy of Music° be added to them as an *orchestra*; and that Mr Figg° with his prize-fighters, and Violante° with the rope-dancers, be admitted in partnership.

2. THAT a spacious building be erected at the public expense, capable of containing at least ten thousand spectators, which is become absolutely necessary by the great addition of children and nurses to the audience, since the new entertainments. That there be a stage as large as the Athenian, which was near ninety thousand geometrical paces square, and separate divisions for the two Houses of Parliament, my Lords the judges, the honourable the Directors of the Academy, and the Court of Aldermen, who shall all have their places frank.°

3. IF Westminster Hall be not allotted to this service (which by reason of its proximity to the two chambers of parliament above mentioned, seems not altogether improper), it is left to the wisdom of the nation whether Somerset House° may not be demolished, and a theatre built upon that site, which lies convenient to receive spectators from the County of Surrey, who may be wafted thither by water-carriage, esteemed by all projectors° the cheapest whatsoever. To this may be added, that the River Thames may in the readiest manner convey those eminent personages from courts beyond the seas, who may be drawn either by curiosity to behold some of our most celebrated pieces, or by affection to see their countrymen the harlequins and eunuchs;° of which convenient notice may be given for two or three months before, in the public prints.

4. THAT the theatre abovesaid be environed with a fair quadrangle of buildings, fitted for the accommodation of decayed critics and poets; out of whom six of the most aged (their age to be computed from the year wherein their first work was published) shall be elected to manage the affairs of the society, provided nevertheless that the Laureate for the time being, may be always one. The head or president over all, (to prevent disputes, but too frequent among the learned) shall be the *oldest poet* and *critic* to be found in the whole island.

5. THE *male-players* are to be lodged in the garrets of the said quadrangle, and to attend the persons of the *poets*, dwelling under them, by brushing their apparel, drawing on their shoes, and the like. The *actresses* are to make their beds, and wash their linen.

6. A LARGE room shall be set apart for a *library*, to consist of all the modern dramatic poems, and all the criticisms extant. In the midst of this room shall be a round table for the Council of SIX to sit and deliberate on the merits of *plays*. The *majority* shall determine the dispute; and if it should happen that *three* and *three* should be of each side, the president shall have a *casting voice*, unless where the contention may run so high as to require a decision by *single combat*.

7. IT may be convenient to place the Council of SIX in some conspicuous situation in the theatre, where after the manner usually practised by composers in music, they may give *signs* (before settled and agreed upon) of dislike or approbation. In consequence of these signs the whole audience shall be required to *clap* or *hiss*, that the town may learn certainly when and how far they ought to be pleased.

8. IT is submitted whether it would not be proper to distinguish the Council of SIX by some particular habit or gown of an honourable shape and colour, to which might be added a square cap and a white wand.

9. THAT to prevent unmarried actresses making away with their infants, a competent provision be allowed for the nurture of them, who shall for that reason be deemed the *children of the society*; and that they may be educated according to the genius of their parents, the said actresses shall declare upon oath (as far as their memory will allow) the true names and qualities of their several fathers. A private gentleman's son shall at the public expense be brought up a page to attend the Council of SIX. A more ample provision shall be made for the son of a *poet*; and a greater still for the son of a *critic*.

10. IF it be discovered that any actress is got with child, during the interludes of any play, wherein she hath a part, it shall be reckoned a neglect of her business, and she shall *forfeit* accordingly. If any actor for the future shall commit *murder*, except upon the stage, he shall be left to the laws of the land; the like is to be understood of *robbery* and *theft*. In all other cases, particularly in those of *debt*, it is proposed that this, like the other courts of Whitehall and St James's, may be held a *place of privilege.*° And whereas it has been found, that an obligation to satisfy *paltry creditors* has been a discouragement to *men of letters*, if any person of quality or others shall send for any *poet* or *critic* of this society to any remote quarter of the town, the said *poet* or *critic* shall freely pass and repass without being liable to an *arrest*.

11. THE fore-mentioned scheme in its several regulations may be supported by profits arising from every third night throughout the year. And as it would be hard to suppose that so many persons could live without any food (though from the former course of their lives, a *very little* will be sufficient) the masters of calculation will, we believe, agree, that out of those profits, the said persons might be subsisted in a sober and decent manner. We will venture to affirm farther, that not only the proper magazines of thunder and lightning, but *paint, diet-drinks, spitting-pots*, and all other *necessaries* of *life*, may in like manner fairly be provided for.

12. IF some of the articles may at first view seem liable to objections, particularly those that give so vast a power to the Council of SIX (which is indeed larger than any entrusted to the great officers of state) this may be obviated, by swearing those *six* persons of his Majesty's Privy Council, and obliging them to pass every thing of moment *previously* at that most honourable board.

Vale & Fruere.°

MAR. SCRIB.

POPE TO JONATHAN SWIFT
28 November 1729

This letter (like all mine) will be a rhapsody;° it is many years ago since I wrote as a wit.° How many occurrencies or informations must one omit, if one determined to say nothing that one could not say prettily? I lately received from the widow of one dead correspondent, and the father of another, several of my own letters of about fifteen or twenty years old; and it was not unentertaining to myself to observe, how and by what degrees I ceased to be a witty writer; as either my experience grew on the one hand, or my affection to my correspondents on the other. Now as I love you better than most I have ever met with in the world, and esteem you too the more the longer I have compared you with the rest of the world; so inevitably I write to you more negligently, that is more openly, and what all but such as love another will call writing worse. I smile to think how Curll would be bit, were our epistles to fall into his hands,° and how gloriously they would fall short of every ingenious reader's expectations?

You can't imagine what a vanity it is to me, to have something to rebuke you for in the way of economy? I love the man that builds a house *subito ingenio,*° and makes a wall for a horse; then cries, 'We wise men must think of nothing but getting ready money.' I am glad you approve my annuity; all we have in this world is no more than an annuity, as to our own enjoyment. But I will increase your regard for my wisdom, and tell you, that this annuity includes also the life of another,° whose concern ought to be as near me as my own, and with whom my whole prospects ought to finish. I throw my javelin of hope no farther, *Cur brevi fortes jaculamur aevo*°—etc.

The second (as it is called, but indeed the eighth) edition of *The Dunciad*, with some additional notes and epigrams, shall be sent you if I know any opportunity; if they reprint it with you, let them by all means follow that octavo edition.—The *Drapier's Letters* are again printed here, very laudably as to paper, print, etc. for you know I disapprove Irish politics (as my commentator tells you) being a strong and jealous subject of England. The lady you mention, you ought not to complain of for not acknowledging your present; she having just now received a much richer present from Mr Knight of the South Sea; and you are sensible she cannot ever return it, to one in the condition of an outlaw: it's certain as he can never expect any favour, his motive must be wholly disinterested.° Will not this reflexion make you blush? Your continual deplorings of Ireland, make me wish, you were here long enough to forget those scenes that so afflict you. I am only in fear if you were, you would grow such a patriot here too, as not to be quite at ease, for your love of old England. It is very possible, your journey, in the time I compute, might exactly tally with my intended one to you; and if you must soon again go back, you would not be unattended. For the poor woman° decays perceptibly every week; and the winter may too probably put an end to a very long, and a very irreproachable, life. My constant attendance on her does indeed affect my mind very much, and lessen extremely my desires of long life; since I see the best that can come of it is a miserable benediction at most: so that I look upon myself to be many years older in two years since you saw me. The natural imbecility° of my body, joined now to this acquired old age of the mind, makes me at least as old as you, and we are the fitter to crawl down the hill together; I only desire I may be able to keep pace with you. My first friendship at sixteen, was contracted with a man of seventy, and I found him not grave enough or consistent enough for me, though we lived well to his death. I speak of old Mr Wycherley; some letters of whom (by the by) and of mine, the booksellers have got and printed not without the concurrence of a noble friend° of mine and yours, I don't much approve of it; though there is nothing for me to be ashamed of, because I will not be ashamed of anything I do not do myself, or of anything that is not immoral but merely dull (as for instance, if they printed this letter I am now writing, which they easily may, if the underlings at the Post Office please to take a copy of it.) I admire on this consideration, your sending your last to me quite open, without a seal, wafer, or any closure whatever, manifesting the utter openness of the writer. I would do the same by this, but fear it would look like affectation to send two letters so together.—I will fully represent to our friend° (and I doubt not it will touch his heart) what you so feelingly set forth as to the badness of your burgundy, etc. He is an extreme honest man, and indeed ought to be so, considering how very indiscreet and unreserved he is. But I do not approve this part of his character, and will never join with him in any of his idlenesses in the way of wit. You know my maxim to keep clear of all offence, as I am clear of all interest in either party. I was once displeased before at you, for complaining to Mr Dodington° of my not having a pension, and am so again at your naming it to a certain Lord.° I have given some proofs in the course of my whole life, (from the time when I was in the friendship of Lord Bolingbroke and Mr Craggs° even to this, when I am civilly treated by Sir R. Walpole) that I never thought myself so warm in any party's cause as to deserve their money; and therefore would never have accepted it; but give me leave to tell you, that of all mankind the two persons I would least have accepted any favour from, are those very two, to whom you have unluckily spoken of it. I desire you to take off any impressions which that dialogue may have left on his Lordship's mind, as if I ever had any thought of being beholden to him, or any other, in that way. And yet you know I am no enemy to the present constitution; I believe, as sincere a well-wisher to it, nay even to the church established, as any minister in, or out of employment, whatever; or any bishop of England or Ireland. Yet am I of the religion of Erasmus, a Catholic; so I live; so I shall die; and hope one day to meet you, Bishop Atterbury, poor Craggs, Dr Garth, Dean Berkeley,° and Mr Hutchinson,° in that place, to which God of his infinite mercy bring us, and everybody!

Lord B's° answer to your letter I have just received, and join it to this packet. The work he speaks of with such abundant partiality, is a system of ethics° in the Horatian way.

EPITAPH
Intended for Sir ISAAC NEWTON
In Westminster-Abbey
ISAACUS NEWTONUS:

Quem Immortalem
Testantur *Tempus, Natura, Coelum:*
Mortalem
Hoc marmor fatetur.

Nature and Nature's Laws lay hid in Night.
GOD said, *Let Newton be!* and all was Light.

AN EPISTLE
TO
Richard Boyle, Earl of *Burlington*

ARGUMENT°
Of the Use of RICHES

The vanity of expense in people of wealth and quality. The abuse of the word taste, v. 13. *That the first principle and foundation, in this as in everything else, is* good sense, v. 40. *The chief proof of it is to* follow nature, *even in works of mere luxury and elegance. Instanced in* architecture *and* gardening, *where all must be adapted to the* genius *and* use *of the* place, *and the beauties not forced into it, but resulting from it, v. 50. How men are disappointed in their most expensive undertakings, for want of this true foundation, without which nothing can please long, if at all; and the best* examples *and* rules *will but be perverted into something* burdensome *or* ridiculous, v. 65, &c. to 92. A description of the* false taste *of* magnificence; *the first grand error* *of which is to imagine that* greatness *consists in the* size *and* dimension, *instead of the* proportion *and* harmony *of the* whole, v. 97, *and the second, either in joining together* parts incoherent, *or too* minutely resembling, *or in the* repetition *of the* same *too frequently,* v. 105, &c. *A word or two of false taste in* books, *in* music, *in* painting, *even in* preaching *and* prayer, *and lastly in* entertainments, v. 133, &c. *Yet* PROVIDENCE *is justified in giving wealth to be squandered in this manner, since it is dispersed to the poor and laborious part of mankind,* v. 169 [*recurring to what is laid down in the first book, Ep.* ii. *and in the Epistle preceding this,* v. 159, &c.] *What are the* proper objects *of magnificence, and a proper field for the expense of* great men, v. 177, &c. *and finally, the great and public works which become a* prince, v. 191, *to the end.*

'Tis strange, the miser should his cares employ   1
To gain those riches he can ne'er enjoy.
Is it less strange, the prodigal should waste
His wealth, to purchase what he ne'er can taste?
Not for himself he sees, or hears, or eats;
Artists° must choose his pictures, music, meats:
He buys for Topham,° drawings and designs,
For Pembroke° statues, dirty gods, and coins;
Rare monkish manuscripts for Hearne° alone,
And books for Mead,° and butterflies for Sloane.°   10
Think we all these are for himself? no more
Than his fine wife, alas! or finer whore.
    For what has Virro painted, built, and planted?
Only to show, how many tastes he wanted.
What brought Sir Visto's° ill got wealth to waste?
Some demon whispered, 'Visto! have a taste.'
Heaven visits with a taste the wealthy fool,
And needs no rod but Ripley° with a rule.
See! sportive fate, to punish awkward pride,
Bids Bubo° build, and sends him such a guide: 20

7. *Topham*] A gentleman famous for a judicious collection of drawings.

10. *Mead—Sloane.*] Two eminent physicians; the one had an excellent library, the other the finest collection in Europe of natural curiosities; both men of great learning and humanity.

18. *Ripley*] This man was a carpenter, employed by a first minister, who raised him to an architect, without any genius in the art; and after some wretched proofs of his insufficiency in public buildings, made him Comptroller of the Board of Works.

A standing sermon, at each year's expense,
That never coxcomb reached magnificence!
    You show us, Rome was glorious, not profuse,
And pompous buildings once were things of use.
Yet shall (my Lord) your just, your noble rules
Fill half the land with imitating fools;
Who random drawings from your sheets shall take,
And of one beauty many blunders make;
Load some vain church with old theatric state,
Turn arcs of triumph to a garden-gate;   30
Reverse your ornaments, and hang them all
On some patched dog-hole° eked with ends of wall,
Then clap four slices of pilaster on't,
That, laced with bits of rustic,° makes a front:
Or call the winds through long arcades to roar,
Proud to catch cold at a Venetian door;
Conscious they act a true Palladian part,
And if they starve, they starve by rules of art.
    Oft have you hinted to your brother peer,
A certain truth, which many buy too dear: 40
Something there is, more needful than expense,
And something previous ev'n to taste—'tis sense:
Good sense, which only is the gift of heaven,
And though no science, fairly worth the seven,
A light, which in yourself you must perceive;
Jones and Le Nôtre° have it not to give.
    To build, to plant, whatever you intend,
To rear the column, or the arch to bend,
To swell the terrace, or to sink the grot;
In all, let nature never be forgot.   50
But treat the goddess like a modest fair,
Nor over-dress, nor leave her wholly bare;
Let not each beauty everywhere be spied,
Where half the skill is decently to hide.

23. The Earl of Burlington was then publishing the designs of Inigo Jones, and the Antiquities of Rome by Palladio.

36. *Venetian door*] A door or window, so called, from being much practised at Venice by Palladio and others.°

46. Inigo Jones the celebrated architect, and M. Le Nôtre, the designer of the best gardens of France.

He gains all points, who pleasingly confounds,
Surprises, varies, and conceals the bounds.
    Consult the genius of the place° in all;
That tells the waters or to rise, or fall,
Or helps th'ambitious hill the heavens to scale,
Or scoops in circling theatres the vale;   60
Calls in the country, catches opening glades,
Joins willing woods, and varies shades from shades;
Now breaks, or now directs, th' intending° lines,
Paints as you plant, and as you work, designs.
    Still follow sense, of every art the soul,
Parts answering parts shall slide into a whole,
Spontaneous beauties all around advance,
Start ev'n from difficulty, strike from chance;
Nature shall join you; time shall make it grow
A work to wonder at—perhaps a STOWE.°   70
    Without it, proud Versailles! thy glory falls,
And Nero's terraces° desert their walls:
The vast parterres° a thousand hands shall make,
Lo! COBHAM comes, and floats them with a lake:
Or cut wide views through mountains to the plain,
You'll wish your hill or sheltered seat again.
Ev'n in an ornament its place remark,
Nor in an hermitage° set Dr Clarke.
    Behold Villario's ten-years' toil complete;
His arbours darken, his espaliers° meet;   80
The wood supports the plain, the parts unite,
And strength of shade contends with strength of light:
A waving glow the bloomy beds display,
Blushing in bright diversities of day,
With silver-quivering rills meandered o'er—
Enjoy them, you! Villario can no more;
Tired of the scene parterres and fountains yield,

70. The seat and gardens of the Lord Viscount Cobham in Buckinghamshire.

75. This was done in Hertfordshire, by a wealthy citizen, at the expense of above £5000 by which means (merely to overlook a dead plain) he let in the north-wind upon his house and parterre, which were before adorned and defended by beautiful woods.

78. Dr S. Clarke's busto placed by the Queen in the Hermitage, while the Dr duly frequented the Court.

He finds at last he better likes a field.

　　Through his young woods how pleased Sabinus strayed
Or sat delighted in the thickening shade,   90
With annual joy the reddening shoots to greet,
Or see the stretching branches long to meet.
His son's fine taste an opener vista loves,
Foe to the dryads of his father's groves,
One boundless green, or flourished carpet views,
With all the mournful family of yews;
The thriving plants ignoble broomsticks made,
Now sweep those alleys they were born to shade.

　　At Timon's villa° let us pass a day,
Where all cry out, 'What sums are thrown away!'   100
So proud, so grand, of that stupendous air,
Soft and agreeable come never there.
Greatness, with Timon, dwells in such a draught
As brings all Brobdignag before your thought.
To compass this, his building is a town,
His pond an ocean, his parterre a down:
Who but must laugh, the master when he sees?
A puny insect, shivering at a breeze.
Lo! what huge heaps of littleness around!
The whole, a laboured quarry above ground.   110
Two cupids squirt before: a lake behind
Improves the keenness of the northern wind.
His gardens next your admiration call,
On every side you look, behold the wall!
No pleasing intricacies intervene,
No artful wildness to perplex the scene;
Grove nods at grove, each alley has a brother,

---

95. The two extremes in parterres, which are equally faulty; a *boundless green*, large and naked as a field, or a *flourished carpet*, where the greatness and nobleness of the piece is lessened by being divided into too many parts, with scrolled works and beds, of which the examples are frequent.

96. Touches upon the ill taste of those who are so fond of evergreens (particularly yews, which are the most tonsile) as to destroy the nobler forest-trees, to make way for such little ornaments as pyramids of dark-green continually repeated, not unlike a funeral procession.

99. This description is intended to comprise the principles of a false taste of magnificence, and to exemplify what was said before, that nothing but good sense can attain it.

And half the platform just reflects the other.
The suffering eye inverted nature sees,
Trees cut to statues, statues thick as trees,   120
With here a fountain, never to be played,
And there a summer-house, that knows no shade.
Here Amphitrite° sails through myrtle bowers;
There gladiators fight, or die, in flowers;
Un-watered see the drooping sea-horse mourn,
And swallows roost in Nilus'° dusty urn.
  My Lord advances with majestic mien,
Smit with the mighty pleasure, to be seen:
But soft—by regular approach—not yet—
First through the length of yon hot terrace sweat,   130
And when up ten steep slopes you've dragged your thighs,
Just at his study-door he'll bless your eyes.
  His study! with what authors is it stored?
In books, not authors, curious is my lord;
To all their dated backs he turns you round:
These Aldus° printed, those Du Suëil° has bound.
Lo some are vellum, and the rest as good
For all his Lordship knows, but they are wood.
For Locke or Milton 'tis in vain to look,
These shelves admit not any modern book.   140
  And now the chapel's silver bell you hear,
That summons you to all the pride of prayer:
Light quirks of music, broken and uneven,
Make the soul dance upon a jig to heaven.

124. The two statues of the *Gladiator pugnans* and *Gladiator moriens*.°

130. The *approaches* and *communication* of house with garden, or of one part with another, ill judged, and inconvenient.

133. The false taste in books; a satire on the vanity in collecting them, more frequent in men of fortune than the study to understand them. Many delight chiefly in the elegance of the print, or of the binding; some have carried it so far, as to cause the upper shelves to be filled with painted books of wood; others pique themselves so much upon books in a language they do not understand, as to exclude the most useful in one they do.

143. The false taste in music, improper to the subjects, as of light airs in churches, often practised by the organists, &c.

On painted ceilings you devoutly stare,
Where sprawl the saints of Verrio° or Laguerre,°
On gilded clouds in fair expansion lie,
And bring all paradise before your eye.
To rest, the cushion and soft dean° invite,
Who never mentions hell to ears polite. 150
    But hark! the chiming clocks to dinner call;
A hundred footsteps scrape the marble hall:
The rich buffet well-coloured serpents grace,
And gaping Tritons spew to wash your face.
Is this a dinner? this a genial° room?
No, 'tis a temple, and a hecatomb,
A solemn sacrifice, performed in state,
You drink by measure, and to minutes eat.
So quick retires each flying course, you'd swear
Sancho's dread doctor° and his wand were there. 160
Between each act the trembling salvers ring,
From soup to sweet-wine, and 'God bless the King'.
In plenty starving, tantalized in state,
And complaisantly helped to all I hate,
Treated, caressed, and tired, I take my leave,
Sick of his civil pride from morn to eve;
I curse such lavish cost, and little skill,
And swear no day was ever passed so ill.

145.—And in painting (from which even Italy is not free) of naked figures in churches, &c. which has obliged some Popes to put draperies on some of those of the best masters.

146. Verrio (Antonio) painted many ceilings, &c. at Windsor, Hampton Court, &c. and Laguerre at Blenheim Castle, and other places.

150. This is a fact; a reverend dean preaching at court, threatened the sinner with punishment in 'a place which he thought it not decent to name in so polite an assembly'.

153. Taxes the incongruity of *ornaments* (though sometimes practised by the ancients) where an open mouth ejects the water into a fountain, or where the shocking images of serpents, &c. are introduced in grottos or buffets.

155. The proud festivals of some men are here set forth to ridicule, where pride destroys the ease, and formal regularity all the pleasurable enjoyment of the entertainment.

160. See *Don Quixote*, chap. xlvii.

Yet hence the poor are clothed, the hungry fed;
Health to himself, and to his infants bread   170
The labourer bears: what his hard heart denies,
His charitable vanity supplies.
　　Another age shall see the golden ear
Imbrown the slope,° and nod on the parterre,
Deep harvests bury all his pride has planned,
And laughing Ceres° reassume the land.
　　Who then shall grace, or who improve the soil?
Who plants like BATHURST,° or who builds like BOYLE.°
'Tis use alone that sanctifies expense,
And splendour borrows all her rays from sense.   180
　　His father's acres who enjoys in peace,
Or makes his neighbours glad, if he increase;
Whose cheerful tenants bless their yearly toil,
Yet to their Lord owe more than to the soil;
Whose ample lawns are not ashamed to feed
The milky heifer and deserving steed;
Whose rising forests, not for pride or show,
But future buildings, future navies grow:
Let his plantations stretch from down to down,
First shade a country,° and then raise a town.   190
　　You too proceed! make falling arts your care,
Erect new wonders, and the old repair;
Jones and Palladio° to themselves restore,
And be whate'er Vitruvius° was before:
Till kings call forth th' ideas of your mind,

169. The *moral* of the whole, where PROVIDENCE is justified in giving wealth to
those who squander it in this manner. A bad taste employs more hands, and diffuses
expense more than a good one. This recurs to what is laid down in Book i. Epist.
II. v. 230–7, and in the Epistle preceding this, v. 161, &c.

195, 197, &c. The poet after having touched upon the proper objects of magnifi-
cence and expense, in the private works of great men, comes to those great and
public works which become a prince. This poem was published in the year 1732,
when some of the new-built churches, by the Act of Queen Anne, were ready to
fall, being founded in boggy land (which is satirically alluded to in our author's
imitation of Horace, *Lib.* ii. *Sat. 2. Shall half the new-built churches round thee fall*),
others were vilely executed, through fraudulent cabals between undertakers, officers,
&c. Dagenham Breach had done very great mischiefs; many of the highways through-
out England were hardly passable; and most of those which were repaired by turn-
pikes were made jobs for private lucre, and infamously executed, even to the
entrances of London itself. The proposal of building a bridge at Westminster had
been petitioned against and rejected; but in two years after the publication of this
poem, an Act for building a bridge passed through both houses. After many debates

(Proud to accomplish what such hands designed,)
Bid harbours open, public ways extend,
Bid temples, worthier of the god, ascend,
Bid the broad arch the dangerous flood contain,
The mole° projected break the roaring main;   200
Back to his bounds their subject sea command,
And roll obedient rivers through the land:
These honours, peace to happy Britain brings,
These are imperial works, and worthy kings.

AN EPISTLE
TO
Allen Lord *Bathurst*

ARGUMENT
Of the Use *of* RICHES

That it is known to few, most falling into one of the extremes, avarice or profusion, v. 1, &c. The point discussed, whether the invention of money has been more commodious, or pernicious to mankind, v. 21 to 77. That riches, either to the avaricious or the prodigal, cannot afford happiness, scarcely necessaries, v. 85 to 106. That avarice is an absolute frenzy, without an end or purpose, v. 107 &c. Conjectures about the motives of avaricious men, v. 113 to 153. That the conduct of men, with respect to riches, can only be accounted for by the ORDER OF PROVIDENCE, which works the general good out of extremes, and brings all to its great end by perpetual revolutions, v. 161 to 178. How a miser acts upon principles which appear to him reasonable, v. 179. How a prodigal does the same, v. 199. The due medium, and true use of riches, v. 219. The Man of Ross, v. 250. The fate of the profuse and the covetous, in two examples; both miserable in life and in death, v. 300, &c. The story of Sir Balaam, v. 339 to the end.

in the committee, the execution was left to the carpenter above-mentioned, who would have made it a wooden one, to which our author alludes in these lines,

> *Who builds a bridge that never drove a pile?*
> *Should Ripley venture, all the world would smile.*

See the notes on that place.°

Who shall decide, when doctors° disagree,   1
And soundest casuists doubt, like you and me?
You hold the word, from Jove to Momus° given,
That man was made the standing jest of heaven;
And gold but sent to keep the fools in play,
For some to heap, and some to throw away.

But I, who think more highly of our kind,
(And surely, heaven and I are of a mind)
Opine, that nature, as in duty bound,
Deep hid the shining mischief under ground: 10
But when by man's audacious labour won,
Flamed forth this rival to its sire the sun,
Then careful heaven supplied two sorts of men,
To squander these, and those to hide again.

Like doctors thus, when much dispute has passed,
We find our tenets just the same at last.
Both fairly owning, riches in effect
No grace of heaven or token of th'elect;
Given to the fool, the mad, the vain, the evil,
To Ward, to Waters, Chartres,° and the devil.   20

20. JOHN WARD of Hackney Esq., Member of Parliament, being prosecuted by the Duchess of Buckingham, and convicted of forgery, was first expelled the House, and then stood in the pillory on the 17th of March 1727. He was suspected of joining in a conveyance with Sir John Blunt, to secrete fifty thousand pounds of that director's estate, forfeited to the South Sea Company by Act of Parliament. The Company recovered the fifty thousand pounds against Ward; but he set up prior conveyances of his real estate to his brother and son, and concealed all his personal, which was computed to be one hundred and fifty thousand pounds. These conveyances being also set aside by a bill in Chancery, Ward was imprisoned, and hazarded the forfeiture of his life, by not giving in his effects till the last day, which was that of his examination. During his confinement, his amusement was to give poison to dogs and cats, and see them expire by slower or quicker torments. To sum up the *worth* of this gentleman, at the several eras of his life; at his standing in the pillory he was *worth above two hundred thousand pounds*; at his commitment to prison, he was *worth one hundred and fifty thousand*; but has been since so far diminished in his reputation, as to be thought a *worse man* by *fifty or sixty thousand*.

FR. CHARTRES, a man infamous for all manner of vices. When he was an ensign in the army, he was drummed out of the regiment for a cheat; he was next banished Brussels, and drummed out of Ghent on the same account. After a hundred tricks at the gaming-tables, he took to lending of money at exorbitant interest and on great penalties, accumulating premium, interest, and capital into a new capital, and seizing to a minute when the payments became due; in a word, by a constant attention to the vices, wants, and follies of mankind, he acquired an immense fortune. His house was a perpetual bawdy house. He was twice condemned for rapes, and pardoned;

What nature wants, commodious gold bestows,

but the last time not without imprisonment in Newgate, and large confiscations. He
died in Scotland in 1731, aged 62. The populace at his funeral raised a great riot,
almost tore the body out of the coffin, and cast dead dogs, etc. into the grave
along with it. The following Epitaph contains his character very justly drawn by Dr
Arbuthnot:

HERE continueth to rot
The Body of FRANCIS CHARTRES,
Who with an INFLEXIBLE CONSTANCY,
and INIMITABLE UNIFORMITY of Life,
PERSISTED,
In spite of AGE and INFIRMITIES,
In the Practice of EVERY HUMAN VICE;
Excepting PRODIGALITY and HYPOCRISY:
His insatiable AVARICE exempted him from the first,
His matchless IMPUDENCE from the second.
Nor was he more singular
in the undeviating *Pravity* of his *Manners*,
Than successful
In *Accumulating* WEALTH,
For, without TRADE or PROFESSION,
Without TRUST of PUBLIC MONEY,
And without BRIBE-WORTHY Service,
He acquired, or more properly created,
A MINISTERIAL ESTATE.
He was the only Person of his Time,
Who could CHEAT without the Mask of HONESTY,
Retain his Primeval MEANNESS
When possessed of TEN THOUSAND a Year,
And having daily deserved the GIBBET for what he *did*,
Was at last condemned to it for what he *could* not *do*.
Oh Indignant Reader!
Think not his Life useless to Mankind!
PROVIDENCE connived at his execrable Designs,
To give to After-ages
A conspicuous PROOF and EXAMPLE,
Of how small Estimation is EXORBITANT WEALTH
in the Sight of GOD,
By his bestowing it on the most UNWORTHY of ALL MORTALS.

This gentleman was *worth seven thousand pounds a year* estate in land, and about
one hundred thousand in money.

Mr WATERS, the third of these worthies, was a man no way resembling the former
in his military, but extremely so in his civil capacity; his great fortune having been
raised by the like diligent attendance on the necessities of others. But this gentleman's
history must be deferred till his death, when his *worth* may be known more certainly.

21. *What nature wants*, commodious *gold bestows*,] The epithet *commodious* gives us
the very proper idea of a *bawd* or *pander*; and this thought produced the two following
lines, which were in all the former editions, but, for their bad reasoning omitted,

'Tis thus we eat the bread another sows:
But how unequal it bestows, observe,
'Tis thus we riot, while who sow it, starve.
What nature wants (a phrase I much distrust)
Extends to luxury, extends to lust:
Useful, I grant, it serves what life requires,
But dreadful too, the dark assassin hires:
Trade it may help, society extend; .
But lures the pirate, and corrupts the friend: 30
It raises armies in a nation's aid,
But bribes a senate, and the land's betrayed.
In vain may heroes fight, and patriots rave;
If secret gold saps° on from knave to knave.
Once, we confess, beneath the patriot's cloak,
From the cracked bag the dropping guinea spoke,
And gingling down the backstairs, told the crew,
'Old Cato is as great a rogue as you.'
Blessed paper-credit! last and best supply!°
That lends corruption lighter wings to fly!   40
Gold imped° by thee, can compass hardest things,
Can pocket states, can fetch or carry kings;
A single leaf shall waft an army o'er,
Or ship off senates to a distant shore;
A leaf, like sibyls,° scatter to and fro
Our fates and fortunes, as the winds shall blow:
Pregnant with thousands flits the scrap unseen,
And silent sells a king, or buys a queen.
    Oh! that such bulky bribes as all might see,

And if we count amongst the needs of life
Another's toil, why not another's wife!

35. This is a true story, which happened in the reign of William III to an unsuspec-
ted old patriot, who coming out at the back-door from having been closeted by the
king, where he had received a large bag of guineas, the bursting of the bag discovered
his business there.

42. In our author's time, many princes had been sent about the world, and great
changes of kings projected in Europe. The partition treaty had disposed of Spain;
France had set up a king for England, who was sent to Scotland, and back again;
King Stanislaus was sent to Poland, and back again; the Duke of Anjou was sent to
Spain, and Don Carlos to Italy.

44. Alludes to several ministers, counsellors, and patriots banished in our times
to Siberia, and to that MORE GLORIOUS FATE of the PARLIAMENT of PARIS, banished
to Pontoise in the year 1720.

Still, as of old, incumbered villainy!   50
Could France or Rome° divert our brave designs,
With all their brandies or with all their wines?
What could they more than knights and squires
         confound,°
Or water all the quorum° ten miles round?
A statesman's slumbers how this speech would spoil!
'Sir, Spain has sent a thousand jars of oil;
Huge bales of British cloth blockade the door;
A hundred oxen at your levee roar.'
    Poor avarice one torment more would find;
Nor could profusion squander all, in kind.   60
Astride his cheese Sir Morgan might we meet,
And Worldly° crying coals from street to street,
Whom with a wig so wild, and mien so mazed,
Pity mistakes for some poor tradesman crazed.
Had Colepepper's° whole wealth been hops and hogs,
Could he himself have sent it to the dogs?
His Grace will game: to White's° a bull be led,
With spurning heels and with a butting head.
To White's° be carried, as to ancient games,
Fair coursers, vases, and alluring dames.   70
Shall then Uxorio, if the stakes he sweep,
Bear home six whores, and make his lady weep?
Or soft Adonis,° so perfumed and fine,
Drive to St James's a whole herd of swine?
Oh filthy check on all industrious skill,
To spoil the nation's last great trade, quadrille!°
Since then, my Lord, on such a world we fall,
What say you? 'Say? Why take it, gold and all.'
    What riches give us let us then enquire:

---

62. Some misers of great wealth, proprietors of the coal mines, had entered at this time into an association to keep up coals to an extravagant price, whereby the poor were reduced almost to starve, till one of them taking the advantage of underselling the rest, defeated the design. One of these misers was *worth ten thousand*, another *seven thousand* a year.

65. Sir WILLIAM COLEPEPPER, Bart. a person of an ancient family, and ample fortune, without one other quality of a gentleman, who, after ruining himself at the gaming table, past the rest of his days in sitting there to see the ruin of others; preferring to subsist upon borrowing and begging, rather than to enter into any reputable method of life, and refusing a post in the army which was offered him.

Meat, fire, and clothes, what more? Meat, clothes, and
fire.   80
Is this too little? would you more than live?
Alas! 'tis more than Turner° finds they give.
Alas! 'tis more than (all his visions passed)
Unhappy Wharton,° waking, found at last!
What can they give? to dying Hopkins,° heirs;
To Chartres, vigour;° Japhet,° nose and ears?
Can they, in gems bid pallid Hippia° glow,
In Fulvia's buckle ease the throbs below;
Or heal, old Narses, thy obscener ail,
With all th'embroidery plastered at thy tail?   90
They might (were Harpax° not too wise to spend)
Give Harpax self the blessing of a friend;
Or find some doctor that would save the life
Of wretched Shylock, spite of Shylock's wife:
But thousands die, without or this or that,
Die, and endow a college, or a cat:°

82. *Turner*] One, who, being possessed of three hundred thousand pounds, laid
down his coach, because interest was reduced from five to four *per cent.* and then
put seventy thousand into the Charitable Corporation for better interest; which sum
having lost, he took it so much to heart, that he kept his chamber ever after. It is
thought he would not have outlived it, but that he was heir to another considerable
estate, which he daily expected, and that by this course of life he saved both clothes
and all other expenses.

84. *Unhappy Wharton.*] A nobleman of great qualities, but as unfortunate in the
application of them, as if they had been vices and follies. See his character in the
first Epistle [*Epistle to Cobham*].

85. *Hopkins,*] A citizen, whose rapacity obtained him the name of Vulture Hop-
kins. He lived worthless, but died *worth three hundred thousand pounds*, which he
would give to no person living, but left it so as not to be inherited till after the second
generation. His counsel representing to him how many years it must be, before this
could take effect, and that his money could only lie at interest all that time, he
expressed great joy thereat, and said, 'They would then be as long in spending, as
he had been in getting it.' But the Chancery afterwards set aside the will, and gave
it to the heir at law.

86. *Japhet, nose and ears*] JAPHET CROOK, alias Sir Peter Stranger, was punished
with the loss of those parts, for having forged a conveyance of an estate to himself,
upon which he took up several thousand pounds. He was at the same time sued in
Chancery for having fraudulently obtained a will, by which he possessed another
considerable estate, in wrong of the brother of the deceased. By these means he
was *worth* a great sum, which (in reward for the small loss of his ears) he enjoyed
in prison till his death, and quietly left to his executor.

96. *Die, and endow a college, or a cat.*] A famous Duchess of R. in her last will left
considerable legacies and annuities to her cats.

To some, indeed, heaven grants the happier fate,
T'enrich a bastard, or a son they hate.
 Perhaps you think the poor might have their part?
Bond° damns the poor, and hates them from his heart: 100
The grave Sir Gilbert° holds it for a rule,
That 'every man in want is knave or fool:'
'God cannot love' (says Blunt,° with tearless eyes)
'The wretch he starves'—and piously denies:
But the good bishop, with a meeker air,
Admits, and leaves them, Providence's care.
 Yet, to be just to these poor men of pelf,°
Each does but hate his neighbour as himself:
Damned to the mines, an equal fate betides
The slave that digs it, and the slave that hides.   110
Who suffer thus, mere charity should own,
Must act on motives powerful, though unknown:
Some war, some plague, or famine they foresee,
Some revelation hid from you and me.
Why Shylock wants a meal, the cause is found,
He thinks a loaf will rise to fifty pound.
What made directors cheat in South Sea year?°
To live on venison when it sold so dear.
Ask you why Phryne the whole auction buys?
Phryne foresees a general excise.°   120
Why she and Sappho raise that monstrous sum?
Alas! they fear a man will cost a plum.°
 Wise Peter° sees the world's respect for gold,

 100. This epistle was written in the year 1730, when a corporation was established
to lend money to the poor upon pledges, by the name of the Charitable Corporation,
but the whole was turned only to an iniquitous method of enriching particular people,
to the ruin of such numbers, that it became a parliamentary concern to endeavour
the relief of those unhappy sufferers, and three of the managers, who were members
of the house, were expelled. By the report of the Committee, appointed to enquire
into that iniquitous affair, it appears, that when it was objected to the intended
removal of the office, that the poor, for whose use it was erected, would be hurt by
it, Bond, one of the directors, replied, *Damn the poor.* That 'God hates the poor,'
and, 'That every man in want is knave or fool,' &c. were the genuine apothegms of
some of the persons here mentioned.

 118. In the extravagance and luxury of the South Sea year, the price of a haunch
of venison was from three to five pounds.

 120. Many people about the year 1733, had a conceit that such a thing was
intended, of which it is not improbable this lady might have some intimation.

 123. PETER WALTER, a person not only eminent in the wisdom of his profession,
as a dexterous attorney, but allowed to be a good, if not a safe, conveyancer; extremely

And therefore hopes this nation may be sold:
Glorious ambition! Peter, swell thy store,
And be what Rome's great Didius was before.
   The crown of Poland,° venal twice an age,
To just three millions stinted modest Gage.°
But nobler scenes Maria's dreams unfold,
Hereditary realms, and worlds of gold.   130
Congenial souls! whose life one avarice joins,
And one fate buries in th'Asturian mines.
   Much injured Blunt!° why bears he Britain's hate?
A wizard told him in these words our fate:
'At length corruption, like a general flood,
(So long by watchful ministers withstood)
Shall deluge all; and avarice creeping on,
Spread like a low-born mist, and blot the sun;
Statesman and patriot° ply alike the stocks,
Peeress and butler share alike the box,°   140
And judges job,° and bishops bite° the town,
And mighty dukes pack° cards for half a crown.
See Britain sunk in lucre's sordid charms,
And France revenged of ANNE's and EDWARD's arms!'°
'Twas no court-badge, great scrivener!° fired thy brain,

respected by the nobility of this land, though free from all manner of luxury and ostentation: his wealth was never seen, and his bounty never heard of, except to his own son, for whom he procured an employment of considerable profit, of which he gave him as much as was *necessary*. Therefore the taxing this gentleman with any ambition, is certainly a great wrong to him.

126. A Roman lawyer, so rich as to purchase the Empire when it was set to sale upon the death of Pertinax.

127. The two persons here mentioned were of quality, each of whom in the Mississippi despised to realise above *three hundred thousand pounds*; the gentleman with a view to the purchase of the crown of Poland, the lady on a vision of the like royal nature. They since retired into Spain, where they are still in search of gold in the mines of the Asturies.

133. Sir JOHN BLUNT, originally a scrivener, was one of the first projectors of the South Sea company, and afterwards one of the directors and chief managers of the famous scheme in 1720. He was also one of those who suffered most severely by the bill of pains and penalties on the said directors. He was a dissenter of a most religious deportment, and professed to be a great believer. Whether he did really credit the prophecy here mentioned is not certain, but it was constantly in this very style he declaimed against the corruption and luxury of the age, the partiality of Parliaments, and the misery of party-spirit. He was particularly eloquent against *avarice* in great and noble persons, of which he had indeed lived to see many miserable examples. He died in the year 1732.

Nor lordly luxury, nor city gain:
No, 'twas thy righteous end, (ashamed to see
Senates degenerate, patriots disagree,
And nobly wishing party-rage to cease)
To buy both sides, and give thy country peace.   150
  'All this is madness,' cries a sober sage:
But who, my friend, has reason in his rage?
'The ruling passion, be it what it will,
The ruling passion conquers reason still.'
Less mad the wildest whimsy we can frame,
That ev'n that passion, if it has no aim;
For though such motives folly you may call,
The folly's greater to have none at all.
  Hear then the truth: ' 'Tis heaven each passion sends,
And different men directs to different ends.   160
Extremes in nature equal good produce,
Extremes in man concur to general use.'°
Ask we what makes one keep, and one bestow?
That POWER who bids the ocean ebb and flow;
Bids seed-time, harvest, equal course maintain,
Through reconciled extremes of drought and rain;
Builds life on death, on change° duration founds,
And gives th'eternal wheels to know their rounds.
  Riches, like insects, when concealed they lie,
Wait but for wings, and in their season fly.   170
Who sees pale Mammon pine amidst his store,
Sees but a backward steward for the poor;
This year a reservoir, to keep and spare;
The next, a fountain, spouting through his heir,
In lavish streams to quench a country's thirst,
And men and dogs shall drink him till they burst.
  Old Cotta shamed his fortune and his birth,
Yet was not Cotta void of wit or worth:
What though (the use of barbarous spits forgot)
His kitchen vied in coolness with his grot?   180
His court with nettles, moats with cresses stored,
With soups unbought and salads blessed his board?
If Cotta lived on pulse,° it was no more
Than Brahmins, saints, and sages did before;
To cram the rich was prodigal expense,

182—dapibus mensas onerabat inemptis. VIRGIL.

And who would take the poor from Providence?
Like some lone Chartreux° stands the good old hall,
Silence without, and fasts within the wall;
No raftered roofs with dance and tabor sound,
No noontide-bell invites the country round: 190
Tenants with sighs the smokeless towers survey,
And turn th'unwilling steeds another way:
Benighted wanderers, the forest o'er,
Curse the saved candle, and unopening door;
While the gaunt mastiff growling at the gate,
Affrights the beggar whom he longs to eat.°
  Not so his son, he marked this oversight,
And then mistook reverse of wrong for right.
(For what to shun will no great knowledge need,
But what to follow, is a task indeed.)   200
Yet sure, of qualities deserving praise,
More go to ruin fortunes, than to raise.
Whole slaughtered hecatombs,° and floods of wine,
Fill the capacious squire, and deep divine!
Yet no mean motive this profusion draws,
His oxen perish in his country's cause;
'Tis GEORGE and LIBERTY that crowns the cup,
And zeal for that great house° which eats him up.
The woods recede around the naked seat,
The sylvans groan—no matter—for the fleet:°   210
Next goes his wool—to clothe our valiant bands,
Last, for his country's love, he sells his lands.
To town he comes, completes the nation's hope,
And heads the bold train-bands,° and burns a Pope.°
And shall not Britain now reward his toils,
Britain, that pays her patriots with her spoils?
In vain at court the bankrupt pleads his cause,
His thankless country leaves him to her laws.
  The sense to value riches, with the art
T'enjoy them, and the virtue to impart,   220
Not meanly, nor ambitiously pursued,
Not sunk by sloth, not raised by servitude;
To balance fortune by a just expense,
Join with economy, magnificence;
With splendour, charity; with plenty, health;
Oh teach us, BATHURST! yet unspoiled by wealth!

That secret rare, between th' extremes to move
Of mad good nature, and of mean self-love.
    To worth or want well-weighed, be bounty given,
And ease, or emulate, the care of heaven;   230
(Whose measure full o'erflows on human race)
Mend fortune's fault, and justify her grace.
Wealth in the gross is death, but life diffused;
As poison heals, in just proportion used:
In heaps, like ambergris,° a stink it lies,
But well-dispersed, is incense to the skies.
    Who starves by nobles, or with nobles eats?
The wretch that trusts them, and the rogue that cheats.
Is there a lord, who knows a cheerful noon
Without a fiddler, flatterer, or buffoon?   240
Whose table, wit, or modest merit share,
Un-elbowed by a gamester, pimp, or player?
Who copies yours, or OXFORD's° better part,
To ease th'oppressed, and raise the sinking heart?
Where'er he shines, oh fortune, gild the scene,
And angels guard him in the golden mean!
There, English bounty yet awhile may stand,
And honour linger e'er it leaves the land.
    But all our praises why should lords engross?
Rise, honest Muse! and sing the MAN of ROSS:°   250
Pleased Vaga° echoes through her winding bounds,
And rapid Severn hoarse applause resounds.
Who hung with woods yon mountain's sultry brow?
From the dry rock who bade the waters flow?
Not to the skies in useless columns tossed,
Or in proud falls magnificently lost,
But clear and artless, pouring through the plain
Health to the sick, and solace to the swain.

243. Edward Harley, Earl of Oxford. The son of Robert, created Earl of Oxford
and Earl Mortimer by Queen Anne. This nobleman died regretted by all men of
letters, great numbers of whom had experienced his benefits. He left behind him
one of the most noble libraries in Europe.

250. The person here celebrated, who with a small estate actually performed all
these good works, and whose true name was almost lost (partly by the title of the
Man of Ross given him by way of eminence, and partly by being buried without so
much as an inscription) was called Mr John Kyrle. He died in the year 1724, aged
90, and lies interred in the chancel of the church of Ross in Herefordshire.

Whose causeway parts the vale with shady rows?
Whose seats the weary traveller repose?   260
Who taught that heaven-directed spire to rise?
'The MAN of ROSS,' each lisping babe replies.
Behold the market-place with poor o'erspread!
The MAN of ROSS divides the weekly bread:
He feeds yon alms-house, neat, but void of state,
Where age and want sit smiling at the gate:
Him portioned° maids, apprenticed orphans blessed,
The young who labour, and the old who rest.
Is any sick? the MAN of ROSS relieves,
Prescribes, attends, the medicine makes, and gives.   270
Is there a variance? enter but his door,
Balked are the courts, and contest is no more.
Despairing quacks with curses fled the place,
And vile attorneys, now an useless race.
    'Thrice happy man! enabled to pursue
What all so wish, but want the power to do!
Oh say, what sums that generous hand supply?
What mines, to swell that boundless charity?'
    Of debts, and taxes, wife and children clear,
This man possessed—five hundred pounds a year.   280
Blush, grandeur, blush! proud courts, withdraw your blaze!
Ye little stars!° hide your diminished rays.
    'And what? no monument, inscription, stone?
His race, his form, his name almost unknown?'
    Who builds a church to God, and not to fame,
Will never mark the marble with his name:
Go search it there, where to be born and die,
Of rich and poor makes all the history;
Enough, that virtue filled the space between;
Proved, by the ends of being, to have been.   290
When Hopkins dies, a thousand lights attend
The wretch, who living saved a candle's end:
Shouldering God's altar a vile image stands,
Belies his features, nay extends his hands;
That livelong wig which Gorgon's self might own,
Eternal buckle° takes in Parian stone.°

287. The parish register.
    296. The poet ridicules the wretched taste of carving large periwigs on bustos,
of which there are several vile examples in the tombs at Westminster and elsewhere.

Behold what blessings wealth to life can lend!
And see, what comfort it affords our end.

   In the worst inn's worst room, with mat half-hung,
The floors of plaster, and the walls of dung,   300
On once a flock-bed,° but repaired with straw,
With tape-tied curtains, never meant to draw,
The George and garter° dangling from that bed
Where tawdry yellow strove with dirty red,
Great Villers lies—alas! how changed from him,
That life of pleasure, and that soul of whim!
Gallant and gay, in Cliveden's proud alcove,
The bower of wanton Shrewsbury and love;
Or just as gay, at council, in a ring
Of mimicked statesmen, and their merry king.°   310
No wit to flatter, left of all his store!
No fool to laugh at, which he valued more.
There, victor of his health, of fortune, friends,
And fame, this lord of useless thousands ends.

   His Grace's fate sage Cutler° could foresee,
And well (he thought) advised him, 'Live like me.'
As well his Grace replied, 'Like you, Sir John?
That I can do, when all I have is gone.'
Resolve me, reason, which of these is worse,
Want with a full, or with an empty purse?   320
Thy life more wretched, Cutler, was confessed,
Arise, and tell me, was thy death more blessed?
Cutler saw tenants break, and houses fall,
For very want; he could not build a wall.
His only daughter in a stranger's power,
For very want; he could not pay a dower.
A few grey hairs his reverend temples crowned,
'Twas very want that sold them for two pound.

305. This lord, yet more famous for his vices than his misfortunes, after having
been possessed of about £50,000 a year, and passed through many of the highest
posts in the kingdom, died in the year 1687, in a remote inn in Yorkshire, reduced
to the utmost misery.°

307. *Cliveden*] A delightful palace, on the banks of the Thames, built by the Duke
of Buckingham.

308. *Shrewsbury*] The Countess of Shrewsbury, a woman abandoned to gallan-
tries. The Earl her husband was killed by the Duke of Buckingham in a duel; and
it has been said, that during the combat she held the Duke's horses in the habit of
a page.°

What ev'n denied a cordial at his end,
Banished the doctor, and expelled the friend?   330
What but a want, which you perhaps think mad,
Yet numbers feel, the want of what he had!
Cutler and Brutus, dying both exclaim,
'Virtue! and wealth! what are ye but a name!'
    Say, for such worth are other worlds prepared?
Or are they both, in this, their own reward?
A knotty point! to which we now proceed.
But you are tired—I'll tell a tale——'Agreed.'
    Where London's column, pointing at the skies,
Like a tall bully, lifts the head, and lies;   340
There dwelt a citizen of sober fame,
A plain good man, and Balaam° was his name;
Religious, punctual, frugal, and so forth;
His word would pass for more than he was worth.
One solid dish his weekday meal affords,
An added pudding solemnized the Lord's:
Constant at church, and Change; his gains were sure,
His givings rare, save farthings to the poor.
    The devil was piqued such saintship to behold,
And longed to tempt him like good Job of old: 350
But Satan now is wiser than of yore,
And tempts by making rich, not making poor.
    Roused by the prince of air, the whirlwinds sweep
The surge, and plunge his father in the deep;
Then full against his Cornish lands they roar,
And two rich shipwrecks bless the lucky shore.
    Sir Balaam now, he lives like other folks,
He takes his chirping° pint, and cracks his jokes:
'Live like yourself,' was soon my Lady's word;
And lo! two puddings smoked upon the board.   360
    Asleep and naked as an Indian lay,

339. The Monument, built in memory of the fire of London, with an inscription, importing that city to have been burnt by the Papists.

355. The author has placed the scene of these shipwrecks in Cornwall, not only from their frequency on that coast, but from the inhumanity of the inhabitants to those to whom that misfortune arrives. When a ship happens to be stranded there, they have been known to bore holes in it, to prevent its getting off; to plunder, and sometimes even to massacre the people. Nor has the Parliament of England been yet able wholly to suppress these barbarities.

An honest factor° stole a gem° away:
He pledged it to the knight; the knight had wit,
So kept the diamond, and the rogue was bit.°
Some scruple rose, but thus he eased his thought,
'I'll now give sixpence where I gave a groat;
Where once I went to church, I'll now go twice—
And am so clear too of all other vice.'

    The tempter saw his time; the work he plied;
Stocks and subscriptions pour on every side,   370
Till all the demon makes his full descent
In one abundant shower of cent per cent,
Sinks deep within him, and possesses whole,
Then dubs director, and secures his soul.

    Behold Sir Balaam, now a man of spirit,
Ascribes his gettings to his parts and merit;
What late he called a blessing, now was wit,
And God's good Providence, a lucky hit.°
Things change their titles, as our manners turn:
His counting house employed the Sunday morn;   380
Seldom at church ('twas such a busy life)
But duly sent his family and wife.
There (so the devil ordained) one Christmas-tide
My good old Lady catched° a cold, and died.

    A nymph of quality admires our knight;
He marries, bows at court, and grows polite:
Leaves the dull cits, and joins (to please the fair)
The well-bred cuckolds in St James's air:°
First, for his son a gay commission buys,
Who drinks, whores, fights, and in a duel dies: 390
His daughter flaunts a viscount's tawdry wife;
She bears a coronet and p—x for life.
In Britain's senate he a seat obtains,
And one more pensioner St Stephen° gains.
My Lady falls to play; so bad her chance,
He must repair it; takes a bribe from France;
The House impeach him; Coningsby° harangues;
The court forsake him, and Sir Balaam hangs:
Wife, son, and daughter, Satan! are thy own,
His wealth, yet dearer, forfeit to the crown: 400
The devil and the king divide the prize,
And sad Sir Balaam curses God and dies.

THE
FIRST SATIRE
OF THE
SECOND BOOK
OF
HORACE IMITATED
To Mr FORTESCUE°

Advertisement

The occasion of publishing these *Imitations* was the clamour raised on
some of my *Epistles*. An answer from *Horace* was both more full, and of
more dignity, than any I could have made in my own person; and the
example of much greater freedom in so eminent a divine as Dr Donne,
seemed a proof with what indignation and contempt a Christian may
treat vice or folly, in ever so low, or ever so high, a station. Both these
authors were acceptable to the princes and ministers under whom they
lived: the satires of Dr Donne I versified at the desire of the Earl of
Oxford while he was Lord Treasurer, and of the Duke of Shrewsbury
who had been Secretary of State; neither of whom looked upon a satire
on vicious courts as any reflection on those they served in. And indeed
there is not in the world a greater error, than that which fools are so apt
to fall into, and knaves with good reason to encourage, the mistaking a
satirist for a *libeller*; whereas to a *true satirist* nothing is so odious as a
libeller, for the same reason as to a man *truly virtuous* nothing is so
hateful as a *hypocrite*.

—*Uni aequus Virtuti atque ejus Amicis.*

P. There are (I scarce can think it, but am told)   1
There are, to whom my satire seems too bold:
Scarce to wise Peter complaisant° enough,
And something said of Chartres° much too rough.
The lines are weak, another's pleased to say,
Lord Fanny° spins a thousand such a day.

Timorous by nature, of the rich in awe,
I come to counsel° learned in the law:
You'll give me, like a friend both sage and free,
Advice; and (as you use) without a fee.   10
    F. I'd write no more.
                  P. Not write? but then I think,
And for my soul I cannot sleep a wink.
I nod in company, I wake at night,
Fools rush into my head, and so I write.
    F. You could not do a worse thing for your life.
Why, if the nights seem tedious—take a wife:
Or rather truly, if your point be rest,
Lettuce° and cowslip-wine; *probatum est.*
But talk with Celsus,° Celsus will advise
Hartshorn,° or something that shall close your eyes.   20
Or, if you needs must write, write CAESAR's° praise,
You'll gain at least a *knighthood,* or the *bays.*°
    P. What? like Sir Richard,° rumbling, rough, and
      fierce,
With ARMS, and GEORGE, and BRUNSWICK° crowd the
      verse,
Rend with tremendous sound your ears asunder,
With gun, drum, trumpet, blunderbuss, and thunder?
Or nobly wild, with Budgell's° fire and force,
Paint angels trembling round his falling horse?
    F. Then all your muse's softer art display,
Let CAROLINA° smooth the tuneful lay,   30
Lull with AMELIA's° liquid name the nine,°
And sweetly flow through all the royal line.
    P. Alas! few verses touch their nicer ear;
They scarce can bear their *Laureate* twice a year;°
And justly CAESAR scorns the poet's lays,
It is to *history* he trusts for praise.
    F. Better be Cibber, I'll maintain it still,
Than ridicule all taste, blaspheme quadrille,°
Abuse the city's best good men in metre,
And laugh at peers that put their trust in Peter.°   40
Ev'n those you touch not, hate you.
                  P. What should ail them?
    F. A hundred smart in Timon° and in Balaam:°
The fewer still you name, you wound the more;

Bond° is but one, but Harpax° is a score.
  P. Each mortal has his pleasure: none deny
Scarsdale° his bottle, Darty° his ham-pie;
Ridotta° sips and dances, till she see
The doubling lustres dance as fast as she;
Fox° loves the senate, Hockley Hole° his brother,
Like in all else, as one egg to another.   50
I love to pour out all myself, as plain
As downright SHIPPEN,° or as old Montaigne:
In them, as certain to be loved as seen,
The soul stood forth, nor kept a thought within;
In me what spots (for spots I have) appear,
Will prove at least the medium must be clear.
In this impartial glass, my muse intends
Fair to expose myself, my foes, my friends;
Publish the present age; but where my text
Is vice too high, reserve it for the next: 60
My foes shall wish my life a longer date,
And every friend the less lament my fate.
My head and heart thus flowing through my quill,
Verse-man or prose-man, term me which you will,
Papist or Protestant, or both between,
Like good Erasmus in an honest mean,
In moderation placing all my glory,
While Tories call me Whig, and Whigs a Tory.
    Satire's my weapon, but I'm too discreet
To run amuck, and tilt at all I meet;   70
I only wear it in a land of Hectors,°
Thieves, supercargoes,° sharpers, and directors.°
Save but our *army!* and let Jove incrust
Swords, pikes, and guns, with everlasting rust!
Peace is my dear delight—not FLEURY's° more:
But touch me, and no minister so sore.
Whoe'er offends, at some unlucky time
Slides into verse, and hitches in a rhyme,
Sacred to ridicule his whole life long,
And the sad burden° of some merry song.   80
    Slander or poison, dread from Delia's rage,
Hard words or hanging, if your judge be Page.°
From furious Sappho° scarce a milder fate,
P-xed by her love, or libelled by her hate.

Its proper power to hurt, each creature feels;
Bulls aim their horns, and asses lift their heels;
'Tis a bear's talent not to kick, but hug;
And no man wonders he's not stung by Pug.
So drink with Walter,° or with Chartres eat,
They'll never poison you, they'll only cheat.   90

    Then, learned Sir! (to cut the matter short)
Whate'er my fate, or well or ill at court,
Whether old age, with faint but cheerful ray,
Attends to gild the evening of my day,
Or death's black wing already be displayed,
To wrap me in the universal shade;
Whether the darkened room to muse invite,
Or whitened wall provoke the skewer to write:
In durance, exile, Bedlam, or the Mint,
Like Lee° or Budgell,° I will rhyme and print.   100
    F. Alas young man! your days can ne'er be long,
In flower of age you perish for a song!
Plums° and directors, Shylock and his wife,
Will club their testers,° now, to take your life!
    P. What, armed for virtue when I point the pen,
Brand the bold front of shameless, guilty men;
Dash the proud gamester in his gilded car;
Bare the mean heart that lurks beneath a *star*;°
Can there be wanting, to defend her cause,
Lights of the church, or guardians of the laws?   110
Could pensioned Boileau lash in honest strain
Flatterers and bigots ev'n in Louis'° reign?
Could Laureate Dryden pimp and friar° engage,
Yet neither Charles nor James be in a rage?
And I not strip the gilding off a knave,
Unplaced, unpensioned, no man's heir, or slave?
I will, or perish in the generous cause:
Hear this, and tremble! you, who 'scape the Laws.
Yes, while I live, no rich or noble knave
Shall walk the world, in credit, to his grave.   120
To VIRTUE ONLY and HER FRIENDS, A FRIEND,
The world beside may murmur, or commend.
Know, all the distant din that world can keep,
Rolls o'er my grotto, and but soothes my sleep.
There, my retreat the best companions grace,

Chiefs out of war, and statesmen out of place.
There ST JOHN° mingles with my friendly bowl
The feast of reason and the flow of soul:
And HE, whose lightning pierced th' Iberian lines,°
Now forms my quincunx,° and now ranks my vines,   130
Or tames the genius of the stubborn plain,
Almost as quickly as he conquered Spain.

　Envy must own, I live among the great,
No pimp of pleasure, and no spy of state,
With eyes that pry not, tongue that ne'er repeats,
Fond to spread friendships, but to cover heats;
To help who want, to forward who excel;
This, all who know me, know; who love me, tell;
And who unknown defame me, let them be
Scribblers or peers, alike are *mob* to me.   140
This is my plea, on this I rest my cause—
What saith my counsel learned in the laws?

　F. Your plea is good; but still I say, beware!
Laws are explained by men—so have a care.
It stands on record, that in Richard's° times
A man was hanged for very honest rhymes.
Consult the statute: *quart.* I think, it is,
Edwardi sext. or *prim. et quint. Eliz.*°
See *Libels, Satires*—here you have it—read.

　P. Libels and *Satires!* lawless things indeed!   150
But grave *Epistles*, bringing vice to light,
Such as a king might read, a bishop write,
Such as Sir ROBERT° would approve—
　　　　　　　　　　F. Indeed?
The case is altered—you may then proceed;
In such a cause the plaintiff will be hissed,
My lords the judges laugh, and you're dismissed.

129. Charles Mordaunt Earl of Peterborough, who in the year 1705 took Bar-
celona, and in the winter following with only 280 horse and 900 foot enterprised
and accomplished the conquest of Valencia.

ESSAY on MAN

FOUR EPISTLES

TO

H. St John Lord Bolingbroke

THE DESIGN

Having proposed to write some pieces on human life and manners, such as (to use my Lord Bacon's expression) 'come home to men's business and bosoms', I thought it more satisfactory to begin with considering *Man* in the abstract, his *Nature* and his *State*; since, to prove any moral duty, to enforce any moral precept, or to examine the perfection or imperfection of any creature whatsoever, it is necessary first to know what *condition* and *relation* it is placed in, and what is the proper *end* and *purpose* of its *being*.

The science of human nature is, like all other sciences, reduced to a *few clear points*: there are not *many certain truths* in this world. It is therefore in the anatomy of the mind as in that of the body; more good will accrue to mankind by attending to the large, open, and perceptible parts, than by studying too much such finer nerves and vessels, the conformations and uses of which will for ever escape our observation. The *disputes* are all upon these last, and, I will venture to say, they have less sharpened the *wits* than the *hearts* of men against each other, and have diminished the practice, more than advanced the theory, of morality. If I could flatter myself that this Essay has any merit, it is in steering betwixt the extremes of doctrines seemingly opposite, in passing over terms utterly unintelligible, and in forming a *temperate* yet not *inconsistent*, and a *short* yet not *imperfect* system of ethics.

This I might have done in prose; but I chose verse, and even rhyme, for two reasons. The one will appear obvious; that principles, maxims, or precepts so written, both strike the reader more strongly at first, and are more easily retained by him afterwards. The other may seem odd, but is true, I found I could express them more *shortly* this way than in prose itself; and nothing is more certain, than that much of the *force* as well as *grace* of arguments or instructions, depends on their *conciseness*. I was unable to treat this part of my subject more in *detail*, without becoming dry and tedious; or more *poetically*, without sacrificing perspicuity to ornament, without wandering from the precision, or breaking the chain of reasoning. If any man can unite all these without diminution of any of them, I freely confess he will compass a thing above my capacity.

What is now published, is only to be considered as a *general map* of MAN, marking out no more than the *greater parts*, their *extent*, their *limits*, and their *connection*, but leaving the particular to be more fully delineated in the charts which are to follow. Consequently, these Epistles in their progress (if I have health and leisure to make any progress) will be less dry, and more susceptible of poetical ornament. I am here only opening the *fountains*, and clearing the passage. To deduce the *rivers*, to follow them in their course, and to observe their effects, may be a task more agreeable.

EPISTLE I

ARGUMENT

Of the Nature and State of Man with respect to the UNIVERSE

Of Man *in the abstract.*—I. *That we can judge only with regard to our own* system, *being ignorant of the* relations *of systems and things,* v. 17, &c. II. *That Man is not to be deemed* imperfect, *but a being suited to his* place *and* rank *in the creation, agreeable to the* general order *of things, and conformable to* ends *and* relations *to him unknown,* v. 35, &c. III. *That it is partly upon his* ignorance *of future* events, *and partly upon the* hope *of a* future state, *that all his happiness in the present depends,* v. 77, &c. IV. *The* pride *of aiming at more knowledge, and pretending to more perfection, the cause of Man's error and misery. The* impiety *of putting himself in the place of* God, *and judging of the fitness or unfitness, perfection or imperfection, justice or injustice of his dispensations,* v. 113, &c. V. *The* absurdity *of conceiting himself the* final cause *of the creation, or expecting that perfection in the* moral world, *which is not in the* natural, v. 131, &c. VI. *The* unreasonableness *of his complaints against* Providence, *while on the one hand he demands the perfections of the angels, and on the other the bodily qualifications of the brutes; though, to possess any of the* sensitive faculties *in a higher degree, would render him miserable,* v. 173, &c. VII. *That throughout the whole visible world, an universal* order *and* gradation *in the sensual and mental faculties is observed, which causes a* subordination *of creature to creature, and of all creatures to Man. The gradations of* sense, instinct, thought, reflection, reason; *that reason alone countervails all the other faculties,* v. 207. VIII. *How much farther this* order *and* subordination *of living creatures may extend, above and below us; were any part of which broken, not that part only, but the whole connected* creation *must be destroyed,* v. 233. IX. *The* extravagance, madness, *and* pride *of such a desire,* v. 259. X. *The consequence of all, the* absolute submission *due to Providence, both as to our* present *and* future state, v. 281, &c. *to the end.*

Awake, my ST JOHN!° leave all meaner things   1
To low ambition, and the pride of kings.
Let us (since life can little more supply
Than just to look about us and to die)
Expatiate° free o'er all this scene of Man;
A mighty maze! but not° without a plan;
A wild, where weeds and flowers promiscuous shoot,
Or garden, tempting with forbidden fruit.
Together let us beat this ample field,
Try what the open, what the covert yield;°   10
The latent tracts, the giddy heights explore
Of all who blindly creep, or sightless soar;
Eye nature's walks, shoot folly as it flies,
And catch the manners living as they rise;
Laugh where we must, be candid° where we can;
But vindicate the ways of God to Man.
　　I. Say first, of God above, or Man below,
What can we reason, but from what we know?
Of Man what see we, but his station here,
From which to reason, or to which refer?   20
Through worlds unnumbered though the God be known,
'Tis ours to trace him only in our own.
He, who through vast immensity can pierce,
See worlds on worlds compose one universe,

---

17 f. He can reason only from things known, and judge only with regard to his own system.

Observe how system into system runs,
What other planets circle other suns,
What varied being peoples every star,
May tell why Heaven has made us as we are.
But of this frame the bearings, and the ties,
The strong connections, nice dependencies,   30
Gradations just, has thy pervading soul
Looked through? or can a part contain the whole?
    Is the great chain,° that draws all to agree,
And drawn supports, upheld by God, or thee?
II. Presumptuous Man! the reason wouldst thou find,
Why formed so weak, so little, and so blind!
First, if thou canst, the harder reason guess,
Why formed no weaker, blinder, and no less!
Ask of thy mother earth, why oaks are made
Taller or stronger than the weeds they shade?   40
Or ask of yonder argent fields above,
Why JOVE's satellites° are less than JOVE?
    Of systems possible, if 'tis confessed
That wisdom infinite must form the best,
Where all must full or not coherent be,
And all that rises, rise in due degree;
Then, in the scale of reasoning life, 'tis plain
There must be, somewhere, such a rank as Man;
And all the question (wrangle e'er so long)
Is only this, if God has placed him wrong?   50
    Respecting Man, whatever wrong we call,
May, must be right, as relative to all.
In human works, though laboured on with pain,
A thousand movements scarce one purpose gain;
In God's, one single can its end produce;
Yet serves to second too some other use.
So Man, who here seems principal alone,
Perhaps acts second to some sphere unknown,
Touches some wheel, or verges to some goal;
'Tis but a part we see, and not a whole.°   60
    When the proud steed shall know why Man restrains
His fiery course, or drives him o'er the plains;

---

35 f. He is not therefore a judge of his own perfection or imperfection, but is
certainly such a being as is suited to his place and rank in the creation.

When the dull ox, why now he breaks the clod,
Is now a victim, and now Egypt's god:°
Then shall Man's pride and dulness comprehend
His actions', passions', being's, use and end;
Why doing, suffering, checked, impelled; and why
This hour a slave, the next a deity.

    Then say not Man's imperfect, Heaven in fault;
Say rather, Man's as perfect as he ought: 70
His knowledge measured to his state and place,
His time a moment, and a point his space.
If to be perfect in a certain sphere,
What matter, soon or late, or here or there?
The blessed to-day is as completely so,
As who began a thousand years ago.

    III. Heaven from all creatures hides the book of fate,°
All but the page prescribed, their present state;
From brutes what men, from men what spirits know:
Or who could suffer being here below?   80
The lamb thy riot° dooms to bleed today,
Had he thy reason, would he skip and play?
Pleased to the last, he crops the flowery food,
And licks the hand just raised to shed his blood.
Oh blindness to the future! kindly given,
That each may fill the circle marked by Heaven;
Who sees with equal eye, as God of all,
A hero perish, or a sparrow fall,°
Atoms or systems into ruin hurled,
And now a bubble burst, and now a world.   90

    Hope humbly then; with trembling pinions soar;
Wait the great teacher death, and God adore!
What future bliss, he gives not thee to know,
But gives that hope to be thy blessing now.
Hope springs eternal in the human breast:
Man never is, but always to be blest:
The soul, uneasy and confined from home,
Rests and expatiates° in a life to come.

77. His happiness depends on his ignorance to a certain degree.
79. See this pursued in Epist. 3, vv. 70 &c., 83 &c.
91. And on his hope of a relation to a future state.
94. Further opened in Epist. 2, v. 283; Epist. 3, v. 74; Epist. 4, v. 346 &c.

Lo! the poor Indian,° whose untutored mind
Sees God in clouds, or hears him in the wind;   100
His soul proud science never taught to stray
Far as the solar walk, or milky way;
Yet simple nature to his hope has given,
Behind the cloud-topped hill, an humbler heaven;
Some safer world in depth of woods embraced,
Some happier island in the watery waste,
Where slaves once more their native land behold,
No fiends torment, no Christians thirst for gold!
To be, contents his natural desire,
He asks no angel's wing, no seraph's fire;°   110
But thinks, admitted to that equal° sky,
His faithful dog shall bear him company.
    IV. Go, wiser thou! and in thy scale of sense
Weigh thy opinion against providence;
Call imperfection what thou fanciest such,
Say, here he gives too little, there too much;
Destroy all creatures for thy sport or gust,°
Yet cry, 'If Man's unhappy, God's unjust';
If Man alone engross not heaven's high care,
Alone made perfect here, immortal there: 120
Snatch from his hand the balance° and the rod,
Re-judge his justice, be the GOD of GOD!
    In pride, in reasoning pride, our error lies;
All quit their sphere, and rush into the skies.
Pride still is aiming at the blessed abodes,
Men would be angels, angels would be gods.
Aspiring to be gods, if angels fell,
Aspiring to be angels, men rebel;
And who but wishes to invert the laws
Of ORDER, sins against th' eternal cause.   130
    V. Ask for what end the heavenly bodies shine,
Earth for whose use? Pride answers, ' 'Tis for mine:
For me kind Nature wakes her genial° power,

113 f. The pride of aiming at more knowledge and perfection, and the impiety
of pretending to judge of the dispensations of Providence, the causes of his error
and misery.

131 f. The absurdity of conceiving himself the final cause of the creation, or
expecting that perfection in the moral world which is not in the natural.

Suckles each herb, and spreads out every flower;
Annual for me, the grape, the rose renew
The juice nectareous, and the balmy dew;
For me, the mine a thousand treasures brings;
For me, health gushes from a thousand springs;
Seas roll to waft me, suns to light me rise;
My footstool earth, my canopy the skies.'   140
    But errs not nature from this gracious end,
From burning suns when livid deaths descend,°
When earthquakes swallow, or when tempests sweep
Towns to one grave, whole nations to the deep?
'No' ('tis replied) 'the first almighty cause
Acts not by partial, but by general laws;
Th'exceptions few; some change since all began,
And what created perfect?'—Why then Man?
If the great end be human happiness
Then nature deviates; and can Man do less?   150
As much that end a constant course requires
Of showers and sunshine, as of Man's desires;
As much eternal springs and cloudless skies,
As men for ever temperate, calm, and wise.
If plagues or earthquakes break not heaven's design,
Why then a Borgia,° or a Catiline?°
Who knows but he, whose hand the lightning forms,
Who heaves old ocean, and who wings the storms;
Pours fierce ambition in a Caesar's mind,
Or turns young Ammon° loose to scourge mankind?   160
From pride, from pride, our very reasoning springs;
Account for moral, as for natural things:
Why charge we heaven in those, in these acquit?
In both, to reason right is to submit.
    Better for us, perhaps, it might appear,
Were there all harmony, all virtue here;
That never air or ocean felt the wind;
That never passion discomposed the mind:
But ALL subsists by elemental strife;
And passions are the elements of life.   170
The general ORDER, since the whole began,
Is kept in nature, and is kept in Man.

170. See this subject extended in Epist. 2 from v. 93–133, 161 &c.

    VI. What would this Man? Now upward will he soar,
And little less than angel,° would be more;
Now looking downwards, just as grieved appears
To want the strength of bulls, the fur of bears.
Made for his use all creatures if he call,
Say what their use, had he the powers of all?
Nature to these, without profusion kind,
The proper organs, proper powers assigned;   180
Each seeming want compensated° of course,
Here with degrees of swiftness, there of force;
All in exact proportion to the state;
Nothing to add, and nothing to abate.
Each beast, each insect, happy in its own;
Is Heaven unkind to Man, and Man alone?
Shall he alone, whom rational we call,
Be pleased with nothing, if not blessed with all?
    The bliss of Man (could pride that blessing find)
Is not to act or think beyond mankind;   190
No powers of body or of soul to share,
But what his nature and his state can bear.
Why has not Man a microscopic eye?
For this plain reason, Man is not a fly.
Say what the use, were finer optics given,
T'inspect a mite, not comprehend the heaven?
Or touch, if tremblingly alive all o'er,
To smart and agonize at every pore?
Or quick effluvia darting through the brain,
Die of a rose in aromatic pain?   200
If nature thundered in his opening ears,
And stunned him with the music of the spheres,
How would he wish that Heaven had left him still
The whispering zephyr, and the purling rill?
Who finds not Providence all good and wise,
Alike in what it gives, and what denies?

173 f. The unreasonableness of the complaints against Providence; and that to possess more faculties would make us miserable.

182. It is a certain axiom in the anatomy of creatures, that in proportion as they are formed for strength, their swiftness is lessened; or as they are formed for swiftness, their strength is abated.

185. Vid. Epist. 3, v. 79 &c. and 109 &c.

    VII. Far as creation's ample range extends,
The scale of sensual, mental powers ascends:
Mark how it mounts, to Man's imperial race,
From the green myriads in the peopled grass: 210
What modes of sight betwixt each wide extreme,
The mole's dim curtain, and the lynx's beam:
Of smell, the headlong lioness° between,
And hound sagacious° on the tainted° green:
Of hearing, from the life that fills the flood,
To that which warbles through the vernal wood:
The spider's touch, how exquisitely fine!
Feels at each thread, and lives along the line:
In the nice° bee, what sense so subtly true
From poisonous herbs extracts the healing dew: 220
How instinct varies in the grovelling swine,
Compared, half-reasoning elephant, with thine:
'Twixt that, and reason, what a nice barrier;°
For ever separate, yet for ever near!
Remembrance and reflection how allied;
What thin partitions sense from thought divide:
And middle natures, how they long to join,
Yet never pass th'insuperable line!
Without this just gradation, could they be
Subjected these to those, or all to thee?   230
The powers of all subdued by thee alone,
Is not thy reason all these powers in one?
    VIII. See, through this air, this ocean, and this earth,
All matter quick, and bursting into birth.

    207 f. There is an universal ORDER and GRADATION through the whole visible world, of the sensible and mental faculties which causes the subordination of creature to creature, and of all creatures to Man, whose reason alone countervails all the other faculties.

    The extent, limits, and use of human reason and science, the author designed as the subject of his next book of Ethic Epistles.

    213. The manner of the lions hunting their prey in the deserts of Africa is this: at their first going out in the night-time they set up a loud roar, and then listen to the noise made by the beasts in their flight, pursuing them by the ear, and not by the nostril. It is probable, the story of the jackal's hunting for the lion was occasioned by observation of this defect of scent in that terrible animal.

    233 f. How much farther this gradation and subordination may extend: were any part of which broken, the whole connected creation must be destroyed.

Above, how high, progressive life may go!
Around, how wide! how deep extend below!
Vast chain of being, which from God began,
Natures ethereal, human, angel, man,
Beast, bird, fish, insect! what no eye can see,
No glass° can reach! from infinite to thee,   240
From thee to nothing!—On superior powers
Were we to press, inferior might on ours:
Or in the full creation leave a void,°
Where, one step broken, the great scale's destroyed:
From Nature's chain whatever link you strike,
Tenth or ten thousandth, breaks the chain alike.

    And if each system in gradation roll,
Alike essential to th'amazing° whole;
The least confusion but in one, not all
That system only, but the whole must fall.   250
Let earth unbalanced from her orbit fly,
Planets and suns run lawless through the sky,
Let ruling angels from their spheres be hurled,
Being on being wrecked, and world on world,
Heaven's whole foundations to their centre nod,
And Nature tremble to the throne of God:
All this dread ORDER break—for whom? for thee?
Vile worm!—oh madness, pride, impiety!

    IX. What if the foot, ordained the dust to tread,
Or hand to toil, aspired to be the head?   260
What if the head, the eye, or ear repined
To serve mere engines to the ruling mind?
Just as absurd for any part to claim
To be another, in this general frame:
Just as absurd, to mourn the tasks or pains
The great directing MIND of ALL ordains.

    All are but parts of one stupendous whole,
Whose body Nature is, and God the soul;
That, changed through all, and yet in all the same,
Great in the earth, as in th'ethereal frame,   270
Warms in the sun, refreshes in the breeze,
Glows in the stars, and blossoms in the trees,

258. The extravagance, impiety, and pride of such a desire.
265. See the prosecution and application of this in Ep. 4. v. 162.

Lives through all life, extends through all extent,
Spreads undivided, operates unspent,
Breathes in our soul, informs our mortal part,
As full, as perfect, in a hair as heart;
As full, as perfect, in vile Man that mourns,
As the rapt seraph that adores and burns;°
To him no high, no low, no great, no small;
He fills, he bounds, connects, and equals all.°   280
   X. Cease then, nor ORDER imperfection name:
Our proper bliss depends on what we blame.
Know thy own point: this kind,° this due degree
Of blindness, weakness, Heaven bestows on thee.
Submit—in this, or any other sphere,°
Secure to be as blest as thou canst bear:
Safe in the hand of one disposing power,
Or in the natal, or the mortal hour.
All nature is but art, unknown to thee;
All chance, direction, which thou canst not see;   290
All discord, harmony, not understood;
All partial evil, universal good:
And, spite of pride, in erring reason's spite,
One truth is clear, 'Whatever is, is RIGHT.'°

EPISTLE II

ARGUMENT

Of the Nature and State of Man *with respect to* Himself,
as an Individual

I. *The business of Man not to pry into* God, *but to study* himself. *His*
Middle Nature; *his powers and frailties,* v. 1 to 18. *The limits of his*
capacity, v. 19, &c. II. *The two principles of Man,* Self-love *and* Reason,
both necessary, v. 53, &c. Self-love *the stronger, and why,* v. 67, &c. *Their*
end the same, v. 81, &c. III. *The* PASSIONS, *and their use,* v. 93 to 130.
The predominant passion, *and its force,* v. 131 to 160. *Its necessity, in*

281 f. The consequence of all, the absolute submission due to Providence, both
as to our present and future state.
   Ep. II. Of the NATURE and STATE of MAN as an INDIVIDUAL.

directing men to different purposes, v. 165, &c. *Its providential use, in fixing our principle, and ascertaining our virtue,* v. 177. IV. *Virtue and* Vice *joined in our* mixed nature; *the limits near, yet the things* separate *and* evident: *What is the office of* reason, v. 203 to 216. V. *How odious* vice *in itself, and how we deceive ourselves into it,* v. 217. VI. *That, however, the* ends of Providence *and* general good *are answered in our passions and imperfections,* v. 238, &c. *How usefully these are distributed to all* orders of Men, v. 241. *How useful they are to* Society, v. 249. *And to the* Individuals, v. 261. *In every* state, *and every* age *of life,* v. 271, &c.

> Know then thyself, presume not God to scan;°   1
> The proper study of mankind is Man.
> Placed on this isthmus of a middle state,
> A being darkly wise, and rudely great:
> With too much knowledge for the sceptic side,
> With too much weakness for the stoic's pride,
> He hangs between; in doubt to act, or rest,
> In doubt to deem himself a god, or beast;
> In doubt his mind or body to prefer,
> Born but to die, and reasoning but to err;   10
> Alike in ignorance, his reason such,
> Whether he thinks too little, or too much:
> Chaos of thought and passion, all confused;
> Still by himself abused, or disabused;
> Created half to rise, and half to fall;
> Great lord of all things, yet a prey to all;
> Sole judge of truth, in endless error hurled:
> The glory, jest, and riddle of the world!
>
>   Go, wondrous creature! mount where science guides,
> Go, measure earth, weigh air, and state the tides;   20
> Instruct the planets in what orbs to run,
> Correct old time, and regulate the sun;
> Go, soar with Plato to th'empyreal sphere,°
> To the first good, first perfect, and first fair;
> Or tread the mazy round his followers trod,
> And quitting sense call imitating God;
> As Eastern priests in giddy circles run,
> And turn their heads to imitate the sun.

---

1 f. The business of Man not to pry into God, but to study himself. His middle nature, his powers, frailties, and the limits of his capacity.

Go, teach eternal wisdom how to rule—
Then drop into thyself, and be a fool!   30

   Superior beings, when of late they saw
A mortal man unfold all nature's law,
Admired such wisdom in an earthly shape,
And showed a NEWTON as we show an ape.

   Could he, whose rules the rapid comet bind,
Describe or fix one movement of his mind?
Who saw its fires here rise, and there descend,
Explain his own beginning, or his end?
Alas what wonder! Man's superior part
Unchecked may rise, and climb from art to art: 40
But when his own great work is but begun,
What reason weaves, by passion is undone.

   Trace science then, with modesty thy guide;
First strip off all her equipage° of pride,
Deduct what is but vanity, or dress,
Or learning's luxury, or idleness;
Or tricks to show the stretch of human brain,
Mere curious pleasure, or ingenious pain:
Expunge the whole, or lop th'excrescent parts
Of all, our vices have created arts: 50
Then see how little the remaining sum,
Which served the past, and must the times to come!

   II. Two principles in human nature reign;
Self-love, to urge, and reason, to restrain;
Nor this a good, nor that a bad we call,
Each works its end, to move or govern all:
And to their proper operation still,
Ascribe all good; to their improper, ill.

   Self-love, the spring of motion, acts° the soul;
Reason's comparing balance rules the whole.   60
Man, but for that, no action could attend,
And, but for this, were active to no end;
Fixed like a plant on his peculiar° spot,
To draw nutrition, propagate, and rot;
Or, meteor-like, flame lawless through the void,
Destroying others, by himself destroyed.

53 f. The TWO PRINCIPLES of MAN, SELF-LOVE and REASON, both necessary,
59. Self-love the stronger, and why? 67. their end the same, 81.

  Most strength the moving principle requires;
Active its task, it prompts, impels, inspires.
Sedate and quiet the comparing lies,
Formed but to check, deliberate, and advise.   70
Self-love still stronger, as its objects nigh;
Reasons at distance, and in prospect lie:
That sees immediate good by present sense;
Reason, the future and the consequence.
Thicker than arguments, temptations throng,
At best more watchful this, but that more strong.
The action of the stronger to suspend
Reason still use, to reason still attend:
Attention, habit and experience gains,
Each strengthens reason, and self-love restrains.   80
  Let subtle schoolmen teach these friends to fight,
More studious to divide than to unite,
And grace and virtue, sense and reason split,
With all the rash dexterity of wit:
Wits, just like fools, at war about a name,
Have full as oft no meaning, or the same.
Self-love and reason to one end aspire,
Pain their aversion, pleasure their desire;
But greedy that,° its object would devour,
This taste the honey, and not wound the flower: 90
Pleasure, or wrong or° rightly understood,
Our greatest evil, or our greatest good.
  III. Modes of self-love the passions we may call:
'Tis real good, or seeming, moves them all:
But since not every good we can divide,
And reason bids us for our own provide;
Passions, though selfish, if their means be fair,
List under reason, and deserve her care;
Those, that imparted,° court a nobler aim,
Exalt their kind, and take some virtue's name.   100
  In lazy apathy let Stoics boast
Their virtue fixed; 'tis fixed as in a frost,
Contracted all, retiring to the breast;
But strength of mind is exercise, not rest:
The rising tempest puts in act the soul,

93 f. The PASSIONS, and their use.

Parts it may ravage, but preserves the whole.
On life's vast ocean diversely we sail,
Reason the card,° but passion is the gale;
Nor God alone in the still calm we find,
He mounts the storm, and walks upon the wind.   110
   Passions, like elements, though born to fight,
Yet, mixed and softened, in his work unite:°
These 'tis enough to temper and employ;
But what composes Man, can Man destroy?
Suffice that reason keep to nature's road,
Subject, compound them, follow her and God.
Love, hope, and joy, fair pleasure's smiling train,
Hate, fear, and grief, the family of pain;
These mixed with art, and to due bounds confined,
Make and maintain the balance of the mind: 120
The lights and shades, whose well accorded strife
Gives all the strength and colour of our life.
   Pleasures are ever in our hands or eyes,
And when in act they cease, in prospect rise;
Present to grasp, and future still to find,
The whole employ of body and of mind.
All spread their charms, but charm not all alike;
On different senses different objects strike;
Hence different passions more or less inflame,
As strong or weak, the organs of the frame;   130
And hence one master passion in the breast,
Like Aaron's serpent,° swallows up the rest.
   As Man, perhaps, the moment of his breath,
Receives the lurking principle of death;
The young disease, that must subdue at length,
Grows with his growth, and strengthens with his strength:
So, cast and mingled with his very frame,
The mind's disease, its ruling passion came;
Each vital humour which should feed the whole,
Soon flows to this, in body and in soul.   140
Whatever warms the heart, or fills the head,
As the mind opens, and its functions spread,
Imagination plies her dangerous art,

133 f. The PREDOMINANT PASSION and its force. The use of this doctrine, as
applied to the knowledge of mankind, is one of the subjects of the second book.

And pours it all upon the peccant° part.
   Nature its mother, habit is its nurse;
Wit, spirit, faculties, but make it worse;
Reason itself but gives it edge and power;
As Heaven's blessed beam turns vinegar more sour;
We, wretched subjects though to lawful sway,
In this weak queen, some favourite still obey.   150
Ah! if she lends not arms, as well as rules,
What can she more than tell us we are fools?
Teach us to mourn our nature, not to mend,
A sharp accuser, but a helpless friend!
Or from a judge turn pleader, to persuade
The choice we make, or justify it made;
Proud of an easy conquest all along,
She but removes weak passions for the strong:
So, when small humours gather to a gout,
The doctor fancies he has driven them out.°   160
   Yes, Nature's road must ever be preferred;°
Reason is here no guide, but still a guard:
'Tis hers to rectify, not overthrow,
And treat this passion more as friend than foe:
A mightier power the strong direction sends,
And several men impels to several ends.
Like varying winds, by other passions tossed,
This drives them constant to a certain coast.
Let power or knowledge, gold or glory, please,
Or (oft more strong than all) the love of ease;   170
Through life 'tis followed, ev'n at life's expense;
The merchant's toil, the sage's indolence,
The monk's humility, the hero's pride,
All, all alike, find reason on their side.
   Th' eternal art educing good from ill,
Grafts on this passion our best principle:
'Tis thus the mercury of Man° is fixed,
Strong grows the virtue with his nature mixed;
The dross cements what else were too refined,

165 f. Its necessity, in directing men to different purposes. The particular application of this to the several pursuits of men, and the general good resulting thence, falls also into the succeeding books.

175 f. Its providential use, in fixing our PRINCIPLE, and ascertaining our VIRTUE.

And in one interest body acts with mind.

    As fruits ungrateful° to the planter's care
On savage stocks inserted learn to bear;
The surest virtues thus from passions shoot,
Wild nature's vigour working at the root.
What crops of wit and honesty appear
From spleen, from obstinacy, hate, or fear!
See anger, zeal and fortitude supply;
Ev'n avarice, prudence; sloth, philosophy;
Lust, through some certain strainers well refined,
Is gentle love, and charms all womankind: 190
Envy, to which th'ignoble mind's a slave,
Is emulation in the learned or brave:
Nor virtue, male or female, can we name,
But what will grow on pride, or grow on shame.°

    Thus Nature gives us (let it check our pride)
The virtue nearest to our vice allied:
Reason the bias° turns to good from ill,
And Nero reigns a Titus,° if he will.
The fiery soul abhorred in Catiline,
In Decius° charms, in Curtius° is divine.   200
The same ambition can destroy or save,
And makes a patriot as it makes a knave.

    IV. This light and darkness in our chaos joined,
What shall divide? The God within the mind.°

    Extremes in Nature equal ends produce,
In Man they join to some mysterious use;
Though each by turns the other's bound invade,
As, in some well-wrought picture, light and shade,
And oft so mix, the difference is too nice
Where ends the virtue, or begins the vice.   210

    Fools! who from hence into the notion fall,
That vice or virtue there is none at all.
If white and black blend, soften, and unite
A thousand ways, is there no black or white?
Ask your own heart, and nothing is so plain;
'Tis to mistake them, costs the time and pain.

---

195 f. Virtue and Vice joined in our mixed nature; the limits near, yet the things separate, and evident. The office of reason.

V. Vice is a monster of so frightful mien,
As, to be hated, needs but to be seen;
Yet seen too oft, familiar with her face,
We first endure, then pity, then embrace.   220
But where th'extreme of vice, was ne'er agreed:
Ask where's the North? at York, 'tis on the Tweed;
In Scotland, at the Orcades;° and there,
At Greenland, Zembla,° or the Lord knows where:
No creature owns it in the first degree,
But thinks his neighbour farther gone than he.
Ev'n those who dwell beneath its very zone,
Or never feel the rage, or never own;
What happier natures shrink at with affright,
The hard inhabitant contends is right.   230
VI. Virtuous and vicious every man must be,
Few in th'extreme, but all in the degree;
The rogue and fool by fits is fair and wise,
And ev'n the best, by fits, what they despise.
'Tis but by parts we follow good or ill,
For, vice or virtue, self directs it still;
Each individual seeks a several° goal;
But HEAVEN's great view is one, and that the whole:
That counter-works each folly and caprice;
That disappoints th'effect of every vice: 240
That happy frailties to all ranks applied,
Shame to the virgin, to the matron pride,
Fear to the statesman, rashness to the chief,
To kings presumption, and to crowds belief:
That virtue's ends from vanity can raise,
Which seeks no interest, no reward but praise;
And build on wants, and on defects of mind,
The joy, the peace, the glory of mankind.
Heaven forming each on other to depend,
A master, or a servant, or a friend,   250
Bids each on other for assistance call,

217 f. VICE odious in itself, and how we deceive ourselves into it.

231 f. The ENDS of PROVIDENCE and general good answered in our passions and imperfections. How usefully these are distributed to all orders of men.

249 f. How useful these are to SOCIETY in general, and to INDIVIDUALS in particular, in every STATE, 261, and every AGE of life, 271.

Till one man's weakness grows the strength of all.
Wants, frailties, passions, closer still ally
The common interest, or endear the tie:
To these we owe true friendship, love sincere,
Each home-felt joy that life inherits here:
Yet from the same we learn, in its decline,
Those joys, those loves, those interests to resign:
Taught half by reason, half by mere decay,
To welcome death, and calmly pass away.   260

Whate'er the passion, knowledge, fame, or pelf,°
Not one will change his neighbour with himself.
The learned is happy nature to explore,
The fool is happy that he knows no more;
The rich is happy in the plenty given,
The poor contents him with the care of Heaven.
See the blind beggar dance, the cripple sing,
The sot a hero, lunatic a king;
The starving chemist° in his golden views
Supremely blessed, the poet in his muse.   270

See some strange comfort every state attend,
And pride bestowed on all, a common friend;
See some fit passion every age supply,
Hope travels through, nor quits us when we die.

Behold the child, by Nature's kindly law,
Pleased with a rattle, tickled with a straw:
Some livelier plaything gives his youth delight,
A little louder, but as empty quite:
Scarves,° garters,° gold, amuse his riper stage;
And beads° and prayer-books are the toys of age: 280
Pleased with this bauble still, as that before;
Till tired he sleeps, and life's poor play is o'er!°

Meanwhile opinion gilds with varying rays
Those painted clouds that beautify our days;
Each want of happiness by hope supplied,
And each vacuity of sense by pride:
These build as fast as knowledge can destroy;
In folly's cup still laughs the bubble,° joy;
One prospect lost, another still we gain;

283 f. See farther, of the use of this principle in Man, Epist. 3, vv. 121, 124,
135, 145, 199 f., 318. And Epist. 4, vv. 358 and 368.

And not a vanity is given in vain; 290
Ev'n mean self-love becomes, by force divine,
The scale to measure others wants by thine.
See! and confess, one comfort still must rise,
'Tis this, though Man's a fool, yet GOD IS WISE.

EPISTLE III

ARGUMENT

Of the Nature and State of Man with respect to Society

I. *The whole universe one system of society*, v. 7, &c. *Nothing made wholly for itself, nor yet wholly for* another, v. 27. *The happiness of animals mutual*, v. 49. II. *Reason or* instinct *operate alike to the good of each individual*, v. 79. *Reason or* instinct *operate also to Society, in all animals*, v. 109. III. *How far* Society *carried by instinct*, v. 115. *How much farther by reason*, v. 131. IV. *Of that which is called the* State of Nature, v. 147. *Reason instructed by instinct in the invention of Arts*, v. 171, *and in the forms of* Society, v. 179. V. *Origin of political societies*, v. 199. *Origin of monarchy*, v. 209. *Patriarchal government*, v. 215. VI. *Origin of true religion and government, from the same principle, of love*, v. 231, &c. *Origin of superstition and tyranny, from the same principle, of fear*, v. 241, &c. *The influence of self-love operating to the* social *and* public *good*, v. 269. *Restoration of true religion and government on their first principle*, v. 283. *Mixed government*, v. 294. *Various forms of each, and the true end of all*, v. 303, &c.

Here then we rest: 'The universal cause   1
Acts to one end, but acts by various laws.'
In all the madness of superfluous health,
The trim of pride, the impudence of wealth,
Let this great truth be present night and day;
But most be present, if we preach or pray.
  Look round our world; behold the chain of love
Combining all below and all above.
See plastic nature° working to this end,

Ep. III. Of the NATURE and STATE of Man with respect to SOCIETY.
1 f. The whole universe one system of society.

The single atoms each to other tend,   10
Attract, attracted to, the next in place
Formed and impelled its neighbour to embrace.
See matter next, with various life endued,
Press to one centre still, the general good.
See dying vegetables life sustain,
See life dissolving vegetate again:
All forms that perish other forms supply,
(By turns we catch the vital breath, and die)
Like bubbles on the sea of matter borne,
They rise, they break, and to that sea return.   20
Nothing is foreign: parts relate to whole;
One all-extending, all-preserving soul
Connects each being, greatest with the least;
Made beast in aid of man, and man of beast;
All served, all serving! nothing stands alone;
The chain holds on, and where it ends, unknown.
    Has God, thou fool! worked solely for thy good,
Thy joy, thy pastime, thy attire, thy food?
Who for thy table feeds the wanton fawn,
For him as kindly spread the flowery lawn.   30
Is it for thee the lark ascends and sings?
Joy tunes his voice, joy elevates his wings:
Is it for thee the linnet pours his throat?
Loves of his own and raptures swell the note:
The bounding steed you pompously bestride,
Shares with his lord the pleasure and the pride:
Is thine alone the seed that strews the plain?
The birds of heaven shall vindicate° their grain:
Thine the full harvest of the golden year?
Part pays, and justly, the deserving steer: 40
The hog, that ploughs not nor obeys thy call,
Lives on the labours of this lord of all.
    Know, Nature's children all divide her care;
The fur that warms a monarch, warmed a bear.
While Man exclaims, 'See all things for my use!'
'See man for mine!' replies a pampered goose;
And just as short of reason he must fall,

27 f. Nothing made wholly for itself, nor yet wholly for another, but the happiness
of all animals mutual.

Who thinks all made for one, not one for all.
    Grant that the powerful still the weak control;
Be Man the wit and tyrant of the whole: 50
Nature that tyrant checks; he only knows,
And helps, another creature's wants and woes.
Say, will the falcon, stooping° from above,
Smit with her varying plumage, spare the dove?
Admires the jay the insect's gilded wings?
Or hears the hawk when Philomela° sings?
Man cares for all: to birds he gives his woods,
To beasts his pastures, and to fish his floods;
For some his interest prompts him to provide,
For more his pleasure, yet for more his pride: 60
All feed on one vain patron, and enjoy
Th'extensive blessing of his luxury.
That very life his learned hunger craves,
He saves from famine, from the savage° saves;
Nay, feasts the animal he dooms his feast,
And, till he ends the being, makes it blest;
Which sees no more the stroke, or feels the pain,
Than favoured Man by touch ethereal slain.
The creature had his feast of life before;
Thou too must perish, when thy feast is o'er.   70
    To each unthinking being, Heaven a friend,
Gives not the useless knowledge of its end:
To Man imparts it; but with such a view
As, while he dreads it, makes him hope it too:
The hour concealed, and so remote the fear,
Death still draws nearer, never seeming near.
Great standing miracle! that Heaven assigned
Its only thinking thing this turn of mind.
    II. Whether with reason, or with instinct blessed,
Know, all enjoy that power which suits them best;   80
To bliss alike by that direction tend,
And find the means proportioned to their end.
Say, where full instinct is th'unerring guide,

68. Several of the ancients, and many of the Orientals since, esteemed those who were struck by lightning as sacred persons, and the particular favourites of Heaven.

79 f. Reason or instinct alike operate to the good of each individual, and operate also to society, in all animals.

What Pope or Council° can they need beside?
Reason, however able, cool at best,
Cares not for service, or but serves when pressed,°
Stays till we call, and then not often near;
But honest instinct comes a volunteer;
Sure never to o'er-shoot, but just to hit,
While still too wide or short is human wit;   90
Sure by quick nature happiness to gain,
Which heavier reason labours at in vain.
This too serves always, reason never long;
One must go right, the other may go wrong.
See then the acting and comparing powers
One in their nature, which are two in ours,
And reason raise o'er instinct as you can,
In this 'tis God directs, in that 'tis Man.

   Who taught the nations of the field and wood
To shun their poison, and to choose their food?   100
Prescient, the tides or tempests to withstand,
Build on the wave, or arch beneath the sand?°
Who made the spider parallels design,
Sure as De Moivre,° without rule or line?
Who bid the stork, Columbus-like, explore
Heavens not his own, and worlds unknown before?
Who calls the council, states the certain day,
Who forms the phalanx, and who points the way?

   III. God, in the nature of each being, founds
Its proper bliss, and sets its proper bounds: 110
But as he framed a whole, the whole to bless,
On mutual wants built mutual happiness:
So from the first eternal ORDER ran,
And creature linked to creature, man to man.
Whate'er of life all-quickening ether keeps,
Or breathes through air, or shoots beneath the deeps,
Or pours profuse on earth; one nature feeds
The vital flame, and swells the genial° seeds.
Not man alone, but all that roam the wood,
Or wing the sky, or roll along the flood,   120
Each loves itself, but not itself alone,

104. De Moivre, an eminent mathematician.
115 f. How far SOCIETY carried by INSTINCT.

Each sex desires alike, till two are one.
Nor ends the pleasure with the fierce embrace;
They love themselves, a third time, in their race.
Thus beast and bird their common charge attend,
The mothers nurse it, and the sires defend;
The young dismissed to wander earth or air,
There stops the instinct, and there ends the care;
The link dissolves, each seeks a fresh embrace,
Another love succeeds, another race.   130
A longer care Man's helpless kind demands;
That longer care contracts more lasting bands:
Reflection, reason, still the ties improve,
At once extend the interest, and the love;
With choice we fix, with sympathy we burn;
Each virtue in each passion takes its turn;
And still new needs, new helps, new habits rise,
That graft benevolence on charities.
Still as one brood, and as another rose,
These natural love maintained, habitual those: 140
The last, scarce ripened into perfect Man,
Saw helpless him from whom their life began:
Memory and forecast just returns engage,
That pointed back to youth, this on to age;
While pleasure, gratitude, and hope, combined,
Still spread the interest, and preserved the kind.°
     IV. Nor think, in NATURE'S STATE they blindly trod;
The state of nature was the reign of God:
Self-love and social at her birth began,
Union the bond of all things, and of Man.   150
Pride then was not; nor arts, that pride to aid;
Man walked with beast, joint tenant of the shade;
The same his table, and the same his bed;
No murder clothed him, and no murder fed.
In the same temple, the resounding wood,
All vocal beings hymned their equal God:
The shrine with gore unstained, with gold undressed,
Unbribed, unbloody, stood the blameless priest:
Heaven's attribute was universal care,

131 f. How much farther SOCIETY is carried by REASON.
147 f. Of the STATE of NATURE: That it was SOCIAL.

And Man's prerogative to rule, but spare.   160
Ah! how unlike the man of times to come!
Of half that live the butcher and the tomb;
Who, foe to Nature, hears the general groan,
Murders their species, and betrays his own.
But just disease to luxury succeeds,
And every death its own avenger breeds;
The fury-passions from that blood began,
And turned on Man a fiercer savage, Man.
   See him from nature rising slow to art!
To copy instinct then was reason's part;   170
Thus then to Man the voice of Nature spake—
'Go, from the creatures thy instructions take:
Learn from the birds what food the thickets yield;
Learn from the beasts the physic of the field;
Thy arts of building from the bee receive;
Learn of the mole to plough, the worm to weave;
Learn of the little nautilus to sail,
Spread the thin oar, and catch the driving gale.
Here too all forms of social union find,
And hence let reason, late, instruct mankind: 180
Here subterranean works and cities see;
There towns aerial on the waving tree.
Learn each small people's genius, policies,
The ant's republic, and the realm of bees;°
How those in common all their wealth bestow,
And anarchy without confusion know;
And these for ever, though a monarch reign,
Their separate cells and properties maintain.
Mark what unvaried laws preserve each state,
Laws wise as nature, and as fixed as fate.   190
In vain thy reason finer webs shall draw,
Entangle justice in her net of law,

169 f. Reason instructed by instinct in the invention of ARTS, and in the FORMS of society.

177. Oppian. Halieut. lib. i. describes this fish in the following manner: 'They swim on the surface of the sea, on the back of their shells, which exactly resembles the hulk of a ship; they raise two feet like masts, and extend a membrane between, which serves as a sail, the other two feet they employ as oars at the side. They are usually seen in the Mediterranean.'

And right, too rigid, harden into wrong;
Still for the strong too weak, the weak too strong.
Yet go! and thus o'er all the creatures sway,
Thus let the wiser make the rest obey,
And for those arts mere instinct could afford,
Be crowned as monarchs, or as gods adored.'
   V. Great Nature spoke; observant men obeyed;
Cities were built, societies were made: 200
Here rose one little state; another near
Grew by like means, and joined, through love or fear.
Did here the trees with ruddier burdens bend,
And there the streams in purer rills descend?
What war could ravish, commerce could bestow,
And he returned a friend, who came a foe.
Converse and love mankind might strongly draw,
When love was liberty, and nature law.
Thus states were formed; the name of king unknown,
Till common interest placed the sway in one.   210
'Twas VIRTUE ONLY (or in arts or arms,
Diffusing blessings, or averting harms)
The same which in a sire the sons obeyed,
A prince the father of a people made.
   VI. Till then, by Nature crowned, each patriarch sate,
King, priest, and parent of his growing state;
On him, their second Providence, they hung,
Their law his eye, their oracle his tongue.
He from the wondering furrow called the food,
Taught to command the fire, control the flood,   220
Draw forth the monsters of th'abyss profound,
Or fetch th'aerial eagle to the ground.°
Till drooping, sickening, dying they began
Whom they revered as God to mourn as Man:
Then, looking up from sire to sire, explored
One great first father, and that first adored.
Or plain tradition that this all begun,
Conveyed unbroken faith from sire to son,
The worker from the work distinct was known,

199 f. Origin of POLITICAL SOCIETIES.
210 f. Origin of MONARCHY.
215 f. Origin of PATRIARCHAL GOVERNMENT.

And simple reason never sought but one: 230
E'er wit oblique had broke that steady light.
Man, like his Maker, saw that all was right,°
To virtue, in the paths of pleasure, trod,
And owned a Father when he owned a God.
LOVE all the faith, and all th'allegiance then;
For Nature knew no right divine in men,
No ill could fear in God; and understood
A sovereign being but a sovereign good.
True faith, true policy, united ran,
That was but love of God, and this of Man.   240

    Who first taught souls enslaved, and realms undone,
Th' enormous° faith of many made for one;
That proud exception to all Nature's laws,
T'invert the world, and counter-work its cause?
Force first made conquest, and that conquest, law;
Till superstition taught the tyrant awe,
Then shared the tyranny, then lent it aid,
And gods of conquerors, slaves of subjects made:
She, 'midst the lightning's blaze, and thunder's sound,
When rocked the mountains, and when groaned the ground,
She taught the weak to bend, the proud to pray,   251
To power unseen, and mightier far than they:
She, from the rending earth and bursting skies,
Saw gods descend, and fiends infernal rise:
Here fixed the dreadful, there the blessed abodes;
Fear made her devils, and weak hope her gods;
Gods partial, changeful, passionate, unjust,
Whose attributes were rage, revenge, or lust;
Such as the souls of cowards might conceive,
And, formed like tyrants, tyrants would believe.   260
Zeal then, not charity, became the guide,
And hell was built on spite, and heaven on pride.
Then sacred seemed th'ethereal vault no more;
Altars grew marble then, and reeked with gore:
Then first the flamen° tasted living food;
Next his grim idol smeared with human blood;

235 f. Origin of TRUE RELIGION and GOVERNMENT from the principle of LOVE:
and of SUPERSTITION and TYRANNY, from that of FEAR.

With Heaven's own thunders shook the world below,
And played the God an engine on his foe.
　So drives self-love, through just and through unjust,
To one man's power, ambition, lucre, lust:　　　　　　270
The same self-love, in all, becomes the cause
Of what restrains him, government and laws.
For, what one likes if others like as well,
What serves one will, when many wills rebel?
How shall he keep, what, sleeping or awake,
A weaker may surprise, a stronger take?
His safety must his liberty restrain:
All join to guard what each desires to gain.
Forced into virtue thus by self-defence,
Ev'n kings learned justice and benevolence:　　　　　280
Self-love forsook the path it first pursued,
And found the private in the public good.
　'Twas then, the studious head or generous mind,
Follower of God or friend of humankind,
Poet or patriot, rose but to restore
The faith and moral,° Nature gave before;
Relumed her ancient light, not kindled new;
If not God's image, yet his shadow drew:
Taught power's due use to people and to kings,
Taught nor to slack, nor strain its tender strings,　　290
The less, or greater, set so justly true,
That touching° one must strike the other too;
Till jarring interests of themselves create
Th'according music of a well-mixed state.
Such is the world's great harmony, that springs
From order, union, full consent of things!
Where small and great, where weak and mighty, made
To serve, not suffer, strengthen, not invade,
More powerful each as needful to the rest,
And, in proportion as it blesses, blessed,　　　　　　300
Draw to one point, and to one centre bring

269 f. The influence of SELF-LOVE operating to the SOCIAL and Public Good.

283 f. Restoration of true religion and government on their first principle. Mixed governments; with the various forms of each, and the TRUE USE OF ALL. The deduction and application of the foregoing principles, with the use or abuse of civil and ecclesiastical policy, was intended for the subject of the third book.

Beast, man, or angel, servant, lord, or king.
   For forms of government let fools contest;
Whate'er is best administered is best:
For modes of faith let graceless zealots fight;
His can't be wrong whose life is in the right:
In faith and hope the world will disagree,
But all mankind's concern is charity:
All must be false that thwart this one great end,
And all of God, that bless mankind or mend.   310
   Man, like the generous° vine, supported lives;
The strength he gains is from th'embrace he gives.
On their own axis as the planets run,
Yet make at once their circle round the sun:
So two consistent motions act° the soul;
And one regards itself, and one the whole.
   Thus God and Nature linked the general frame,
And bade self-love and social be the same.

EPISTLE IV

ARGUMENT

Of the Nature and State of Man with respect to Happiness

I. *False notions of happiness, philosophical and popular, answered from* v. 19
to 76. II. *It is the end of all men, and attainable by all,* v. 29. *God intends
happiness to be* equal; *and to be so, it must be* social, *since all particular
happiness depends on general, and since he governs by* general, *not particular
laws,* v. 35. *As it is necessary for* order, *and the peace and welfare of* society,
that external goods *should be* unequal, *happiness is not made to consist in
these,* v. 49. *But, notwithstanding that inequality, the* balance *of happiness
among mankind is kept even by Providence, by the two passions of* Hope *and*
Fear, v. 67. III. *What the happiness of* Individuals *is, as far as is consistent
with the constitution of this world; and that the* good Man *has here the
advantage,* v. 77. *The error of imputing to* Virtue *what are only the calamities
of* Nature, *or of* Fortune, v. 93. IV. *The folly of expecting that God should
alter his general laws in favour of particulars,* v. 111. V. *That we are not
judges who are good; but that, whoever they are, they must be happiest,* v. 131,

Ep. IV. Of the Nature and State of MAN, with respect to HAPPINESS.

&c. VI. *That* external goods *are not the proper rewards, but often inconsistent with, or destructive of virtue,* v. 167. *That even these can make no man happy without virtue: Instanced in* Riches, v. 185. Honours, v. 193. Nobility, v. 205. Greatness, v. 217. Fame, v. 237. Superior Talents, v. 259, &c. *With pictures of human infelicity in men possessed of them all,* v. 269, &c. VII. *That* Virtue only *constitutes a happiness, whose object is* universal, *and whose prospect* eternal, v. 309, &c. *That the* perfection *of* Virtue *and* Happiness *consists in a* conformity *to the* ORDER *of* PROVIDENCE *here, and a* Resignation *to it here and hereafter,* v. 327, &c.

Oh happiness! our being's end and aim!   1
Good, pleasure, ease, content! whate'er thy name:
That something still which prompts th'eternal sigh,
For which we bear to live, or dare to die,
Which still so near us, yet beyond us lies,
O'erlooked, seen double, by the fool, and wise.
Plant of celestial seed! if dropped below,
Say, in what mortal soil though deignst to grow?
Fair opening to some court's propitious shine,
Or deep with diamonds in the flaming mine?°   10
Twined with the wreaths Parnassian laurels yield,
Or reaped in iron harvests of the field?
Where grows?—where grows it not?—If vain our toil,
We ought to blame the culture, not the soil:
Fixed to no spot is happiness sincere,°
'Tis nowhere to be found, or everywhere;
'Tis never to be bought, but always free,
And fled from monarchs, ST JOHN! dwells with thee.
    Ask of the learned the way, the learned are blind,
This bids to serve, and that to shun mankind;   20
Some place the bliss in action, some in ease,
Those call it pleasure, and contentment these;
Some sunk to beasts, find pleasure end in pain;
Some swelled to gods, confess ev'n virtue vain;
Or indolent, to each extreme they fall,
To trust in everything, or doubt of all.
    Who thus define it, say they more or less
Than this, that happiness is happiness?
    II. Take Nature's path, and mad opinion's leave;

29 f. HAPPINESS the END of all men, and attainable by all.

All states can reach it, and all heads conceive;   30
Obvious her goods, in no extreme they dwell,
There needs but thinking right, and meaning well;
And mourn our various portions as we please,
Equal is common sense, and common ease.

Remember, Man, 'the universal cause
Acts not by partial, but by general laws;'
And makes what happiness we justly call
Submit not in the good of one, but all.
There's not a blessing individuals find,
But some way leans and hearkens to the kind.   40
No bandit fierce, no tyrant mad with pride,
No caverned hermit, rests self-satisfied;
Who most to shun or hate mankind pretend,
Seek an admirer, or would fix a friend.
Abstract what others feel, what others think,
All pleasures sicken, and all glories sink:
Each has his share; and who would more obtain,
Shall find, the pleasure pays not half the pain.

ORDER is Heaven's first law; and this confessed,
Some are, and must be, greater than the rest,   50
More rich, more wise; but who infers from hence
That such are happier, shocks all common sense.
Heaven to mankind impartial we confess,
If all are equal in their happiness;
But mutual wants this happiness increase;
All Nature's difference keeps all Nature's peace.
Condition, circumstance is not the thing;
Bliss is the same in subject or in king,
In who obtain defence, or who defend,
In him who is, or him who finds a friend: 60
Heaven breathes through every member of the whole
One common blessing, as one common soul.
But fortune's gifts if each alike possessed,
And each were equal, must not all contest?
If then to all men happiness was meant,

35 f. GOD governs by general not particular laws; intends happiness to be equal; and to be so, it must be social, since all particular happiness depends on general.

49. It is necessary for ORDER and the common peace, that external goods be unequal, therefore happiness is not constituted in these.

God in externals could not place content.
    Fortune her gifts may variously dispose,
And these be happy called, unhappy those;
But Heaven's just balance equal will appear,
While those are placed in hope, and these in fear: 70
Not present good or ill, the joy or curse,
But future views of better, or of worse.
    Oh sons of earth! attempt ye still to rise,
By mountains piled on mountains, to the skies?
Heaven still with laughter the vain toil surveys,
And buries madmen in the heaps they raise.°
    III. Know, all the good that individuals find,
Or God and Nature meant to mere mankind,
Reason's whole pleasure, all the joys of sense,
Lie in three words, health, peace, and competence.°   80
But health consists with temperance alone;
And peace, oh virtue! Peace is all thy own.
The good or bad the gifts of fortune gain;
But these less taste them, as they worse obtain.
Say, in pursuit of profit or delight,
Who risk the most, that take wrong means, or right?
Of vice or virtue, whether blest or cursed,
Which meets contempt, or which compassion first?
Count all th'advantage prosperous vice attains,
'Tis but what virtue flies from and disdains: 90
And grant the bad what happiness they would,
One they must want, which is, to pass for good.
    Oh blind to truth, and God's whole scheme below,
Who fancy bliss to vice, to virtue woe!
Who sees and follows that great scheme the best,
Best knows the blessing, and will most be blessed.
But fools, the good alone unhappy call,
For ills or accidents that chance to all.

67 f. The balance of human happiness kept equal (notwithstanding externals) by Hope and Fear. The exemplification of this truth, by a view of the equality of happiness in the several particular stations of life, were designed for the subject of a future Epistle.

77 f. In what the happiness of individuals consists, and that the Good Man has the advantage, even in this world.

93 f. That no man is unhappy through Virtue.

See FALKLAND° dies, the virtuous and the just!
See god-like TURENNE° prostrate on the dust!   100
See SIDNEY° bleeds amid the martial strife!
Was this their virtue, or contempt of life?
Say, was it virtue, more though Heaven ne'er gave,
Lamented DIGBY!° sunk thee to the grave?
Tell me, if virtue made the son expire,
Why, full of days and honour, lives the sire?
Why drew Marseille's good bishop° purer breath,
When Nature sickened, and each gale was death!
Or why so long (in life if long can be)
Lent Heaven a parent° to the poor and me?   110
     IV. What makes all physical or moral ill?
There deviates Nature, and here wanders will.
God sends not ill; if rightly understood,
Or partial ill is universal good,
Or change admits, or Nature lets it fall,
Short, and but rare, till Man improved it all.
We just as wisely might of Heaven complain
That righteous Abel° was destroyed by Cain;
As that the virtuous son is ill at ease
When his lewd father gave the dire disease.°   120
Think we, like some weak prince, th'eternal cause,
Prone for his favourites to reverse his laws?
     Shall burning Etna, if a sage° requires,
Forget to thunder, and recall her fires?
On air or sea new motions be impressed,
Oh blameless Bethel!° to relieve thy breast?
When the loose mountain trembles from on high,
Shall gravitation cease, if you go by?
Or some old temple, nodding to its fall,
For Charters'° head reserve the hanging wall?   130
     V. But still this world (so fitted for the knave)
Contents us not. A better shall we have?
A kingdom of the just then let it be:
But first consider how those just agree.
The good must merit God's peculiar care;
But who, but God, can tell us who they are?
One thinks on Calvin Heaven's own spirit fell,
Another deems him instrument of hell;
If Calvin feel Heaven's blessing, or its rod,

This cries there is, and that, there is no God.   140
What shocks one part will edify the rest,
Nor with one system can they all be blest.
The very best will variously incline,
And what rewards your virtue, punish mine.
'Whatever IS, is RIGHT'—This world, 'tis true,
Was made for Caesar°—but for Titus too:
And which more blessed? who chained his country, say,
Or he whose virtue sighed to lose a day?
   'But sometimes virtue starves, while vice is fed.'
What then? Is the reward of virtue bread?   150
That, vice may merit; 'tis the price of toil;
The knave deserves it, when he tills the soil,
The knave deserves it, when he tempts the main,
Where folly fights for kings, or dives for gain.
The good man may be weak, be indolent;
Nor is his claim to plenty, but content.
But grant him riches, your demand is o'er?
'No—shall the good want health, the good want power?'
Add health, and power, and every earthly thing;
'Why bounded power? why private? why no king?'   160
Nay, why external for internal given?
Why is not Man a God, and earth a heaven?
Who ask and reason thus, will scarce conceive
God gives enough, while he has more to give:
Immense the power, immense were the demand;
Say, at what part of nature will they stand?
   VI. What nothing earthly gives, or can destroy,
The soul's calm sunshine, and the heartfelt joy,
Is virtue's prize: a better would you fix?
Then give humility a coach and six,   170
Justice a conqueror's sword, or truth a gown,°
Or public spirit its great cure, a crown.
Weak, foolish man! will Heaven reward us there
With the same trash mad mortals wish for here?
The boy and man an individual makes,

---

167 f. That external goods are not the proper rewards of virtue; often inconsistent
with or destructive of it; but that all these can make no man happy without virtue.
Instanced in each of them. 1. Riches. 2. Honours. 3. Titles. 4. Birth. 5. Greatness.
6. Fame. 7. Superior Parts.

Yet sighst thou now for apples and for cakes?
Go, like the Indian, in another life
Expect thy dog, thy bottle, and thy wife:
As well as dream such trifles are assigned,
As toys and empires, for a god-like mind.   180
Rewards, that either would to virtue bring
No joy, or be destructive of the thing:
How oft by these at sixty are undone
The virtues of a saint at twenty-one!
To whom can riches give repute, or trust,
Content, or pleasure, but the good and just?
Judges and senates have been bought for gold,
Esteem and love were never to be sold.
Oh fool! to think God hates the worthy mind,
The lover and the love of humankind,   190
Whose life is healthful, and whose conscience clear;
Because he wants a thousand pounds a year.

　　Honour and shame from no condition rise;
Act well your part, there all the honour lies.
Fortune in men has some small difference made,
One flaunts in rags, one flutters in brocade;
The cobbler aproned, and the parson gowned,
The friar hooded, and the monarch crowned.
'What differ more' (you cry) 'than crown and cowl?'
I'll tell you, friend! a wise man and a fool.   200
You'll find, if once the monarch° acts the monk,
Or, cobbler-like, the parson will be drunk,
Worth makes the man, and want of it, the fellow;
The rest is all but leather or prunella.°

　　Stuck o'er with titles and hung round with strings,°
That thou mayst be by kings, or whores of kings.
Boast the pure blood of an illustrious race,
In quiet flow from Lucrece to Lucrece:
But by your father's worth if yours you rate,
Count me those only who were good and great.   210
Go! if your ancient, but ignoble blood
Has crept through scoundrels ever since the flood,
Go! and pretend your family is young;
Nor own, your fathers have been fools so long.
What can ennoble sots, or slaves, or cowards?
Alas! not all the blood of all the HOWARDS.°

Look next on greatness; say where greatness lies?
'Where, but among the heroes and the wise?'
Heroes are much the same, the point's agreed,
From Macedonia's madman° to the Swede;°   220
The whole strange purpose of their lives, to find
Or make, an enemy of all mankind!
Not one looks backward, onward still he goes,
Yet ne'er looks forward farther than his nose.
No less alike the politic and wise;
All sly slow things, with circumspective eyes:
Men in their loose unguarded hours they take,
Not that themselves are wise, but others weak.
But grant that those can conquer, these can cheat;
'Tis phrase absurd to call a villain great: 230
Who wickedly is wise, or madly brave,
Is but the more a fool, the more a knave.
Who noble ends by noble means obtains,
Or failing, smiles in exile or in chains,
Like good Aurelius° let him reign, or bleed
Like Socrates, that Man is great indeed.

What's fame? a fancied life in others' breath,
A thing beyond us, ev'n before our death.
Just what you hear, you have, and what's unknown
The same (my Lord) if Tully's,° or your own.   240
All that we feel of it begins and ends
In the small circle of our foes or friends;
To all beside as much an empty shade,
An Eugene° living, as a Caesar dead,
Alike or when, or where, they shone, or shine,
Or on the Rubicon, or on the Rhine.
A wit's a feather, and a chief a rod;°
An honest man's the noblest work of God.
Fame but from death a villain's name can save,
As justice tears his body from the grave,°   250
When what t'oblivion better were resigned,
Is hung on high, to poison half mankind.
All fame is foreign, but of true desert,
Plays round the head, but comes not to the heart:
One self-approving hour whole years outweighs
Of stupid starers, and of loud huzzas;
And more true joy Marcellus° exiled feels,

Than Caesar with a senate at his heels.
　　In parts superior what advantage lies?
Tell (for you can) what is it to be wise?   260
'Tis but to know how little can be known;
To see all others faults, and feel our own:
Condemned in business or in arts to drudge,
Without a second, or without a judge:
Truths would you teach, or save a sinking land?
All fear, none aid you, and few understand.
Painful preeminence! yourself to view
Above life's weakness, and its comforts too.
　　Bring then these blessings to a strict account,
Make fair deductions, see to what they mount.   270
How much of other each is sure to cost;
How each for other oft is wholly lost;
How inconsistent greater goods with these;
How sometimes life is risked, and always ease:
Think, and if still the things thy envy call,
Say, wouldst thou be the man to whom they fall?
To sigh for ribbons° if thou art so silly,
Mark how they grace Lord Umbra, or Sir Billy:
Is yellow dirt the passion of thy life?
Look but on Gripus,° or on Gripus' wife: 280
If parts allure thee, think how Bacon shined,
The wisest, brightest, meanest of mankind,
Or ravished with the whistling of a name,
See Cromwell, damned to everlasting fame!
If all, united, thy ambition call,
From ancient story learn to scorn them all.
There, in the rich, the honoured, famed, and great,
See the false scale of happiness complete!
In hearts of kings, or arms of queens who lay,
How happy! those to ruin, these betray.   290
Mark by what wretched steps their glory grows,
From dirt and seaweed as proud Venice rose;
In each how guilt and greatness equal ran,
And all that raised the hero, sunk the man:
Now Europe's laurels on their brows behold,
But stained with blood, or ill exchanged for gold:
Then see them broke with toils, or sunk in ease,
Or infamous for plundered provinces.

Oh wealth ill-fated! which no act of fame
E'er taught to shine, or sanctified from shame!   300
What greater bliss attends their close of life?
Some greedy minion, or imperious wife,
The trophied arches, storied halls invade
And haunt their slumbers in the pompous shade.
Alas! not dazzled with their noontide ray,
Compute the morn and evening to the day;
The whole amount of that enormous° fame,
A tale, that blends their glory with their shame!°
   VII. Know then this truth (enough for Man to know)
'Virtue alone is happiness below.'   310
The only point where human bliss stands still,
And tastes the good without the fall to ill;
Where only merit constant pay receives,
Is blessed in what it takes, and what it gives;
The joy unequalled, if its end it gain,
And if it lose, attended with no pain:
Without satiety, though e'er so blessed,
And but more relished as the more distressed:
The broadest mirth unfeeling folly wears,
Less pleasing far than virtue's very tears.   320
Good, from each object, from each place acquired,
For ever exercised, yet never tired;
Never elated, while one man's oppressed;
Never dejected, while another's blessed;
And where no wants, no wishes can remain,
Since but to wish more virtue, is to gain.
   See the sole bliss Heaven could on all bestow!
Which who but feels can taste, but thinks can know:
Yet poor with fortune, and with learning blind,
The bad must miss; the good, untaught, will find;   330
Slave to no sect, who takes no private road,
But looks through Nature, up to Nature's God;
Pursues that chain which links th'immense design,
Joins heaven and earth, and mortal and divine;

---

309 f. That VIRTUE only constitutes a happiness, whose object is universal, and
whose prospect eternal.

327 f. That the perfection of happiness consists in a conformity to the order of
Providence here, and a resignation to it, here and hereafter.

Sees, that no being any bliss can know,
But touches some above, and some below;
Learns, from this union of the rising whole,
The first, last purpose of the human soul;
And knows where faith, law, morals, all began,
All end, in LOVE OF GOD, and LOVE OF MAN.   340

    For him alone, hope leads from goal to goal,
And opens still, and opens on his soul,
Till lengthened on to faith, and unconfined,
It pours the bliss that fills up all the mind.
He sees, why Nature plants in Man alone
Hope of known bliss, and faith in bliss unknown:
(Nature, whose dictates to no other kind
Are given in vain, but what they seek they find)
Wise is her present; she connects in this
His greatest virtue with his greatest bliss;   350
At once his own bright prospect to be blessed,
And strongest motive to assist the rest.

    Self-love thus pushed to social, to divine,
Gives thee to make thy neighbour's blessing thine.
Is this too little for the boundless heart?
Extend it, let thy enemies have part:
Grasp the whole worlds of reason, life, and sense,
In one close system of benevolence:
Happier as kinder, in whate'er degree,
And height of bliss but height of charity.   360

    God loves from whole to parts: but human soul
Must rise from individual to the whole.
Self-love but serves the virtuous mind to wake,
As the small pebble stirs the peaceful lake;
The centre moved, a circle straight succeeds,
Another still, and still another spreads;
Friend, parent, neighbour, first it will embrace,
His country next, and next all human race;
Wide and more wide, th' o'erflowings of the mind
Take every creature in, of every kind;   370
Earth smiles around, with boundless bounty blest,
And Heaven beholds its image in his breast.

    Come then, my friend, my genius,° come along,
Oh master of the poet, and the song!
And while the Muse now stoops, or now ascends,

To Man's low passions, or their glorious ends,
Teach me, like thee, in various nature wise,
To fall with dignity, with temper° rise;
Formed by thy converse, happily to steer
From grave to gay, from lively to severe;   380
Correct with spirit, eloquent with ease,
Intent to reason, or polite to please.
Oh! while along the stream of time thy name
Expanded flies, and gathers all its fame,
Say, shall my little bark attendant sail,
Pursue the triumph, and partake the gale?
When statesmen, heroes, kings, in dust repose,
Whose sons shall blush their fathers were thy foes,
Shall then this verse to future age pretend°
Thou wert my guide, philosopher, and friend?   390
That urged by thee, I turned the tuneful art
From sounds to things, from fancy to the heart;
For wit's false mirror held up Nature's light;
Showed erring pride, 'WHATEVER IS, IS RIGHT';
That REASON, PASSION, answer one great aim;
That true SELF-LOVE and SOCIAL are the same;
That VIRTUE only makes our bliss below;
And all our knowledge is, OURSELVES TO KNOW.

POPE TO JONATHAN SWIFT
20 April 1733

You say truly, that death is only terrible to us as it separates us from
those we love, but I really think those have the worst of it who are left
by us, if we are true friends. I have felt more (I fancy) in the loss of
poor Mr Gay, than I shall suffer in the thought of going away myself
into a state that can feel none of this sort of losses. I wished vehemently
to have seen him in a condition of living independent, and to have lived
in perfect indolence the rest of our days together, the two most idle,
most innocent, undesigning poets of our age. I now as vehemently wish,
you and I might walk into the grave together, by as slow steps as you
please, but contentedly and cheerfully: whether that ever can be, or in

what country, I know no more, than into what country we shall walk
out of the grave. But it suffices me to know it will be exactly what
region or state our Maker appoints, and that whatever *Is*, is *Right*.° Our
poor friend's papers are partly in my hands, and for as much as is so,
I will take care to suppress things unworthy of him. As to the epitaph,°
I am sorry you gave a copy, for it will certainly by that means come into
print, and I would correct it more, unless you will do it for me (and
that I shall like as well). Upon the whole I earnestly wish your coming
over hither, for this reason among many others, that your influence
may be joined with mine to suppress whatever we may judge proper of
his papers. To be plunged in my neighbours and my papers, will be
your inevitable fate as soon as you come. That I am an author whose
characters are thought of some weight, appears from the great noise
and bustle that the court and town make about any I give: and I will
not render them less important or interesting, by sparing Vice and
Folly, or by betraying the cause of Truth and Virtue. I will take care
they shall be such as no man can be angry at but the persons I would
have angry. You are sensible with what decency and justice I paid
homage to the royal family, at the same time that I satirized false
courtiers, and spies, etc. about 'em. I have not the courage however
to be such a satirist as you, but I would be as much, or more, a
philosopher. You call your satires, libels; I would rather call my satires,
epistles. They will consist more of morality than wit, and grow graver,
which you will call duller. I shall leave it to my antagonists to be witty
(if they can) and content myself to be useful, and in the right. Tell me
your opinion as to Lady M—'s or Lord H—'s performance?° they are
certainly the top wits of the court, and you may judge by that single
piece what can be done against me; for it was laboured, corrected,
præcommended and post-disapproved, so far as to be dis-owned by
themselves, after each had highly cried it up for the others. I have
met with some complaints, and heard at a distance of some threats,
occasioned by my satires: I sent fair messages to acquaint them where
I was to be found in town, and to offer to call at their houses to satisfy
them, and so it dropped. It is very poor in anyone to rail and threaten
at a distance, and have nothing to say to you when they see you.—I
am glad you persist and abide by so good a thing as that poem, in which
I am immortal for my morality: I never took any praise so kindly, and
yet I think I deserve that praise better than I do any other.—When
does your collection° come out, and what will it consist of? I have but
last week finished another of my *Epistles*,° in the order of the system;
and this week (*exercitandi gratia*) I have translated, or rather parodied,

another of Horace's,° in which I introduce you advising me about my
expenses, house-keeping, etc. But these things shall lie by, till you
come to carp at 'em, and alter rhymes, and grammar, and triplets, and
cacophonies of all kinds. Our parliament will sit till midsummer, which
I hope may be a motive to bring you rather in summer than so late as
autumn: you use to love what I hate, a hurry of politics, etc. Courts I
see not, courtiers I know not, kings I adore not, queens I compliment
not; so I am never like to be in fashion, nor in dependance. I heartily
join with you in pitying our poor lady° for her unhappiness, and should
only pity her more, if she had more of what they at court call happiness.
Come then, and perhaps we may go all together into France at the end
of the season, and compare the liberties of both kingdoms. Adieu.
Believe me dear Sir, (with a thousand warm wishes, mixed with short
sighs) ever yours.

THE FOURTH SATIRE OF DR JOHN DONNE VERSIFIED

Well, if it be my time to quit the stage,   1
Adieu to all the follies of the age!
I die in charity with fool and knave,
Secure of peace at least beyond the grave.
I've had my purgatory here betimes,
And paid for all my satires, all my rhymes:
The poet's hell, its tortures, fiends, and flames,
To this were trifles, toys and empty names.
   With foolish pride my heart was never fired,
Nor the vain itch t'admire, or be admired;   10
I hoped for no commission from his Grace;
I bought no benefice, I begged no place;
Had no new verses, or new suit to show;
Yet went to court!—the devil would have it so.
But, as the fool that in reforming days
Would go to mass in jest (as story says)
Could not but think, to pay his fine° was odd,
Since 'twas no formed design of serving God;
So was I punished, as if full as proud,

As prone to ill, as negligent of good.   20
As deep in debt, without a thought to pay, ⎞
As vain, as idle, and as false, as they   ⎬
Who live at court, for going once that way! ⎠
Scarce was I entered, when, behold! there came
A thing which Adam had been posed to name;
Noah had refused it lodging in his ark,
Where all the race of reptiles might embark:
A verier monster, than on Afric's shore
The sun e'er got, or slimy Nilus bore,
Or Sloane or Woodward's wondrous shelves° contain,   30
Nay, all that lying travellers can feign.
The watch would hardly let him pass at noon,
At night, would swear him dropped out of the moon.
One whom the mob, when next we find or make°
A Popish plot, shall for a Jesuit take,
And the wise justice starting from his chair
Cry, 'By your priesthood tell me what you are?'
    Such was the wight: th' apparel on his back
Though coarse, was reverend, and though bare, was
        black:
The suit, if by the fashion one might guess,   40
Was velvet in the youth of good Queen *Bess*,°
But mere tuftaffeta° what now remained;
So time, that changes all things, had ordained!
Our sons shall see it leisurely decay,
First turn plain rash,° then vanish quite away.
    This thing has travelled, speaks each language too,
And knows what's fit for every state to do;
Of whose best phrase and courtly accent joined,
He forms one tongue, exotic and refined.
Talkers I've learned to bear; Motteux I knew,   50
Henley himself I've heard, and Budgell too.°
The Doctor's wormwood style,° the hash of tongues
A pedant makes, the storm of Gonson's° lungs,
The whole artillery of the terms of war,
And (all those plague in one) the bawling bar:
These I could bear; but not a rogue so civil,
Whose tongue will compliment you to the devil.
A tongue, that can cheat widows, cancel scores,°
Make Scots speak treason, cozen° subtlest whores,

With royal favourites in flattery vie,   60
And Oldmixon and Burnet° both outlie.
    He spies me out. I whisper, 'Gracious God!
What sin of mine could merit such a rod?
That all the shot of dulness now must be
From this thy blunderbuss discharged on me!'
'Permit,' he cries, 'no stranger to your fame
To crave your sentiment, if —'s your name.
What *speech* esteem you most?' 'The *King's*,'° said I.
'But the best *words*?'—'O Sir, the *Dictionary*.'
'You miss my aim; I mean the most acute   70
And perfect *Speaker*?'—'Onslow,° past dispute.'
'But, Sir, of writers?' 'Swift, for closer° style,
But Hoadly° for a period of a mile.'
'Why yes, 'tis granted, these indeed may pass
Good common linguists, and so Panurge° was;
Nay troth, th' apostles (though perhaps too rough)
Had once a pretty gift of tongues° enough:
Yet these were all poor gentlemen! I dare
Affirm, 'twas travel made them what they were.'
    Thus others' talents having nicely shown,   80
He came by sure transition to his own:
Till I cried out, 'You prove yourself so able,
Pity! you was not druggerman° at Babel;
For had they found a linguist half so good,
I make no question but the Tower had stood.'
    'Obliging sir! for courts you sure were made:
Why then for ever buried in the shade?
Spirits like you, should see and should be seen,
The King would smile on you—at least the Queen.'
'Ah gentle sir! you courtiers so cajole us—   90
But Tully° has it, *Nunquam minus solus*:
And as for courts, forgive me, if I say
No lessons now are taught the Spartan way:
Though in his pictures lust be full displayed,
Few are the converts Aretine° has made;
And though the court show vice exceeding clear,
None should, by my advice, learn virtue there.'
    At this entranced, he lifts his hands and eyes,
Squeaks like a high-stretched lutestring, and replies:
'Oh 'tis the sweetest of all earthly things   100

To gaze on princes, and to talk of kings!'
'Then, happy man who shows the tombs!'° said I,
'He dwells amidst the royal family;
He every day, from king to king can walk,
Of all our Harries, all our Edwards talk,
And get by speaking truth of monarchs dead,
What few can of the living, ease and bread.'
'Lord, sir, a mere mechanic!° strangely low,
And coarse of phrase,—your English all are so.
How elegant your Frenchmen?' 'Mine, d'ye mean?   110
I have but one, I hope the fellow's clean.'
'Oh! sir, politely so! nay, let me die,
Your only wearing is your paduasoy.'°
'Not, Sir, my only, I have better still,
And this you see is but my dishabille'—
Wild to get loose, his patience I provoke,
Mistake, confound, object at all he spoke.
But as coarse iron, sharpened, mangles more,
And itch most hurts when angered to a sore;
So when you plague a fool, 'tis still the curse,   120
You only make the matter worse and worse.

     He passed it o'er; affects an easy smile
At all my peevishness, and turns his style.
He asks, 'What news?' I tell him of new plays,
New eunuchs, harlequins, and operas.°
He hears, and as a still with simples in it,
Between each drop it gives, stays half a minute,
Loth to enrich me with too quick replies,
By little, and by little, drops his lies.
Mere household trash! of birth-nights,° balls, and shows,   130
More than ten Holinsheds, or Halls, or Stows.°
When the Queen° frowned, or smiled, he knows; and
     what
A subtle minister may make of that:
Who sins with whom: who got his pension rug.°
Or quickened a reversion by a drug:
Whose place is quartered out, three parts in four,
And whether to a bishop, or a whore:
Who having lost his credit, pawned his rent,
Is therefore fit to have a government:
Who in the secret, deals in stocks secure,   140

And cheats th' unknowing widow and the poor:
Who makes a trust or charity° a job,
And gets an Act of Parliament to rob:
Why turnpikes rise, and now no cit nor clown°
Can gratis see the country, or the town:
Shortly no lad shall chuck,° or lady vole,°
But some excising° courtier will have toll.
He tells what strumpet places sells for life,
What squire his lands, what citizen his wife:
And last (which proves him wiser still than all)   150
What lady's face is not a whited wall.°
    As one of Woodward's patients,° sick, and sore,
I puke, I nauseate,—yet he thrusts in more:
Trims Europe's balance,° tops the statesman's part,
And talks *Gazettes* and *Post Boys*° o'er by heart.
Like a big wife at sight of loathsome meat,
Ready to cast,° I yawn, I sigh, and sweat.
Then as a licensed spy, whom nothing can
Silence or hurt, he libels the great man;°
Swears every place entailed for years to come,   160
In sure succession to the day of doom:
He names the price° for every office paid,
And says our wars thrive ill, because delayed:
Nay hints, 'tis by connivance of the court,
That Spain robs on,° and Dunkirk's° still a port.
Not more amazement seized on Circe's guests,°
To see themselves fall endlong into beasts,
Than mine, to find a subject stayed and wise
Already half turned traitor by surprise.
I felt th' infection slide from him to me,   170
As in the pox, some give it to get free;
And quick to swallow me, methought I saw
One of our giant statutes ope its jaw.
    In that nice moment, as another lie
Stood just atilt,° the minister came by.
To him he flies, and bows, and bows again,
Then, close as Umbra, joins the dirty train.
Not Fannius'° self more impudently near,
When half his nose is in his prince's ear.
I quaked at heart; and still afraid to see   180
All the court filled with stranger things than he,

Ran out as fast, as one that pays his bail
And dreads more actions,° hurries from a jail.
   Bear me, some god, oh quickly bear me hence
To wholesome solitude, the nurse of sense:
Where contemplation preens her ruffled wings,
And the free soul looks down to pity kings!
There sober thought pursued th' amusing theme,
Till fancy coloured it, and formed a dream.
A vision hermits can to hell transport,   190
And forced ev'n me to see the damned at court.
Not Dante dreaming all th' infernal state,
Beheld such scenes of envy, sin, and hate.
Base fear becomes the guilty, not the free;
Suits tyrants, plunderers, but suits not me:
Shall I, the terror of this sinful town,
Care, if a liveried lord or smile or frown?
Who cannot flatter, and detest who can,
Tremble before a noble serving-man?
O my fair mistress, truth! shall I quit thee   200
For huffing, braggart, puffed nobility?
Thou, who since yesterday hast rolled o'er all
The busy, idle blockheads of the ball,
Hast thou, oh sun! beheld an emptier sort,
Than such as swell this bladder of a court?
Now pox on those who show a *court in wax!*
It ought to bring all courtiers on their backs:
Such painted puppets! such a varnished race
Of hollow gewgaws, only dress and face!
Such waxen noses, stately, staring things—   210
No wonder some folks bow, and think them kings.
   See! where the British youth, engaged no more
At Figg's,° at White's,° with felons, or a whore,
Pay their last duty to the court, and come
All fresh and fragrant, to the drawing-room;
In hues as gay, and odours as divine,
As the fair fields they sold to look so fine.

---

206. *Court in wax!*] A famous show of the court of France, in waxwork.°

213. White's was a noted gaming-house: Figg's, a prizefighter's academy, where
the young nobility received instruction in those days. It was also customary for the
nobility and gentry to visit the condemned criminals in Newgate.

'That's velvet for a king!' the flatterer swears;
'Tis true, for ten days hence 'twill be King Lear's.
Our court may justly to our stage give rules,   220
That helps it both to fool's coats and to fools.
And why not players strut in courtiers' clothes?°
For these are actors too, as well as those:
Wants reach all states; they beg but better dressed,
And all is splendid poverty at best.
 Painted for sight, and essenced for the smell,
Like frigates fraught with spice and cochineal,
Sail in the ladies: how each pirate eyes
So weak a vessel, and so rich a prize!
Top-gallant he, and she in all her trim,   230
He boarding her, she striking sail to him:
'Dear Countess! you have charms all hearts to hit!'
And 'Sweet Sir Fopling!° you have so much wit!'
Such wits and beauties are not praised for nought,
For both the beauty and the wit are bought.
'Twould burst ev'n Heraclitus° with the spleen,
To see those antics, Fopling and Courtin:
The presence° seems, with things so richly odd,
The mosque of Mahound,° or some queer pagod.°
See them survey their limbs by Dürer's rules,°   240
Of all beau-kind the best proportioned fools!
Adjust their clothes, and to confession draw
Those venial sins, an atom, or a straw;
But oh! what terrors must distract the soul
Convicted of that mortal crime, a hole;
Or should one pound of powder less bespread
Those monkey tails that wag behind their head.
Thus finished, and corrected to a hair,
They march, to prate their hour before the fair.
So first to preach a white-gloved chaplain goes,   250
With band° of lily, and with cheek of rose,
Sweeter than Sharon,° in immaculate trim,
Neatness itself impertinent in him.
Let but the ladies smile, and they are blessed:
Prodigious! how the things *protest, protest:*°
Peace, fools, or Gonson will for papists seize you,
If once he catch you at your '*Jesu! Jesu!*'
 Nature made every fop to plague his brother,

Just as one beauty mortifies another.
But here's the captain that will plague them both,   260
Whose air cries 'Arm!', whose very look's an oath:
The captain's honest, sirs, and that's enough,
Though his soul's bullet, and his body buff.°
He spits fore-right; his haughty chest before,
Like battering rams, beats open every door:
And with a face as red, and as awry,
As Herod's hangdogs° in old tapestry,°
Scarecrow to boys, the breeding woman's curse,
Has yet a strange ambition to look worse;
Confounds the civil, keeps the rude in awe,   270
Jests like a licensed fool, commands like law.
      Frighted, I quit the room, but leave it so
As men from gaols to execution go;
For hung with deadly sins I see the wall,
And lined with giants deadlier than 'em all:
Each man an Askapart, of strength to toss
For quoits, both Temple Bar and Charing Cross.°
Scared at the grisly forms, I sweat, I fly,
And shake all o'er, like a discovered spy.
      Courts are too much for wits so weak as mine: 280
Charge them with heaven's artillery, bold divine!
From such alone the great rebukes endure,
Whose satire's sacred, and whose rage secure:
'Tis mine to wash a few light stains, but theirs
To deluge sin, and drown a court in tears.
Howe'er what's now Apocrypha, my wit,
In time to come, may pass for holy writ.

274. The room hung with old tapestry, representing the seven deadly sins.
276. A giant famous in romances.

AN EPISTLE
TO
Sir *Richard Temple*, Lord *Cobham*

ARGUMENT

Of the Knowledge *and* Characters *of* MEN

That it is not sufficient for this knowledge to consider Man in the abstract: books *will not serve the purpose, nor yet our own* experience *singly*, v. 1. *General maxims, unless they be formed upon* both, *will be but notional*, v. 10. *Some peculiarity in every man, characteristic to himself, yet varying from himself*, v. 15. *Difficulties arising from our own passions, fancies, faculties*, &c. v. 31. *The shortness of life, to observe in, and the uncertainty of the* principles of action *in men, to observe by*, v. 37, &c. *Our own principle of action often hid from ourselves*, v. 41. *Some few characters plain, but in general confounded, dissembled, or inconsistent*, v. 51. *The same man utterly different in different places and seasons*, v. 71. *Unimaginable weaknesses in the greatest*, v. 70, &c. *Nothing constant and certain but* God *and* Nature, v. 95. *No judging of the* motives *from the actions; the same actions proceeding from contrary motives, and the same motives influencing contrary actions*, v. 100. II. *Yet to form* characters, *we can only take the* strongest actions *of a man's life, and try to make them* agree. *The utter uncertainty of this, from* Nature *itself, and from* policy, v. 120. *Characters given according to the* rank *of men of the world*, v. 135. *And some reason for it*, v. 140. Education *alters the* nature, *or at least* character *of many*, v. 149. Actions, passions, opinions, manners, humours, *or* principles *all subject to change. No judging by* Nature, *from* v. 158 *to* 178. III. *It only remains to find (if we can) his* RULING PASSION. *That will certainly influence all the rest, and can reconcile the seeming or real inconsistency of all his actions*, v. 175. *Instanced in the extraordinary character of* Clodio, v. 179. *A caution against mistaking* second qualities *for* first, *which will destroy all possibility of the knowledge of mankind*, v. 210. *Examples of the strength of the* ruling passion, *and its continuation to the last breath*, v. 222, &c.

Yes, you despise the man to books confined,
Who from his study rails at human kind; 1

Though what he learns, he speaks, and may advance
Some general maxims, or be right by chance.
The coxcomb bird, so talkative and grave,
That from his cage cries cuckold, whore, and knave,
Though many a passenger° he rightly call,
You hold him no philosopher at all.
    And yet the fate of all extremes is such,
Men may be read, as well as books, too much.   10
To observations which ourselves we make,
We grow more partial for th'observer's sake;
To written wisdom, as another's, less:
Maxims are drawn from notions, these from guess.
There's some peculiar in each leaf and grain,
Some unmarked fibre, or some varying vein:
Shall only man be taken in the gross?
Grant but as many sorts of mind, as moss.
    That each from other differs, first confess;
Next, that he varies from himself no less: 20
Add nature's, custom's, reason's, passion's strife,
And all opinion's colours cast on life.
    Our depths who fathoms, or our shallows finds,
Quick whirls, and shifting eddies, of our minds?
On human actions reason though you can,
It may be reason, but it is not man:
His principle of action once explore,
That instant 'tis his principle no more.
Like following life through creatures you dissect,
You lose it in the moment you detect.   30
    Yet more; the difference is as great between
The optics seeing, as the objects seen.
All manners take a tincture from our own;
Or come discoloured through our passions shown.
Or fancy's beam enlarges, multiplies,
Contracts, inverts, and gives ten thousand dyes.
    Nor will life's stream for observation stay,
It hurries all too fast to mark their way:
In vain sedate reflections we would make,
When half our knowledge we must snatch, not take.   40

18. There are about 300 sorts of moss observed by naturalists.

Oft, in the passions' wild rotation tossed,
Our spring of action to ourselves is lost:
Tired, not determined, to the last we yield,
And what comes then is master of the field.
As the last image of that troubled heap,
When sense° subsides, and fancy sports in sleep,
(Though past the recollection of the thought)
Becomes the stuff of which our dream is wrought;
Something, as dim to our internal view,
Is thus perhaps the cause of most we do.   50

   True, some are open, and to all men known;
Others so very close, they're hid from none;
(So darkness strikes the sense no less than light)
Thus gracious CHANDOS° is beloved at sight;
And every child hates Shylock,° though his soul
Still sits at squat,° and peeps not from its hole.
At half mankind when generous° Manly° raves,
All know 'tis virtue, for he thinks them knaves:
When universal homage Umbra° pays,
All see 'tis vice, and itch of vulgar praise.   60
When flattery glares, all hate it in a queen,
While one there is who charms us with his spleen.°

   But these plain characters we rarely find;
Though strong the bent, yet quick the turns of mind:
Or puzzling contraries confound the whole,
Or affectations quite reverse the soul.
The dull, flat falsehood serves for policy,
And in the cunning, truth itself's a lie:
Unthought-of frailties cheat us in the wise;
The fool lies hid in inconsistencies.   70

   See the same man, in vigour, in the gout;
Alone, in company; in place, or out;
Early at business, and at hazard° late;
Mad at a fox-chase, wise at a debate;
Drunk at a borough, civil at a ball;
Friendly at Hackney, faithless at Whitehall.°

   Catius° is ever moral, ever grave,
Thinks who endures a knave, is next a knave,
Save just at dinner—then prefers, no doubt,
A rogue with venison to a saint without.   80

   Who would not praise Patritio's high desert,

His hand unstained, his uncorrupted heart,
His comprehensive head? all interests weighed,
All Europe saved, yet Britain not betrayed.
He thanks you not, his pride is in picquette,
Newmarket°-fame, and judgment at a bet.
    What made (say Montaigne, or more sage Charron!)°
Otho° a warrior, Cromwell a buffoon?
A perjured prince a leaden saint revere?
A godless regent tremble at a star?   90
The throne a bigot keep, a genius quit,
Faithless through piety, and duped through wit?
Europe a woman, child, or dotard rule,°
And just her ablest monarch made a fool?
    Know, GOD and NATURE only are the same:
In man, the judgment shoots at flying game,
A bird of passage! gone as soon as found,
Now in the moon perhaps, now under ground.
    In vain the sage, with retrospective eye,
Would from th'apparent what conclude the why,   100
Infer the motive from the deed, and show
That what we chanced, was what we meant to do.
Behold! If fortune or a mistress frowns,
Some plunge in business, others shave their crowns:°
To ease the soul of one oppressive weight,
This quits an empire, that embroils a state:
The same adust° complexion has impelled
Charles to the convent, Philip to the field.°
    Not always actions show the man: we find
Who does a kindness, is not therefore kind;   110
Perhaps prosperity becalmed his breast,

After v. 86, in the former editions,
> Triumphant leaders, at an army's head,
> Hemmed round with glories, pilfer cloth or bread;
> As meanly plunder as they bravely fought,
> Now save a people, and now save a groat.

89. Louis XI of France wore in his hat a leaden image of the Virgin Mary, which when he swore by, he feared to break his oath.

91. Philip V of Spain, who, after renouncing the throne for religion, resumed it to gratify his queen; and Victor Amadeus II, King of Sardinia, who resigned the crown, and trying to reassume it, was imprisoned till his death.

108. Charles V and Philip II.

Perhaps the wind just shifted from the east:
Not therefore humble he who seeks retreat,
Pride guides his steps, and bids him shun the great:
Who combats bravely is not therefore brave,
He dreads a death-bed like the meanest slave:
Who reasons wisely is not therefore wise,
His pride in reasoning, not in acting lies.
    But grant that actions best discover man;
Take the most strong, and sort them as you can.   120
The few that glare, each character must mark,
You balance not the many in the dark.
What will you do with such as disagree?
Suppress them, or miscall them policy?
Must then at once (the character to save)
The plain rough hero turn a crafty knave?
Alas! in truth the man but changed his mind,
Perhaps was sick, in love, or had not dined.
Ask why from Britain Caesar would retreat?
Caesar himself might whisper he was beat.   130
Why risk the world's great empire for a punk?°
Caesar perhaps might answer he was drunk.
But, sage historians! 'tis your task to prove
One action, conduct;° one, heroic love.
    'Tis from high life high characters are drawn;
A saint in crape° is twice a saint in lawn;°
A judge is just, a chancellor juster still;
A gownman, learned; a bishop, what you will;
Wise, if a minister; but, if a king,
More wise, more learned, more just, more everything.   140
Court-virtues bear, like gems,° the highest rate,
Born where heaven's influence scarce can penetrate:
In life's low vale, the soil the virtues like,
They please as beauties, here as wonders strike.
Though the same sun with all-diffusive rays
Blush in the rose, and in the diamond blaze,
We prize the stronger effort of his power,
And justly set the gem above the flower.
    'Tis education forms the common mind,
Just as the twig is bent, the tree's inclined.   150
Boastful and rough, your first son is a squire;
The next a tradesman, meek, and much a liar;

Tom struts a soldier, open, bold, and brave;
Will sneaks a scrivener,° an exceeding knave:
Is he a churchman? then he's fond of power: ⎫
A quaker? sly: a presbyterian? sour: ⎬
A smart freethinker? all things in an hour. ⎭

Ask men's opinions: Scoto° now shall tell
How trade increases, and the world goes well;
Strike off his pension, by the setting sun,   160
And Britain, if not Europe, is undone.

That gay freethinker, a fine talker once,
What turns him now a stupid silent dunce?
Some god, or spirit he has lately found;
Or chanced to meet a minister that frowned.

Judge we by nature? Habit can efface,
Interest o'ercome, or policy take place:°
By actions? those uncertainty divides:
By passions? these dissimulation hides:
Opinions? they still take a wider range: 170
Find, if you can, in what you cannot change.

Manners with fortunes, humours° turn with climes.
Tenets with books, and principles with times.

Search then the RULING PASSION: there, alone,
The wild are constant, and the cunning known;
The fool consistent, and the false sincere;
Priests, princes, women, no dissemblers here.
This clue° once found, unravels all the rest,
The prospect clears, and Wharton° stands confessed.
Wharton, the scorn and wonder of our days,   180
Whose ruling passion was the lust of praise:
Born with whate'er could win it from the wise,
Women and fools must like him or he dies;
Though wondering senates hung on all he spoke,
The club must hail him master of the joke.
Shall parts so various aim at nothing new?
He'll shine a Tully and a Wilmot too.
Then turns repentant, and his God adores
With the same spirit that he drinks and whores;

187. John Wilmot, Earl of Rochester, famous for his wit and extravagancies in the time of Charles the Second.

Enough if all around him but admire,   190
And now the punk applaud, and now the friar.
Thus, with each gift of nature and of art,
And wanting nothing but an honest heart;
Grown all to all, from no one vice exempt,
And most contemptible, to shun contempt;
His passion still, to covet general praise,
His life, to forfeit it a thousand ways;
A constant bounty, which no friend has made;
An angel tongue, which no man can persuade;
A fool, with more of wit than half mankind,   200
Too rash for thought, for action too refined;
A tyrant to the wife his heart approves;
A rebel to the very king he loves;
He dies, sad outcast of each church and state,
And, harder still! flagitious, yet not great.
Ask you why Wharton broke through every rule?
'Twas all for fear the knaves should call him fool.

  Nature well known, no prodigies remain,
Comets are regular and Wharton plain.

  Yet, in this search, the wisest may mistake,   210
If second qualities for first they take.
When Catiline° by rapine swelled his store;
When Caesar made a noble dame° a whore;
In this the lust, in that the avarice
Were means, not ends; ambition was the vice.
That very Caesar, born in Scipio's° days,
Had aimed, like him, by chastity at praise.
Lucullus,° when frugality could charm,
Had roasted turnips in the Sabine farm.
In vain th' observer eyes the builder's toil,°   220
But quite mistakes the scaffold for the pile.

  In this one passion man can strength enjoy,
As fits give vigour, just when they destroy.
Time, that on all things lays his lenient hand,
Yet tames not this; it sticks to our last sand.°
Consistent in our follies and our sins,
Here honest Nature ends as she begins.

  Old politicians chew on wisdom past,
And totter on in business to the last;
As weak, as earnest; and as gravely out,   230

As sober Lanesborough° dancing in the gout.
    Behold a reverend sire, whom want of grace
Has made the father of a nameless race,
Shoved from the wall perhaps, or rudely pressed
By his own son, that passes by unblessed:
Still to his wench he crawls on knocking knees,
And envies every sparrow that he sees.
    A salmon's belly, Helluo,° was thy fate;
The doctor called, declares all help too late:
'Mercy!' cries Helluo, 'mercy on my soul!   240
Is there no hope?—Alas!—then bring the jowl.'
    The frugal crone, whom praying priests attend,
Still tries to save the hallowed taper's end,
Collects her breath, as ebbing life retires,
For one puff more, and in that puff expires.
    'Odious!° in woollen! 'twould a saint provoke',
(Were the last words that poor Narcissa° spoke)
'No, let a charming chintz, and Brussels lace
Wrap my cold limbs, and shade my lifeless face:
One would not, sure, be frightful when one's dead—   250
And—Betty°—give this cheek a little red.'
    The courtier smooth, who forty years had shined
An humble servant to all human kind,
Just brought out this, when scarce his tongue could stir,
'If—where I'm going—I could serve you, Sir?'
    'I give and I devise' (old Euclio said,
And sighed) 'my lands and tenements to Ned.'
Your money, Sir; 'My money, Sir, what all?
Why,—if I must'—(then wept) 'I give it Paul.'
The manor, Sir?—'The manor! hold,' he cried,   260
'Not that—I cannot part with that'—and died.
    And you! brave COBHAM, to the latest breath
Shall feel your ruling passion strong in death:

---

231. *Lanesborough.*] An ancient nobleman, who continued this practice long after his legs were disabled by the gout. Upon the death of Prince George of Denmark, he demanded an audience of the Queen to advise her to preserve her health and dispel her grief by *dancing.*

247. This story, as well as the others, is founded on fact, though the author had the goodness not to mention the names. Several attribute this in particular to a very celebrated actress, who, in detestation of the thought of being buried in woollen, gave these her last orders with her dying breath.

Such in those moments as in all the past,
'Oh, save my country, Heaven!' shall be your last.

THE

SECOND SATIRE

OF THE

SECOND BOOK

OF

HORACE IMITATED

To Mr BETHEL

What, and how great, the virtue and the art   1
To live on little with a cheerful heart,
(A doctrine sage, but truly none of mine)
Let's talk, my friends, but talk before we dine:
Not when a gilt buffet's reflected pride
Turns you from sound philosophy aside,
Not when from plate to plate your eyeballs roll,
And the brain dances to the mantling° bowl.
Hear BETHEL's sermon, one not versed in schools,°
But strong in sense, and wise without the rules.   10
   'Go work, hunt, exercise!' he thus began,
'Then scorn a homely dinner, if you can.
Your wine locked up, your butler strolled abroad,
Or fish denied (the river yet unthawed)
If then plain bread and milk will do the feat,
The pleasure lies in you, and not the meat.
   Preach as I please, I doubt our curious° men
Will choose a pheasant still before a hen;
Yet hens of Guinea° full as good I hold,
Except you eat the feathers, green and gold.   20
Of carps and mullets why prefer the great,
(Though cut in pieces 'ere my Lord can eat)
Yet for small turbots such esteem profess?

Because God made these large, the other less.
Oldfield,° with more than harpy throat endued,
Cries "Send me, gods! a whole hog barbecued!"
Oh blast it, south-winds! till a stench exhale
Rank as the ripeness of a rabbit's tail.
By what criterion do ye eat, d'ye think,
If this is prized for sweetness, that for stink?   30
When the tired glutton labours through a treat,°
He finds no relish in the sweetest meat;
He calls for something bitter, something sour,
And the rich feast concludes extremely poor:
Cheap eggs, and herbs, and olives still we see;
Thus much is left of old simplicity!
The robin-redbreast till of late had rest,
And children sacred held a martin's nest,°
Till beccaficos° sold so devilish dear
To one that was, or would have been a peer.   40
Let me extol a cat, on oysters fed,
I'll have a party at the Bedford Head;
Or ev'n to crack live crawfish recommend;
I'd never doubt at court to make a friend.
    'Tis yet in vain, I own, to keep a pother
About one vice, and fall into the other:
Between excess and famine lies a mean;
Plain, but not sordid; though not splendid, clean.
    Avidien° or his wife (no matter which,
For him you'll call a dog, and her a bitch)   50
Sell their presented partridges, and fruits,
And humbly live on rabbits and on roots:
One half-pint bottle serves them both to dine,
And is at once their vinegar and wine.
But on some lucky day (as when they found
A lost bank-bill, or heard their son° was drowned)
At such a feast, old vinegar to spare,
Is what two souls so generous cannot bear:
Oil, though it stink, they drop by drop impart,
But souse the cabbage with a bounteous heart.   60

26. *barbecued*]° A West Indian term of gluttony, a hog roasted whole, stuffed with
spice, and basted with Madeira wine.

42. *Bedford Head*]° A famous eating house.

He knows to live, who keeps the middle state,
And neither leans on this side, nor on that:
Nor stops, for one bad cork, his butler's pay,
Swears, like Albutius, a good cook away;
Nor lets, like Naevius, every error pass,
The musty wine, foul cloth, or greasy glass.
    'Now hear what blessings temperance can bring:'
(Thus said our friend, and what he said I sing)
'First health: the stomach (crammed from every dish,
A tomb of boiled and roast, and flesh and fish,   70
Where bile, and wind, and phlegm, and acid jar,
And all the man is one intestine war)
Remembers oft the schoolboy's simple fare,
The temperate sleeps, and spirits light as air.
    How pale, each worshipful and reverend guest
Rise from a clergy, or a city feast!
What life in all that ample body, say?
What heavenly particle inspires the clay?
The soul subsides, and wickedly inclines
To seem but mortal, ev'n in sound divines.   80
    On morning wings how active springs the mind
That leaves the load of yesterday behind?
How easy every labour it pursues?
How coming° to the poet every muse?
Not but we may exceed, some holy time,
Or tired in search of truth, or search of rhyme.
Ill health some just indulgence may engage,
And more, the sickness of long life, old age;
For fainting age what cordial drop° remains,
If our intemperate youth the vessel drains?   90
    Our fathers praised rank venison. You suppose
Perhaps, young men! our fathers had no nose?
Not so: a buck was then a week's repast,
And 'twas their point, I ween, to make it last;
More pleased to keep it till their friends could come,
Than eat the sweetest by themselves at home.
Why had not I in those good times my birth,
Ere coxcomb-pies° or coxcombs were on earth?
    Unworthy he, the voice of fame to hear,
That sweetest music to an honest ear;   100
(For 'faith, Lord Fanny!° you are in the wrong,

The world's good word is better than a song)
Who has not learned, fresh sturgeon and ham-pie
Are no rewards for want, and infamy!
When luxury has licked up all thy pelf,°
Cursed by thy neighbours, thy trustees, thyself,
To friends, to fortune, to mankind a shame,
Think how posterity will treat thy name;
And buy a rope, that future times may tell
Thou hast at least bestowed one penny well.   110
   "Right," cries his Lordship, "for a rogue in need
To have a taste, is insolence indeed:
In me 'tis noble, suits my birth and state,
My wealth unwieldy, and my heap too great."
Then, like the sun, let bounty spread her ray,
And shine that superfluity away.
Oh impudence of wealth! with all thy store,
How darest thou let one worthy man be poor?
Shall half the new-built churches° round thee fall?
Make quays, build bridges,° or repair Whitehall:°   120
Or to thy country let that heap be lent,
As Marlborough's was, but not at five per cent.
   Who thinks that fortune cannot change her mind,
Prepares a dreadful jest for all mankind.
And who stands safest? tell me, is it he
That spreads and swells in puffed prosperity,
Or blessed with little, whose preventing° care
In peace provides fit arms against a war?'
Thus BETHEL spoke, who always speaks his thought,
And always thinks the very thing he ought: 130
His equal° mind I copy what I can,
And as I love, would imitate the man.
In South Sea days not happier, when surmised
The lords of thousands, than if now *excised*;°
In forest° planted by a father's hand,
Than in five acres° now of rented land.
Content with little, I can piddle° here
On broccoli and mutton, round the year;
But ancient friends (though poor, or out of play)°
That touch my bell, I cannot turn away.   140
'Tis true, no turbots dignify my boards,
But gudgeons, flounders, what my Thames affords:

To Hounslow Heath I point and Banstead Down,°
Thence comes your mutton, and these chicks my own:
From yon old walnut-tree a shower shall fall;
And grapes, long lingering on my only wall,
And figs, from standard and espalier join;
The devil is in you if you cannot dine:
Then cheerful healths (your mistress shall have place)
And, what's more rare, a poet shall say grace.   150
    Fortune not much of humbling me can boast;
Though double taxed,° how little have I lost?
My life's amusements have been just the same,
Before, and after standing armies° came.
My lands are sold, my father's house is gone;
I'll hire another's; is not that my own,
And yours, my friends? through whose free-opening gate
None comes too early, none departs too late;
(For I, who hold sage Homer's rule° the best,
Welcome the coming, speed the going guest.)   160
'Pray heaven it last!' cries SWIFT, 'as you go on;
I wish to God this house had been your own:
Pity! to build, without a son or wife:
Why, you'll enjoy it only all your life.'
Well, if the use be mine, can it concern one,
Whether the name belong to Pope or Vernon?°
What's *property?* dear Swift! you see it alter
From you to me, from me to Peter Walter;
Or, in a mortgage, prove a lawyer's share;
Or, in a jointure,° vanish from the heir;   170
Or in pure equity° (the case not clear)
The Chancery takes your rents for twenty year:
At best, it falls to some ungracious son,
Who cries, 'My father's damned, and all's my own.'
Shades,° that to BACON could retreat afford,
Become the portion of a booby lord;
And Helmsley, once proud Buckingham's delight,°
Slides to a scrivener or a city knight.
Let lands and houses have what lords they will,
Let us be fixed, and our own masters still.   180

THE
SECOND SATIRE
OF THE
FIRST BOOK
OF
HORACE

Imitated in the manner of Mr POPE

The tribe of templars, players, apothecaries,   1
Pimps, poets, wits, Lord Fanny's, Lady Mary's,°
And all the court in tears, and half the town,
Lament dear charming Oldfield,° dead and gone!
Engaging Oldfield! who, with grace and ease,
Could join the arts, to ruin, and to please.
    Not so, who of ten thousand gulled her knight,
Then asked ten thousand for a second night:
The gallant too, to whom she paid it down,
Lived to refuse that mistress half a crown.   10
    Con. Philips° cries, 'A sneaking dog I hate.'
That's all three lovers have for their estate!
'Treat on, treat on,' is her eternal note,
And lands and tenements go down her throat.
Some damn the jade, and some the cullies blame,
But not Sir Herbert,° for he does the same.
    With all a woman's virtues but the p—x,
Fufidia° thrives in money, land, and stocks;
For interest, ten per cent. her constant rate is;
Her body? hopeful heirs may have it *gratis*.   20
She turns her very sister to a job,°
And, in the happy minute, picks your fob:°
Yet starves herself, so little her own friend,
And thirsts and hungers only at one end:
A self-tormentor,° worse than (in the play)

The wretch, whose avarice drove his son away.
　　But why all this? I'll tell ye, 'tis my theme:
'Women and fools are always in extreme.'
Rufa's° at either end a common shore,°
Sweet Moll and Jack are civet-cat° and boar:°　　　　30
Nothing in nature is so lewd as Peg,
Yet, for the world, she would not show her leg!
While bashful Jenny, ev'n at morning prayer,
Spreads her fore-buttocks to the navel bare.°
But different taste in different men prevails,
And one is fired by heads, and one by tails;
Some feel no flames but at the court or ball,
And others hunt white aprons in the Mall.
　　My Lord of London,° chancing to remark
A noted dean° much busied in the Park,　　　　　　40
'Proceed', he cried, 'proceed, my reverend brother,
'Tis *fornicatio simplex*, and no other:
Better than lust for boys, with Pope and Turk,
Or others' spouses, like my Lord of York'.°
　　'May no such praise', cries Jefferies, 'e'er be mine!'
Jefferies, who bows at Hillsborough's hoary shrine.
　　All you, who think the city ne'er can thrive,
Till every cuckold-maker's flayed alive;
Attend, while I their miseries explain,
And pity men of pleasure still in pain!　　　　　　50
Survey the pangs they bear, the risks they run,
Where the most lucky are but last undone.
See! wretched Monsieur° flies to save his throat,
And quits his mistress, money, ring, and note!
See good Sir George of ragged livery stripped,
By worthier footmen pissed upon and whipped!
Plundered by thieves, (or lawyers, which is worse)
One bleeds in person, and one bleeds in purse;
This meets a blanket, and that meets a cudgel——
And all applaud the justice—All, but Budgell.°　　　60
　　How much more safe, dear countrymen! his state,
Who trades in frigates of the second rate?
And yet some care of Sallust° should be had;
Nothing so mean for which he can't run mad;
His wit confirms him but a slave the more,
And makes a princess whom he found a whore:

The youth might save much trouble and expense,
Were he a dupe of only common sense.
But here's his point; 'A wench' (he cries) 'for me!
I never touch a dame of quality.'   70
  To Palmer's° bed no actress comes amiss,
He courts the whole *personae dramatis:*
He too can say, 'With wives I never sin.'
But singing-girls and mimics draw him in.
Sure, worthy sir, the difference is not great,
With whom you lose your credit and estate?
This, or that person, what avails to shun?
What's wrong is wrong, wherever it be done;
The ease, support, and lustre of your life,
Destroyed alike with strumpet, maid, or wife.   80
  What pushed poor Ellis° on th' imperial whore?
'Twas but to be where CHARLES had been before.
The fatal steel unjustly was applied,
When not his lust offended, but his pride:
Too hard a penance for defeated sin,
Himself shut out, and Jacob Hall let in.
  Suppose that honest part that rules us all,
Should rise, and say,—'Sir Robert!° or Sir Paul!°
Did I demand, in my most vigorous hour,
A thing descended from the Conqueror?   90
Or when my pulse beat highest, ask for any
Such nicety, as Lady, or Lord Fanny?'——
What would you answer? could you have the face, ⎫
When the poor sufferer humbly mourned his case, ⎬
To cry, 'You weep the favours of her GRACE?'   ⎭
  Hath not indulgent nature spread a feast,
And given enough for man, enough for beast?
But man corrupt, perverse in all his ways,
In search of vanities, from nature strays:
Yea, though the blessing's more than he can use,   100
Shuns the permitted, the forbid pursues!
Weigh well the cause from whence these evils spring,
'Tis in thyself, and not in God's good thing:
Then, lest repentance punish such a life,
Never, ah, never! kiss thy neighbour's wife.
  First, silks and diamonds veil no finer shape,
Or plumper thigh, than lurk in humble crape:

And secondly, how innocent a belle
Is she who shows what ware she has to sell?
Not ladylike, displays a milk-white breast,   110
And hides, in sacred sluttishness, the rest.
    Our ancient kings (and sure those kings were wise,
Who judged themselves, and saw with their own eyes)
A warhorse never for the service chose,
But eyed him round, and stripped off all the clothes;
For well they knew, proud trappings serve to hide
A heavy chest, thick neck, or heaving side.
But fools are ready chaps,° agog to buy,
Let but a comely forehand strike the eye:
No eagle sharper, every charm to find,   120
To all defects, Tyrawley° not so blind:
Goose-rumped, hawk-nosed, swan-footed is my dear?
They'll praise her elbow, heel, or tip o'th' ear.
    A lady's face is all you see undressed;
(For none but Lady Mary shows the rest)
But if to charms more latent you pretend,
What lines encompass, and what works defend!
Dangers on dangers! Obstacles by dozens!
Spies, guardians, guests, old women, aunts, and cousins!°
Could you directly to her person go,   130
Stays will obstruct above, and hoops below,
And if the dame says yes, the dress says no.
Not thus at Needham's;° your judicious eye
May measure there the breast, the hip, the thigh!
And will you run to perils, sword, and law,
All for a thing you ne'er so much as saw?
'The hare once seized, the hunter heeds no more
The little scut° he so pursued before;
Love follows flying game (as Suckling° sings)
And 'tis for that the wanton boy has wings.'   140
Why let him sing—but when you're in the wrong,
Think ye to cure the mischief with a song?
Has nature set no bounds to wild desire?
No sense to guide, no reason to enquire,
What solid happiness, what empty pride,
And what is best indulged, or best denied?
If neither gems adorn, nor silver tip
The flowing bowl, will you not wet your lip?

When sharp with hunger, scorn you to be fed
Except on pea-chicks, at the Bedford Head?°   150
Or, when a tight neat girl will serve the turn,
In errant pride, continue stiff and burn?
I'm a plain man, whose maxim is professed,
'The thing at hand is of all things the best.'
But her who will, and then will not comply,
Whose word is, 'If', 'Perhaps', and 'By-and-by',
'Z——ds! let some eunuch or Platonic take——'
So Bathurst cries, philosopher and rake!
Who asks no more (right reasonable peer)
Than not to wait too long, nor pay too dear.   160
Give me a willing nymph! ('tis all I care,)
Extremely clean, and tolerably fair;
Her shape her own, whatever shape she have,
And just that white and red which Nature gave:
Her I transported touch, transported view,
And call her angel! goddess! Montague!
No furious husband thunders at the door;
No barking dog, no household in a roar;
From gleaming swords no shrieking women run;
No wretched wife cries out, 'Undone! undone!'   170
Seized in the fact, and in her cuckold's power,
She kneels, she weeps, and worse! resigns her dower.
Me, naked me, to posts,° to pumps° they draw,
To shame eternal, or eternal law.
Oh love! be deep tranquillity my luck,
No Mistress Heysham near, no Lady Buck:°
For, to be taken, is the devil in hell;
This truth let Liddel,° Jefferies,° Onslow° tell.

Epistle to Dr Arbuthnot

Neque sermonibus Vulgi dederis te, nec in Praemiis humanis spem posueris rerum tuarum: suis te oportet illecebris ipsa Virtus trahat

ad verum decus. Quid de te alii loquantur, ipsi videant, sed
loquentur tamen.

TULLY [*De Re Publica*, vi. 23].

Advertisement

This paper is a sort of bill of complaint, begun many years since, and
drawn up by snatches, as the several occasions offered. I had no
thoughts of publishing it, till it pleased some persons of rank and
fortune° [the authors of *Verses to the Imitator of Horace*, and of an *Epistle
to a Doctor of Divinity from a Nobleman at Hampton Court*] to attack in a
very extraordinary manner, not only my writings (of which being public
the public judge) but my *person, morals*, and *family*, whereof to those
who know me not, a truer information may be requisite. Being divided
between the necessity to say something of *myself*, and my own laziness
to undertake so awkward a task, I thought it the shortest way to put
the last hand to this epistle. If it have any thing pleasing, it will be that
by which I am most desirous to please, the *truth* and the *sentiment*; and
if any thing offensive, it will be only to those I am least sorry to offend,
the *vicious* or *the ungenerous*.

Many will know their own pictures in it, there being not a circum-
stance but what is true; but I have, for the most part spared their *names*,
and they may escape being laughed at, if they please.

I would have some of them know, it was owing to the request of the
learned and candid friend to whom it is inscribed, that I make not as
free use of theirs as they have done of mine. However I shall have this
advantage, and honour, on my side, that whereas by their proceeding,
any abuse may be directed at any man, no injury can possibly be done
by mine, since a nameless character can never be found out, but by its
truth and *likeness*.

'Shut, shut the door, good John!',° fatigued I said,   1
'Tie up the knocker, say I'm sick, I'm dead.'
The dog-star° rages! nay 'tis past a doubt,
All Bedlam, or Parnassus, is let out:
Fire in each eye, and papers in each hand,
They rave, recite, and madden round the land.
    What walls can guard me, or what shades can hide?
They pierce my thickets, through my grot° they glide,

By land, by water, they renew the charge,
They stop the chariot, and they board the barge.   10
No place is sacred, not the church is free,
Ev'n Sunday shines no sabbath day° to me:
Then from the Mint walks forth the man of rhyme,
Happy! to catch me, just at dinner time.

    Is there a parson,° much bemused in beer,
A maudlin poetess, a rhyming peer,
A clerk, foredoomed his father's soul to cross,
Who pens a stanza, when he should *engross*?°
Is there, who, locked from ink and paper, scrawls
With desperate charcoal round his darkened walls?   20
All fly to TWIT'NAM, and in humble strain
Apply to me, to keep them mad or vain.
Arthur,° whose giddy son neglects the laws,
Imputes to me and my damned works the cause:
Poor Cornus° sees his frantic wife elope,
And curses wit, and poetry, and Pope.

    Friend to my life! (which did not you prolong,
The world had wanted many an idle song)
What *drop*° or *nostrum* can this plague remove?
Or which must end me, a fool's wrath or love?   30
A dire dilemma! either way I'm sped,
If foes, they write, if friends, they read me dead.
Seized and tied down to judge, how wretched I!
Who can't be silent, and who will not lie:
To laugh, were want of goodness and of grace,
And to be grave, exceeds all power of face.
I sit with sad civility, I read
With honest anguish, and an aching head;
And drop at last, but in unwilling ears,
This saving counsel, 'Keep your piece nine years.'°   40

    'Nine years!', cries he, who high° in Drury Lane°
Lulled by soft zephyrs through the broken pane,
Rhymes ere he wakes, and prints before *term*° ends,
Obliged by hunger, and request of friends:
'The piece, you think, is incorrect? why take it,
I'm all submission, what you'd have it, make it.'

    Three things another's modest wishes bound,
My friendship, and a prologue, and ten pound.

Pitholeon sends to me: 'You know his Grace,
I want a patron; ask him for a place.'   50
Pitholeon libelled me—'but here's a letter
Informs you, sir, 'twas when he knew no better.
Dare you refuse him? Curll° invites to dine,
He'll write a *Journal*, or he'll turn divine.'
    Bless me! a packet—' 'Tis a stranger sues,
A virgin tragedy, an orphan muse.'
If I dislike it, 'Furies, death and rage!'
If I approve, 'Commend it to the stage.'
There (thank my stars) my whole commission ends,
The players and I are, luckily, no friends.   60
Fired that the house reject him, ' 'Sdeath I'll print it,
And shame the fools—your interest, sir, with Lintot.'°
Lintot, dull rogue! will think your price too much:
'Not, sir, if you revise it, and retouch.'
All my demurs but double his attacks;
At last he whispers, 'Do, and we go snacks.'°
Glad of a quarrel, straight I clap the door,
Sir, let me see your works and you no more.
    'Tis sung, when Midas' ears began to spring,
(Midas, a sacred person and a king)   70
His very minister who spied them first,
(Some say his queen) was forced to speak, or burst.
And is not mine, my friend, a sorer case,
When every coxcomb perks them in my face?
    'Good friend forbear! you deal in dangerous things.
I'd never name queens, ministers, or kings;
Keep close to ears, and those let asses prick,
'Tis nothing'—Nothing? if they bite and kick?
Out with it, *Dunciad*! let the secret pass,
That secret to each fool, that he's an ass: 80
The truth once told (and wherefore should we lie?)
The queen of Midas slept, and so may I.
    You think this cruel? take it for a rule,

---

49. *Pitholeon*] The name taken from a foolish poet of Rhodes, who pretended
much to Greek. Schol. in Horat. lib. i. Dr Bentley pretends, that this Pitholeon
libelled Caesar also. See notes on Horace *Sat.* 10. l. i.

72. The story is told, by some, of his barber, but by Chaucer of his queen. See
Wife of Bath's Tale in Dryden's *Fables*.°

No creature smarts so little as a fool.
Let peals of laughter, Codrus!° round thee break,
Thou unconcerned canst hear the mighty crack:
Pit, box, and gallery in convulsions hurled,
Thou standst unshook amidst a bursting world.
Who shames a scribbler? break one cobweb through,
He spins the slight, self-pleasing thread anew: 90
Destroy his fib or sophistry; in vain,
The creature's at his dirty work again,
Throned in the centre of his thin designs,
Proud of a vast extent of flimsy lines!
Whom have I hurt? has poet yet, or peer,
Lost the arched eyebrow, or Parnassian sneer?
And has not Colley° still his lord, and whore?
His butchers Henley,° his freemasons° Moore?
Does not one table Bavius° still admit?
Still to one bishop° Philips seem a wit?   100
Still Sappho—'Hold! for God sake—you'll offend,
No names—be calm—learn prudence of a friend:
I too could write, and I am twice as tall;
But foes like these'—One flatterer's worse than all;
Of all mad creatures, if the learned are right,
It is the slaver° kills, and not the bite.
A fool quite angry is quite innocent:
Alas! 'tis ten times worse when they *repent*.
    One dedicates in high heroic prose,
And ridicules beyond a hundred foes: 110
One from all Grub Street will my fame defend,
And more abusive, calls himself my friend.
This prints my *Letters*,° that expects a bribe,
And others roar aloud, 'Subscribe, subscribe.'
    There are, who to my person pay their court:
I cough like Horace, and, though lean, am short,
Ammon's great son° one shoulder had too high,
Such Ovid's nose, and 'Sir! you have an eye—'
Go on, obliging creatures, make me see
All that disgraced my betters, met in me.   120

88. Alluding to Horace,
      Si fractus illabatur orbis,
      Impavidum ferient ruinae.

Say for my comfort, languishing in bed,
'Just so immortal Maro° held his head:'
And when I die, be sure you let me know
Great Homer died three thousand years ago.
  Why did I write? what sin to me unknown
Dipped me in ink, my parents', or my own?
As yet a child, nor yet a fool to fame,
I lisped in numbers, for the numbers came.
I left no calling for this idle trade,
No duty broke, no father disobeyed.   130
The Muse but served to ease some friend, not wife,
To help me through this long disease, my life,
To second, ARBUTHNOT! thy art and care,
And teach, the being you preserved, to bear.
  But why then publish? Granville° the polite,
And knowing Walsh,° would tell me I could write;
Well-natured Garth° inflamed with early praise,
And Congreve loved, and Swift endured my lays;
The courtly Talbot,° Somers,° Sheffield° read,
Ev'n mitred Rochester° would nod the head,   140
And St John's° self (great Dryden's friends before)
With open arms received one poet more.
Happy my studies, when by these approved!
Happier their author, when by these beloved!
From these the world will judge of men and books,
Not from the Burnets, Oldmixons, and Cookes.°
  Soft were my numbers; who could take offence
While pure description held the place of sense?
Like gentle Fanny's° was my flowery theme,
A painted mistress, or a purling stream.   150

---

139. All these were patrons or admirers of Mr Dryden; though a scandalous libel against him, entitled, *Dryden's Satyr to his Muse*, has been printed in the name of the Lord Somers, of which he was wholly ignorant.

These are the persons to whose account the author charges the publication of his first pieces: persons with whom he was conversant (and he adds beloved) at 16 or 17 years of age; an early period for such acquaintance. The catalogue might be made yet more illustrious, had he not confined it to that time when he writ the *Pastorals* and *Windsor Forest*, on which he passes a sort of censure in the lines following, *While pure description held the place of sense? &c.*

146. Authors of secret and scandalous history.

150. *A painted meadow, or a purling stream* is a verse of Mr Addison.

Yet then did Gildon° draw his venal quill;
I wished the man a dinner, and sate still:
Yet then did Dennis° rave in furious fret;
I never answered, I was not in debt:
If want provoked, or madness made them print,
I waged no war with Bedlam or the Mint.
   Did some more sober critic come abroad?
If wrong, I smiled; if right, I kissed the rod.°
Pains, reading, study, are their just pretence,
And all they want is spirit, taste, and sense.   160
Commas and points they set exactly right,
And 'twere a sin to rob them of their mite.
Yet ne'er one sprig of laurel graced these ribalds,°
From slashing Bentley down to piddling Tibbalds:°
Each wight who reads not, and but scans and spells,
Each word-catcher that lives on syllables,
Ev'n such small critics some regard may claim,
Preserved in Milton's or in Shakespeare's name.
Pretty! in amber to observe the forms
Of hairs, or straws, or dirt, or grubs, or worms!   170
The things, we know, are neither rich nor rare,
But wonder how the devil they got there?
   Were others angry? I excused them too;
Well might they rage, I gave them but their due.
A man's true merit 'tis not hard to find,
But each man's secret standard in his mind,
That casting-weight pride adds to emptiness,
This, who can gratify? for who can *guess*?
The bard whom pilfered pastorals° renown,
Who turns a Persian tale for half a crown,   180
Just writes to make his barrenness appear,
And strains from hard-bound brains, eight lines a year;
He, who still wanting, though he lives on theft,
Steals much, spends little, yet has nothing left:
And he, who now to sense, now nonsense leaning,
Means not, but blunders round about a meaning:
And he, whose fustian's so sublimely bad,
It is not poetry, but prose run mad:
All these, my modest satire bad *translate*,

180. Amb. Philips translated a book called the *Persian Tales*.

And owned that nine such poets made a Tate.°   190
How did they fume, and stamp, and roar, and chafe!
And swear, not ADDISON himself was safe.
   Peace to all such! but were there one° whose fires
True genius kindles, and fair fame inspires;
Blessed with each talent and each art to please,
And born to write, converse, and live with ease:
Should such a man, too fond to rule alone,
Bear, like the Turk, no brother near the throne,
View him with scornful, yet with jealous eyes,
And hate for arts that caused himself to rise;   200
Damn with faint praise, assent with civil leer,
And without sneering, teach the rest to sneer;
Willing to wound, and yet afraid to strike,
Just hint a fault, and hesitate dislike;
Alike reserved to blame, or to commend,
A timorous foe, and a suspicious friend;
Dreading ev'n fools, by flatterers besieged,
And so obliging, that he ne'er obliged;
Like Cato,° give his little senate laws,
And sit attentive to his own applause;   210
While wits and templars° every sentence raise,
And wonder with a foolish face of praise—
Who but must laugh, if such a man there be?
Who would not weep, if ATTICUS° were he!
   What though my name stood rubric° on the walls,
Or plastered posts, with claps,° in capitals?
Or smoking forth, a hundred hawkers load,
On wings of winds came flying all abroad?
I sought no homage from the race that write;
I kept, like Asian monarchs, from their sight: 220
Poems I heeded (now berhymed so long)
No more than thou, great GEORGE! a birthday song.°
I ne'er with wits or witlings passed my days,
To spread about the itch of verse and praise;

214. ATTICUS] It was a great falsehood, which some of the libels reported, that
this character was written after the gentleman's death; which see refuted in the
testimonies prefixed to the *Dunciad*. But the occasion of writing it was such as he
would not make public out of regard to his memory: and all that could further be
done was to omit the name, in the editions of his Works.

218. *On wings of winds came flying all abroad?*] Hopkins, in the civ[th] Psalm.

Nor like a puppy daggled through the town,
To fetch and carry singsong up and down;
Nor at rehearsals sweat, and mouthed, and cried,
With handkerchief and orange at my side;
But sick of fops, and poetry, and prate,
To Bufo° left the whole Castalian° state.   230

    Proud as Apollo on his forked hill,
Sate full-blown Bufo, puffed by every quill;
Fed with soft dedication all day long,
Horace and he went hand in hand in song.
His library (where busts of poets dead
And a true Pindar stood without a head)
Received of wits an undistinguished race,
Who first his judgment asked, and then a place:
Much they extolled his pictures, much his seat,
And flattered every day, and some days eat: 240
Till grown more frugal in his riper days,
He paid some bards with port, and some with praise.
To some a dry rehearsal was assigned,
And others (harder still) he paid in kind.
Dryden alone (what wonder?) came not nigh,
Dryden alone escaped this judging eye:
But still the great have kindness in reserve,
He helped to bury whom he helped to starve.

    May some choice patron bless each gray goose quill!
May every Bavius have his Bufo still!   250
So when a statesman wants a day's defence,
Or envy holds a whole week's war with sense,
Or simple pride for flattery makes demands,
May dunce by dunce be whistled off my hands!
Blessed be the great! for those they take away,
And those they left me; for they left me GAY;
Left me to see neglected genius bloom,
Neglected die, and tell it on his tomb:
Of all thy blameless life the sole return
My verse, and QUEENSBERRY° weeping o'er thy urn!   260

---

236. Ridicules the affectation of antiquaries, who frequently exhibit the headless *trunks* and *terms* of statues, for Plato, Homer, Pindar, &c. *Vide* Fulv. Ursin, &c.

248. Mr Dryden, after having lived in exigencies, had a magnificent funeral bestowed upon him by the contribution of several persons of quality.

Oh let me live my own, and die so too!
(To live and die is all I have to do:)
Maintain a poet's dignity and ease,
And see what friends, and read what books I please:
Above a patron, though I condescend
Sometimes to call a minister my friend:
I was not born for courts or great affairs;
I pay my debts, believe, and say my prayers;
Can sleep without a poem in my head,
Nor know, if Dennis be alive or dead.   270

  Why am I asked what next shall see the light?
Heavens! was I born for nothing but to write?
Has life no joys for me? or (to be grave)
Have I no friend to serve, no soul to save?
'I found him close with Swift'—'Indeed? no doubt'
(Cries prating Balbus) 'something will come out.'
'Tis all in vain, deny it as I will.
'No, such a genius never can lie still;'
And then for mine obligingly mistakes
The first lampoon Sir Will.° or Bubo° makes.   280
Poor guiltless I! and can I choose but smile,
When every coxcomb knows me by my *style?*°

  Cursed be the verse, how well soe'er it flow,
That tends to make one worthy man my foe,
Give virtue scandal, innocence a fear,
Or from the soft-eyed virgin steal a tear!
But he who hurts a harmless neighbour's peace,
Insults fallen worth, or beauty in distress,
Who loves a lie, lame slander helps about,
Who writes a libel, or who copies out: 290
That fop, whose pride affects a patron's name,
Yet absent, wounds an author's honest fame:
Who can *your* merit *selfishly* approve,
And show the *sense* of it without the *love*;
Who has the vanity to call you friend,
Yet wants the honour, injured, to defend;
Who tells whate'er you think, whate'er you say,
And, if he lie not, must at least betray:
Who to the dean and *silver bell* can swear,

299. *Dean.*] See the *Epistle to the Earl of Burlington.*

And sees at Cannons what was never there;   300
Who reads, but with a lust to misapply,
Make satire a lampoon, and fiction lie.
A lash like mine no honest man shall dread,
But all such babbling blockheads in his stead.
　　Let Sporus° tremble—'What? that thing of silk,
Sporus, that mere white curd of ass's milk?°
Satire or sense, alas! can Sporus feel?
Who breaks a butterfly upon a wheel?'
　　Yet let me flap this bug° with gilded wings,
This painted child° of dirt, that stinks and stings;   310
Whose buzz the witty and the fair annoys,
Yet wit ne'er tastes, and beauty ne'er enjoys:
So well-bred spaniels civilly delight
In mumbling of the game they dare not bite.
Eternal smiles his emptiness betray,
As shallow streams run dimpling all the way.
Whether in florid impotence he speaks,
And, as the prompter° breathes, the puppet° squeaks;
Or at the ear of Eve,° familiar toad,
Half froth, half venom, spits himself abroad,   320
In puns, or politics, or tales, or lies,
Or spite, or smut, or rhymes, or blasphemies.
His wit all seesaw, between *that* and *this*,
Now high, now low, now master up, now miss,°
And he himself one vile antithesis.
Amphibious thing! that acting either part,
The trifling head, or the corrupted heart,
Fop at the toilet, flatterer at the board,
Now trips a lady, and now struts a lord.
Eve's tempter thus the rabbins° have expressed,   330
A cherub's face, a reptile all the rest,
Beauty that shocks you, parts that none will trust,
Wit that can creep, and pride that licks the dust.
　　Not fortune's worshipper, nor fashion's fool,
Not lucre's madman, nor ambition's tool,
Not proud, nor servile; be one poet's praise,
That, if he pleased, he pleased by manly ways:
That flattery, ev'n to kings, he held a shame,

319. See Milton, Book iv.

And thought a lie in verse or prose the same:
That not in fancy's maze he wandered long,   340
But stooped° to truth, and moralized his song:
That not for fame, but virtue's better end,
He stood° the furious foe, the timid friend,
The damning critic, half approving wit,
The coxcomb hit, or fearing to be hit;
Laughed at the loss of friends he never had,
The dull, the proud, the wicked, and the mad;
The distant threats of vengeance on his head,
The blow unfelt, the tear he never shed;
The tale revived, the lie so oft o'erthrown;   350
Th' imputed trash, and dulness not his own;
The morals blackened when the writings 'scape,
The libelled person, and the pictured shape;°
Abuse, on all he loved, or loved him, spread,
A friend in exile,° or a father, dead;
The whisper, that to greatness still too near,
Perhaps, yet vibrates on his SOVEREIGN's ear—
Welcome for thee, fair virtue! all the past:
For thee, fair virtue! welcome ev'n the *last!*
    'But why insult the poor, affront the great?'   360
A knave's a knave, to me, in every state:
Alike my scorn, if he succeed or fail,
Sporus at court, or Japhet° in a jail,
A hireling scribbler, or a hireling peer,
Knight of the post° corrupt, or of the shire;
If on a pillory, or near a throne,
He gain his prince's ear, or lose his own.
    Yet soft by nature, more a dupe than wit,
Sappho can tell you how this man was bit:

---

350. *the lie so oft o'erthrown*] As that he received subscriptions for Shakespeare, that he set his name to Mr Broome's verses, &c. which, though publicly disproved, were nevertheless shamelessly repeated in the libels, and even in that called the *Nobleman's Epistle.*

351. *Th' imputed trash*] Such as profane *Psalms, Court Poems,* and other scandalous things, printed in his name by Curll and others.

354. Namely on the Duke of Buckingham, the Earl of Burlington, Lord Bathurst, Lord Bolingbroke, Bishop Atterbury, Dr Swift, Dr Arbuthnot, Mr Gay, his friends, his parents, and his very nurse, aspersed in printed papers, by James Moore, G. Ducket, L. Welsted, Tho. Bentley, and other obscure persons.

This dreaded satirist Dennis will confess   370
Foe to his pride, but friend to his distress:°
So humble, he has knocked at Tibbald's door,
Has drunk with Cibber, nay has rhymed for Moore.
Full ten years slandered, did he once reply?
Three thousand suns went down on Welsted's° lie.
To please a mistress, one aspersed his life;
He lashed him not, but let her be his wife:
Let Budgell° charge low Grub Street on his quill,
And write whate'er he pleased, except his will;
Let the two Curlls° of town and court, abuse   380
His father, mother, body, soul, and muse.
Yet why? that father held it for a rule,
It was a sin to call our neighbour fool:°
That harmless mother thought no wife a whore:
Hear this, and spare his family, James Moore!

374. *ten years*] It was so long after many libels before the author of the *Dunciad*
published that poem, till when, he never writ a word in answer to the many scurrilities
and falsehoods concerning him.

375. *Welsted's lie.*] This man had the impudence to tell in print, that Mr P. had
occasioned a *lady's death*, and to name a person he never heard of. He also published
that he libelled the Duke of Chandos; with whom (it was added) that he had lived
in familiarity, and received from him a present of *five hundred pounds*: the falsehood
of both which is known to his Grace. Mr P. never received any present, farther than
the subscription for Homer, from him, or from *Any great Man* whatsoever.

378. Budgell, in a weekly pamphlet called the *Bee*, bestowed much abuse on him,
in the imagination that he writ some things about the *Last Will* of Dr Tindal, in the
Grubstreet Journal; a paper wherein he never had the least hand, direction, or supervi-
sal, nor the least knowledge of its author.

381. In some of Curll's and other pamphlets, Mr Pope's father was said to be a
mechanic, a hatter, a farmer, nay a bankrupt. But, what is stranger, a nobleman (if
such a reflection could be thought to come from a nobleman) had dropped an
allusion to that pitiful untruth, in a paper called an *Epistle to a Doctor of Divinity*: and
the following line,

> *Hard as thy heart, and as thy birth obscure,*

had fallen from a like *courtly* pen, in certain *Verses to the Imitator of Horace*. Mr Pope's
father was of a gentleman's family in Oxfordshire, the head of which was the Earl
of Downe, whose sole heiress married the Earl of Lindsey—His mother was the
daughter of William Turner, Esq. of York. She had three brothers, one of whom
was killed, another died in the service of King Charles; the eldest following his
fortunes, and becoming a general officer in Spain, left her what estate remained
after the sequestrations and forfeitures of her family—Mr Pope died in 1717, aged
75; she in 1733, aged 93, a very few weeks after this poem was finished. The

Unspotted names, and memorable long!
If there be force in virtue, or in song.
   Of gentle blood (part shed in honour's cause,
While yet in Britain honour had applause)
Each parent sprung—'What fortune, pray?'—Their own,   390
And better got, than Bestia's° from the throne.
Born to no pride, inheriting no strife,
Nor marrying discord in a noble wife,
Stranger to civil and religious rage,
The good man walked innoxious through his age.
No courts he saw, no suits would ever try,
Nor dared an oath,° nor hazarded a lie:
Unlearned, he knew no schoolman's subtle art,
No language, but the language of the heart.
By nature honest, by experience wise,   400
Healthy by temperance, and by exercise;
His life, though long, to sickness past unknown,
His death was instant, and without a groan.
O grant me, thus to live, and thus to die!
Who sprung from kings shall know less joy than I.°
   O friend! may each domestic bliss be thine!
Be no unpleasing melancholy mine:
Me, let the tender office long engage
To rock the cradle of reposing age,
With lenient° arts extend a mother's breath,   410
Make languor smile, and smooth the bed of death,
Explore the thought, explain the asking eye,
And keep a while one parent from the sky!
On cares like these if length of days attend,

following inscription was placed by their son on their monument in the parish of
Twickenham, in Middlesex.

D. O. M.
ALEXANDRO. POPE. VIRO. INNOCVO. PROBO. PIO.
QVI. VIXIT. ANNOS. LXXV. OB. MDCCXVII.
ET. EDITHAE. CONIVGI. INCVLPABILI.
PIENTISSIMAE. QVAE. VIXIT. ANNOS.
XCIII. OB. MDCCXXXIII.
PARENTIBVS. BENEMERENTIBVS. FILIVS. FECIT.
ET. SIBI.°

May heaven, to bless those days, preserve my friend,
Preserve him social, cheerful, and serene,
And just as rich as when he served a QUEEN.°
Whether that blessing be denied or given,
Thus far was right, the rest belongs to heaven.

AN EPISTLE
TO
A LADY
Of the Characters *of* WOMEN

Nothing so true as what you once let fall,   1
'Most women have no characters at all.'
Matter too soft a lasting mark to bear,
And best distinguished by black, brown, or fair.
    How many pictures of one nymph we view,
All how unlike each other, all how true!
Arcadia's Countess,° here, in ermined pride,
Is there, Pastora° by a fountain side.
Here Fannia,° leering on her own good man,
And there, a naked Leda with a swan.   10
Let then the fair one beautifully cry,
In Magdalen's° loose hair and lifted eye,
Or dressed in smiles of sweet Cecilia shine,
With simpering angels, palms, and harps divine;
Whether the charmer sinner it, or saint it,

1. Of the CHARACTERS of WOMEN, *treating of this sex only as contradistinguished from the other.*
    That their particular characters are not so strongly marked as those of men, seldom so fixed, and still more inconsistent with themselves.

7, 8, 10, &c. *Arcadia's Countess,—Pastora by a fountain—Leda with a swan.— Magdalen—Cecilia—*] Attitudes in which several ladies affected to be drawn, and sometimes one lady in them all—The poet's politeness and compliance to the sex is observable in this instance, amongst others, that, whereas in the *Characters of Men* he has sometimes made use of real names, in the *Characters of Women* always fictitious.

If folly grow romantic,° I must paint it!
   Come then, the colours and the ground prepare!
Dip in the rainbow, trick her off° in air;
Choose a firm cloud before it fall, and in it
Catch, e'er she change, the Cynthia° of this minute.   20

   Rufa,° whose eye quick-glancing o'er the park,
Attracts each light gay meteor of a spark,
Agrees as ill with Rufa studying Locke,
As Sappho's diamonds with her dirty smock;
Or Sappho at her toilet's greasy task,
With Sappho fragrant at an evening mask:°
So morning insects that in muck begun,
Shine, buzz, and fly-blow in the setting-sun.

   How soft is Silia! fearful to offend,
The frail one's advocate, the weak one's friend: 30
To her, Calista proved her conduct nice,°
And good Simplicius asks of her advice.
Sudden, she storms! she raves! You tip the wink,
But spare your censure; Silia does not drink.
All eyes may see from what the change arose,
All eyes may see—a pimple on her nose.

   Papillia,° wedded to her amorous spark,
Sighs for the shades—'How charming° is a park!'
A park is purchased; but the fair he sees
All bathed in tears—'Oh odious, odious trees!'   40

   Ladies like variegated tulips show;
'Tis to their changes half their charms we owe;
Their happy spots the nice admirer take,
Fine by defect, and delicately weak.
'Twas thus Calypso° once each heart alarmed,
Awed without virtue, without beauty charmed;
Her tongue bewitched as oddly as her eyes,
Less wit than mimic, more a wit than wise;
Strange graces still, and stranger flights she had,
Was just not ugly, and was just not mad;   50

---

21. Instances of contrarieties, given even from such characters as are most
strongly marked, and seemingly, therefore most consistent: as, I. In the *Affected*,
v. 21, &c.

29–40. II. Contrarieties in the *soft-natured*.

45. III. Contrarieties in the *cunning* and *artful*.

Yet ne'er so sure our passion to create,
As when she touched the brink of all we hate.
   Narcissa's nature, tolerably mild,
To make a wash,° would hardly stew a child;
Has ev'n been proved to grant a lover's prayer,
And paid a tradesman once to make him stare;
Gave alms at Easter, in a Christian trim,°
And made a widow happy, for a whim.
Why then declare good nature is her scorn,
When 'tis by that alone she can be born?   60
Why pique all mortals, yet affect a name?
A fool to pleasure, yet a slave to fame:
Now deep in Taylor° and the Book of Martyrs,°
Now drinking citron° with his Grace and Chartres:°
Now conscience chills her, and now passion burns;
And atheism and religion take their turns;
A very heathen in the carnal part,
Yet still a sad, good Christian at her heart.
   See sin in state, majestically drunk;
Proud as a peeress, prouder as a punk;°   70
Chaste to her husband, frank to all beside,
A teeming mistress, but a barren bride.
What then? let blood and body bear the fault,°
Her head's untouched, that noble seat of thought:
Such this day's doctrine—in another fit
She sins with poets through pure love of wit.
What has not fired her bosom or her brain?
Caesar and Tallboy,° Charles° and Charlemagne.
As Helluo,° late dictator of the feast,
The nose of hautgout,° and the tip of taste,   80
Critiqued your wine, and analyzed your meat,
Yet on plain pudding deigned at home to eat;
So Philomedé,° lecturing all mankind
On the soft passion, and the taste refined,
Th'address, the delicacy—stoops at once,
And makes her hearty meal upon a dunce.
   Flavia's a wit, has too much sense to pray;

53. IV. In the *whimsical.*
69. V. In the *lewd* and *vicious.*
87. VI. Contrarieties in the *witty* and *refined.*

To toast our wants and wishes, is her way;
Nor asks of God, but of her stars, to give
The mighty blessing, 'while we live, to live.' 90
Then all for death, that opiate of the soul!
Lucretia's dagger, Rosamonda's bowl.°
Say, what can cause such impotence of mind?
A spark too fickle, or a spouse too kind.
Wise wretch! with pleasures too refined to please,
With too much spirit to be e'er at ease,
With too much quickness ever to be taught,
With too much thinking to have common thought:
You purchase pain with all that joy can give,
And die of nothing but a rage to live. 100
    Turn then from wits; and look on Simo's° mate,
No ass so meek, no ass so obstinate:
Or her, that owns her faults, but never mends,
Because she's honest, and the best of friends:
Or her, whose life the church and scandal share,
For ever in a passion, or a prayer:
Or her, who laughs at hell, but (like her Grace)
Cries, 'Ah! how charming if there's no such place!'
Or who in sweet vicissitude appears
Of mirth and opium, ratafee° and tears, 110
The daily anodyne, and nightly draught,
To kill those foes to fair ones, time and thought.
Woman and fool are two hard things to hit;
For true no-meaning puzzles more than wit.
    But what are these to great Atossa's° mind?
Scarce once herself, by turns all womankind!
Who, with herself, or others, from her birth
Finds all her life one warfare upon earth:
Shines, in exposing knaves, and painting fools,
Yet is, whate'er she hates and ridicules. 120
No thought advances, but her eddy brain
Whisks it about, and down it goes again.
Full sixty years the world has been her trade,
The wisest fool much time has ever made.
From loveless youth to unrespected age,
No passion gratified except her rage.
So much the fury still outran the wit,
The pleasure missed her, and the scandal hit.

Who breaks with her, provokes revenge from hell,
But he's a bolder man who dares be well.   130
Her every turn with violence pursued,
Nor more a storm her hate than gratitude:
To that each passion turns, or soon or late;
Love, if it makes her yield, must make her hate:
Superiors? death! and equals? what a curse!
But an inferior not dependant? worse.
Offend her, and she knows not to forgive;
Oblige her, and she'll hate you while you live:
But die, and she'll adore you—Then the bust
And temple rise—then fall again to dust.   140
Last night, her lord was all that's good and great;
A knave this morning, and his will a cheat.°
Strange! by the means defeated of the ends,
By spirit robbed of power, by warmth of friends,
By wealth of followers! without one distress
Sick of herself through very selfishness!
Atossa, cursed with every granted prayer,
Childless with all her children, wants an heir.
To heirs unknown descends th'unguarded store
Or wanders, heaven-directed, to the poor.   150

　　Pictures like these, dear Madam, to design,
Asks no firm hand, and no unerring line;
Some wandering touches, some reflected light,
Some flying stroke alone can hit 'em right:
For how should equal colours do the knack?°
Chameleons who can paint in white and black?

　　'Yet Cloe° sure was formed without a spot'—
Nature in her then erred not, but forgot.
'With every pleasing, every prudent part,
Say, what can Cloe want?'—She wants a heart.   160
She speaks, behaves, and acts just as she ought;
But never, never, reached one generous thought.
Virtue she finds too painful an endeavour,
Content to dwell in decencies for ever.
So very reasonable, so unmoved,
As never yet to love, or to be loved.
She, while her lover pants upon her breast,
Can mark the figures on an Indian chest;
And when she sees her friend in deep despair,

Observes how much a chintz exceeds mohair.   170
Forbid it heaven, a favour or a debt
She e'er should cancel—but she may forget.
Safe is your secret still in Cloe's ear;
But none of Cloe's shall you ever hear.
Of all her dears she never slandered one,
But cares not if a thousand are undone.
Would Cloe know if you're alive or dead?
She bids her footman put it in her head.
Cloe is prudent—Would you too be wise?
Then never break your heart when Cloe dies.   180
     One certain portrait may (I grant) be seen,
Which heaven has varnished out, and made a Queen:°
THE SAME FOR EVER! and described by all
With truth and goodness, as with crown and ball.°
Poets heap virtues, painters gems at will,
And show their zeal, and hide their want of skill,
'Tis well—but, artists! who can paint or write,
To draw the naked is your true delight.
That robe of quality so struts and swells,
None see what parts or nature it conceals: 190
Th'exactest traits of body or of mind,
We owe to models of an humble kind.
If QUEENSBERRY° to strip there's no compelling,
'Tis from a handmaid we must take a Helen.
From peer or bishop 'tis no easy thing
To draw the man who loves his God, or king:
Alas! I copy (or my draught would fail)
From honest Mah'met, or plain Parson Hale.°
     But grant, in public men sometimes are shown,
A woman's seen in private life alone: 200
Our bolder talents in full light displayed;
Your virtues open fairest in the shade.
Bred to disguise, in public 'tis you hide;
There, none distinguish 'twixt your shame or pride,
Weakness or delicacy; all so nice,
That each may seem a virtue, or a vice.

198. *Mah'met*, servant to the late king, said to be the son of a Turkish Bassa,
whom he took at the Siege of Buda, and constantly kept about his person.

  In men, we various ruling passions find;
In women, two almost divide the kind;
Those, only fixed, they first or last obey,
The love of pleasure, and the love of sway.   210
  That, nature gives; and where the lesson taught
Is but to please, can pleasure seem a fault?
Experience, this; by man's oppression cursed,
They seek the second not to lose the first.
  Men, some to business, some to pleasure take;
But every woman is at heart a rake:
Men, some to quiet, some to public strife;
But every lady would be queen for life.
  Yet mark the fate of a whole sex of queens!
Power all their end, but beauty all the means: 220
In youth they conquer with so wild a rage,
As leaves them scarce a subject in their age:
For foreign glory, foreign joy, they roam;
No thought of peace or happiness at home.
But wisdom's triumph is well-timed retreat,
As hard a science to the fair as great!
Beauties, like tyrants, old and friendless grown,
Yet hate repose, and dread to be alone,
Worn out in public, weary every eye,
Nor leave one sigh behind them when they die.   230
  Pleasures the sex, as children birds, pursue,
Still out of reach, yet never out of view;
Sure, if they catch, to spoil the toy at most,
To covet flying, and regret when lost:
At last, to follies youth could scarce defend,
It grows their age's prudence to pretend;
Ashamed to own they gave delight before,
Reduced to feign it, when they give no more:
As hags° hold sabbaths, less for joy than spite,

---

 207. The former part having shown, that the *particular characters* of women are more various than those of men, it is nevertheless observed, that the *general* characteristic of the sex, as to the *ruling passion*, is more uniform.

 211. This is occasioned partly by their *nature*, partly their *education*, and in some degree by *necessity*.

 219. What are the *aims* and the *fate* of this sex?—I. As to *power*.

 231.—II. As to *pleasure*.

So these their merry, miserable night;   240
Still round and round° the ghosts of beauty glide,
And haunt the places where their honour died.
  See how the world its veterans rewards!
A youth of frolics, an old age of cards;
Fair to no purpose, artful to no end,
Young without lovers, old without a friend;
A fop their passion, but their prize a sot,
Alive, ridiculous, and dead, forgot!
  Ah! friend!° to dazzle let the vain design;
To raise the thought, and touch the heart be thine!   250
That charm shall grow, while what fatigues the ring
Flaunts and goes down, an unregarded thing:
So when the sun's broad beam has tired the sight,
All mild ascends the moon's more sober light,
Serene in virgin modesty she shines,
And unobserved the glaring orb declines.
  Oh! blessed with temper,° whose unclouded ray
Can make tomorrow cheerful as today;
She, who can love a sister's charms, or hear
Sighs for a daughter with unwounded ear;   260
She, who ne'er answers till a husband cools,
Or, if she rules him, never shows she rules;
Charms by accepting, by submitting sways,
Yet has her humour most, when she obeys;
Let fops or fortune fly which way they will;
Disdains all loss of tickets,° or codille;°
Spleen, vapours, or smallpox,° above them all,
And mistress of herself, though China fall.
  And yet, believe me, good as well as ill,
Woman's at best a contradiction still.   270
Heaven, when it strives to polish all it can
Its last best work, but forms a softer man;
Picks from each sex, to make the favourite blest,
Your love of pleasure, our desire of rest:
Blends, in exception to all general rules,
Your taste of follies, with our scorn of fools,
Reserve with frankness, art with truth allied,

249. Advice for their true interest.
269. The picture of an estimable woman, with the best kind of contrarieties.

Courage with softness, modesty with pride,
Fixed principles, with fancy ever new;
Shakes all together, and produces—You.   280
   Be this a woman's fame: with this unblessed,
Toasts live a scorn, and queens may die a jest.
This Phoebus promised (I forget the year)°
When those blue eyes first opened on the sphere;
Ascendant° Phoebus watched that hour with care,
Averted half your parents' simple prayer,
And gave you beauty, but denied the pelf
That buys your sex a tyrant o'er itself.
The generous God, who wit and gold refines,°
And ripens spirits as he ripens mines,   290
Kept dross for duchesses, the world shall know it,
To you gave sense, good humour, and a poet.

THE SECOND SATIRE OF DR JOHN DONNE
VERSIFIED

Yes; thank my stars! as early as I knew   1
This town, I had the sense to hate it too:
Yet here, as even in hell, there must be still
One giant-vice, so excellently ill,
That all beside, one pities, not abhors;
As who knows Sappho, smiles at other whores.
   I grant that poetry's a crying sin;
It brought (no doubt) th' Excise° and Army° in:
Catched like the plague, or love, the Lord knows how,
But that the cure is starving, all allow.   10
Yet like the papist's, is the poet's state,
Poor and disarmed,° and hardly worth your hate!
   Here a lean bard, whose wit could never give
Himself a dinner, makes an actor live:
The thief condemned, in law already dead,
So prompts, and saves a rogue who cannot read.°
Thus as the pipes of some carved organ move,
The gilded puppets dance and mount above.

Heaved by the breath th' inspiring bellows blow:
Th' inspiring bellows lie and pant below.   20

   One sings the fair; but songs no longer move;
No rat is rhymed° to death, nor maid to love:
In love's, in nature's spite, the siege they hold,
And scorn the flesh, the devil,° and all but gold.

   These write to lords, some mean reward to get,
As needy beggars sing at doors for meat.
Those write because all write, and so have still
Excuse for writing, and for writing ill.

   Wretched indeed! but far more wretched yet
Is he who makes his meal on others' wit: 30
'Tis changed, no doubt, from what it was before;
His rank digestion makes it wit no more:
Sense, passed through him, no longer is the same;
For food digested takes another name.

   I pass o'er all those confessors° and martyrs,
Who live like Sutton,° or who die like Chartres,°
Outcant old Esdras,° or outdrink his heir,
Out-usure Jews, or Irishmen outswear;
Wicked as pages, who in early years
Act sins which Prisca's° confessor° scarce hears.   40
Ev'n those I pardon, for whose sinful sake
Schoolmen new tenements in hell must make;
Of whose strange crimes no canonist° can tell
In what commandment's large contents they dwell.

   One, one man only breeds my just offence;
Whom crimes gave wealth, and wealth gave impudence:
Time, that at last matures a clap° to pox,°
Whose gentle progress makes a calf an ox,
And brings all natural events to pass,
Hath made him an attorney of an ass.   50
No young divine, new-beneficed, can be
More pert, more proud, more positive than he.
What further could I wish the fop to do,
But turn a wit, and scribble verses too;
Pierce the soft labyrinth of a lady's ear
With rhymes of this *per cent.* and that *per year?*
Or court a wife, spread out his wily parts,
Like nets or lime-twigs,° for rich widows' hearts?
Call himself barrister to every wench,

And woo in language of the Pleas and Bench?°   60
Language, which Boreas might to Auster° hold
More rough than forty Germans when they scold.
  Cursed be the wretch! so venal and so vain;
Paltry and proud, as drabs in Drury Lane.°
'Tis such a bounty as was never known,
If PETER° deigns to help you to your *own:*
What thanks, what praise, if Peter but supplies,
And what a solemn face if he denies!
Grave, as when prisoners shake the head and swear
'Twas only suretyship° that brought 'em there.   70
His *office* keeps your parchment fates entire,
He starves with cold to save them from the fire;
For you he walks the streets through rain or dust,
For not in chariots Peter puts his trust;
For you he sweats and labours at the laws,
Takes God to witness he affects° your cause,
And lies to every lord in everything.°
Like a king's favourite—or like a king.
These are the talents that adorn them all,
From wicked Waters ev'n to godly * *°   80
Not more of simony beneath black gowns,
Nor more of bastardy in heirs to crowns.
In shillings and in pence at first they deal;
And steal so little, few perceive they steal;
Till, like the sea, they compass all the land,
From Scots to Wight, from Mount to Dover strand:
And when rank widows purchase luscious nights,
Or when a duke° to Jansen punts at White's,°
Or city-heir in mortgage melts away;
Satan himself feels far less joy than they.   90
Piecemeal they win this acre first, then that,
Glean on, and gather up the whole estate.
Then strongly fencing° ill-got wealth by law,
Indentures, covenants, articles they draw,
Large as the fields themselves, and larger far
Than civil codes, with all their glosses, are;
So vast, our new divines, we must confess,
Are fathers of the church for writing less.
But let them write for you, each rogue impairs
The deeds, and dextrously omits, *ses heires:*   100

No commentator can more slily pass
O'er a learned, unintelligible place;°
Or, in quotation, shrewd divines leave out
Those words, that would against them clear the doubt.
    So Luther thought the Paternoster long,
When doomed to say his beads° and evensong;
But having cast his cowl, and left those laws,
Adds to Christ's prayer, the 'power and glory' clause.°
    The lands are bought; but where are to be found
Those ancient woods, that shaded all the ground?   110
We see no new-built palaces aspire,
No kitchens emulate the vestal fire.
Where are those troops of poor, that thronged of yore
The good old landlord's hospitable door?
Well, I could wish, that still in lordly domes
Some beasts were killed, though not whole hecatombs;
That both extremes were banished from their walls,
Carthusian° fasts, and fulsome bacchanals;
And all mankind might that just mean observe,
In which none e'er could surfeit, none could starve.   120
These as good works, 'tis true, we all allow;
But oh! these works are not in fashion now:
Like rich old wardrobes,° things extremely rare,
Extremely fine, but what no man will wear.
    Thus much I've said, I trust, without offence;
Let no court sycophant pervert my sense,
Nor sly informer watch these words to draw
Within the reach of treason, or the law.

POPE TO JONATHAN SWIFT
25 March 1736

If ever I write more epistles in verse, one of them shall be addressed
to you.° I have long concerted it, and begun it, but I would make what
bears your name as finished as my last work ought to be, that is to say,
more finished than any of the rest. The subject is large, and will divide
into four epistles,° which naturally follow the *Essay on Man, viz.* 1. Of

the extent and limits of human reason, and science, 2. A view of the useful and therefore attainable, and of the un-useful and therefore unattainable, arts. 3. Of the nature, ends, application, and the use of different capacities. 4. Of the use of *learning*, of the *science* of the *world*, and of *wit*. It will conclude with a satire against the misapplication of all these, exemplified by pictures, characters, and examples.

But alas! the task is great, and *non sum qualis eram*!° My understanding indeed, such as it is, is extended rather than diminished: I see things more in the whole, more consistent, and more clearly deduced from, and related to, each other. But what I gain on the side of philosophy, I lose on the side of poetry: the flowers are gone, when the fruits begin to ripen, and the fruits perhaps will never ripen perfectly. The climate (under our heaven of a court) is but cold and uncertain: the winds rise, and the winter comes on. I find myself but little disposed to build a new house; I have nothing left but to gather up the relics of a wreck, and look about me to see what friends I have! Pray whose esteem or admiration should I desire now to procure by my writings? whose friendship or conversation to obtain by 'em? I am a man of desperate fortunes, that is a man whose friends are dead: for I never aimed at any other fortune than in friends. As soon as I had sent my last letter, I received a most kind one from you, expressing great pain for my late illness at Mr Cheselden's.° I conclude you was eased of that friendly apprehension in a few days after you had dispatched yours, for mine must have reached you then. I wondered a little at your query, who Cheselden was? it shows that the truest merit does not travel so far any way as on the wings of poetry; he is the most noted, and most deserving man, in the whole profession of chirurgery; and has saved the lives of thousands by his manner of cutting for the stone.—I am now well, or what I must call so.

I have lately seen some writings of Lord B's,° since he went to France. Nothing can depress his genius: whatever befalls him, he will still be the greatest man in the world, either in his own time, or with posterity.

Every man you know or care for here, enquires of you, and pays you the only devoir he can, that of drinking your health. Here are a race sprung up of young patriots,° who would animate you. I wish you had any motive to see this kingdom. I could keep you, for I am rich, that is, I have more than I want. I can afford you room for yourself and two servants; I have indeed room enough, nothing but myself at home! the kind and hearty housewife° is dead! the agreeable and instructive neighbour is gone! yet my house is enlarged, and the gardens extend

and flourish, as knowing nothing of the guests they have lost. I have
more fruit-trees and kitchen-garden than you have any thought of; nay
I have good melons and pineapples of my own growth. I am as much
a better gardener, as I'm a worse poet, than when you saw me: but
gardening is near akin to philosophy, for Tully° says *Agricultura
proxima sapientiae*. For God's sake, why should not you, (that are a step
higher than a philosopher, a divine, yet have too much grace and wit
than to be a bishop) e'en give all you have to the poor of Ireland (for
whom you have already done everything else) so quit the place, and
live and die with me? And let *Tales Animae Concordes*° be our motto and
our epitaph.

THE

SECOND EPISTLE

OF THE

SECOND BOOK

OF

HORACE IMITATED

Ludentis speciem dabit et torquebitur.

HORACE.

Dear Colonel,° COBHAM's and your country's friend!   1
You love a verse, take such as I can send.
A Frenchman comes, presents you with his boy,
Bows and begins—'This lad, sir, is of Blois:°
Observe his shape how clean! his locks how curled!
My only son, I'd have him see the world:
His French is pure; his voice too—you shall hear—
Sir, he's your slave, for twenty pound a year.
Mere wax as yet, you fashion him with ease,
Your barber, cook, upholsterer,° what you please: 10
A perfect genius at an opera song—
To say too much, might do my honour wrong.

Take him with all his virtues, on my word;
His whole ambition was to serve a lord;
But, sir, to you, with what would I not part?
Though faith, I fear 'twill break his mother's heart.
Once (and but once) I caught him in a lie,
And then, unwhipped, he had the grace to cry:
The fault he has I fairly shall reveal,
(Could you o'erlook but that) it is, to steal.'   20

    If, after this, you took the graceless lad,
Could you complain, my friend, he proved so bad?
Faith, in such case, if you should prosecute,
I think Sir Godfrey should decide the suit;
Who sent the thief that stole the cash away,
And punished him that put it in his way.

    Consider then, and judge me in this light;
I told you when I went, I could not write;
You said the same; and are you discontent
With laws, to which you gave your own assent?   30
Nay worse, to ask for verse at such a time!
D'ye think me good for nothing but to rhyme?

    In ANNA's wars,° a soldier poor and old
Had dearly earned a little purse of gold:
Tired with a tedious march, one luckless night,
He slept, poor dog! and lost it, to a doit.°
This put the man in such a desperate mind, ⎫
Between revenge, and grief, and hunger joined ⎬
Against the foe, himself, and all mankind, ⎭
He leapt the trenches, scaled a castle-wall,   40
Tore down a standard, took the fort and all.
'Prodigious well', his great commander cried,
Gave him much praise, and some reward beside.
Next pleased his Excellence a town to batter;
(Its name I know not, and it's no great matter)
'Go on, my friend,' he cried, 'see yonder walls!
Advance and conquer! go where glory calls!
More honours, more rewards, attend the brave.'
Don't you remember what reply he gave?
'D'ye think me, noble general, such a sot?   50

---

24. *Sir Godfrey*. An eminent Justice of Peace, who decided much in the manner of Sancho Pança.°

Let him take castles who has ne'er a groat."°
   Bred up at home, full early I begun
To read in Greek the wrath of Peleus' son.°
Besides, my father taught me from a lad,
The better art to know the good from bad:
(And little sure imported to remove,
To hunt for truth in Maudlin's° learned grove.)
But knottier points we knew not half so well,
Deprived us soon of our paternal cell;
And certain laws, by sufferers thought unjust,   60
Denied all posts of profit or of trust:
Hopes after hopes of pious papists failed,
While mighty WILLIAM's thundering arm prevailed.
For right hereditary taxed and fined,
He stuck to poverty with peace of mind;
And me, the muses helped to undergo it;
Convict° a papist he, and I a poet.°
But (thanks to Homer)° since I live and thrive,
Indebted to no prince or peer alive,
Sure I should want the care of ten Munroes,°   70
If I would scribble, rather than repose.

   Years following years, steal something every day,
At last they steal us from ourselves away;
In one our frolics, one amusements end,
In one a mistress drops, in one a friend:
This subtle thief of life, this paltry time,
What will it leave me, if it snatch my rhyme?
If every wheel of that unwearied mill
That turned ten thousand verses, now stands still.°   80

   But after all, what would you have me do?
When out of twenty I can please not two;
When this heroics only deigns to praise,
Sharp satire that, and that Pindaric lays?
One likes the pheasant's wing, and one the leg;
The vulgar boil, the learned roast an egg;
Hard task! to hit the palate of such guests,
When Oldfield° loves, what Dartineuf° detests.

   But grant I may relapse, for want of grace,
Again to rhyme; can London be the place?

70. Dr Munroe, physician to Bedlam Hospital.

Who there his muse, or self, or soul attends,   90
In crowds, and courts, law, business, feasts and friends?
My counsel sends to execute a deed:
A poet begs me, I will hear him read:
'In Palace Yard at nine you'll find me there—
At ten for certain, sir, in Bloomsbury Square—
Before the Lords at twelve my cause comes on—
There's a rehearsal, Sir, exact at one.'—°
'Oh but a wit can study in the streets,
And raise his mind above the mob he meets.'
Not quite so well however as one ought;   100
A hackney coach may chance to spoil a thought;
And then a nodding beam, or pig° of lead,
God knows, may hurt the very ablest head.
Have you not seen, at Guildhall's narrow pass,°
Two aldermen dispute it with an ass?
And peers give way, exalted as they are,
Ev'n to their own s–r–v—nce° in a car?°
    Go, lofty poet! and in such a crowd,
Sing thy sonorous verse—but not aloud.
Alas! to grottoes° and to groves we run,   110
To ease and silence, every muse's son:
Blackmore himself, for any grand effort,
Would drink and doze at Tooting or Earl's Court.
How shall I rhyme in this eternal roar?
How match the bards whom none e'er matched before?
The man, who, stretched in Isis' calm retreat,°
To books and study gives seven years complete,
See! strowed with learned dust, his nightcap on,
He walks, an object new beneath the sun!
The boys flock round him, and the people stare: \
So stiff, so mute! some statue you would swear, } 120
Stepped from its pedestal to take the air!   /
And here, while town, and court, and city roars,
With mobs, and duns,° and soldiers, at their doors;
Shall I, in London, act this idle part?
Composing songs, for fools to get by heart?
    The Temple late two brother serjeants° saw,
Who deemed each other oracles of law;

113. Two villages within a few miles of London.

With equal talents, these congenial souls
One lulled th' Exchequer, and one stunned the Rolls;°   130
Each had a gravity would make you split,
And shook his head at Murray,° as a wit.
'Twas, 'Sir, your law'—and 'Sir, your eloquence'
'Yours, Cowper's° manner—and yours, Talbot's° sense.'
    Thus we dispose of all poetic merit,
Yours Milton's genius, and mine Homer's spirit.
Call Tibbald° Shakespeare, and he'll swear the nine°
(Dear Cibber!) never matched one ode of thine.
Lord! how we strut through Merlin's Cave,° to see
No poets there, but Stephen,° you, and me.   140
Walk with respect behind, while we at ease
Weave laurel crowns, and take what names we please.
'My dear Tibullus!'° if that will not do,
'Let me be Horace, and be Ovid you:
Or, I'm content, allow me Dryden's strains,
And you shall rise up Otway for your pains.'
Much do I suffer, much, to keep in peace
This jealous, waspish, wronghead, rhyming race;
And much must flatter, if the whim should bite
To court applause by printing what I write: 150
But let the fit pass o'er, I'm wise enough,
To stop my ears to their confounded stuff.
    In vain, bad rhymers all mankind reject,
They treat themselves with most profound respect;
'Tis to small purpose that you hold your tongue,
Each praised within, is happy all day long,
But how severely with themselves proceed
The men, who write such verse as we can read?
Their own strict judges, not a word they spare
That wants or force, or light, or weight, or care,   160
Howe'er unwillingly it quits its place,
Nay though at court (perhaps) it may find grace:
Such they'll degrade; and sometimes, in its stead,
In downright charity revive the dead;
Mark where a bold expressive phrase appears,
Bright through the rubbish of some hundred years;
Command old words that long have slept, to wake,
Words, that wise Bacon, or brave Raleigh spake;
Or bid the new be English, ages hence,

(For use will father what's begot by sense)   170
Pour the full tide of eloquence along,
Serenely pure, and yet divinely strong,
Rich with the treasures of each foreign tongue;
Prune the luxuriant, the uncouth refine
But show no mercy to an empty line:
Then polish all, with so much life and ease,
You think 'tis nature, and a knack to please:
'But ease in writing flows from art, not chance;
As those move easiest who have learned to dance.'°

  If such the plague and pains to write by rule,   180
Better (say I) be pleased, and play the fool;
Call, if you will, bad rhyming a disease,
It gives men happiness, or leaves them ease.
There lived *in primo Georgii* (they record)
A worthy member, no small fool, a lord;
Who, though the House was up, delighted sate,
Heard, noted, answered, as in full debate:
In all but this, a man of sober life,
Fond of his friend, and civil to his wife;
Not quite a madman, though a pasty fell,   190
And much too wise to walk into a well:
Him, the damned doctors and his friends immured,
They bled, they cupped,° they purged; in short, they
        cured:
Whereat the gentleman began to stare—
'My friends?' he cried, 'p—x take you for your care!
That from a patriot° of distinguished note,
Have bled and purged me to a simple vote.'

  Well, on the whole, plain prose must be my fate:
Wisdom (curse on it) will come soon or late.
There is a time when poets will grow dull: 200
I'll e'en° leave verses to the boys at school:
To rules of poetry no more confined,
I learn to smooth and harmonize my mind,
Teach every thought within its bounds to roll,
And keep the equal measure of the soul.

  Soon as I enter at my country door,
My mind resumes the thread it dropped before;
Thoughts, which at Hyde Park Corner° I forgot,
Meet and rejoin me, in the pensive grot.

There all alone, and compliments apart,   210
I ask these sober questions of my heart.

If, when the more you drink, the more you crave,
You tell the doctor; when the more you have,
The more you want, why not with equal ease
Confess as well your folly, as disease?
The heart resolves this matter in a trice,
'Men only feel the smart, but not the vice.'

When golden angels cease to cure the evil,°
You give all royal witchcraft to the devil:
When servile chaplains cry, that birth and place   220
Endue a peer with honour, truth, and grace,
Look in that breast, most dirty Duke! be fair,
Say, can you find out one such lodger there?
Yet still, not heeding what your heart can teach,
You go to church to hear these flatterers preach.

Indeed, could wealth bestow or wit or merit,
A grain of courage, or a spark of spirit,
The wisest man might blush, I must agree,
If Devonshire° loved sixpence, more than he.

If there be truth in law, and use can give   230
A property, that's yours on which you live.
Delightful Abscourt,° if its fields afford
Their fruits to you, confesses you its lord:
All Worldly's° hens, nay partridge, sold to town,
His venison too, a guinea makes your own:
He bought at thousands, what with better wit
You purchase as you want, and bit by bit;
Now, or long since, what difference will be found?
You pay a penny, and he paid a pound.

Heathcote° himself, and such large-acred men,   240
Lords of fat Evesham, or of Lincoln fen,°
Buy every stick of wood that lends them heat,
Buy every pullet they afford to eat.
Yet these are wights, who fondly call their own
Half that the devil o'erlooks from Lincoln town.°
The laws of God, as well as of the land,
Abhor, a perpetuity° should stand:
Estates have wings, and hang in fortune's power
Loose on the point of every wavering hour,
Ready, by force, or of your own accord,   250

By sale, at least by death, to change their lord.
Man? and *for ever?* wretch! what wouldst thou have?
Heir urges heir, like wave impelling wave.
All vast possessions (just the same the case
Whether you call them villa, park, or chase)
Alas, my BATHURST! what will they avail?°
Join Cotswold hills to Sapperton's° fair dale,
Let rising granaries and temples here,
There mingled farms and pyramids appear,
Link towns to towns with avenues of oak,   260
Enclose whole downs in walls, 'tis all a joke!
Inexorable Death shall level all,
And trees, and stones, and farms, and farmer fall.

   Gold, silver, ivory, vases sculptured high,
Paint, marble, gems, and robes of Persian dye,
There are who have not—and thank heaven there are,
Who, if they have not, think not worth their care.

   Talk what you will of taste, my friend, you'll find,
Two of a face, as soon as of a mind.
Why, of two brothers, rich and restless one   270
Ploughs, burns, manures, and toils from sun to sun;
The other slights, for women, sports, and wines,
All Townshend's° turnips, and all Grosvenor's° mines:
Why one like Bubb° with pay and scorn content,
Bows and votes on, in court and parliament;
One, driven by strong benevolence of soul,
Shall fly, like Oglethorpe,° from pole to pole:
Is known alone to that directing power,
Who forms the genius in the natal hour;
That God of nature, who, within us still,   280
Inclines our action, not constrains our will;
Various of temper, as of face or frame,
Each individual: His great end the same.

   Yes, sir, how small soever be my heap,°
A part I will enjoy, as well as keep.
My heir may sigh, and think it want of grace
A man so poor would live without a place:
But sure no statute in his favour says,
How free, or frugal, I shall pass my days:
I, who at some times spend, at others spare,   290
Divided between carelessness and care.

'Tis one thing madly to disperse my store:
Another, not to heed to treasure more;
Glad, like a boy, to snatch the first good day,
And pleased, if sordid want be far away.
　　What is't to me (a passenger, God wot)
Whether my vessel be first-rate or not?
The ship itself may make a better figure,
But I that sail, am neither less nor bigger.
I neither strut° with every favouring breath,   300
Nor strive with all the tempest in my teeth.
In power, wit, figure, virtue, fortune, placed
Behind the foremost, and before the last.
　　'But why all this of avarice? I have none.'
I wish you joy, sir, of a tyrant gone;
But does no other lord it at this hour,
As wild and mad? the avarice of power?
Does neither rage inflame, nor fear appal?
Not the black fear of death, that saddens all?
With terrors round, can reason hold her throne,   310
Despise the known, nor tremble at th' unknown!
Survey both worlds, intrepid and entire,
In spite of witches, devils, dreams, and fire?
Pleased to look forward, pleased to look behind,
And count each birthday with a grateful mind?
Has life no sourness, drawn so near its end?
Canst thou endure a foe, forgive a friend?
Has age but melted the rough parts away,
As winter-fruits grow mild e'er they decay?
Or will you think, my friends, your business done,   320
When, of a hundred thorns, you pull out one?
　　Learn to live well, or fairly make your will;
You've played, and loved, and eat,° and drunk your fill:
Walk sober off; before a sprightlier age
Comes tittering on, and shoves you from the stage:
Leave such to trifle with more grace and ease,
Whom folly pleases, and whose follies please.

THE
FIRST EPISTLE
OF THE
SECOND BOOK
OF
HORACE IMITATED
To Augustus

Advertisement

The reflections of *Horace*, and the judgments passed in his *Epistle to Augustus*, seemed so seasonable to the present times, that I could not help applying them to the use of my own country. The author thought them considerable enough to address them to his prince; whom he paints with all the great and good qualities of a monarch, upon whom the Romans depended for the increase of an *absolute empire*. But to make the poem entirely English, I was willing to add one or two of those which contribute to the happiness of a *free people*, and are more consistent with the welfare of *our neighbours*.

This Epistle will show the learned world to have fallen into two mistakes: one, that *Augustus was a patron of poets in general*; whereas he not only prohibited all but the best writers to name him, but recommended that care even to the civil magistrate: *Admonebat praetores,°
ne paterentur nomen suum obsolefieri*, etc.° The other, that this piece was only a *general discourse of poetry*; whereas it was an *apology for the poets*, in order to render *Augustus* more their patron. *Horace* here pleads the cause of his contemporaries, first against the taste of the *town*, whose humour it was to magnify the authors of the preceding age; secondly against the *court* and *nobility*, who encouraged only the writers for the theatre; and lastly against the Emperor himself, who had conceived them of little use to the government. He shows (by a view of the progress of learning, and the change of taste among the Romans) that the introduction of the polite arts of Greece had given the writers of

his time great advantages over their predecessors; that their *morals* were
much improved, and the license of those ancient poets restrained: that
satire and *comedy* were become more just and useful; that whatever
extravagancies were left on the stage, were owing to the *ill taste* of the
nobility; that poets, under due regulations, were in many respects useful
to the *state*, and concludes, that it was upon them the Emperor himself
must depend, for his fame with posterity.

We may farther learn from this Epistle, that Horace made his court
to this great prince by writing with a decent freedom toward him, with
a just contempt of his low flatterers, and with a manly regard to his
own character.

While you, great patron of mankind! sustain   1
The balanced world, and open all the main;°
Your country, chief, in arms° abroad defend,
At home, with morals, arts, and laws amend;
How shall the muse, from such a monarch, steal
An hour, and not defraud the public weal?°
    Edward and Henry, now the boast of fame,
And virtuous Alfred,° a more sacred name,
After a life of generous toils endured,
The Gaul subdued, or property secured,   10
Ambition humbled, mighty cities stormed,
Or laws established, and the world reformed;
Closed their long glories with a sigh, to find
Th' unwilling gratitude of base mankind!
All human virtue, to its latest breath,
Finds envy never conquered, but by death.
The great Alcides,° every labour past,
Had still this monster to subdue at last.
Sure fate of all, beneath whose rising ray
Each star of meaner merit fades away!   20
Oppressed we feel the beam directly beat,
Those suns of glory please not till they set.
    To thee, the world its present homage pays,
The harvest early, but mature the praise:°
Great friend of LIBERTY! in *kings* a name
Above all Greek, above all Roman fame:
Whose word is truth, as sacred and revered,
As heaven's own oracles from altars heard.
Wonder of kings! like whom, to mortal eyes

None e'er has risen, and none e'er shall rise.   30
　　Just in one instance, be it yet confessed
Your people, sir, are partial in the rest:
Foes to all living worth except your own,
And advocates for folly dead and gone.
Authors, like coins, grow dear as they grow old;
It is the rust we value, not the gold.
Chaucer's worst ribaldry is learned by rote,
And beastly Skelton heads of houses quote:
One likes no language but the *Faery Queene*;
A Scot will fight for *Christ's Kirk o' the Green*;   40
And each true Briton is to Ben so civil,
He swears the muses met him at the Devil.
　　Though justly Greece her eldest sons admires,
Why should not we be wiser than our sires?
In every public virtue we excel;
We build, we paint, we sing, we dance as well,
And learned Athens to our art must stoop,
Could she behold us tumbling through a hoop.
　　If time improve our wit as well as wine,
Say at what age a poet grows divine?   50
Shall we, or shall we not, account him so,
Who died, perhaps, an hundred years ago?
End all dispute; and fix the year precise
When British bards begin t'immortalize?
　　'Who lasts a century can have no flaw,
I hold that wit a classic, good in law.'
　　Suppose he wants a year, will you compound?°
And shall we deem him ancient, right and sound,
Or damn to all eternity at once,
At ninety nine, a modern and a dunce?   60
　　'We shall not quarrel for a year or two;
By courtesy of England,° he may do.'
　　Then, by the rule that made the horse-tail bare,
I pluck out year by year, as hair by hair,

---

38. Skelton, Poet Laureate to Henry VIII, a volume of whose verses has been lately reprinted, consisting almost wholly of ribaldry, obscenity, and scurrilous language.°

40. *Christ's Kirk o' the Green*;] A ballad made by a king of Scotland.°

42. The Devil Tavern, where Ben Jonson held his poetical club.°

And melt down ancients like a heap of snow:
While you, to measure merits, look in Stow,°
And estimating authors by the year,
Bestow a garland only on a bier.
    Shakespeare (whom you and every playhouse bill
Style the divine, the matchless, what you will)   70
For gain, not glory, winged his roving flight,
And grew immortal in his own despite.
Ben, old and poor, as little seemed to heed
The life to come, in every poet's creed.
Who now reads Cowley?° If he pleases yet,
His moral pleases, not his pointed wit;
Forgot his epic, nay Pindaric art,
But still I love the language of his heart.
    'Yet surely, surely, these were famous men!
What boy but hears the sayings of old Ben?   80
In all debates where critics bear a part,
Not one but nods, and talks of Jonson's art,
Of Shakespeare's nature, and of Cowley's wit;
How Beaumont's judgment checked what Fletcher writ;
How Shadwell hasty, Wycherley was slow;
But, for the passions, Southerne sure and Rowe.°
These, only these, support the crowded stage,
From eldest Heywood° down to Cibber's age.'
    All this may be; the people's voice is odd,
It is, and it is not, the voice of God.   90
To *Gammer Gurton* if it give the bays,
And yet deny *The Careless Husband*° praise,
Or say our fathers never broke a rule;

69. Shakespeare and Ben Jonson may truly be said not much to have thought of this immortality, the one in many pieces composed in haste for the stage; the other in his latter works in general, which Dryden called his *dotages*.

77. *Pindaric art*] which has much more merit than his epic, but very unlike the character, as well as numbers, of Pindar.

85. Nothing was less true than this particular: but the whole paragraph has a mixture of irony, and must not altogether be taken for Horace's own judgment, only the common chat of the pretenders to criticism; in some things right, in others, wrong; as he tells us in his answer,

    Interdum vulgus rectum videt: est ubi peccat.

91. *Gammer Gurton*] A piece of very low humour, one of the first printed plays in English, and therefore much valued by some antiquaries.°

Why then, I say, the public is a fool.
But let them own, that greater faults than we
They had, and greater virtues, I'll agree.
Spenser himself affects the obsolete,°
And Sidney's verse halts ill on Roman feet:°
Milton's strong pinion now not heaven can bound,
Now serpent-like, in prose he sweeps the ground,   100
In quibbles, angel and archangel join,
And God the Father turns a school-divine.
Not that I'd lop the beauties from his book,
Like slashing Bentley with his desperate hook;°
Or damn all Shakespeare, like th' affected fool
At court, who hates whate'er he read at school.
    But for the wits of either Charles's days,
The mob of gentlemen who wrote with ease;
Sprat, Carew, Sedley,° and a hundred more,
(Like twinkling stars the miscellanies o'er)   110
One simile, that solitary shines
In the dry desert of a thousand lines,
Or lengthened thought that gleams through many a page,
Has sanctified whole poems for an age.
I lose my patience, and I own it too,
When works are censured, not as bad, but new;
While if our elders break all reason's laws,
These fools demand not pardon, but applause.
    On Avon's bank, where flowers eternal blow,
If I but ask, if any weed° can grow?   120
One tragic sentence if I dare deride
Which Betterton's° grave action dignified,
Or well-mouthed Booth with emphasis proclaims,
(Though but, perhaps, a muster-roll of names)
How will our fathers rise up in a rage,
And swear, all shame is lost in George's age!
You'd think no fools disgraced the former reign,
Did not some grave examples yet remain,
Who scorn a lad should teach his father skill,

97. Particularly in the *Shepherd's Calendar*, where he imitates the unequal measures, as well as the language, of Chaucer.

124. An absurd custom of several actors, to pronounce with emphasis the mere *proper names* of Greeks or Romans, which (as they call it) *fill the mouth* of the player.

And, having once been wrong, will be so still.   130
He, who to seem more deep than you or I,
Extols old bards, or Merlin's prophecy,°
Mistake him not; he envies, not admires,
And to debase the sons, exalts the sires.
Had ancient times conspired to disallow
What then was new, what had been ancient now?
Or what remained, so worthy to be read
By learned critics, of the mighty dead?
    In days of ease, when now the weary sword
Was sheathed, and *luxury* with Charles restored;   140
In every taste of foreign courts improved,
'All, by the King's example, lived and loved.'
Then peers grew proud in horsemanship t'excel,
Newmarket's° glory rose, as Britain's fell;
The soldier breathed the gallantries of France,
And every flowery courtier writ romance.
Then marble, softened into life, grew warm,
And yielding metal flowed to human form:
Lely° on animated canvas stole
The sleepy eye, that spoke the melting soul.   150
No wonder then, when all was love and sport,
The willing muses were debauched at court:
On each enervate string they taught the note
To pant, or tremble through an eunuch's throat.°
    But Britain, changeful as a child at play,
Now calls in princes, and now turns away.
Now Whig, now Tory, what we loved we hate;
Now all for pleasure, now for church and state;
Now for prerogative, and now for laws;
Effects unhappy! from a noble cause.°   160
      Time was, a sober Englishman would knock
His servants up, and rise by five o'clock,
Instruct his family in every rule,

142. A verse of the Lord Lansdowne.°

143. The Duke of Newcastle's book of Horsemanship: the romance of *Parthenissa*, by the Earl of Orrery, and most of the French romances translated by Persons of Quality.

153. *On each enervate string etc.*] *The Siege of Rhodes* by Sir William Davenant, the first opera sung in England.°

And send his wife to church, his son to school.
To worship like his fathers, was his care;
To teach their frugal virtues to his heir;
To prove, that luxury could never hold;
And place, on good security, his gold.
Now times are changed, and one poetic itch
Has seized the court and city, poor and rich: 170
Sons, sires, and grandsires, all will wear the bays,
Our wives read Milton, and our daughters plays,
To theatres, and to rehearsals throng,
And all our grace at table is a song.
I, who so oft renounce the muses, lie,
Not —'s self° e'er tells more *fibs* than I;
When sick of muse, our follies we deplore,
And promise our best friends to rhyme no more;
We wake next morning in a raging fit,
And call for pen and ink to show our wit.   180
      He served a 'prenticeship, who sets up shop;
Ward tried on puppies, and the poor, his drop;
Ev'n Radcliffe's° doctors travel first to France,
Nor dare to practise till they've learned to dance.
Who builds a bridge that never drove a pile?
(Should Ripley° venture, all the world would smile)
But those who cannot write, and those who can,
All rhyme, and scrawl, and scribble, to a man.
      Yet, sir, reflect, the mischief is not great;
These madmen never hurt the church or state: 190
Sometimes the folly benefits mankind;
And rarely avarice taints the tuneful mind.
Allow him but his plaything of a pen,
He ne'er rebels, or plots, like other men:
Flight of cashiers,° or mobs, he'll never mind;
And knows no losses while the muse is kind.
To cheat a friend, or Ward, he leaves to Peter;°
The good man heaps up nothing but mere metre,
Enjoys his garden and his book in quiet;
And then—a perfect hermit in his diet.°   200
      Of little use the man you may suppose,

----

182. *Ward.* A famous empiric, whose pill and drop had several surprising effects,
and were one of the principal subjects of writing and conversation at this time.°

Who says in verse what others say in prose;
Yet let me show, a poet's of some weight,
And (though no soldier) useful to the state.
What will a child learn sooner than a song?
What better teach a foreigner° the tongue?
What's long or short, each accent where to place,
And speak in public with some sort of grace.
I scarce can think him such a worthless thing,
Unless he praise some monster of a king;   210
Or virtue, or religion turn to sport,
To please a lewd, or unbelieving° court.
Unhappy Dryden!—In all Charles's days,
Roscommon° only boasts unspotted bays;
And in our own (excuse some courtly stains)
No whiter page than Addison remains.
He, from the taste obscene reclaims our youth,
And sets the passions on the side of truth,
Forms the soft bosom with the gentlest art,
And pours each human virtue in the heart.   220
Let Ireland tell, how wit upheld her cause,
Her trade supported, and supplied° her laws;
And leave on Swift this grateful verse engraved,
The rights a court attacked, a poet saved.
Behold the hand that wrought a nation's cure,
Stretched to relieve the idiot and the poor,
Proud vice to brand, or injured worth adorn,
And stretch the ray to ages yet unborn.°
Not but there are, who merit other palms;
Hopkins and Sternhold° glad the heart with Psalms: 230
The boys and girls whom charity° maintains,
Implore your help in these pathetic strains:

204. Horace had not acquitted himself much to his credit in this capacity (*non bene relicta parmula*) in the battle of Philippi. It is manifest he alludes to himself, in this whole account of a poet's character; but with an intermixture of irony: *Vivit siliquis et pane secundo* has a relation to his Epicurism; *Os tenerum pueri*, is ridicule. The nobler office of a poet follows, *Torquet ab obscoenis—Mox etiam pectus—Recte facta refert, etc.* which the imitator has applied where he thinks it more due than to himself. He hopes to be pardoned, if, as he is sincerely inclined to praise what deserves to be praised, he arraigns what deserves to be arraigned, in the 210, 211, and 212th verses.

226. A foundation for the maintenance of idiots, and a fund for assisting the poor, by lending small sums of money on demand.°

How could devotion touch the country pews,
Unless the gods bestowed a proper muse?
Verse cheers their leisure, verse assists their work,
Verse prays for peace, or sings down Pope and Turk.°
The silenced preacher yields to potent strain,
And feels that grace his prayer besought in vain;
The blessing thrills through all the labouring throng,
And heaven is won by violence of song.   240
    Our rural ancestors, with little blessed,
Patient of labour when the end was rest,
Indulged the day that housed their annual grain,
With feasts, and offerings, and a thankful strain:
The joy their wives, their sons, and servants share,
Ease of their toil, and partners of their care:
The laugh, the jest, attendants on the bowl,
Smoothed every brow, and opened every soul:
With growing years the pleasing licence grew,
And taunts alternate innocently flew.   250
But times corrupt, and nature, ill-inclined,
Produced the point that left a sting behind;
Till friend with friend, and families at strife,
Triumphant malice raged through private life.
Who felt the wrong, or feared it, took th' alarm,
Appealed to law, and justice lent her arm.
At length, by wholesome dread of statutes bound,
The poets learned to please, and not to wound:
Most warped to flattery's side; but some, more nice,°
Preserved the freedom, and forbore the vice.   260
Hence satire rose, that just the medium hit.
And heals with morals what it hurts with wit.
    We conquered France, but felt our captive's charms;
Her arts victorious triumphed o'er our arms:
Britain to soft refinements less a foe,
Wit grew polite, and numbers learned to flow.
Waller was smooth; but Dryden taught to join ⎫
The varying verse, the full-resounding line,   ⎬
The long majestic march, and energy divine.°   ⎭

267. Mr Waller, about this time, with the Earl of Dorset, Mr Godolphin, and others, translated the *Pompey* of Corneille; and the more correct French poets began to be in reputation.

Though still some traces of our rustic vein   270
And splay-foot verse, remained, and will remain.
Late, very late, correctness grew our care,
When the tired nation breathed from civil war.
Exact Racine, and Corneille's noble fire
Showed us that France had something to admire.
Not but the tragic spirit was our own,
And full in Shakespeare, fair in Otway° shone:
But Otway failed to polish or refine,
And fluent Shakespeare scarce effaced a line.°
Ev'n copious Dryden wanted, or forgot,   280
The last and greatest art, the art to blot.
Some doubt, if equal pains, or equal fire
The humbler muse of comedy require?
But in known images of life, I guess
The labour greater, as th' indulgence less.
Observe how seldom ev'n the best succeed:
Tell me if Congreve's fools are fools indeed?
What pert, low dialogue has Farquhar° writ!
How Van° wants grace, who never wanted wit!
The stage how loosely does Astraea° tread,   290
Who fairly puts all characters to bed!
And idle Cibber, how he breaks the laws,
To make poor Pinky° eat with vast applause!
But fill their purse, our poet's work is done,
Alike to them, by pathos or by pun.
    O you! whom vanity's light bark conveys
On fame's mad voyage by the wind of praise,
With what a shifting gale your course you ply,
For ever sunk too low, or borne too high!
Who pants for glory finds but short repose,   300
A breath revives him, or a breath o'erthrows.
Farewell the stage! if just as thrives the play,
The silly bard grows fat, or falls away.
    There still remains, to mortify a wit,
The many-headed monster of the pit:
A senseless, worthless, and unhonoured crowd;
Who, to disturb their betters mighty proud,

---

290. *Astraea.* A name taken by Mrs Behn, authoress of several obscene plays, *etc.*

Clattering their sticks before ten lines are spoke,
Call for the farce, the bear,° or the 'Black Joke'.°
What dear delight to Britons farce affords!   310
Ever the taste of mobs, but now of lords;
(Taste, that eternal wanderer, which flies
From heads to ears, and now from ears to eyes.)
The play stands still; damn action and discourse,
Back fly the scenes,° and enter foot and horse;
Pageants on pageants, in long order drawn,
Peers, heralds, bishops, ermine, gold and lawn;°
The Champion° too! and, to complete the jest,
Old Edward's armour beams on Cibber's breast!
With laughter sure Democritus had died,   320
Had he beheld an audience gape so wide.
Let bear or elephant be e'er so white,
The people, sure, the people are the sight!
Ah luckless poet! stretch thy lungs and roar,
That bear or elephant shall heed thee more;
While all its throats the gallery extends,
And all the thunder of the pit ascends!
Loud as the wolves, on Orcas' stormy steep,
Howl to the roarings of the northern deep.
Such is the shout, the long-applauding note,   330
At Quin's° high plume, or Oldfield's petticoat;
Or when from court a birthday suit° bestowed,
Sinks the lost actor in the tawdry load.
Booth enters—hark! the universal peal!
'But has he spoken?' Not a syllable.
'What shook the stage, and made the people stare?'
Cato's° long wig, flowered gown, and lacquered chair.
    Yet lest you think I rally° more than teach,
Or praise malignly arts I cannot reach,
Let me for once presume t'instruct the times,   340
To know the poet from the man of rhymes:

319. 'The Coronation of Henry VIII and Queen Anne Boleyn', in which the
playhouses vied with each other to represent all the pomp of a coronation. In this
noble contention, the armour of one of the Kings of England was borrowed from
the Tower, to dress the Champion.°

328. *Orcas' stormy steep*.] The farthest northern promontory of Scotland, opposite
to the Orcades.

'Tis he, who gives my breast a thousand pains,
Can make me feel each passion that he feigns;
Enrage, compose, with more than magic art,
With pity, and with terror, tear my heart;
And snatch me, o'er the earth, or through the air,
To Thebes, to Athens,° when he will, and where.

But not this part of the poetic state
Alone, deserves the favour of the great:
Think of those authors, sir, who would rely   350
More on a reader's sense, than gazer's eye.
Or who shall wander where the muses sing?
Who climb their mountain,° or who taste their spring?°
How shall we fill a library with wit,
When Merlin's Cave is half unfurnished yet?
My liege! why writers little claim your thought,
I guess; and, with their leave, will tell the fault:
We poets are (upon a poet's word)
Of all mankind, the creatures most absurd:
The season, when to come, and when to go,   360
To sing, or cease to sing, we never know;
And if we will recite nine hours in ten,
You lose your patience, just like other men.
Then too we hurt ourselves, when to defend
A single verse, we quarrel with a friend;
Repeat unasked; lament, the wit's too fine
For vulgar eyes, and point out every line.
But most, when straining with too weak a wing
We needs will write epistles to the King;
And from the moment we oblige the town,   370
Expect a place, or pension from the crown;
Or dubbed historians° by express command,
T' enroll your triumphs o'er the seas and land;
Be called to court to plan some work divine,
As once for LOUIS, Boileau and Racine.

Yet think, great sir! (so many virtues shown)
Ah think, what poet best may make them known?
Or choose at least some minister° of grace,

354. *a library*] *Munus Apolline dignum.* The Palatine Library then building by Augustus.

355. *Merlin's Cave*] A building in the Royal Gardens of Richmond, where is a small but choice collection of books.°

Fit to bestow the laureate's weighty place.

    Charles, to late times to be transmitted fair,   380
Assigned his figure to Bernini's° care;
And great Nassau to Kneller's° hand decreed
To fix him graceful on the bounding steed;
So well in paint and stone they judged of merit:
But kings in wit may want discerning spirit.
The hero William, and the martyr Charles,
One knighted Blackmore,° and one pensioned Quarles;°
Which made old Ben, and surly Dennis swear,
'No lord's anointed, but a Russian bear.'

    Not with such majesty, such bold relief,   390
The forms august of king, or conquering chief,
E'er swelled on marble; as in verse have shined
(In polished verse) the manners and the mind.
Oh! could I mount on the Maeonian wing,°
Your arms, your actions, your repose to sing!
What seas you traversed, and what fields you fought!
Your country's peace,° how oft, how dearly bought!
How barbarous rage subsided at your word,
And nations wondered while they dropped the sword!
How, when you nodded, o'er the land and deep,   400
Peace stole her wing, and wrapped the world in sleep;
Till earth's extremes your mediation own,
And Asia's tyrants tremble at your throne—
But verse, alas! your Majesty disdains;°
And I'm not used to panegyric strains:
The zeal of fools offends at any time,
But most of all, the zeal of fools in rhyme,
Besides, a fate attends on all I write,
That when I aim at praise, they say I bite.
A vile encomium doubly ridicules: 410
There's nothing blackens like the ink of fools.
If true, a woeful likeness; and if lies,
'Praise undeserved is scandal in disguise:'
Well may he blush, who gives it, or receives;
And when I flatter, let my dirty leaves
(Like journals, odes, and such forgotten things
As Eusden, Philips, Settle,° writ of kings)
Clothe spice, line trunks, or fluttering in a row,
Befringe the rails of Bedlam and Soho.°

THE

SIXTH EPISTLE
OF THE
FIRST BOOK
OF
HORACE IMITATED
To Mr MURRAY

'Not to admire,° is all the art I know,   1
To make men happy, and to keep them so.'
(Plain truth, dear MURRAY,° needs no flowers of speech,
So take it in the very words of Creech.)°
    This vault of air, this congregated ball,
Self-centred sun, and stars that rise and fall,
There are, my friend! whose philosophic eyes
Look through, and trust the ruler with his skies,
To him commit the hour, the day, the year,
And view this dreadful all without a fear.   10
Admire we then what earth's low entrails hold, ⎤
Arabian shores, or Indian seas enfold?   ⎥
All the mad trade of fools and slaves for gold? ⎦
Or popularity, or stars and strings?°
The mob's applauses, or the gifts of kings?
Say with what eyes we ought at courts to gaze,
And pay the great our homage of amaze?
    If weak the pleasure that from these can spring,
The fear to want them is as weak a thing:
Whether we dread, or whether we desire,   20
In either case, believe me, we admire;
Whether we joy or grieve, the same the curse,
Surprised at better, or surprised at worse.

---

4. *Creech*. From whose translation of Horace the two first lines are taken.

Thus good or bad, to one extreme betray
Th' unbalanced mind, and snatch the man away;
For virtue's self may too much zeal be had;
The worst of madmen is a saint run mad.

  Go then, and if you can, admire the state
Of beaming diamonds, and reflected plate;
Procure a TASTE to double the surprise,   30
And gaze on Parian° charms with learnèd eyes:
Be struck with bright brocade, or Tyrian dye,°
Our birthday nobles' splendid livery.°
If not so pleased, at council-board rejoice,
To see their judgments hang upon thy voice;
From morn to night, at senate,° Rolls,° and Hall,°
Plead much, read more, dine late, or not at all.
But wherefore all this labour, all this strife?
For fame, for riches, for a noble wife?
Shall one whom nature, learning, birth, conspired   40
To form, not to admire but be admired,
Sigh, while his Chloe, blind to wit and worth,
Weds the rich dulness of some son of earth?°
Yet time ennobles, or degrades each line;
It brightened CRAGG's,° and may darken thine:
And what is fame? the meanest have their day,
The greatest can but blaze, and pass away.
Graced as thou art, with all the power of words,
So known, so honoured, at the House of Lords:
Conspicuous scene! another° yet is nigh,   50
(More silent far) where kings and poets lie;
Where MURRAY (long enough his country's pride)
Shall be no more than TULLY, or than HYDE!°

  Racked with sciatics, martyred with the stone,
Will any mortal let himself alone?
See Ward° by battered beaux invited over,
And desperate misery lays hold on Dover.°
The case is easier in the mind's disease;
There all men may be cured, whene'er they please.
Would ye be blessed? despise low joys, low gains;   60
Disdain whatever CORNBURY° disdains;
Be virtuous, and be happy for your pains.

  But art thou one, whom new opinions sway,
One who believes as Tindal° leads the way,

Who virtue and a church alike disowns,
Thinks that but words, and this but brick and stones?
Fly then, on all the wings of wild desire,
Admire whate'er the maddest can admire.
Is wealth thy passion? Hence! from pole to pole,
Where winds can carry, or where waves can roll,   70
For Indian spices, for Peruvian gold,
Prevent° the greedy, and outbid the bold:
Advance thy golden mountain to the skies;
On the broad base of fifty thousand rise,
Add one round hundred, and (if that's not fair)
Add fifty more, and bring it to a square.
For, mark th' advantage; just so many score
Will gain a wife with half as many more,
Procure her beauty, make that beauty chaste,
And then such friends—as cannot fail to last.   80
A man of wealth is dubbed a man of worth,
Venus shall give him form, and Anstis° birth.
(Believe me, many a German prince is worse,
Who proud of pedigree, is poor of purse.)°
His wealth brave Timon gloriously confounds;
Asked for a groat,° he gives a hundred pounds;
Or if three ladies like a luckless play,
Takes the whole house upon the poet's day.°
Now, in such exigencies not to need,
Upon my word, you must be rich indeed;   90
A noble superfluity it craves,
Not for yourself, but for your fools and knaves;
Something, which for your honour they may cheat,
And which it much becomes you to forget.
If wealth alone then make and keep us blessed,
Still, still be getting, never, never rest.
    But if to power and place your passion lie,
If in the pomp of life consist the joy;°
Then hire a slave, or (if you will) a lord
To do the honours, and to give the word;   100
Tell at your levee, as the crowds approach,
To whom to nod, whom take into your coach,
Whom honour with your hand: to make remarks,
Who rules in Cornwall,° or who rules in Berks:
'This may be troublesome, is near the chair:°

That makes three members, this can choose a mayor.'
Instructed thus, you bow, embrace, protest,° ⎫
Adopt him son, or cousin at the least, ⎬
Then turn about, and laugh at your own jest. ⎭

    Or if your life be one continued treat,   110
If to live well means nothing but to eat;
Up, up! cries gluttony, 'tis break of day,
Go drive the deer, and drag the finny prey;
With hounds and horns go hunt an appetite—
So Russell° did, but could not eat at night,
Called happy dog! the beggar at his door,
And envied thirst and hunger to the poor.

    Or shall we every decency confound,
Through taverns, stews, and bagnios° take our round,
Go dine with Chartres,° in each vice outdo   120
Kinnoul's° lewd cargo, or Tyrawley's° crew,
From Latian° sirens, French Circean° feasts,
Return well travelled, and transformed to beasts,
Or for a titled punk,° or foreign flame,
Renounce our country, and degrade our name?

    If, after all, we must with Wilmot° own,
The cordial drop of life is love alone,
And SWIFT cry wisely, 'Vive la bagatelle!'°
The man that loves and laughs, must sure do well.
Adieu—if this advice appear the worst,   130
E'en take the counsel which I gave you first:
Or better precepts if you can impart,
Why do, I'll follow them with all my heart.

THE
FIRST EPISTLE
OF THE
FIRST BOOK
OF
HORACE IMITATED
To Lord Bolingbroke

St John,° whose love indulged my labours past,   1
Matures my present, and shall bound my last!
Why will you break the sabbath° of my days?
Now sick alike of envy and of praise.
Public too long, ah let me hide my age!
See modest Cibber now has left the stage:
Our generals now, retired to their estates,
Hang their old trophies o'er the garden gates,
In life's cool evening satiate of applause,
Nor fond of bleeding, ev'n in Brunswick's cause.°   10
   A voice there is, that whispers in my ear,
('Tis reason's voice, which sometimes one can hear)
'Friend Pope! be prudent, let your Muse take breath,
And never gallop Pegasus to death;
Lest stiff, and stately, void of fire or force,
You limp, like Blackmore, on a Lord Mayor's horse.'
   Farewell then verse, and love, and every toy,
The rhymes and rattles of the man or boy;
What right, what true, what fit we justly call,°

16. The fame of this heavy poet, however problematical elsewhere, was univer-
sally received in the City of London. His versification is here exactly described: stiff,
and not strong; stately and yet dull, like the sober and slow-paced animal generally
employed to mount the Lord Mayor; and therefore here humorously opposed to
Pegasus.°

Let this be all my care—for this is all: 20
To lay this harvest up, and hoard with haste
What every day will want, and most, the last.
　　But ask not, to what doctors° I apply?
Sworn to no master, of no sect am I:
As drives the storm, at any door I knock:
And house with Montaigne now, or now with Locke.°
Sometimes a patriot,° active in debate,
Mix with the world, and battle for the state,
Free as young Lyttelton,° her cause pursue,
Still true to virtue, and as warm as true: 30
Sometimes with Aristippus,° or St Paul,°
Indulge my candour,° and grow all to all;
Back to my native moderation slide,
And win my way by yielding to the tide.
　　Long, as to him who works for debt, the day;
Long as the night to her whose love's away;
Long as the year's dull circle seems to run,
When the brisk minor pants for twenty-one:
So slow th' unprofitable moments roll,
That lock up all the functions of my soul;   40
That keep me from myself; and still delay
Life's instant business to a future day:
That task, which as we follow, or despise,
The eldest is a fool, the youngest wise;
Which done, the poorest can no wants endure,
And which not done, the richest must be poor.
　　Late as it is, I put myself to school,
And feel some comfort, not to be a fool.
Weak though I am of limb, and short of sight,
Far from a lynx,° and not a giant quite;   50
I'll do what Mead° and Cheselden° advise,
To keep these limbs, and to preserve these eyes.
Not to go back, is somewhat to advance,
And men must walk at least before they dance.
　　Say, does thy blood rebel, thy bosom move
With wretched avarice, or as wretched love?
Know, there are words. and spells, which can control°
Between the fits this fever of the soul:

31. Omnis Aristippum decuit color, & status, & res.

Know, there are rhymes, which fresh and fresh applied
Will cure the arrant'st puppy of his pride.   60
Be furious, envious, slothful, mad, or drunk,
Slave to a wife, or vassal to a punk,
A Switz, a High Dutch, or a Low Dutch bear;°
All that we ask is but a patient ear.
   'Tis the first virtue, vices to abhor;
And the first wisdom, to be fool no more.
But to the world no bugbear is so great,
As want of figure, and a small estate.
To either India° see the merchant fly,
Scared at the spectre of pale poverty!   70
See him, with pains of body, pangs of soul,
Burn through the Tropic, freeze beneath the Pole!
Wilt thou do nothing for a nobler end,
Nothing, to make philosophy thy friend?
To stop thy foolish views, thy long desires,
And ease thy heart of all that it admires?
   Here, wisdom calls: 'Seek virtue first, be bold!
As gold to silver, virtue is to gold.'
There, London's voice: 'Get money, money still!
And then let virtue follow, if she will.'   80
This, this the saving doctrine, preached to all,
From low St James's° up to high St Paul;°
From him whose quills stand quivered at his ear,
To him who notches sticks° at Westminster.
   Barnard° in spirit, sense, and truth abounds;
'Pray then, what wants he?' Fourscore thousand pounds;
A pension, or such harness° for a slave
As Bug° now has, and Dorimant° would have.
Barnard,° thou art a cit,° with all thy worth;
But Bug and D *l,° their *honours*, and so forth.   90
   Yet every child another song will sing,
'Virtue, brave boys! 'tis virtue makes a king.'
True, conscious honour is to feel no sin,
He's armed without that's innocent within;
Be this thy screen, and this thy wall of brass;°
Compared to this, a minister's an ass.
   And say, to which shall our applause belong,
This new court jargon, or the good old song?
The modern language of corrupted peers,

Or what was spoke at CRESSY and POITIERS?°   100
Who counsels best? who whispers, 'Be but great,
With praise or infamy, leave that to fate;
Get place and wealth, if possible, with grace;
If not, by any means get wealth and place.'
For what? to have a box where eunuchs° sing,
And foremost in the circle eye a king.
Or he, who bids thee face with steady view   ⎫
Proud fortune, and look shallow greatness through: ⎬
And, while he bids thee, sets th' example too?   ⎭
If such a doctrine, in St James's air,°   110
Should chance to make the well-dressed rabble
        stare;
If honest Schutz° take scandal at a spark,
That less admires the palace than the park;
Faith I shall give the answer Reynard gave:
'I cannot like, dread sir, your royal cave;
Because I see, by all the tracks about,
Full many a beast goes in, but none come out.'
Adieu to virtue if you're once a slave:
Send her to court, you send her to her grave.°
    Well, if a king's a lion, at the least   120
The people are a many-headed beast:
Can they direct what measures to pursue,
Who know themselves so little what to do?
Alike in nothing but one lust of gold,
Just half the land would buy, and half be sold:
Their country's wealth our mightier misers drain,
Or cross, to plunder provinces, the main;
The rest, some farm° the poor-box, some the pews;
Some keep assemblies, and would keep the stews;
Some with fat bucks on childless dotards fawn;   130
Some win rich widows by their chine and brawn;°
While with the silent growth of ten per cent,
In dirt and darkness hundreds stink content.
    Of all these ways, if each pursues his own,
Satire be kind, and let the wretch alone:
But show me one who has it in his power
To act consistent with himself an hour.
Sir Job° sailed forth, the evening bright and still,
'No place on earth' (he cried) 'like Greenwich Hill!'

Up starts a palace, lo th' obedient base ⎫
Slopes at its foot, the woods its sides embrace, ⎬
The silver Thames reflects its marble face. ⎭

Now let some whimsy, or that devil within ⎫
Which guides all those who know not what they mean, ⎬
But give the knight (or give his lady) spleen; ⎭
'Away, away! take all your scaffolds down,
For snug's the word.° My dear! we'll live in town.'
   At amorous Flavio is the stocking° thrown?
That very night he longs to lie alone.
   The fool, whose wife elopes some thrice a quarter, 150
For matrimonial solace dies a martyr.
Did ever Proteus, Merlin, any witch, ⎫
Transform themselves so strangely as the rich? ⎬
Well, but the poor—the poor have the same itch; ⎭
They change their weekly barber, weekly news,
Prefer a new japanner° to their shoes,
Discharge° their garrets, move their beds, and run
(They know not whither) in a chaise and one;°
They hire their sculler,° and when once aboard,
Grow sick, and damn the climate—like a lord. 160
   You laugh, half beau, half sloven if I stand,
My wig all powder, and all snuff my band;°
You laugh, if coat and breeches strangely vary,
White gloves, and linen worthy Lady Mary!°
But when no prelate's lawn with hair-shirt lined,
Is half so incoherent as my mind,
When (each opinion with the next at strife,
One ebb and flow of follies all my life)
I plant, root up; I build, and then confound;°
Turn round to square, and square again to round; 170
You never change one muscle of your face,
You think this madness but a common case,
Nor once to Chancery, nor to Hales° apply;
Yet hang your lip, to see a seam awry!
Careless how ill I with myself agree,
Kind to my dress, my figure, not to me.
Is this my guide, philosopher, and friend?°
This, he who loves me, and who ought to mend?

173. *Hales*] The doctor of Bedlam.

Who ought to make me (what he can, or none,)
That man divine whom wisdom calls her own;   180
Great without title,° without fortune blessed;
Rich ev'n when plundered,° honoured while oppressed;
Loved without youth, and followed without power;
At home, though exiled; free, though in the Tower:°
In short, that reasoning, high, immortal thing,
Just less than Jove, and much above a king,
Nay, half in heaven—except (what's mighty odd)
A fit of vapours clouds this demigod.

EPILOGUE
TO THE
SATIRES
Written in MDCCXXXVIII
DIALOGUE I

Fr. Not twice a twelve-month you appear in print,   1
And when it comes, the court see nothing in't.
You grow *correct*, that once with rapture writ,
And are, besides, too *moral* for a wit.
Decay of parts, alas! we all must feel—
Why now, this moment, don't I see you steal?
'Tis all from Horace; Horace long before ye
Said, 'Tories called him Whig, and Whigs a Tory,'°
And taught his Romans, in much better metre,
'To laugh at fools who put their trust in Peter.'   10
    But Horace, sir, was delicate, was nice;°
Bubo observes, he lashed no sort of *vice:*

1, 2. These two lines are from Horace; and the only lines that are so in the whole
poem; being meant to give a handle to that which follows in the character of an
impertinent censurer,

'Tis all from Horace; etc.°

12. *Bubo observes*] Some guilty person very fond of making such an observation.°

Horace would say, Sir Billy° *served the crown,*
Blunt° could *do business,* Huggins° *knew the town,*
In Sappho° touch the *failings of the sex,*
In reverend bishops note some *small neglects,*
And own, the Spaniard did a *waggish thing,*
Who cropped our ears, and sent them to the King.
His sly, polite, insinuating style
Could please at Court, and make AUGUSTUS smile: 20
An artful manager, that crept between
His friend and shame, and was a kind of *screen.*
But 'faith your very friends will soon be sore;
Patriots there are, who wish you'd jest no more—
And where's the glory? 'twill be only thought
The great man never offered you a groat.
Go see Sir ROBERT—
                     P. See Sir ROBERT!—hum—
And never laugh—for all my life to come?
Seen him I have, but in his happier hour
Of social pleasure, ill-exchanged for power;   30
Seen him, uncumbered with the venal tribe,
Smile without art, and win without a bribe.
Would he oblige me? let me only find,
He does not think me what he thinks mankind.°
Come, come, at all I laugh he laughs, no doubt;
The only difference is, I dare laugh out.

---

14. *Huggins*] Formerly gaoler of the Fleet prison, enriched himself by many exactions, for which he was tried and expelled.

18. *Who cropped our ears*] Said to be executed by the captain of a Spanish ship on one Jenkins, a captain of an English one. He cut off his ears, and bid him carry them to the King, his master.°

22. *His friend,* etc.]

> *Omne vafer vitium ridenti Flaccus amico*
> *Tangit, et admissus circum praecordia ludit.*
>   Persius.°

Screen.] A metaphor peculiarly appropriated to a certain person in power.°

24. *Patriots*] This appellation was generally given to those in opposition to the court. Though some of them (which our author hints at) had views too mean and interested to deserve that name.

26. *The great man*] A phrase, by common use, appropriated to the first minister.°

31–32. These two verses were originally in the poem, though omitted in all the first editions.

F. Why yes: with *scripture* still you may be free;
A horse-laugh, if you please, at *honesty*;
A joke on JEKYLL, or some odd *Old Whig*
Who never changed his principle, or wig:°   40
A patriot is a fool in every age,
Whom all Lord Chamberlains° allow the stage:
These nothing hurts; they keep their fashion still,
And wear their strange old virtue as they will.

If any ask you, 'Who's the man, so near
His prince, that writes in verse, and has his ear?'
Why, answer LYTTELTON, and I'll engage
The worthy youth shall ne'er be in a rage:
But were his verses vile, his whisper base,
You'd quickly find him in Lord Fanny's° case.   50
Sejanus, Wolsey, hurt not honest FLEURY,
But well may put some statesmen in a fury.

Laugh then at any, but at fools or foes;
These you but anger, and you mend not those.
Laugh at your friends, and, if your friends are sore,
So much the better, you may laugh the more.
To vice and folly to confine the jest,
Sets half the world, God knows, against the rest;
Did not the sneer of more impartial men
At sense and virtue, balance all again.   60
Judicious wits spread wide the ridicule,
And charitably comfort knave and fool.

P. Dear sir, forgive the prejudice of youth:
Adieu distinction, satire, warmth, and truth!
Come, harmless characters that no one hit;

---

39. Sir Joseph Jekyll, Master of the Rolls, a true Whig in his principles, and a man of the utmost probity. He sometimes voted against the court, which drew upon him the laugh here described of ONE who bestowed it equally upon religion and honesty. He died a few months after the publication of this poem.°

47. George Lyttelton, Secretary to the Prince of Wales, distinguished both for his writings and speeches in the spirit of liberty.°

51. *Sejanus, Wolsey*] The one the wicked minister of Tiberius; the other, of Henry VIII. The writers against the court usually bestowed these and other odious names on the minister, without distinction, and in the most injurious manner. See Dial. II. 137.°

Fleury] Cardinal: and Minister to Louis XV. It was a patriot fashion, at that time, to cry up his wisdom and honesty.°

Come, Henley's oratory, Osborne's° wit!
The honey dropping from Favonio's tongue,
The flowers of Bubo, and the flow of Young!
The gracious dew of pulpit eloquence,
And all the well-whipped cream of courtly sense,   70
That first was Hervey's, Fox's next, and then
The senate's, and then Hervey's once again.
O come, that easy Ciceronian style,
So Latin, yet so English all the while,
As, though the pride of Middleton and Bland,°
All boys may read, and girls may understand!
Then might I sing, without the least offence,
And all I sung should be the *nation's sense*;
Or teach the melancholy muse to mourn,
Hang the sad verse on CAROLINA's urn,   80
And hail her passage to the realms of rest,
All parts performed, and *all* her children blessed!°
So—satire is no more—I feel it die—
No *gazetteer*° more innocent than I—
And let, a-God's name, every fool and knave
Be graced through life, and flattered in his grave.
   F. Why so? if satire knows its time and place,
You still may lash the greatest—in disgrace:
For merit will by turns forsake them all;
Would you know when? exactly when they fall.   90
But let all satire in all changes spare
Immortal Selkirk, and grave De la Ware!°
Silent and soft, as saints remove to heaven,

66. *Henley—Osborne*] See them in their places in the *Dunciad.*

69. Alludes to some court sermons, and florid panegyrical speeches; particularly one very full of puerilities and flatteries; which afterwards got into an address in the same pretty style; and was lastly served up in an epitaph, between Latin and English, published by its author.°

80. *Carolina*] Queen consort to King George II. She died in 1737. Her death gave occasion, as is observed above, to many indiscreet and mean performances unworthy of her memory, whose last moments manifested the utmost courage and resolution.

92. *Immortal Selkirk, and grave De la Ware!*] A title given *that* Lord by King James II. He was of the Bedchamber to King William; he was so to King George I; he was so to King George II. *This* Lord was very skilful in all the forms of the House, in which he discharged himself with great gravity.

All ties dissolved, and every sin forgiven,
These may some gentle, ministerial wing
Receive, and place for ever near a king!
There, where no passion, pride, or shame transport,
Lulled with the sweet nepenthe° of a court;
There, where no father's, brother's, friend's disgrace
Once break their rest, or stir them from their place: 100
But past the sense of human miseries,
All tears are wiped for ever from all eyes;°
No cheek is known to blush, no heart to throb,
Save when they lose a question,° or a job.°
    P. Good heaven forbid, that I should blast their glory,
Who know how like Whig ministers to Tory,
And when three sovereigns died, could scarce be vexed,
Considering what a *gracious Prince*° was next.
Have I, in silent wonder, seen such things
As pride in slaves, and avarice in kings;   110
And at a peer, or peeress, shall I fret,
Who starves a sister, or forswears a debt?
Virtue, I grant you, is an empty boast;
But shall the dignity of *Vice* be lost?
Ye Gods! shall Cibber's son,° without rebuke,
Swear like a lord, or Rich° out-whore a duke?
A favourite's porter with his master vie,
Be bribed as often, and as often lie?
Shall Ward° draw contracts with a statesman's skill?
Or Japhet° pocket, like his Grace,° a will?   120
Is it for Bond,° or Peter° (paltry things)
To pay their debts, or keep their faith, like kings?
If Blount° dispatched himself, he played the man,
And so mayst thou, illustrious Passeran!°
But shall a printer, weary of his life,
Learn, from their books, to hang himself and wife?

115, 116. *Cibber's son,—Rich*] Two players: look for them in the *Dunciad.*

123. *Blount*] Author of a book entitled *The Oracles of Reason,* who being in love with a near kinswoman of his, and rejected, gave himself a stab in the arm, as pretending to kill himself, of the consequence of which he really died.

124. *Passeran!*] Author of another, called *A philosophical discourse on death.*

125. A fact that happened in London a few years past. The unhappy man left behind him a paper justifying his action by the reasonings of some of these authors.°

This, this, my friend, I cannot, must not bear;
Vice thus abused, demands a nation's care:
This calls the church to deprecate our sin.
And hurls the thunder of the laws on *gin.*°   130
     Let modest FOSTER,° if he will, excel
Ten metropolitans in preaching well;
A simple Quaker, or a Quaker's wife,°
Outdo Llandaff in doctrine,—yea in life:
Let humble ALLEN,° with an awkward shame,
Do good by stealth, and blush to find it fame.
Virtue may choose the high or low degree,
'Tis just alike to Virtue,° and to me;
Dwell in a monk, or light upon a king,
She's still the same, beloved, contented thing.   140
Vice is undone, if she forgets her birth,
And stoops from angels to the dregs of earth:
But 'tis the *fall* degrades her to a whore;
Let *Greatness* own her, and she's mean no more:
Her birth, her beauty, crowds and courts confess,
Chaste matrons praise her, and grave bishops bless;
In golden chains the willing world she draws,
And hers the gospel is, and hers the laws,
Mounts the tribunal, lifts her scarlet head,°
And sees pale Virtue carted° in her stead.   150
Lo! at the wheels of her triumphal car,
Old England's genius, rough with many a scar,
Dragged in the dust! his arms hang idly round,
His flag inverted° trails along the ground!
Our youth, all liveried o'er with foreign gold,
Before her dance: behind her, crawl the old!
See thronging millions to the pagod° run,
And offer country, parent, wife, or son!
Hear her black trumpet through the land proclaim,
That 'not to be corrupted is the shame.'   160
In soldier, churchman, patriot, man in power,
'Tis avarice all, ambition is no more!
See, all our nobles begging to be slaves!

---

130. *Gin*] A spirituous liquor, the exorbitant use of which had almost destroyed the lowest rank of the people till it was restrained by an act of Parliament in 1736.

134. *Llandaff*] A poor bishopric in Wales, as poorly supplied.°

See, all our fools aspiring to be knaves!
The wit of cheats, the courage of a whore,
Are what ten thousand envy and adore:
All, all look up, with reverential awe,
At crimes that 'scape, or triumph o'er the law:
While truth, worth, wisdom, daily they decry—
'Nothing is sacred now but villainy.'   170
    Yet may this verse (if such a verse remain)
Show, there was one who held it in disdain.

EPILOGUE
TO THE
SATIRES
DIALOGUE II

Fr. 'Tis all a libel—Paxton,° sir, will say.   I
    P. Not yet, my friend! tomorrow 'faith it may;
And for that very cause I print today.
How should I fret, to mangle every line,
In reverence to the sins of Thirty-nine!
Vice with such giant strides comes on amain,°
Invention° strives to be before in vain;
Feign what I will, and paint it e'er so strong,
Some rising genius sins up to my song.
    F. Yet none but you by name the guilty lash;   10
Ev'n Guthrie saves half Newgate by a dash.
Spare then the person, and expose the vice.
    P. How, sir! not damn the sharper, but the dice?
Come on then, satire! general, unconfined,
Spread thy broad wing, and souze° on all the kind.
Ye statesmen, priests, of one religion all!
Ye tradesmen vile, in army, court, or hall!°
Ye reverend atheists. *F.* Scandal! name them, who?

---

11. *Guthrie*] The Ordinary of Newgate, who publishes the memoirs of the malefactors.°

P. Why that's the thing you bid me not to do.
'Who starved a sister, who forswore a debt,'°   20
I never named; the town's enquiring yet.
The poisoning dame°—*F.* You mean—*P.* I don't. *F.* You
    do.
    P. See, now I keep the secret, and not you!
The bribing statesman—*F.* Hold, too high you go.
    P. The bribed elector—*F.* There you stoop too low.
    P. I fain would please you, if I knew with what;
Tell me, which knave is lawful game, which not?
Must great offenders, once escaped the crown,
Like royal harts,° be never more run down?
Admit your law to spare the knight requires,   30
As beasts of nature may we hunt the squires?
Suppose I censure—you know what I mean—
To save a bishop, may I name a dean?
    F. A dean, sir? no: his fortune is not made,
You hurt a man that's rising in the trade.
    P. If not the tradesman who set up today,
Much less the prentice who tomorrow may.
Down, down, proud satire! though a realm be spoiled,
Arraign no mightier thief than wretched Wild;°
Or, if a court or country's made a job,   40
Go drench° a pickpocket, and join the mob.
    But, sir, I beg you (for the love of vice!)
The matter's weighty, pray consider twice:
Have you less pity for the needy cheat,
The poor and friendless villain, than the great?
Alas! the small discredit of a bribe
Scarce hurts the lawyer, but undoes the scribe.
Then better sure it charity becomes
To tax directors,° who (thank God) have plums;°
Still better, ministers; or, if the thing   50
May pinch ev'n there—why lay it on a king.
    F. Stop! stop!
                P. Must satire, then, nor rise nor fall?
Speak out, and bid me blame no rogues at all.
    F. Yes, strike that Wild, I'll justify the blow.

39. Jonathan Wild, a famous thief, and thief-impeacher, who was at last caught
in his own train and hanged.

P. Strike? why the man was hanged ten years ago:
Who now that obsolete example fears?
Ev'n Peter° trembles only for his ears.
   F. What always Peter? Peter thinks you mad,
You make men desperate if they once are bad:
Else might he take to virtue some years hence—   60
   P. As Selkirk,° if he lives, will love the PRINCE.
   F. Strange spleen to Selkirk!
                  P. Do I wrong the man?
God knows, I praise a courtier where I can.
When I confess, there is who feels for fame,
And melts to goodness, need I SCARBOROUGH° name?
Pleased let me own, in Esher's peaceful grove
(Where Kent° and nature vie for PELHAM's° love)
The scene, the master, opening to my view,
I sit and dream I see my CRAGGS anew!
   Ev'n in a bishop I can spy desert;   70
Secker is decent, Rundle has a heart,
Manners with candour are to Benson° given,
To Berkeley,° every virtue under heaven.
   But does the court a worthy man remove?
That instant, I declare, he has my love:
I shun his zenith, court his mild decline;
Thus SOMERS once, and HALIFAX° were mine.
Oft, in the clear, still mirror of retreat,

---

57. Peter had, the year before this, narrowly escaped the pillory for forgery: and got off with a severe rebuke only from the bench.

65. *Scarborough*] Earl of; and Knight of the Garter, whose personal attachments to the king appeared from his steady adherence to the royal interest, after his resignation of his great employment of Master of the Horse; and whose known honour and virtue made him esteemed by all parties.

66. The house and gardens of Esher in Surrey, belonging to the Honourable Mr Pelham, brother of the Duke of Newcastle. The author could not have given a more amiable idea of his character than in comparing him to Mr Craggs.

77. *Somers*] John Lord Somers died in 1716. He had been Lord Keeper in the reign of William III, who took from him the seals in 1700. The author had the honour of knowing him in 1706. A faithful, able, and incorrupt minister; who, to the qualities of a consummate statesman, added those of a man of learning and politeness.

Halifax] A peer, no less distinguished by his love of letters than his abilities in Parliament. He was disgraced in 1710, on the change of Queen Anne's ministry.

I studied SHREWSBURY, the wise and great:
CARLETON's calm sense, and STANHOPE's° noble flame,   80
Compared, and knew their generous end the same:
How pleasing ATTERBURY's softer hour!
How shined the soul, unconquered in the Tower!
How can I PULTENEY, CHESTERFIELD forget,
While Roman spirit charms, and Attic wit:
ARGYLL, the state's whole thunder born to wield,
And shake alike the senate and the field:
Or WYNDHAM, just to freedom and the throne,
The master of our passions, and his own.°
Names, which I long have loved, nor loved in vain,   90
Ranked with their friends, not numbered with their
        train:
And if yet higher the proud list should end,
Still let me say, 'No follower, but a friend.'
    Yet think not, friendship only prompts my lays;
I follow *virtue*; where she shines, I praise:
Point she to priest or elder, Whig or Tory,
Or round a Quaker's beaver cast a glory.
I never (to my sorrow I declare)
Dined with the MAN of ROSS,° or my LORD MAYOR.
Some, in their choice of friends (nay, look not grave)   100
Have still a secret bias to a knave:
To find an honest man I beat about,
And love him, court him, praise him, in or out.
    F. Then why so few commended?
                        P. Not so fierce;

79. *Shrewsbury,*] Charles Talbot, Duke of Shrewsbury, had been Secretary of State, Ambassador in France, Lord Lieutenant of Ireland, Lord Chamberlain, and Lord Treasurer. He several times quitted his employments, and was often recalled. He died in 1718.

80. *Carleton*] Henry Boyle, Lord Carleton (nephew of the famous Robert Boyle) who was Secretary of State under William III, and President of the Council under Queen Anne.
    Stanhope] James Earl Stanhope. A nobleman of equal courage, spirit, and learning. General in Spain, and Secretary of State.

88. *Wyndham*] Sir William Wyndham, Chancellor of the Exchequer under Queen Anne, made early a considerable figure; but since a much greater both by his ability and eloquence, joined with the utmost judgment and temper.

99. *my Lord Mayor.*] Sir John Barnard.

Find you the virtue, and I'll find the verse.
But random praise—the task can ne'er be done;
Each mother asks it for her booby son,
Each widow asks it for *the best of men*,
For him she weeps, and him she weds again.
Praise cannot stoop,° like satire, to the ground;   110
The number° may be hanged, but not be crowned.
Enough for half the greatest of these days,
To 'scape my censure, not expect my praise.
Are they not rich? what more can they pretend?
Dare they to hope a poet for their friend?
What RICHELIEU wanted, LOUIS° scarce could gain,
And what young AMMON° wished, but wished in vain.
No power the muse's friendship can command;
No power, when virtue claims it, can withstand:
To Cato, Virgil paid one honest line;°   120
O let my country's friends illumine mine!
—What are you thinking? *F.* Faith the thought's no sin,
I think your friends are out, and would be in.
    P. If merely to come in, sir, they go out,
The way they take is strangely round about.
    F. They too may be corrupted, you'll allow?
    P. I only call those knaves who are so now.
    Is that too little? Come then, I'll comply—
Spirit of *Arnall!*° aid me while I lie.
COBHAM'S° a coward, POLWARTH° is a slave,   130
And LYTTELTON a dark, designing knave,
ST JOHN has ever been a wealthy fool—
But let me add, Sir ROBERT's mighty dull,
Has never made a friend in private life,
And was, besides, a tyrant to his wife.
    But pray, when others praise him, do I blame?
Call Verres,° Wolsey, any odious name?
Why rail they then, if but a wreath of mine,
Oh all-accomplished ST JOHN! deck thy shrine?
    What? shall each spur-galled hackney of the day,   140
When Paxton gives him double pots and pay,

130. *Polwarth*] The Hon. Hugh Hume, son of Alexander, Earl of Marchmont, grandson of Patric, Earl of Marchmont, and distinguished, like them, in the cause of liberty.

Or each new-pensioned sycophant, pretend°
To break my windows, if I treat a friend?
Then wisely plead, to me they meant no hurt,
But 'twas my guest at whom they threw the dirt?
Sure, if I spare the minister, no rules
Of honour bind me, not to maul his tools;
Sure, if they cannot cut, it may be said
His saws are toothless, and his hatchets lead.

It angered TURENNE,° once upon a day,   150
To see a footman kicked that took his pay:
But when he heard th' affront the fellow gave,
Knew one a man of honour, one a knave;
The prudent general turned it to a jest,
And begged, he'd take the pains to kick the rest:
Which not at present having time to do—
    F. Hold sir! for God's sake where's th' affront to you?
Against your worship when had Selkirk writ?
Or Page° poured forth the torrent of his wit?
Or grant the bard° whose distich all commend   160
'*In power a servant, out of power a friend*'
To Walpole guilty of some venial sin;
What's that to you who ne'er was out nor in?

The priest whose flattery bedropped the crown,
How hurt he you? he only stained the gown.
And how did, pray, the florid youth° offend,
Whose speech you took, and gave it to a friend?
    P. Faith, it imports not much from whom it came, ⎫
Whoever borrowed, could not be to blame,   ⎬
Since the whole House did afterwards the same.   ⎭   170
Let courtly wits to wits afford supply,
As hog to hog in huts of Westphaly;°
If one, through nature's bounty or his lord's,
Has what the frugal, dirty soil affords,
From him the next receives it, thick or thin,
As pure a mess almost as it came in;
The blessed benefit, not there confined,
Drops to the third, who nuzzles close behind;

160. A verse taken out of a poem to Sir R. W.
164. Spoken not of any particular priest, but of many priests.
166. This seems to allude to a complaint made v. 71. of the preceding Dialogue.

From tail to mouth, they feed and they carouse:
The last full fairly gives it to the House.   180
    F. This filthy simile, this beastly line
Quite turns my stomach—

                        P. So does flattery mine;
And all your courtly civet-cats° can vent,
Perfume to you, to me is excrement.
But hear me further—Japhet, 'tis agreed,
Writ not, and Chartres° scarce could write or read,
In all the courts of Pindus° guiltless quite;
But pens can forge, my friend, that cannot write;
And must no egg in Japhet's face be thrown,
Because the deed he forged was not my own?   190
Must never patriot then declaim at gin,°
Unless, good man! he has been fairly in?°
No zealous pastor blame a failing spouse,
Without a staring reason on his brows?°
And each blasphemer quite escape the rod,
Because the insult's not on man, but God?
    Ask you what provocation I have had?
The strong antipathy of good to bad.
When truth or virtue an affront endures,
Th'affront is mine, my friend, and should be yours.   200
Mine, as a foe professed to false pretence,
Who think a coxcomb's honour like his sense;
Mine, as a friend to every worthy mind;
And mine as man, who feel for all mankind.°
    F. You're strangely proud.

                  P. So proud, I am no slave:⎫
So impudent, I own myself no knave: ⎬
So odd, my country's ruin makes me grave. ⎭
Yes, I am proud; I must be proud to see
Men not afraid of God, afraid of me:
Safe from the bar, the pulpit, and the throne,   210
Yet touched and shamed by ridicule alone.
    O sacred weapon! left for truth's defence,
Sole dread of folly, vice, and insolence!
To all but heaven-directed hands denied,

185–6. *Japhet—Chartres*] See the *Epistle to Lord Bathurst.*
204. From Terence: 'Homo sum: humani nihil a me alienum puto.'

The muse may give thee, but the God must guide:
Reverent I touch thee! but with honest zeal;
To rouse the watchmen of the public weal,
To virtue's work provoke the tardy Hall,°
And goad the prelate slumbering in his stall.
Ye tinsel insects! whom a court maintains,   220
That counts your beauties only by your stains,
Spin all your cobwebs o'er the eye of day!
The muse's wing shall brush you all away:
All his Grace preaches, all his Lordship sings,
All that makes saints of queens, and gods of kings,
All, all but truth, drops dead-born from the press,
Like the last Gazette,° or the last address.°
    When black ambition stains a public cause,
A monarch's sword when mad vainglory draws,
Not Waller's wreath° can hide the nation's scar,   230
Nor Boileau turn the feather to a star.°
    Not so, when diademed with rays divine,
Touched with the flame that breaks from virtue's shrine,
Her priestess muse forbids the good to die,
And opes the temple of eternity.
There, other trophies deck the truly brave,
Than such as Anstis casts into the grave;
Far other stars than * and * *° wear,
And may descend to Mordington° from STAIR:°
(Such as on HOUGH's unsullied mitre shine,   240

222. *Cobwebs*] Weak and slight sophistry against virtue and honour. Thin colours over vice, as unable to hide the light of truth, as cobwebs to shade the sun.

228. The case of Cromwell in the Civil War of England; and (229) of Louis XIV in his conquest of the Low Countries.

231. *Nor Boileau turn the feather to a star.*] See his *Ode on Namur*, where (to use his own words) 'il a fait un Astre de la Plume blanche que le Roy porte ordinairement à son Chapeau, et qui est en effet une espece de Comete, fatale à nos ennemis.'

237. *Anstis*] The chief Herald at Arms. It is the custom, at the funeral of great peers, to cast into the grave the broken staves and ensigns of honour.°

239. *Stair*] John Dalrymple, Earl of Stair, Knight of the Thistle; served in all the wars under the Duke of Marlborough; and afterwards as Ambassador in France.

240, 241. *Hough and Digby*] Dr John Hough, Bishop of Worcester, and the Lord Digby. The one an assertor of the Church of England in opposition to the false measures of King James II. The other as firmly attached to the cause of that king. Both acting out of principle, and equally men of honour and virtue.

Or beam, good DIGBY,° from a heart like thine)
Let envy howl, while heaven's whole chorus sings,
And bark at honour not conferred by kings;
Let flattery sickening see the incense rise,
Sweet to the world, and grateful to the skies:
Truth guards the poet, sanctifies the line,
And makes immortal, verse as mean as mine.

    Yes, the last pen for freedom let me draw,
When truth stands trembling on the edge of law;
Here, last of Britons! let your names be read;   250
Are none, none living? let me praise the dead,
And for that cause° which made your fathers shine,
Fall by the votes of their degenerate line.
    F. Alas! alas! pray end what you began,
And write next winter more *Essays on Man.*

EPIGRAM

*Engraved on the Collar of a Dog which
I gave to his Royal Highness*

I am his Highness' dog at Kew;
Pray tell me, sir, whose dog are you?

255. This was the last poem of the kind printed by our author, with a resolution
to publish no more; but to enter thus, in the most plain and solemn manner he
could, a sort of PROTEST against that insuperable corruption and depravity of
manners, which he had been so unhappy as to live to see. Could he have hoped to
have amended any, he had continued those attacks; but bad men were grown so
shameless and so powerful, that ridicule was become as unsafe as it was ineffectual.
The poem raised him, as he knew it would, some enemies; but he had reason to be
satisfied with the approbation of good men, and the testimony of his own conscience.

EPITAPH

For One who would not be buried in Westminster Abbey

Heroes, and kings! your distance keep:
In peace let one poor poet sleep,
Who never flattered folks like you:
Let Horace blush, and Virgil too.

POPE TO HUGH BETHEL
19 March 1744

I am very solicitous to know how you proceed in your health, and these inveterate north-easterly winds give me much apprehension for yours, as they very greatly affect mine. Within these three weeks I have been excessive ill. The asthma in every symptom increased, with a swelling in my legs and a low fever. I have been so long and yet am confined to my chamber at Twitnam and the whole business of my two servants night and day to attend me. Dr Burton° is very watchful over me, he changed the warm pills into a cooler regimen. I drink no wine, and take scarce any meat. Asses' milk° twice a day. My only medicines are millepedes and garlic,° and horehound° tea. He is against crude quicksilver till he is sure there is no fever, but prescribes alkalized mercury° in five pills a day: and proposes an issue, which I fear may drain and waste me too much, it can't be imagined how weak I am, and how unable to move, or walk, or use any exercise, but going in a coach, for which the weather is yet too cold. These are all discouraging things, to cure me of buying houses, so I've determined not to purchase this, which will cost me £1200 and instead of it to lay out three upon a cheap one° in London, seated in an airy high place. If I live but five months I shall never be able to live about, as I used, in other peoples houses, but quite at ease, to keep my own hours, and with my own servants: and if I don't live there, it will do for a friend, which Twitnam would not suit at all. Give me leave therefore to pay in to your brother° what I don't want of the sum I drew upon him by your kind order.—

I told you in my last how very welcome was your kind present of your picture which he transmitted very safe. The last thing I did before I was confined, was to sit the first time to Mr Kent,° for you: it wants but one sitting more, and pray tell me, where, or with whom it shall be left for you?

Now I have said a great deal, all I could, of my own state, pray be as particular as to yours. I every morning and night see you in my bedchamber° and think of you: nothing can be more resembling, but I wish your complexion be in reality as healthy. Dear Sir, if you are not worse, do not let me wait long for the comfort of knowing it, though you employ any hand, and spare your own eyes. Above all, what is your scheme, as to coming to London, and when? Me you cannot miss; and we may truly say of each other, that we shall be friends to the last breath. Pray remember me to Mr Moyser.°

Ever yours
A. Pope

Twitnam
March 19th
I must desire you to say nothing of what I tell you concerning my purchase of the house in town, which is done in another's name.

THE
DUNCIAD
IN
FOUR BOOKS
Printed according to the complete Copy
found in the Year 1742

WITH THE
PROLEGOMENA OF SCRIBLERUS
AND
NOTES VARIORUM

To which are added SEVERAL NOTES now first pub-
lished, the HYPERCRITICS of ARISTARCHUS, and
his *Dissertation* on the HERO of the POEM

Tandem *Phoebus* adest, morsusque inferre parantem Congelat, et
patulos, ut erant, indurat hiatus.

OVID.°

By AUTHORITY

By virtue of the Authority in Us vested by the Act for subjecting Poets to the power of a Licenser, we have revised this Piece; where finding the style and appellation of KING to have been given to a certain Pretender, Pseudo-Poet, or Phantom, of the name of TIBBALD;° and apprehending the same may be deemed in some sort a Reflection on Majesty, or at least an insult on that Legal Authority which has bestowed on another person the Crown of Poesy: We have ordered the said Pretender, Pseudo-Poet, or Phantom, utterly to vanish, and evaporate out of this work: And do declare the said Throne of Poesy from henceforth to be abdicated and vacant, unless duly and lawfully supplied by the LAUREATE himself. And it is hereby enacted, that no other person do presume to fill the same.

ƆC. Ch.°

MARTINUS SCRIBLERUS

HIS

Prolegomena and Illustrations

TO THE

DUNCIAD

WITH THE

Hyper-critics of ARISTARCHUS

LETTER

TO THE

PUBLISHER

Occasioned by the first correct
EDITION of the DUNCIAD

It is with pleasure I hear, that you have procured a correct copy of the *Dunciad*, which the many surreptitious ones have rendered so necessary; and it is yet with more, that I am informed it will be attended with a COMMENTARY: a work so requisite, that I cannot think the author himself would have omitted it, had he approved of the first appearance of this poem.

Such notes as have occurred to me I herewith send you. You will oblige me by inserting them amongst those which are, or will be, transmitted to you by others; since not only the author's friends, but even strangers, appear engaged by humanity, to take some care of an orphan of so much genius and spirit, which its parent seems to have abandoned from the very beginning, and suffered to step into the world naked, unguarded, and unattended.

It was upon reading some of the abusive papers lately published, that my great regard to a person, whose friendship I esteem as one of the chief honours of my life, and a much greater respect to truth, than to him or any man living, engaged me in enquiries, of which the enclosed notes are the fruit.

I perceived, that most of these authors had been (doubtless very wisely) the first aggressors. They had tried, till they were weary, what was to be got by railing at each other: nobody was either concerned or surprised, if this or that scribbler was proved a dunce. But everyone was curious to read what could be said to prove Mr POPE one, and was ready to pay something for such a discovery: a stratagem, which would they fairly own, it might not only reconcile them to me, but screen them from the resentment of their lawful superiors, whom they daily abuse, only (as I charitably hope) to get that *by* them, which they cannot get *from* them.

I found this was not all: ill success in that had transported them to personal abuse, either of himself, or (what I think he could less forgive) of his friends. They had called men of virtue and honour bad men, long before he had either leisure or inclination to call them bad writers: and some had been such old offenders, that he had quite forgotten their persons as well as their slanders, till they were pleased to revive them.

Now what had Mr POPE done before, to incense them? He had published those works which are in the hands of everybody, in which not the least mention° is made of any of them. And what has he done since? He has laughed, and written the *Dunciad*. What has that said of them? A very serious truth, which the public had said before, that they were dull. And what it had no sooner said, but they themselves were at great pains to procure or even purchase room in the prints, to testify under their hands to the truth of it.

I should still have been silent, if either I had seen any inclination in my friend to be serious with such accusers, or if they had only meddled with his writings; since whoever publishes, puts himself on his trial by his country. But when his moral character was attacked, and in a manner from which neither truth nor virtue can secure the most innocent, in a manner, which, though it annihilates the credit of the accusation with the just and impartial, yet aggravates very much the guilt of the accusers; I mean by authors *without names:* then I thought, since the danger was common to all, the concern ought to be so; and that it was an act of justice to detect the authors, not only on this account, but as many of them are the same who for several years past have made free with the greatest names in church and state, exposed to the world the private misfortunes of families, abused all, even to women, and whose prostituted papers (for one or other party, in the unhappy divisions of their country) have insulted the fallen, the friendless, the exiled, and the dead.

Besides this, which I take to be a public concern, I have already confessed I had a private one. I am one of that number who have long loved and esteemed Mr POPE; and had often declared it was not his capacity or writings (which we ever thought the least valuable part of his character) but the honest, open, and beneficent man, that we most esteemed, and loved in him. Now, if what these people say were believed, I must appear to all my friends either a fool, or a knave; either imposed on myself, or imposing on them; so that I am as much interested in the confutation of these calumnies, as he is himself.

I am no author, and consequently not to be suspected either of jealousy or resentment against any of the men, of whom scarce one is known to me by sight; and as for their writings, I have sought them (on this one occasion) in vain, in the closets and libraries of all my acquaintance. I had still been in the dark, if a gentleman° had not procured me (I suppose from some of themselves, for they are generally much more dangerous friends than enemies) the passages I send you. I solemnly protest I have added nothing to the malice or absurdity of them; which it behoves me to declare, since the vouchers themselves will be so soon and so irrecoverably lost. You may in some measure prevent it, by preserving at least their titles, and discovering (as far as you can depend on the truth of your information) the names of the concealed authors.

The first objection I have heard made to the poem is, that the persons are too *obscure* for satire. The persons themselves, rather than allow the objection, would forgive the satire; and if one could be tempted to afford it a serious answer, were not all assassinates, popular insurrections, the insolence of the rabble without doors, and of domestics within, most wrongfully chastised, if the meanness of offenders indemnified them from punishment? On the contrary, obscurity renders them more dangerous, as less thought of: law can pronounce judgment only on open facts; morality alone can pass censure on intentions of mischief; so that for secret calumny, or the arrow flying in the dark, there is no public punishment left, but what a good writer inflicts.

The next objection is, that these sort of authors are *poor*. That might be pleaded as an excuse at the Old Bailey, for lesser crimes than defamation, (for 'tis the case of almost all who are tried there) but sure it can be none: for who will pretend that the robbing another of his reputation supplies the want of it in himself? I question not but such authors are poor, and heartily wish the objection were removed by any honest livelihood. But poverty is here the accident, not the subject: he who describes malice and villainy to be pale and meagre, expresses not the least anger against paleness or leanness, but against malice and villainy. The apothecary° in *Romeo and Juliet* is poor; but is he therefore justified in vending poison? Not but poverty itself becomes a just subject of satire, when it is the consequence of vice, prodigality, or neglect of one's lawful calling: for then it increases the public burden, fills the streets and highways with robbers, and the garrets with clippers, coiners, and weekly journalists.

But admitting that two or three of these offend less in their morals, than in their writings; must poverty make nonsense sacred? If so, the fame of bad authors would be much better consulted than that of all the good ones in the world; and not one of an hundred had ever been called by his right name.

They mistake the whole matter: it is not charity to encourage them in the way they follow, but to get them out of it; for men are not bunglers because they are poor, but they are poor because they are bunglers.

Is it not pleasant enough, to hear our authors crying out on the one hand, as if their persons and characters were too sacred for satire; and the public objecting on the other, that they are too mean even for ridicule? But whether bread or fame be their end, it must be allowed, our author, by and in this poem, has mercifully given them a little of both.

There are two or three, who by their rank and fortune have no benefit from the former objections, supposing them good, and these I was sorry to see in such company. But if, without any provocation, two or three gentlemen will fall upon one, in an affair wherein his interest and reputation are equally embarked; they cannot certainly, after they have been content to print themselves his enemies, complain of being put into the number of them.

Others, I am told, pretend to have been once his friends. Surely they are their enemies who say so, since nothing can be more odious than to treat a friend as they have done. But of this I cannot persuade myself, when I consider the constant and eternal aversion of all bad writers to a good one.

Such as claim a merit from being his admirers I would gladly ask, if it lays him under a personal obligation? At that rate he would be the most obliged humble servant in the world. I dare swear for these in particular, he never desired them to be his admirers, nor promised in return to be theirs: that had truly been a sign he was of their acquaintance; but would not the malicious world have suspected such an approbation of some motive worse than ignorance, in the author of the *Essay on Criticism*? Be it as it will, the reasons of their admiration and of his contempt are equally subsisting,° for his works and theirs are the very same that they were.

One, therefore, of their assertions I believe may be true, 'That he has a contempt for their writings.' And there is another, which would probably be sooner allowed by himself than by any good judge beside, 'That his own have found too much success with the public'. But as it cannot consist with his modesty to claim this as a justice, it lies not on him, but entirely on the public, to defend its own judgment.

There remains what in my opinion might seem a better plea for these people, than any they have made use of. If obscurity or poverty were to exempt a man from satire, much more should folly or dulness, which are still more involuntary; nay, as much so as personal deformity. But even this will not help them: deformity becomes an object of ridicule when a man sets up for being handsome; and so must dulness when he sets up for a wit. They are not ridiculed because ridicule in itself is, or ought to be, a pleasure; but because it is just to undeceive and vindicate the honest and unpretending part of mankind from imposition, because particular interest ought to yield to general, and a great number who are not naturally fools, ought never to be made so, in complaisance to a few who are. Accordingly we find that in all ages, all vain pretenders, were they ever so poor or ever so dull, have been constantly the topics of the most candid satirists, from the Codrus° of JUVENAL to the Damon° of BOILEAU.

Having mentioned BOILEAU, the greatest poet and most judicious critic of his age and country, admirable for his talents, and yet perhaps more admirable for his judgment in the proper application of them; I cannot help remarking the resemblance betwixt him and our author, in qualities, fame, and fortune; in the distinctions shown them by their superiors, in the general esteem of their equals, and in their extended reputation amongst foreigners; in the latter of which ours has met with the better fate, as he has had for his translators° persons of the most eminent rank and abilities in their respective nations. But the resemblance holds in nothing more, than in their being equally abused by the ignorant pretenders to poetry of their times; of which not the least memory will remain but in their own writings, and in the notes made upon them. What BOILEAU has done in almost all his poems, our author has only in this: I dare answer for him he will do it in no more; and on this principle, of attacking few but who had slandered him, he could not have done it at all, had he been confined from censuring obscure and worthless persons, for scarce any other were his enemies. However, as the parity is so remarkable, I hope it will continue to the last; and if ever he shall give us an edition of this poem himself, I may see some of them treated as gently, on their repentance or better merit, as Perrault° and Quinault° were at last by BOILEAU.

In one point I must be allowed to think the character of our English poet the more amiable. He has not been a follower of fortune or success; he has lived with the great without flattery; been a friend to men in power, without pensions, from whom, as he asked, so he received no favour, but what was done him in his friends. As his satires were the more just for being delayed, so were his panegyrics; bestowed only on such persons as he had familiarly known, only for such virtues as he had long observed in them, and only at such times as others cease to praise, if not begin to calumniate them, I mean when out of power or out of fashion.[1] A satire, therefore, on writers so notorious for the contrary practice, became no man so well as himself; as none, it is plain, was so little in their friendships, or so much in that of those whom they had most abused, namely the greatest and best of all parties. Let me add a further reason, that, though engaged in their friendships, he never espoused their animosities; and can almost singly challenge this honour, not to have written a line of any man, which, through guilt, through shame, or through fear, through variety of fortune, or change of interests, he was ever unwilling to own.

I shall conclude with remarking what a pleasure it must be to every reader of humanity, to see all along, that our author in his very laughter is not indulging his own ill-nature, but only punishing that of others. As to his poem, those alone are capable of doing it justice, who, to use the words of a great writer, know how hard it is (with regard both to his subject and his manner) VETUSTIS DARE NOVITATEM, OBSOLETIS NITOREM, OBSCURIS LUCEM, FASTIDITIS GRATIAM.° I am

Your most humble servant,
WILLIAM CLELAND.[2]

St James's
Dec. 22, 1728.

MARTINUS SCRIBLERUS
of the POEM

This poem, as it celebrateth the most grave and ancient of things, Chaos, Night, and Dulness; so is it of the most grave and ancient kind.

---

[1] As Mr Wycherley,° at the time the town declaimed against his book of poems; Mr Walsh, after his death; Sir William Trumbull, when he had resigned the office of Secretary of State; Lord Bolingbroke, at his leaving England after the Queen's death; Lord Oxford in his last decline of life; Mr Secretary Craggs, at the end of the South Sea year, and after his death: others only in epitaphs.

[2] This gentleman was of Scotland, and bred at the University of Utrecht, with the Earl of Mar. He served in Spain under Earl Rivers. After the Peace, he was made one of the Commissioners of the Customs in Scotland, and then of Taxes in England, in which having shown himself for twenty years diligent, punctual, and incorruptible, though without any other assistance of fortune, he was suddenly displaced by the Minister in the sixty-eighth year of his age; and died two months after, in 1741. He was a person of universal learning, and an enlarged conversation; no

Homer, saith Aristotle, was the first who gave the *form*, and, saith Horace, who adapted the *measure*, to heroic poesy. But even before this, may be rationally presumed from what the ancients have left written, was a piece by Homer° composed, of like nature and matter with this of our poet. For of epic sort it appeareth to have been, yet of matter surely not unpleasant, witness what is reported of it by the learned archbishop Eustathius,° in *Odyss.* x. And accordingly Aristotle, in his *Poetics*, chap. iv, doth further set forth, that as the *Iliad* and *Odyssey* gave example to tragedy, so did this poem to comedy its first idea.

From these authors also it should seem, that the hero, or chief personage of it was no less *obscure*, and his understanding and sentiments no less quaint and strange (if indeed not more so) than any of the actors of our poem. MARGITES was the name of this personage, whom antiquity recordeth to have been *Dunce the first*; and surely from what we hear of him, not unworthy to be the root of so spreading a tree, and so numerous a posterity. The poem therefore celebrating him was properly and absolutely a *Dunciad*; which though now unhappily lost, yet is its nature sufficiently known by the infallible tokens aforesaid. And thus it doth appear, that the first *Dunciad* was the first epic poem, written by Homer himself, and anterior even to the *Iliad* or *Odyssey*.

Now, forasmuch as our poet had translated those two famous works of Homer which are yet left, he did conceive it in some sort his duty to imitate that also which was lost: and was therefore induced to bestow on it the same form which Homer's is reported to have had, namely that of epic poem; with a title also framed after the ancient Greek manner, to wit, that of *Dunciad*.

Wonderful it is, that so few of the moderns have been stimulated to attempt some *Dunciad*! since, in the opinion of the multitude, it might cost less pain and oil than an imitation of the greater epic. But possible it is also, that, on due reflection, the maker might find it easier to paint a Charlemagne, a Brute,° or a Godfrey,° with just pomp and dignity heroic, than a Margites, a Codrus, or a Flecknoe.°

We shall next declare the occasion and the cause which moved our poet to this particular work. He lived in those days, when (after Providence had permitted the invention of printing as a scourge for the sins of the learned) paper also became so cheap, and printers so numerous, that a deluge of authors covered the land: whereby not only the peace

man had a warmer heart for his friend, or a sincerer attachment to the constitution of his country.

of the honest unwriting subject was daily molested, but unmerciful demands were made of his applause, yea of his money, by such as would neither earn the one, nor deserve the other. At the same time, the licence of the press was such, that it grew dangerous to refuse them either; for they would forthwith publish slanders unpunished, the authors being anonymous, and skulking under the wings of publishers, a set of men who never scrupled to vend either calumny or blasphemy, as long as the town would call for it.

[a]Now our author, living in those times, did conceive it an endeavour well worthy an honest satirist, to dissuade the dull, and punish the wicked, *the only way that was left*. In that public-spirited view he laid the plan of this poem, as the greatest service he was capable (without much hurt, or being slain) to render his dear country. First, taking things from their original, he considereth the causes creative of such authors, namely *dulness* and *poverty*; the one born with them, the other contracted by neglect of their proper talents, through self-conceit of greater abilities. This truth he wrapped in an *allegory*[b] (as the construction of epic poesy requireth) and feigns that one of these goddesses had taken up her abode with the other, and that they jointly inspired all such writers and such works.[c] He proceedeth to show the *qualities* they bestow on these authors, and the *effects* they produce[d]: then the *materials*, or *stock*, with which they furnish them[e]; and (above all) that *self-opinion*[f] which causeth it to seem to themselves vastly greater than it is, and is the prime motive of their setting up in this sad and sorry merchandise. The great power of these goddesses acting in alliance (whereof as the one is the mother of industry, so is the other of plodding) was to be exemplified in some *one*, *great* and *remarkable action*[g]. And none could be more so than that which our poet hath chosen, viz. the restoration of the reign of Chaos and Night, by the ministry of Dulness their daughter, in the removal of her imperial seat from the city to the polite world; as the action of the *Aeneid* is the restoration of the empire of Troy, by the removal of the race from thence to Latium. But as Homer singing only the *wrath* of Achilles, yet includes in his poem the whole history of the Trojan war; in like manner our author hath drawn into this *single action* the whole history of Dulness and her children.

A *person* must next be fixed upon to support this action. This *phantom*

---

[a] Vide Bossu, *Du Poème Épique*, ch. viii.   [b] Bossu, chap. vii.
[c] Book I. v. 32, &c.   [d] Ver. 45 to 54.   [e] Ver. 57 to 77.   [f] Ver. 80.
[g] Ibid. chap. vii, viii.

in the poet's mind must have a *name*[h]. He finds it to be °—; and he
becomes of course the hero of the poem.

The *fable*° being thus, according to the best example, one and entire,
as contained in the proposition;° the *machinery* is a continued chain of
allegories, setting forth the whole power, ministry, and empire of Dul-
ness, extended through her subordinate instruments, in all her various
operations.

This is branched into *episodes*,° each of which hath its moral apart,
though all conducive to the main end. The crowd assembled in the
second book, demonstrates the design to be more extensive than to bad
poets only, and that we may expect other episodes of the patrons,
encouragers, or paymasters of such authors, as occasion shall bring
them forth. And the third book, if well considered, seemeth to embrace
the whole world. Each of the games relateth to some or other vile class
of writers. The first concerneth the plagiary, to whom he giveth the
name of More;° the second the libellous novelist, whom he styleth
Eliza;° the third, the flattering dedicator; the fourth, the bawling critic,
or noisy poet; the fifth, the dark and dirty party-writer; and so of the
rest; assigning to each some *proper name* or other, such as he could
find.

As for the *characters*, the public hath already acknowledged how justly
they are drawn. The manners are so depicted, and the sentiments so
peculiar to those to whom applied, that surely to transfer them to any
other or wiser personages, would be exceeding difficult. And certain it
is that every person concerned, being consulted apart, hath readily
owned the resemblance of every portrait, his own excepted. So Mr
Cibber calls them, 'a parcel of *poor wretches*, so many '*silly flies*'[i]: but
adds, 'our author's wit is remarkably more bare and barren, whenever
it would fall foul on Cibber, than upon any other person whatever.'

The *descriptions* are singular, the *comparisons* very quaint, the *narration*
various, yet of one colour. The purity and chastity of *diction* is so
preserved, that in the places most suspicious, not the *words* but only
the *images* have been censured, and yet are those images no other than
have been sanctified by ancient and classical authority, (though, as was
the manner of those good times, not so curiously wrapped up) yea, and
commented upon by most grave doctors, and approved critics.

As it beareth the name of *epic*, it is thereby subjected to such severe
indispensable rules as are laid on all neoterics,° a strict imitation of

[h] Ibid. chap. viii. Vide Aristotle, *Poetics*, cap. ix.
[i] Cibber's *Letter to Mr P.* pag. 9, 12, 41.

the ancients; insomuch that any deviation, accompanied with whatever poetic beauties, hath always been censured by the sound critic. How exact that imitation hath been in this piece, appeareth not only by its general structure, but by particular allusions infinite, many whereof have escaped both the commentator and poet himself; yea divers by his exceeding diligence are so altered and interwoven with the rest, that several have already been, and more will be, by the ignorant abused, as altogether and originally his own.

In a word, the whole poem proveth itself to be the work of our author, when his faculties were in full vigour and perfection; at that exact time when years have ripened the judgment, without diminishing the imagination: which, by good critics, is held to be punctually at *forty*.° For, at that season it was that Virgil finished his *Georgics*; and Sir Richard Blackmore at the like age composing his *Arthurs*, declared the same to be the very *acme* and pitch of life for epic poesy: though since he hath altered it to *sixty*, the year in which he published his *Alfred*[k]. True it is, that the talents for *criticism*, namely smartness, quick censure, vivacity of remark, certainty of asseveration, indeed all but acerbity, seem rather the gifts of youth than of riper age. But it is far otherwise in *poetry*; witness the works of Mr Rymer° and Mr Dennis, who beginning with criticism, became afterwards such poets as no age hath paralleled. With good reason therefore did our author choose to write his *Essay* on that subject at twenty,° and reserve for his maturer years this great and wonderful work of the *Dunciad*.

RICARDUS ARISTARCHUS
OF THE
HERO of the POEM°

Of the nature of *Dunciad* in general, whence derived, and on what authority founded, as well as of the art and conduct of this our poem in particular, the learned and laborious Scriblerus hath, according to his manner, and with tolerable share of judgment, dissertated. But when he cometh to speak of the *person* of the *hero* fitted for such poem, in truth he miserably halts and hallucinates. For, misled by one

[k] See his *Essays*.

Monsieur Bossu,° a Gallic critic, he prateth of I cannot tell what *phan-tom of a hero*, only raised up to support the fable. A putid° conceit! As if Homer and Virgil, like modern undertakers,° who first build their house and then seek out for a tenant, had contrived the story of a war and a wandering, before they once thought either of Achilles or Aeneas. We shall therefore set our good brother and the world also right in this particular, by giving our word, that in the *greater epic*, the prime intention of the muse is to exalt heroic virtue, in order to propagate the love of it among the children of men; and consequently that the poet's first thought must needs be turned upon a real subject meet for laud and celebration; not one whom he is to make, but one whom he may find, truly illustrious. This is the *primum mobile* of his poetic world, whence everything is to receive life and motion. For this subject being found, he is immediately ordained, or rather acknowledged, an *hero*, and put upon such action as befitteth the dignity of his character.

But the muse ceases not here her eagle-flight. Sometimes, satiated with the contemplation of these *suns* of glory, she turneth downward on her wing, and darts like lightning on the *goose* and *serpent* kind. For we may apply to the muse in her various moods, what an ancient master of wisdom affirmeth of the gods in general: *Si Dii non irascuntur impiis et injustis, nec pios utique justosque diligunt. In rebus enim diversis, aut in utramque partem moveri necesse est, aut in neutram. Itaque qui bonos diligit, & malos odit; & qui malos non odit, nec bonos diligit. Quia & diligere bonos ex odio malorum venit; & malos odisse ex bonorum caritate descendit.*° Which in the vernacular idiom may be thus interpreted: 'If the gods be not provoked at evil men, neither are they delighted with the good and just. For contrary objects must either excite contrary affections, or no affections at all. So that he who loveth good men, must at the same time hate the bad; and he who hateth not bad men, cannot love the good; because to love good men proceedeth from an aversion to evil, and to hate evil men from a tenderness to the good.' From this delicacy of the muse arose the *little epic*,° (more lively and choleric than her elder sister, whose bulk and complexion incline her to the phlegmatic) and for this some notorious vehicle of vice and folly was sought out, to make thereof an example. An early instance of which (nor could it escape the accurate Scriblerus) the father of epic poem himself afford-eth us. From him the practice descended to the Greek dramatic poets, his offspring; who in the composition of their *tetralogy*, or set of four pieces, were wont to make the last a *satiric tragedy*. Happily one of these ancient *Dunciads* (as we may well term it) is come down to us amongst the tragedies of Euripides.° And what doth the reader think may be the

subject? Why truly, and it is worth his observation, the unequal conten-
tion of an *old, dull, debauched, buffoon Cyclops*, with the heaven-directed
favourite of Minerva; who after having quietly borne all the monster's
obscene and impious ribaldry, endeth the farce in punishing him with
the mark of an indelible brand in his *forehead*. May we not then be
excused, if for the future we consider the epics of Homer, Virgil, and
Milton, together with this our poem, as a complete *tetralogy*, in which
the last worthily holdeth the place or station of the *satiric* piece?

Proceed we therefore in our subject. It hath been long, and alas for
pity! still remaineth a question, whether the hero of the *greater epic*
should be an *honest man?* or, as the French critics express it, *un honnête
homme*[a]; but it never admitted of any doubt but that the hero of the
little epic should *not* be so. Hence, to the advantage of our *Dunciad*, we
may observe how much juster the *moral* of that poem must needs be,
where so important a question is previously decided.

But then it is not every knave, nor (let me add) fool, that is a fit subject
for a *Dunciad*. There must still exist some analogy, if not resemblance of
qualities, between the heroes of the two poems; and this in order to
admit what neoteric critics call the *parody*, one of the liveliest graces of
the little epic. Thus it being agreed that the constituent qualities of the
greater epic hero, are *wisdom, bravery*, and *love*, from whence springeth
heroic virtue; it followeth that those of the lesser epic hero, should be
vanity, impudence, and *debauchery*, from which happy assemblage resul-
teth *heroic dulness*, the never-dying subject of this our poem.

This being confessed, come we now to particulars. It is the character
of true *wisdom*, to seek its chief support and confidence within itself; and
to place that support in the resources which proceed from a conscious
rectitude of will.—And are the advantages of *vanity*, when arising to
the heroic standard, at all short of this self-complacence? Nay, are they
not, in the opinion of the enamoured owner, far beyond it? 'Let the
world' (will such an one say) 'impute to me what folly or weakness they
please; but till *wisdom* can give me something that will make me more
heartily happy, I am content to be GAZED AT[b].' This we see is *vanity*
according to the *heroic* gauge or measure; not that low and ignoble
species which pretendeth to *virtues* we *have not*, but the laudable
ambition of being *gazed at* for glorying in those *vices* which all the world
know *we have*. 'The world may ask' (says he) 'why I make my follies

---

[a] Si un Heros Poëtique doit être un honnête homme. Bossu, *du Poème Épique*,
lib. v. ch. 5.

[b] Dedication to the *Life* of Colley Cibber.

public? Why not? I have passed my time very pleasantly with them^c.' In short, there is no sort of vanity such a hero would scruple, but that which might go near to degrade him from his high station in this our *Dunciad*; namely, 'Whether it would not be *vanity* in him, to take shame to himself for *not being* a *wise man*^d?'

Bravery, the second attribute of the true hero, is courage manifesting itself in every limb; while, in its correspondent virtue in the mock hero, that courage is all collected into the *face*. And as power when drawn together, must needs be more strong than when dispersed, we generally find this kind of courage in so high and heroic a degree, that it insults not only men, but gods. Mezentius° is without doubt the bravest character in all the *Aeneis*; but how? His bravery, we know, was an high courage of blasphemy. And can we say less of this brave man's, who having told us that he placed 'his *summum bonum* in those follies, which he was not content barely to possess but would likewise glory in,' adds, '*If I am misguided,* 'TIS NATURE'S FAULT, *and I follow* HER^e.' Nor can we be mistaken in making this happy quality a species of *courage*, when we consider those illustrious marks of it, which made his *face* 'more known' (as he justly boasteth) 'than most in the kingdom,' and his *language* to consist of what we must allow to be the most *daring* figure of speech, that which is taken from the *name of God*.

Gentle love, the next ingredient in the true hero's composition, is a mere bird of passage, or (as Shakespeare calls it) *summer-teeming lust,*° and evaporates in the heat of *youth*; doubtless by that refinement it suffers in passing through those *certain strainers*° which our poet somewhere speaketh of. But when it is let alone to work upon the *lees*, it acquireth strength by *old age*; and becometh a standing ornament to the little epic. It is true indeed, there is one objection to its fitness for such an use: for not only the ignorant may think it *common*, but it is admitted to be so, even by him who best knoweth its nature. 'Don't you think', saith he, 'to say only *a man has his whore*, ought to go for little or nothing? Because *defendit numerus*, take the first ten thousand men you meet, and I believe you would be no loser if you betted ten to one, that every single sinner of them, one with another, had been guilty of the same frailty^f.' But here he seemeth not to have done himself justice: the man is sure enough a hero, who has his lady at fourscore.° How doth his modesty herein lessen the merit of a *whole well-spent* life: not taking to himself the commendation (which Horace

^c *Life*, p. 2. octavo ed.   ^d *Life*, ibid.
^e *Life*, p. 23. octavo.   ^f *Letter to Mr P.*, p. 46.

accounted the greatest in a theatrical character) of continuing to the very *dregs*, the same he was from the beginning,

> ——*Servetur ad* IMUM
> *Qualis ab incepto processerat*°——

But let us farther remark, that the calling her *his* whore, implieth she was *his own*, and not his *neighbour*'s. Truly a commendable continence! and such as Scipio himself must have applauded. For how much self-denial was necessary not to covet his neighbour's whore? And what disorders must the coveting her have occasioned, in that society, where (according to this political calculator) *nine* in *ten* of all ages have their *concubines?*

We have now, as briefly as we could devise, gone through the three constituent qualities of either hero. But it is not in any, or all of these, that heroism properly or essentially resideth. It is a lucky result rather from the collision of these lively qualities against one another. Thus, as from wisdom, bravery, and love, ariseth *magnanimity*, the object of *admiration*, which is the aim of the greater epic; so from vanity, impudence, and debauchery, springeth *buffoonery*, the source of *ridicule*, that 'laughing ornament,' as he well termeth it[g], of the little epic.

He is not ashamed (God forbid he ever should be ashamed!) of this character; who deemeth, that not *reason* but *risibility* distinguisheth the human species from the brutal. 'As Nature' (saith this profound philosopher) 'distinguished our species from the mute creation by our risibility, her design MUST have been by *that faculty* as evidently to raise our HAPPINESS, as by OUR *os sublime* (OUR ERECTED FACES) to lift the dignity of our FORM above them[h].' All this considered, how complete a hero must he be, as well as how *happy* a man, whose risibility lieth not barely in his *muscles* as in the common sort, but (as himself informeth us) in his very *spirits?* And whose *os sublime* is not simply an *erect face*, but a brazen head, as should seem by his comparing it with one of iron, said to belong to the late king of Sweden[i]!°

But whatever personal qualities a hero may have, the examples of Achilles and Aeneas show us, that all those are of small avail, without the constant *assistance of the* GODS: for the subversion and erection of empires have never been judged the work of man. How greatly soever then we may esteem of his high talents, we can hardly conceive his personal prowess alone sufficient to restore the decayed empire of

[g] *Letter to Mr P.*, p. 31.   [h] *Life*, p. 23, 24.   [i] *Letter*, p. 8.

Dulness. So weighty an achievement must require the particular favour
and protection of the GREAT: who being the natural patrons and sup-
porters of *letters*, as the ancient gods were of Troy, must first be drawn
off and engaged in another interest, before the total subversion of them
can be accomplished. To surmount, therefore, this last and greatest
difficulty, we have in this excellent man a professed favourite and
intimado of the great. And look of what force ancient piety was to draw
the gods into the party of Aeneas, that, and much stronger is modern
incense, to engage the great in the party of Dulness.

Thus have we essayed to portray or shadow out this noble imp of
fame. But now the impatient reader will be apt to say, if so many and
various graces go to the making up of a hero, what mortal shall suffice
to bear this character? Ill hath he read, who sees not in every trace of
this picture, that *individual*, ALL-ACCOMPLISHED PERSON, in whom
these rare virtues and lucky circumstances have agreed to meet and
concentre with the strongest lustre and fullest harmony.

The good Scriblerus indeed, nay the world itself might be imposed
on in the late spurious editions, by I can't tell what *sham-hero*, or
phantom. But it was not so easy to impose on HIM whom this egregious
error most of all concerned. For no sooner had the fourth book laid
open the high and swelling scene, but he recognized his own heroic
acts: and when he came to the words,

Soft on her lap her laureate son reclines,

(though *laureate* imply no more than *one crowned with laurel*, as befitteth
any associate or consort in empire) he ROARED (like a lion) and VINDI-
CATED HIS RIGHT OF FAME. Indeed not without cause, he being there
represented as *fast asleep*; so unbeseeming the eye of empire, which,
like that of Providence, should never slumber. 'Hah!', saith he, 'fast
asleep it seems! that's a little too strong. Pert and dull at least you
might have allowed me, but as seldom asleep as any fool[k].' However,
the injured hero may comfort himself with this reflexion, that though
it be *sleep*, yet it is not the *sleep of death*, but of *immortality*. Here he
will[l] *live* at least, though not *awake*; and in no worse condition than
many an enchanted warrior before him. The famous Durandarte,[o] for
instance, was, like him, cast into a long slumber by Merlin the British
bard and necromancer: and his example, for submitting to it with so
good a grace, might be of use to our hero. For this disastrous knight

---

[k] *Letter*, p. 53.   [l] *Letter*, p. 1.

being sorely pressed or driven to make his answer by several *persons of quality*, only replied with a sigh, '*Patience, and shuffle the cards*'.[m]

But now, as nothing in this world, no not the most sacred or perfect things either of religion or government, can escape the teeth or tongue of envy, methinks I already hear these carpers objecting to the clear title of our hero.

'It would never' (say they) 'have been esteemed sufficient to make an hero for the *Iliad* or *Aeneis*, that Achilles was brave enough to overturn one empire, or Aeneas pious enough to raise another, had they not been goddess-born, and princes bred. What then did this author mean, by erecting a player instead of one of his patrons, (a person "never a hero even on the stage,[n]") to this dignity of colleague in the empire of Dulness, and achiever of a work that neither old Omar,° Attila, nor John of Leiden° could entirely compass.'

To all this we have, as we conceive, a sufficient answer from the Roman historian,° *Fabrum esse suae quemque fortunae: Every man is the Smith of his own fortune*. The politic Florentine Nicholas Machiavel° goeth still farther, and affirms that a man needs but to *believe himself a hero* to be one of the best. 'Let him', saith he, 'but fancy himself capable of the highest things, and he will of course be able to achieve them.' Laying this down as a principle, it will certainly and incontestably follow, that, if ever hero *was* such a character, OURS *is:* for if ever man *thought* himself such, OURS *doth*. Hear how he constantly paragons himself, at one time to ALEXANDER the Great and CHARLES the XII of SWEDEN, for the excess and delicacy of his ambition°; to HENRY the IV of FRANCE, for honest policy[p]; to the first BRUTUS, for love of liberty[q]; and to Sir ROBERT WALPOLE, for good government while in power[r]: at another time, to the godlike SOCRATES, for his diversions and amusements[s]; to HORACE, MONTAIGNE, and Sir WILLIAM TEMPLE, for an elegant vanity that makes them for ever read and admired[t]; to TWO Lord CHANCELLORS, for law, from whom, when confederate against him at the bar, he carried away the prize of eloquence[v]; and, to say all in a word, to the right reverend the Lord BISHOP of LONDON himself, in the art of writing *pastoral letters*[w].

Nor did his *actions* fall short of the sublimity of his conceptions. In

[m] *Don Quixote*, Part ii. Book ii. ch. 22.
[n] See *Life*, p. 148. [o] *Life*, p. 149. [p] P. 424.
[q] P. 366. [r] P. 457. [s] P. 18.
[t] P. 425. [v] P. 436, 437. [w] P. 52.

his early youth he *met the Revolution* at Nottingham[x] face to face, at a time when his betters contented themselves with *following* her. But he shone in courts as well as camps: he was *called up* when *the nation fell in labour* of this *Revolution*[y]: and was a gossip at her christening, with the Bishop and the ladies[z].

As to his *birth*, it is true he pretendeth no relation either to heathen god or goddess; but, what is as good, he was descended from a *maker* of both[a]. And that he did not pass himself on the world for a hero, as well by birth as education, was his own fault: for, his lineage he bringeth into his life as an anecdote, and is sensible he had it in his power *to be thought nobody's son at all*[b]: and what is that but coming into the world a hero?

There is in truth another objection of greater weight, namely. 'That this hero still existeth, and hath not yet finished his earthly course. For if Solon° said well, that no man could be called happy till his death, surely much less can anyone, till then, be pronounced a hero: this species of men being far more subject than others to the caprices of fortune and humour.' But to this also we have an answer, that will be deemed (we hope) decisive. It cometh from *himself*, who, to cut this dispute short, hath solemnly protested that *he will never change or amend*.

With regard to his *vanity*, he declareth that nothing shall ever part them. 'Nature', saith he, 'hath amply supplied me in vanity; a pleasure which neither the pertness of wit, nor the gravity of wisdom, will ever persuade me to part with[c].' Our poet had charitably endeavoured to administer a cure to it: but he telleth us plainly, 'My superiors perhaps may be mended by him; but for my part I own myself incorrigible. I look upon my follies as the best part of my fortune.[d]' And with good reason: we see to what they have brought him!

Secondly, as to *buffoonery*, 'Is it', saith he, 'a time of day for me to leave off these fooleries, and set up a new character? I can no more put off my follies than my skin; I have often tried, but they stick too close to me; nor am I sure my friends are displeased with them, for in this light I afford them frequent matter of mirth, etc. etc.[e]' Having then so publicly declared himself *incorrigible*, he is become *dead in law*, (I mean the *law epopoeian*)° and descendeth to the poet as his property: who may take him, and deal with him, as if he had been dead as long as an old Egyptian hero; that is to say, *embowel* and *embalm him for posterity*.

[x] P. 47.   [y] P. 57.   [z] P. 58, 59.   [a] A statuary.°
[b] *Life*, p. 6.   [c] P. 424.   [d] P. 19.   [e] P. 17.

Nothing therefore (we conceive) remains to hinder his own prophecy of himself from taking immediate effect. A rare felicity! and what few prophets have had the satisfaction to see, alive! Nor can we conclude better than with that extraordinary one of his, which is conceived in these oraculous words, 'MY DULNESS WILL FIND SOMEBODY TO DO IT RIGHT'.

ARGUMENT
TO
BOOK the FIRST

The proposition, the invocation, and the inscription. Then the original of the great empire of Dulness, and cause of the continuance thereof. The college of the Goddess in the City, with her private academy for poets in particular, the governors of it, and the four cardinal virtues. Then the poem hastes into the midst of things,° presenting her, on the evening of a Lord Mayor's day, revolving the long succession of her sons, and the glories past and to come. She fixes her eye on Bays to be the instrument of that great event which is the subject of the poem. He is described pensive among his books, giving up the cause, and apprehending the period of her empire. After debating whether to betake himself to the church, or to gaming, or to party-writing, he raises an altar of proper books, and (making first his solemn prayer and declaration) purposes thereon to sacrifice all his unsuccessful writings. As the pile is kindled, the Goddess beholding the flame from her seat, flies and puts it out by casting upon it the poem of Thule. She forthwith reveals herself to him, transports him to her temple, unfolds her arts, and initiates him into her mysteries; then announcing the death of Eusden the Poet Laureate, anoints him, carries him to court, and proclaims him successor.

ᶠ Ibid. p. 243. octavo edit.

THE
DUNCIAD
TO
Dr JONATHAN SWIFT
BOOK the FIRST

The Mighty Mother,° and her son who brings   1

The DUNCIAD, sic MS. It may well be disputed whether this be a right reading. Ought it not rather to be spelled *Dunceiad*, as the etymology evidently demands? *Dunce* with an *e*, therefore *Dunceiad* with an *e*. That accurate and punctual man of letters, the restorer of Shakespeare, constantly observes the preservation of this very letter *e*, in spelling the name of his beloved author, and not like his common careless editors, with the omission of one, nay sometimes of two *ee*'s [as Shakspear] which is utterly unpardonable. 'Nor is the neglect of a *single letter* so trivial as to some it may appear; the alteration whereof in a learned language is an achievement that brings honour to the critic who advances it; and Dr Bentley will be remembered to posterity for his performances of this sort, as long as the world shall have any esteem for the remains of Menander and Philemon.' THEOBALD.

This is surely a slip in the learned author of the foregoing note; there having been since produced by an accurate antiquary, an *autograph* of *Shakspeare* himself, whereby it appears that he spelled his own name without the first *e*. And upon this authority it was, that those most critical curators of his monument in Westminster Abbey erased the former wrong reading, and restored the true spelling on a new piece of old Egyptian granite. Nor for this only do they deserve our thanks, but for exhibiting on the same monument the first specimen of an *edition* of an author in *marble*; where (as may be seen on comparing the tomb with the book) in the space of five lines, two words and a whole verse are changed, and it is to be hoped will there stand, and outlast whatever hath been hitherto done in paper; as for the future, our learned sister university (the other eye of England) is taking care to perpetuate a *total new Shakespeare*, at the Clarendon Press. BENTLEY.

It is to be noted, that this great critic also has omitted one circumstance; which is, that the inscription with the name of Shakespeare was intended to be placed on the marble scroll to which he points with his hand; instead of which it is now placed behind his back, and that specimen of an edition is put on the scroll, which indeed Shakespeare hath great reason to point at. ANON.

Though I have as just a value for the letter *E*, as any grammarian living, and the same affection for the name of this poem as any critic for that of his author; yet cannot it induce me to agree with those who would add yet another *e* to it, and call it the *Dunceiade*; which being a French and foreign termination, is no way proper to a word entirely English, and vernacular. One *e* therefore in this case is right, and two *e*'s wrong. Yet upon the whole I shall follow the manuscript, and print it without any *e* at all; moved thereto by authority (at all times, with critics, equal, if not superior to reason.) In which method of proceeding, I can never enough praise my good friend, the exact Mr Tho. Hearne; who if any word occur, which to him and all mankind is evidently wrong, yet keeps he it in the text with due reverence, and only remarks in the margin *sic MS.* In like manner we shall not amend this error in the title itself, but only note it *obiter*, to evince to the learned that it was not our fault, nor any effect of our ignorance or inattention. SCRIBLERUS.

This poem was written in the year 1726. In the next year an imperfect edition was published at Dublin, and reprinted at London in twelves; another at Dublin, and another at London in octavo; and three others in twelves the same year. But there was no perfect edition before that of London in quarto; which was attended with notes. SCHOL. VET.

It was expressly confessed in the preface to the first edition, that this poem was not published by the author himself. It was printed originally in a foreign country. And what foreign country? Why, one notorious for blunders; where finding blanks only instead of proper names, these blunderers filled them up at their pleasure.

The very *hero* of the poem hath been mistaken to this hour; so that we are obliged to open our notes with a discovery who he really was. We learn from the former editor, that this piece was presented by the hands of Sir Robert Walpole to King George II. Now the author directly tells us, his hero is the man

———*who brings*
The Smithfield muses to the ear of kings.

And it is notorious who was the person on whom this Prince conferred the honour of the *laurel*.

It appears as plainly from the *apostrophe* to the *great* in the third verse, that Tibbald could not be the person, who was never an author in fashion, or caressed by the great; whereas this single characteristic is sufficient to point out the true hero; who, above all other poets of his time, was the *peculiar delight* and *chosen companion* of the nobility of England; and wrote, as he himself tells us, certain of his works at the *earnest desire* of *persons of quality*.

Lastly, the sixth verse affords full proof; this poet being the only one who was universally known to have had a *son* so exactly like him, in his poetical, theatrical, political, and moral capacities, that it could justly be said of him

Still Dunce the second reigned like Dunce the first. BENTLEY.

1. The reader ought here to be cautioned, that the *mother*, and not the *son*, is the principal agent of this poem: the latter of them is only chosen as her colleague (as was anciently the custom in Rome before some great expedition) the main action of the poem being by no means the coronation of the Laureate, which is performed in the very first book, but the restoration of the empire of Dulness in Britain, which is not accomplished till the last.

Wonderful is the stupidity of all the former critics and commentators on this work! It breaks forth at the very first line. The author of the critique prefixed to *Sawney*, a Poem, p. 5 hath been so dull as to explain *the man who brings. &c.* not of the hero of the piece, but of our poet himself, as if he vaunted that *kings* were to be his readers; an honour which though this poem hath had, yet knoweth he how to receive it with more modesty.

We remit this ignorant to the first lines of the *Aeneid*, assuring him that Virgil there speaketh not of himself, but of Aeneas:

The Smithfield muses° to the ear of kings,
I sing. Say you, her instruments the great!
Called to this work by Dulness, Jove, and Fate;
You by whose care, in vain decried and cursed,
Still Dunce the second reigns like Dunce the first;°
Say how the Goddess bade Britannia sleep,
And poured her spirit o'er the land and deep.

   In eldest time, e'er mortals writ or read,
E'er Pallas issued from the Thunderer's° head,   10
Dulness o'er all possessed her ancient right,
Daughter of Chaos and eternal Night:
Fate in their dotage this fair idiot gave,
Gross as her sire, and as her mother grave,
Laborious, heavy, busy, bold, and blind,

     Arma virumque cano, Trojae qui primus ab oris
     Italiam, fato profugus, Lavinaque venit
     Littora: multum ille & terris jactatus & alto, &c.

I cite the whole three verses, that I may by the way offer a *conjectural emendation*, purely my own, upon each: first, *oris* should be read *aris*, it being, as we see *Aen*. ii. 513. from the *altar* of *Jupiter Hercaeus* that Aeneas fled as soon as he saw Priam slain. In the second line I would read *flatu* for *fato*, since it is most clear it was by *winds* that he arrived at the *shore* of Italy. *Jactatus*, in the third, is surely as improperly applied to *terris*, as proper to *alto*; to say a man *is tossed on land*, is much at one with saying *he walks at sea: Risum teneatis, amici?* Correct it, as I doubt not it ought to be, *vexatus*. SCRIBLERUS.

   2. *Smithfield* is the place where Bartholomew Fair was kept, whose shows, machines, and dramatical entertainments, formerly agreeable only to the taste of the rabble, were, by the hero of this poem and others of equal genius, brought to the theatres of Covent Garden, Lincoln's Inn Fields, and the Haymarket, to be the reigning pleasures of the court and town. This happened in the reigns of King George I and II. See Book 3.

   4. *By Dulness, Jove, and Fate:*] i.e. By their *judgments*, their *interests*, and their *inclinations*.

   12. The beauty of this whole allegory being purely of the poetical kind, we think it not our proper business, as a scholiast, to meddle with it: but leave it (as we shall in general all such) to the reader; remarking only, that *Chaos* (according to *Hesiod*'s Θεογονία) was the progenitor of all the gods. SCRIBLERUS.

   15. I wonder the learned Scriblerus has omitted to advertise the reader, at the opening of this poem, that Dulness here is not to be taken contractedly for mere stupidity, but in the enlarged sense of the word, for all slowness of apprehension, shortness of sight, or imperfect sense of things. It includes (as we see by the poet's own words) labour, industry, and some degree of activity and boldness: a ruling principle not inert, but turning topsy-turvy the understanding, and inducing an anarchy or confused state of mind. This remark ought to be carried along with the reader throughout the work; and without this caution he will be apt to mistake the importance of many of the characters, as well as of the design of the poet. Hence it

She ruled, in native anarchy, the mind.
　　Still her old empire to restore she tries,
For, born a goddess, Dulness never dies.
　　O thou! whatever title please thine ear,
Dean,° Drapier, Bickerstaff, or Gulliver!   20
Whether thou choose Cervantes' serious air,
Or laugh and shake in Rabelais' easy chair,
Or praise the court, or magnify mankind,
Or thy grieved country's copper chains unbind;
From thy Boeotia° though her power retires,
Mourn not, my SWIFT, at ought our realm acquires,
Here pleased behold her mighty wings out-spread
To hatch a new Saturnian age of lead.
　　Close to those walls where Folly holds her throne,
And laughs to think Monroe would take her down,°   30
Where o'er the gates, by his famed father's hand

is that some have complained he chooses too mean a subject, and imagined he employs himself, like Domitian, in killing flies; whereas those who have the true key will find he sports with nobler quarry, and embraces a larger compass; or (as one saith, on a like occasion)

　　　　Will see his work, like Jacob's ladder, rise,
　　　　Its foot in dirt, its head amid the skies.
　　　　　　　　　　　　　　　　　　BENTLEY.

16. *The native anarchy of the mind* is that state which precedes the time of reason's assuming the rule of the passions. But in that state, the uncontrolled violence of the passions would soon bring things to confusion, were it not for the intervention of Dulness in this absence of reason; who, though she cannot regulate them like reason, yet blunts and deadens their vigour, and, indeed, produces some of the good effects of it: hence it is that Dulness has often the appearance of reason. This is the only good she ever did; and the poet takes particular care to tell it in the very introduction of his poem. It is to be observed indeed, that this is spoken of the universal rule of Dulness in ancient days, but we may form an idea of it from her partial government in later times.

17. This restoration makes the completion of the poem. *Vide* Book 4.

23. *Ironicè*, alluding to Gulliver's representations of both.—The next line relates to the papers of the Drapier against the currency of Wood's copper coin in Ireland, which, upon the great discontent of the people, his Majesty was graciously pleased to recall.

28. The ancient Golden Age is by poets styled Saturnian; but in the chemical language Saturn is lead. She is said here only to be spreading her wings to hatch this age; which is not produced completely till the fourth book.

31. *By his famed father's hand*] Mr Caius Gabriel Cibber, father of the Poet Laureate. The two statues of the lunatics over the gates of Bedlam Hospital were done by him, and (as the son justly says of them) are no ill monuments of his fame as an artist.

Great Cibber's brazen, brainless brothers stand;
One cell there is, concealed from vulgar eye,
The cave of poverty and poetry.
Keen, hollow winds howl through the bleak recess,
Emblem of music caused by emptiness.
Hence bards, like Proteus long in vain tied down,

33. The cell of poor poetry is here very properly represented as a little *unendowed hall* in the neighbourhood of the magnific College of Bedlam; and as the surest seminary to supply those learned walls with professors. For there cannot be a plainer indication of madness than in men's persisting to starve themselves and offend the public by scribbling,

Escape in monsters, and amaze the town.

when they might have benefited themselves and others in profitable and honest employments. The *qualities* and *productions* of the students of this private academy are afterwards described in this first book; as are also their *actions* throughout the second; by which it appears, how near allied dulness is to madness. This naturally prepares us for the subject of the third book, where we find them in union, and acting in conjunction to produce the catastrophe of the fourth; a mad poetical sibyl leading our hero through the regions of vision, to animate him in the present undertaking, by a view of the past triumphs of barbarism over science.

34. I cannot here omit a remark that will greatly endear our author to everyone, who shall attentively observe that humanity and candour, which everywhere appears in him towards those unhappy objects of the ridicule of all mankind, the bad poets. He here imputes all scandalous rhymes, scurrilous weekly papers, base flatteries, wretched elegies, songs, and verses (even from those sung at court to ballads in the streets) not so much to malice or servility as to Dulness; and not so much to Dulness as to necessity. And thus, at the very commencement of his satire, makes an apology for all that are to be satirized.

37.   *Sunt quibus in plures jus est transire figuras:*
            Ut tibi, complexi terram maris incola, Proteu;
            Nunc violentus aper, nunc quem tetigisse timerent,
            Anguis eras, modo te faciebant cornua Taurum,
            Saepe Lapis poteras.

                                        Ovid, *Met.* viii.

Neither Palaephatus, Phurnutus, nor Heraclides give us any steady light into the mythology of this mysterious fable. If I be not deceived in a part of learning which has so long exercised my pen, by *Proteus* must certainly be meant a hackneyed town scribbler; and by his transformations, the various disguises such a one assumes, to elude the pursuit of his irreconcilable enemy, the bailiff. Proteus is represented as one bred of the mud and slime of Egypt, the original soil of arts and letters. And what is a town-scribbler, but a creature made up of the excrements of luxurious science? By the change then into a *boar* is meant his character of a *furious and dirty party-writer*; the *snake* signifies a *libeller*; and the *horns of the bull*, the *dilemmas of a polemical answerer*. These are the three great parts he acts under; and when he has completed his circle, he sinks back again, as the last change into a *stone* denotes, into his natural state of immovable stupidity. If I may expect thanks of the learned

Escape in monsters, and amaze the town.
Hence miscellanies° spring, the weekly boast
Of Curll's chaste press, and Lintot's rubric post: 40
Hence hymning Tyburn's elegiac lines,
Hence *Journals, Medleys, Merc'ries, Magazines:*°
Sepulchral lies, our holy walls to grace,
And New Year odes, and all the Grub Street° race.
In clouded majesty here Dulness shone;

world for this discovery, I would by no means deprive that excellent critic of his
share, who discovered before me, that in the character of Proteus was designed
Sophistam, Magum, Politicum, praesertim rebus omnibus sese accommodantem. Which in
English is, *A political writer, a libeller, and a disputer, writing indifferently for or against
every party in the state, every sect in religion, and every character in private life.* See my
Fables of Ovid explained. ABBÉ BANIER.

40. *Curll's chaste press, and Lintot's rubric post:*] Two booksellers, of whom see
Book 2. The former was fined by the Court of King's Bench for publishing obscene
books; the latter usually adorned his shop with titles in red letters.

41, 42.   ——*Genus unde Latinum,*
                    Albanique patres, atque altae moenia Romae.
                                        Virgil, *Aen.* i.

41. It is an ancient English custom for the malefactors to sing a psalm at their
execution at Tyburn; and no less customary to print elegies on their deaths, at the
same time, or before.

42. *Magazines,*] Miscellanies in prose and verse, in which at some times
                    —*new-born nonsense first is taught to cry;*
at others, dead-born Dulness appears in a thousand shapes. These were thrown out
weekly and monthly by every miserable scribbler; or picked up piece-meal and stolen
from anybody, under the title of papers, essays, queries, verses, epigrams, riddles,
etc. equally the disgrace of human wit, morality, and decency.

43. *Sepulchral lies,*] Is a just satire on the flatteries and falsehoods admitted to be
inscribed on the walls of churches, in epitaphs.

44. *New Year odes*] Made by the Poet Laureate for the time being, to be sung at
court on every New Year's day, the words of which are happily drowned in the
voices and instruments. The *New Year odes* of the hero of this work were of a cast
distinguished from all that preceded him, and made a conspicuous part of his
character as a writer, which doubtless induced our author to mention them here so
particularly.

45.   ——*the moon*
                    Rising in clouded majesty——
                                        Milton, Book iv.

See this cloud removed, or rolled back, or gathered up to her head, book iv. ver.
17, 18. It is worthwhile to compare this description of the majesty of Dulness in a
state of peace and tranquillity, with that more busy scene where she mounts the
throne in triumph, and is not so much supported by her own virtues, as by the
princely consciousness of having destroyed all other. SCRIBL.

Four guardian virtues,° round, support her throne:
Fierce champion Fortitude, that knows no fears
Of hisses, blows, or want, or loss of ears:
Calm Temperance, whose blessings those partake
Who hunger, and who thirst for scribbling sake:°   50
Prudence, whose glass presents th' approaching gaol.
Poetic justice, with her lifted scale,
Where, in nice balance, truth with gold she weighs,
And solid pudding against empty praise.
 Here she beholds the chaos dark and deep,
Where nameless somethings in their causes sleep,
Till genial Jacob,° or a warm third day,°
Call forth each mass, a poem, or a play:
How hints, like spawn, scarce quick in embryo lie,
How new-born nonsense first is taught to cry,   60
Maggots half-formed in rhyme exactly meet,
And learn to crawl upon poetic feet.
 Here one poor word an hundred clenches makes,

---

48. *Quem neque pauperies, neque mors, neque vincula terrent.* Horace.

50. 'This is an allusion to a text in scripture, which shows, in Mr *Pope*, a delight in prophaneness,' said Curll upon this place. But it is very familiar with Shakespeare to allude to passages of scripture: out of a great number I will select a few, in which he not only alludes to, but quotes the very texts from holy writ. In *All's Well that Ends Well*, 'I am no great Nebuchadnezzar, I have not much skill in grass.' Ibid. '*They are for the flowery way that leads to the broad gate and the great fire.*' Mat. vii. 13. In *Much Ado About Nothing*, '*All, all, and moreover God saw him when he was hid in the garden.*' Gen. iii. 8. (in a very jocose scene.) In *Love's Labour Lost*, he talks of Samson's carrying the gates on his back; in the *Merry Wives of Windsor*, of Goliath and the weaver's beam; and in *Henry IV*, Falstaff's soldiers are compared to Lazarus and the prodigal son.

The first part of this note is Mr CURLL's, the rest is Mr THEOBALD's, Appendix to *Shakespeare Restored*, p. 144.

55, 56. That is to say, unformed things, which are either made into poems or plays, as the booksellers or the players bid most. These lines allude to the following in Garth's *Dispensary*, Cant. vi.

> *Within the chambers of the globe they spy*
> *The beds where sleeping vegetables lie,*
> *Till the glad summons of a genial ray*
> *Unbinds the glebe, and calls them out to day.*

63. It may not be amiss to give an instance or two of these operations of Dulness out of the works of her sons, celebrated in the poem. A great critic formerly held these clenches in such abhorrence, that he declared 'he that would pun would pick a pocket.' Yet Mr Dennis's works afford us notable examples in this kind: 'Alexander

And ductile dulness new meanders takes;
There motley images her fancy strike,
Figures ill paired, and similes unlike.
She sees a mob of metaphors advance,
Pleased with the madness of the mazy dance:
How tragedy and comedy embrace;
How farce and epic get a jumbled race; 70
How time himself stands still at her command,
Realms shift their place, and ocean turns to land.
Here gay description Egypt glads with showers,
Or gives to Zembla° fruits, to Barca° flowers;
Glittering with ice here hoary hills are seen,
There painted valleys of eternal green,
In cold December fragrant chaplets blow,
And heavy harvests nod beneath the snow.
　　All these, and more, the cloud-compelling Queen
Beholds through fogs, that magnify the scene. 80
She, tinselled o'er in robes of varying hues,
With self-applause her wild creation views;
Sees momentary monsters rise and fall,
And with her own fools-colours gilds them all.

Pope hath sent abroad into the world as many *bulls* as his namesake Pope *Alexander.*
—Let us take the initial and final letters of his name, *viz. A. P—E,* and they give
you the idea of an *ape.*—*Pope* comes from the Latin word *Popa,* which signifies a
little wart; or from *poppysma,* because he was continually *popping* out squibs of wit,
or rather *Popysmata,* or *Popisms.*' DENNIS on *Hom.* and *Daily Journal,* June 11, 1728.

64. A parody on a verse in Garth, Cant. I.
　　　　How ductile matter new meanders takes.

70, etc. Allude to the transgressions of the *unities* in the plays of such poets. For
the miracles wrought upon *time* and *place,* and the mixture of tragedy and comedy,
farce and epic, see *Pluto and Proserpine, Penelope,* etc. if yet extant.

73. In the lower Egypt rain is of no use, the overflowing of the Nile being sufficient
to impregnate the soil.—These six verses represent the inconsistencies in the
descriptions of poets, who heap together all glittering and gaudy images, though
incompatible in one season, or in one scene.
　　See the *Guardian,* Nº. 40. parag. 6. See also Eusden's whole works, if to be found.
It would not have been unpleasant to have given examples of all these species of bad
writing from these authors, but that it is already done in our treatise of the *Bathos.*
　　　　　　　　　　　　　　　　　　　　　　　　　　　　　　　　SCRIBL.

79. From Homer's epithet of Jupiter, νεφεληγερέτα Ζεύς.

'Twas on the day, when * * rich and grave,°
Like Cimon, triumphed both on land and wave:
(Pomps without guilt, of bloodless swords and maces,
Glad chains, warm furs, broad banners, and broad faces)
Now night descending, the proud scene was o'er,
But lived, in Settle's numbers, one day more.   90
Now mayors and shrieves° all hushed and satiate lay,
Yet eat, in dreams, the custard of the day;
While pensive poets painful vigils keep,
Sleepless themselves, to give their readers sleep.
Much to the mindful Queen the feast recalls
What city swans once sung within the walls;
Much she revolves their arts, their ancient praise,
And sure succession down from Heywood's days.
She saw, with joy, the line immortal run,
Each sire impressed and glaring in his son: 100
So watchful Bruin° forms, with plastic care,
Each growing lump, and brings it to a bear.

85, 86. Viz. a Lord Mayor's Day; his name the author had left in blanks, but
most certainly could never be that which the editor foisted in formerly, and which
no way agrees with the chronology of the poem. BENTLEY.
    The procession of a Lord Mayor is made partly by land, and partly by water.—
Cimon, the famous Athenian general, obtained a victory by sea, and another by land,
on the same day, over the Persians and Barbarians.

88. Glad chains] The ignorance of these moderns! This was altered in one edition
to Gold chains, showing more regard to the metal of which the chains of alderman
are made, than to the beauty of the Latinism and Graecism, nay of figurative speech
itself: Laetas segetes, glad, for making glad, &c. SCRIBL.

90. A beautiful manner of speaking, usual with poets in praise of poetry, in which
kind nothing is finer than those lines of Mr Addison:

> Sometimes, misguided by the tuneful throng,
> I look for streams immortalized in song,
> That lost in silence and oblivion lie,
> Dumb are their fountains, and their channels dry;
> Yet run for ever by the muses' skill,
> And in the smooth description murmur still.

    Settle was poet of the City of London. His office was to compose yearly panegyrics
upon the Lord Mayors, and verses to be spoken in the pageants: but that part of the
shows being at length frugally abolished, the employment of city-poet ceased; so
that upon Settle's demise there was no successor to that place.

98. John Heywood, whose interludes were printed in the time of Henry VIII.

She saw old Prynne in restless Daniel shine,
And Eusden eke out Blackmore's endless line;

103. The first edition had it,

> *She saw in Norton all his father shine:*

a great mistake! for Daniel Defoe had parts, but Norton Defoe was a wretched writer, and never attempted poetry. Much more justly is Daniel himself made successor to W. Prynne, both of whom wrote verses as well as politics; as appears by the poem *De jure divino, &c.* of Defoe, and by these lines in Cowley's *Miscellanies*, on the other:

> ——*One lately did not fear*
> *(Without the muses leave) to plant verse here,*
> *But it produced such base, rough, crabbed, hedge-*
> *Rhymes, as e'en set the hearers ears on edge:*
> *Written by* William Prynne Esquire, *the*
> *Year of our Lord, six hundred thirty three.*
> *Brave Jersey muse! and he's for his high style*
> *Called to this day the Homer of the isle.*

And both these authors had a resemblance in their fates as well as writings, having been alike sentenced to the pillory.

104. Laurence Eusden, Poet Laureate. Mr Jacob gives a catalogue of some few only of his works, which were very numerous. Mr Cooke, in his *Battle of Poets*, saith of him,

> *Eusden, a laurelled bard, by fortune raised,*
> *By very few was read, by fewer praised.*

Mr Oldmixon, in his *Arts of Logic and Rhetoric*, p. 413, 414 affirms, 'That of all the galimatia's he ever met with, none comes up to some verses of this poet, which have as much of the ridiculum and the fustian in them as can well be jumbled together, and are of that sort of nonsense, which so perfectly confounds all ideas, that there is no distinct one left in the mind.' Farther he says of him, 'That he hath prophesied his own poetry shall be sweeter than Catullus, Ovid, and Tibullus; but we have little hope of the accomplishment of it, from what he hath lately published.' Upon which Mr Oldmixon has not spared a reflection, 'That the putting the laurel on the head of one who writ such verses, will give futurity a very lively idea of the judgment and justice of those who bestowed it.' Ibid. p. 417. But the well-known learning of that noble person, who was then Lord Chamberlain, might have screened him from this unmannerly reflection. Nor ought Mr Oldmixon to complain, so long after, that the laurel would have better become his own brows, or any others. It were more decent to acquiesce in the opinion of the Duke of Buckingham upon this matter:

> —*In rushed Eusden, and cried, 'Who shall have it,*
> *But I, the true Laureate, to whom the King gave it?'*
> *Apollo begged pardon, and granted his claim,*
> *But vowed that till then he ne'er heard of his name.*
> *Session of Poets.*

The same plea might also serve for his successor, Mr Cibber; and is further strengthened in the following epigram, made on that occasion:

> *In merry old England it once was a rule,*
> *The King had his poet, and also his fool:*

She saw slow Philips creep like Tate's poor page,
And all the mighty mad in Dennis rage.

But now we're so frugal, I'd have you to know it,
That Cibber can serve both for fool and for poet.

Of Blackmore, see Book 2. Of Philips, Book 1. ver. 262. and Book 3. *prope fin.*

Nahum Tate was Poet Laureate, a cold writer, of no invention; but sometimes translated tolerably when befriended by Mr Dryden. In his second part of *Absalom and Achitophel* are above two hundred admirable lines together of that great hand, which strongly shine through the insipidity of the rest. Something parallel may be observed of another author here mentioned.

106. This is by no means to be understood literally, as if Mr Dennis were really mad, according to the *Narrative of Dr Norris* in Swift and Pope's *Miscellanies*, vol. 3. No—it is spoken of that *excellent* and *divine madness*, so often mentioned by Plato; that poetical rage and enthusiasm, with which Mr D. hath, in his time, been highly possessed; and of those *extraordinary hints and motions* whereof he himself so feelingly treats in his preface to the *Rem. on Pr. Arth.* [See notes on Book 2. ver. 268.]

Mr Theobald, in the *Censor*, vol. ii. N. 33. calls Mr Dennis by the name of Furius. 'The modern Furius is to be looked upon as more an object of pity, than of that which he daily provokes, laughter and contempt. Did we really know how much this *poor* man (*I wish that reflection on* poverty *had been spared*) suffers by being contradicted, or, which is the same thing in effect, by hearing another praised; we should, in compassion, sometimes attend to him with a silent nod, and let him go away with the triumphs of his ill nature.—*Poor* Furius (*again*) when any of his contemporaries are spoken well of, quitting the ground of the present dispute, steps back a thousand years to call in the succour of the ancients. His very panegyric is spiteful, and he uses it for the same reason as some ladies do their commendations of a dead beauty, who would never have had their good word, but that a living one happened to be mentioned in their company. His applause is not the tribute of his *heart*, but the sacrifice of his *revenge*,' etc. Indeed his pieces against our poet are somewhat of an angry character, and as they are now scarce extant, a taste of his style may be satisfactory to the curious. 'A young, squab, short gentleman, whose outward form, though it should be that of downright monkey, would not differ so much from human shape as his unthinking immaterial part does from human understanding.—He is as stupid and as venomous as a hunch-backed toad.—A book through which folly and ignorance, those brethren so lame and impotent, do ridiculously look very big and very dull, and strut and hobble, cheek by jowl, with their arms on kimbo, being led and supported, and bully-backed by that blind Hector, Impudence.' Reflect. on the *Essay on Criticism*, p. 26, 29, 30.

It would be unjust not to add his reasons for this fury, they are so strong and so coercive: 'I regard him' (saith he) 'as an *enemy*, not so much to me, as to my king, to my country, to my religion, and to that liberty which has been the sole felicity of my life. A vagary of fortune, who is sometimes pleased to be frolicsome, and the epidemic *madness of the times* have given him *reputation*, and reputation (as Hobbes says) is *power*, and *that has made him dangerous*. Therefore I look on it as my duty to King George, whose faithful subject I am; to my *country*, of which I have appeared a constant lover, to the *laws*, under whose protection I have so long lived; and to the *liberty* of my *country*, more dear to me than life, of which I have now for forty years been a constant assertor, *&c.* I look upon it as my duty, I say, to do—*you shall see*

In each she marks her image full expressed,
But chief in BAYS's° monster-breeding breast;
Bays, formed by nature stage and town to bless,
And act, and be, a coxcomb with success.   110

what—to pull the lion's skin from this little ass, which popular error has thrown round him; and to show that this author, who has been lately so much in vogue, has neither sense in his thoughts, nor English in his expressions.' DENNIS, *Rem. on Hom.* Pref. p. 2. 91, *&c.*

Besides these public-spirited reasons, Mr D. had a private one; which, by his manner of expressing it in p. 92 appears to have been equally strong. He was even in bodily fear of his life from the machinations of the said Mr P. 'The story' (says he) 'is too long to be told, but who would be acquainted with it, may hear it from Mr Curll, my bookseller.—However, what my reason has suggested to me, that I have with a just confidence said, in defiance of his two clandestine weapons, his *slander* and his *poison*.' Which last words of his book plainly discover Mr D.'s suspicion was that of being *poisoned*, in like manner as Mr Curll had been before him; of which fact see *A full and true account of a horrid and barbarous revenge, by poison, on the body of Edmund Curll*, printed in 1716, the year antecedent to that wherein these remarks of Mr Dennis were published. But what puts it beyond all question, is a passage in a very warm treatise, in which Mr D. was also concerned, price two pence, called *A true character of Mr Pope and his writings*, printed for S. Popping, 1716; in the tenth page whereof he is said 'to have insulted people on those calamities and diseases which he himself gave them, by administering *poison* to them;' and is called (p. 4) 'a lurking way-laying coward, and a stabber in the dark.' Which (with many other things most lively set forth in that piece) must have rendered him a terror, not to Mr Dennis only, but to all Christian people.

For the rest; Mr John Dennis was the son of a saddler in London, born in 1657. He paid court to Mr Dryden: and having obtained some correspondence with Mr Wycherley and Mr Congreve, he immediately obliged the public with their letters. He made himself known to the government by many admirable schemes and projects; which the ministry, for reasons best known to themselves, constantly kept private. For his character, as a writer, it is given us as follows: 'Mr Dennis is *excellent* at Pindaric writings, *perfectly regular* in all his performances, and a person of *sound learning*. That he is master of a great deal of *penetration* and *judgment*, his criticisms, (particularly on *Prince Arthur*) do sufficiently demonstrate.' From the same account it also appears that he writ plays 'more to get *reputation* than *money*.' DENNIS of himself. See Giles Jacob's *Lives of Dram. Poets*, p. 68, 69. compared with p. 286.

109. It is hoped the poet here hath done full justice to his hero's character, which it were a great mistake to imagine was wholly sunk in stupidity; he is allowed to have supported it with a wonderful mixture of vivacity. This character is heightened according to his own desire, in a letter he wrote to our author. 'Pert and dull at least you might have allowed me. What! am I only to be dull, and dull still, and again, and for ever?' He then solemnly appealed to his own conscience, that 'he could not think himself so, nor believe that our poet did; but that he spoke worse of him than he could possibly think; and concluded it must be merely to show his *wit*, or for some *profit* or *lucre* to himself.' *Life of C.C.* chap. vii, and *Letter to Mr P.* pag. 15, 40, 53.

Dulness with transport eyes the lively dunce,
Remembring she herself was pertness once.
Now (shame to fortune!) an ill run at play
Blanked his bold visage, and a thin third day:
Swearing and supperless the hero sate,
Blasphemed his gods, the dice, and damned his fate.
Then gnawed his pen, then dashed it on the ground,
Sinking from thought to thought, a vast profound!
Plunged for his sense, but found no bottom there,
Yet wrote and floundered on, in mere despair.   120
Round him much embryo, much abortion lay,
Much future ode, and abdicated play;
Nonsense precipitate, like running lead,
That slipped through cracks and zigzags of the head;
All that on folly frenzy could beget,
Fruits of dull heat, and sooterkins° of wit.
Next, o'er his books his eyes began to roll,
In pleasing memory of all he stole,
How here he sipped, how there he plundered snug
And sucked all o'er, like an industrious bug.   130
Here lay poor Fletcher's half-eat scenes, and here

113. *shame to fortune*] Because she usually shows favour to persons of this charac-
ter, who have a three-fold pretence to it.

115. It is amazing how the sense of this hath been mistaken by all the former
commentators, who most idly suppose it to imply that the hero of the poem wanted
a supper. In truth a great absurdity! Not that we are ignorant that the hero of
Homer's *Odyssey* is frequently in that circumstance, and therefore it can no way
derogate from the grandeur of epic poem to represent such hero under a calamity,
to which the greatest, not only of critics and poets, but of kings and warriors, have
been subject. But much more refined, I will venture to say, is the meaning of our
author: it was to give us, obliquely, a curious precept, or, what Bossu calls, a *disguised
sentence*, that 'Temperance is the life of study.' The language of poesy brings all into
action; and to represent a critic encompassed with books, but without a supper, is a
picture which lively expresseth how much the true critic prefers the diet of the mind
to that of the body, one of which he always castigates, and often totally neglects for
the greater improvement of the other.   SCRIBL.

But since the discovery of the true hero of the poem, may we not add that nothing
was so natural, after so great a loss of money at dice, or of reputation by his play,
as that the poet should have no great stomach to eat a supper? Besides, how well
has the poet consulted his heroic character, in adding that he *swore* all the time?

BENTLEY.

131. *poor Fletcher's half-eat scenes*] A great number of them taken out to patch up
his plays.

The frippery of crucified Molière;
There hapless Shakespeare, yet of Tibbald sore,
Wished he had blotted for himself before.
The rest on outside merit but presume,
Or serve (like other fools) to fill a room;
Such with their shelves as due proportion hold,
Or their fond parents dressed in red and gold;
Or where the pictures for the page atone,
And Quarles is saved by beauties not his own.   140
Here swells the shelf with Ogilby the great;
There, stamped with arms, Newcastle shines complete:
Here all his suffering brotherhood retire,
And 'scape the martyrdom of jakes° and fire:

132. *The frippery*] 'When I fitted up an old play, it was as a good housewife will mend old linen, when she has not better employment.' *Life*, p. 217. octavo.

133. It is not to be doubted but Bays was a subscriber to Tibbald's *Shakespeare*. He was frequently liberal this way; and, as he tells us, 'subscribed to Mr Pope's *Homer*, out of pure generosity and civility; but when Mr Pope did so to his *Nonjuror*, he concluded it could be nothing but a joke.' *Letter to Mr P.*, p. 24.

This Tibbald, or Theobald, published an edition of Shakespeare, of which he was so proud himself as to say, in one of Mist's *Journals*, June 8, 'That to expose any errors in it was impracticable.' And in another, April 27, 'That whatever care might for the future be taken by any other editor, he would still give above five hundred emendations, that *shall* escape them all.'

134. It was a ridiculous praise which the players gave to Shakespeare, 'that he never blotted a line.' Ben Jonson honestly wished he had blotted a thousand; and Shakespeare would certainly have wished the same, if he had lived to see those alterations in his works, which, not the actors only (and especially the daring hero of this poem) have made on the *stage*, but the presumptuous critics of our days in their *editions*.

135. This library is divided into three parts; the first consists of those authors from whom he stole, and whose works he mangled; the second, of such as fitted the shelves, or were gilded for show, or adorned with pictures; the third class our author calls solid learning, old bodies of divinity, old commentaries, old English printers, or old English translations; all very voluminous, and fit to erect altars to Dulness.

141. 'John Ogilby was one, who, from a late initiation into literature, made such a progress as might well style him the prodigy of his time! sending into the world so many *large volumes!* His translations of Homer and Virgil *done to the life*, and *with such excellent sculptures!* And (what added great grace to his works) he printed them all on *special good paper*, and in a *very good letter*.' WINSTANLEY, *Lives of Poets*.

142. 'The Duchess of Newcastle was one who busied herself in the ravishing delights of poetry; leaving to posterity in print three *ample volumes* of her studious endeavours.' WINSTANLEY, ibid. Langbaine reckons up *eight* folios of her Grace's; which were usually adorned with gilded covers, and had her coat of arms upon them.

A Gothic° library! of Greece and Rome°
Well purged, and worthy Settle, Banks, and Broome.
  But, high above, more solid learning shone,
The classics of an age that heard of none;
There Caxton slept, with Wynkyn at his side,
One clasped in wood, and one in strong cow-hide;   150
There, saved by spice, like mummies, many a year,
Dry bodies of divinity appear:
De Lyra there a dreadful front extends,

146. The poet has mentioned these three authors in particular, as they are parallel to our hero in his three capacities: 1. Settle was his brother Laureate; only indeed upon half-pay, for the City instead of the Court; but equally famous for unintelligible flights in his poems on public occasions, such as shows, birthdays, &c. 2. Banks was his rival in *tragedy* though more successful in one of his tragedies, the *Earl of Essex*, which is yet alive: *Anna Boleyn, The Queen of Scots*, and *Cyrus the Great*, are dead and gone. These he dressed in a sort of *beggar's velvet*, or a happy mixture of the *thick fustian* and *thin prosaic*; exactly imitated in *Perella and Isidora, Caesar in Egypt*, and *The Heroic Daughter*. 3. Broome was a serving-man of Ben Jonson, who once picked up a *comedy* from his betters, or from some cast scenes of his master, not entirely contemptible.

147. Some have objected, that books of this sort suit not so well the library of our Bays, which they imagine consisted of novels, plays, and obscene books; but they are to consider, that he furnished his shelves only for ornament, and read these books no more than the *dry bodies of Divinity*, which, no doubt, were purchased by his father when he designed him for the gown. See the note on v. 200.

149. *Caxton*] A printer in the time of Ed. IV. Rich. III. and Hen. VII. Wynkyn de Worde, his successor, in that of Hen. VII. and VIII. The former translated into prose Virgil's *Aeneis*, as a history; of which he speaks, in his proem, in a very singular manner, as of a book hardly known. 'Happened that to my hande cam a lytyl book in frenche, whiche late was translated out of latyn by some noble clerke of fraunce, whiche booke is named *Eneydos* (made in latyn by that noble poete & grete clerk Vyrgyle) whiche booke I sawe over and redde therein, How after the general destruc-cyon of the grete Troy, Eneas departed berynge his olde fader anchises upon his sholdres, his lytyl son yolas on his hande, his wyfe with moche other people fol-lowynge, and how he shipped and departed; wyth alle thystorye of his adventures that he had er he came to the atchievement of his conquest of ytalye, as all alonge shall be shewed in this present booke. In whiche booke I had grete playsyr, by cause of the fayr and honest termes & wordes in frenche, whiche I never saw to fore lyke, ne none so playsaunt ne so well ordred; whiche booke as me semed sholde be moche requysite to noble men to see, as wel for the eloquence as the hystoryes. How wel that many hondred yerys passed was the sayd booke of Eneydos wyth other workes made and lerned dayly in scolis, especyally in ytayle and other places, which historye the sayd Vyrgyle made in metre.'

153. *Nich. de Lyra*, or Harpsfield, a very voluminous commentator, whose works, in five vast folios, were printed in 1472.

And here the groaning shelves Philemon bends.

Of these twelve volumes, twelve of amplest size,
Redeemed from tapers and defrauded pies,
Inspired he seizes: these an altar raise:
An hecatomb of pure, unsullied lays
That altar crowns: a folio commonplace
Founds the whole pile, of all his works the base: 160
Quartos, octavos, shape the lessening pyre;
A twisted birthday ode completes the spire.

Then he: 'Great tamer of all human art!
First in my care, and ever at my heart;
Dulness! whose good old cause I yet defend,
With whom my muse began, with whom shall end;
E'er since Sir Fopling's periwig was praise,
To the last honours of the butt and bays:°
O thou! of business the directing soul!
To this our head like bias to the bowl,   170
Which, as more ponderous, made its aim more true,
Obliquely waddling to the mark in view:
O! ever gracious to perplexed mankind,
Still spread a healing mist before the mind;

---

154. *Philemon Holland*, Doctor in Physic. 'He translated *so many books*, that a man would think he had done *nothing else*; insomuch that he might be called *translator general of his age*. The books alone of his turning into English are sufficient to make a *country gentleman* a *complete library*.' WINSTANLEY.

166. *A te principium, tibi desinet.*——   Virgil, *Ecl.* viii.
   'Εκ Διὸς ἀρχώμεσθα, καὶ εἰς Δία λήγετε, Μοῦσαι.   Theocritus.
   Prima dicte mihi, summa dicende Camoena.   Horace.

167. The first visible cause of the passion of the town for our hero, was a fair flaxen full-bottomed periwig, which, he tells us, he wore in his first play of the *Fool in Fashion*. It attracted, in a particular manner, the friendship of Col. Brett, who wanted to purchase it. 'Whatever contempt', says he, 'Philosophers may have for a fine periwig, my friend, who was not to despise the world but to live in it, knew very well that so material an article of dress upon the head of a man of sense, if it became him, could never fail of drawing to him a more partial regard and benevolence, than could possibly be hoped for in an ill-made one. This perhaps, may soften the grave censure which so youthful a purchase might otherwise have laid upon him. In a word, he made his attack upon this periwig, as your young fellows generally do upon a lady of pleasure, first by a few familiar praises of her person, and then a civil enquiry into the price of it; and we finished our bargain that night over a bottle.' See *Life*, octavo p. 303. This remarkable periwig usually made its entrance upon the stage in a sedan, brought in by two chair-men, with infinite approbation of the audience.

And lest we err by wit's wild dancing light,
Secure us kindly in our native night.
Or, if to wit a coxcomb make pretence,
Guard the sure barrier between that and sense;
Or quite unravel all the reasoning thread,
And hang some curious cobweb in its stead!   180
As, forced from wind-guns, lead itself can fly,
And ponderous slugs cut swiftly through the sky;
As clocks to weight their nimble motion owe,
The wheels above urged by the load below:
Me emptiness, and dulness could inspire,
And were my elasticity, and fire.
Some daemon stole my pen (forgive th'offence)
And once betrayed me into common sense:
Else all my prose and verse were much the same;
This, prose on stilts, that, poetry fallen lame.   190
Did on the stage my fops appear confined?
My life gave ampler lessons to mankind.
Did the dead letter unsuccessful prove?
The brisk example never failed to move.
Yet sure had heaven decreed to save the state,
Heaven had decreed these works a longer date.
Could Troy be saved by any single hand,
This grey-goose weapon must have made her stand.
What can I now? my Fletcher cast aside,

178, 179. *For wit* or *reasoning* are never greatly hurtful to Dulness, but when the first is founded in *truth*, and the other in *usefulness*.

195. *Me si coelicolae voluissent ducere vitam,*
     Has mihi servassent sedes.——
                              Virgil, *Aen*. ii.

197, 198.   ——*Si Pergama dextra*
     Defendi possent, etiam hac defensa fuissent.
                              Virgil, ibid.

199. *my Fletcher*] A familiar manner of speaking, used by modern critics, of a favourite author. Bays might as justly speak thus of Fletcher, as a French wit did of Tully, seeing his works in a library, 'Ah! mon cher Ciceron! je le connois bien; c'est le même que Marc Tulle.' But he had a better title to call Fletcher *his own*, having made so free with him.

Take up the Bible, once my better guide?   200
Or tread the path by venturous heroes trod,
This box° my thunder, this right hand my god?
Or chaired at White's° amidst the doctors sit,
Teach oaths to gamesters, and to nobles wit?
Or bidst thou rather party to embrace?
(A friend to party thou, and all her race;
'Tis the same rope at different ends they twist;
To Dulness Ridpath is as dear as Mist.)
Shall I, like Curtius,° desperate in my zeal,
O'er head and ears plunge for the commonweal?   210
Or rob Rome's ancient geese° of all their glories,

200. When, according to his father's intention, he had been a *clergyman*, or (as he thinks himself) a *bishop* of the Church of England. Hear his own words: 'At the time that the fate of King James, the Prince of Orange and Myself, were on the anvil, Providence thought fit to postpone mine, till theirs were determined. But had my father carried me a month sooner to the university, who knows but that purer fountain might have washed my imperfections into a capacity of writing, instead of plays and annual *odes*, sermons and *pastoral letters?*' *Apology for his Life*, chap. iii.

202.   *Dextra mihi* Deus, *& telum* quod missile libro.
Virgil of the gods of Mezentius.

203. 'These doctors had a modest and fair appearance, and, like true Masters of Arts, were habited in *black* and *white*; they were justly styled *subtiles* and *graves*, but not always *irrefragabiles*, being sometimes examined, laid open, and split.'   SCRIBL.

This learned critic is to be understood allegorically. The *doctors* in this place mean no more than *false dice*, a cant phrase used amongst gamesters, so the meaning of these four sonorous lines is only this, 'Shall I play fair, or foul?'

208. *Ridpath—Mist*] George Ridpath, author of a Whig paper, called the *Flying Post*; Nathanael Mist, of a famous Tory *Journal*.

211. Relates to the well-known story of the geese that saved the Capitol; of which Virgil, *Aen.* viii.

    Atque hic auratis volitans argenteus anser
    Porticibus. Gallos in limine adesse canebat.

A passage I have always suspected. Who sees not the antithesis of *auratis* and *argenteus* to be unworthy the Virgilian majesty? And what absurdity to say a goose *sings? canebat*. Virgil gives a contrary character of the voice of this silly bird, in *Ecl.* ix.

    ——*argutos* interstrepere *anser olores*.

Read it, therefore, *adesse strepebat*. And why *auratis porticibus*? does not the very verse preceding this inform us,

    Romuleoque recens horrebat regia culmo.

Is this *thatch* in one line, and *gold* in another, consistent? I scruple not (*repugnantibus omnibus manuscriptis*) to correct it *auritis*. Horace uses the same epithet in the same sense,

And cackling save the monarchy of Tories?
Hold—to the minister I more incline;
To serve his cause, O Queen! is serving thine.
And see! thy very gazetteers give o'er,
Ev'n Ralph repents, and Henley writes no more.
What then remains? Ourself. Still, still remain
Cibberian forehead, and Cibberian brain.
This brazen brightness, to the 'squire so dear;
This polished hardness, that reflects the peer;   220
This arch absurd, that wit and fool delights;
This mess, tossed up of Hockley Hole° and White's;
Where dukes and butchers join to wreathe my crown,
At once the bear and fiddle° of the town.
　　O born in sin, and forth in folly brought!
Works damned, or to be damned! (your father's fault)
Go, purified by flames ascend the sky,
My better and more Christian progeny!

　　　　　——Auritas *fidibus canoris*
　　　　　Ducere quercus.
And to say that *walls have ears* is common even to a proverb. SCRIBL.

212. Not out of any preference or affection to the Tories. For what Hobbes so ingenuously confesses of himself, is true of all party-writers whatsoever: 'That he defends the supreme powers, as the *geese* by their *cackling* defended the Romans, who held the Capitol; for they favoured them no more than the Gauls their enemies, but were as ready to have defended the Gauls if they had been *possessed of the Capitol.*' Epist. Dedic. to the *Leviathan.*

215. *Gazetteers*] A band of ministerial writers, hired at the price mentioned in the note on book ii. ver. 316. who on the very day their patron quitted his post, laid down their paper, and declared they would never more meddle in politics.

218. *Cibberian forehead*] So indeed all the MSS. read; but I make no scruple to pronounce them all wrong, the Laureate being elsewhere celebrated by our poet for his great *modesty—modest Cibber*—Read, therefore, at my peril, *Cerberian forehead.* This is perfectly classical, and, what is more, *Homerical*; the *dog* was the ancient, as the *bitch* is the modern, symbol of impudence: (Κυνὸς ὄμματ' ἔχων, says Achilles to Agamemnon) which, when in a superlative degree, may well be denominated from *Cerberus*, the *dog with three heads.*—But as to the latter part of this verse, *Cibberian brain*, that is certainly the genuine reading. BENTLEY.

225. This is a tender and passionate apostrophe to his own works, which he is going to sacrifice, agreeable to the nature of man in great affliction; and reflecting like a parent on the many miserable fates to which they would otherwise be subject.

228. 'It may be observable, that my muse and my spouse were equally prolific; that the one was seldom the mother of a child, but in the same year the other made me the father of a play. I think we had a dozen of each sort between us; of both which kinds some *died* in their *infancy*,' etc. *Life of C.C.*, p. 217. 8vo edit.

Unstained, untouched, and yet in maiden sheets;
While all your smutty sisters walk the streets.   230
Ye shall not beg, like gratis-given Bland,
Sent with a pass, and vagrant through the land;
Not sail, with Ward, to ape-and-monkey climes,
Where vile mundungus° trucks for viler rhymes;
Not sulphur-tipped, emblaze an alehouse fire;
Not wrap up oranges, to pelt your sire!
O! pass more innocent, in infant state,
To the mild limbo of our father Tate:
Or peaceably forgot, at once be blessed
In Shadwell's bosom with eternal rest!   240
Soon to that mass of nonsense to return,
Where things destroyed are swept to things unborn.'
    With that, a tear (portentous sign of grace!)
Stole from the master of the sevenfold face:
And thrice he lifted high the birthday brand,

229.   ——*Felix Priameïa virgo!*
Jussa mori: quae sortitus non pertulit ullos,
Nec victoris heri tetigit captiva cubile!
Nos, patria incensa, diversa per aequora vectae, &c.
                      Virgil, *Aen.* iii.

231, 232. It was a practice so to give the *Daily Gazetteer* and ministerial pamphlets (in which this B. was a writer) and to send them *post-free* to all the towns in the kingdom.

233. 'Edward Ward, a very voluminous poet in Hudibrastic verse, but best known by the *London Spy*, in prose. He has of late years kept a public house in the City, (but in a genteel way) and with his wit, humour, and good liquor (ale) afforded his guests a pleasurable entertainment, especially those of the high-church party,' JACOB, *Lives of Poets*, vol. ii. p. 225. Great numbers of his works were yearly sold into the plantations.—Ward, in a book called *Apollo's Maggot*, declared this account to be a great falsity, protesting that his public house was not in the *City*, but in *Moorfields*.

238 & 240. *Tate—Shadwell*] Two of his predecessors in the laurel.

241. Ovid of Althaea on a like occasion, burning her offspring (*Met.* viii.):
        Tum conata quater flammis imponere torrem,
        Coepta quater tenuit.

243. It is to be observed that our poet hath made his hero, in imitation of Virgil's, obnoxious to the tender passions. He was indeed so given to weeping, that he tells us, when Goodman the player swore, if he did not *make a good actor, he'd be damned*; 'the surprise of being commended by one who had been himself so eminent on the stage, and in so *positive a manner*, was more than he could support. In a word' (says he) 'it almost took away my breath and (laugh if you please) fairly drew tears from my eyes.' P. 149. of his *Life*, octavo.

And thrice he dropped it from his quivering hand;
Then lights the structure, with averted eyes:
The rolling smokes involve the sacrifice.
The opening clouds disclose each work by turns,
Now flames the *Cid*, and now *Perolla* burns;   250
Great *Caesar* roars, and hisses in the fires;
King John in silence modestly expires:
No merit now the dear *Nonjuror* claims,°
Molière's old stubble in a moment flames.
Tears gushed again, as from pale Priam's eyes
When the last blaze sent Ilion° to the skies.

250.   ——*Jam Deïphobi dedit ampla ruinam*
              Vulcano superante domus; jam proximus ardet
              Ucalegon.——

                                        Virgil, *Aen.* ii.

In the first notes on the *Dunciad* it was said, that this author was particularly
excellent at tragedy. 'This' (says he) 'is as unjust as to say I could not dance on a
rope.' But certain it is that he had attempted to dance on this rope, and fell most
shamefully, having produced no less than four tragedies (the names of which the
poet preserves in these few lines) the three first of them were fairly printed, acted,
and damned; the fourth suppressed, in fear of the like treatment.

253–4. *the dear Nonjuror—Molière's old stubble*] A comedy threshed out of Mol-
ière's *Tartuffe*, and so much the translator's favourite, that he assures us all our
author's dislike to it could only arise from *disaffection to the government*;

              Qui meprise Cotin, n'estime point son Roi,
              Et n'a, selon Cotin, ni Dieu, ni foi, ni loi.
                                        Boileau.

He assures us, that 'when he had the honour to kiss his Majesty's hand upon
presenting his dedication of it, he was graciously pleased, out of his royal bounty, to
order him two hundred pounds for it. And this he doubts not *grieved* Mr P.'

256. See Virgil, *Aen.* ii. where I would advise the reader to peruse the story of
Troy's destruction, rather than in Wynkyn. But I caution him alike in both to beware
of a most grievous error, that of thinking it was brought about by I know not what
Trojan horse; there never having been any such thing. For, first, it was not *Trojan*,
being made by the *Greeks*; and, secondly, it was not a *horse*, but a *mare*. This is clear
from many verses in Virgil:

              ——*Uterumque armato milite complent.*——
              Inclusos utero *Danaos*——

Can a horse be said *Utero gerere*? Again,

              ——*Uteroque recusso,*
              Insonuere cavae——
              ——*Atque utero sonitum quater arma dedere.*

Nay, is it not expressly said

              Scandit fatalis machina muros
              Foeta armis——

Roused by the light, old Dulness heaved the head;
Then snatched a sheet of Thulè from her bed,
Sudden she flies, and whelms it o'er the pyre;
Down sink the flames, and with a hiss expire.   260
Her ample presence fills up all the place;
A veil of fogs dilates her awful face:
Great in her charms! as when on shrieves and mayors
She looks, and breathes herself into their airs.
She bids him wait her to her sacred dome:
Well pleased he entered, and confessed his home.
So spirits ending their terrestrial race,
Ascend, and recognize their native place.
This the Great Mother dearer held than all
The clubs of quidnuncs, or her own Guildhall: 270
Here stood her opium, here she nursed her owls,
And here she planned th' imperial seat of Fools.
Here to her chosen all her works she shows;
Prose swelled to verse, verse loitering into prose:

How is it possible the word *foeta* can agree with a *horse*? And indeed can it be conceived that the chaste and virgin goddess *Pallas* would employ herself in forming and fashioning the male of that species? But this shall be proved to a demonstration in our *Virgil Restored*. SCRIBL.

258. *Thulè*] An unfinished poem of that name, of which one sheet was printed many years ago, by Amb. Philips, a northern author. It is an usual method of putting out a fire, to cast wet sheets upon it. Some critics have been of opinion that this sheet was of the nature of the asbestos, which cannot be consumed by fire: but I rather think it an allegorical allusion to the coldness and heaviness of the writing.

263, 264. *Alma parens confessa Deam; qualisque videri
Coelicolis, & quanta solet——*
                                Virgil, *Aen.* ii.

Et laetos oculis afflarat honores.
                                Id. *Aen.* i.

265. *sacred dome:*] Where he no sooner enters, but he reconnoitres the place of his original; as Plato says the spirits shall, at their entrance into the celestial regions.

269 &c. *Urbs antiqua fuit——
Quam Juno fertur terris magis omnibus unam
Posthabita coluisse Samo: hic illius arma,
Hic currus fuit: hic regnum Dea gentibus esse
(Si qua fata sinant) jam tum tenditque fovetque.*
                                Virgil, *Aen.* i.

Great Mother] *Magna mater*, here applied to *Dulness*. The *quidnuncs*, a name given to the ancient members of certain political clubs, who were constantly enquiring *quid nunc?* what news?

How random thoughts now meaning chance to find,
Now leave all memory of sense behind:
How prologues into prefaces decay,
And these to notes are frittered quite away:
How index-learning turns no student pale,
Yet holds the eel of science by the tail: 280
How, with less reading than makes felons 'scape,°
Less human genius than God gives an ape,
Small thanks to France, and none to Rome or Greece,
A past, vamped, future, old, revived, new piece,
'Twixt Plautus, Fletcher, Shakespeare, and Corneille,
Can make a Cibber, Tibbald, or Ozell.
    The Goddess then, o'er his anointed head,

286. *Tibbald*] Lewis Tibbald (as pronounced) or Theobald (as written) was bred an attorney, and son to an attorney (says Mr Jacob) of Sittingbourne in Kent. He was author of some forgotten plays, translations, and other pieces. He was concerned in a paper called the *Censor*, and a translation of Ovid. 'There is a notorious idiot, one hight Whachum, who, from an underspurleather to the law, is become an under-strapper to the playhouse, who hath lately burlesqued the *Metamorphoses* of Ovid by a vile translation, etc. This fellow is concerned in an impertinent paper called the *Censor*.' DENNIS, *Rem. on Pope's Hom.* p. 9, 10.

Ibid. *Ozell*] 'Mr John Ozell (if we credit Mr Jacob) did go to school in Leicestershire, where *somebody* left him *something* to live on, when he shall retire from business. He was designed to be sent to Cambridge, in order for priesthood; but he chose rather to be placed in an *office* of *accounts*, in the City, being qualified for the same by his skill in *arithmetic*, and writing the necessary *hands*. He has obliged the world with many translations of French plays.' JACOB, *Lives of Dram. Poets*, p. 198.

Mr Jacob's character of Mr Ozell seems vastly short of his merits, and he ought to have further justice done him, having since fully confuted all sarcasms on his learning and genius, by an advertisement of Sept. 20, 1729. in a paper called the *Weekly Medley*, etc. 'As to my *learning*, everybody knows that the *whole bench of bishops*, not long ago, were pleased to give me a *purse of guineas*, for discovering the erroneous translations of the Common Prayer in Portuguese, Spanish, French, Italian, etc. As for my *genius*, let Mr Cleland show better verses in all Pope's works, than Ozell's version of Boileau's *Lutrin*, which the late Lord Halifax was so pleased with, that he complimented him with leave to dedicate it to him, etc. etc. Let him show better and truer poetry in the *Rape of the Lock*, than in Ozell's *Rape of the Bucket* (*la Secchia rapita*.) And Mr Toland and Mr Gildon publicly declared Ozell's translation of Homer *to be*, as it was *prior*, so likewise *superior* to Pope's.—Surely, surely, every man is free to deserve well of his country!' JOHN OZELL.

We cannot but subscribe to such reverend testimonies, as those of the *bench of bishops*, Mr *Toland*, and Mr *Gildon*.

With mystic words, the sacred opium shed.
And lo! her bird, (a monster of a fowl,
Something betwixt a Heidegger and owl,)   290
Perched on his crown:° 'All hail! and hail again,
My son! the promised land expects thy reign.
Know, Eusden thirsts no more for sack or praise;
He sleeps among the dull of ancient days;
Safe, where no critics damn, no duns molest,
Where wretched Withers, Ward, and Gildon rest,
And high-born Howard, more majestic sire,
With fool of quality° completes the quire.
Thou Cibber! thou, his laurel shalt support,
Folly, my son, has still a friend at court.   300
Lift up your gates, ye princes, see him come!
Sound, sound ye viols, be the catcall dumb!
Bring, bring the madding bay, the drunken vine;
The creeping, dirty, courtly ivy join.
And thou! his aide de camp, lead on my sons,
Light-armed with points,° antitheses, and puns.
Let bawdry, Billingsgate,° my daughters dear,
Support his front, and oaths bring up the rear:

290. *A Heidegger*] A strange bird from Switzerland, and not (as some have supposed) the name of an eminent person who was a man of parts, and, as was said of Petronius, *Arbiter elegantiarum*.

296. *Withers*] 'George Withers was a great pretender to poetical zeal, and abused the greatest personages in power, which brought upon him frequent correction. The Marshalsea and Newgate were no strangers to him.' WINSTANLEY, *Lives of Poets*.

Ibid. *Gildon*] Charles Gildon, a writer of criticisms and libels of the last age, bred at St Omer's with the Jesuits; but renouncing popery, he published Blount's books against the divinity of Christ, the *Oracles of Reason*, etc. He signalized himself as a critic, having written some very bad plays; abused Mr P. very scandalously in an anonymous pamphlet of the *Life of Mr Wycherley*, printed by Curll; in another, called the *New Rehearsal*, printed in 1714; in a third, entituled the *Complete Art of English Poetry*, in two volumes; and others.

297. *Howard*] Hon. Edward Howard, author of the *British Princes*, and a great number of wonderful pieces, celebrated by the late Earls of Dorset and Rochester, Duke of Buckingham, Mr Waller, etc.

And under his, and under Archer's wing,
Gaming and Grub Street skulk behind the king.   310
   O! when shall rise a monarch all our own,
And I, a nursing-mother,° rock the throne,
'Twixt prince and people close the curtain draw,
Shade him from light, and cover him from law;
Fatten the courtier, starve the learned band,
And suckle armies, and dry-nurse the land,
Till senates nod to lullabies divine,
And all be sleep, as at an ode of thine.'

   She ceased. Then swells the Chapel Royal throat:
'God save King Cibber!' mounts in every note.   320
Familiar White's, 'God save King Colley!' cries;
'God save King Colley!' Drury Lane replies:
To Needham's quick the voice triumphal rode,
But pious Needham dropped the name of God;

   309, 310. When the statute against gaming was drawn up, it was represented, that the king, by ancient custom, plays at hazard one night in the year; and therefore a clause was inserted, with an exception as to that particular. Under this pretence, the Groom Porter had a room appropriated to gaming all the summer the court was at Kensington, which his Majesty accidentally being acquainted of, with a just indignation prohibited. It is reported, the same practice is yet continued wherever the court resides, and the hazard table there open to all the professed gamesters in town.

> Greatest *and* justest SOVEREIGN! *know you this?*
> *Alas! no more, than* Thames' *calm* head *can know*
> *Whose meads his* arms *drown, or whose corn o'erflow.*
>   Donne to Queen Eliz.

311. Boileau, *Lutrin*, Chant. 2.

> *Helas! qu'est devenu cet tems, cet heureux tems,*
> *Ou les Rois s'honoroient du nom du Faineans:*
> *S'endormoient sur le trone, & me servant sans honte,*
> *Laissoient leur sceptre au mains ou d'un mair, ou d'un comte:*
> *Aucun soin n'approchoit de leur paisible cour,*
> *On reposoit la nuit, on dormoit tout le jour, &c.*

319. The voices and instruments used in the service of the Chapel Royal being also employed in the performance of the birthday and New Year odes.

324. *But pious Needham*] A matron of great fame, and very religious in her way; whose constant prayer it was, that she might 'get enough by her profession to leave it off in time, and make her peace with God.' But her fate was not so happy; for being convicted, and set in the pillory, she was (to the lasting shame of all her great friends and votaries) so ill used by the populace, that it put an end to her days.

Back to the Devil the last echoes roll,
And 'Coll!' each butcher roars at Hockley Hole.
    So when Jove's block descended from on high
(As sings thy great forefather Ogilby)
Loud thunder to its bottom shook the bog,
And the hoarse nation croaked, 'God save King Log!'°   330

The End of the FIRST BOOK.

325. *Back to the Devil*] The Devil Tavern in Fleet Street, where these odes are usually rehearsed before they are performed at court.

328–330. See Ogilby's *Aesop's Fables*, where, in the story of the frogs and their king this excellent hemistich is to be found.

Our author manifests here, and elsewhere, a prodigious tenderness for the *bad writers*. We see he selects the only good passage, perhaps, in all that ever Ogilby writ; which shows how candid and patient a reader he must have been. What can be more kind and affectionate than these words in the preface to his *Poems*, where he labours to call up all our humanity and forgiveness toward these unlucky men, by the most moderate representation of their case that has ever been given by any author? 'Much may be said to extenuate the fault of bad poets: what we call a *genius* is hard to be distinguished, by a man himself, from a prevalent inclination. And if it be never so great, he can at first discover it no other way than by that strong propensity which renders him the more liable to be mistaken. He has no other method but to make the experiment, by writing, and so appealing to the judgment of others: and if he happens to write ill (which is certainly no sin in itself) he is immediately made the object of ridicule! I wish we had the humanity to reflect, that even the worst authors might endeavour to please us, and, in that endeavour, deserve something at our hands. We have no cause to quarrel with them, but for their obstinacy in persisting, and even that may admit of alleviating circumstances. For their particular friends may be either ignorant, or unsincere; and the rest of the world too well bred to shock them with a truth which generally their booksellers are the first that inform them of.'

But how much all indulgence is lost upon these people may appear from the just reflection made on their constant conduct, and constant fate, in the following epigram:

> *Ye little wits, that gleamed awhile,*
>   *When Pope vouchsafed a ray,*
> *Alas! deprived of his kind smile,*
>   *How soon ye fade away!*
>
> *To compass Phoebus' car about,*
>   *Thus empty vapours rise;*
> *Each lends his cloud, to put him out,*
>   *That reared him to the skies.*
>
> *Alas! those skies are not your sphere;*
>   *There he shall ever burn:*
> *Weep, weep, and fall! for earth ye were,*
>   *And must to earth return.*

THE
DUNCIAD
BOOK the SECOND

ARGUMENT

The King being proclaimed, the solemnity is graced with public games and sports of various kinds; not instituted by the hero, as by Aeneas° in Virgil, but for greater honour by the Goddess in person (in like manner as the games Pythia, Isthmia, etc. were anciently said to be ordained by the gods, and as Thetis herself appearing, according to Homer, Odyss. 24. *proposed the prizes in honour of her son Achilles.) Hither flock the poets and critics, attended, as is but just, with their patrons and booksellers. The Goddess is first pleased, for her disport, to propose games to the booksellers; and setteth up the phantom of a poet, which they contend to overtake. The races described, with their divers accidents. Next, the game for a* poetess. *Then follow the exercises for the* poets, *of* tickling, vociferating, diving: *The first holds forth the arts and practices of* dedicators, *the second of* disputants *and* fustian° *poets, the third of* profound, dark, *and* dirty party-writers. *Lastly, for the* critics, *the Goddess proposes (with great propriety) an exercise, not of their parts, but their patience, in hearing the works of two voluminous authors, one in* verse,

Two things there are, upon the supposition of which the very basis of all verbal criticism is founded and supported: the first, that an author could never fail to use the *best word* on every occasion; the second, that a critic cannot choose but know *which that is.* This being granted, whenever any word doth not fully content us, we take upon us to conclude, first, that the author could *never have used it;* and, secondly, that he must have used *that very one* which we conjecture in its stead.

We cannot, therefore, enough admire the learned Scriblerus for his alteration of the text in the two last verses of the preceding book, which in all the former editions stood thus:

> *Hoarse thunder to its bottom shook the bog,*
> *And the loud nation croaked, 'God save King Log.'*

He has, with great judgment, transposed these two epithets; putting *hoarse* to the nation, and *loud* to the thunder. And this being evidently the true reading, he vouchsafed not so much as to mention the former; for which assertion of the just right of a critic, he merits the acknowledgment of all sound commentators.

and the other in prose, *deliberately read, without sleeping. The various effects of which, with the several degrees and manners of their operation, are here set forth; till the whole number, not of critics only, but of spectators, actors, and all present, fall fast asleep; which naturally and necessarily ends the games.*

> High on a gorgeous seat, that far outshone   1
> Henley's gilt tub, or Flecknoe's Irish throne,
> Or that where on her Curlls the public pours,
> All-bounteous, fragrant grains and golden showers,°
> Great Cibber sate: the proud Parnassian sneer,
> The conscious simper, and the jealous leer,
> Mix on his look: all eyes direct their rays
> On him, and crowds turn coxcombs as they gaze.
> His peers shine round him with reflected grace,

1. *High on a gorgeous seat*] Parody of Milton, book 2.

> *High on a throne of royal state, that far*
> *Outshone the wealth of Ormus and of Ind,*
> *Or where the gorgeous East with richest hand*
> *Showers on her kings barbaric pearl and gold*
> *Satan exalted sate,* ——

2. *Henley's gilt tub*] The pulpit of a dissenter is usually called a tub; but that of Mr Orator Henley was covered with velvet, and adorned with gold. He had also a fair altar, and over it is this extraordinary inscription, *The Primitive Eucharist.* See the history of this person, book 3. v. 199.

Ibid. *or Flecknoe's Irish throne,*] Richard Flecknoe was an Irish priest, but had laid aside (as himself expressed it) the mechanic part of priesthood. He printed some plays, poems, letters, and travels. I doubt not our author took occasion to mention him in respect to the poem of Mr Dryden, to which this bears some resemblance, though of a character more different from it than that of the *Aeneid* from the *Iliad,* or the *Lutrin* of Boileau from the *Defait de Bouts rimées* of Sarazin.

It may be just worth mentioning, that the eminence from whence the ancient sophists entertained their auditors, was called by the pompous name of a throne;— ἐπὶ Θρόνου τινὸς ὑψηλοῦ μάλα σοφιστικῶς καὶ σοβαρῶς. Themistius, Orat. i.

3. Edmund Curll stood in the pillory at Charing Cross, in March 1727–8.

Mr Curll loudly complained of this note, as an untruth; protesting 'that he stood in the pillory, not in March, but in February.' And of another on ver. 152, saying, 'he was not tossed in a *blanket,* but a *rug.' Curlliad,* duodecimo, 1729, p. 19, 25. Much in the same manner Mr Cibber remonstrated that his brothers at Bedlam, mentioned Book i. were not *brazen,* but *blocks;* yet our author let it pass unaltered, as a trifle, that no way lessened the relationship.

New edge their dulness, and new bronze their face.   10
So from the sun's broad beam, in shallow urns
Heaven's twinkling sparks draw light, and point their
        horns.
    Not with more glee, by hands pontific crowned,
With scarlet hats° wide-waving circled round,
Rome in her Capitol saw Querno sit,
Throned on seven hills,° the Antichrist of wit.
    And now the Queen, to glad her sons, proclaims
By herald hawkers, high heroic games.
They summon all her race: an endless band
Pours forth, and leaves unpeopled half the land.   20
A motley mixture! in long wigs, in bags,°
In silks, in crapes,° in garters,° and in rags,
From drawing rooms, from colleges, from garrets,
On horse, on foot, in hacks,° and gilded chariots:
All who true dunces in her cause appeared,
And all who knew those dunces to reward.
    Amid that area° wide they took their stand,
Where the tall maypole once o'erlooked the Strand;
But now (so ANNE and piety ordain)
A church collects the saints of Drury Lane.   30
    With authors, stationers° obeyed the call,
(The field of glory is a field for all).
Glory, and gain, th'industrious tribe provoke;
And gentle Dulness ever loves a joke.

15. Camillo Querno was of Apulia, who hearing the great encouragement which
Leo X gave to poets, travelled to Rome with a harp in his hand, and sung to it twenty
thousand verses of a poem called *Alexias*. He was introduced *as a buffoon* to Leo,
and promoted to the honour of the *laurel*; a jest which the court of Rome and the
Pope himself entered into so far, as to cause him to ride on an elephant to the
Capitol, and to hold a solemn festival on his coronation; at which it is recorded the
poet himself was so transported as to *weep for joy**. He was ever after a constant
frequenter of the Pope's table, drank abundantly, and poured forth verses without
number. PAULUS JOVIUS, *Elog. Vir. doct.*, chap. lxxxii. Some idea of his poetry is given
by Fam. Strada, in his *Prolusions*.

* See *Life of C.C.*, chap. vi. p. 149.

A poet's form she placed before their eyes,
And bade the nimblest racer seize the prize;
No meagre, muse-rid mope, adust° and thin,
In a dun nightgown of his own loose skin;
But such a bulk as no twelve bards could raise,
Twelve starveling bards of these degenerate days.   40
All as a partridge plump, full-fed, and fair,
She formed this image of well-bodied air;
With pert flat eyes she windowed well its head;
A brain of feathers, and a heart of lead;
And empty words she gave, and sounding strain,
But senseless, lifeless! idol void and vain!
Never was dashed out, at one lucky hit,
A fool, so just a copy of a wit;
So like, that critics said, and courtiers swore,

35. This is what Juno does to deceive Turnus, *Aen.* x.

> *Tum Dea nube cava,* tenuem sine viribus umbram
> *In faciem Aeneae (visu mirabile monstrum!)*
> *Dardaniis ornat telis, clypeumque jubasque*
> *Divini assimilat capitis*——
> ——*Dat* inania verba,
> *Dat* sine mente sonum——

The reader will observe how exactly some of these verses suit with their allegorical application here to a plagiary: there seems to me a great propriety in this episode, where such an one is imaged by a phantom that deludes the grasp of the expecting bookseller.

39. *Vix illud lecti bis sex—*
Qualia nunc hominum producit corpora tellus.
                                   Virgil, *Aen.* xii.

44. *A brain of feathers, and a heart of lead;*] i.e.

A trifling head, *and a* contracted heart,

as the poet, book 4. describes the *accomplished* sons of Dulness; of whom this is only an *image*, or scarecrow, and so stuffed out with these corresponding materials.
                                                                        SCRIBL.

47. Our author here seems willing to give some account of the possibility of Dulness making a wit (which could be done no other way than by *chance*.) The fiction is the more reconciled to probability, by the known story of Apelles, who being at a loss to express the foam of Alexander's horse, dashed his pencil in despair at the picture, and happened to do it by that fortunate stroke.

A wit it was, and called the phantom More.°   50

    All gaze with ardour: some a poet's name,
Others a sword-knot and laced suit inflame.
But lofty Lintot in the circle rose:
'This prize is mine; who tempt it are my foes;
With me began this genius, and shall end.'
He spoke: and who with Lintot shall contend?

    Fear held them mute. Alone, untaught to fear,
Stood dauntless Curll; 'Behold that rival here!
The race by vigour, not by vaunts is won;

50. *and called the phantom More.*] CURLL, in his *Key to the Dunciad*, affirmed this to be James Moore Smith esq. and it is probable (considering what is said of him in the *Testimonies*) that some might fancy our author obliged to represent this gentleman as a plagiary, or to pass for one himself. His case indeed was like that of a man I have heard of, who, as he was sitting in company, perceived his next neighbour had stolen his handkerchief. 'Sir' (said the thief, finding himself detected) 'do not expose me, I did it for mere want; be so good but to take it privately out of my pocket again, and say nothing.' The honest man did so, but the other cried out, 'See, gentlemen, what a thief we have among us! look, he is stealing my handkerchief!'

The plagiarisms of this person gave occasion to the following epigram:

> *More always smiles whenever he recites;*
> *He smiles (you think) approving what he writes.*
> *And yet in.this no vanity is shown;*
> *A modest man may like what's not his own.*

His only work was a comedy called *The Rival Modes*; the town condemned it in the action, but he printed it in $17\frac{26}{27}$, with this modest motto,

> *Hic caestus artemque repono.*

50. *the phantom More.*] It appears from hence, that this is not the name of a real person, but fictitious. *More* from μῶρος, *stultus*, μωρία, *stultitia*, to represent the folly of a plagiary. Thus Erasmus, *Admonuit me* Mori *cognomen tibi, quod tam ad* Moriae *vocabulum accedit quam es ipse a re alienus.* Dedication of *Moriae Encomium* to Sir Tho. More; the farewell of which may be our author's to his plagiary, *Vale,* More! *& moriam tuam gnaviter defende.* Adieu, More! and be sure strongly to defend thy own folly. SCRIBL.

53. We enter here upon the episode of the booksellers: persons, whose names being more known and famous in the learned world than those of the authors in this poem, do therefore need less explanation. The action of Mr Lintot here imitates that of Dares in Virgil, rising just in this manner to lay hold on a *bull*. This eminent bookseller printed the *Rival Modes* before mentioned.

58. We come now to a character of much respect, that of Mr Edmund Curll. As a plain repetition of great actions is the best praise of them, we shall only say of this

So take the hindmost, Hell.'—He said, and run.   60
Swift as a bard the bailiff leaves behind,
He left huge Lintot, and out-stripped the wind.
As when a dabchick° waddles through the copse
On feet and wings, and flies, and wades, and hops;

eminent man, that he carried the trade many lengths beyond what it ever before had
arrived at; and that he was the envy and admiration of all his profession. He possessed
himself of a command over all authors whatever; he caused them to write what he
pleased; they could not call their very *names* their own. He was not only famous
among these; he was taken notice of by the *state*, the *church*, and the *law*, and received
particular marks of distinction from each.

It will be owned that he is here introduced with all possible dignity. He speaks
like the intrepid Diomed; he runs like the swift-footed Achilles; if he falls, 'tis like
the beloved Nisus; and (what Homer makes to be the chief of all praises) he is
favoured of the gods; he says but three words, and his prayer is heard; a Goddess
conveys it to the seat of Jupiter. Though he loses the prize, he gains the victory; the
Great Mother herself comforts him, she inspires him with expedients, she honours
him with an immortal present (such as Achilles receives from Thetis, and Aeneas
from Venus) at once instructive and prophetical. After this he is unrivalled and
triumphant.

The tribute our author here pays him is a grateful return for several unmerited
obligations. Many weighty animadversions on the public affairs, and many excellent
and diverting pieces on private persons, has he given to his name. If ever he owed
two verses to any other, he owed Mr Curll some thousands. He was every day
extending his fame, and enlarging his writings: witness innumerable instances; but
it shall suffice only to mention the *Court Poems*, which he meant to publish as the
work of the true writer, a lady of quality; but being first threatened, and afterwards
punished for it by Mr Pope, he generously transferred it from *her* to *him*, and ever
since printed it in his name. The single time that ever he spoke to C. was on that
affair, and to that happy incident he owed all the favours since received from him.
So true is the saying of Dr Sydenham, 'that any one shall be, at some time or other,
the better or the worse, for having but *seen* or *spoken* to a good or bad man.'

60. *Occupet extremum scabies; mihi turpe relinqui est.*   Horace, *de Arte.*

61. *&c.* Something like this is in Homer, *Il.* x. v. 220. of Diomed. Two different
manners of the same author in his similes are also imitated in the two following; the
first, of the bailiff, is short, unadorned, and (as the critics well know) from *familiar
life*; the second, of the water-fowl, more extended, picturesque, and from *rural life*.
The 59th verse is likewise a literal translation of one in Homer.

64, 65.   ——*So eagerly the Fiend*
         O'er bog, o'er steep, thro' strait, rough, dense, or rare,
         With head, hands, wings, or feet pursues his way,
         And swims, or sinks, or wades, or creeps, or flies.
                                        Milton, Book 2.

So labouring on, with shoulders, hands, and head,
Wide as a windmill all his figure spread,
With arms expanded Bernard rows his state,
And left-legged Jacob seems to emulate:
Full in the middle way there stood a lake,
Which Curll's Corinna chanced that morn to make: 70
(Such was her wont, at early dawn to drop
Her evening cates° before his neighbour's shop,)
Here fortuned Curll to slide; loud shout the band,
And 'Bernard! Bernard!' rings through all the Strand.
Obscene with filth the miscreant lies bewrayed,

67, 68. Milton, of the motion of the swan,

> ——rows
> His state with oary feet.

And Dryden, of another's,—*With two left legs*—

70. *Curll's Corinna*] This name, it seems, was taken by one Mrs T[homas], who procured some private letters of Mr Pope's, while almost a boy, to Mr Cromwell, and sold them without the consent of either of those gentlemen to Curll, who printed them in 12mo, 1727. He discovered her to be the publisher, in his *Key*, p. 11. We only take this opportunity of mentioning the manner in which those letters got abroad, which the author was ashamed of as very trivial things, full not only of levities, but of wrong judgments of men and books, and only excusable from the youth and inexperience of the writer.

73.   *Labitur infelix, caesis ut forte juvencis*
                    Fusus humum viridesque super madefecerat herbas—
                    Concidit, immundoque fimo, sacroque cruore.
                                        Virgil, *Aen.* v. of Nisus.

74. —*Ut littus, Hyla, Hyla, omne sonaret.*
                    Virgil, *Ecl.* v.

75. Though this incident may seem too low and base for the dignity of an epic poem, the learned very well know it to be but a copy of Homer and Virgil; the very words ὄνθος and *fimus* are used by them, though our poet (in compliance to modern nicety) has remarkably enriched and coloured his language, as well as raised the versification, in this episode, and in the following one of Eliza. Mr Dryden in *Mack-Fleckno*, has not scrupled to mention the *morning toast* at which the fishes bite in the Thames, *Pissing Alley, Reliques of the bum, &c.* but our author is more grave, and (as a fine writer says of Virgil in his *Georgics*) *tosses about his* dung *with an air of majesty*. If we consider that the exercises of his *authors* could with justice be no higher than *tickling, chattering, braying,* or *diving*, it was no easy matter to invent such games as were proportioned to the meaner degree of *booksellers*. In Homer and Virgil, Ajax and Nisus the persons drawn in this plight are *heroes*; whereas here they are such with whom it had been great impropriety to have joined any but vile ideas; besides the natural connection there is between libellers and common nuisances. Nevertheless I have heard our author own, that this part of his poem was (as it frequently happens) what cost him most trouble and pleased him least; but that he hoped it was excusable, since levelled at such as understand no delicate satire. Thus

Fallen in the plash his wickedness had laid:
Then first (if poets aught of truth declare)
The caitiff vaticide° conceived a prayer.
    'Hear Jove! whose name my bards and I adore,
As much at least as any god's, or more;   80
And him and his, if more devotion warms,
Down with the Bible, up with the Pope's Arms.'°
    A place there is, betwixt earth, air, and seas,
Where, from Ambrosia, Jove retires for ease.
There in his seat two spacious vents appear,
On this he sits, to that he leans his ear.
And hears the various vows of fond mankind;
Some beg an eastern, some a western wind:
All vain petitions, mounting to the sky,
With reams abundant this abode supply;   90
Amused he reads, and then returns the bills
Signed with that Ichor° which from gods distils.
    In office here fair Cloacina stands,
And ministers to Jove with purest hands.
Forth from the heap she picked her votary's prayer,
And placed it next him, a distinction rare!
Oft had the Goddess heard her servant's call,
From her black grottos° near the Temple wall,
Listening delighted to the jest unclean
Of link-boys° vile, and watermen obscene;   100
Where as he fished her nether realms for wit,

the politest men are sometimes obliged to *swear*, when they happen to have to do with
porters and oyster-wenches.
    82. The Bible, Curll's sign; the Cross Keys, Lintot's.
    83. See Lucian's Icaro-Menippus; where this fiction is more extended.
    Ibid. *Orbe locus medio est, inter terrasque, fretumque,*
            Coelestesque plagas—
                                Ovid, *Met.* xii.
    92. Alludes to Homer, *Iliad* v.
            ——ῥέε δ' ἄμβροτον αἷμα Θέοιο,
            Ἰχὼρ, οἷος πέρ τε ῥέει μακάρεσσι Θεοῖσιν.
            A stream of nect'rous humour issuing flowed,
            Sanguine, such as celestial sp'rits may bleed.
                                Milton.
    93. *Cloacina*] The Roman goddess of the common-sewers.
    101. See the preface to Swift's and Pope's *Miscellanies*.

She oft had favoured him, and favours yet.
Renewed by ordure's sympathetic° force,
As oiled with magic juices for the course,
Vigorous he rises; from th' effluvia strong
Imbibes new life, and scours and stinks along;
Repasses Lintot, vindicates° the race,
Nor heeds the brown dishonours of his face.

And now the victor stretched his eager hand
Where the tall nothing stood, or seemed to stand;   110
A shapeless shade, it melted from his sight,
Like forms in clouds, or visions of the night.
To seize his papers, Curll, was next thy care;
His papers light, fly diverse, tossed in air;
Songs, sonnets, epigrams the winds uplift,
And whisk 'em back to Evans, Young, and Swift.
Th'embroidered suit at least he deemed his prey;
That suit an unpaid tailor snatched away.
No rag, no scrap, of all the beau, or wit,

104. Alluding to the opinion that there are ointments used by witches to enable
them to fly in the air, &c.

108. ——faciem ostentabat, & udo
Turpia membra fimo——
                                Virgil, Aen. v.

111.   ——Effugit imago
Par levibus ventis, volucrique simillima somno.
                                Virgil, Aen. vi.

114. Virgil, Aen. vi. of the sibyls' leaves,
Carmina——
Turbata volent rapidis ludibria ventis.

116. Evans, Young, and Swift.] Some of those persons whose writings, epigrams,
or jests he had owned. See note on ver. 50.

118. This line has been loudly complained of in Mist, June 8, Dedic. to Sawney,
and others, as a most inhuman satire on the poverty of poets; but it is thought our
author would be acquitted by a jury of tailors. To me this instance seems unluckily
chosen; if it be a satire on anybody, it must be on a bad paymaster, since the person
to whom they have here applied it, was a man of fortune. Not but poets may well
be jealous of so great a prerogative as non-payment; which Mr Dennis so far asserts,
as boldly to pronounce that 'if Homer himself was not in debt, it was because nobody
would trust him.' Pref. to Rem. on the Rape of the Lock, p. 15.

That once so fluttered, and that once so writ.   120
   Heaven rings with laughter: of the laughter vain,
Dulness, good Queen, repeats the jest again.
Three wicked imps, of her own Grub Street choir,
She decked like Congreve, Addison, and Prior;
Mears, Warner, Wilkins run: delusive thought!
Breval, Bond, Besaleel, the varlets caught.
Curll stretches after Gay, but Gay is gone,
He grasps an empty Joseph° for a John:
So Proteus, hunted in a nobler shape,
Became, when seized, a puppy, or an ape.   130
   To him the Goddess: 'Son! thy grief lay down,
And turn this whole illusion on the town:
As the sage dame, experienced in her trade,
By names of toasts retails each battered jade;
(Whence hapless Monsieur° much complains at Paris
Of wrongs from Duchesses and Lady Maries);
Be thine, my stationer! this magic gift;

<hr/>

124. *like Congreve, Addison, and Prior*] These authors being such whose names will reach posterity, we shall not give any account of them, but proceed to those of whom it is necessary.—Bezaleel Morris was author of some satires on the translators of Homer, with many other things printed in newspapers.—'Bond writ a satire against Mr P—. Capt. Breval was author of *The Confederates*, an ingenious dramatic performance to expose Mr P., Mr Gay, Dr Arb. and some ladies of quality,' says CURLL, *Key*, p. 11.

125. *Mears, Warner, Wilkins*] Booksellers, and printers of much anonymous stuff.

126. *Breval, Bond, Besaleel,*] I foresee it will be objected from this line, that we were in an error in our assertion on ver. 50. of this book, that More was a fictitious name, since these persons are equally represented by the poet as phantoms. So at first sight it may seem; but be not deceived, reader; these also are not real persons. 'Tis true, Curll declares Breval, a captain, author of a piece called *The Confederates*; but the same Curll first said it was written by Joseph Gay. Is his second assertion to be credited any more than his first? He likewise affirms Bond to be one who writ a satire on our poet. But where is such a satire to be found? where was such a writer ever heard of? As for Bezaleel, it carries forgery in the very name; nor is it, as the others are, a surname. Thou mayst depend upon it, no such authors ever lived: all phantoms. SCRIBL.

128. *Joseph Gay*, a fictitious name put by Curll before several pamphlets, which made them pass with many for Mr Gay's.

132. It was a common practice of this bookseller to publish vile pieces of obscure hands under the names of eminent authors.

Cooke shall be Prior, and Concanen, Swift:
So shall each hostile name become our own,
And we too boast our Garth and Addison.'   140
With that she gave him (piteous of his case,

138. *Cooke shall be Prior,*] The man here specified writ a thing called *The Battle of Poets*, in which Philips and Welsted were the heroes, and Swift and Pope utterly routed. He also published some malevolent things in the *British, London*, and *Daily Journals*; and at the same time wrote letters to Mr Pope, protesting his innocence. His chief work was a translation of Hesiod, to which Theobald writ notes and half-notes, which he carefully owned.

138. *and Concanen, Swift*] In the first edition of this poem there were only asterisks in this place, but the names were since inserted, merely to fill up the verse, and give ease to the ear of the reader.

140. Nothing is more remarkable than our author's love of praising good writers. He has in this very poem celebrated Mr Locke, Sir Isaac Newton, Dr Barrow, Dr Atterbury, Mr Dryden, Mr Congreve, Dr Garth, Mr Addison; in a word, almost every man of his time that deserved it; even Cibber himself (presuming him to be author of *The Careless Husband*.) It was very difficult to have that pleasure in a poem on this subject, yet he has found means to insert their panegyric, and has made even Dulness out of her own mouth pronounce it. It must have been particularly agreeable to him to celebrate Dr Garth; both as his constant friend, and as he was his predecessor in this kind of satire. *The Dispensary* attacked the whole body of apothecaries, a much more useful one undoubtedly than that of the bad poets; if in truth this can be a body, of which no two members ever agreed. It also did what Mr Theobald says is unpardonable, drew in *parts* of *private character*, and introduced *persons independent of his subject*. Much more would Boileau have incurred his censure, who left all subjects whatever, on all occasions, to fall upon the bad poets (which, it is to be feared, would have been more immediately his concern.) But certainly next to commending good writers, the greatest service to learning is to expose the bad, who can only that way be made of any use to it. This truth is very well set forth in these lines addressed to our author:

> *The craven rook, and pert jackdaw,*
> *(Though neither birds of moral kind)*
> *Yet serve, if hanged, or stuffed with straw,*
> *To show us which way blows the wind.*
>
> *Thus dirty knaves, or chattering fools,*
> *Strung up by dozens in thy lay,*
> *Teach more by half than Dennis' rules,*
> *And point instruction every way.*
>
> *With Egypt's art thy pen may strive,*
> *One potent drop let this but shed,*
> *And every rogue that stunk alive,*
> *Becomes a precious mummy dead.*

141, 142.   ——*Risit pater optimus illi.*——
Me liceat casus misereri insontis amici——
Sic fatus, tergum Gaetuli immane leonis, &c.
      Virgil, *Aen.* v.

Yet smiling at his rueful length of face)

142. 'The decrepit person or figure of a man are no reflections upon his *genius*: an honest mind will love and esteem a *man of worth*, though he be deformed or poor. Yet the author of the *Dunciad* hath libelled a person for his *rueful length of face!* Mist's *Journal*, June 8. This *genius* and *man of worth*, whom an honest mind should *love*, is Mr Curll. True it is, he stood in the pillory, an incident which will lengthen the face of any man though it were ever so comely, therefore is no reflection on the natural beauty of Mr Curll. But as to reflections on any man's face, or figure, Mr Dennis saith excellently; 'Natural deformity comes not by our fault'; 'tis often occasioned by calamities and diseases, which a man can no more help than a monster can his deformity. There is no one misfortune, and no one disease, but what all the rest of mankind are subject to.—But the deformity of this *author* is visible, present, lasting, unalterable, and peculiar to himself. 'Tis the mark of God and Nature upon him, to give us warning that we should hold no society with him, as a creature not of our original, nor of our species: and they who have refused to take this warning which God and nature have given them, and have in spite of it by a senseless presumption ventured to be familiar with him, have severely suffered, etc. 'Tis certain his original is not from Adam, but from the Devil,' etc. DENNIS, *Charact. of Mr P.* octavo, 1716.

Admirably it is observed by Mr Dennis against Mr Law, p. 33. 'That the language of Billingsgate can never be the language of charity, nor consequently of Christianity.' I should else be tempted to use the language of a critic; for what is more provoking to a commentator, than to behold his author thus portrayed? Yet I consider it really hurts not *him*; whereas to call some others dull, might do them prejudice with a world too apt to believe it: therefore, though Mr D. may call another a *little ass* or a *young toad*, far be it from us to call him a *toothless lion* or an *old serpent*. Indeed, had I written these notes (as was once my intent) in the learned language, I might have given him the appellations of *balatro, calceatum caput, scurra in triviis*, being phrases in good esteem and frequent usage among the best learned: but in our mother-tongue, were I to tax any gentleman of the *Dunciad*, surely it should be in words not to the vulgar intelligible; whereby Christian charity, decency, and good accord among authors, might be preserved. SCRIBL.

The good Scriblerus here, as on all occasions, eminently shows his humanity. But it was far otherwise with the gentlemen of the *Dunciad*, whose scurrilities were always personal, and of that nature which provoked every honest man but Mr Pope; yet never to be lamented, since they occasioned the following amiable Verses:

> *While malice, Pope, denies thy page*
> *Its own celestial fire,*
> *While critics, and while bards in rage,*
> *Admiring, won't admire:*
>
> *While wayward pens thy worth assail,*
> *And envious tongues decry;*
> *These times though many a friend bewail,*
> *These times bewail not I.*
>
> *But when the world's loud praise is thine,*
> *And spleen no more shall blame,*
> *When with thy Homer thou shalt shine*
> *In one established fame:*
>
> *When none shall rail, and every lay*

A shaggy tapestry, worthy to be spread
On Codrus' old, or Dunton's modern bed;
Instructive work! whose wry-mouthed portraiture
Displayed the fates her confessors° endure.
Earless on high, stood unabashed Defoe,°
And Tutchin flagrant from the scourge below.
There Ridpath, Roper, cudgelled might ye view,
The very worsted still looked black and blue.   150

Devote a wreath to thee;
That day (for come it will) that day
Shall I lament to see.

143. A sorry kind of tapestry frequent in old inns, made of worsted or some coarser stuff; like that which is spoken of by Donne—*Faces as frightful as theirs who whip Christ in old hangings.* The imagery woven in it alludes to the mantle of Cloanthus, in *Aen.* v.

144. Of Codrus the poet's bed, see Juvenal, describing his *poverty* very copiously, *Sat.* iii. ver. 203, *&c.*

Lectus erat Codro, &c.

Codrus had but one bed, so short to boot,
That his short wife's short legs hung dangling out.
His cupboard's head six earthen pitchers graced,
Beneath them was his trusty tankard placed;
And to support this noble plate, there lay
A bending Chiron, cast from honest clay.
His few Greek books a rotten chest contained,
Whose covers much of mouldiness complained,
Where mice and rats devoured poetic bread,
And on heroic verse luxuriously were fed.
'Tis true poor Codrus nothing had to boast,
And yet poor Codrus all that nothing lost.

Dryden.

But Mr Concanen, in his dedication of the letters, advertisements, etc. to the author of the *Dunciad,* assures us that 'Juvenal never satirized the poverty of Codrus.'

John Dunton was a broken bookseller and abusive scribbler; he writ *Neck or Nothing,* a violent satire on some ministers of state; a libel on the Duke of Devonshire and the Bishop of Peterborough, etc.

148. John Tutchin, author of some vile verses, and of a weekly paper called the *Observator.* He was sentenced to be whipped through several towns in the west of England, upon which he petitioned King James II to be hanged. When that prince died in exile, he wrote an invective against his memory, occasioned by some humane elegies on his death. He lived to the time of Queen Anne.

149. *There Ridpath, Roper*] Authors of the *Flying Post* and *Post Boy,* two scandalous papers on different sides, for which they equally and alternately deserved to be cudgelled, and were so.

Himself among the storied chiefs he spies,
As from the blanket high in air he flies,
'And oh!' (he cried) 'what street, what lane but knows,
Our purgings, pumpings, blankettings, and blows?
In every loom our labours° shall be seen,
And the fresh vomit run for ever green!'
   See in the circle next, Eliza placed,
Two babes of love close clinging to her waist;
Fair as before her works she stands confessed,
In flowers and pearls by bounteous Kirkall dressed.   160
The Goddess then: 'Who best can send on high
The salient spout, far-streaming to the sky;

151.   *Se quoque principibus permixtum agnovit Achivis—*
      Constitit, & lacrymans: Quis jam locus, inquit, Achate!
      Quae regio in terris nostri non plena laboris?
                              Virgil, *Aen.* i.

151. The history of Curll's being tossed in a blanket, and whipped by the scholars of Westminster, is well known. Of his purging and vomiting, see *A Full and True Account of a horrid Revenge on the body of Edm. Curll*, in Swift and Pope's *Miscell.*

156. A parody on these of a late noble author:

    His bleeding arm had furnished all their rooms,
    And run for ever purple in the looms.

157. In this game is exposed, in the most contemptuous manner, the profligate licentiousness of those shameless scribblers (for the most part of that sex, which ought least to be capable of such malice or impudence) who in libellous memoirs and novels, reveal the faults or misfortunes of both sexes, to the ruin of public fame, or disturbance of private happiness. Our good poet (by the whole cast of his work being obliged not to take off the irony) where he could not show his indignation, hath shown his contempt, as much as possible; having here drawn as vile a picture as could be represented in the colours of epic poesy. SCRIBL.

Ibid. *Eliza Haywood*; this woman was authoress of those most scandalous books called the *Court of Carimania*, and the *New Utopia*. For the *two babes of love*, see CURLL, *Key*, p. 22. But whatever reflection he is pleased to throw upon this lady, surely it was what from him she little deserved, who had celebrated Curll's undertakings for *Reformation of manners*, and declared herself 'to be so perfectly acquainted with the *sweetness of his disposition*, and that *tenderness with which he considered the errors of his fellow creatures*; that, though she should find the *little inadvertencies* of her *own life* recorded in his papers, she was certain it would be done in such a manner as she could not but approve.' Mrs HAYWOOD, *Hist of Clar.* printed in the *Female Dunciad*, p. 18.

158. *Cressa genus, Pholoë, geminique sub ubere nati.* Virgil, *Aen.* v.

160. *Kirkall*, the name of an engraver. Some of this lady's works were printed in four volumes in 12ᵐᵒ, with her picture thus dressed up before them.

His be yon Juno of majestic size,
With cow-like udders, and with ox-like eyes.
This China jordan let the chief o'ercome
Replenish, not ingloriously, at home.'
Osborne and Curll accept the glorious strife,
(Though this his son dissuades, and that his wife.)
One on his manly confidence relies,
One on his vigour and superior size.   170
First Osborne leaned against his lettered post;°
It rose, and laboured to a curve at most.
So Jove's bright bow displays its watery round,
(Sure sign, that no spectator shall be drowned).
A second effort brought but new disgrace,
The wild meander washed the artist's face:

163, 164. In allusion to Homer's Βοῶπις πότνια Ἥρη.

165. *Tertius Argolica hac galea contentus abito.* Virgil, *Aen.* v. 314.

In the games of Homer, *Il.* xxiii. there are set together, as prizes, a lady and a kettle, as in this place Mrs Haywood and a jordan. But there the preference in value is given to the kettle, at which Mad. Dacier is justly displeased. Mrs H. is here treated with distinction, and acknowledged to be the more valuable of the two.

167. *Osborne*] A bookseller in Grays Inn, very well qualified by his impudence to act this part; and therefore placed here instead of a less deserving predecessor. This man published advertisements for a year together, pretending to sell Mr Pope's subscription books of Homer's *Iliad* at half the price: of which books he had none, but cut to the size of them (which was quarto) the common books in folio, without copperplates, on a worse paper, and never above half the value.

Upon this advertisement the *Gazetteer* harangued thus, July 6, 1739. 'How melancholy must it be to a writer to be so unhappy as to see his works hawked for sale in a manner so fatal to his fame! How, with honour to yourself, and justice to your subscribers, can this be done? What an ingratitude to be charged on the *Only honest poet* that lived in 1738! and than whom *virtue* has not had a *shriller trumpeter* for many ages! That you were once *generally admired and esteemed* can be denied by none: but that you and your works are now despised, is verified by *this fact:*' which being utterly false, did not indeed much humble the author, but drew this just chastisement on the bookseller.

169, 170. *Ille melior motu, fretusque juventa;*
        Hic membris & mole valens—
                        Virgil, *Aen.* v.

173, 174. The words of Homer, of the rainbow, in *Iliad* xi.
        ——ἅς τε Κρονίων
        Ἐν νέφεϊ στήριξε, τέρας μερόπων ἀνθρώπων.

Que le fils de Saturn a fondez dans les nües, pour être dans tous les âges une signe à tous les mortels.
                                                    Dacier.

Thus the small jet, which hasty hands unlock,
Spurts in the gardener's eyes who turns the cock.
Not so from shameless Curll; impetuous spread
The stream, and smoking flourished o'er his head.   180
So (famed like thee for turbulence and horns)°
Eridanus his humble fountain scorns;
Through half the heavens he pours th'exalted urn;
His rapid waters in their passage burn.°
    Swift as it mounts, all follow with their eyes:

181, 182. Virgil mentions these two qualifications of Eridanus, *Georg.* iv.

> *Et gemina auratus taurino cornua vultu,*
> *Eridanus, quo non alius per pinguia culta*
> *In mare purpureum violentior effluit amnis.*

The poets fabled of this river Eridanus, that it flowed through the skies. Denham, *Cooper's Hill*:

> *Heaven her Eridanus no more shall boast,*
> *Whose fame in thine, like lesser currents lost;*
> *Thy nobler stream shall visit Jove's abodes,*
> *To shine among the stars, and bathe the gods.*

183. In a manuscript *Dunciad* (where are some marginal corrections of some gentlemen some time deceased) I have found another reading of these lines, thus,

> *And lifts his urn, through half the heavens to flow;*
> *His rapid waters in their passage* glow.

This I cannot but think the right: For first, though the difference between *burn* and *glow* may seem not very material to others, to me I confess the latter has an elegance, a *je ne sçay quoy*, which is much easier to be conceived than explained. Secondly, every reader of our poet must have observed how frequently he uses this word *glow* in other parts of his works: To instance only in his Homer:

(1.) *Iliad.* ix.   v. 726.—*With one resentment glows.*
(2.) *Iliad.* xi.   v. 626.—*There the battle glows.*
(3.) Ibid.   v. 985.—*The closing flesh that instant ceased to glow.*
(4.) *Iliad.* xii.   v. 45.—*Encompassed Hector glows.*
(5.) Ibid.   v. 475.—*His beating breast with generous ardour glows.*
(6.) *Iliad.* xviii. v. 591.—*Another part glowed with refulgent arms.*
(7.) Ibid.   v. 654.—*And curled on silver props in order glow.*

I am afraid of growing too luxuriant in examples, or I could stretch this catalogue to a great extent, but these are enough to prove his fondness for this *beautiful word*, which, therefore, let *all future editions* replace there.

I am aware, after all, that *burn* is the proper word to convey an idea of what was said to be Mr Curll's condition at this time: but from that very reason I infer the direct contrary. For surely every *lover of our author* will conclude he had more *humanity* than to insult a man on such a misfortune or calamity, which could never befall him purely by his *own fault*, but from an unhappy communication with another. This note is half Mr THEOBALD, half SCRIBL.

Still happy impudence obtains the prize.
Thou triumph'st, victor of the high-wrought day,
And the pleased dame, soft-smiling, leadst away.
Osborne, through perfect modesty o'ercome,
Crowned with the jordan, walks contented home.   190
    But now for authors nobler palms remain;
Room for my Lord! three jockeys in his train;
Six huntsmen with a shout precede his chair:
He grins, and looks broad nonsense with a stare.
His honour's meaning Dulness thus expressed,
'He wins this patron, who can tickle best.'
    He chinks his purse, and takes his seat of state:
With ready quills the dedicators wait;
Now at his head the dexterous task commence,
And, instant, fancy feels th' imputed sense;   200
Now gentle touches wanton o'er his face,
He struts Adonis, and affects grimace:
Rolli the feather to his ear conveys,
Then his nice taste directs our operas:
Bentley his mouth with classic flattery opes,

187. *The high-wrought day,*] Some affirm, this was originally, *well p—st day*; but
the poet's decency would not suffer it.

Here the learned Scriblerus manifests great anger; he exclaims against all such
conjectural emendations in this manner: 'Let it suffice, O Pallas! that every noble
Ancient, Greek or Roman, hath suffered the impertinent correction of every Dutch,
German, and Swiss schoolmaster! Let our English at least escape, whose intrinsic
is scarce of marble so solid, as not to be impaired or soiled by such rude and dirty
hands. Suffer them to call their works their own, and after death at least to find rest
and sanctuary from critics! When these men have ceased to *rail*, let them not begin
to do worse, to *comment*! Let them not conjecture into nonsense, correct out of all
correctness, and restore into obscurity and confusion. Miserable fate! which can
befall only the sprightliest wits that have written, and will befall them only from such
dull ones as could never write.' SCRIBL.

203. *Paolo Antonio Rolli,* an Italian poet, and writer of many operas in that lan-
guage, which, partly by the help of his genius, prevailed in England near twenty
years. He taught Italian to some fine gentlemen, who affected to direct the operas.

205. Not spoken of the famous Dr Richard Bentley, but of one Thom. Bentley,
a small critic, who aped his uncle in a *little Horace*. The great one was intended to
be dedicated to the Lord Halifax, but (on a change of the ministry) was given to the
Earl of Oxford; for which reason the little one was dedicated to his son the Lord
Harley. A taste of this *classic elocution* may be seen in his following panegyric on the
Peace of Utrecht. *Cupimus patrem tuum, fulgentissimum illud Orbis Anglicani jubar,*
adorare. *O ingens* Reipublicae *nostrae columen! O fortunatam tanto* Heroe Britanniam!
Illi tali tantoque viro DEUM *per* Omnia *adfuisse, manumque ejus & mentem direxisse,*

And the puffed orator bursts out in tropes.
But Welsted most the poet's healing balm
Strives to extract from his soft, giving palm;
Unlucky Welsted! thy unfeeling master,
The more thou ticklest, gripes his fist the faster.   210
    While thus each hand promotes the pleasing pain,
And quick sensations skip from vein to vein;

CERTISSIMUM EST. Hujus *enim* Unius *ferme opera,* aequissimis & perhonorificis conditionibus, *diuturno, heu nimium! bello, finem impositum videmus. O Diem aeterna memoria dignissimam! qua terrores Patriae omnes excidit,* Pacem*que diu exoptatam toti sere Europae restituit, ille Populi Anglicani Amor, Harleius.*

Thus critically (that is verbally) translated:

'Thy Father, that most refulgent star of the Anglican orb, we much desire to *adore!* Oh mighty column of our *Republic!* Oh Britain, fortunate in such an *hero!* That to such and so great a man GOD was ever present, in *every thing,* and all along directed both his hand and his heart, is a *most absolute certainty!* For it is in a manner by the operation of this *man alone,* that we behold a *war* (alas! how much too long an one!) brought at length to an end, *on the most just and most honourable conditions.* Oh day eternally to be memorated! wherein all the terrors of his country were ended, and a PEACE (long wished for by *almost all Europe*) was restored by HARLEY, the love and delight of the people of England.'

But that this gentleman can write in a different style, may be seen in a letter he printed to Mr Pope, wherein several noble lords are treated in a most extraordinary language, particularly the Lord Bolingbroke abused for that very PEACE which he here makes the *single work of* the Earl of Oxford, directed by *God Almighty.*

207. Leonard Welsted, author of *The Triumvirate,* or a Letter in verse from Palaemon to Celia at Bath, which was meant for a satire on Mr P. and some of his friends, about the year 1718. He writ other things which we cannot remember. Smedley in his *Metamorphosis of Scriblerus,* mentions one, the hymn of a *gentleman* to his *creator:* And there was another in praise either of a cellar, or a garret. L.W. characterized in the treatise Περὶ Βάθους, or the Art of Sinking, as a didapper, and after as an eel, is said to be this person, by Dennis, *Daily Journal* of May 11, 1728. He was also characterized under another animal, a mole, by the author of the ensuing simile, which was handed about at the same time:

> Dear Welsted, mark, in dirty hole,
> That painful animal, a mole:
> Above ground never born to grow;
> What mighty stir it keeps below?
> To make a molehill all this strife!
> It digs, pokes, undermines for life.
> How proud a little dirt to spread;
> Conscious of nothing o'er its head!
> Till, labouring on for want of eyes,
> It blunders into light—and dies.

You have him again in book 3. ver. 169.

A youth unknown to Phoebus, in despair,
Puts his last refuge all in heaven and prayer.
What force have pious vows! The Queen of Love
His sister sends, her votress, from above.
As taught by Venus, Paris learnt the art
To touch Achilles' only tender part;°
Secure, through her, the noble prize to carry,
He marches off, his Grace's secretary.   220
  'Now turn to different sports,' the Goddess cries,
'And learn, my sons, the wondrous power of noise.
To move, to raise, to ravish every heart,
With Shakespeare's nature, or with Jonson's art,
Let others aim: 'tis yours to shake the soul
With thunder rumbling from the mustard bowl,
With horns and trumpets now to madness swell,
Now sink in sorrows with a tolling bell;
Such happy arts attention can command,
When fancy flags, and sense is at a stand.   230
Improve we these. Three catcalls be the bribe
Of him, whose chattering shames the monkey tribe:
And his this drum, whose hoarse heroic bass

213. The satire of this episode being levelled at the base flatteries of authors to
worthless wealth or greatness, concludes here with an excellent lesson to such men:
that although their pens and praises were as exquisite as they conceit of themselves,
yet (even in their own mercenary views) a creature unlettered, who serveth the
passions, or pimpeth to the pleasures, of such vain, braggart, puffed nobility, shall
with those patrons be much more inward, and of them much higher rewarded.
                                                                      SCRIBL.

223, 225.   *To move, to raise, &c.*
               Let others aim: 'Tis yours to shake, &c.]
               Excudent alii spirantia mollius aera,
               Credo equidem, vivos ducent de marmore vultus, &c.
               Tu regere imperio populos, Romane, memento,
               Hae tibi erunt artes——

226. The old way of making thunder and mustard were the same; but since, it is
more advantageously performed by troughs of wood with stops in them. Whether
Mr Dennis was the inventor of that improvement, I know not; but it is certain, that
being once at a tragedy of a new author, he fell into a great passion at hearing some,
and cried, ' 'Sdeath! that is *my* thunder.'°

228. —*with a tolling bell*] A mechanical help to the pathetic, not unuseful to the
modern writers of tragedy.

231. *Three catcalls*] Certain musical instruments used by one sort of critics to
confound the poets of the theatre.

Drowns the loud clarion of the braying ass.'
  Now thousand tongues are heard in one loud din:
The monkey-mimics rush discordant in;
'Twas chattering, grinning, mouthing, jabbering all,
And noise and Norton,° brangling° and Breval,
Dennis and dissonance, and captious art,
And snipsnap° short, and interruption smart,   240
And demonstration thin, and theses thick,
And major, minor, and conclusion quick.°
'Hold', cried the Queen, 'a catcall each shall win;
Equal your merits! equal is your din!
But that this well-disputed game may end,
Sound forth my brayers, and the welkin rend.'
  As when the long-eared milky mothers wait
At some sick miser's triple-bolted gate,
For their defrauded, absent foals they make
A moan so loud, that all the guild awake;   250
Sore sighs Sir Gilbert,° starting at the bray,
From dreams of millions, and three groats to pay.
So swells each wind-pipe; ass intones to ass,
Harmonic twang! of leather, horn, and brass;
Such as from labouring lungs th' enthusiast° blows,
High sound, attempered to the vocal nose;
Or such as bellow from the deep divine;
There Webster! pealed thy voice, and Whitfield! thine.
But far o'er all, sonorous Blackmore's strain;

---

238. *Norton*] See ver. 417.—*J. Durant Breval*, author of a very extraordinary book of travels, and some poems. See before, note on ver. 126.

243. *Non nostrum inter vos tantas componere lites,*
    Et vitula tu dignus, & hic——
                         Virgil, *Ecl.* iii.

247. *As when the, &c.*] A simile with a long tail, in the manner of Homer.

258. *Webster—and Whitfield*] The one the writer of a newspaper called the *Weekly Miscellany*, the other a field preacher. This thought the only means of advancing Christianity was by the new birth of religious madness; that, by the old death of fire and faggot. And therefore they agreed in this, though in no other earthly thing, to abuse all the sober clergy. From the small success of these two extraordinary persons, we may learn how little hurtful *bigotry* and *enthusiasm* are, while the civil magistrate prudently forbears to lend his power to the one, in order to the employing it against the other.

Walls, steeples, skies, bray back to him again.   260
In Tottenham fields, the brethren, with amaze,
Prick all their ears up, and forget to graze;
Long Chancery Lane retentive rolls the sound,
And courts to courts return it round and round;
Thames wafts it thence to Rufus' roaring hall,
And Hungerford re-echoes bawl for bawl.
All hail him victor in both gifts of song,
Who sings so loudly, and who sings so long.°

260. A figure of speech taken from Virgil:

> *Et vox assensu nemorum ingeminata remugit. Georg.* iii
> *He hears his numerous herds low o'er the plain,*
> *While neighbouring hills low back to them again.*
> Cowley.

The poet here celebrated, Sir R.B. delighted much in the word *bray*, which he endeavoured to ennoble by applying it to the sound of *armour*, *war*, etc. In imitation of him, and strengthened by his authority, our author has here admitted it into heroic poetry.

262. *Immemor herbarum quos est mirata juvenca.*   Virgil, *Ecl.* viii.

The progress of the sound from place to place, and the scenery here of the bordering regions, Tottenham Fields, Chancery Lane, the Thames, Westminster Hall, and Hungerford Stairs, are imitated from Virgil, *Aen.* vii. on the sounding the horn of Alecto:

> *Audiit & Triviae longe lacus, audiit amnis*
> *Sulphurea Nar albus aqua, fontesque Velini, &c.*

263. *Long Chancery Lane*] The place where the offices of Chancery are kept. The long detention of clients in that court, and the difficulty of getting out, is humorously allegorized in these lines.

268. A just character of Sir Richard Blackmore knight, who (as Mr Dryden expresseth it)

> *Writ to the rumbling of his coach's wheels.*

and whose indefatigable muse produced no less than six epic poems: *Prince* and *King Arthur*, twenty books; *Eliza*, ten; *Alfred*, twelve; the *Redeemer*, six; besides *Job*, in folio; the whole book of Psalms; the *Creation*, seven books; *Nature of Man*, three books; and many more. 'Tis in this sense he is styled afterwards the *everlasting Blackmore*. Notwithstanding all which, Mr Gildon seems assured, that 'this admirable author did not think himself upon the *same foot* with *Homer*.' *Comp. Art of Poetry*, vol. i. p. 108.

But how different is the judgment of the author of *Characters of the Times*, p. 25, who says, 'Sir Richard Blackmore is unfortunate in happening to mistakè his proper talents; and that he has not for many years been *so much as named*, or even *thought of* among writers.' Even Mr Dennis differs greatly from his friend Mr Gildon: 'Blackmore's *action* (saith he) has neither unity, nor integrity, nor morality, nor universality; and consequently he can have no *fable*, and no *heroic poem*. His narration

This labour past, by Bridewell° all descend,
(As morning prayer, and flagellation end)   270
To where Fleet Ditch with disemboguing° streams
Rolls the large tribute of dead dogs to Thames,

is neither probable, delightful, nor wonderful; his characters have none of the necessary qualifications; the things contained in his narration are neither in their own
nature delightful, nor numerous enough, nor rightly disposed, nor surprising, nor
pathetic.'—Nay he proceeds so far as to say Sir Richard has *no genius*; first laying
down, that 'Genius is caused by a *furious joy* and *pride of soul*, on the conception of
an *extraordinary hint*. Many men (says he) have their *hints*, without these motions of
fury and *pride of soul*, because they want fire enough to agitate their spirits; and these
we call cold writers. Others who have a great deal of fire, but have not excellent
organs, feel the forementioned *motions*, without the *extraordinary hints*; and these we
call fustian writers.' But he declares that 'Sir Richard had neither the *hints*, nor the
motions'. *Remarks on Pr. Arth.*, octavo, 1696. Preface.

This gentleman in his first works abused the character of Mr Dryden; and in his
last, of Mr Pope, accusing him in very high and sober terms of profaneness and
immorality (*Essay on Polite Writing*, vol. ii. p. 270) on a mere report from Edm. Curll,
that he was author of a travesty on the first Psalm. Mr Dennis took up the same
report, but with the addition of what Sir Richard had neglected, an *argument to prove
it*; which being very curious, we shall here transcribe. 'It *was* he who burlesqued the
Psalm of David. It is *apparent* to me that Psalm was burlesqued by a *Popish rhymester*.
Let rhyming persons who have been brought up *Protestants* be otherwise what they
will, let them be rakes, let them be scoundrels, let them be *atheists*, yet education
has made an invincible impression on them in behalf of the sacred writings. But a
Popish rhymester has been brought up with a contempt for those sacred writings; now
show me another *Popish rhymester* but he.' This manner of argumentation is usual
with Mr Dennis; he has employed the same against Sir Richard himself, in a like
charge of *impiety* and *irreligion*. 'All Mr Blackmore's celestial machines, as they
cannot be defended so much as by common received opinion, so are they directly
contrary to the doctrine of the church of England; for the visible descent of an angel
must be a miracle. Now it is the doctrine of the Church of England that miracles
had ceased a long time before Prince Arthur came into the world. Now if the doctrine
of the Church of England be true, as we are obliged to believe, then are all the
celestial machines in Prince Arthur unsufferable, as wanting not only human, but
divine probability. But if the machines are sufferable, that is if they have so much
as divine probability, then it follows of necessity that the doctrine of the Church is
false. So I leave it to every impartial clergyman to consider,' etc. Preface to the
Remarks on Prince Arthur.

270. It is between eleven and twelve in the morning, after church service, that
the criminals are whipped in Bridewell.—This is to mark punctually the *time* of the
day: Homer does it by the circumstance of the judges rising from court, or of the
labourer's dinner; our author by one very proper both to the *persons* and the *scene* of
his poem, which we may remember commenced in the evening of the Lord Mayor's
Day. The first book passed in that *night*; the next *morning* the games begin in the
Strand, thence along Fleet Street (places inhabited by booksellers) then they proceed
by Bridewell toward Fleet Ditch, and lastly through Ludgate to the City and the
Temple of the Goddess.

The King of dykes! than whom no sluice of mud
With deeper sable blots the silver flood.
'Here strip, my children! here at once leap in,
Here prove who best can dash through thick and thin,
And who the most in love of dirt excel,
Or dark dexterity of groping well.
Who flings most filth, and wide pollutes around
The stream, be his the *Weekly Journals* bound,   280
A pig° of lead to him who dives the best;
A peck of coals apiece shall glad the rest.'
    In naked majesty Oldmixon stands,

273.   *Fluviorum rex Eridanus,*
                    ——*quo non alius, per pinguia culta,*
                    In mare purpureum violentior influit amnis.
                                                        Virgil.

276, 277, 278. —*dash through thick and thin,*—*love of dirt*—*dark dexterity*] The
three chief qualifications of party-writers; to stick at nothing, to delight in flinging
dirt, and to slander in the dark by guess.

280. *the Weekly Journals*] Papers of news and scandal intermixed, on different
sides and parties, and frequently shifting from one side to the other, called the
London Journal, British Journal, Daily Journal, etc. the concealed writers of which for
some time were Oldmixon, Roome, Arnall, Concanen, and others; persons never
seen by our author.

282. Our indulgent poet, whenever he has spoken of any dirty or low work,
constantly puts us in mind of the *poverty* of the offenders, as the only extenuation of
such practices. Let anyone but remark, when a thief, a pickpocket, an highwayman,
or a knight of the post are spoken of how much our hate to those characters is
lessened, if they add a *needy* thief, a *poor* pickpocket, an *hungry* highwayman, a *starving*
knight of the post, etc.

283. Mr John Oldmixon, next to Mr Dennis, the most ancient critic of our
nation; an unjust censurer of Mr Addison in his prose *Essay on Criticism*, whom also
in his imitation of Bouhours (called the *Arts of Logic and Rhetoric*) he misrepresents
in plain matter of fact; for in p. 45 he cites the *Spectator* as abusing Dr Swift by
name, where there is not the least hint of it; and in p. 304 is so injurious as to
suggest, that Mr Addison himself writ that *Tatler*, No. 43. which says of his own
simile, that ' 'Tis as great as ever entered into the mind of man.' 'In poetry he was
not so happy as laborious, and therefore characterised by the *Tatler*, No. 62. by the
name of *Omicron* the *unborn poet*,' Curll, *Key*, p. 13. 'He writ dramatic works, and a
volume of poetry, consisting of heroic epistles, etc. some whereof are very well done,'
saith that great judge Mr Jacob, in his *Lives of Poets*, vol. ii. p. 303.

In his *Essay on Criticism*, and the *Arts of Logic and Rhetoric*, he frequently reflects
on our author. But the top of his character was a perverter of history, in that
scandalous one of the Stuarts, in folio, and his *Critical History of England*, two
volumes, octavo. Being employed by Bishop Kennet, in publishing the historians in
his collection, he falsified Daniel's chronicle in numberless places. Yet this very

And Milo-like surveys his arms and hands;
Then sighing, thus, 'And am I now three score?
Ah why, ye gods! should two and two make four?'
He said, and climbed a stranded lighter's° height,
Shot to the black abyss, and plunged downright.
The senior's judgment all the crowd admire,
Who but to sink the deeper, rose the higher.   290
    Next Smedley dived; slow circles dimpled o'er
The quaking mud, that closed, and oped no more.
All look, all sigh, and call on Smedley lost;
'Smedley' in vain resounds through all the coast.

man, in the preface to the first of these books, advanced a *particular fact* to charge three eminent persons of falsifying the Lord Clarendon's *History*; which fact has been disproved by Dr Atterbury, late Bishop of Rochester, then the only survivor of them; and the particular part he pretended to be falsified, produced since, after almost ninety years, in that noble author's original manuscript. He was all his life a virulent party-writer for hire, and received his reward in a small place, which he enjoyed to his death.

He is here likened to Milo, in allusion to that verse of Ovid,

> —*Fletque Milon senior, cum spectat inanes*
> *Herculeis similes, fluidos pendere lacertos;*

either with regard to his age, or because he was undone by trying to pull to pieces an oak that was too strong for him.

> ——*Remember Milo's end*
> *Wedged in that timber which he strove to rend.*
>
> Lord Roscommon.

286. Very reasonably doth this ancient critic complain. Without doubt it was a fault in the constitution of things, For the *world*, as a great writer saith, *being given to man for a subject of disputation*, he might think himself mocked with a penurious gift, were any thing made certain. Hence those superior masters of wisdom, the *Sceptics* and *Academics*, reasonably conclude that *two and two do not make four*.

SCRIBL.

But we need not go so far, to remark what the poet principally intended, the absurdity of complaining of *old age*, which must necessarily happen, as long as we are indulged in our desires of adding one year to another.

291. *Next Smedley dived;*] The person here mentioned, an Irishman, was author and publisher of many scurrilous pieces, a weekly *Whitehall Journal*, in the year 1722, in the name of Sir James Baker; and particularly whole volumes of Billingsgate against Dr Swift and Mr Pope, called *Gulliveriana* and *Alexandriana*, printed in octavo, 1728.

293.   *Alcides wept in vain for Hylas lost,*
          Hylas, in vain, resounds through all the coast.

          Lord Roscommon. Translat. of Virgil's 6th Ecl.

Then *° essayed; scarce vanished out of sight,
He buoys up instant, and returns to light:
He bears no token of the sabler streams,
And mounts far off among the swans of Thames.
True to the bottom, see Concanen creep,
A cold, long-winded, native of the deep: 300
If perseverance gain the diver's prize,
Not everlasting Blackmore this denies:
No noise, no stir, no motion canst thou make,
Th' unconscious stream sleeps o'er thee like a lake.
Next plunged a feeble, but a desperate pack,
With each a sickly brother at his back:
Sons of a day! just buoyant on the flood,
Then numbered with the puppies in the mud.
Ask ye their names? I could as soon disclose
The names of these blind puppies as of those.   310
Fast by, like Niobe° (her children gone)
Sits Mother Osborne,° stupefied to stone!
And monumental brass this record bears,

295. *Then * essayed;*] A gentleman of genius and spirit, who was secretly dipped in some papers of this kind, on whom our poet bestows a panegyric instead of a satire, as deserving to be better employed than in party-quarrels and personal invectives.

299. MATTHEW CONCANEN, an Irishman, bred to the law. Smedley (one of his brethren in enmity to Swift) in his *Metamorphosis of Scriblerus*, p. 7 accuses him of 'having boasted of what he had not written, but others had revised and done for him.' He was author of several dull and dead scurrilities in the *British* and *London Journals*, and in a paper called the *Speculatist*. In a pamphlet, called a *Supplement to the Profound*, he dealt very unfairly with our poet, not only frequently imputing to him Mr Broome's verses (for which he might indeed seem in some degree accountable, having corrected what that gentleman did) but those of the Duke of Buckingham, and others: to this rare piece somebody humorously caused him to take for his motto, *De profundis clamavi*. He was since a hired scribbler in the *Daily Courant*, where he poured forth much Billingsgate against the Lord Bolingbroke, and others; after which this man was surprisingly promoted to administer justice and law in Jamaica.

302. *Nec bonus Eurytion praelato invidit honori, &c.* Virgil, *Aen.* v.

306, 307. These were daily papers, a number of which, to lessen the expense, were printed one on the back of another.

311. *like Niobe*] See the story in Ovid, *Met.* vii., where the miserable petrefaction of this old lady is pathetically described.

312. *Osborne*] A name assumed by the eldest and gravest of these writers, who at last being ashamed of his pupils, gave his paper over, and in his age remained silent.

'These are,—ah no! these were, the *Gazetteers*!'
Not so bold Arnall; with a weight of skull,
Furious he dives, precipitately dull.
Whirlpools and storms his circling arm invest,

314. We ought not to suppress that a modern critic here taxeth the poet with an anachronism, affirming these *Gazetteers* not to have lived within the time of his poem, and challenging us to produce any such paper of that date. But we may with equal assurance assert, these *Gazetteers* not to have lived since, and challenge all the learned world to produce one such paper at this day. Surely therefore, where the point is so obscure, our author ought not to be censured too rashly. SCRIBL.

Notwithstanding this affected ignorance of the good Scriblerus, the *Daily Gazetteer* was a title given very properly to certain papers, each of which lasted but a day. Into this, as a common sink, was received all the trash, which had been before dispersed in several journals, and circulated at the public expense of the nation. The authors were the same obscure men; though sometimes relieved by occasional essays from statesmen, courtiers, bishops, deans, and doctors. The meaner sort were rewarded with money; others with places or benefices, from an hundred to a thousand a year. It appears from the *Report of the Secret Committee for enquiring into the Conduct of R. Earl of O.* 'That no less than *fifty thousand, seventy-seven pounds, eighteen shillings*, were paid to authors and printers of newspapers, such as *Free Britons, Daily Courants, Corn Cutter's Journals, Gazetteers*, and other political papers, between Feb. 10, 1731. and Feb. 10, 1741.' Which shows the benevolence of one minister to have expended, for the current dulness of ten years in Britain, double the sum which gained Louis XIV so much honour, in annual pensions to learned men all over Europe. In which, and in a much longer time, not a pension at Court, nor preferment in the church or universities, of any consideration, was bestowed on any man distinguished for his learning separately from party-merit, or pamphlet-writing.

It is worth a reflection, that of all the panegyrics bestowed by these writers on this great minister, not one is at this day extant or remembered; nor even so much credit done to his personal character by all they have written, as by one short occasional compliment of our author.

> *Seen him I have; but in his happier hour*
> *Of social pleasure, ill exchanged for* power!
> *Seen him, uncumbered by the venal tribe,*
> *Smile without* art, *and win without a* bribe.

315. WILLIAM ARNALL, bred an attorney, was a perfect genius in this sort of work. He began under twenty with furious party-papers; then succeeded Concanen in the *British Journal*. At the first publication of the *Dunciad*, he prevailed on the author not to give him his due place in it, by a letter professing his detestation of such practices as his predecessor's. But since, by the most unexampled insolence, and personal abuse of several great men, the poet's particular friends, he most amply deserved a niche in the temple of infamy: witness a paper, called the *Free Briton*, a dedication intituled 'To the Genuine Blunderer', 1732, and many others. He writ for hire, and valued himself upon it; not indeed without cause, it appearing by the aforesaid REPORT, that he received 'for *Free Britons*, and other writings, in the space of *four years*, no less than *ten thousand nine hundred and ninety-seven pounds, six shillings, and eight pence*, out of the Treasury.'

With all the might of gravitation blessed:
No crab more active in the dirty dance,
Downward to climb, and backward to advance.   320
He brings up half the bottom on his head,
And loudly claims the journals and the lead.

    The plunging prelate, and his ponderous Grace,
With holy envy gave one layman place.
When lo! a burst of thunder shook the flood.
Slow rose a form, in majesty of mud;
Shaking the horrors of his sable brows,
And each ferocious feature grim with ooze.
Greater he looks, and more than mortal stares:
Then thus the wonders of the deep declares.   330

    First he relates, how sinking to the chin,
Smit with his mien, the mud-nymphs sucked him in:
How young Lutetia, softer than the down,
Nigrina black, and Merdamante° brown,
Vied for his love in jetty bowers below,
As Hylas° fair was ravished long ago.
Then sung, how shown him by the nut-brown maids
A branch of Styx here rises from the shades,

329. Virgil, *Aen.* vi. of the Sibyl:

   ——*majorque videri,*
   Nec mortale sonans—

336. *As Hylas fair*] Who was ravished by the water-nymphs and drawn into the river. The story is told at large by Valerius Flaccus, lib. 3. *Argon.* See Virgil, *Ecl.* vi.

338. *A branch of Styx, &c.*] Homer, *Il.* ii. Catal.

   Οἵ τ' ἀμφ' ἱμερτὸν Τιταρήσιον ἔργ' ἐνέμοντο
   Ὅς ῥ' ἐς Πηνειὸν προΐεε καλλίρροον ὕδωρ
   Οὐδ' ὅγε Πηνειῷ συμμίσγεται ἀργυροδίνῃ,
   Ἀλλά τέ μιν καθύπερθεν ἐπιρρέει ἠΰτ' ἔλαιον·
   Ὅρκου γὰρ δεινοῦ Στυγὸς ὕδατός ἐστιν ἀπορρώξ.

Of the land of dreams in the same region, he makes mention, *Odyss.* xxiv. See also Lucian's *True History. Lethe* and the *Land of Dreams* allegorically represent the *stupefaction* and *visionary madness of* poets, equally dull and extravagant. Of Alphaeus' waters gliding secretly under the sea of Pisa, to mix with those of Arethuse in Sicily, see Moschus, *Idyll.* viii., Virgil, *Ecl.* x.

   Sic tibi, cum fluctus subter labere Sicanos,
   Doris amara suam non intermisceat undam.

And again, *Aen.* 3.

   ——*Alphaeum, fama est, huc Elidis amnem*
   Occultas egisse vias, subter mare, qui nunc
   Ore, Arethusa, tuo Siculis confunditur undis.

That tinctured as it runs with Lethe's streams,
And wafting vapours from the land of dreams,   340
(As under seas Alpheus'° secret sluice
Bears Pisa's offerings to his Arethuse)
Pours into Thames: and hence the mingled wave
Intoxicates the pert, and lulls the grave:
Here brisker vapours o'er the Temple creep,
There, all from Paul's to Aldgate° drink and sleep.

　　Thence to the banks where reverend bards repose,
They led him soft; each reverend bard arose;
And Milbourne chief, deputed by the rest,
Gave him the cassock, surcingle,° and vest.   350
'Receive', he said, 'these robes which once were mine,
Dulness is sacred in a sound divine.'

　　He ceased, and spread the robe; the crowd confess,°
The reverend flamen° in his lengthened dress.
Around him wide a sable army stand,
A low-born, cell-bred, selfish, servile band,
Prompt or to guard or stab, to saint or damn,
Heaven's Swiss,° who fight for any god, or man.

347.　　　　*Tum canit errantem Permessi ad flumina Gallum,*
　　　　　　Utque viro Phoebi chorus assurrexerit omnis;
　　　　　　Ut Linus haec illi divino carmine pastor,
　　　　　　Floribus atque apio crines ornatus amaro,
　　　　　　Dixerit, Hos tibi dant calamos, en accipe, Musae,
　　　　　　Ascraeo quos ante seni——&c.

349. *And Milbourne*] Luke Milbourne, a clergyman, the fairest of critics; who, when he wrote against Mr Dryden's Virgil, did him justice in printing at the same time his own translations of him, which were intolerable. His manner of writing has a great resemblance with that of the gentlemen of the *Dunciad* against our author, as will be seen in the parallel of Mr Dryden and him.

355. *Around him wide, etc.*] It is to be hoped that the satire in these lines will be understood in the confined sense in which the author meant it, of such only of the clergy, who, though solemnly engaged in the service of religion, dedicate themselves for venal and corrupt ends to that of ministers or factions; and though educated under an entire ignorance of the world, aspire to interfere in the government of it, and, consequently, to disturb and disorder it; in which they fall short only of their predecessors, when invested with a larger share of power and authority, which they employed indifferently (as is hinted at in the lines above) either in supporting arbitrary power, or in exciting rebellion; in canonizing the vices of tyrants, or in blackening the virtues of patriots; in corrupting religion by superstition, or betraying it by libertinism, as either was thought best to serve the ends of policy, or flatter the follies of the great.

Through Lud's famed gates,° along the well-known
      Fleet
Rolls the black troop, and overshades the street,   360
Till showers of sermons, characters, essays,
In circling fleeces whiten all the ways:
So clouds replenished from some bog below,
Mount in dark volumes, and descend in snow.
Here stopped the Goddess; and in pomp proclaims
A gentler exercise to close the games.
      'Ye critics! in whose heads, as equal scales,
I weigh what author's heaviness prevails;
Which most conduce to soothe the soul in slumbers,
My Henley's periods, or my Blackmore's numbers;   370
Attend the trial we propose to make:
If there be man, who o'er such works can wake,
Sleep's all-subduing charms who dares defy,
And boasts Ulysses' ear with Argus' eye;°
To him we grant our amplest powers to sit
Judge of all present, past, and future wit;
To cavil, censure, dictate, right or wrong,
Full and eternal privilege of tongue.'
      Three college sophs,° and three pert templars° came,
The same their talents, and their tastes the same;   380
Each prompt to query, answer, and debate,
And smit with love of poesy and prate.
The ponderous books two gentle readers bring;
The heroes sit, the vulgar form a ring.

---

359. 'King Lud repairing the City, called it, after his own name, Lud's Town;
the strong gate which he built in the west part he likewise, for his own honour,
named Ludgate. In the year 1260. this gate was beautified with images of Lud and
other Kings. Those images in the reign of Edward VI. had their heads smitten off,
and were otherwise defaced by unadvised folks. Queen Mary did set new heads
upon their old bodies again. The 28th of Queen Elizabeth the same gate was clean
taken down, and newly and beautifully builded, with images of Lud and others, as
afore.' *Stow*'s Survey of London.

374. See Homer, *Odyss.* xii. Ovid, *Met.* i.

380, 381. *Ambo florentes aetatibus, Arcades ambo,*
            Et cantare pares, & respondere parati.
                              Virgil, *Ecl.* vii.

382. *Smit with the love of sacred song—* Milton.

384. *Consedere duces, & vulgi stante corona.* Ovid, *Met.* xiii.

The clamorous crowd is hushed with mugs of mum,°
Till all tuned equal, send a general hum.
Then mount the clerks, and in one lazy tone
Through the long, heavy, painful page drawl on;
Soft creeping, words on words, the sense compose,
At every line they stretch, they yawn, they doze.   390
As to soft gales top-heavy pines bow low
Their heads, and lift them as they cease to blow:
Thus oft they rear, and oft the head decline,
As breathe, or pause, by fits, the airs divine.
And now to this side, now to that they nod,
As verse, or prose, infuse the drowsy god.
Thrice Budgell aimed to speak, but thrice suppressed
By potent Arthur,° knocked his chin and breast.
Toland and Tindal, prompt at priests to jeer,
Yet silent bowed to Christ's no kingdom° here.   400
Who sate the nearest, by the words o'ercome,
Slept first; the distant nodded to the hum.
Then down are rolled the books; stretched o'er 'em lies
Each gentle clerk, and muttering seals his eyes.
As what a Dutchman plumps into the lakes,

388. 'All these lines very well imitate the slow drowsiness with which they pro-ceed. It is impossible to anyone, who has a poetical ear, to read them without perceiving the heaviness that lags in the verse, to imitate the action it describes. The simile of the pines is very just and well adapted to the subject;' says an enemy, in his *Essay on the Dunciad*, p. 21.

397. *Budgell*] Famous for his speeches on many occasions about the South Sea scheme, etc. 'He is a very ingenious gentleman, and hath written some excellent epilogues to plays, and *one small* piece on love, which is very pretty.' Jacob, *Lives of Poets*, vol. ii. p. 289. But this gentleman since made himself much more eminent, and personally well-known to the greatest statesmen of all parties, as well as to all the courts of law in this nation.

399. *Toland and Tindal*] Two persons, not so happy as to be obscure, who writ against the religion of their country.

400. This is said by Curll, *Key to Dunc.*, to allude to a sermon of a reverend bishop.

405. It is a common and foolish mistake, that a ludicrous parody of a grave and celebrated passage is a ridicule to that passage. The reader therefore, if he will, may call this a parody of the author's own similitude in the *Essay on Man*, Ep. iv.

As the small pebble, &c.

but will anybody therefore suspect the one to be a ridicule of the other? A ridicule indeed there is in every parody; but when the image is transferred from one subject to another, and the subject is not a *poem burlesqued* (which Scriblerus hopes the

One circle first, and then a second makes;
What Dulness dropped among her sons impressed
Like motion from one circle to the rest;
So from the midmost the nutation° spreads
Round and more round, o'er all the sea of heads.   410
At last Centlivre felt her voice to fail,
Motteux himself unfinished left his tale,
Boyer the state, and Law the stage gave o'er,
Morgan and Mandeville could prate no more;

reader will distinguish from a *burlesque poem*) there the ridicule falls not on the thing *imitated*, but *imitating*. Thus, for instance, when

> *Old Edward's armour beams on Cibber's breast,*

it is, without doubt, an object ridiculous enough. But I think it falls neither on old king Edward, nor his armour, but on his *armour-bearer* only. Let this be said to explain our author's parodies (a figure that has always a good effect in a mock epic poem) either from profane or sacred writers.

410. *A waving sea of heads was round me spread,*
     And still fresh streams the gazing deluge fed.
                         Blackmore, *Job.*

411. Mrs Susannah Centlivre, wife to Mr Centlivre, Yeoman of the Mouth to his Majesty. She writ many plays, and a song (says Mr Jacob, vol. i. p. 32) before she was seven years old. She also writ a ballad against Mr Pope's Homer, before he begun it.

413. A. Boyer, a voluminous compiler of annals, political collections, *&c.*—William Law, A. M. wrote with great zeal against the stage; Mr Dennis answered with as great: their books were printed in 1726. Mr Law affirmed, that 'The playhouse is the temple of the devil; the peculiar pleasure of the devil; where all they who go, yield to the devil; where all the laughter is a laughter among devils; and all who are there are hearing music in the very porch of hell.' To which Mr Dennis replied, that 'There is every jot as much difference between a true play, and one made by a poetaster, as between two *religious books*, the *Bible* and the *Alcoran.*' Then he demonstrates, that 'All those who had written against the stage were *Jacobites* and *Non-jurors*; and did it always at a time when something was to be done for the *Pretender*. Mr Collier published his *Short View* when France declared for the Chevalier; and his dissuasive, just at the *great storm*, when the devastation which that hurricane wrought, had amazed and astonished the minds of men, and made them obnoxious to melancholy and desponding thoughts. Mr Law took the opportunity to attack the stage upon the great preparations he heard were making abroad, and which the *Jacobites* flattered themselves were designed in their favour. And as for Mr Bedford's *Serious Remonstrance*, though I know nothing of the time of publishing it, yet I dare to lay odds it was either upon the Duke d'Aumont's being at Somerset House, or upon the *late Rebellion.*' DENNIS, *Stage defended against Mr Law*, p. ult.

414. *Morgan*] A writer against religion, distinguished no otherwise from the rabble of his tribe than by the pompousness of his title; for having stolen his morality from Tindal, and his philosophy from Spinoza, he calls himself, by the courtesy of England, a *moral philosopher.*

Norton, from Daniel and Ostroea sprung,
Blessed with his father's front,° and mother's tongue,
Hung silent down his never-blushing head;
And all was hushed, as folly's self lay dead.

    Thus the soft gifts of sleep conclude the day,
And stretched on bulks,° as usual, poets lay.   420
Why should I sing what bards the nightly muse
Did slumbering visit, and convey to stews;
Who prouder marched, with magistrates in state,
To some famed round-house,° ever open gate!
How Henley lay inspired beside a sink,°
And to mere mortals seemed a priest in drink:
While others, timely, to the neighbouring Fleet°
(Haunt of the muses) made their safe retreat.

The End of the SECOND BOOK

Ibid. *Mandeville*] This writer, who prided himself as much in the reputation of an *immoral philosopher*, was author of a famous book called the *Fable of the Bees*; which may seem written to prove, that moral virtue is the invention of knaves, and Christian virtue the imposition of fools; and that vice is necessary, and alone sufficient to render society flourishing and happy.

415. Norton Defoe, offspring of the famous Daniel. *Fortes creantur fortibus*. One of the authors of the *Flying Post*, in which well-bred work Mr P. had sometime the honour to be abused with his betters; and of many hired scurrilities and daily papers, to which he never set his name.

418. Alludes to Dryden's verse in the *Indian Emperor*:

> *All things are hushed, as Nature's self lay dead.*

426. This line presents us with an excellent moral, that we are never to pass judgment merely by *appearances*; a lesson to all men who may happen to see a reverend person in the like situation, not to determine too rashly; since not only the poets frequently describe a bard inspired in this posture,

> (*On Cam's fair bank, where Chaucer lay inspired*,

and the like) but an eminent casuist tells us, that 'if a priest be seen in any indecent action, we ought to account it a deception of sight, or illusion of the devil, who sometimes takes upon him the shape of holy men on purpose to cause scandal.'

                                                 SCRIBL.

427. *Fleet*] A prison for insolvent debtors on the bank of the Ditch.

THE

DUNCIAD

BOOK the THIRD

ARGUMENT

*After the other persons are disposed in their proper places of rest, the Goddess
transports the King to her temple, and there lays him to slumber with his
head on her lap; a position of marvellous virtue,° which causes all the visions
of wild enthusiasts, projectors, politicians, inamoratos, castle-builders, chem-
ists, and poets. He is immediately carried on the wings of fancy, and led by a
mad poetical sibyl, to the Elysian shade; where, on the banks of Lethe, the
souls of the dull are dipped by Bavius, before their entrance into this world.
There he is met by the ghost of Settle, and by him made acquainted with the
wonders of the place, and with those which he himself is destined to perform.
He takes him to a mount of vision, from whence he shows him the past
triumphs of the empire of Dulness, then the present, and lastly the future:
how small a part of the world was ever conquered by science, how soon those
conquests were stopped, and those very nations again reduced to her dominion.
Then distinguishing the island of Great Britain, shows by what aids, by what
persons, and by what degrees it shall be brought to her empire. Some of the
persons he causes to pass in review before his eyes, describing each by his proper
figure, character, and qualifications. On a sudden the scene shifts, and a vast
number of miracles and prodigies appear, utterly surprising and unknown to
the King himself, till they are explained to be the wonders of his own reign
now commencing. On this subject Settle breaks into a congratulation, yet not
unmixed with concern, that his own times were but the types of these. He
prophesies how first the nation shall be overrun with farces, operas, and shows;
how the throne of Dulness shall be advanced over the theatres, and set up
even at* court: then how her sons shall preside in the seats of* arts *and*
sciences: *giving a glimpse, or Pisgah-sight of the future fullness of her glory,
the accomplishment whereof is the subject of the fourth and last book.*

> But in her temple's last recess enclosed,   1
> On Dulness' lap th' anointed head reposed.

Him close she curtains round with vapours blue,
And soft besprinkles with Cimmerian° dew.
Then raptures high the seat of sense o'erflow,
Which only heads refined from reason° know.
Hence, from the straw where Bedlam's prophet nods,
He hears loud oracles, and talks with gods:
Hence the fool's paradise, the statesman's scheme,
The air-built castle, and the golden dream,   10
The maid's romantic wish, the chemist's flame,°
And poet's vision of eternal fame.
 And now, on fancy's easy wing conveyed,
The King descending, views th' Elysian shade.°
A slipshod sibyl led his steps along,
In lofty madness meditating song;
Her tresses staring from poetic dreams,
And never washed, but in Castalia's streams.°

5, 6, *etc.* Hereby is intimated that the following vision is no more than the chimera of the dreamer's brain, and not a real or intended satire on the present age, doubtless more learned, more enlightened, and more abounding with great geniuses in divinity, politics, and whatever arts and sciences, than all the preceding. For fear of any such mistake of our poet's honest meaning, he hath again at the end of the vision repeated this monition, saying that it all passed through the *ivory gate*, which (according to the ancients) denoteth falsity. SCRIBL.

How much the good Scriblerus was mistaken, may be seen from the fourth book, which, it is plain from hence, he had never seen. BENTLEY.

7, 8. *Et varias audit voces, fruiturque deorum*
 Colloquio——
       Virgil, *Aen.* vii.

15. This allegory is extremely just, no conformation of the mind so much subjecting it to real *madness*, as that which produces real *dulness*. Hence we find the religious (as well as the poetical) enthusiasts of all ages were ever, in their natural state, most heavy and lumpish; but on the least application of *heat*, they run like lead, which of all metals falls quickest into fusion. Whereas *fire* in a genius is truly Promethean, it hurts not its constituent parts, but only fits it (as it does well-tempered steel) for the necessary impressions of art. But the common people have been taught (I do not know on what foundation) to regard lunacy as a mark of *wit*, just as the Turks and our modern Methodists do of *holiness*. But if the cause of madness assigned by a great philosopher be true, it will unavoidably fall upon the dunces. He supposes it to be the *dwelling over long on one object or idea*: now as this attention is occasioned either by grief or study, it will be fixed by dulness; which hath not quickness enough to comprehend what it seeks, nor force and vigour enough to divert the imagination from the object it laments.

Taylor, their better Charon, lends an oar,
(Once swan of Thames, though now he sings no more.)   20
Benlowes, propitious still to blockheads, bows;
And Shadwell nods the poppy on his brows.
Here, in a dusky vale where Lethe rolls,
Old Bavius sits, to dip poetic souls,
And blunt the sense, and fit it for a skull
Of solid proof,° impenetrably dull:
Instant, when dipped, away they wing their flight,

19. John Taylor the Water Poet, an honest man, who owns he learned not so much as the accidence: a rare example of modesty in a poet!

> *I must confess I do want eloquence,*
> *And never scarce did learn my accidence;*
> *For having got from* possum *to* posset,
> *I there was gravelled, could no farther get.*

He wrote fourscore books in the reign of James I and Charles I and afterwards (like Edward Ward) kept an alehouse in Long Acre. He died in 1654.

21. *Benlowes*] A country gentleman, famous for his own bad poetry, and for patronizing bad poets, as may be seen from many dedications of Quarles and others to him. Some of these anagrammed his name, *Benlowes* into *Benevolus*, to verify which, he spent his whole estate upon them.

22. Shadwell took opium for many years, and died of too large a dose, in the year 1692.

23.   ——*Videt Aeneas in valle reducta*
Seclusum nemus——
Lethaeumque domos placidas qui praenatat amnem, &c.
Hunc circum innumerae gentes, etc.

Virgil, *Aen.* vi.

24. Alluding to the story of Thetis dipping Achilles to render him impenetrable:

> *At pater Anchises penitus convalle virenti*
> *Inclusas animas, superumque ad lumen ituras,*
> *Lustrabat*——

Virgil, *Aen.* vi.

Bavius was an ancient poet, celebrated by Virgil for the like cause as Bays by our author, though not in so Christian-like a manner: for heathenishly it is declared by Virgil of Bavius, that he ought to be *hated* and *detested* for his evil works; *Qui Bavium non odit*; whereas we have often had occasion to observe our poet's great *good nature* and *mercifulness* through the whole course of this poem. SCRIBL.

Mr Dennis warmly contends, that Bavius was no inconsiderable author; nay, that 'He and Maevius had (even in Augustus's days) a very formidable party at Rome, who thought them much superior to Virgil and Horace: for', saith he 'I cannot believe they would have fixed that eternal brand upon them, if they had not been coxcombs in more than ordinary credit.' *Rem. on Pr. Arthur*, part ii. c. 1. An argument which, if this poem should last, will conduce to the honour of the gentlemen of the *Dunciad*.

Where Brown and Mears unbar the gates of Light,
Demand new bodies, and in calf's array,
Rush to the world, impatient for the day. 30
Millions and millions on these banks he views,
Thick as the stars of night, or morning dews,
As thick as bees o'er vernal blossoms fly,
As thick as eggs at Ward in pillory.
 Wondering he gazed: when lo! a sage appears,
By his broad shoulders known, and length of ears,

---

28. *Brown and Mears*] Booksellers, printers for anybody.—The allegory of the souls of the dull coming forth in the form of books, dressed in calf's leather, and being let abroad in vast numbers by booksellers, is sufficiently intelligible.
Unbar the gates of Light] An hemistich of Milton.

31, 32.   *Quam multa in sylvis autumni frigore primo*
    Lapsa cadunt folia, aut ad terram gurgite ab alto
    Quam multae glomerantur aves. etc.
             Virgil, *Aen.* vi.

34. John Ward of Hackney Esq., Member of Parliament, being convicted of forgery, was first expelled the House, and then sentenced to the pillory on the 17th of February 1727. Mr Curll (having likewise stood there) looks upon the mention of such a gentleman in a satire, as a *great act of barbarity*, *Key to the Dunc.* 3rd edit. p. 16. And another author reasons thus upon it. *Durgen.* 8vo. p. 11, 12. 'How unworthy is it of *Christian charity* to animate the *rabble* to abuse a *worthy man* in such a situation? what could move the poet thus to mention a *brave sufferer*, a *gallant prisoner*, exposed to the view of all mankind! It was laying aside his *senses*, it was committing a *crime*, for which the *law is deficient* not to punish him! nay, a crime which *man can scarce forgive*, or *time efface!* Nothing surely could have induced him to it but being bribed by a great Lady, *etc.*' (to whom this brave, honest, worthy gentleman was guilty of no offence but forgery, proved in open court.) But it is evident this verse could not be meant of him; it being notorious, that no *eggs* were thrown at that gentleman. Perhaps therefore it might be intended of Mr Edward Ward the poet when he stood there.

36. *And length of ears,*] This is a *sophisticated* reading. I think I may venture to affirm all the copyists are mistaken here: I believe I may say the same of the critics; Dennis, Oldmixon, Welsted have passed it in silence. I have also stumbled at it, and wondered how an error so manifest could escape such accurate persons. I dare assert it proceeded originally from the inadvertency of some transcriber, whose head run on the *pillory*, mentioned two lines before; it is therefore amazing that Mr Curll himself should overlook it! Yet that *scholiast* takes not the least notice hereof. That the learned Mist also read it thus, is plain from his ranging this passage among those in which our author was blamed for *personal satire* on a *man's face* (whereof doubtless he might take the *ear* to be a part;) so likewise Concanen, Ralph, the *Flying Post*, and all the herd of commentators.—*Tota armenta sequuntur.*
 A very little sagacity (which all these gentlemen therefore wanted) will restore us to the true sense of the poet, thus,
    By his broad shoulders known, and length of years.
See how easy a change; of one single letter! That Mr Settle was old, is most certain;

Known by the band° and suit which Settle wore
(His only suit) for twice three years before:
All as the vest, appeared the wearer's frame,
Old in new state, another yet the same.   40
Bland and familiar as in life, begun
Thus the great father to the greater son.
    'Oh, born to see what none can see awake!
Behold the wonders of th' oblivious lake.
Thou, yet unborn, hast touched this sacred shore;
The hand of Bavius drenched thee o'er and o'er.
But blind to former as to future fate,
What mortal knows his pre-existent state?
Who knows how long thy transmigrating soul
Might from Boeotian to Boeotian roll?   50
How many Dutchmen she vouchsafed to thrid?°
How many stages through old monks she rid?
And all who since, in mild benighted days,

but he was (happily) a stranger to the *pillory*. This note partly Mr THEOBALD's, partly
SCRIBL.

37. Elkanah Settle was once a writer in vogue, as well as Cibber, both for dramatic
poetry and politics. Mr Dennis tells us that 'he was a formidable rival to Mr
Dryden, and that in the University of Cambridge there were those who gave him
the *preference*.' Mr Welsted goes yet farther in his behalf: 'Poor Settle was formerly
the *mighty rival* of Dryden; nay, for *many years*, bore his reputation *above* him.' Pref.
to his *Poems*, 8vo. p. 31. And Mr Milbourne cried out, 'How little was Dryden able,
even when his blood run high, to defend himself against Mr Settle!' *Notes on Dryd.
Virg.* p. 175. These are comfortable opinions! and no wonder some authors indulge
them.

He was author or publisher of many noted pamphlets in the time of King Charles
II. He answered all Dryden's political poems; and being cried up on *one side*, suc-
ceeded not a little in his tragedy of the *Empress of Morocco* (the first that was ever
printed with cuts.) 'Upon this he grew insolent, the wits writ against his play, he
replied, and the town judged he had the better. In short, Settle was then thought a
very formidable rival to Mr Dryden; and not only the town but the University of
Cambridge was divided which to prefer; and in both places the younger sort inclined
to Elkanah.' DENNIS. Pref. to *Rem. on Hom.*

50. Boeotia lay under the ridicule of the wits formerly, as Ireland does now;
though it produced one of the greatest poets and one of the greatest generals of
Greece:

> *Boeotum crasso jurares aere natum.*
>   Horace.

Mixed the owl's ivy° with the poet's bays.
As man's meanders to the vital spring
Roll all their tides, then back their circles bring;
Or whirligigs, twirled round by skilful swain,
Suck the thread in, then yield it out again:
All nonsense thus, of old or modern date,
Shall in thee centre, from thee circulate.　　　　　　60
For this our Queen unfolds to vision true
Thy mental eye, for thou hast much to view:
Old scenes of glory, times long cast behind
Shall, first recalled, rush forward to thy mind:
Then stretch thy sight o'er all her rising reign,
And let the past and future fire thy brain.

Ascend this hill, whose cloudy point commands
Her boundless empire over seas and lands.
See, round the poles where keener spangles shine,
Where spices smoke beneath the burning line,°　　　70
(Earth's wide extremes) her sable flag displayed,
And all the nations covered in her shade!

Far eastward cast thine eye, from whence the sun
And orient science° their bright course begun:

54.　　——sine tempora circum
Inter victrices hederam tibi serpere lauros.
　　　　　　　　Virgil, Ecl. viii.

61, 62. This has a resemblance to that passage in Milton, book xi. where the angel

To nobler sights from Adam's eye removed
The film; then purged with euphrasie and rue
The visual nerve—For he had much to see.

There is a general allusion in what follows to that whole episode.

67. The scenes of this vision are remarkable for the order of their appearance. First, from ver. 67 to 73, those places of the globe are shown where science never rose; then from ver. 73 to 83, those where she was destroyed by tyranny; from ver. 85 to 95, by inundations of barbarians; from ver. 96 to 106, by superstition. Then Rome, the mistress of arts, described in her degeneracy; and lastly Britain, the scene of the action of the poem; which furnishes the occasion of drawing out the progeny of Dulness in review.

69. See round the poles, &c.] Almost the whole Southern and Northern continent wrapped in ignorance.

73. Our author favours the opinion that all sciences came from the Eastern nations.

One godlike monarch all that pride confounds,
He, whose long wall the wandering Tartar bounds;
Heavens! what a pile! whole ages perish there,
And one bright blaze turns learning into air.

Thence to the south extend thy gladdened eyes;
There rival flames with equal glory rise, 80
From shelves to shelves see greedy Vulcan roll,
And lick up all their physic of the soul.

How little, mark! that portion of the ball,
Where, faint at best, the beams of science fall:
Soon as they dawn, from Hyperborean° skies
Embodied dark, what clouds of Vandals rise!
Lo! where Maeotis° sleeps, and hardly flows
The freezing Tanais through a waste of snows,
The North by myriads pours her mighty sons,
Great nurse of Goths, of Alans and of Huns! 90
See Alaric's° stern port! the martial frame
Of Genseric!° and Attila's° dread name!
See the bold Ostrogoths° on Latium° fall;
See the fierce Visigoths° on Spain and Gaul!
See, where the morning gilds the palmy shore
(The soil that arts and infant letters bore)
His conquering tribes th' Arabian prophet draws,
And saving igrorance enthrones by laws.
See Christians, Jews, one heavy sabbath keep,
And all the western world believe and sleep. 100

Lo! Rome herself, proud mistress now no more
Of arts, but thundering against heathen lore;

75. Chi Ho-am-ti Emperor of China, the same who built the great wall between China and Tartary, destroyed all the books and learned men of that empire.

81, 82. The Caliph, Omar I, having conquered Egypt, caused his general to burn the Ptolemaean library, on the gates of which was this inscription, ΨΥΧΗΣ ΙΑΤΡΕΙΟΝ, the physic of the soul.

96. Phoenicia, Syria, *etc.* where letters are said to have been invented. In these countries Mahomet began his conquests.

102. 'A strong instance of this pious rage is placed to Pope Gregory's account. John of Salisbury gives a very odd encomium of this Pope, at the same time that he mentions one of the strangest effects of this excess of zeal in him: *Doctor sanctissimus ille Gregorius, qui melleo praedicationis imbre totam rigavit & inebriavit ecclesiam; non modo Mathesin jussit ab aula, sed, ut traditur a majoribus, incendio dedit probatae lectionis scripta, Palatinus quaecunque tenebat Apollo.* And in another place: *Fertur beatus Gregorius bibliothecam combussisse gentilem; quo divinae paginae gratior esset locus, & major*

Her grey-haired synods damning books unread,
And Bacon trembling for his brazen head.
Padua, with sighs, beholds her Livy° burn,
And ev'n th' Antipodes Vigilius° mourn.
See, the cirque° falls, th' unpillared temple nods,
Streets paved with heroes, Tiber choked with gods;
Till Peter's keys some christened Jove adorn,
And Pan to Moses lends his pagan horn;   110
See graceless Venus to a Virgin turned,
Or Phidias broken, and Apelles° burned.

Behold yon isle, by palmers, pilgrims trod,
Men bearded, bald, cowled, uncowled, shod, unshod,
Peeled, patched and piebald, linsey-wolsey° brothers,
Grave mummers! sleeveless some, and shirtless others.
That once was Britain—Happy! had she seen
No fiercer sons, had Easter never been.
In peace, great Goddess, ever be adored;
How keen the war, if Dulness draw the sword!   120
Thus visit not thy own! on this blessed age
Oh spread thy influence, but restrain thy rage.

And see, my son! the hour is on its way,
That lifts our Goddess to imperial sway;
This favourite isle, long severed from her reign,

authoritas, et diligentia studiosior. Desiderius Archbishop of Vienna was sharply reproved by him for teaching grammar and literature, and explaining the poets; because (says this Pope) *In uno se ore cum Jovis laudibus Christi laudes non capiunt: Et quam grave nefandumque sit Episcopis canere quod nec Laico religioso conveniat, ipse considera.* He is said, among the rest, to have burned Livy; *Quia in superstitionibus et sacris Romanorum perpetuo versatur.* The same Pope is accused by Vossius, and others, of having caused the noble monuments of the old Roman magnificence to be destroyed, lest those who came to Rome should give more attention to triumphal arches, *etc.* than to holy things.' Bayle, *Dict.*

109. After the government of Rome devolved to the Popes, their zeal was for some time exerted in demolishing the heathen temples and statues, so that the Goths scarce destroyed more monuments of antiquity out of rage, than these out of devotion. At length they spared some of the temples, by converting them to churches; and some of the statues, by modifying them into images of saints. In much later times, it was thought necessary to change the statues of Apollo and Pallas, on the tomb of Sannazarius, into David and Judith; the lyre easily became a harp, and the Gorgon's head turned to that of Holofernes.

117, 118. *Happy!—had Easter never been!*] Wars in England anciently, about the right time of celebrating Easter.

    Et fortunatam, si nunquam armenta fuissent. Virgil, *Ecl.* vi.

Dovelike, she gathers to her wings again.
Now look through fate! behold the scene she draws!
What aids, what armies to assert her cause!
See all her progeny, illustrious sight!
Behold, and count them, as they rise to light.   130
As Berecynthia,° while her offspring vie
In homage to the mother of the sky,
Surveys around her, in the blessed abode,
An hundred sons, and every son a god:
Not with less glory mighty Dulness crowned,
Shall take through Grub Street her triumphant round;
And her Parnassus glancing o'er at once,
Behold an hundred sons, and each a Dunce.
     Mark first that youth who takes the foremost place,
And thrusts his person full into your face.   140
With all thy Father's virtues blessed, be born!

126. This is fulfilled in the fourth book.

127, 129.   *Nunc age, Dardaniam prolem quae deinde sequatur*
                 Gloria, qui maneant Itala de gente nepotes,
                 Illustres animas, nostrumque in nomen ituras,
                 Expediam.

                                             Virgil, *Aen.* vi.

128. *What aids, what armies to assert her cause!*] i.e. of poets, antiquaries, critics,
divines, freethinkers. But as this revolution is only here set on foot by the first of
these classes, the poets, they only are here particularly celebrated, and they only
properly fall under the care and review of this colleague of Dulness, the Laureate.
The others, who finish the great work, are reserved for the fourth book, when the
Goddess herself appears in full glory.

131.   *Felix prole virûm, qualis Berecynthia mater*
                Invehitur curru Phrygias turrita per urbes,
                Laeta deûm partu, centum complexa nepotes,
                Omnes coelicolas, omnes supera alta tenentes.
                                             Virgil, *Aen.* vi.

139. *Ille vides, pura juvenis qui nititur hasta,*
     Proxima sorte tenet lucis loca——
                        Virgil, *Aen.* vi.

141. A manner of expression used by Virgil, *Ecl.* viii.

              Nascere! praeque diem veniens, age, Lucifer—

As also that of *patriis virtutibus, Ecl.* iv.

It was very natural to show to the hero, before all others, his own son, who had
already begun to emulate him in his theatrical, poetical, and even political capacities.
By the attitude in which he here presents himself, the reader may be cautioned
against ascribing wholly to the father the merit of the epithet *Cibberian*, which is
equally to be understood with an eye to the son.

And a new Cibber° shall the stage adorn.

A second see, by meeker manners known,
And modest as the maid that sips alone;
From the strong fate of drams if thou get free,
Another Durfey, Ward! shall sing in thee.
Thee shall each alehouse, thee each gillhouse° mourn,
And answering gin-shops sourer sighs return.

Jacob, the scourge of grammar, mark with awe,
Nor less revere him, blunderbuss of Law.   150
Lo Popple's brow, tremendous to the town,
Horneck's fierce eye, and Roome's funereal frown.

---

145. ——*si qua fata aspera rumpas,*
Tu Marcellus eris!——
Virgil, *Aen.* vi.

147. *Te nemus Angitiae, vitrea te Fucinus unda,*
Te liquidi flevere lacus.
Virgil, *Aen.* viii.

Virgil again, *Ecl.* x.
Illum etiam lauri, illum flevere myricae, etc.

149, 150. 'This *gentleman* is son of a *considerable maltster* of Romsey in South-amptonshire, and bred to the law under a *very eminent attorney:* who, between his *more laborious* studies, has *diverted* himself with poetry. He is a great admirer of poets and their works, which has occasioned him to try his genius that way.—He has writ in prose the *Lives of the Poets, Essays*, and a great many law books, *The Accomplished Conveyancer, Modern Justice, etc.*' GILES JACOB of himself, *Lives of Poets*, vol. 1. He very grossly, and unprovoked, abused in that book the author's friend, Mr Gay. There may seem some error in these verses, Mr Jacob having proved our author to have a *respect* for him, by this undeniable argument. 'He had once a *regard* for my *judgment;* otherwise he would never have subscribed *two guineas* to me, for one small book in octavo.' Jacob's *Letter to Dennis*, printed in Dennis's *Remarks on the Dunciad*, pag. 49. Therefore I should think the appellation of *blunderbuss* to Mr Jacob, like that of *thunderbolt* to Scipio, was meant in his honour.

Mr Dennis argues the same way. 'My writings having made great impression on the minds of all sensible men, Mr P. *repented*, and to *give proof of his repentance*, subscribed to my two volumes of select works, and afterward to my two volumes of letters.' Ibid. pag. 80. We should hence believe, the name of Mr Dennis hath also crept into this poem by some mistake. But from hence, gentle reader! thou mayst beware, when thou givest thy money to such authors, not to flatter thyself that thy motives are good nature or charity.

150. Virgil, *Aen.* vi.   ——*duo fulmina belli*
Scipiadas, cladem Libyae!

152. *Horneck and Roome*] These two were virulent party-writers, worthily coupled together, and one would think prophetically, since, after the publishing of this piece, the former dying, the latter succeeded him in *honour* and *employment*. The first was Philip Horneck, author of a Billingsgate paper called *The High German Doctor*.

Lo sneering Goode, half malice and half whim,
A fiend in glee, ridiculously grim.
Each cygnet sweet of Bath and Tunbridge race,
Whose tuneful whistling makes the waters pass:
Each songster, riddler, every nameless name,
All crowd, who foremost shall be damned to fame.
Some strain in rhyme; the muses, on their racks,
Scream like the winding of ten thousand jacks:°   160
Some free from rhyme or reason, rule or check,
Break Priscian's head,° and Pegasus's neck;
Down, down they larum,° with impetuous whirl,
The Pindars, and the Miltons of a Curll.
  Silence, ye wolves! while Ralph to Cynthia howls,
And makes night hideous—Answer him, ye owls!
  Sense, speech, and measure, living tongues and dead,
Let all give way—and Morris may be read.

Edward Roome was son of an undertaker for funerals in Fleet Street, and writ some of the papers called *Pasquin*, where by malicious innuendos he endeavoured to represent our author guilty of malevolent practices with a great man then under prosecution of Parliament. Popple was the author of some vile plays and pamphlets. He published abuses on our author in a paper called the *Prompter*.

  153. *Goode*] An ill-natured critic, who writ a satire on our author, called *The mock Aesop*, and many anonymous libels in newspapers for hire.

  156. There were several successions of these sort of minor poets, at Tunbridge, Bath, etc. singing the praise of the annuals flourishing for that season; whose names indeed would be nameless, and therefore the poet slurs them over with others in general.

  165. James Ralph, a name inserted after the first editions, not known to our author till he writ a swearing-piece called *Sawney*, very abusive of Dr Swift, Mr Gay, and himself. These lines allude to a thing of his, entitled, *Night*, a poem:

> ——*Visit thus the glimpses of the moon,*
> *Making night hideous*——
>
> Shakesp.

This low writer attended his own works with panegyrics in the journals, and once in particular praised himself highly above Mr Addison, in wretched remarks upon that author's account of English poets, printed in a *London Journal*, Sept. 1728. He ended at last in the common sink of all such writers, a political newspaper, to which he was recommended by his friend Arnall, and received a small pittance for pay.

  168. *Morris*] *Bezaleel*, see Book 2.

Flow Welsted, flow! like thine inspirer, beer,
Though stale, not ripe; though thin, yet never clear;   170
So sweetly mawkish, and so smoothly dull;
Heady, not strong; o'erflowing, though not full.
    Ah Dennis! Gildon ah! what ill-starred rage
Divides a friendship long confirmed by age?
Blockheads with reason wicked wits abhor,
But fool with fool is barbarous civil war.
Embrace, embrace my sons! be foes no more!

169. Parody on Denham, *Cooper's Hill.*

> *O could I flow like thee, and make thy stream*
> *My great example, as it is my theme:*
> *Though deep, yet clear; though gentle, yet not dull;*
> *Strong without rage; without o'erflowing, full.*

Welsted] Of this author see the remark on Book 2. ver. 209. But (to be impartial)
add to it the following different character of him:

'Mr *Welsted* had, in his youth, raised so great expectations of his future genius,
that there was a *kind of struggle* between the most eminent in the two Universities,
which should have the *honour* of his education. To *compound* this, he (*civilly*) became
a member of both, and after having passed some time at the one, he removed to the
other. From thence he returned to town, where he became the *darling expectation* of
all the polite writers, whose encouragement he acknowledged in his occasional
poems, in a manner that *will make no small part of the fame* of his protectors. It also
appears from his works, that he was happy in the patronage of the most illustrious
characters of the present age—encouraged by such a *combination* in his favour, he
—published a book a poems, some in the Ovidian, some in the Horatian manner,
in both which the most exquisite judges pronounce he even *rivalled his masters*—His
love verses have rescued that way of writing from contempt—In his translations, he
has given us the very soul and spirit of his author. His ode—his epistle—his verses
—his love tale—all, are the *most perfect things in all poetry.*' WELSTED of himself, *Char.
of the Times,* 8vo 1728. *pag.* 23, 24. It should not be forgot to his honour, that he
received at one time the sum of 500 pounds for secret service, among the other
excellent authors hired to write anonymously for the ministry. See *Report of the Secret
Committee,* etc. in 1742.

173. The reader, who has seen through the course of these notes, what a constant
attendance Mr Dennis paid to our author and all his works, may perhaps wonder
he should be mentioned but twice, and so slightly touched, in this poem. But in
truth he looked upon him with some esteem, for having (more generously than all
the rest) *set his name* to such writings. He was also a very old man at this time. By
his own account of himself in Mr Jacob's *Lives,* he must have been above three
score, and happily lived many years after. So that he was senior to Mr Durfey, who
hitherto of all our poets enjoyed the longest bodily life.

177. Virgil, *Aen.* vi.

> ——*Ne tanta animis assuescite bella,*
> *Neu patriae validas in viscera vertite vires:*
> *Tuque prior, tu parce—sanguis meus!*——

Nor glad vile poets with true critics' gore.

Behold yon pair,° in strict embraces joined;
How like in manners, and how like in mind!   180
Equal in wit, and equally polite,
Shall this a *Pasquin*, that a *Grumbler* write;
Like are their merits, like rewards they share,
That shines a consul, this commissioner.

179. Virgil, *Aen.* vi.

> *Illae autem paribus quas fulgere cernis in armis,*
> *Concordes animae—*

And in the fifth,

> *Euryalus, forma insignis viridique juventa,*
> *Nisus amore pio pueri.*

179. *Behold yon pair, etc.*] One of these was author of a weekly paper called *The Grumbler*, as the other was concerned in another called *Pasquin*, in which Mr Pope was abused with the Duke of Buckingham and Bishop of Rochester. They also joined in a piece against his first undertaking to translate the *Iliad*, entitled *Homerides*, by Sir Iliad Doggrel, printed 1715.

Of the other works of these gentlemen the world has heard no more, than it would of Mr Pope's, had their united laudable endeavours discouraged him from pursuing his studies. How few good works had ever appeared (since men of true merit are always the least presuming) had there been always such champions to stifle them in their conception? And were it not better for the public, that a million of monsters should come into the world, which are sure to die as soon as born, than that the serpents should strangle one Hercules in his cradle?   C.

After many editions of this poem, the author thought fit to omit the names of these two persons, whose injury to him was of so old a date. In the verses he omitted, it was said that one of them had a *pious passion* for the other. It was a literal translation of Virgil, *Nisus amore pio pueri*—and there, as in the original, applied to friendship: that between Nisus and Euryalus is allowed to make one of the most amiable episodes in the world, and surely was never interpreted in a perverse sense. But it will astonish the reader to hear, that on no other occasion than this line, a dedication was written to that gentleman to induce him to think something further. 'Sir, you are known to have all that affection for the beautiful part of the creation which God and Nature designed.—Sir, you have a very fine lady—and, Sir, you have eight very fine children,'—*etc.* [*Dedic.* to Dennis, *Rem. on the Rape of the Lock.*] The truth is, the poor dedicator's brain was turned upon this article: he had taken into his head, that ever since some books were written against the stage, and since the Italian Opera had prevailed, the nation was infected with a vice not fit to be named. He went so far as to print upon the subject, and concludes his argument with this remark, 'That he cannot help thinking the obscenity of plays excusable at this juncture; since, when that execrable sin is spread so wide, it may be of use to the reducing men's minds to the natural desire of women.' DENNIS, *Stage defended against* Mr *Law*, p. 20. Our author solemnly declared, he never heard any creature but the dedicator mention that vice and this gentleman together.

184. Such places were given at this time to such sort of writers.

'But who is he, in closet close y-pent,
Of sober face, with learned dust besprent?'
Right well mine eyes arede the myster wight,°
On parchment scraps y-fed, and Wormius hight.

185. Virgil, *Aen.* vi. questions and answers in this manner, of Numa:

> *Quis procul ille autem ramis insignis olivae,*
> *Sacra ferens?—nosco crines, incanaque menta, etc.*

187. *arede*] Read, or *peruse*; though sometimes used for *counsel*. 'READE THY READ, *take thy Counsaile*. Thomas Sternhold, in his translation of the first Psalm into English metre, hath *wisely* made use of this word,

> *The man is blest that hath not bent*
> *To wicked READ his ear.*

But in the last spurious editions of the singing Psalms the word READ is changed into *men*. I say *spurious* editions, because not only here, but quite throughout the whole book of Psalms, are *strange alterations*, all for the worse; and yet the title-page stands as it used to do! and all (which is *abominable* in any book, much more in a sacred work) is ascribed to Thomas Sternhold, John Hopkins, and others; I am confident, were Sternhold and Hopkins now living they would proceed against the innovators as cheats.—A liberty, which to say no more of their intolerable alterations, ought by no means to be permitted or approved of by such as are for *uniformity*, and have any regard for the *old* English Saxon tongue.' HEARNE, Gloss. on *Rob. of Gloc.* artic. REDE.

I do herein agree with Mr Hearne: little is it of avail to object, that such words are become *unintelligible*; since they are *truly English*, men ought to understand them; and such as are for *uniformity* should think all alterations in a language, *strange*, *abominable*, and *unwarrantable*. Rightly therefore, I say, again, hath our poet used ancient words, and poured them forth as a precious ointment upon good old Wormius in this place. SCRIBL.

Ibid. *myster wight*] Uncouth mortal.

188. *Wormius hight*] Let not this name, purely fictitious, be conceited to mean the learned Olaus Wormius; much less (as it was unwarrantably foisted into the surreptitious editions) our own antiquary Mr Thomas Hearne, who had no way aggrieved our poet, but on the contrary published many curious tracts which he hath to his great contentment perused.

Most rightly are *ancient words* here employed, in speaking of such who so greatly delight in the same. We may say not only rightly, but *wisely*, yea *excellently*, inasmuch as for the like practice the like praise is given by Mr Hearne himself. Glossar. to *Rob. of Gloucester*, artic. BEHETT; 'Others say BEHIGHT, *promised*, and so it is used *excellently well* by Thomas Norton, in his translation into metre of the 116th Psalm, ver. 14.

> *I to the Lord will pay my vows,*
> *That I to him BEHIGHT.*

Where the modern innovators, not understanding the propriety of the word (which is *truly English*, from the Saxon) have most *unwarrantably* altered it thus,

> *I to the Lord will pay my vows*
> *With joy and great delight.*'

188. *hight*.] 'In Cumberland they say to *hight*, for to *promise*, or *vow*; but HIGHT

To future ages may thy dulness last,
As thou preserv'st the dulness of the past!   190
   There, dim in clouds, the poring scholiasts mark,
Wits, who like owls, see only in the dark,
A lumberhouse of books in every head,
For ever reading, never to be read!
   But, where each science lifts its modern type,°
History her pot,° divinity her pipe,
While proud philosophy repines to show,
Dishonest sight! his breeches rent below;
Imbrowned with native bronze, lo! Henley stands,

usually signifies *was called*; and so it does in the North even to this day, notwithstanding what is done in Cumberland.' Hearne, ibid.

192. These few lines exactly describe the right verbal critic: the darker his author is, the better he is pleased; like the famous quack doctor, who put up in his bills, *he delighted in matters of difficulty*. Somebody said well of these men, that their heads were *libraries out of order*.

199. J. Henley the Orator; he preached on the Sundays upon theological matters, and on the Wednesdays upon all other sciences. Each auditor paid one shilling. He declaimed some years against the greatest persons, and occasionally did our author that honour. WELSTED, in *Oratory Transactions*, No. 1. published by Henley himself, gives the following account of him. 'He was born at Melton Mowbray in Leicestershire. From his own parish school he went to St John's College in Cambridge. He began there to be uneasy; for it *shocked* him to find he was *commanded to believe* against his own judgment in points of religion, philosophy, etc. for his genius leading him freely to *dispute all propositions*, and *call all points to account*, he was impatient under those fetters of the freeborn mind.—Being admitted to priest's orders, he found the examination very short and superficial, and that it was not *necessary to conform to the Christian religion*, in order either to *deaconship*, or *priesthood*.' He came to town, and after having for some years been a writer for booksellers, he had an ambition to be so for ministers of state. The only reason he did not rise in the Church, we are told, 'was the envy of others, and a disrelish entertained of him, because *he was not qualified to be a complete spaniel*.' However he offered the service of his pen to two great men, of opinions and interests directly opposite; by both of whom being rejected, he set up a new project, and styled himself the *restorer of ancient eloquence*. He thought 'it as lawful to take a licence from the King and Parliament at one place, as another; at Hickes' Hall, as at Doctors Commons; so set up his Oratory in Newport Market, Butcher Row. There,' says his friend, 'he had the *assurance* to form a plan, which no mortal ever thought of; he had success against all opposition; challenged his adversaries to fair disputations, and *none would dispute* with him; writ, read, and studied twelve hours a day; composed three dissertations a week on all subjects; undertook to teach in *one year* what schools and universities teach in *five*; was not terrified by menaces, insults, or satires, but still proceeded, matured his bold scheme, and put the *Church*, and *all that*, in *danger*.' WELSTED, Narrative in *Orat. Transact.* No. 1.

After having stood some prosecutions, he turned his rhetoric to buffoonery upon

Tuning his voice, and balancing his hands.   200
How fluent nonsense trickles from his tongue!
How sweet the periods, neither said, nor sung!
Still break the benches, Henley! with thy strain,
While Sherlock, Hare, and Gibson preach in vain.
Oh great restorer of the good old stage,
Preacher at once, and zany of thy age!
Oh worthy thou of Egypt's wise abodes,
A decent priest, where monkeys were the gods!
But fate with butchers placed thy priestly stall,
Meek modern faith to murder, hack, and maul;   210
And bade thee live, to crown Britannia's praise,
In Toland's, Tindal's, and in Woolston's days.
   Yet oh, my sons! a father's words attend:
(So may the fates preserve the ears you lend)
'Tis yours, a Bacon or a Locke to blame,
A Newton's genius, or a Milton's flame:
But oh! with one, immortal one dispense,
The source of Newton's light, of Bacon's sense!
Content, each emanation of his fires
That beams on earth, each virtue he inspires,   220
Each art he prompts, each charm he can create,
Whate'er he gives, are given for you to hate.
Persist, by all divine in man unawed,

all public and private occurrences. All this passed in the same room; where some-
times he broke jests, and sometimes that bread which he called the *Primitive Euchar-
ist.*—This wonderful person struck medals, which he dispersed as tickets to his
subscribers: the device, a star rising to the meridian, with this motto, AD SUMMA;
and below, INVENIAM VIAM AUT FACIAM. This man had an hundred pounds a year
given him for the secret service of a weekly paper of unintelligible nonsense, called
the *Hyp Doctor.*

   204. *Sherlock, Hare, Gibson*] Bishops of Salisbury, Chichester, and London.

   212. *Of Toland* and *Tindal*, see book 2. *Tho. Woolston* was an impious madman,
who wrote in a most insolent style against the miracles of the Gospel, in the years
1726, etc.

   213. The caution against blasphemy here given by a departed son of Dulness to
his yet existing brethren, is, as the poet rightly intimates, not out of tenderness to
the ears of others, but their own. And so we see that when that danger is removed,
on the open establishment of the Goddess in the fourth book, she encourages her
sons, and they beg assistance to pollute the source of light itself, with the same
virulence they had before done the purest emanations from it.

But, "Learn, ye DUNCES! not to scorn your GOD".'
   Thus he, for then a ray of reason stole
Half through the solid darkness of his soul;
But soon the cloud returned—and thus the sire:
'See now, what Dulness and her sons admire!
See what the charms, that smite the simple heart
Not touched by nature, and not reached by art.'   230
   His never-blushing head he turned aside,
(Not half so pleased when Goodman prophesied)
And looked, and saw a sable sorcerer° rise,
Swift to whose hand a winged volume flies:
All sudden, gorgons hiss, and dragons glare,
And ten-horned fiends and giants rush to war.
Hell rises, Heaven descends, and dance on earth:
Gods, imps, and monsters, music, rage, and mirth,
A fire, a jig, a battle, and a ball,
Till one wide conflagration swallows all.   240
   Thence a new world to nature's laws unknown,
Breaks out refulgent, with a heaven its own:
Another Cynthia° her new journey runs,
And other planets circle other suns.
The forests dance, the rivers upward rise,
Whales sport in woods, and dolphins in the skies;

---

224. Virgil, *Aen.* vi. puts this precept into the mouth of a wicked man, as here of a stupid one.

Discite justitiam moniti, & non temnere divos!

Ibid. '*not to scorn your God*'] See this subject pursued in Book 4.

232. Mr Cibber tells us, in his *Life*, p. 149. that Goodman being at the rehearsal of a play, in which he had a part, clapped him on the shoulder, and cried, 'If he does not make a good actor, I'll be d—d—.' And, says Mr Cibber, 'I make it a question, whether Alexander himself, or Charles the twelfth of Sweden, when at the head of their first victorious armies, could feel a greater transport in their bosoms than I did in mine.'

233. *a sable sorcerer*] Dr Faustus, the subject of a set of farces, which lasted in vogue two or three seasons, in which both playhouses strove to outdo each other for some years. All the extravagancies in the sixteen lines following were introduced on the stage, and frequented by persons of the first quality in England, to the twentieth and thirtieth time.

237. This monstrous absurdity was actually represented in Tibbald's *Rape of Proserpine*.

244.   ——*solemque* suum, sua *sidera norunt*——   Virgil, *Aen.* vi.

246.   *Delphinum sylvis appingit, fluctibus aprum.*   Horace.

And last, to give the whole creation grace,
Lo! one vast egg produces human race.
   Joy fills his soul, joy innocent of thought;
'What power,' he cries, 'what power these wonders
        wrought?   250
Son; what thou seekst is in thee! Look, and find
Each monster meets his likeness in thy mind.
Yet wouldst thou more? In yonder cloud behold,
Whose sarsenet° skirts are edged with flamey gold,
A matchless youth! his nod these worlds controls,
Wings the red lightning, and the thunder rolls.
Angel of Dulness, sent to scatter round
Her magic charms o'er all unclassic ground:
Yon stars, yon suns, he rears at pleasure higher,
Illumes their light, and sets their flames on fire.   260
Immortal Rich! how calm he sits at ease
'Mid snows of paper, and fierce hail of pease;
And proud his mistress' orders to perform,
Rides in the whirlwind, and directs the storm.°
   But lo! to dark encounter in mid air

248. In another of these farces Harlequin is hatched upon the stage, out of a large egg.

251.   *Quod petis in te est——*
              ——*Ne te quaesiveris extra.*
                      Persius.

256. Like Salmoneus in *Aen.* vi.
          Dum flammas Jovis, & sonitus imitatur Olympi.
          ——*nimbos, & non imitabile fulmen,*
          Aere & cornipedum cursu simularat equorum.

258. Alludes to Mr Addison's verse, in the praises of Italy:
          Poetic fields encompass me around,
          And still I seem to tread on classic ground.

As ver. 264 is a parody on a noble one of the same author in *The Campaign*; and ver. 259, 260. on two sublime verses of Dr Y[oung].

261. Mr John Rich, master of the Theatre Royal in Covent Garden, was the first that excelled this way.

New wizards rise; I see my Cibber there!
Booth in his cloudy tabernacle shrined,
On grinning dragons thou shalt mount the wind.
Dire is the conflict, dismal is the din,
Here shouts all Drury, there all Lincoln's Inn;   270
Contending theatres our empire raise,
Alike their labours, and alike their praise.
　　And are these wonders, son, to thee unknown?
Unknown to thee? These wonders are thy own.
These fate reserved to grace thy reign divine,
Foreseen° by me, but ah! withheld from mine.
In Lud's old walls though long I ruled, renowned
Far as loud Bow's° stupendous bells resound;
Though my own aldermen conferred the bays,
To me committing their eternal praise,   280
Their full-fed heroes, their pacific mayors,
Their annual trophies, and their monthly wars:
Though long my party built on me their hopes,

266. *I see my Cibber there!*] The history of the foregoing absurdities is versified by himself, in these words (*Life*, chap. xv.) 'Then sprung forth that succession of monstrous medleys that have so long infested the stage, which arose upon one another alternately at both houses, outvying each other in expense.' He then proceeds to excuse his own part in them, as follows: 'If I am asked why I assented? I have no better excuse for my error than to confess I did it against my conscience, and had not virtue enough to starve. Had Henry IV of France a better for changing his religion? I was still in my heart, as much as he could be, on the side of truth and sense; but with this difference, that I had their leave to quit them when they could not support me.—But let the question go which way it will, Harry IVth has *always been allowed a great man.*' This must be confessed a full answer, only the question still seems to be, 1. How the doing a thing against one's conscience is an excuse for it? and, 2ndly, It will be hard to prove how he got the leave of truth and sense to quit their service, unless he can produce a certificate that he ever was in it.

266, 267. *Booth* and *Cibber* were joint managers of the Theatre in Drury Lane.

268. In his *Letter to Mr P.*, Mr C. solemnly declares this not to be *literally true*. We hope therefore the reader will understand it *allegorically* only.

282. *Annual trophies*, on the Lord Mayor's day; and *monthly wars* in the Artillery Ground.

283. Settle, like most party-writers, was very uncertain in his political principles. He was employed to hold the pen in the *Character of a popish successor*, but afterwards printed his *Narrative* on the other side. He had managed the ceremony of a famous Pope-burning on Nov. 17, 1680, then became a trooper in King James's army, at Hounslow Heath. After the Revolution he kept a booth at Bartholomew Fair, where, in the droll called *St George for England*, he acted in his old age in a dragon of green leather of his own invention; he was at last taken into the Charterhouse, and there died, aged sixty years.

For writing pamphlets, and for roasting popes;
Yet lo! in me what authors have to brag on!
Reduced at last to hiss in my own dragon.
Avert it heaven! that thou, my Cibber, e'er
Shouldst wag a serpent-tail in Smithfield Fair!
Like the vile straw that's blown about the streets,
The needy poet sticks to all he meets,   290
Coached, carted,° trod upon, now loose, now fast,
And carried off in some dog's tail at last.
Happier thy fortunes! like a rolling stone,
Thy giddy dulness still shall lumber on,
Safe in its heaviness, shall never stray,
But lick up every blockhead in the way.
Thee shall the patriot, thee the courtier taste,
And every year be duller than the last.
Till raised from booths,° to theatre, to court,
Her seat imperial Dulness shall transport.   300
Already opera° prepares the way,
The sure forerunner of her gentle sway:
Let her thy heart, next drabs and dice, engage,
The third mad passion of thy doting age.
Teach thou the warbling Polypheme to roar,
And scream thyself as none e'er screamed before!
To aid our cause, if heaven thou canst not bend,
Hell thou shalt move; for Faustus is our friend:
Pluto with Cato thou for this shalt join,

297. It stood in the first edition with blanks, ** *and* **. Concanen was sure 'they must needs mean nobody but *King GEORGE* and *Queen CAROLINE*; and said he would insist it was so, till the poet cleared himself by filling up the blanks otherwise, agreeably to the context, and consistent with his *allegiance*.' Pref. to a *Collection of verses, essays, letters, etc. against Mr P.*, printed for A. Moore, p. 6.

305. *Polypheme*] He translated the Italian opera of *Polifemo*; but unfortunately lost the whole jest of the story. The Cyclops asks Ulysses his *name*, who tells him his name is Noman: after his eye is put out, he roars and calls the brother Cyclops to his aid. They enquire *who has hurt him?* he answers *Noman*; whereupon they all go away again. Our ingenious translator made Ulysses answer, *I take no name*, whereby all that followed became unintelligible. Hence it appears that Mr Cibber (who values himself on subscribing to the English translation of Homer's *Iliad*) had not that merit with respect to the *Odyssey*, or he might have been better instructed in the Greek pun-nology.

308, 309. *Faustus, Pluto, etc.*] Names of miserable farces which it was the custom to act at the end of the best tragedies, to spoil the digestion of the audience.

And link the *Mourning Bride* to *Proserpine.*   310
Grub Street! thy fall should men and gods conspire.
Thy stage shall stand, ensure it but from fire.
Another Aeschylus appears! prepare
For new abortions, all ye pregnant fair!
In flames, like Semele's,° be brought to bed,
While opening hell spouts wildfire at your head.
   Now Bavius take the poppy from thy brow,
And place it here! here all ye heroes bow!
This, this is he, foretold by ancient rhymes:
Th' Augustus born to bring Saturnian times.   320
Signs following signs lead on the mighty year!
See! the dull stars roll round and reappear.
See, see, our own true Phoebus wears the bays!
Our Midas° sits Lord Chancellor of Plays!
On poets' tombs see Benson's titles writ!

312. In the farce of *Proserpine* a cornfield was set on fire: whereupon the other playhouse had a barn burnt down for the recreation of the spectators. They also rivalled each other in showing the burnings of hell-fire, in *Dr Faustus.*

313. It is reported of Aeschylus, that when his tragedy of the *Furies* was acted, the audience were so terrified that the children fell into fits, and the big-bellied women miscarried.

315. See Ovid, *Met.* iii.

319, 320.   *Hic vir, hic est! tibi quem promitti saepius audis,*
                      Augustus Caesar, divum genus; aurea condet
                      Secula qui rursus Latio, regnata per arva
                      Saturno quondam—

                                                    Virgil, *Aen.* vi.

Saturnian here relates to the age of *lead,* mentioned book 1. ver. 26.

325. William Benson (Surveyor of the Buildings to his Majesty King George I.) gave in a report to the Lords, that their House and the Painted Chamber adjoining were in immediate danger of falling. Whereupon the Lords met in a committee to appoint some other place to sit in, while the house should be taken down. But it being proposed to cause some other builders first to inspect it, they found it in very good condition. The Lords, upon this, were going upon an address to the King against Benson, for such a misrepresentation; but the Earl of Sunderland, then secretary, gave them an assurance that his Majesty would remove him, which was done accordingly. In favour of this man, the famous Sir Christopher Wren, who had been architect to the crown for above fifty years, who built most of the churches in London, laid the first stone of St Paul's, and lived to finish it, had been displaced from his employment at the age of near ninety years.

Lo! Ambrose Philips is preferred for wit!
See under Ripley rise a new Whitehall,°
While Jones' and Boyle's° united labours fall:
While Wren with sorrow to the grave descends,
Gay dies unpensioned with a hundred friends.   330

326. *Ambrose Philips*] He was, saith Mr JACOB, 'one of the wits at Button's, and a justice of the peace;' but he hath since met with higher preferment in Ireland: and a much greater character we have of him in Mr Gildon's *Complete Art of Poetry*, vol. 1. p. 157. 'Indeed he confesses, he dares not set him *quite on the same foot with Virgil*, lest it should *seem* flattery; but he is much mistaken if posterity does not afford him a *greater esteem* than he *at present enjoys.*' He endeavoured to create some misunderstanding between our author and Mr Addison, whom also soon after he abused as much. His constant cry was, that Mr P. was an *enemy to the government*; and in particular he was the avowed author of a report very industriously spread, that he had a hand in a party-paper called the *Examiner*: a falsehood well known to those yet living, who had the direction and publication of it.

328. At the time when this poem was written, the banqueting house of Whitehall, the church and piazza of Covent Garden, and the palace and chapel of Somerset House, the works of the famous Inigo Jones, had been for many years so neglected, as to be in danger of ruin. The portico of Covent Garden church had been just then restored and beautified at the expense of the Earl of Burlington; who, at the same time, by his publication of the designs of that great master and Palladio, as well as by many noble buildings of his own, revived the true taste of architecture in this kingdom.

330. See Mr Gay's fable of the *Hare and many Friends*. This gentleman was early in the friendship of our author, which continued to his death. He wrote several works of humour with great success, the *Shepherd's Week*, *Trivia*, the *What-d'ye-call-it*, *Fables*, and lastly, the celebrated *Beggar's Opera*; a piece of satire which hit all tastes and degrees of men, from those of the highest quality to the very rabble. That verse of Horace

Primores populi arripuit, populumque tributim,

could never be so justly applied as to this. The vast success of it was unprecedented, and almost incredible: what is related of the wonderful effects of the ancient music or tragedy hardly came up to it: Sophocles and Euripides were less followed and famous. It was acted in London sixty-three days, uninterrupted; and renewed the next season with equal applauses. It spread into all the great towns of England, was played in many places to the thirtieth and fortieth time, at Bath and Bristol fifty, etc. It made its progress into Wales, Scotland, and Ireland, where it was performed twenty-four days together: it was lastly acted in Minorca. The fame of it was not confined to the author only; the ladies carried about with them the favourite songs of it in fans; and houses were furnished with it in screens. The person who acted Polly, till then obscure, became all at once the favourite of the town; her pictures were engraved, and sold in great numbers; her life written, books of letters and verses to her, published; and pamphlets made even of her sayings and jests.

Furthermore, it drove out of England, for that season, the Italian opera, which had carried all before it for ten years. That idol of the nobility and the people, which the great critic Mr Dennis by the labours and outcries of a whole life could not

Hibernian politics,° O Swift! thy fate;
And Pope's, ten years to comment and translate.
   Proceed, great days! till Learning fly the shore,
Till Birch shall blush with noble blood no more,
Till Thames see Eton's sons for ever play,
Till Westminster's° whole year be holiday,
Till Isis' elders° reel, their pupils sport,
And alma mater lie dissolved in port!'
   'Enough! enough!' the raptured monarch cries;
And through the ivory gate° the vision flies.   340

The End of the THIRD BOOK

overthrow, was demolished by a single stroke of this gentleman's pen. This happened in the year 1728. Yet so great was his modesty, that he constantly prefixed to all the editions of it this motto, *Nos haec novimus esse nihil.*

331. See book 1. ver. 26.

332. The author here plainly laments that he was so long employed in translating and commenting. He began the *Iliad* in 1713, and finished it in 1719. The edition of Shakespeare (which he undertook merely because nobody else would) took up near two years more in the drudgery of comparing impressions, rectifying the scenery, etc. and the translation of half the *Odyssey* employed him from that time to 1725.

333. It may perhaps seem incredible, that so great a revolution in learning as is here prophesied, should be brought about by such *weak instruments* as have been described in our poem: but do not thou, gentle reader, rest too secure in thy contempt of these instruments. Remember what the Dutch stories somewhere relate, that a great part of their provinces was once overflowed, by a small opening made in one of their dykes by a single *water-rat.*

However, that such is not seriously the judgment of our poet, but that he conceiveth better hopes from the diligence of our schools, from the regularity of our universities, the discernment of our great men, the accomplishments of our nobility, the encouragement of our patrons, and the genius of our writers in all kinds (notwithstanding some few exceptions in each) may plainly be seen from his conclusion; where causing all this vision to pass through the ivory gate, he expressly, in the language of poesy, declares all such imagination to be wild, ungrounded, and fictitious. SCRIBL.

340.   *Sunt geminae Somni portae; quarum altera fertur*
        Cornea, qua veris facilis datur exitus umbris;
        Altera candenti perfecta nitens elephanto,
        Sed falsa ad coelum mittunt insomnia manes.
                              Virgil, *Aen.* vi.

THE
DUNCIAD
Book the Fourth

ARGUMENT

*The poet being, in this book, to declare the completion of the prophecies
mentioned at the end of the former, makes a new invocation; as the greater
poets are wont, when some high and worthy matter is to be sung. He shows
the Goddess coming in her majesty, to destroy order and science, and to
substitute the Kingdom of the Dull upon earth. How she leads captive the
sciences, and silenceth the muses; and what they be who succeed in their
stead. All her children, by a wonderful attraction, are drawn about her; and
bear along with them divers others, who promote her empire by connivance,
weak resistance, or discouragement of arts; such as half-wits, tasteless
admirers, vain pretenders, the flatterers of dunces, or the patrons of them. All
these crowd round her; one of them offering to approach her, is driven back
by a rival, but she commends and encourages both. The first who speak in
form are the genius's of the schools, who assure her of their care to advance
her cause, by confining youth to words, and keeping them out of the way of
real knowledge. Their address, and her gracious answer; with her charge to
them and the universities. The universities appear by their proper deputies,
and assure her that the same method is observed in the progress of education;
the speech of Aristarchus on this subject. They are driven off by a band of
young gentlemen returned from travel with their tutors; one of whom delivers
to the Goddess, in a polite oration, an account of the whole conduct and fruits
of their travels: presenting to her at the same time a young nobleman perfectly
accomplished. She receives him graciously, and endues him with the happy*

The DUNCIAD, Book IV.] This book may properly be distinguished from the
former, by the name of the GREATER DUNCIAD, not so indeed in size, but in subject;
and so far contrary to the distinction anciently made of the *greater* and *lesser Iliad.*
But much are they mistaken who imagine this work in any wise inferior to the former,
or of any other hand than of our poet; of which I am much more certain than that
the *Iliad* itself was the work of Solomon, or the *Batrachomuomachia* of Homer, as
Barnes hath affirmed. BENTLEY.

quality of want of shame. *She sees loitering about her a number of* indolent persons *abandoning all business and duty, and dying with laziness: to these approaches the antiquary Annius, entreating her to make them* virtuosos, *and assign them over to him: but Mummius, another antiquary, complaining of his fraudulent proceeding, she finds a method to reconcile their difference. Then enter a troop of people fantastically adorned, offering her strange and exotic presents: amongst them, one stands forth and demands justice on another, who had deprived him of one of the greatest curiosities in nature: but he justifies himself so well, that the Goddess gives them both her approbation. She recommends to them to find proper employment for the* indolents *before-mentioned, in the study of* butterflies, shells, birds' nests, moss, etc. *but with particular caution, not to proceed beyond* trifles, *to any useful or extensive views of nature, or of the author of nature. Against the last of these apprehensions, she is secured by a hearty address from the* minute philosophers *and* freethinkers, *one of whom speaks in the name of the rest. The youth thus instructed and principled, are delivered to her in a body, by the hands of Silenus; and then admitted to taste the cup of the* Magus *her high priest, which causes a total oblivion of all obligations, divine, civil, moral, or rational. To these her adepts she sends* priests, attendants, *and* comforters, *of various kinds; confers on them* orders *and* degrees; *and then dismissing them with a speech, confirming to each his* privileges *and telling what she expects from each, concludes with a* yawn *of extraordinary virtue: the progress and effects whereof on all orders of men, and the consummation of all, in the restoration of* Night *and* Chaos, *conclude the poem.*

> Yet, yet a moment, one dim ray of light   1
> Indulge, dread Chaos, and eternal Night!
> Of darkness visible° so much be lent,
> As half to show, half veil the deep intent.

1, &c.] This is an invocation of much piety. The poet willing to approve himself a genuine son, beginneth by showing (what is ever agreeable to Dulness) his high respect for *antiquity* and a *great family*, how dull, or dark soever: next declareth his love for *mystery* and *obscurity*; and lastly his impatience to be *reunited* to her.   SCRIBL.

2. *dread Chaos, and eternal Night!*] Invoked, as the restoration of their empire is the action of the poem.

4. This is a great propriety, for a dull poet can never express himself otherwise than by *halves*, or imperfectly.   SCRIBL.

I understand it very differently; the author in this work had indeed a *deep intent*; there were in it *mysteries* or ἀπόρρητα which he durst not fully reveal, and doubtless in divers verses (according to Milton)

——*more is meant than meets the ear.*   BENTLEY.

Ye powers! whose mysteries restored I sing,
To whom time bears me on his rapid wing,
Suspend a while your force inertly strong,
Then take at once the poet and the song.

Now flamed the dog-star's° unpropitious ray,
Smote every brain, and withered every bay;   10
Sick was the sun, the owl forsook his bower,
The moonstruck prophet felt the madding hour:
Then rose the seed of Chaos, and of Night,
To blot out order, and extinguish light,
Of dull and venal a new world to mould,

6. Fair and softly, good poet! (cries the gentle Scriblerus on this place.) For sure in spite of his unusual modesty, he shall not travel so fast toward oblivion, as divers others of more confidence have done. For when I revolve in my mind the catalogue of those who have the most boldly promised to themselves immortality, *viz.* Pindar, Luis Gongora, Ronsard, Oldham, lyrics; Lycophron, Statius, Chapman, Blackmore, heroics; I find the one half to be already dead, and the other in utter darkness. But it becometh not us, who have taken upon us the office of commentator, to suffer our poet thus prodigally to cast away his life; contrariwise, the more hidden and abstruse is his work, and the more remote its beauties from common understanding, the more is it our duty to draw forth and exalt the same, in the face of men and angels. Herein shall we imitate the laudable spirit of those who have (for this very reason) delighted to comment on the fragments of *dark* and *uncouth* authors, preferred Ennius to Virgil, and chosen to turn the dark lanthorn of Lycophron, rather than to trim the everlasting lamp of Homer. SCRIBL.

7. *Force inertly strong*] Alluding to the *Vis inertiae of matter*, which, though it really be no power, is yet the foundation of all the qualities and attributes of that sluggish substance.

11, 12. The poet introduceth this, (as all great events are supposed by sage historians to be preceded) by an *eclipse of the sun*; but with a peculiar propriety, as the sun is the *emblem* of that intellectual light which dies before the face of Dulness. Very apposite likewise is it to make this *eclipse*, which is occasioned by the *moon's predominancy*, the very time when *dulness* and *madness* are in *conjunction*; whose relation and influence on each other the poet hath shown in many places, Book 1. ver. 22. Book 3. ver. 5, & seq.

14. *To blot out order, and extinguish light*] The two great ends of her mission; the one in quality of daughter of Chaos, the other as daughter of Night. Order here is to be understood extensively, both as civil and moral, the distinctions between high and low in society, and true and false in individuals: light, as intellectual only, wit, science, arts.

15. *Of dull and venal*] The allegory continued; *dull* referring to the extinction of light or science, *venal* to the destruction of order, or the truth of things.

Ibid. *a new world*] In allusion to the Epicurean opinion, that from the dissolution of the natural world into Night and Chaos, a new one should arise; this the poet alluding to, in the production of a new moral world, makes it partake of its original principles.

And bring Saturnian days of lead and gold.

    She mounts the throne: her head a cloud concealed,
In broad effulgence all below revealed,
('Tis thus aspiring Dulness ever shines)
Soft on her lap her laureate son reclines.   20

    Beneath her footstool, Science° groans in chains,
And Wit° dreads exile, penalties and pains.
There foamed rebellious Logic, gagged and bound,
There, stripped, fair Rhetoric languished on the ground;

16. *lead and gold*] *i.e.* dull and venal.

18. *all below revealed*] Vet. Adag.° 'The higher you climb, the more you show your A——.' Verified in no instance more than in Dulness aspiring. Emblematized also by an ape climbing and exposing his posteriors. SCRIBL.

20. *her laureate son reclines.*] With great judgment it is imagined by the poet, that such a colleague as Dulness had elected, should sleep on the throne, and have very little share in the action of the poem. Accordingly he hath done little or nothing from the day of his anointing; having passed through the second book without taking part in anything that was transacted about him, and through the third in profound sleep. Nor ought this, well considered, to seem strange in our days, when so many *king-consorts* have done the like. SCRIBL.

This verse our excellent laureate took so to heart, that he appealed to all mankind, 'if he was not as *seldom asleep as any fool?*' But it is hoped the poet hath not injured him, but rather verified his prophecy (p. 243. of his own *Life*, 8vo. ch. ix.) where he says '*the reader will be as much pleased to find me a* dunce *in my* old age, *as he was to prove me a* brisk blockhead *in my* youth.' Wherever there was any room for briskness, or alacrity of any sort, *even in sinking*, he hath had it allowed him; but here, where there is nothing for him to do but to take his natural rest, he must permit his historian to be silent. It is from their *actions* only that princes have their character, and poets from their *works*: and if in *those* he be *as much asleep as any fool*, the poet must leave him and them to *sleep to all eternity*. BENTLEY.

Ibid. *her laureate*] 'When I find my name in the satirical works of this poet, I never look upon it as any malice meant to me, but PROFIT to himself. For he considers that *my face* is more *known* than most in the nation; and therefore *a lick at the laureate* will be a sure bait *ad captandum vulgus*, to catch little readers.' *Life of Colley Cibber*, chap. ii.

Now if it be certain, that the works of our poet have owed their success to this ingenious expedient, we hence derive an unanswerable argument, that this fourth DUNCIAD, as well as the former three, hath had the author's last hand, and was by him intended for the press: or else to what purpose hath he crowned it, as we see, by this finishing stroke, the profitable *lick* at the *laureate?* BENTLEY.

21, 22. We are next presented with the pictures of those whom the Goddess leads in captivity. *Science* is only depressed and confined so as to be rendered useless; but *wit* or *genius*, as a more dangerous and active enemy, punished, or driven away: Dulness being often reconciled in some degree with learning, but never upon any terms with wit. And accordingly it will be seen that she admits something *like* each science, as casuistry, sophistry, etc.

His blunted arms by Sophistry are borne,
And shameless Billingsgate her robes adorn.
Morality, by her false guardians drawn,
Chicane in furs, and Casuistry in lawn,°
Gasps, as they straiten at each end the cord,
And dies, when Dulness gives her Page the word.   30
Mad Mathesis° alone was unconfined,
Too mad for mere material chains to bind,
Now to pure space lifts her ecstatic stare,
Now running round the circle, finds it square.
But held in tenfold bonds the muses lie,
Watched both by envy's and by flattery's eye:
There to her heart sad Tragedy addressed
The dagger wont to pierce the tyrant's breast;
But sober History restrained her rage,

27. *Morality* is the daughter of *Astraea*. This alludes to the mythology of the ancient poets; who tell us that in the *gold* and *silver* ages, or in the *state of nature*, the gods cohabited with men here on earth; but when by reason of human degeneracy men were forced to have recourse to a *magistrate*, and that the ages of *brass* and *iron* came on, (that is, when laws were wrote on brazen tablets and enforced by the sword of justice) the celestials soon retired from earth, and Astraea last of all; and then it was she left this her orphan daughter in the hands of the *guardians* aforesaid.

SCRIBL.

30. *gives her Page the word.*] There was a judge of this name, always ready to hang any man, of which he was suffered to give a hundred miserable examples during a long life, even to his dotage.—Though the candid Scriblerus imagined *Page* here to mean no more than a *page* or *mute*, and to allude to the custom of strangling state criminals in Turkey by mutes or pages. A practice more decent than that of *our Page*, who before he hanged any person, loaded him with reproachful language. SCRIBL.

31. *Mad Mathesis*] Alluding to the strange conclusions some mathematicians have deduced from their principles concerning the *real quantity of matter*, the *reality of space*, etc.

33. *pure space*] i.e. pure and defecated from matter.—*ecstatic stare*, the action of men who look about with full assurance of seeing what does not exist, such as those who expect to find *space* a real being.

34. Regards the wild and fruitless attempts of *squaring the circle*.

36. One of the misfortunes falling on authors, from the Act for subjecting plays to the power of a *licenser*, being the false representations to which they were exposed, from such as either gratified their envy to merit, or made their court to greatness, by perverting general reflections against vice into libels on particular persons.

39. History attends on Tragedy, Satire on Comedy, as their substitutes in the

And promised vengeance on a barbarous age.   40
There sunk Thalia,° nerveless, cold, and dead,
Had not her sister Satire held her head:
Nor couldst thou, CHESTERFIELD! a tear refuse,
Thou wept'st, and with thee wept each gentle muse.
   When lo! a harlot form soft sliding by,
With mincing step, small voice, and languid eye;
Foreign her air, her robe's discordant pride
In patchwork fluttering, and her head aside:
By singing peers upheld on either hand,
She tripped and laughed, too pretty much to stand;   50

discharge of their distinct functions: the one in high life, recording the crimes and
punishments of the great; the other in low, exposing the vices or follies of the
common people. But it may be asked, How came History and Satire to be admitted
with impunity to minister comfort to the muses, even in the presence of the Goddess,
and in the midst of all her triumphs? A question, says Scriblerus, which we thus
resolve: History was brought up in her infancy by Dulness herself; but being after-
wards espoused into a noble house, she forgot (as is usual) the humility of her birth,
and the cares of her early friends. This occasioned a long estrangement between
her and Dulness. At length, in process of time, they met together in a monk's cell,
were reconciled, and became better friends than ever. After this they had a second
quarrel, but it held not long, and are now again on reasonable terms, and so are like
to continue. This accounts for the connivance shown to History on this occasion.
But the boldness of Satire springs from a very different cause: for the reader ought
to know, that she alone of all the sisters is unconquerable, never to be silenced,
when truly inspired and animated (as should seem) from above, for this very purpose,
to oppose the kingdom of Dulness to her last breath.

   43. This noble person in the year 1737, when the Act aforesaid was brought into
the House of Lords, opposed it in an excellent speech (says Mr Cibber) 'with a
lively spirit and uncommon eloquence.' This speech had the honour to be answered
by the said Mr Cibber, with a lively spirit also, and in a manner very uncommon, in
the 8th chapter of his *Life and Manners*. And here, gentle reader, would I gladly
insert the other speech, whereby thou mightest judge between them: but I must
defer it on account of some differences not yet adjusted between the noble author
and myself, concerning the *true reading* of certain passages.   SCRIBL.

   45. The attitude given to this phantom represents the nature and genius of the
Italian opera; its affected airs, its effeminate sounds, and the practice of patching up
these operas with favourite songs, incoherently put together. These things were
supported by the subscriptions of the nobility. This circumstance that opera should
prepare for the opening of the grand sessions, was prophesied of in Book 3. ver.
304.

   Already Opera prepares the way,
   The sure forerunner of her gentle sway.

Cast on the prostrate nine a scornful look,
Then thus in quaint recitativo spoke.
    'O *Cara! Cara!* silence all that train:
Joy to great Chaos! let division reign:
Chromatic tortures soon shall drive them hence,
Break all their nerves, and fritter all their sense:
One trill shall harmonize joy, grief, and rage,
Wake the dull church, and lull the ranting stage;
To the same notes thy sons shall hum, or snore,
And all thy yawning daughters cry, *encore*.   60
Another Phoebus, thy own Phoebus, reigns,
Joys in my jigs, and dances in my chains.
But soon, ah soon rebellion will commence,
If music meanly borrows aid from sense:
Strong in new arms, lo! giant Handel stands,
Like bold Briareus,° with a hundred hands;
To stir, to rouse, to shake the soul he comes,
And Jove's own thunders follow Mars's drums.
Arrest him, Empress; or you sleep no more'—
She heard, and drove him to th' Hibernian shore.   70

54. *let division reign*] Alluding to the false taste of playing tricks in music with numberless divisions, to the neglect of that harmony which conforms to the sense, and applies to the passions. Mr Handel had introduced a great number of hands, and more variety of instruments into the orchestra, and employed even drums and cannon to make a fuller chorus; which proved so much too manly for the fine gentlemen of his age, that he was obliged to remove his music into Ireland. After which they were reduced, for want of composers, to practise the patchwork above mentioned.

55. That species of the ancient music called the *chromatic* was a variation and embellishment, in odd irregularities, of the *diatonic* kind. They say it was invented about the time of Alexander, and that the Spartans forbad the use of it, as languid and effeminate.

61. *Thy own Phoebus reigns*] *Tuus jam regnat Apollo.*
                                        Virgil.

Not the ancient Phoebus, the God of harmony, but a modern Phoebus of French extraction, married to the Princess Galimathia, one of the handmaids of Dulness, and an assistant to Opera. Of whom see Bouhours, and other critics of that nation.
SCRIBL.

And now had Fame's posterior trumpet blown,
And all the nations summoned to the throne.
The young, the old, who feel her inward sway,
One instinct seizes, and transports away.
None need a guide, by sure attraction led,
And strong impulsive gravity of head:
None want a place, for all their centre found,
Hung to the Goddess, and cohered around.
Not closer, orb in orb, conglobed are seen
The buzzing bees about their dusky queen.   80
The gathering number, as it moves along,
Involves a vast involuntary throng,

71. *Posterior*, viz. her *second* or *more certain* report: unless we imagine this word *posterior* to relate to the position of one of her trumpets, according to *Hudibras*:

> She blows not both with the same wind,
> But one before and one behind;
> And therefore modern authors name
> One good, and t'other evil fame.

75. *None need a guide,—None want a place*,] The sons of Dulness want no instructors in study, nor guides in life: they are their own masters in all sciences, and their own heralds and introducers into all places.

76 to 101. It ought to be observed that here are three classes in this assembly. The first of men absolutely and avowedly dull, who naturally adhere to the Goddess, and are imaged in the simile of the bees about their queen. The second involuntarily drawn to her, though not caring to own her influence; from ver. 81 to 90. The third of such, as, though not members of her state, yet advance her service by flattering Dulness, cultivating mistaken talents, patronizing vile scribblers, discouraging living merit, or setting up for wits, and men of taste in arts they understand not; from ver. 91 to 101. In this new world of Dulness each of these three classes hath its appointed station, as best suits its nature, and concurs to the harmony of the system. The *first* drawn only by the strong and simple impulse of attraction, are represented as falling directly down into her; as conglobed into her substance, and resting in her centre.

> ——*All their centre found,*
> *Hung to the Goddess, and cohered around.*

The *second*, though within the sphere of her attraction, yet having at the same time a different motion, they are carried, by the composition of these two, in planetary revolutions round her centre, some nearer to it, some further off:

> Who gently drawn, and struggling less and less,
> Roll in her vortex, and her power confess.

The *third* are properly *eccentrical*, and no constant members of her state or system: sometimes at an immense distance from her influence, and sometimes again almost on the surface of her *broad effulgence*. Their use in their perihelion, or nearest approach to Dulness, is the same in the moral world, as that of *comets* in the natural, namely to refresh and recreate the dryness and decays of the system; in the manner marked out from ver. 91 to 98.

Who gently drawn, and struggling less and less,
Roll in her vortex, and her power confess.
Not those alone who passive own her laws,
But who, weak rebels, more advance her cause.
Whate'er of dunce in college or in town
Sneers at another, in toupee or gown;
Whate'er of mongrel no one class admits,
A wit with dunces, and a dunce with wits.   90

    Nor absent they, no members of her state,
Who pay her homage in her sons, the great;
Who false to Phoebus, bow the knee to Baal;°
Or impious, preach his word without a call.
Patrons, who sneak from living worth to dead,
Withhold the pension, and set up the head;°
Or vest dull flattery in the sacred gown;
Or give from fool to fool the laurel crown.
And (last and worst) with all the cant of wit,
Without the soul, the muse's hypocrite.   100
There marched the bard and blockhead, side by side,
Who rhymed for hire, and patronized for pride.
Narcissus,° praised with all a parson's power,
Looked a white lily sunk beneath a shower.
There moved Montalto° with superior air;
His stretched-out arm displayed a volume fair;
Courtiers and patriots in two ranks divide,
Through both he passed, and bowed from side to side:
But as in graceful act, with awful eye
Composed he stood, bold Benson thrust him by: 110

93. *false to Phoebus*] Spoken of the ancient and true Phoebus, not the French Phoebus, who hath no chosen priests or poets, but equally inspires any man that pleaseth to sing or preach.   SCRIBL.

99, 100. In this division are reckoned up 1. The idolizers of Dulness in the great —2. ill judges,—3. ill writers,—4. ill patrons. But the *last and worst*, as he justly calls him, is the *muse's hypocrite*, who is as it were the epitome of them all. He who thinks the only end of poetry is to amuse, and the only business of the poet to be witty; and consequently who cultivates only such trifling talents in himself, and encourages only such in others.

110. *bold Benson*] This man endeavoured to raise himself to fame by erecting monuments, striking coins, setting up heads, and procuring translations, of Milton; and afterwards by a great passion for Arthur Johnston, a Scotch physician's version of the Psalms, of which he printed many fine editions. See more of him, Book 3. ver. 325.

On two unequal crutches propped he came,
Milton's on this, on that one Johnston's name.
The decent knight retired with sober rage,
Withdrew his hand, and closed the pompous page.

```
    *       *       *       *       *       *       *
    *       *       *       *       *       *       *
    *       *       *       *       *       *       *
    *       *       *       *       *       *       *
```

When Dulness, smiling—'Thus revive the wits!
But murder first, and mince them all to bits;   120
As erst Medea° (cruel, so to save!)
A new edition of old Aeson gave,
Let standard-authors, thus, like trophies born,
Appear more glorious as more hacked and torn,
And you, my critics! in the chequered shade,
Admire new light through holes yourselves have made.
    Leave not a foot of verse, a foot of stone,
A page, a grave, that they can call their own;
But spread, my sons, your glory thin or thick,
On passive paper, or on solid brick.   130
So by each bard an alderman shall sit,
A heavy lord shall hang at every wit,
And while on Fame's triumphal car they ride,
Some slave of mine be pinioned to their side.'

113. *The decent knight.*] An eminent person, who was about to publish a very pompous edition of a great author, *at his own expense.*

119. The Goddess applauds the practice of tacking the obscure names of persons not eminent in any branch of learning, to those of the most distinguished writers; either by printing *editions* of their works with impertinent alterations of their text, as in the former instances, or by setting up *monuments* disgraced with their own vile names and inscriptions, as in the latter.

122. *old* Aeson] Of whom Ovid (very applicable to these restored authors)

> Aeson *miratur,*
> Dissimilemque animum *subiit—*

128. For what less than a grave can be granted to a dead author? or what less than a page can be allowed a living one?

Ibid. *A page*] *Pagina,* not *Pedissequus.* A page of a book, not a servant, follower, or attendant; no poet having had a *page* since the death of Mr Thomas Durfey.
                                                                 SCRIBL.

131. Vide the *Tombs of the Poets,* Editio Westmonasteriensis.

Now crowds on crowds around the Goddess press,
Each eager to present the first address.
Dunce scorning dunce beholds the next advance,
But fop shows fop superior complaisance.
When lo! a spectre° rose, whose index-hand
Held forth the virtue of the dreadful wand;   140
His beavered brow° a birchen garland wears,
Dropping with infant's blood, and mother's tears.
O'er every vein a shuddering horror runs;
Eton and Winton° shake through all their sons.
All flesh is humbled, Westminster's bold race
Shrink, and confess the genius of the place:
The pale boy-senator yet tingling stands,
And holds his breeches close with both his hands.
     Then thus: 'Since man from beast by words is known,
Words are man's province, words we teach alone.   150
When reason doubtful, like the Samian letter,
Points him two ways, the narrower is the better.
Placed at the door of learning, youth to guide,

137, 138. This is not to be ascribed so much to the different manners of a court
and college, as to the different effects which a pretence to learning, and a pretence
to wit, have on blockheads. For as judgment consists in finding out the *differences* in
things, and wit in finding out their *likenesses*, so the dunce is all discord and dissen-
sion, and constantly busied in *reproving, examining, confuting*, etc. while the fop
flourishes in peace, with songs and hymns of praise, *addresses, characters, epithalamiums*,
etc.

140. *the dreadful wand*] A cane usually borne by schoolmasters, which drives the
poor souls about like the wand of Mercury. SCRIBL.

148. An effect of fear somewhat like this, is described in the 7th *Aeneid*,

> *Contremuit nemus——*
> *Et trepidae matres pressere ad pectora natos.*

nothing being so natural in any apprehension, as to lay close hold on whatever is
supposed to be most in danger. But let it not be imagined the author would insinuate
these youthful senators (though so lately come from school) to be under the undue
influence of any *master*. SCRIBL.

151. *like the Samian letter*] The letter Y, used by Pythagoras as an emblem of the
different roads of virtue and vice.

> *Et tibi quae Samios diduxit litera ramos.* Persius.

153. This circumstance of the *genius loci* (with that of the index-hand before)
seems to be an allusion to the *Table of Cebes*, where the genius of human nature
points out the road to be pursued by those entering into life. Ὁ δὲ γέρων ὁ ἄνω
ἑστηκὼς ἔχων χάρτην τινά ἐν τῇ χειρί, καὶ τῇ ἑτέρᾳ ὥσπερ δεικνύων τί
οὗτος Δαίμων καλεῖται, &c.

We never suffer it to stand too wide.
To ask, to guess, to know, as they commence,
As fancy opens the quick springs of sense,
We ply the memory, we load the brain,
Bind rebel wit, and double chain on chain,
Confine the thought, to exercise the breath;
And keep them in the pale of words till death.   160
Whate'er the talents, or howe'er designed,
We hang one jingling padlock on the mind:
A poet the first day, he dips his quill;
And what the last? a very poet still.
Pity! the charm works only in our wall,
Lost, lost too soon in yonder house or hall.
There truant WYNDHAM every muse gave o'er,
There TALBOT sunk, and was a wit no more!
How sweet an Ovid, MURRAY was our boast!
How many Martials were in PULTENEY lost!   170
Else sure some bard, to our eternal praise,
In twice ten thousand rhyming nights and days,
Had reached the work, the all that mortal can;
And South beheld that masterpiece of man.'
     'Oh,' cried the Goddess, 'for some pedant reign!

159. *to exercise the breath*] By obliging them to get the classic poets by heart, which furnishes them with endless matter for conversation, and verbal amusement for their whole lives.

162. For youth being used like packhorses and beaten on under a heavy load of words, lest they should tire, their instructors contrive to make the words jingle in rhyme or metre.

166. *in yonder house or hall.*] Westminster Hall and the House of Commons.

174. *that masterpiece of man.*] viz. an *epigram*. The famous Dr South declared a perfect epigram to be as difficult a performance as an epic poem. And the critics say, 'an epic poem is the greatest work human nature is capable of.'

175. The matter under debate is how to confine men to words for life. The instructors of youth show how well they do their parts; but complain that when men come into the world they are apt to forget their learning, and turn themselves to useful knowledge. This was an evil that wanted to be redressed. And this the Goddess assures them will need a more extensive tyranny than that of grammar schools. She therefore points out to them the remedy, in her wishes for *arbitrary powers*; whose interest it being to keep men from the study of *things*, will encourage the propagation of *words* and *sounds*; and to make all sure, she wishes for another *pedant monarch*. The sooner to obtain so great a blessing, she is willing even for once to violate the fundamental principle of her politics, in having her sons taught at least *one thing*; but that sufficient, the *doctrine of divine right*.

Nothing can be juster than the observation here insinuated, that no branch of

Some gentle JAMES, to bless the land again;
To stick the doctor's chair into the throne,
Give law to words, or war with words alone,
Senates and courts with Greek and Latin rule,
And turn the council° to a grammar school!   180
For sure, if Dulness sees a grateful day,

learning thrives well under arbitrary government but *verbal*. The reasons are evident. It is unsafe under such governments to cultivate the study of things of importance. Besides, when men have lost their public virtue, they naturally delight in trifles, if their private morals secure them from being vicious. Hence so great a cloud of scholiasts and grammarians so soon overspread the learning of Greece and Rome, when once those famous communities had lost their liberties. Another reason is the *encouragement* which arbitrary governments give to the study of *words*, in order to busy and amuse active geniuses, who might otherwise prove troublesome and inquisitive. So when Cardinal Richelieu had destroyed the poor remains of his country's liberties, and made the supreme court of Parliament merely *ministerial*, he instituted the French Academy. What was said upon that occasion, by a brave magistrate, when the letters-patent of its erection came to be verified in the Parliament of Paris, deserves to be remembered: he told the assembly, that *this adventure put him in mind after what manner an Emperor of Rome once treated his senate; who when he had deprived them of the cognizance of public matters, sent a message to them in form for their opinion about the best sauce for a turbot.*

176. *Some gentle JAMES, etc.*] Wilson tells us that this king, James the first, took upon himself to teach the Latin tongue to Carr, Earl of Somerset; and that Gondomar the Spanish ambassador would speak false Latin to him, on purpose to give him the pleasure of correcting it, whereby he wrought himself into his good graces.

This great prince was the first who assumed the title of Sacred Majesty, which his loyal clergy transferred from God to him. 'The principles of passive obedience and non-resistance', says the author of the *Dissertation on Parties*, Letter 8, 'which before his time had skulked perhaps in some old homily, were talked, written, and preached into vogue in that inglorious reign.'

181, 182. And grateful it is in Dulness to make this confession. I will not say she alludes to that celebrated verse of Claudian,

———*nunquam* Libertas *gratior extat*
Quam sub Rege *pia*———

But this I will say, that the words *liberty* and *monarchy* have been frequently confounded and mistaken one for the other by the gravest authors. I should therefore conjecture, that the genuine reading of the forecited verse was thus,

———*nunquam* Libertas *gratior exstat*
Quam sub Lege *pia*———

and that *Rege* was the reading only of Dulness herself: and therefore she might allude to it.   SCRIBL.

I judge quite otherwise of this passage: the genuine reading is *libertas*, and *rege*: so Claudian gave it. But the error lies in the first verse: it should be *exit*, not *exstat*, and then the meaning will be, that liberty was never *lost*, or *went away* with so good a grace, as under a good king: it being without doubt a tenfold shame to lose it

'Tis in the shade of arbitrary sway.
O! if my sons may learn one earthly thing,
Teach but that one, sufficient for a king;
That which my priests, and mine alone, maintain,
Which as it dies, or lives, we fall, or reign:
May you, may Cam, and Isis° preach it long!
The RIGHT DIVINE of kings to govern wrong.'
    Prompt at the call, around the Goddess roll
Broad hats, and hoods, and caps, a sable shoal: 190
Thick and more thick the black blockade extends,
A hundred head of Aristotle's friends.

under a bad one.

This farther leads me to animadvert upon a most grievous piece of nonsense to be found in all the editions of the author of the *Dunciad* himself. A most capital one it is, and owing to the confusion above mentioned by Scriblerus, of the two words *liberty* and *monarchy. Essay on Crit.*

> *Nature, like* monarchy, *is but restrained*
> *By the same laws herself at first ordained.*

Who sees not, it should be, *Nature like* liberty? Correct it therefore *repugnantibus omnibus* (even though the author himself should oppugn) in all the impressions which have been, or shall be, made of his works.   BENTLEY.

192. The philosophy of Aristotle had suffered a long disgrace in this learned university: being first expelled by the Cartesian, which, in its turn, gave place to the Newtonian. But it had all this while some faithful followers in secret, who never bowed the knee to Baal, nor acknowledged any strange god in philosophy. These, on this new appearance of the Goddess, come out like confessors, and make an open profession of the ancient faith in the *ipse dixit* of their master. Thus far SCRIBLERUS.

But the learned Mr Colley Cibber takes the matter quite otherwise; and that this *various fortune of Aristotle* relates not to his *natural*, but his *moral* philosophy. For speaking of that university in his time, he says, *they seemed to have as implicit a reverence for Shakespeare and Jonson, as formerly for the* ETHICS *of Aristotle.* See his *Life*, p. 385. One would think this learned professor had mistaken *ethics* for *physics*; unless he might imagine the morals too were grown into disuse, from the relaxation they admitted of during the time he mentions, *viz.* while he and the players were at Oxford.

Ibid. *A hundred head etc.*] It appears by this the Goddess has been careful of keeping up a succession, according to the rule,

> *Semper enim refice: ac ne post amissa requiras,*
> *Anteveni; & sobolem* armento *sortire* quotannis.

It is remarkable with what dignity the poet here describes the *friends* of this ancient philosopher. Horace does not observe the same decorum with regard to those of another sect, when he says *Cum ridere voles Epicuri de grege Porcum.* But the word *drove, Armentum,* here understood, is a word of honour, as the most noble *Festus* the *Grammarian* assures us, *Armentum id genus pecoris appellatur quod est idoneum opus* armorum. And alluding to the temper of this *warlike breed,* our poet very appositely calls them *a hundred head.*   SCRIBL.

Nor wert thou, Isis! wanting to the day,
[Though Christ Church long kept prudishly away.]
Each staunch polemic, stubborn as a rock,
Each fierce logician, still expelling Locke,
Came whip and spur, and dashed through thin and thick
On German Crousaz,° and Dutch Burgersdyck.°
As many quit the streams that murmuring fall
To lull the sons of Margaret and Clare Hall,°   200
Where Bentley late tempestuous wont to sport
In troubled waters, but now sleeps in port.
Before them marched that awful aristarch;
Ploughed was his front with many a deep remark:
His hat, which never vailed to human pride,
Walker° with reverence took, and laid aside.
Low bowed the rest: he, kingly, did but nod;
So upright Quakers please both man and God.
'Mistress! dismiss that rabble from your throne:

194. This line is doubtless spurious, and foisted in by the impertinence of the editor; and accordingly we have put it between hooks. For I affirm this college came as early as any other, by its *proper deputies*; nor did any college pay homage to Dulness in its *whole body*. BENTLEY.

196. In the year 1703 there was a meeting of the heads of the University of Oxford to censure Mr Locke's *Essay on Human Understanding*, and to forbid the reading it. See his *Letters* in the last edit.

198. There seems to be an improbability that the doctors and heads of houses should ride on horseback, who of late days, being gouty or unwieldy, have kept their coaches. But these are horses of great strength, and fit to carry any weight, as their German and Dutch extraction may manifest; and very famous we may conclude, being honoured with *names*, as were the horses Pegasus and Bucephalus. SCRIBL.

199. *the streams*] The River Cam, running by the walls of these colleges, which are particularly famous for their skill in disputation.

202. *sleeps in port.*] viz. 'now retired into harbour, after the tempests that had long agitated his society.' So Scriblerus. But the learned Scipio Maffei understands it of a certain wine called *port*, from Oporto a city of Portugal, of which this professor invited him to drink abundantly. SCIP. MAFF. *de Compotationibus Academicis.*

205 to 208. The hat-worship, as the Quakers call it, is an abomination to that sect: yet, where it is necessary to pay that respect to man (as in the courts of justice and houses of parliament) they have, to avoid offence, and yet not violate their conscience, permitted other people to uncover them.

207. Milton,
    —*He, kingly, from his state*
    Declined not——

Avaunt——is Aristarchus yet unknown?   210
Thy mighty scholiast, whose unwearied pains
Made Horace dull, and humbled Milton's strains.
Turn what they will to verse, their toil is vain,
Critics like me shall make it prose again.
Roman and Greek grammarians! know your better:
Author of something yet more great than letter;
While towering o'er your alphabet, like Saul,°
Stands our digamma, and o'ertops them all.
'Tis true, on words is still our whole debate,
Disputes of *me* or *te*, of *aut* or *at*,   220
To sound or sink in *cano*, O or A,
Or give up Cicero to C or K.°
Let Freind affect to speak as Terence spoke,
And Alsop never but like Horace joke:
For me, what Virgil, Pliny may deny,

---

210.   ——*Sic notus* Ulysses?   Virgil.
                 Dost thou not feel me, Rome?   Ben Jonson.

Aristarchus] A famous commentator, and corrector of Homer, whose name has been frequently used to signify a complete critic. The compliment paid by our author to this eminent professor, in applying to him so great a name, was the reason that he hath omitted to comment on this part which contains his own praises. We shall therefore supply that loss to our best ability.   SCRIBL.

215. Imitated from Propertius speaking of the *Aeneid*.

          Cedite, Romani *scriptores*, *cedite* Graii!
          Nescio quid majus *nascitur Iliade*.

217, 218. Alludes to the boasted restoration of the Aeolic digamma, in his long-projected edition of Homer. He calls it *something more than letter*, from the enormous figure it would make among the other letters, being one gamma set upon the shoulders of another.

220. *of me or te*,] It was a serious dispute, about which the learned were much divided, and some treatises written: had it been about *meum* or *tuum* it could not be more contested, than whether at the end of the first Ode of Horace, to read, Me *doctarum hederae praemia frontium*, or, Te *doctarum hederae*—.

222. Grammatical disputes about the manner of pronouncing Cicero's name in Greek. It is a dispute whether in Latin the name of Hermagoras should end in *as* or *a*. Quintilian quotes Cicero as writing it *Hermagora*, which Bentley rejects, and says Quintilian must be mistaken, Cicero could not write it so, and that in this case he would not believe Cicero himself. These are his very words: *Ego vero Ciceronem ita scripsisse ne Ciceroni quidem affirmanti crediderim.*—*Epist. ad Mill. in fin Frag. Menand. et Phil.*

223, 224. Dr Robert Freind, master of Westminster School, and canon of Christ Church—Dr Anthony Alsop, a happy imitator of the Horatian style.

Manilius° or Solinus° shall supply:
For Attic phrase in Plato let them seek,
I poach in Suidas for unlicensed Greek.
In ancient sense if any needs will deal,
Be sure I give them fragments, not a meal;   230
What Gellius or Stobaeus hashed before,
Or chewed by blind old scholiasts o'er and o'er.
The critic eye, that microscope of wit,
Sees hairs and pores, examines bit by bit:
How parts relate to parts, or they to whole,
The body's harmony, the beaming soul,
Are things which Kuster,° Burman,° Wasse° shall see,
When man's whole frame is obvious to a *flea*.

    Ah, think not, mistress! more true Dulness lies
In folly's cap, than wisdom's grave disguise.   240
Like buoys, that never sink into the flood,
On learning's surface we but lie and nod.
Thine is the genuine head of many a house,°

226. Some critics having had it in their choice to comment either on Virgil or Manilius, Pliny or Solinus, have chosen the worse author, the more freely to display their critical capacity.

228, *etc. Suidas, Gellius, Stobaeus*] The first a dictionary-writer, a collector of impertinent facts and barbarous words; the second a minute critic; the third an author, who gave his commonplace book to the public, where we happen to find much mincemeat of old books.

232. *Or chewed by blind old scholiasts o'er and o'er.*] These taking the same things eternally from the mouth of one another.

239, 240. By this it would seem the dunces and fops mentioned ver. 139, 140 had a contention of rivalship for the Goddess's favour on this great day. Those got the start, but these make it up by their spokesmen in the next speech. It seems as if Aristarchus here first saw him advancing with his fair pupil. SCRIBL.

241, 242. So that the station of a Professor is only a kind of legal noticer to inform us where the *shattered hulk* of learning lies at anchor; which after so long unhappy navigation, and now without either master or patron, we may wish, with Horace, may *lie there still.*

      ——*Nonne vides, ut*
    Nudum remigio latus?
      ——*non tibi sunt integra lintea;*
    Non Di, *quos iterum pressa voces malo.*
      Quamvis pontica pinus,
      Sylvae filia nobilis,
    Jactes & genus, & nomen inutile. Horace.

                                            SCRIBL.

And much divinity without a *Noῦς*.
Nor could a BARROW work on every block,
Nor has one ATTERBURY spoiled the flock.
See! still thy own, the heavy canon roll,
And metaphysic smokes involve the pole.
For thee we dim the eyes, and stuff the head
With all such reading as was never read: 250
For thee explain a thing till all men doubt it,
And write about it, Goddess, and about it:
So spins the silk-worm small its slender store,
And labours till it clouds itself all o'er.

244. *Noῦς*] A word much affected by the learned Aristarchus in common conver-
sation, to signify *genius* or natural *acumen*. But this passage has a farther view: *Noῦς*
was the Platonic term for *mind*, or the *first cause*, and that system of divinity is here
hinted at which terminates in blind nature without a *Noῦς*: such as the poet after-
wards describes (speaking of the dreams of one of these later Platonists)

> *Or that* bright image *to our fancy draw,*
> *Which* Theocles *in raptured vision saw,*
> *That* Nature——*&c.*

245, 246. Isaac Barrow Master of Trinity, Francis Atterbury Dean of Christ
Church, both great genius's and eloquent preachers; one more conversant in the
sublime geometry, the other in classical learning; but who equally made it their care
to advance the polite arts in their several societies.

247. *the heavy canon*] Canon here, if spoken of *artillery*, is in the plural number;
if of the *canons of the house*, in the singular, and meant only of *one*: in which case I
suspect the *pole* to be a false reading, and that it should be the *poll*, or *head* of that
canon. It may be objected, that this is a mere *paranomasia* or *pun*. But what of that?
Is any figure of speech more apposite to our gentle Goddess, or more frequently
used by her, and her children, especially of the university? Doubtless it better suits
the character of Dulness, yea of a doctor, than that of an angel; yet Milton feared
not to put a considerable quantity into the mouths of his. It hath indeed been
observed, that they were the devil's angels, as if he did it to suggest the devil was
the author as well of false wit, as of false religion, and that the father of lies was
also the father of puns. But this is idle: it must be owned a Christian practice, used
in the primitive times by some of the fathers, and in later by most of the sons of
the church; till the debauched reign of Charles the second, when the shameful
passion for *wit* overthrew everything: and even then the best writers admitted it,
provided it was obscene, under the name of the *double entendre*. SCRIBL.

248. Here the learned Aristarchus ending the first member of his harangue in
behalf of *words*; and entering on the other half, which regards the teaching of *things*;
very artfully connects the two parts in an encomium on METAPHYSICS, a kind of
middle nature between words and things: communicating, in its obscurity with *sub-
stance*, and in its emptiness with *names*. SCRIBL.

What though we let some better sort of fool
Thrid every science, run through every school?
Never by tumbler through the hoops was shown
Such skill in passing all, and touching none.
He may indeed (if sober all this time)
Plague with dispute, or persecute with rhyme.   260
We only furnish what he cannot use,
Or wed to what he must divorce, a muse:
Full in the midst of Euclid dip at once,
And petrify a genius to a dunce:
Or set on metaphysic ground to prance,
Show all his paces, not a step advance.
With the same cement, ever sure to bind,
We bring to one dead level every mind.
Then take him to develop, if you can,
And hew the block off, and get out the man.   270

---

255 to 271. Hitherto Aristarchus hath displayed the art of teaching his pupils
words, without things. He shows greater skill in what follows, which is to teach
things, without profit. For with the *better sort of fool* the first expedient is, ver. 254
to 258, to run him so swiftly through the circle of the sciences that he shall stick at
nothing, nor nothing stick with him; and though some little, both of words and
things, should by chance be gathered up in his passage, yet he shows, ver. 255 to
260. that it is never more of the one than just to enable him to *persecute with rhyme*,
or of the other than to *plague with dispute*. But, if after all, the pupil will needs *learn*
a science, it is then provided by his careful directors, ver. 261, 262, that it shall
either be such as he can never *enjoy* when he comes out into life, or such as he will
be obliged to *divorce*. And to make all sure, ver. 263 to 268, the useless or pernicious
sciences, thus taught, are still applied perversely; the man of wit *petrified* in Euclid,
or *trammelled* in metaphysics; and the man of judgment *married*, without his parents'
consent, to a *muse*. Thus far the particular arts of modern education, used partially,
and diversified according to the subject and the occasion: but there is one general
method, with the encomium of which the great Aristarchus ends his speech, ver.
266 to 268, and that is AUTHORITY, the universal *cement*, which fills all the cracks
and chasms of *lifeless* matter, shuts up all the pores of *living* substance, and brings
all human minds to *one dead level*. For if nature should chance to struggle through
all the entanglements of the foregoing ingenious expedients to *bind rebel wit*, this
claps upon her one sure and entire cover. So that well may Aristarchus defy all
human power to *get the man out* again from under so impenetrable a crust. The poet
alludes to this masterpiece of the schools in ver. 501, where he speaks of *vassals to
a name*.

264. Those who have no genius, employed in works of imagination; those who
have, in abstract sciences.

270. A notion of Aristotle, that there was originally in every block of marble, a
statue, which would appear on the removal of the superfluous parts.

But wherefore waste I words? I see advance
Whore, pupil, and laced governor° from France.
Walker! our hat'——nor more he deigned to say,
But, stern as Ajax' spectre, strode away.
   In flowed at once a gay embroidered race,
And tittering pushed the pedants off the place:
Some would have spoken, but the voice was drowned
By the French horn, or by the opening° hound.
The first came forwards, with as easy mien,
As if he saw St James's and the Queen.   280
When thus th'attendant orator begun:
'Receive, great Empress! thy accomplished son:
Thine from the birth, and sacred° from the rod,
A dauntless infant! never scared with God.
The sire saw, one by one, his virtues wake:

272. *laced governor*] Why laced? Because gold and silver are necessary trimming to denote the dress of a person of rank, and the governor must be supposed so in foreign countries, to be admitted into courts and other places of fair reception. But how comes Aristarchus to know by sight that this governor came from France? Why, by the laced coat. SCRIBL.

Ibid. *Whore, pupil, and laced governor*] Some critics have objected to the order here, being of opinion that the governor should have the precedence before the whore, if not before the pupil. But were he so placed, it might be thought to insinuate that the governor led the pupil to the whore: and were the pupil placed first, he might be supposed to lead the governor to her. But our impartial poet, as he is drawing their picture, represents them in the order in which they are generally seen; namely, the pupil between the whore and the governor; but placeth the whore first, as she usually governs both the other.

274. *stern as Ajax' spectre,*] See Homer, *Odyss.* xi. where the ghost of Ajax turns sullenly from Ulysses. A passage extremely admired by Longinus.

276. *And tittering pushed, &c.*] Horace.
              Rideat & pulset lasciva decentiùs aetas.

279. This forwardness or pertness is the certain consequence, when the children of Dulness are spoiled by too great fondness of their parent.

280. Reflecting on the disrespectful and indecent behaviour of several forward young persons in the presence, so offensive to all serious men, and to none more than the good Scriblerus.

281. *th'attendant orator*] The governor abovesaid. The poet gives him no particular name; being unwilling, I presume, to offend or do injustice to any, by celebrating one only with whom this character agrees, in preference to so many who equally deserve it. SCRIBL.

284. *A dauntless infant! never scared with God.*] Horace.
              ——*sine Dis Animosus Infans.*

The mother begged the blessing of a rake.
Thou gavest that ripeness, which so soon began,
And ceased so soon, he ne'er was boy, nor man.
Through school and college, thy kind cloud o'ercast,
Safe and unseen the young Aeneas passed: 290
Thence bursting glorious, all at once let down,
Stunned with his giddy larum half the town.
Intrepid then, o'er seas and lands he flew:
Europe he saw, and Europe saw him too.
There all thy gifts and graces we display,
Thou, only thou, directing all our way!
To where the Seine, obsequious as she runs,
Pours at great Bourbon's° feet her silken sons;
Or Tiber, now no longer Roman, rolls,
Vain of Italian arts, Italian souls: 300
To happy convents, bosomed deep in vines,
Where slumber abbots, purple as their wines:
To isles of fragrance, lily-silvered vales,
Diffusing languor in the panting gales:
To lands of singing, or of dancing slaves,
Love-whispering woods, and lute-resounding waves.
But chief her shrine where naked Venus keeps,
And Cupids ride the lion of the deeps;

288. Nature hath bestowed on the human species two states or conditions, *infancy* and *manhood*. Wit sometimes makes the *first* disappear, and folly the *latter*; but true Dulness annihilates *both*. For, want of *apprehension* in boys, not suffering that conscious ignorance and inexperience which produce the awkward bashfulness of youth, makes them *assured*; and want of *imagination* makes them *grave*. But this *gravity* and *assurance*, which is beyond *boyhood*, being neither wisdom nor knowledge, do never reach to *manhood*. SCRIBL.

290. See Virgil, *Aen.* i.

> *At Venus obscuro gradientes aëre sepsit,*
> *Et multo nebulae circum Dea fudit amictu,*
>
> *Cernere ne quis eos;*—1. *neu quis contingere possit;*
> 2. *Molirive moram;*—*aut* 3. *veniendi poscere causas.*

Where he enumerates the causes why his mother took this care of him: to wit, 1. that nobody might touch or correct him: 2. might stop or detain him: 3. examine him about the progress he had made, or so much as guess why he came there.

303. *lily-silvered vales,*] Tuberoses.

308. The winged lion, the arms of Venice. This Republic heretofore the most considerable in Europe, for her naval force and the extent of her commerce; now illustrious for her *carnivals*.

Where, eased of fleets, the Adriatic main
Wafts the smooth eunuch and enamoured swain.   310
Led by my hand, he sauntered Europe round,
And gathered every vice on Christian ground;
Saw every court, heard every king declare
His royal sense, of operas or the fair;
The stews and palace equally explored,
Intrigued with glory, and with spirit whored;
Tried all *hors d'oeuvres*, all *liqueurs* defined,
Judicious drank, and greatly daring dined;
Dropped the dull lumber of the Latin store,
Spoiled his own language, and acquired no more;   320
All classic learning lost on classic ground;
And last turned *air*,° the echo of a sound!
See now, half-cured, and perfectly well-bred,
With nothing but a solo in his head;
As much estate, and principle, and wit,
As Jansen, Fleetwood, Cibber shall think fit;
Stolen from a duel, followed by a nun,
And, if a borough choose him, not undone;°
See, to my country happy I restore
This glorious youth, and add one Venus more.   330

318. *greatly daring dined;*] It being indeed no small risk to eat through those extraordinary compositions, whose disguised ingredients are generally unknown to the guests, and highly inflammatory and unwholesome.

322. Yet less a body than echo itself; for echo reflects *sense* or *words* at least, this gentleman only *airs* and *tunes*:

—Sonus *est, qui vivit in* illo.   Ovid, *Met.*

So that this was not a metamorphosis either in one or the other, but only a resolution of the soul into its true principles, its real essence being harmony; according to the doctrine of Orpheus, the inventor of opera, who first performed to a choice assembly of beasts.   SCRIBL.

324. With nothing but a *solo?* Why, if it be a *solo*, how should there be anything else? Palpable tautology! Read boldly an opera, which is enough of conscience for such a head as has lost all its Latin.   BENTLEY.

326. *Jansen, Fleetwood, Cibber*] Three very eminent persons, all managers of *plays*; who, though not governors by profession, had, each in his way, concerned themselves in the education of youth; and regulated their wits, their morals, or their finances, at that period of their age which is the most important, their entrance into the polite world. Of the last of these, and his talents for this end, see Book 1. ver. 199, *&c.*

Her too receive (for her my soul adores)
So may the sons of sons of sons of whores,
Prop thine, O Empress! like each neighbour throne,
And make a long posterity thy own.'
    Pleased, she accepts the hero, and the dame,
Wraps in her veil, and frees from sense of shame.
    Then looked, and saw a lazy, lolling sort,
Unseen at church, at senate, or at court,
Of ever-listless loiterers, that attend
No cause, no trust, no duty, and no friend.   340
Thee too, my Paridel! she marked thee there,
Stretched on the rack of a too easy chair,
And heard thy everlasting yawn confess
The pains and penalties of idleness.
She pitied! but her pity only shed
Benigner influence on thy nodding head.
    But Annius,° crafty seer, with ebon wand,
And well dissembled emerald on his hand,
False as his gems, and cankered as his coins,

---

331. This confirms what the learned Scriblerus advanced in his note on ver. 272, that the governor, as well as the pupil, had a particular interest in this lady.

332. *So may the sons of sons, etc.*] Virgil.

> *Et nati natorum, et qui nascentur ab illis.*   *Aen.* iii.

Ibid. *sons of whores,*] For such have been always esteemed the ablest supports of the throne of *Dulness*, even by the confession of those her most *legitimate* sons, who have unfortunately wanted that advantage. The illustrious Vanini in his divine encomium on our Goddess, entitled *De Admirandis Naturae Reginae Deaeque Mortalium Arcanis*, laments that he was not born a bastard: *O utinam extra legitimum ac connubialem thorum essem procreatus! etc.* He expatiates on the prerogatives of a *free birth*, and on what he would have done for the *Great Mother* with those advantages; and then sorrowfully concludes, *At quia Conjugatorum sum soboles his orbatus sum bonis.*

341. *Thee too, my Paridel!*] The poet seems to speak of this young gentleman with great affection. The name is taken from Spenser, who gives it to a *wandering courtly squire*, that travelled about for the same reason, for which many young squires are now fond of travelling, and especially to Paris.

342, etc. Virgil, *Aen.* vi.

> *Sedet,* aeternumque sedebit,
> *Infelix Theseus, Phlegyasque* miserrimus *omnes*
> *Admonet——*

347. *Annius*] The name taken from Annius the monk of Viterbo, famous for many impositions and forgeries of ancient manuscripts and inscriptions, which he was prompted to by mere vanity, but our Annius had a more substantial motive.

Came, crammed with capon, from where Pollio dines.   350
Soft, as the wily fox is seen to creep,
Where bask on sunny banks the simple sheep,
Walk round and round, now prying here, now there;
So he; but pious, whispered first his prayer.
      'Grant, gracious Goddess! grant me still to cheat,
O may thy cloud still cover the deceit!
Thy choicer mists on this assembly shed,
But pour them thickest on the noble head.
So shall each youth, assisted by our eyes,
See other Caesars, other Homers rise;   360
Through twilight ages hunt th' Athenian fowl,
Which Chalcis gods, and mortals call an owl,
Now see an Attys, now a Cecrops clear,
Nay, Mahomet!° the pigeon at thine ear;
Be rich in ancient brass, though not in gold,
And keep his Lares,° though his house be sold;
To headless Phoebe° his fair bride postpone,
Honour a Syrian prince above his own;
Lord of an Otho,° if I vouch it true;
Blessed in one Niger,° till he knows of two.'   370
      Mummius o'erheard him; Mummius, fool-renowned,

355, 356. Horace.
                    ——Da, pulchra Laverna,
        Da mihi fallere——
        Noctem peccatis & fraudibus objice nubem.

Ibid. *still to cheat,*] Some read *skill,* but that is frivolous, for Annius hath that skill
already; or if he had not, *skill* were not wanting to cheat such persons.   BENTLEY.

361. *hunt th' Athenian fowl,*] The owl stamped on the reverse of the ancient money
of Athens.

        Which Chalcis gods, and mortals call an owl
is the verse by which Hobbes renders that of Homer,
        Χαλκίδα κικλήσκουσι Θεοί, ἄνδρες δὲ Κύμινδιν.

363. *Attys and Cecrops.*] The first kings of Athens, of whom it is hard to suppose
any coins are extant; but not so improbable as what follows, that there should be
any of Mahomet, who forbad all images. Nevertheless one of these Anniuses made
a counterfeit one, now in the collection of a learned nobleman.

371. *Mummius*] This name is not merely an allusion to the mummies he was so
fond of, but probably referred to the Roman general of that name, who burned
Corinth, and committed the curious statues to the captain of a ship, assuring him,
'that if any were lost or broken, he should procure others to be made in their
stead:' by which it should seem (whatever may be pretended) that Mummius was no
virtuoso.

Who like his Cheops stinks above the ground,
Fierce as a startled adder, swelled, and said,
Rattling an ancient sistrum° at his head:
   'Speakst thou of Syrian princes? Traitor base!
Mine, Goddess! mine is all the horned race.
True, he had wit, to make their value rise;
From foolish Greeks to steal them, was as wise;
More glorious yet, from barbarous hands to keep,
When Sallee rovers° chased him on the deep.   380
Then taught by Hermes, and divinely bold,
Down his own throat he risked the Grecian gold;
Received each demigod, with pious care,
Deep in his entrails—I revered them there,
I bought them, shrouded in that living shrine,
And, at their second birth, they issue mine.'
   'Witness great Ammon! by whose horns I swore,'
Replied soft Annius, 'this our paunch before
Still bears them, faithful; and that thus I eat,

372. *Cheops*] A king of Egypt, whose body was certainly to be known, as being buried alone in his pyramid, and is therefore more genuine than any of the Cleopatras. This royal mummy, being stolen by a wild Arab, was purchased by the consul of Alexandria, and transmitted to the museum of Mummius; for proof of which he brings a passage in Sandys's *Travels*, where that accurate and learned voyager assures us that he saw the sepulchre empty, which agrees exactly (saith he) with the time of the theft above mentioned. But he omits to observe that Herodotus tells the same thing of it in his time.

375. The strange story following which may be taken for a fiction of the poet, is justified by a true relation in Spon's *Voyages*. Vaillant (who wrote the history of the Syrian Kings as it is to be found on medals) coming from the Levant, where he had been collecting various coins, and being pursued by a corsair of Sallee, swallowed down twenty gold medals. A sudden borasco freed him from the rover, and he got to land with them in his belly. On his road to Avignon he met two physicians, of whom he demanded assistance. One advised purgations, the other vomits. In this uncertainty he took neither, but pursued his way to Lyons, where he found his ancient friend, the famous physician and antiquary Dufour, to whom he related his adventure. Dufour first asked him *whether the medals were of the higher Empire?* He assured him they were. Dufour was ravished with the hope of possessing such a treasure, he bargained with him on the spot for the most curious of them, and was to recover them at his own expense.

383. *each demigod*] They are called Θεῖοι on their coins.

387. Jupiter Ammon is called to witness, as the father of Alexander, to whom those kings succeeded in the division of the Macedonian empire, and whose *horns* they wore on their medals.

Is to refund the medals with the meat.   390
To prove me, Goddess! clear of all design,
Bid me with Pollio sup, as well as dine:
There all the learned shall at the labour stand,
And Douglas lend his soft, obstetric hand.'
  The Goddess smiling seemed to give consent;
So back to Pollio, hand in hand, they went.
  Then thick as locusts blackening all the ground,
A tribe,° with weeds and shells fantastic crowned,
Each with some wondrous gift approached the power,
A nest, a toad, a fungus, or a flower.   400
But far the foremost, two, with earnest zeal,
And aspect ardent to the throne appeal.
  The first thus opened: 'Hear thy suppliant's call,
Great Queen, and common Mother of us all!
Fair from its humble bed I reared this flower,
Suckled, and cheered, with air, and sun, and shower,
Soft on the paper ruff its leaves I spread,
Bright with the gilded button tipped its head,
Then throned in glass, and named it CAROLINE:
Each maid cried, 'Charming!' and each youth, 'Divine!' 410
Did nature's pencil ever blend such rays,
Such varied light in one promiscuous blaze?
Now prostrate! dead! behold that Caroline:

394. *Douglas*] A physician of great learning and no less taste; above all curious in
what related to Horace, of whom he collected every edition, translation, and com-
ment, to the number of several hundred volumes.

397. The similitude of *locusts* does not refer more to the numbers than to the
qualities of the virtuosi: who not only devour and lay waste every tree, shrub, and
green leaf in their *course*, i.e. of experiments; but suffer neither a moss nor fungus
to escape untouched. SCRIBL.

405 to 414. These verses are translated from Catullus, *Epith.*

> *Ut flos in septis secretus nascitur hortis,*
> *Quem mulcent aurae, firmat Sol, educat imber,*
> *Multi illum pueri, multae optavere puellae;*
> *Idem quum tenui carptus defloruit ungui,*
> *Nulli illum pueri, nullae optavere puellae, etc.*

409. It is a compliment which the florists usually pay to princes and great persons,
to give their names to the most curious flowers of their raising. Some have been
very jealous of vindicating this honour, but none more than that ambitious gardener
at Hammersmith, who caused his favourite to be painted on his sign, with this
inscription, *This is My Queen Caroline.*

No maid cries, 'Charming!' and no youth, 'Divine!'
And lo the wretch! whose vile, whose insect lust
Laid this gay daughter of the spring in dust.
Oh punish him, or to th' Elysian shades
Dismiss my soul, where no carnation fades.'
    He ceased, and wept. With innocence of mien,
Th' accused stood forth, and thus addressed the
        Queen: 420
    'Of all th' enamelled race,° whose silvery wing
Waves to the tepid zephyrs of the spring,
Or swims along the fluid atmosphere,
Once brightest shined this child of heat and air.
I saw, and started from its vernal bower
The rising game, and chased from flower to flower.
It fled, I followed; now in hope, now pain;
It stopped, I stopped; it moved, I moved again.
At last it fixed, 'twas on what plant it pleased,
And where it fixed, the beauteous bird I seized: 430
Rose or carnation was below my care;
I meddle, Goddess! only in my sphere.
I tell the naked fact without disguise,
And, to excuse it, need but show the prize;
Whose spoils this paper offers to your eye,
Fair ev'n in death! this peerless *butterfly*.'
    'My sons!', she answered, 'both have done your parts:
Live happy both, and long promote our arts.
But hear a mother, when she recommends
To your fraternal care, our sleeping friends.   440
The common soul, of heaven's more frugal make,
Serves but to keep fools pert, and knaves awake:
A drowsy watchman, that just gives a knock,

---

421. The poet seems to have an eye to Spenser, *Muiopotmos*.
                Of all the race of silver-winged flies
                Which do possess the empire of the air.
427, 428.   *It fled, I followed*, &c.
                        —*I started back,*
            It started back; but pleased I soon returned,
            Pleased it returned as soon——
                                        Milton.
440. *our sleeping friends*] Of whom see ver. 345 above.

And breaks our rest, to tell us what's o'clock.
Yet by some object every brain is stirred;
The dull may waken to a humming bird;
The most recluse, discreetly opened, find
Congenial matter in the cockle-kind;
The mind, in metaphysics at a loss,
May wander in a wilderness of moss;   450
The head that turns at super-lunar things,
Poised with a tail, may steer on Wilkins' wings.°

  O! would the sons of men once think their eyes
And reason given them but to study *flies!*
See nature in some partial narrow shape,
And let the author of the whole escape:
Learn but to trifle; or, who most observe,
To wonder at their maker, not to serve.'

  'Be that my task', replies a gloomy clerk,°
Sworn foe to mystery,° yet divinely dark;   460
Whose pious hope aspires to see the day
When moral evidence shall quite decay,

450. *a wilderness of moss*] Of which the naturalists count I can't tell how many
hundred species.

452. *Wilkins' wings*] One of the first projectors of the Royal Society, who, among
many enlarged and useful notions, entertained the extravagant hope of a possibility
to fly to the moon; which has put some volatile geniuses upon making wings for
that purpose.

453. This is the third speech of the Goddess to her supplicants, and completes
the whole of what she had to give in instruction on this important occasion, concern-
ing learning, civil society, and religion. In the first speech, ver. 119, to her editors
and conceited critics, she directs how to deprave wit and discredit fine writers. In
her second, ver. 175, to the educators of youth, she shows them how all civil duties
may be extinguished, in that one doctrine of divine hereditary right. And in this
third, she charges the investigators of nature to amuse themselves in trifles, and
rest in second causes, with a total disregard of the first. This being all that Dulness
can wish, is all she needs to say; and we may apply to her (as the poet hath managed
it) what hath been said of true wit, that *She neither says too little, nor too much.*

459. The epithet gloomy in this line may seem the same with that of dark in the
next. But *gloomy* relates to the uncomfortable and disastrous condition of an irre-
ligious sceptic, whereas *dark* alludes only to his puzzled and embroiled systems.

462. Alluding to a ridiculous and absurd way of some mathematicians, in calculat-

And damns implicit faith,° and holy lies,
Prompt to impose, and fond to dogmatize:
'Let others creep by timid steps, and slow,
On plain experience lay foundations low,
By common sense to common knowledge bred,
And last, to nature's cause through nature led.
All-seeing in thy mists, we want no guide,
Mother of arrogance, and source of pride!   470
We nobly take the high *priori* road,
And reason downward, till we doubt of God:

ing the gradual decay of moral evidence by mathematical proportions: according to which calculation, in about fifty years it will be no longer probable that Julius Caesar was in Gaul, or died in the Senate House. See Craig's *Theologiae Christianae Principia Mathematica*. But as it seems evident, that facts of a thousand years old, for instance, are now as probable as they were five hundred years ago; it is plain that if in fifty more they quite disappear, it must be owing, not to their arguments, but to the extraordinary power of our Goddess; for whose help therefore they have reason to pray.

465 to 468. In these lines are described the *disposition* of the rational *inquirer*, and the *means* and *end* of *knowledge*. With regard to his *disposition*, the contemplation of the works of God with human faculties, must needs make a modest and sensible man timorous and fearful; and that will naturally direct him to the right *means* of acquiring the little knowledge his faculties are capable of, namely *plain and sure experience*; which though supporting only an humble *foundation*, and permitting only a very slow progress, yet leads, surely, to the *end*, the discovery of the *God of nature*.

471. Those who, from the effects in this visible world, deduce the eternal power and godhead of the First Cause though they cannot attain to an adequate idea of the Deity, yet discover so much of him, as enables them to see the end of their creation, and the means of their happiness: whereas they who take this high *priori* road (such as Hobbes, Spinoza, Descartes, and some better reasoners) for one that goes right, ten lose themselves in mists, or ramble after visions which deprive them of all sight of their end, and mislead them in the choice of wrong means.

472. This was in fact the case of those who, instead of reasoning from a *visible world* to an *invisible God*, took the other road; and from an *invisible God* (to whom they had given attributes agreeable to certain metaphysical principles formed out of their own imaginations) reasoned *downwards* to a *visible world* in theory, of man's creation; which not agreeing, as might be expected, to that of God's, they began, from their inability to account for *evil* which they saw in his world, to doubt of that God, whose being they had admitted, and whose attributes they had deduced *a priori*, on weak and mistaken principles.

Make nature still encroach upon his plan:
And shove him off as far as e'er we can:
Thrust some mechanic cause into his place;
Or bind in matter, or diffuse in space.
Or, at one bound o'er-leaping all his laws,
Make God man's image, man the final cause,
Find virtue local,° all relation scorn,
See all in *self*, and but for self be born: 480
Of nought so certain as our *reason* still,
Of nought so doubtful as of *soul* and *will*.
Oh hide the God still more! and make us see
Such as Lucretius drew,° a God like thee:
Wrapped up in self, a God without a thought,
Regardless of our merit or default.

473. This relates to such as being ashamed to assert a mere mechanic cause, and yet unwilling to forsake it entirely, have had recourse to a certain *Plastic Nature, Elastic Fluid, Subtle Matter, etc.*

475 to 476. The first of these follies is that of Descartes, the second of Hobbes, the third of some succeeding philosophers.

477. These words are very significant: in their physical and metaphysical reasonings it was a *chain* of pretended *demonstrations* that drew them into all these absurd conclusions. But their errors in morals rest only on bold and impudent *assertions*, without the least shadow of proof, in which they *o'er-leap* all the laws of argument as well as truth.

478, etc. Here the poet, from the errors relating to a deity in natural philosophy, descends to those in moral. Man was made according to *God's image*; this false theology, measuring his attributes by ours, makes God after *man's image*. This proceeds from the imperfection of his *reason*. The next, of imagining himself the final cause, is the effect of his *pride*: as the making virtue and vice arbitrary, and morality the imposition of the magistrate, is of the *corruption* of his *heart*. Hence he centres everything in *himself*. The progress of dulness herein differing from that of madness; one ends in *seeing all in God*, the other in *seeing all in self*.

481. *Of nought so certain as our reason still*] Of which we have most cause to be diffident. *Of nought so doubtful as of* soul *and* will: two things the most self-evident, the existence of our soul, and the freedom of our will.

484. *Such as Lucretius drew*] Lib. 1. ver. 57.

> *Omnis enim per se Divom natura necesse'st*
> *Immortali aevo summa cum pace fruatur,*
> *Semota ab nostris rebus, summotaque longe—*
> *Nec bene pro meritis capitur, nec tangitur ira.*

From whence the two verses following are translated, and wonderfully agree with the character of our Goddess. SCRIBL.

Or that bright image to our fancy draw,
Which Theocles° in raptured vision saw,
While through poetic scenes the genius roves,
Or wanders wild in academic groves;   490
That NATURE our society adores,
Where Tindal dictates, and Silenus snores.'
   Roused at his name, up rose the boozy sire,
And shook from out his pipe the seeds of fire;
Then snapped his box, and stroked his belly down:
Rosy and reverend, though without a gown.

487. *Bright image* was the title given by the later Platonists, to that idea of *Nature*, which they had formed in their fancy, so bright that they called it Αὐτοπτον Ἄγαλμα, or the *Self-seen image*, i.e. seen by its own light.

488. Thus this philosopher calls upon his friend, to partake with him in these visions:

> 'To-morrow, when the Eastern sun
> With his first beams adorns the front
> Of yonder hill, if you're content
> To wander with me in the woods you see,
> We will pursue those loves of ours,
> By favour of the sylvan nymphs:

and invoking first the *genius* of the *place*, we'll try to obtain at least some faint and distant view of the *sovereign genius* and *first beauty*.' *Charact.* Vol. 2. pag. 245.
This *genius* is thus apostrophized (pag. 345.) by the same philosopher:

> '—O glorious *Nature!*
> Supremely fair, and sovereignly good!
> All-loving, and all-lovely! all divine!
> Wise substitute of Providence! *empowered*
> *Creatress!* or *empowering Deity,*
> *Supreme Creator!*
> Thee I invoke, and thee alone adore.'

Sir Isaac Newton distinguishes between these two in a very different manner. [*Princ. Schol. gen. sub fin.*]—*Hunc cognoscimus solummodo per proprietates suas & attributa, & per sapientissimas & optimas rerum structuras, & causas finales; veneramur autem, & colimus ob dominium.* Deus *etenim sine dominio, providentia, & causis finalibus, nihil aliud est quam* Fatum & Natura.

489, 490. 'Above all things I loved *ease*, and of all philosophers those who reasoned most *at their ease*, and were never angry or disturbed, as those called *sceptics* never were. I looked upon this kind of philosophy as the *prettiest, agreeablest, roving exercise of the mind*, possible to be imagined.' Vol. 2. p. 206.

492. Silenus was an Epicurean philosopher, as appears from Virgil, *Eclog.* 6. where he sings the principles of that philosophy in his drink.

494. *seeds of fire;*] The Epicurean language, *Semina rerum*, or atoms. Virgil, *Eclog.* 6. *Semina ignis—semina flammae—*.

Bland and familiar to the throne he came,
Led up the youth, and called the Goddess *Dame*.
Then thus: 'From priestcraft happily set free,
Lo! every finished son returns to thee: 500
First slave to words, then vassal to a name,
Then dupe to party; child and man the same;
Bounded by nature, narrowed still by art,
A trifling head, and a contracted heart.
Thus bred, thus taught, how many have I seen,
Smiling on all, and smiled on by a queen.
Marked out for honours, honoured for their birth,
To thee the most rebellious things on earth:
Now to thy gentle shadow all are shrunk,
All melted down, in pension, or in punk!   510
So Kent, so Berkeley° sneaked into the grave,
A monarch's half, and half a harlot's slave.
Poor Warwick nipped in folly's broadest bloom,
Who praises now? his chaplain on his tomb.
Then take them all, oh take them to thy breast!
Thy *Magus*,° Goddess! shall perform the rest.'
    With that, a WIZARD OLD his *cup* extends;
Which whoso tastes, forgets his former friends,

499, 500. The learned Scriblerus is here very whimsical. It would seem, says he, by this, as if the *priests* (who are always plotting and contriving mischief against the *law of nature*) had inveigled these harmless youths from the bosom of their mother, and kept them in open rebellion to her, till Silenus broke the charm, and restored them to her indulgent arms. But this is so singular a fancy, and at the same time so unsupported by proof, that we must in justice acquit them of all suspicions of this kind.

501 etc. A recapitulation of the whole course of modern education described in this book, which confines youth to the study of *words* only in schools, subjects them to the authority of *systems* in the universities, and deludes them with the names of *party-distinctions* in the world. All equally concurring to narrow the understanding, and establish slavery and error in literature, philosophy, and politics. The whole finished in modern freethinking; the completion of whatever is vain, wrong, and destructive to the happiness of mankind, as it establishes *self-love* for the sole principle of action.

517. Here beginneth the celebration of the *greater mysteries* of the Goddess, which the poet in his invocation ver. 5. promised to sing. For when now each aspirant, as was the custom, had proved his qualification and claim to a participation, the high

Sire, ancestors, himself. One casts his eyes
Up to a *star,*° and like Endymion dies: 520
A *feather*° shooting from another's head,
Extracts his brain, and principle is fled,
Lost is his God, his country, everything;
And nothing left but homage to a king!
The vulgar herd turn off to roll with hogs,
To run with horses, or to hunt with dogs;
But, sad example! never to escape

priest of Dulness first initiateth the assembly by the usual way of *libation*. And then
each of the initiated, as was always required, putteth on a *new nature*, described from
ver. 518 to 529. When the high priest and Goddess have thus done their parts, each
of them is delivered into the hands of his conductor, an inferior minister or *hiero-
phant*, whose names are *impudence, stupefaction, self-conceit, self-interest, pleasure, Epi-
curism, etc.* to lead them through the several apartments of her mystic dome or palace.
When all this is over, the sovereign Goddess, from ver. 565 to 600 conferreth her
titles and *degrees*; rewards inseparably attendant on the *participation* of the *mysteries*;
which made the ancient Theon say of them—κάλλιστα μὲν οὖν, καὶ τῶν
μεγίστων ἀγαθῶν, τὸ Μυστηρίων μετέχειν. Hence being enriched with so many
various gifts and graces, *initiation* into the mysteries was anciently, as well as in these
our times, esteemed a necessary qualification for every high office and employment,
whether in church or state. Lastly the great Mother shutteth up the solemnity with
her gracious benediction, which concludeth in drawing the curtain, and laying all
her children to rest. It is to be observed that Dulness, before this her restoration,
had her pontiffs *in partibus*; who from time to time held her mysteries in secret, and
with great privacy. But now, on her re-establishment, she celebrateth them, like
those of the Cretans (the most ancient of all mysteries) in open day, and offereth
them to the inspection of all men. SCRIBL.

Ibid. The *cup* of *self-love*, which causes a total oblivion of the obligations of
friendship, or honour, and of the service of God or our country; all sacrificed to
vainglory, court-worship, or yet meaner considerations of lucre and brutal pleasures.
From ver. 520 to 528.

518, 519. *Which whoso tastes, forgets his former friends,—Sire, etc.*] Homer of the
Nepenthe, *Odyss.* 4.

Αὐτίκ' ἄρ' εἰς οἶνον βάλε φάρμακον ἔνθεν ἔπινον
Νηπενθές τ' ἀχολόν τε, κακῶν ἐπίληθον ἁπάντων.

523, 524. So strange as this must seem to a mere English reader, the famous
Mons. de la Bruyère declares it to be the character of every good subject in a
monarchy: 'Where', says he, '*there is no such thing as love of our country*, the interest,
the glory and service of the Prince supply its place.' *De la République*, chap. 10.

Their infamy, still keep the human shape.
  But she, good Goddess, sent to every child
Firm impudence, or stupefaction mild;   530
And straight succeeded, leaving shame no room,
Cibberian forehead, or Cimmerian gloom.
  Kind self-conceit to some her glass applies,
Which no one looks in with another's eyes:
But as the flatterer or dependant paint,
Beholds himself a patriot, chief, or saint.
  On others interest her gay livery flings,
Interest, that waves on party-coloured wings:
Turned to the sun, she casts a thousand dyes,
And, as she turns, the colours fall or rise.   540
  Others the siren sisters warble round,
And empty heads console with empty sound.
No more, alas! the voice of Fame they hear,
The balm of Dulness trickling in their ear.
Great Cowper, Harcourt, Parker, Raymond, King,
Why all your toils? your sons have learned to sing.
How quick ambition hastes to ridicule!
The sire is made a peer, the son a fool.
  On some, a priest succinct in amice white°
Attends; all flesh is nothing in his sight!   550
Beeves, at his touch, at once to jelly turn,
And the huge boar is shrunk into an urn:

528. The effects of the Magus's cup are just contrary to that of Circe. Hers took
away the shape, and left the human mind: this takes away the mind, and leaves the
human shape.

529. The only comfort such people can receive, must be owing in some shape or
other to Dulness; which makes some stupid, others impudent, gives self-conceit to
some, upon the flatteries of their dependants, presents the false colours of interest
to others, and busies or amuses the rest with idle pleasures or sensuality, till they
become easy under any infamy. Each of which species is here shadowed under
allegorical persons.

544. The true *balm of Dulness*, called by the Greek physician Κολακεία, is a
sovereign remedy, and has its name from the Goddess herself. Its ancient dispensators
were *her poets*; but it is now got into as many hands as Goddard's Drops or Daffy's
Elixir. It is prepared by the *clergy*, as appears from several places of this poem: and
by ver. 534, 535, it seems as if the *nobility* had it made up in their own houses. This,
which *opera* is here said to administer, is but a spurious sort. See my dissertation
on the *Silphium* of the *ancients*. BENTLEY.

The board with specious miracles he loads,
Turns hares to larks, and pigeons into toads.
Another (for in all what one can shine?)
Explains the *Sève* and *Verdeur* of the vine.
What cannot copious sacrifice atone?
Thy truffles, Perigord! thy hams, Bayonne!
With French libation, and Italian strain,
Wash Bladen white, and expiate Hays's stain.   560
Knight lifts the head, for what are crowds undone°
To three essential partridges in one?
Gone every blush, and silent all reproach,

553. Scriblerus seems at a loss in this place. *Speciosa miracula* (says he) according
to Horace, were the monstrous fables of the Cyclops, Laestrygons, Scylla, etc. What
relation have these to the transformation of hares into larks, or of pigeons into toads?
I shall tell thee. The Laestrygons spitted men upon spears, as we do larks upon
skewers: and the fair pigeon turned to a toad is similar to the fair virgin Scylla ending
in a filthy beast. But here is the difficulty, why pigeons in so shocking a shape should
be brought to a table. Hares indeed might be cut into larks at a second dressing,
out of frugality: yet that seems no probable motive, when we consider the extrava-
gance before mentioned, of dissolving whole oxen and boars into a small vial of jelly;
nay it is expressly said, that *all flesh is nothing in his sight.* I have searched in Apicius,
Pliny, and the *Feast of Trimalchio*, in vain: I can only resolve it into some mysterious
superstitious rite, as it is said to be done by a *priest*, and soon after called a *sacrifice*,
attended (as all ancient sacrifices were) with *libation* and *song*. SCRIBL.
    This good scholiast, not being acquainted with modern luxury, was ignorant that
these were only the miracles of *French cookery*, and that particularly *Pigeons en crapeau*
were a common dish.

555. *in all what one can shine?*] Alludes to that of Virgil, *Ecl.* 8.
        —*non omnia possumus omnes.*

556. *Sève and* Verdeur] French terms relating to wines. St Evremond has a very
pathetic letter to a *nobleman in disgrace*, advising him to seek comfort in a *good table*,
and particularly to be attentive to *these qualities* in his champagne.

560. *Bladen—Hays*] Names of gamesters. Bladen is a black man. Robert Knight
Cashier of the South Sea Company, who fled from England in 1720, (afterwards
pardoned in 1742.)—These lived with the utmost magnificence at Paris, and kept
open tables frequented by persons of the first quality of England, and even by princes
of the blood of France.
    Ibid. *Bladen*, etc.] The former note of *Bladen is a black man*, is very absurd. The
manuscript here is partly obliterated, and doubtless could only have been, *Wash
blackmoors white*, alluding to a known proverb. SCRIBL.

562. *three essential partridges in one?*] i.e. two dissolved into quintessence to make
sauce for the third. The honour of this invention belongs to France, yet has it been
excelled by our native luxury, an hundred squab turkeys being not unfrequently
deposited in one pie in the Bishopric of Durham: to which our author alludes in
ver. 593 of this work.

Contending princes mount them in their coach.
  Next bidding all draw near on bended knees,
The Queen confers her *titles* and *degrees*.
Her children first of more distinguished sort,
Who study Shakespeare at the Inns of Court,
Impale a glowworm, or vertù profess,
Shine in the dignity of F. R. S.   570
Some, deep freemasons, join the silent race
Worthy to fill Pythagoras's place:
Some botanists, or florists at the least,
Or issue members of an annual feast.
Nor passed the meanest unregarded, one
Rose a Gregorian, one a Gormogon.
The last, not least in honour or applause,
Isis and Cam made doctors of her laws.
  Then blessing all, 'Go children of my care!
To practice now from theory repair.   580
All my commands are easy, short, and full:
My sons! be proud, be selfish, and be dull.
Guard my prerogative, assert my throne:

571. The poet all along expresses a very particular concern for this silent race. He has here provided, that in case they will not waken or open (as was before proposed) to a *humming-bird* or *cockle*, yet at worst they may be made freemasons; where *taciturnity* is the *only* essential qualification, as it was the *chief* of the disciples of Pythagoras.

576. *a Gregorian, one a Gormogon*] A sort of lay-brothers, *slips* from the root of the freemasons.

581, 582. We should be unjust to the reign of Dulness not to confess that hers has one advantage in it rarely to be met with in modern governments, which is, that the public *education* of her youth sits and prepares them for the observance of her *laws*, and the exertion of those virtues she recommends. For what makes men *prouder* than the empty *knowledge of words*; more *selfish* than the freethinker's *system of morals*; or *duller* than the profession of true *virtuosoship*? Nor are her *institutions* less admirable in themselves than in the fitness of these their several relations, to promote the harmony of the whole. For she tells her sons, and with great truth, that 'all her commands are *easy*, *short*, and *full*.' For is anything in nature more *easy* than the exertion of *pride*, more *short* and *simple* than the principle of *selfishness*, or more full and ample than the sphere of *Dulness*? Thus birth, education, and wise policy all concurring to support the throne of our Goddess, great must be the strength thereof.

This nod confirms each privilege your own.
The cap and switch° be sacred to his Grace;
With staff and pumps° the Marquis lead the race;
From stage to stage the licensed Earl may run,
Paired with his fellow-charioteer the sun;
The learned baron butterflies design,
Or draw to silk Arachne's subtle line;   590
The judge to dance his brother sergeant call;
The senator at cricket° urge the ball;
The bishop° stow (pontific luxury!)
An hundred souls of turkeys in a pie;
The sturdy squire to Gallic masters stoop,
And drown his lands and manors in a soup.
Others import yet nobler arts from France,
Teach kings to fiddle, and make senates dance.
Perhaps more high some daring son may soar,
Proud to my list to add one monarch more;   600
And nobly conscious, princes are but things
Born for first ministers,° as slaves for kings,
Tyrant supreme! shall three estates° command,
And MAKE ONE MIGHTY DUNCIAD OF THE LAND!'
   More she had spoke, but yawned—all nature nods:
What mortal can resist the yawn of gods?

584. This speech of Dulness to her sons at parting may possibly fall short of the reader's expectation; who may imagine the Goddess might give them a charge of more consequence, and, from such a theory as is before delivered, incite them to the practice of something more extraordinary, than to personate running-footmen, jockeys, stage coachmen, etc.

But if it be well considered, that whatever inclination they might have to do mischief, her sons are generally rendered harmless by their inability; and that it is the common effect of Dulness (even in her greatest efforts) to defeat her own design; the poet, I am persuaded, will be justified, and it will be allowed that these worthy persons, in their several ranks, do as much as can be expected from them.

590. This is one of the most ingenious employments assigned, and therefore recommended only to peers of learning. Of weaving stockings of the webs of spiders, see the *Phil. Trans.*

591. Alluding perhaps to that ancient and solemn *dance* entitled *A Call of Sergeants*.

598. *Teach kings to fiddle*] An ancient amusement of sovereign princes, (viz.) Achilles, Alexander, Nero; though despised by Themistocles, who was a republican—*Make senates dance*, either after their Prince, or to Pontoise, or Siberia.

606. This verse is truly Homerical; as is the conclusion of the action, where the great Mother composes all, in the same manner as Minerva at the period of the *Odyssey*.—It may indeed seem a very singular epitasis of a poem, to end as this does,

Churches and chapels instantly it reached;
(St James's first, for leaden Gilbert preached)
Then catched the schools; the Hall° scarce kept awake;
The Convocation° gaped, but could not speak: 610
Lost was the nation's sense, nor could be found,
While the long solemn unison went round:
Wide, and more wide, it spread o'er all the realm;
Ev'n Palinurus° nodded at the helm:
The vapour mild o'er each committee crept;
Unfinished treaties in each office slept;
And chiefless armies dozed out the campaign;
And navies yawned for orders on the main.
    O Muse! relate (for you can tell alone,

with a *great yawn*; but we must consider it as the *yawn of a god*, and of powerful effects. It is not out of nature, most long and grave counsels concluding in this very manner: nor without authority, the incomparable Spenser having ended one of the most considerable of his works with a *roar*, but then it is the *roar of a lion*, the effects whereof are described as the catastrophe of his poem.

607. The progress of this yawn is judicious, natural, and worthy to be noted. First it seizeth the churches and chapels; then catcheth the schools, where, though the boys be unwilling to sleep, the masters are not. Next Westminster Hall, much more hard indeed to subdue, and not totally put to silence even by the Goddess. Then the Convocation, which though extremely desirous to speak, yet cannot: even the House of Commons, justly called the sense of the nation, is *lost* (that is to say *suspended*) during the yawn (far be it from our author to suggest it could be lost any longer!) but it spreadeth at large over all the rest of the kingdom, to such a degree, that Palinurus himself (though as incapable of sleeping as Jupiter) yet noddeth for a moment: the effect of which, though ever so momentary, could not but cause some relaxation, for the time, in all public affairs. SCRIBL.

608. *leaden*] An epithet from the *age* she had just then restored, according to that sublime custom of the Easterns, in calling new-born princes after some great and recent event. SCRIBL.

610. Implying a great desire so to do, as the learned scholiast on the place rightly observes. Therefore beware reader lest thou take this *gape* for a *yawn*, which is attended with no desire but to go to rest: by no means the disposition of the Convocation; whose melancholy case in short is this: she was, it is *reported*, infected with the general influence of the Goddess, and while she was yawning at her ease, a wanton courtier took her at this advantage, and in the very nick clapped a *gag* into her mouth. Well therefore may she be distinguished by her *gaping*; and this distressful posture it is our poet would describe, just as she stands at this day, a sad example of the effects of dulness and malice unchecked and despised. BENTLEY.

614, 618. These verses were written many years ago, and may be found in the *State Poems* of that time. So that Scriblerus is mistaken, or whoever else have imagined this poem of a fresher date.

Wits have short memories, and dunces none)   620
Relate, who first, who last resigned to rest;
Whose heads she partly, whose completely blest;
What charms could faction, what ambition lull,
The venal quiet, and entrance the dull;
Till drowned was sense, and shame, and right, and
    wrong—
O sing, and hush the nations with thy song!

       *   *   *   *   *   *

In vain, in vain,—the all-composing hour
Resistless falls: the Muse obeys the power.
She comes! she comes! the sable throne behold
Of *Night* primeval, and of *Chaos* old!   630
Before her, Fancy's gilded clouds decay,
And all its varying rainbows die away.
Wit shoots in vain its momentary fires,
The meteor drops, and in a flash expires.

620. This seems to be the reason why the poets, whenever they give us a cata-
logue, constantly call for help on the muses, who, as the daughters of Memory, are
obliged not to forget anything. So Homer, *Iliad* 2.

    Πληθὺν δ' οὐκ ἂν ἐγὼ μυθήσομαι, οὐδ' ὀνομήνω,
    Εἰ μὴ Ὀλυμπιάδες Μοῦσαι, Διὸς αἰγιόχοιο
    Θυγατέρες, μνησαίαθ'—

And Virgil, *Aen.* vii.

    Et meministis enim, Divae, & memorare potestis;
    Ad nos vix tenuis famae perlabitur aura.

But our poet had yet another reason for putting this task upon the Muse, that all
besides being *asleep*, she only could relate what passed. SCRIBL.

624. It would be a problem worthy the solution of Aristarchus himself, (and per-
haps not of less importance than some of those weighty questions so long and warmly
disputed amongst Homer's scholiasts, as, *in which hand Venus was wounded*, and *what
Jupiter whispered in the ear of Juno*) to inform us, which required the greatest effort
of our Goddess's power, to *entrance the dull*, or to *quiet the venal*. For though the
venal may be more unruly than the *dull*, yet, on the other hand, it demands a much
greater expense of her virtue to *entrance* than barely to *quiet*. SCRIBL.

629. The sable thrones of Night and Chaos, here represented as advancing to
extinguish the light of the sciences, in the first place blot out the colours of Fancy,
and damp the fire of Wit, before they proceed to their greater work.

As one by one, at dread Medea's° strain,
The sickening stars fade off th'ethereal plain;
As Argus' eyes by Hermes' wand oppressed,°
Closed one by one to everlasting rest;
Thus at her felt approach, and secret might,
Art after Art goes out, and all is Night.   640
See skulking Truth to her old cavern fled,
Mountains of casuistry heaped o'er her head!
Philosophy, that leaned on heaven before,
Shrinks to her second cause, and is no more.
Physic of Metaphysic begs defence,

637.   *Et quamvis sopor est oculorum parte receptus,*
                    Parte tamen vigilat——
                    ——Vidit Cyllenius omnes
                    Succubuisse oculos, &c.

                                        Ovid, *Met.* 1.

641. Alluding to the saying of Democritus, that truth lay at the bottom of a deep well, from whence he had drawn her: though Butler says, *He first put her in, before he drew her out.*

643. *Philosophy, that leaned on heaven*] Philosophy has at length brought things to that pass, as to have it esteemed unphilosophical to rest in the *first cause*; as if its ends were an endless indagation of cause after cause, without ever coming to the first. So that to avoid this unlearned disgrace, some of the propagators of our best philosophy have had recourse to the contrivance here hinted at. For this philosophy, which is founded in the principle of *gravitation*, first considered that property in matter, as something extrinsical to it, and impressed immediately by God upon it. Which fairly and modestly coming up to the first cause, was pushing natural enquiries as far as they should go. But this stopping, though at the extent of our ideas, was mistaken by foreign philosophers as recurring to the *occult* qualities of the Peripatetics. To avoid which imaginary discredit to the new theory, it was thought proper to seek for the *cause* of gravitation in a certain *elastic fluid*, which pervaded all body. By this means, instead of really advancing in natural enquiries, we were brought back again by this ingenious expedient to an unsatisfactory *second cause*: for it might still, by the same kind of objection, be asked, what was the *cause* of that *elasticity*? See this folly censured, ver. 475.

645, 646. Certain writers, as Malebranche, Norris, and others, have thought it of importance, in order to secure the existence of the *soul*, to bring in question the reality of *body*; which they have attempted to do by a very refined *metaphysical* reasoning: while others of the same party, in order to persuade us of the necessity of a revelation which promises immortality, have been as anxious to prove that those qualities which are commonly supposed to belong only to an immaterial being, are but the result from the sensations of matter, and the soul naturally mortal. Thus between these different reasonings, they have left us neither soul nor body: nor the sciences of physics and metaphysics the least support, by making them depend upon and go a-begging to one another.

And Metaphysic calls for aid on Sense!
See Mystery to Mathematics fly!
In vain! they gaze, turn giddy, rave, and die.
Religion blushing veils her sacred fires,
And unawares Morality expires.   650
Nor *public* flame, nor *private*, dares to shine;
Nor *human* spark is left, nor glimpse *divine!*
Lo! thy dread empire, CHAOS! is restored;
Light dies before thy uncreating word:
Thy hand, great Anarch! lets the curtain fall;
And universal darkness buries all.°

FINIS

647. A sort of men (who make human reason the adequate measure of all truth) having pretended that whatsoever is not fully comprehended by it, is contrary to it; certain defenders of religion, who would not be outdone in a paradox, have gone as far in the opposite folly, and attempted to show that the mysteries of religion may be mathematically demonstrated; as the authors of philosophic, or astronomic principles, natural and revealed.

649. *Religion blushing veils her sacred fires*] *Blushing,* not only at the view of these her false supports in the *present* overflow of dulness, but at the memory of the *past;* when the barbarous learning of so many ages was solely employed in corrupting the simplicity, and defiling the purity of religion. Amidst the extinction of all other lights, she is said only to withdraw hers; as hers alone in its own nature is unextinguishable and eternal.

650. It appears from hence that our poet was of very different sentiments from the author of the *Characteristics,* who has written a formal treatise on virtue, to prove it not only real but durable, without the support of religion. The word *unawares* alludes to the confidence of those men who suppose that morality would flourish best without it, and consequently to the surprise such would be in (if any such there are) who indeed love virtue, and yet do all they can to root out the religion of their country.

APPENDIX

I
PREFACE

Prefixed to the five first imperfect Editions of the DUNCIAD, in three books, printed at DUBLIN and LONDON, in octavo and duodecimo, 1727.°

The PUBLISHER[1] to the READER.

[1] *The Publisher*] Who he was is uncertain; but Edward Ward tells us, in his preface to *Durgen*, 'that most judges are of opinion this preface is not of English extraction, but Hibernian,' etc. He means it was written by Dr Swift, who, whether publisher or not, may be said in a sort to be author of the poem: for when he, together with Mr Pope (for reasons specified in the preface to their *Miscellanies*) determined to own the most trifling pieces in which they had any hand, and to destroy all that remained in their power; the first sketch of this poem was snatched from the fire by Dr Swift, who persuaded his friend to proceed in it, and to him it was therefore inscribed. But the occasion of printing it was as follows.

There was published in those *Miscellanies*, a Treatise of the Bathos, or *Art of Sinking in Poetry*, in which was a chapter, where the species of bad writers were ranged in classes, and initial letters of names prefixed, for the most part at random. But such was the number of poets eminent in that art, that someone or other took every letter to himself. All fell into so violent a fury, that for half a year, or more, the common newspapers (in most of which they had some property, as being hired writers) were filled with the most abusive falsehoods and scurrilities they could possibly devise: a liberty no ways to be wondered at in those people, and in those papers, that, for many years, during the uncontrolled licence of the press, had aspersed almost all the great characters of the age; and this with impunity, their own persons and names being utterly secret and obscure. This gave Mr Pope the thought, that he had now some opportunity of doing good, by detecting and dragging into light these common enemies of mankind; since to invalidate this universal slander, it sufficed to show what contemptible men were the authors of it. He was not without hopes, that by manifesting the dulness of those who had only malice to recommend them, either the booksellers would not find their account in employing them; or the men themselves, when discovered, want courage to proceed in so unlawful an occupation. This it was that gave birth to the *Dunciad*; and he thought it an happiness, that by the late flood of slander on himself, he had acquired such a peculiar right over their names as was necessary to his design.

It will be found a true observation, though somewhat surprising, that when any scandal is vented against a man of the highest distinction and character, either in the state or in literature, the public in general afford it a most quiet reception; and the larger part accept it as favourably as if it were some kindness done to themselves: whereas if a known scoundrel or blockhead but chance to be touched upon, a whole legion is up in arms, and it becomes the common cause of all scribblers, booksellers, and printers whatsoever.

Not to search too deeply into the reason hereof, I will only observe as a fact, that every week for these two months past, the town has been persecuted with[1] pamphlets, advertisements, letters, and weekly essays, not only against the wit and writings, but against the character and person of Mr Pope. And that of all those men who have received pleasure from his works, which by modest computation may be about a[2] hundred thousand in these kingdoms of England and Ireland (not to mention Jersey, Guernsey, the Orcades,° those in the new world, and foreigners who have translated him into their languages); of all this number not a man hath stood up to say one word in his defence.

The only exception is the [3]author of the following poem, who doubtless had either a better insight into the grounds of this clamour, or a better opinion of Mr Pope's integrity, joined with a greater personal love for him, than any other of his numerous friends and admirers.

Farther, that he was in his peculiar intimacy, appears from the knowledge he manifests of the most private authors of all the anonymous pieces against him, and from his having in this poem attacked[4] no man

[1] *Pamphlets, advertisements,* etc.] See the list of those anonymous papers, with their dates and authors annexed, inserted before the poem.

[2] *About a hundred thousand*] It is surprising with what stupidity this preface, which is almost a continued irony, was taken by those authors. All such passages as these were understood by Curll, Cooke, Cibber, and others, to be serious. Hear the Laureate (*Letter to Mr Pope*, p. 9.) 'Though I grant the *Dunciad* a better poem of its kind than ever was writ; yet, when I read it with those *vainglorious* encumbrances of notes and remarks upon it, *etc.*—it is amazing, that you, who have writ with such masterly spirit upon the ruling passion, should be so blind a slave to your own, as not to see how far a *low avarice of praise*', *etc.* (taking it for granted that the notes of Scriblerus and others, were the author's own.)

[3] *The author of the following poem,* etc.] A very plain irony, speaking of Mr Pope himself.

[4] The publisher in these words went a little too far: but it is certain whatever names the reader finds that are unknown to him, are of such; and the exception is only of two or three, whose dulness, impudent scurrility, or self-conceit, all mankind agreed to have justly entitled them to a place in the *Dunciad*.

living, who had not before printed, or published, some scandal against this gentleman.

How I came possessed of it, is no concern to the reader; but it would have been a wrong to him had I detained the publication; since those names which are its chief ornaments die off daily so fast, as must render it too soon unintelligible. If it provoke the author to give us a more perfect edition, I have my end.

Who he is I cannot say, and (which is great pity) there is certainly[1] nothing in his style and manner of writing which can distinguish or discover him: for if it bears any resemblance to that of Mr Pope, 'tis not improbable but it might be done on purpose, with a view to have it pass for his. But by the frequency of his allusions to Virgil, and a laboured (not to say affected) *shortness* in imitation of him, I should think him more an admirer of the Roman poet than of the Grecian, and in that not of the same taste with his friend.

I have been well informed, that this work was the labour of full[2] six years of his life, and that he wholly retired himself from all the avocations and pleasures of the world, to attend diligently to its correction and perfection; and six years more he intended to bestow upon it, as it should seem by this verse of Statius which was cited at the head of his manuscript,

> *Oh mihi bissenos multum vigilata per annos,*
> *Duncia*[3]*!*

Hence also we learn the true title of the poem; which with the same

---

[1] *There is certainly nothing in his style, etc.*] This irony had small effect in concealing the author. The *Dunciad*, imperfect as it was, had not been published two days, but the whole town gave it to Mr Pope.

[2] *The labour of full six years, etc.*] This also was honestly and seriously believed by divers gentlemen of the *Dunciad*. J. Ralph, pref. to *Sawney*. 'We are told it was the labour of six years, with the utmost assiduity and application: it is no great compliment to the author's sense, to have employed so large a part of his life, etc.' So also Ward, pref. to *Durgen*, 'The *Dunciad*, as the publisher very wisely confesses, cost the author six years' retirement from all the pleasures of life; though it is somewhat difficult to conceive, from either its bulk or beauty, that it could be so long in hatching, etc. But the length of time and closeness of application were mentioned to prepossess the reader with a good opinion of it.'
They just as well understood what Scriblerus said of the poem.

[3] The prefacer to Curll's *Key*, p. 3. took this word to be really in Statius: 'By a quibble on the word *Duncia*, the *Dunciad* is formed.' Mr Ward also follows him in the same opinion.

certainty as we call that of Homer the *Iliad*, of Virgil the *Aeneid*, of Camoens the *Lusiad*,° we may pronounce could have been, and can be no other than

The DUNCIAD.

It is styled *heroic*, as being *doubly* so; not only with respect to its nature, which according to the best rules of the ancients, and strictest ideas of the moderns, is critically such; but also with regard to the heroical disposition and high courage of the writer, who dared to stir up such a formidable, irritable, and implacable race of mortals.

There may arise some obscurity in chronology from the *names* in the poem, by the inevitable removal of some authors, and insertion of others, in their niches. For whoever will consider the unity of the whole design, will be sensible, that the *poem was not made for these authors, but these authors for the poem*. I should judge that they were clapped in as they rose, fresh and fresh, and changed from day to day; in like manner as when the old boughs wither, we thrust new ones into a chimney.

I would not have the reader too much troubled or anxious, if he cannot decipher them; since when he shall have found them out, he will probably know no more of the persons than before.

Yet we judged it better to preserve them as they are, than to change them for fictitious names; by which the satire would only be multiplied, and applied to many instead of one. Had the hero, for instance, been called Codrus, how many would have affirmed him to have been Mr T.,° Mr E., Sir R.B., etc. but now all that unjust scandal is saved by calling him by a name, which by good luck happens to be that of a real person.

II
ADVERTISEMENT
To the FIRST EDITION with Notes, in Quarto, 1729

It will be sufficient to say of this edition, that the reader has here a much more correct and complete copy of the DUNCIAD, than has hitherto appeared. I cannot answer but some mistakes may have slipped into it, but a vast number of others will be prevented by the names being now not only set at length, but justified by the authorities and reasons given. I make no doubt, the author's own motive to use real rather than feigned names, was his care to preserve the innocent from any false application; whereas in the former editions, which had no more than the initial letters, he was made, by keys printed here, to hurt the inoffensive; and (what was worse) to abuse his friends, by an impression at Dublin.

The commentary which attends this poem was sent me from several hands, and consequently must be unequally written; yet will have one advantage over most commentaries, that it is not made upon conjectures, or at a remote distance of time. And the reader cannot but derive one pleasure from the very *obscurity* of the persons it treats of, that it partakes of the nature of a *secret*, which most people love to be let into, though the men or the things be ever so inconsiderable or trivial.

Of the *persons* it was judged proper to give some account: for since it is only in this monument that they must expect to survive (and here survive they will, as long as the English tongue shall remain such as it was in the reigns of Queen ANNE and King GEORGE,) it seemed but humanity to bestow a word or two upon each, just to tell what he was, what he writ, when he lived, and when he died.

If a word or two more are added upon the chief offenders, 'tis only as a paper pinned upon the breast, to mark the enormities for which they suffered; lest the correction only should be remembered, and the crime forgotten.

In some articles it was thought sufficient, barely to transcribe from Jacob, Curll, and other writers of their own rank, who were much better acquainted with them than any of the authors of this comment can pretend to be. Most of them had drawn each other's characters on certain occasions; but the few here inserted are all that could be saved from the general destruction of such works.

Of the part of Scriblerus I need say nothing; his manner is well enough known, and approved by all but those who are too much concerned to be judges.

The imitations of the ancients are added, to gratify those who either never read, or may have forgotten them; together with some of the parodies and allusions to the most excellent of the moderns. If, from the frequency of the former, any man think the poem too much a cento, our poet will but appear to have done the same thing in jest which Boileau° did in earnest; and upon which Vida,° Fracastorius,° and many of the most eminent Latin poets, professedly valued themselves.

III

THE

GUARDIAN

Being a continuation of some former Papers on the
Subject of PASTORALS

Monday, April 27, 1713

Compulerantque greges Corydon & Thyrsis in unum.—
Ex illo Corydon, Corydon est tempore nobis.°

I designed to have troubled the reader with no farther discourse of
pastoral; but being informed that I am taxed of partiality, in not men-
tioning an author° whose eclogues are published in the same volume
with Mr Philips's; I shall employ this paper in observations upon him,
written in the free spirit of criticism, and without any apprehension of
offending that gentleman, whose character it is, that he takes the great-
est care of his works before they are published, and has the least
concern for them afterwards.

I have laid it down as the first rule of pastoral, that its idea should
be taken from the manners of the Golden Age, and the moral formed
upon the representation of innocence; 'tis therefore plain that any
deviations from that design degrade a poem from being truly pastoral.
In this view it will appear that Virgil can only have two of his *Eclogues*
allowed to be such: his first and ninth must be rejected, because they
describe the ravages of armies, and oppressions of the innocent; Cory-
don's criminal passion for Alexis throws out the second; the calumny
and railing in the third are not proper to that state of concord; the
eighth represents unlawful ways of procuring love by enchantments,
and introduces a shepherd whom an inviting precipice tempts to self-
murder. As to the fourth, sixth, and tenth, they are given up by Hein-
sius,° Salmasius,° Rapin,° and the critics in general. They likewise
observe that but eleven of all the *Idyllia* of Theocritus are to be admitted
as pastorals; and even out of that number the greater part will be
excluded for one or other of the reasons above mentioned. So that when

I remarked in a former paper, that Virgil's *Eclogues* taken altogether are rather select poems than pastorals; I might have said the same thing with no less truth of Theocritus. The reason of this I take to be yet unobserved by the critics, viz. they never meant them all for pastorals.

Now it is plain Philips hath done this, and in that particular excelled both Theocritus and Virgil.

As simplicity is the distinguishing characteristic of pastoral, Virgil hath been thought guilty of too courtly a style; his language is perfectly pure, and he often forgets he is among peasants. I have frequently wondered that since he was so conversant in the writings of Ennius,° he had not imitated the rusticity of the Doric,° as well by the help of the old obsolete Roman language, as Philips hath by the antiquated English. For example, might not he have said *quoi* instead of *cui*, *quoijum* for *cujum*, *volt* for *vult*, etc. as well as our modern hath *welladay* for *alas*, *whilome* for *of old*, *make mock* for *deride*, and *witless younglings* for *simple lambs*, etc. by which means he had attained as much of the air of Theocritus, as Philips hath of Spenser.

Mr Pope hath fallen into the same error with Virgil. His clowns do not converse in all the simplicity proper to the country; his names are borrowed from Theocritus and Virgil, which are improper to the scene of his pastorals. He introduces Daphnis, Alexis, and Thyrsis on British plains, as Virgil hath done before him on the Mantuan. Whereas Philips, who hath the strictest regard to propriety, makes choice of names peculiar to the country, and more agreeable to a reader of delicacy, such as Hobbinol, Lobbin, Cuddy, and Colin Clout.

So easy as pastoral writing may seem (in the simplicity we have described it) yet it requires great reading, both of the ancients and moderns, to be a master of it. Philips hath given us manifest proofs of his knowledge of books. It must be confessed his competitor hath imitated *some single thoughts* of the ancients well enough (if we consider he had not the happiness of an university education) but he hath dispersed them, here and there, without that order and method which Mr Philips observes, whose *whole* third pastoral is an instance how well he hath studied the fifth of Virgil, and how judiciously reduced Virgil's thoughts to the standard of pastoral; as his contention of Colin Clout and the nightingale shows with what exactness he hath imitated every line in Strada.°

When I remarked it as a principal fault to introduce fruits and flowers of a foreign growth, in the descriptions where the scene lies in our own country, I did not design that observation should extend also to animals, or the sensitive life;° for Mr Philips hath with great judgment described wolves in England° in his first pastoral. Nor would I have a poet slavishly confine himself (as Mr Pope hath done) to one particular season of the year, one certain time of the day, and one unbroken scene in each eclogue. 'Tis plain Spenser neglected this pedantry, who in his pastoral of November mentions the mournful song of the nightingale.

> *Sad Philomel her song in tears doth steep.*

And Mr Philips, by a poetical creation, hath raised up finer beds of flowers than the most industrious gardener; his roses, endives, lilies, king-cups, and daffodils blow all in the same season.

But the better to discover the merits of our two contemporary pastoral writers, I shall endeavour to draw a parallel of them, by setting several of their particular thoughts in the same light, whereby it will be obvious how much Philips hath the advantage. With what simplicity he introduces two shepherds singing alternately!

> Hobb.   *Come, Rosalind, O come, for without thee*
> *What pleasure can the country have for me!*
> *Come, Rosalind, O come; my brinded kine,*
> *My snowy sheep, my farm, and all are thine.*

> Lanq.   *Come, Rosalind, O come; here shady bowers,*
> *Here are cool fountains, and here springing flowers,*
> *Come, Rosalind; here ever let us stay,*
> *And sweetly waste our live-long time away.*

Our other pastoral writer, in expressing the same thought, deviates into downright poetry:

> Streph.   *In spring, the fields, in autumn, hills I love;*
> *At morn the plains, at noon the shady grove;*
> *But Delia always; forced from Delia's sight,*
> *Nor plains at morn, nor groves at noon delight.*

> Daph.   *Sylvia's like autumn ripe, yet mild as May,*
> *More bright than noon, yet fresh as early day;*
> *Ev'n spring displeases when she shines not here,*
> *But blessed with her 'tis spring throughout the year.*

In the first of these authors, two shepherds thus innocently describe the behaviour of their mistresses:

Hobb. *As Marian bathed, by chance I passed by,*
   She blushed, and at me cast a side-long eye;
   Then swift beneath the crystal wave she tried
   Her beauteous form, but all in vain to hide.

Lanq. *As I to cool me bathed one sultry day,*
   Fond Lydia lurking in the sedges lay;
   The wanton laughed, and seemed in haste to fly;
   Yet often stopped, and often turned her eye.

The other modern (who, it must be confessed, hath a knack of versifying) hath it as follows:

Streph. *Me gentle Delia beckons from the plain,*
   Then, hid in shades, eludes her eager swain;
   But feigns a laugh, to see me search around,
   And by that laugh the willing fair is found.

Daph. *The sprightly Sylvia trips along the green,*
   She runs, but hopes she does not run unseen,
   While a kind glance at her pursuer flies,
   How much at variance are her feet and eyes!

There is nothing the writers of this kind of poetry are fonder of, than descriptions of pastoral presents. Philips says thus of a sheep-hook:

   Of seasoned elm, where studs of brass appear,
   To speak the giver's name, the month and year;
   The hook of polished steel, the handle turned,
   And richly by the graver's skill adorned.

The other of a bowl embossed with figures:

   ————*where wanton ivy twines,*
   And swelling clusters bend the curling vines;
   Four figures rising from the work appear,
   The various seasons of the rolling year;
   And what is that which binds the radiant sky,
   Where twelve bright signs in beauteous order lie?

The simplicity of the swain in this place, who forgets the name of the zodiac, is no ill imitation of Virgil: but how much more plainly and unaffectedly would Philips have dressed this thought in his Doric?

And what that hight which girds the welkin sheen,
Where twelve gay signs in meet array are seen?

If the reader would indulge his curiosity any farther in the comparison of particulars, he may read the first pastoral of Philips with the second of his contemporary; and the fourth and sixth of the former with the fourth and first of the latter; where several parallel places will occur to everyone.

Having now shown some parts in which these two writers may be compared, it is a justice I owe to Mr Philips, to discover those in which no man can compare with him. First, that beautiful rusticity, of which I shall only produce two instances of an hundred not yet quoted:

> *O woeful day! O day of woe! quoth he;*
> *And woeful I, who live the day to see!*

The simplicity of the diction, the melancholy flowing of the numbers, the solemnity of the sound, and the easy turn of the words in this dirge (to make use of our author's expression) are extremely elegant.

In another of his pastorals, a shepherd utters a dirge not much inferior to the former, in the following lines:

> *Ah me, the while! ah me! the luckless day!*
> *Ah luckless lad! the rather might I say!*
> *Ah silly I! more silly than my sheep,*
> *Which on the flowery plain I once did keep.*

How he still charms the ear with these artful repetitions of the epithets; and how significant is the last verse! I defy the most common reader to repeat them without feeling some motions of compassion.

In the next place I shall rank his proverbs, in which I formerly observed he excels. For example:

> *A rolling stone is ever bare of moss;*
> *And, to their cost, green years old proverbs cross.*

> *—He that late lies down, as late will rise,*
> *And, sluggard-like, till noon-day snoring lies.*

> *—Against ill luck all cunning foresight fails;*
> *Whether we sleep or wake, it nought avails.*

—Nor fear, from upright sentence, wrong.

Lastly, his elegant dialect, which alone might prove him the eldest born of Spenser, and our only true Arcadian. I should think it proper for the several writers of pastoral to confine themselves to their several counties. Spenser seems to have been of this opinion; for he hath laid the scene of one of his pastorals° in Wales; where with all the simplicity natural to that part of our island, one shepherd bids the other good-morrow, in an unusual and elegant manner:

> *Diggon Davy, I bid hur God-day;*
> *Or Diggon hur is, or I mis-say.*

Diggon answers,

> *Hur was hur while it was day-light;*
> *But now hur is a most wretched wight, etc.*

But the most beautiful example of this kind that I ever met with, is in a very valuable piece which I chanced to find among some old manuscripts, entituled a *Pastoral Ballad*; which I think, for its nature and simplicity, may (notwithstanding the modesty of the title) be allowed a perfect pastoral. It is composed in the Somersetshire dialect, and the names such as are proper to the country people. It may be observed, as a farther beauty of this pastoral, the words nymph, dryad, naiad, fawn, cupid, or satyr, are not once mentioned throughout the whole. I shall make no apology for inserting some few lines of this excellent piece. Cicily breaks thus into the subject as she is going a-milking:

> Cicily. *Rager, go vetch tha kee¹, or else tha zun*
>   *Will quite be go, bevore c'have half a don.*
>
> Roger. *Thou shouldst not ax ma tweece, but I've a bee*
>   *To dreave our bull to bull tha parson's kee.*

It is to be observed, that this whole dialogue is formed upon the passion of *jealousy*; and his mentioning the parson's kine naturally revives the jealousy of the shepherdess Cicily, which she expresses as follows:

---

¹ That is, the *kine*, or *cows*.

Cicily.   *Ah Rager, Rager! ches was zore avraid*
          When in yon vield you kissed the parson's maid;
          Is this the love that once to me you zed,
          When from tha wake thou brought'st me ginger-bread!

Roger.   *Cicily, thou charg'st me valse,—I'll zwear to thee*
          Tha parson's maid is still a maid for me.

In which answer of his are expressed at once that spirit of religion, and that innocence of the Golden Age, so necessary to be observed by all writers of pastoral.

At the conclusion of this piece, the author reconciles the lovers, and ends the eclogue the most simply in the world:

          So Rager parted, vor to vetch tha kee;
          And vor her bucket in went Cicily.

I am loath to show my fondness for antiquity so far as to prefer this ancient British author to our present English writers of pastoral; but I cannot avoid making this obvious remark, that Philips hath hit into the same road with this old West Country bard of ours.

After all that hath been said, I hope none can think it any injustice to Mr Pope, that I forbore to mention him as a pastoral writer; since upon the whole, he is of the same class with Moschus and Bion,° whom we have excluded that rank; and of whose eclogues, as well as some of Virgil's, it may be said, that (according to the description we have given of this sort of poetry) they are by no means pastorals, but something better.

IV

OF THE

POET LAUREATE

19 *November* 1729

The time of the election of a Poet Laureate being now at hand, it may be proper to give some account of the *rites* and *ceremonies* anciently used at that solemnity, and only discontinued through the neglect and degeneracy of later times. These we have extracted from an historian of undoubted credit, a reverend bishop, the learned Paulus Jovius; and are the same that were practised under the pontificate of Leo X,° the great restorer of learning.

As we now see an *age* and a *court*, that for the encouragement of poetry rivals, if not exceeds, that of this famous Pope, we cannot but wish a restoration of all its *honours* to *poesy*; the rather, since there are so many parallel circumstances in the *person* who was then honoured with the laurel, and in *him*, who (in all probability) is now to wear it.

I shall translate my author exactly as I find it in the 82nd chapter of his *Elogia Vir. Doct.* He begins with the character of the poet himself, who was the original and father of all laureates, and called Camillo. He was a plain countryman of Apulia, whether a *shepherd* or *thresher*, is not material. 'This man', says Jovius, 'excited by the fame of the great encouragement given to poets at court, and the high honour in which they were held, came to the city, bringing with him a strange kind of lyre in his hand, and at least some *twenty thousand of verses*. All the wits and critics of the court flocked about him, delighted to see a *clown*, with a ruddy, hale complexion, and in his own long hair, so top full of poetry; and at the first sight of him all agreed he was born to be *Poet Laureate*[1]. He had a most hearty welcome in an *island* of the river Tiber (an agreeable place, not unlike our Richmond) where he was first made to *eat* and *drink plentifully*, and *to repeat his verses to everybody*. Then they adorned him with a new and elegant garland, composed of *vine-leaves*, *laurel*, and *brassica* (a sort of cabbage) so composed, says my author, emblematically, *ut tam sales, quam lepida ejus temulentia, Brassicae remedio cohibenda, notaretur.* He was then saluted by common consent with the title of *archi-poeta*, or *arch-poet*, in the style of those days, in ours, *Poet Laureate*. This honour the poor man received with the most sensible demonstrations of joy, his eyes drunk with tears and gladness[2]. Next the public acclamation was expressed in a *canticle*, which is transmitted to us, as follows:

> *Salve, brassicea virens corona,*
> *Et lauro, archipoeta, pampinoque!*
> *Dignus principis auribus Leonis.*

---

[1] Apulus praepingui vultu alacer, & prolixe comatus, omnino dignus festa laurea videretur.

[2] Manantibus prae gaudio oculis.

All hail, arch-poet without peer!
Vine, bay, or cabbage fit to wear,
And worthy of the prince's ear.

From hence he was conducted in pomp to the *Capitol* of Rome, mounted on an *elephant*, through the shouts of the populace, where the ceremony ended.'

The historian tells us farther, 'That at his introduction to Leo, he not only poured forth verses innumerable, like a torrent, but also *sung* them with *open mouth*. Nor was he only *once* introduced, or on *stated* days (like our laureates) but made a *companion* to his *master*, and entertained as one of the instruments of his *most elegant pleasures*. When the prince was at table, the poet had his place at the window. When the prince had ¹half eaten his meat, he gave with his own hands the rest to the poet. When the poet drank, it was out of the prince's own flagon, insomuch (says the historian) that through so great food eating and drinking he contracted a most terrible gout.' Sorry I am to relate what follows, but that I cannot leave my reader's curiosity unsatisfied in the catastrophe of this extraordinary man. To use my author's words, which are remarkable, *mortuo Leone, profligatisque poetis etc.* 'When Leo died, and poets were no more' (for I would not understand *profligatis* literally, as if poets then were *profligate*) this unhappy Laureate was forthwith reduced to return to his country, where, oppressed with *old age* and *want*, he miserably perished in a *common hospital*.

We see from this sad conclusion (which may be of example to the poets of our time) that it were happier to meet with no encouragement at all, to remain at the plough, or other lawful occupation, than to be elevated above their condition, and taken out of the common means of life, without a surer support than the *temporary*, or, at best, *mortal* favours of the great. It was doubtless for this consideration, that when the royal bounty was lately extended to a *rural genius*,° care was taken to *settle it upon him for life*. And it hath been the practice of our princes, never to remove from the station of Poet Laureate any man who hath once been chosen, though never so much greater geniuses might arise in his time. A noble instance, how much the *charity* of our monarchs hath exceeded their *love of fame*.

To come now to the intent of this paper. We have here the whole ancient *ceremonial* of the laureate. In the first place the crown is to be

¹ Semesis opsoniis.

mixed with *vine-leaves*, as the vine is the plant of Bacchus, and full as essential to the honour, as the *butt of sack* to the salary.

Secondly, the *brassica* must be made use of as a qualifier of the former. It seems the *cabbage* was anciently accounted a remedy for *drunkenness*; a power the French now ascribe to the onion, and style a soup made of it, *soupe d'Yvronge*. I would recommend a large mixture of the *brassica* if Mr Dennis be chosen; but if Mr Tibbald, it is not so necessary, unless the cabbage° be supposed to signify the same thing with respect to *poets* as to *tailors*, viz. *stealing*. I should judge it not amiss to add another plant to this garland, to wit, *ivy:* not only as it anciently belonged to poets in general; but as it is emblematical of the three virtues of a court poet in particular; it is *creeping*, *dirty*, and *dangling*.

In the next place, a *canticle* must be composed and sung in laud and praise of the new poet. If Mr CIBBER be laureated, it is my opinion no man can *write* this but himself: and no man, I am sure, can *sing* it so affectingly. But what this canticle should be, either in his or the other candidates' case, I shall not pretend to determine.

Thirdly, there ought to be a *public show*, or entry of the poet: to settle the order or procession of which, Mr Anstis° and Mr DENNIS ought to have a conference. I apprehend here two difficulties: one, of procuring an *elephant*; the other of teaching the poet to ride him: therefore I should imagine the next animal in size or dignity would do best; either a *mule* or a large *ass*; particularly if that noble one could be had, whose portraiture makes so great an ornament of the *Dunciad*, and which (unless I am misinformed) is yet in the park of a nobleman near this city—unless Mr CIBBER be the man; who may, with great propriety and beauty, ride on a *dragon*, if he goes by land; or if he choose the water, upon one of his own *swans* from *Caesar in Egypt*.°

We have spoken sufficiently of the *ceremony*; let us now speak of the *qualifications* and *privileges* of the laureate. First, we see he must be able to make verses *extempore*, and to pour forth innumerable, if required. In this I doubt Mr TIBBALD. Secondly, he ought to *sing*, and intrepidly, *patulo ore:* here, I confess the excellency of Mr CIBBER. Thirdly, he ought to carry a *lyre* about with him: if a large one be thought too cumbersome, a small one may be contrived to hang about the neck, like an order, and be very much a grace to the person. Fourthly, he ought to have a good *stomach*, to eat and drink whatever his betters think fit; and therefore it is in this high office as in many others, no puny constitution can discharge it. I do not think CIBBER or TIBBALD here so happy: but rather a staunch, vigorous, seasoned, and dry *old gentleman*, whom I have in my eye.

I could also wish at this juncture, such a person as is truly jealous of the *honour* and *dignity* of *poetry*; no joker, or trifler; but a bard in *good earnest*; nay, not amiss if a critic, and the better if a little *obstinate*. For when we consider what great privileges have been lost from this office (as we see from the forecited authentic record of Jovius) namely those of *feeding* from the *prince's table, drinking* out of his *own flagon*, becoming even his *domestic* and *companion*; it requires a man warm and resolute, to be able to claim and obtain the restoring of these high honours. I have cause to fear the most of the candidates would be liable, either through the influence of ministers, or for rewards or favours, to give up the glorious rights of the laureate: yet I am not without hopes, there is *one*, from whom a *serious* and *steady* assertion of these privileges may be expected; and, if there be such a one, I must do him the justice to say, it is Mr DENNIS the worthy president of our society.°

INDEX

OF

PERSONS celebrated in this POEM

The first number shows the Book, the second the Verse

Epitaph on Bounce

Ah Bounce! ah gentle beast! why wouldst thou die,
When thou hadst meat enough, and Orrery?

CONVERSATIONS WITH JOSEPH SPENCE

(a) When I had done with my priests I took to reading by myself, for which I had a very great eagerness and enthusiasm, especially for poetry. In a few years I had dipped into a great number of the English, French, Italian, Latin and Greek poets. This I did without any design but that of pleasing myself, and got the languages by hunting after the stories in the several poets I read, rather than read the books to get the languages. I followed everywhere as my fancy led me, and was like a boy gathering flowers in the woods and fields just as they fall in his way. I still look upon these five or six years as the happiest part of my life.

(June 1739)

(b) I learned versification wholly from Dryden's works, who had improved it much beyond any of our former poets, and would probably have brought it to perfection, had not he been unhappily obliged to write so often in haste.

(March 1743)

(c) The great matter to write well is 'to know thoroughly what one writes about' and 'not to be affected'.

(December 1743)

(d) A poem on a slight subject requires the greater care to make it considerable enough to be read. [Just after speaking of his *Dunciad*.]

(1728?)

(e) After writing a poem one should correct it all over with one single view at a time. Thus for language, if an elegy: 'these lines are very good, but are not they of too heroical a strain?', and so vice versa. It appears very plainly from comparing parallel passages touched both in the *Iliad* and *Odyssey* that Homer did this, and 'tis yet plainer that Virgil did so, from the distinct styles he uses in his three sorts of poems. It always answers in him, and so constant an effect could not be the effect of chance.

(May 1730)

(f) I have nothing to say for rhyme, but that I doubt whether a poem can support itself without it in our language, unless it be stiffened with such strange words as are likely to destroy our language itself.

The high style that is affected so much in blank verse would not have been borne even in Milton, had not his subject turned so much on such strange out-of-the-world things as it does.

(June 1739)

(g) 'Tis easy to mark the general course of our poetry. Chaucer, Spenser, Milton, and Dryden are the great landmarks for it.

(1736)

(h) Donne had no imagination, but as much wit I think as any writer can possibly have.

(1734?)

(i) All the rules of gardening are reducible to three heads: the contrasts, the management of surprises, and the concealment of the bounds.

(1742)

(j) A tree is a nobler object than a prince in his coronation robes.

(1728?)

(k) I *must* make a perfect edition of my works, and then I shall have nothing to do but to die.

(January 1744)

(l) On the fifteenth, on Mr Lyttelton's coming in to see him, he said, 'Here am I, dying of a hundred good symptoms.'

(15 May 1744)

NOTES

THERE is no end to the making of notes on Pope, so dense is the texture of his verse. Severe discipline has had to be exercised in an attempt to keep these notes as short as possible. In particular: (1) Major individual figures are entered in the Biographical Index. A few persons are omitted who are mentioned briefly in poems packed with names such as *The Dunciad*. Many of these can be found in works of biographical reference: others will be found in the biographical appendix to volumes of *TE*, e.g. v. 341–92. (2) Biographical facts are supplied only where the text of the poem fails to make complete sense without such information. (3) Straightforward references to stock mythology, e.g. to Orpheus and his lyre, are not explained. (4) Allusions to earlier poets, classical and native, are indicated only where a strong local point is made, e.g. by heavy parody. Similarly, cross-references to Pope's own poetry are not routinely signalized. However, certain categories of allusion are glossed more freely. These include biblical quotations and proverbs, neither of which are well covered in any previous edition of Pope, and which can easily pass by a modern reader without being recognized for what they are. Only minimal information is given on bibliographical matters: the history of Pope's text is a complicated one, still not entirely cleared up in every detail, and seldom bears inescapably on the meaning of the poems.

For fuller discussion of editorial principles and choices, see the Note on the Text, pp. xxvii–xxix. Where possible, the weight of annotation is lightened by presenting key facts in the headnote to each poem.

ABBREVIATIONS

Ault	Norman Ault, *New Light on Pope* (1949)
CH	*Pope: The Critical Heritage*, ed. John Barnard (Harmondsworth, 1973)
Corr.	*The Correspondence of Alexander Pope*, ed. George Sherburn (5 vols., Oxford, 1956)
DNB	*Dictionary of National Biography*
EC	*The Works of Alexander Pope*, ed. W. Elwin and W. J. Courthope (10 vols.; 1871–89)
Johnson	Samuel Johnson, *A Dictionary of the English Language* (1755)
L&GA	Maynard Mack, *The Last and Greatest Art* (Newark, Del., 1984)
Mack, *Life*	Maynard Mack, *Alexander Pope: A Life* (1985)
MLN	*Modern Language Notes*
OED	*Oxford English Dictionary*
P	Alexander Pope
Prose	*The Prose Works of Alexander Pope*, vol. i, ed. Norman Ault (Oxford, 1936); vol. ii, ed. Rosemary Cowler (Oxford, 1986)
RES	*Review of English Studies*

Sherburn   George Sherburn, *The Early Career of Alexander Pope* (Oxford,
                1966)
Spence   J. Spence, *Observations, Anecdotes, and Characters of Books and
                Men*, ed. J. M. Osborn (2 vols.; Oxford, 1966).
TE   The Twickenham Edition of *The Poems of Alexander Pope*, ed.
                John Butt *et al.* (11 vols.; 1939–69)
Tilley   Morris P. Tilley, *A Dictionary of the Proverb in England in the
                Sixteenth and Seventeenth Centuries* (Ann Arbor, Mich., 1950)

1 *Pastorals*. When these poems first appeared in Tonson's *Miscellanies* in
1709, they marked P's first major appearance as a published author. They
were reprinted in 1716 and again in P's *Works* of 1717. In the last of these,
they were accompanied by a prose 'Discourse on Pastoral Poetry', omitted
here; for the text, see *TE*, i. 23–33. The date of composition cannot be
fixed with complete accuracy: P's note to 'Spring', l. 1, characteristically
simplifies the story. The poems must have existed by about 1705 or 1706
('Autumn' being the last completed) and were known to a circle of literary
men. Of the figures mentioned in P's note, it was perhaps William Walsh
who gave the young poet most help (see Biographical Index). A period of
revision followed in 1706 and 1707. Together with a version of Chaucer's
Merchant's Tale, they were submitted to the leading publisher Jacob Ton-
son, who paid P the sum of ten guineas in March 1708. They came at the
end of the *Miscellanies* and were preceded in the early part of the volume
by the rival pastorals of Ambrose Philips.

A manuscript survives of a slightly earlier version of the poem than the
one which appeared in 1709, and this was the one which was circulated to
P's advisers. It is written out with extreme care in P's most finished hand.
The manuscript has been edited by M. Mack (*L&GA*, 19–71). It is worth
noting one of the divergences: the holograph omits the brief dedication to
three of P's friends, which occurs near the start of 'Spring', 'Summer', and
'Autumn' (presumably 'Winter' would have been given to Walsh, who died
in 1708). If these passages were left out from the printed text, they would
run to 366 lines, a figure of obvious numerological significance in a work
dealing with the seasons of the year. See Pat Rogers, 'Rhythm and Recoil in
Pope's *Pastorals*,' *Eighteenth-Century Studies*, 14 (1980), 1–17.

P's introductory discourse addresses a number of issues thrown up in
some intense recent debate on the status of the pastoral form. Many of
the matters under review are connected with the ongoing *querelle* over the
respective merits of ancients and moderns, which had split both France
and England: Swift's *Battle of the Books* is the best-known outcome as far
as literature is concerned. P carried on the debate in later periodical essays
(notably *Guardian*, no. 40, in 1713), implicitly defending his practice as a
true follower of the ancient pastoralists as against the 'modern' Ambrose
Philips. For the background to this dispute, see J. E. Congleton, *Theories
of Pastoral Poetry in England, 1684–1798* (1952). In practice, P draws on
the standard models of bucolic verse: Theocritus, Virgil, Bion, and

Spenser's *Shepheardes Calendar*. Of these, Virgil was ultimately the most important, in part because P was already modelling his career on that of the Roman poet. The *Pastorals* constituted a diploma piece and were meant to gain P attention as a craftsman and as a new force on the poetic scene. (Hence his consultations with the group of mentors, and hence too the exaggerated care with which the verses were revised and transcribed.)

Virgil. Eclogues, ii. 485–6: 'May the countryside and the irrigating streams in the valleys be my pleasure; and may the woods and rivers be my love, as I live in quiet obscurity.'

'SPRING'

Trumbull. See Biographical Index.

l. 1 note. See headnote for composition, and Biographical Index for persons named.

2   l. 4. *Sicilian.* Because Theocritus, the first pastoral poet, came from Sicily.

l. 5. *osiers.* Willows.

l. 10. *illustriously.* Resplendently, brilliantly.

l. 11. *inspire.* Literally, fill with air, but hinting at the modern sense.

3   l. 26. *Philomel.* The nightingale.

l. 27. *Phosphor.* The morning star, Venus.

l. 28. *Purple.* Lat. *purpureus*, vivid in colour.

l. 32. *breathing.* Fragrant.

l. 37. *rising.* Carved in relief.

l. 40. *twelve fair signs.* The Zodiac.

4   l. 46. *Granville.* See *Windsor Forest*, headnote, and Biographical Index.

l. 48. *spurns.* Tramples on, kicks at.

5   l. 61. *Pactolus.* A river in Lydia, famous for the gold-dust in its water.

l. 62. *And trees . . . Po.* Recalls an episode in *Metamorphoses*, Book II, in which the sisters of Phaethon were transformed into poplars which wept tears of amber.

l. 65. *Idalia.* A town in Cyprus consecrated to the 'heavenly' Aphrodite.

l. 66. *Cynthus.* A mountain on Delos, said to be the birthplace of Diana.   *Hybla.* A mountain in Sicily, whose bountiful stores made it a fit emblem of Ceres, the goddess of growth and fertility.

6   l. 86 note. The escape of Charles II in 1651 gave rise to a royalist mythology surrounding the oak in which he hid; the anniversary of Charles's restoration became known as Oak-apple Day.

l. 90 note. The riddle seems to refer to the victory at Blenheim, with the thistle representing the English and the lily the French. Queen Anne had revived the Order of the Thistle in 1703; by the time the poem appeared, the parliaments as well as the crowns of England and Scotland were united. The royal arms were consequently changed in 1707, giving prominence to the Scottish emblem of the thistle. See *TE*, i. 39–40.

7 l. 102. *Pleiades*. The seven daughters of Atlas, who were transformed into a constellation and associated with the vernal equinox.

'SUMMER'

Note the shift to high noon (from the morning scene in 'Spring'), to be followed by sunset in 'Autumn' and midnight in 'Winter'. Moreover, the boyish games of spring are replaced by the adolescent love plaint, to be followed by the autumnal melancholy of deserted lovers and the final elegiac statement of winter. The diction of each item matches the season, the time of day, and the stage in life; thus the vocabulary of 'Spring' is sweet, vernal, and sanguine; that of 'Summer' fierce, ardent, and choleric; with 'Autumn' plangent and melancholy; and 'Winter' damp, chill, and phlegmatic. The dominant element of spring is the air (ll. 5, 113–16, 39–40, 69–76); in summer it is fire (ll. 14, 20–1, 85–92); in autumn it is the earth (ll. 49–50, 57–96); and in winter it is water (ll. 1–4, 15–16, 21–4, 29–32, 65–8, 85–9).

l. 9 note. For earth, see also Biographical Index.

8 l. 21. *Sirius*. The dog-star, believed to be connected with the heat of summer and attendant maladies: see *Epistle to Arbuthnot*, l. 3.

l. 25. *Isis*. By metonymy Oxford (the river flowing through the city, just as the Cam in the next line symbolizes Cambridge).

l. 36. *share*. Shear. (The spelling indicates P's pronunciation of the word.)

9 l. 41. *Alexis*. Pointing at Alexander Pope as poetic successor to Spenser.

l. 52. *turtles*. Turtle-doves (as in, for example, Song of Solomon 2: 12).

l. 56. *join*. Also a good rhyme in P's day.

10 ll. 73–6. *Where'er . . . eyes*. Celebrated in their setting by Handel for *Semele* (1744), based on a text by Congreve; it was probably Newburgh Hamilton who introduced the passage from P.

ll. 79–80 note. In fact wolves had been found in England as late as the sixteenth century.

'AUTUMN'

l. 1. *displays*. Causes to be observed or perceived (*OED*).

11 ll. 3–4. *This mourned . . . Grove*. Hylas had originally mourned rather a male lover, Thyrsis, but in the *Works* of 1736 and subsequently P yielded to modern decorum by substituting a heterosexual passion.

l. 5. *Mantuan*. Applicable to Virgil, a native of Mantua.

l. 7 note. See also Biographical Index.

ll. 7–8. *Thou ... fire.* Writers of Greek and Latin comedies; the 'nine' are the Muses.

l. 19. *turtle.* See 'Summer', l. 52.

12 l. 44. *pain.* Labour (poetic).

13 l. 72. *Arcturus.* 'According to the ancients, the weather was stormy for a few days when Arcturus rose with the sun, which took place in September, and Pope apparently means that the rain at this crisis was beneficial to the standing corn' (*EC*, i. 289). Cf. *Windsor Forest*, l. 119.

l. 74. *grateful clusters.* P had a vineyard in his own garden at Twickenham.

'WINTER'

14 P's general note indicates the reasons for addressing the poem to the memory of the obscure Mrs Tempest; otherwise it might reasonably have been dedicated to his early mentor William Walsh (see headnote to *Pastorals* and Biographical Index). The great storm took place on 26 November 1703; it was unequalled in its ferocity, esp. in southern England, until 1987. Rather than alluding directly to the storm, P expresses a general sense of 'the year's midnight', as Donne puts it, involving a pervasive breakdown of the natural order and an overriding presence of death and decay. These were common attributes both of elegy and of 'winter' themes (see 'Summer' above), but P turns them to the circumstance of a woman named Tempest, celebrated by Walsh, who died on the very night of the storm almost at midwinter. The work thus becomes a kind of elegiac nocturnal, identifying the decay of human life with the shrivelled world of winter.

l. 12. *dryads.* Wood-nymphs.

l. 14. *willows.* Symbol of mourning (as with cypresses, l. 22).

15 l. 22. *sylvans.* Forest deities.

l. 23. *myrtles.* Associated with Venus and hence with love.

l. 26. *relenting.* Melting.

ll. 29–36. *'Tis done ... no more.* Here and in succeeding sections there are many recollections of Moschus's lament for the death of Bion, one of the most important pastoral elegies from the ancient world.

l. 41. *sweet Echo.* Itself an echo (deliberately) of Milton, *Comus*, l. 229.

l. 52. *sweetness is no more.* The conceit perhaps recalls the aromatic leaves of the laurel, since the original Daphne was transformed into a bay-tree (Ovid, *Metamorphoses*, i. 452–567).

16 l. 73. *amaranthine.* Alluding to the amaranth, 'an imaginary flower reputed never to fade; a fadeless flower (as a poetic concept)' (*OED*).

17 l. 85. *Orion.* 'The rising and setting of the constellation Orion was thought to bring storm and rain' (*TE*, i. 95).

l. 88. *Time obey*. Recalling Virgil, *Eclogues*, x. 69: 'omnia vincit Amor; et nos cedamus Amori' (with time substituted for love).

ll. 89–92 note. Similarly Spenser had ended *The Shepheardes Calendar* with six resumptive lines.

An Essay on Criticism. Published in 1711; P gave different dates for the year of composition, but in print generally stuck to 1709. The renown of the poem was spread principally through a highly commendatory notice by Addison in *Spectator*, no. 253 (20 December 1711), which likened the work to Horace's *Art of Poetry* in its orderly but not mechanically regular development of the critical argument. Horace is certainly a prime model for the *Essay*, although P also recalled Boileau's *Art poétique* (1674) and English verse treatises of the Restoration era by John Sheffield (later Duke of Buckingham, whose collected works P was to edit) and the Earl of Roscommon. More generally he is indebted to a host of critics both ancient and modern, ranging from Quintilian and Longinus to Dryden and the recent French authorities such as Rapin and Le Bossu. P's aim lay not so much in novelty of ideas as in the sparkle, compression, and literary energy of their embodiment in poetry.

The three-part structure, as set out in the table of contents, was not explicitly indicated until the poem appeared in the octavo *Works* of 1736. However, the broad pattern had been clear all along: ll. 1–200 work towards establishing the primacy of the ancients, most directly stated in ll. 181–200; ll. 201–559 anatomize the faults of the moderns, whilst ll. 560–744 set out a programme of reform and offer a brief history of criticism (one of the first attempted at this level of discrimination). Underlying the various stages of the argument are the disputes over artistic achievement, history, and the possibility of human progress which collectively made up the international 'battle of the books' or grand *querelle*, which had been raging for almost twenty years. The most up-to-date and incisive survey of this wide-ranging cultural debate will be found in Joseph M. Levine, *Ancients and Moderns* (1991).

18 *Horace. Epistles*, i. vi. 67–8: 'If you know any more correct rules than these, share them frankly with me; if not, use these as I do.'

19 l. 8. *in prose*. Thomas Rymer had written in 1674, 'Till of late years England was as free from critics as it is free from wolves'; the new visibility of criticism as a major branch of literary activity is one of P's incentives towards writing the poem.

ll. 13–14. *Both must . . . write*. Playing with the tag *poeta nascitur, non fit*.

l. 20 note. Cicero is no longer accepted as the author of the rhetorical treatise P cites.

l. 26. *schools*. Academic pedantry.

ll. 27–8. *And some . . . sense*. Three crucial concepts are introduced, with the rich and complex words *wit* (intelligence, literary skill, inventiveness, creative zest); *nature* (order, universally accepted principles, the actual state of the world, but also innate reality, the unmediated truth of things); and *sense* (judgement, taste, good humour, and a feeling for proportion). Each individual occurrence of these words needs careful attention to see which overtone is predominant.

l. 34. *Maevius.* The proverbial type of an untalented poetaster, deriving his name from a real writer mentioned by Virgil and Horace.   *In Apollo's spite.* In contempt of the rules of good writing prescribed by the god of poetry, Apollo.

20 l. 43. *equivocal.* Spontaneous, because insects (which then included frogs and snakes) were believed to be hatched along the flooded banks of the Nile. The word also suggests 'of nondescript status' and 'of dubious parentage'.

l. 44. *tell.* Count.

l. 61. *art.* The realm of learning.

l. 67. *stoop.* Condescend to apply oneself to.

l. 69. *still.* Always.

l. 76. *informing.* Animating.

l. 77. *spirits.* Subtle fluids permeating the body through the bloodstream and directing the key functions of life (the old psychological explanation of human personality).

21 l. 84. *the Muse's steed.* Pegasus, the winged horse.

l. 86. *generous.* Mettlesome.

ll. 108–11. *So modern . . . fools.* Referring to the controversy surrounding the proposal for a public dispensary which underlay a famous mock-heroic poem, *The Dispensary* (1699) by P's friend Samuel Garth. The project, initiated by the physicians, was opposed by the apothecaries, who had established a lucrative business by taking on cases which the licensed medical profession had previously ignored. P implicitly takes the side of the physicians, although today it could be argued that the apothecaries were performing a useful function.

l. 109. *bills.* Prescriptions, but punning on modern sense of 'charges'.

l. 115. *receipts.* Recipes.

22 l. 120. *fable.* Plot.

ll. 123–4 note. P identifies Zoilus (the ancient critic who had been most severe on Homer) with Charles Perrault, who had opened up the campaign of the moderns with strictures on the most revered ancient, Homer (see headnote).

l. 129. *comment.* Commentary.   *Mantuan Muse.* Virgil.

l. 130. *young Maro.* Virgil (P. Virgilius Maro). For a full exposition of this passage, and of P's note, see Roger Savage, 'Antiquity as Nature: Pope's Fable of "Young Maro" in *An Essay on Criticism*', in C. Nicholson (ed.), *Alexander Pope: Essays for the Tercentenary* (1988), 83-116.

l. 138. *the Stagyrite*. Aristotle (from his birthplace, Stagira in Macedonia).

l. 141. *declare*. Make clear.

l. 142. *happiness*. Spontaneous felicity or grace.

23 l. 155. *art*. For a discussion of the implications of this famous line, see S. H. Monk, 'A Grace beyond the Reach of Art', *Journal of the History of Ideas*, 5 (1944), 131-50.

l. 168. *seizes*. Takes possession of (as by a legal order).

l. 170. *faults*. Pronounced 'fawtes' in P's day and thus a good rhyme.

l. 180. *Homer nods*. Recalling a famous line in Horace, *Art of Poetry*, 349.

24 ll. 183-4. *Secure . . . age*. The flames are those of fires such as that which destroyed the library of Alexandria; the envy that of malevolent critics like Zoilus; the wars those mounted by invading barbarians; and the age, according to Warburton, means 'the long reign of ignorance and superstition in the cloisters'.

l. 186. *consenting*. In concord.

l. 187. *joined*. 'Jined' was then the pronunciation.

l. 206. *recruits*. Supplies.

l. 208. *wants*. Is deficient.

l. 216. *Pierian spring*. A spring sacred to the muses, who were called the Pierides from a district on the slopes of Mt Olympus.

l. 220. *tempt*. Attempt.

25 l. 224. *science*. Knowledge.

ll. 247-8. *Thus when . . . Rome*. Referring to the cupola of St Peter's, Rome.

26 l. 261. *verbal critic*. Pedant, esp. of a philological cast, who concentrates on the textual letter rather than the spirit.

ll. 267-84. The story derives from a spurious continuation to *Don Quixote*, which had recently been translated into English.

l. 270. *Dennis*. John Dennis (see Biographical Dictionary) is named on account of his pronounced emphasis on 'regularity' in dramatic composition. This was the start of a prolonged quarrel between P and Dennis.

l. 273. *nice*. Fastidious.

l. 276. *unities*. The prescribed limitations of time and place in the action of a play.

ll. 289-96. *Some . . . of art*. Aimed at the then unfashionable metaphysicals and other baroque writers of the seventeenth century.

27 l. 308. *upon content*. Without question.

l. 321. *clown*. Yokel.

l. 323. *court*. The appropriate forms to the three settings are respectively pastoral, satire, and epic.

28 l. 328. *Fungoso*. P mistook the play by Ben Jonson; Fungoso is a character who follows the fashion at a distance.

l. 337. *numbers*. Versification.

l. 345. *open vowels*. A hiatus caused in this line by *though/oft, the/ear, the/ open*.

l. 357. *length along*. Itself an Alexandrine or twelve-syllable line.

29 l. 361. *strength*. Represented by the work of Sir John Denham (1615–69) and suggesting forceful, concise language.   *sweetness*. Belongs to Edmund Waller (1606–87), equally renowned for the highly flavoured diction and skilful use of ornament in his verse. They were regarded as the founding fathers of Augustan poetry.

l. 372. *Camilla*. A Volscian warrior maiden who figures in the *Aeneid*: P recalls a passage at vii. 808–11.

l. 374. *Timotheus*. A poet and musician from the Ionian city of Miletus (447–357 BC).

l. 376. *Libyan Jove*. Alexander the Great visited the oracle of Ammon at an oasis in the Libyan desert in 331 BC and was proclaimed the son of God.

l. 390. *turn*. A piece of embellished language, or a specially worked phrase.

l. 398. *blessing*. Recalling Matt. 5: 45: 'He maketh his sun to rise on the evil and the good.'

30 l. 400. *sublimes*. Either 'exalts' or synonymous with 'ripens' in l. 401.

l. 415. *quality*. Social eminence.

l. 419. *sonneteer*. A writer of trifles.

l. 428. *schismatics*. Stress on first syllable.

31 l. 440. *school-divines*. Scholastic theologians.

l. 441. *sentences*. Theological maxims.

l. 444. *Scotists and Thomists*. Referring to disputes between the thirteenth-century founders of distinct religious philosophies, Duns Scotus and St Thomas Aquinas.

l. 445 note. A frequent metonym in Augustan satire for the book trade and for unwanted literature.

l. 454. *fondly*. Foolishly.

l. 459. *parsons, critics, beaux*. Parsons such as Jeremy Collier, who assailed Dryden's 'immorality'; critics such as Gerald Langbaine, who disparaged his plays; and beaux such as George Villiers, Duke of Buckingham, who satirized him in *The Rehearsal*.

l. 463. *Milbournes*. For Sir Richard Blackmore and Revd Luke Milbourne, who had criticized respectively Dryden's pretensions to wit and his abilities as a translator, see Biographical Index.

l. 465. *Zoilus*. Greek grammarian of the fourth century BC, who had filled nine books with animadversions on Homer, and had become the type of the carping critic.

33 l. 521. *sacred*. Accursed (Lat. *sacer*).

l. 525. *divine*. P's statement is the most famous expression of an idea which had occasionally been found earlier, e.g. Plautus, *Mercator*, II. ii. 46, 'Humanum errare est, humanum autem ignoscere est' ('it is human to err, but it is human to excuse it').

l. 536. *monarch*. Charles II.

l. 541. *mask*. A woman who wore a mask at the theatre, often suggesting a prostitute.

l. 544. *a foreign reign*. That of William III.

l. 545. *Socinus*. The founder of what came in England to take the form of Unitarianism, i.e. the rejection of the Trinity and denial of the divinity of Christ. Lelio Sozzini (1525–62) was an Italian theologian.

34 ll. 550–1. *flatterer there*. A thrust at the liberal clergyman and future bishop, White Kennett, who had pronounced an adulatory funeral sermon for a dissipated nobleman in 1708.

l. 552. *wit's Titans*. Deists, rebels against the truths of the Church.

l. 553. *licensed blasphemies*. The lapse of the Licensing Act in 1695 led to a much more free press and the appearance of heterodox works which would formerly have been censored.

l. 563. *candour*. Kindliness.

l. 580. *complacence*. Anxiety to please.

l. 585. *Appius*. Certainly intended to point to John Dennis (see P's note), who had written an unsuccessful tragedy called *Appius and Virginia* (1709). Dennis was famous for his glaring gaze and for his fondness for the word 'tremendous'. He appears as 'Sir Tremendous', a critic in the Scriblerian play *Three Hours after Marriage* (1717).

35 l. 591. *degrees*. These were freely bestowed by the two English universities on peers without any academic requirements.

l. 592. *satires*. Pronounced 'sate-ers'.

l. 601. *tops*. 'A top sleeps when it moves with such velocity . . . that its motion is imperceptible' (*OED*).

l. 617. *Durfey*. Thomas Durfey, a popular miscellaneous writer: see Biographical Index.

36 l. 623. *Paul's church yard*. A headquarters of the book trade; all kinds of business meetings and stray assignations were held within the cathedral itself.

l. 648. *Maeonian Star*. Homer, whose birthplace was sometimes given as Lydia or Maeonia; hence his sobriquet Maeonides.

37 l. 665. *Dionysius*. Dionysius of Halicarnassus, a Greek critic who lived in Rome at the time of Augustus.

l. 667. *Petronius*. Petronius Arbiter (d. AD 65), Roman author of the *Satyricon*, noted for his polished manners and good taste.

l. 669. *Quintilian*. M. Fabius Quintilianus (*c.* AD 35–*c.*95), author of *Institutio Oratoria*, the major textbook of ancient rhetoric.

l. 675. *Longinus*. The hugely influential author of a treatise on the sublime, a Greek work of unknown date and origin. The work exercised a powerful impact on English criticism and poetry in P's time and beyond: see S. H. Monk, *The Sublime* (1935).

l. 684. *her eagles*. The Roman standards in battle.

l. 686. *Rome*. Pronounced to rhyme with *doom*.

38 l. 693. *injured name*. P refers to the criticism Erasmus had received from his fellow members of the Roman Catholic Church.

l. 697. *Leo's golden days*. The high point of the Renaissance was thought to have been reached under Pope Leo X, who reigned 1513–21.

l. 705 note. The Renaissance Latin poet Vida had written an art of poetry which was one of P's models for the *Essay*.

40 *Sappho to Phaon*. First published in March 1712, in the eighth edition of a collective translation of *Ovid's Epistles*, first put out in 1680 by Jacob Tonson, with contributions by Dryden, Otway, Aphra Behn, Settle, Rymer, Nahum Tate, and others. P's version was designed to supplement (though it did not supplant) an incomplete translation of the same epistle by Sir Carr Scrope, in the same volume. Reprinted in successive editions of the *Works*: in 1736 P stated that he had included the translations 'done by the author in his youth' as 'a sort of exercises, while he was improving himself in the languages'. The text here is based on Warburton (1751).

The exact date of composition is uncertain. A manuscript survives with P's own statement, 'Written first 1707', but the manuscript itself seems to date from shortly before publication. There are marginal comments, possibly by P's friend Henry Cromwell (1659–1728). For a transcription of this manuscript and full discussion, see *L&GA*, 72–89. It is a relatively free translation: for a comparison with the original, see *TE*, i. 343–6.

Sappho to Phaon is placed as no. 15 in editions of Ovid's *Heroides*, an early work consisting of twenty-one letters from legendary heroines to their lovers (some of the series may be spurious). This particular item is not found in the earliest manuscripts and owes its present position in the sequence to Daniel Heinsius. P may have known the edition by Heinsius (1629). For the contemporary surge of interest in the theme of the abandoned woman, inspired by the *Heroides* and more recent imitations, see *Eloisa to Abelard*, headnote (p. 620 below). Sappho's life, loves, and poetry had furnished an unceasing body of myth in later literature, art, and music: see D. M. Robinson, *Sappho and her Influence* (1963). The 'patently mythological' story of her association with Phaon is discussed by Robinson, 37–43. In *Spectator*, no. 233 (17 November 1711), Addison had given a comic version of Sappho's desperate leap.

l. 1. *Say . . . command.* There is nothing in the Latin corresponding to this opening line.

l. 5. *new numbers.* That is, the elegiac verses used by Ovid, rather than the lyric forms associated with the Lesbian poet (especially Sapphics, a stanza of three longer lines and a shorter last line).

l. 11. *retires.* The (wholly unsubstantiated) legend was that Sappho had fallen in love with a boatman of Mytilene: he had been granted youth and beauty by Aphrodite. Spurning her love, he had fled to Sicily.

l. 14. *peaceful minds.* P may be remembering Congreve's line, 'Music has charms to soothe a savage breast' (*The Mourning Bride*).

l. 17. *Lesbian dames.* P omits Ovid's listing of the former lovers, both female and male, of Sappho. The prime sense of 'Lesbian' is geographic, although there were associations of homosexuality with the island, inspired by the story of Sappho herself.

l. 28. *Cretan dame.* Ariadne, daughter of King Minos, abandoned by Theseus on the island of Naxos and there wedded by Dionysus (Bacchus).

l. 29. *nymphs.* A general usage, for fair women.

41 l. 33. *Alcaeus.* The other great Lesbian poet, contemporary with Sappho.

l. 38. *wit.* Creativity, poetic genius.

l. 39. *short my stature.* A writer of the second century AD described her as 'small and dark', and even her name may be derived from *psafos*, Doric for 'a little stone': see Robinson, 35–6.

l. 41. *Ethiopian dame.* Andromeda, daughter of the king of Ethiopia, found chained to a rock by Perseus, who rescued her and later married her.

l. 70. *Venus.* Ovid had used her epithet Erycina, from Mount Eryx in Sicily, where a temple was dedicated to her.

42 l. 75. *my brother.* Charaxus, who became entangled with an Egyptian courtesan named Dircha (see Herodotus, *History*, ii. 135).

l. 84. *Arabian dews.* Perfumes.

l. 88. *only.* Modifying 'whom'.

l. 90. *Still . . . to love.* Mimicking the wordplay in Ovid: 'et semper causa est, cur ego semper amem.'

l. 91. *the sisters.* The Fates.

l. 97. *Cephalus.* A hunter loved by the goddess of dawn, Aurora or Eos, thus causing dissension between Cephalus and his wife Procris.

l. 98. *conscious.* Feeling guilt.

l. 99. *Cynthia.* Another name for the moon-goddess Diana, beloved of the shepherd Endymion.

43 l. 121. *the Nine.* The Muses.

l. 133. *not fiercer pangs.* An epic formula: cf. *Rape of the Lock*, iii. 157.

44 l. 159. *Fury.* One of the Furies, the feared avengers.

l. 166. *Parian stone.* Marble from Phrygia and stone from Paros were much used in statues and architecture.

l. 178. *Tereus.* Philomela was raped by Tereus, King of Sparta, the husband of her sister Procne. Ultimately she was transformed into a nightingale and Procne into a swallow.

l. 181. *lotus.* A North African shrub, perhaps the jujube, whose fruit was said to cause oblivion if tasted.

l. 184. *genius of the place.* Or *genius loci*, the tutelary deity who guarded a locality: see *Epistle to Burlington*, l. 57.

l. 188. *Leucadian main.* Leucadia (now Leucas), an island off the western coast of Greece, with a towering cliff off which despairing lovers were alleged to throw themselves (see Addison's essay, cited in the headnote, for a number of such stories).

l. 189. *impending.* Overhanging.

l. 190. *fane.* Temple.

l. 193. *fury burned.* In the Greek version of the story of the Flood, only Deucalion and his wife Pyrrha survived.

45 l. 201. *prove.* Experience, put to the test.

l. 227. *loves.* Cupids.

46 l. 244. *numbers.* Verses.

An Epistle to Miss Blount, with the Works of Voiture. First published in May 1712, as *To a Young Lady.* P did not introduce the name of 'Miss Blount' until 1735, when he certainly meant the younger sister Martha. But, if it was originally addressed to either, Teresa is the likelier (Valerie Rumbold, *Women's Place in Pope's World* (Cambridge, 1989), 52–3). The probable date of composition is 1710, though P placed it earlier; he had met the Blounts around 1707. See further Ault, 49–56.

Vincent de Voiture (1598–1648) was a French poet who had become best known for his letters of wit and gallantry.

l. 1. *Loves*. Cupids.

47 l. 26. *regular*. Strictly bound by the (dramatic) rules.

l. 28. *time and place*. Carrying on the metaphor drawn from the neo-classic rules of drama, here relating to the so-called 'unities' limiting the extent of time and space in a well-made play.

l. 31. *forms*. This time the rules of social propriety.

l. 35. *fame*. Reputation.

l. 49. *Pamela*. Pronounced with accent on second syllable.

48 l. 53. *the Ring*. See note to *Rape of the Lock*, i. 44.

l. 62. *still*. Continually.

l. 67. *this*. Good humour (as in subsequent uses).

l. 69 note. The daughter of a court official.

l. 70. *Monthausier*. The Duchesse de Montausier, who was a daughter of the Marquise de Rambouillet (see l. 76), and an object of Voiture's devotion.

l. 73. *myrtle*. Sacred to Venus and an emblem of love.

49 *Windsor Forest*. First published in 1713, when P received £32. 5s. from Bernard Lintot for the poem. The full composition history is extremely involved, and P's note to l. 1 obscures as much as it clarifies. The work certainly existed in one shape or form by 1707, and most of the second section (beginning at l. 290) probably dates from 1712. It foreshadows the Peace of Utrecht, ending the long Marlborough wars, which was signed on 11 April 1713. But revision had started earlier and seemingly went on up to the time of publication. Even after this there were significant alterations introduced in the *Works* of 1717 and subsequently. The text here is based on the 1751 collection, but correcting some small errors introduced by the editor Warburton.

A holograph version of the poem, which has been written out with great care, survives from 1712. It has a number of important divergences from the printed text: for a full analysis, see the edition by R. M. Schmitz (1952).

The work belongs to a tradition of topographical poetry using local detail to encode historical, political, and moral issues. The classic exemplar is Denham's *Cooper's Hill* (1642), whose setting is in fact very close to that of P's poem, and whose intellectual structure gave P a *point d'appui*. But there are other literary models. A pervasive Georgic strain reminds us that P had moved from his *Pastorals* as Virgil had gone on from *Eclogues* to

Georgics (see note to l. 434). Echoes of Spenser, Drayton, Milton, and William Camden are among the more noticeable strands of allusion. The work embraces 'the matter of England', and its political celebration of a Tory peace draws on many elements of traditional patriotic and celebratory verse.

Lansdowne. P may have originally intended to dedicate the poem to his mentor Sir William Trumbull, but transferred the honour to Lord Lansdowne, a poet, a member of the Tory ministry, and a supporter of P for several years. See Frances M. Clements, 'Lansdowne, Pope, and the Unity of *Windsor-Forest*', *Modern Language Quarterly*, 33 (1972), 44–53.

Virgil. Eclogues, vi. 9–12: 'My song is no self-appointed task; all the grove of our tamarisk shrubs shall sing of you, Varus, nor is any page more agreeable to Apollo than that which is heralded by the name of Varus.' The tamarisk was sacred to Apollo.

l. 1. *Windsor.* P had grown up at Binfield, in Windsor Forest, about ten miles from the town of Windsor. The castle had first been sited there by William I. The Order of the Garter had first been instituted by Edward III at Windsor on St George's Day in 1349, and the castle was remodelled under the supervision of William of Wykeham, to serve as a meeting-place for knights of the order. See l. 290. For the poets who made the district a home of the muses, see ll. 259–95.

l. 5. *Granville.* Lord Lansdowne (see note to dedication).

ll. 7–10. *The groves . . . fame.* Referring explicitly to the re-creation of Eden by Milton in *Paradise Lost*, Books IV–V, esp.

l. 14. *harmoniously confused.* Opening up the theme of *discors concordia*, a concept derived from Ovid, *Metamorphoses*, i. 433. The fullest application of this idea to the poem is by Earl R. Wasserman, *The Subtler Language* (1959), 113–28.

50 l. 21. *lawns.* Clearings.

l. 26. *desert.* 'Formerly applied . . . to any wild, uninhabited region, including forest' (*OED*).

l. 27. *tufted trees.* Trees in small clumps.

l. 31. *borne.* Referring to the oak-built ships which carried rich spices and other goods from the East, providing the foundations of Britain's overseas empire.

l. 37. *Pomona.* Goddess of fruits. (Pan is here the god of shepherds and flocks.)

l. 38. *enamelled ground.* Referring to the practice of enamelling a base coat on metals as a background for painting. The phrase opens up a strand of imagery connected with heraldic and emblematic art: see Pat Rogers, 'The Enamelled Ground: The Language of Heraldry and Natural Description in *Windsor-Forest*', in M. Mack and J. A. Winn (eds.), *Pope: Recent Essays* (1980), 159–76.

l. 42. *a Stuart*. Queen Anne, who was to die within a year from the appearance of the poem. As early as this, P is relating the beauties of Windsor to the harmonious arrangement of politics under the last Stuart monarch, and linking the quiet prosperity of the district to the beneficent peace brought about by the Tory ministry. Lines 42−90 describe the creation of royal hunting-grounds by the Normans (most of the detail relating in fact to the New Forest), and the destruction of the local environment and community this involved. By association this is extended to the unpopular Dutch invader of more recent times, William III. See J. R. Moore, '*Windsor-Forest* and William III', *MLN* 66 (1951), 451−4.

l. 45 note. The 'forest laws' covered areas specifically excluded from the common law and subject to particularly severe restrictions. See E. P. Thompson, *Whigs and Hunters* (1975), 1−54.

51   l. 61. *Nimrod*. The 'mighty hunter' (Gen. 10: 9), who had come to be regarded as the type of a tyrant.

l. 65 note. P drew much of his materials on this from Camden's *Britannica*, which had been translated and re-edited in 1695, and was one of the key books of the age. The 'monkish writer' in the note is drawn from this source.

l. 67. *fanes*. Temples or shrines. P's imagination has leapt forward from the Norman yoke to the destruction of abbeys during the Reformation.

l. 71. *obscene*. Filthy, foul, disgusting.

ll. 79−80. *But see . . . a grave*. The burial of William I was delayed because a knight who held the patrimony of the chosen spot raised objections.

52   l. 81 note. Richard, the second son of William I, was killed by a stag whilst hunting in the New Forest.

ll. 83−4. *Lo Rufus . . . hart*. William II, nicknamed 'Rufus' was shot accidentally by Walter Tyrrel in 1100, once more during the chase in the New Forest. P recalls in this passage the death of William III in 1702, hastened if not caused by a hunting accident. The parallel works to identify the oppressive 'Dutch' influence (people associated with the incomer, notably City magnates and Whig war-lords) with the depredations of the Norman invaders.

l. 90. *conscious*. Previous editors follow the *OED* citation of this usage and define 'witting, well aware'. It may mean rather 'observing, witnessing', or possibly 'embarrassed by his joy'.

ll. 91−2. *Fair Liberty . . . years*. Identifies liberty and prosperity with the rule of Anne.

ll. 93−4. *Ye vigorous . . . flood*. Refers to an abundance of healthy 'animal spirit', the forces which circulated in the blood, directing bodily exercise (as distinct from vital and natural spirits).

l. 101. *tainted.* 'Imbued with scent of an animal' (*OED*). 'Tainted gales' is one of several phrases P borrowed, with a suspicion of malicious enjoyment, from Addison's *Campaign* (1705).

ll. 106–10. *When Albion . . . flies.* Recalling recent British military exploits, such as the capture of Gibraltar (1704).

53 l. 119. *Arcturus.* See *Pastorals*, 'Autumn', l. 72.

l. 135. *genial.* Pleasantly warm (*OED*, sense 3), but also including sense 1, 'generative'.

l. 142. *Tyrian dye.* Crimson, as in the dye anciently made in Tyre (capital of Phoenicia).

l. 143. *volumes.* Coils of a serpent.

54 l. 147. *fiery car.* Apollo's chariot, that is the sun, enters the constellation of Gemini around 21 May (see original version in P's note), and then the constellation of the Crab around 22 June: thus midsummer begins under the astrological sign of Cancer.

l. 150. *opening.* 'Of hounds: [beginning] to cry when in pursuit of a scent' (*OED*).

l. 162. *a Queen.* P identifies Diana with Queen Anne, whose interest in hunting was noted by Swift (*Journal to Stella*, 31 July 1711).

l. 166. *Cynthus.* A mountain of the Ovidian *Metamorphoses*.

l. 176. *crescent.* i.e. the moon, Diana's emblem.   *zone.* girdle (epic diction).

l. 178. *fillet.* A headband or ribbon.

l. 186. *liquid.* Pure or transparent (Lat. *liquidus*).

55 l. 207 note. The Loddon flows into Thames not far from P's boyhood home at Binfield.

l. 221. *honours.* Adornments, that is leaves.

56 ll. 227–8. *Nor Po . . . strays.* The Eridanus, a river in classical mythology, was identified by Ovid with the Po; it is also the name of a constellation in the southern hemisphere whose shape was seen as that of a winding river.

l. 243. *exalts.* In alchemy, raises a substance to a higher power. For this aspect of the poem, see Douglas Brooks-Davies, ' "Thoughts of Gods": Messianic Alchemy in *Windsor-Forest*', *Yearbook of English Studies*, 13 (1988), 125–42.

l. 244. *draws.* Extracts.

l. 246. *figured worlds. TE* (i. 172) suggests 'perhaps the Zodiac, or a globe of the world'. The former is more in keeping with the hermetic cast of the passage.

l. 255. *kindred.* Possessing similar substance to that of the soul.

l. 257. *Scipio*. Scipio Africanus the elder (*c.*265–*c.*183 BC) retired to his estate in Campania after the successful outcome of the Second Punic War.

l. 258. *Atticus*. Pomponius Atticus (109–32 BC), the friend of Cicero, retired to Athens and held himself aloof from public events. Like Scipio, a type of the hero in retirement. For Trumbull, see Biographical Index.

57 l. 264. *Cooper's Hill*. An eminence alongside the Thames near Egham, about five miles from Windsor, and celebrated in Denham's famous poem (see headnote).

l. 272 note. The poet Abraham Cowley died at the Thames-side town of Chertsey in 1667.

ll. 273–4. *O early lost . . . led*. Cowley was only 49 at his death; his body was floated down the river by barge prior to his funeral at Westminster Abbey.

l. 275. *expire*. See *Rape of the Lock*, v. 66.

ll. 289–90. *To sing . . . star*. P suggests that his dedicatee Granville deserved to be made a knight of the Garter, just as he had recently been elevated to the peerage (see headnote). The star refers to the insignia of the Garter.

l. 290 note. See headnote for the more complex truth.

58 l. 291 note. Surrey (*c.*1517–47) is mentioned specifically because of love poems supposed to have been written while he was imprisoned in Windsor Castle in 1537.

l. 297. *Geraldine*. Surrey's poetic mistress, sometimes identified with Lady Elizabeth Fitzgerald, daughter of the Earl of Kildare.

l. 298. *Myra*. The name Granville had used for his poetic mistress.

l. 300. *winding shore*. P follows the etymological hints of Camden's *Britannia*, where the name Windsor is derived from 'winding banks'.

l. 303 note. Edward III (born 1312) had remodelled the castle and founded the Order of the Garter: see headnote. Other kings had either been born at Windsor or were buried there.

l. 305. *monarchs chained*. David II of Scotland and Jean le Bon of France, both held captive at Windsor during the reign of Edward III.   *Cressi*. The battle of Crécy in 1346, one of the major English victories in the Hundred Years War.

l. 306. *shield*. In 1340 Edward III 'assumed the title of king of France, and quartered the lilies of France with the leopards of France' (*DNB*). Another link in the chain of heraldic imagery and allusion.

l. 307. *Verrio's colours*. The Italian decorative artist Antonio Verrio (1639–1707) had been employed by Charles II to paint scenes of victories on the ceilings at Windsor. For Defoe's comment on some of this work, see his *Tour through Great Britain* (1724–6), letter iv.

l. 311. *Henry*. Henry VI, murdered near the end of the Wars of the Roses in 1471, and subsequently buried at Windsor, near to Edward IV, his adversary, who died in 1483 (see l. 314).

l. 316. *Belerium*. Land's End, in Cornwall; there seems to be a distant echo of Milton, *Lycidas*, ll. 159–60.

ll. 319–20. *Make sacred . . . stone*. After his execution in 1649, Charles I had been buried at Windsor without ceremony.

l. 321. *fact*. Crime.

ll. 323–6. *She saw . . . scars*. P refers to the Great Plague in 1665, the Great Fire of 1666 consuming the 'domes' or buildings of London, and the struggles almost amounting to civil war in the reign of James II, culminating in the arrival of William III in 1689. These disasters are imputed to the martyrdom of Charles I (more clearly so in the manuscript version) and point to a possible Jacobite interpretation of seventeenth-century history.   *dishonest*. Dishonourable.

59 l. 327. *cease*. An allusion to the forthcoming Treaty of Utrecht (see head-note), couched in the form of a parody of Gen. 1: 3.

ll. 329–54. There are many literary antecedents for this masque-like scene but the closest in many ways is an anonymous Latin poem, *De connubio*, which had been translated in Camden's *Britannia* (1695 edn.). See Pat Rogers, 'Windsor-Forest, Britannia, and River Poetry', *Studies in Philology*, 77 (1980), 283–99. 'Oozy bed' is one of P's sly borrowings from Addison's *Campaign* (1704).

l. 332. Horns of a bull were a conventional attribute of river gods in iconography.

l. 336. *Augusta*. London (poetic).

l. 340. *Thame*. The marriage of the Thame and Isis to produce the infant Thames was a common poetic topos; see the poem in *Britannia* (as at ll. 329–54 note).

l. 343. *Cole*. The Colne, which flows south through the district west of London.

l. 345. *Vandalis*. The Wandle, which flows northwards through what is now south London.

l. 346. *gulphy*. Eddying.

l. 347. *diving flood*. For the apparent disappearance of the River Mole underground, near Dorking in Surrey, see Defoe's *Tour*, letter ii.

l. 348. *blood*. Probably alluding to the battle of Otford (1016), which is mentioned by Camden in connection with the Darent.

60 l. 358. *Hermus*. A river in Lydia with sands, according to legend, covered in gold.

l. 359. *Nilus flows*. The Nile's seven mouths; its source was still unknown.

l. 363. *Volga's banks*. Referring to the course of the war between Charles XII of Sweden against Peter the Great of Russia; Charles had invaded Muscovy but had suffered defeat at Poltava in 1709.

l. 365. *Ganges*. Referring to Moghul wars in recent years.

l. 368. *Iber's sands*. The Ebro in Spain; P refers to the victories in the Iberian campaign in 1710.   *Ister*. The Danube. The reference is to Britain's greatest recent victory, at Blenheim in 1704.

l. 378 note. Queen Anne had promoted the building of fifty churches in London, but in the end no more than twelve were built.

l. 379. *two fair cities*. London and Westminster, situated on a sweeping bend in the Thames.

l. 380. *Whitehall*. Most of the historic Whitehall Palace had been burnt down in 1698. There were several plans for restoration, never implemented.

ll. 381–422. Pervasively drawing on Isa. 60: see M. Mack, *Collected in Himself* (1983), 21–3.

l. 384. *once more*. As in the time of Elizabeth I.

l. 387. *her cross*. The red cross of St George: a possible Rosicrucian strand of allusion surfaces here.

l. 389. *Tempt*. Risk or attempt.

61 l. 396. *gold*. The sun was thought to ripen precious metals in the earth.

l. 404. *side*. Recalling a famous recent event, when four Iroquois chiefs visited London in 1710.

l. 409. *freed Indians*. South American natives, liberated from the dominion of Spain.

l. 411. *race of kings*. The Incas.

l. 420. *wheel*. The wheel of torture.

62 l. 434. *sylvan strains*. Just as Virgil had concluded his *Georgics* with a recollection of the opening of the *Eclogues*, so P echoes the first line of his own *Pastorals*.

Guardian, no. 173. Richard Steele set up the daily journal the *Guardian* in March 1713 as the immediate successor to the *Spectator*. It ran for 175 numbers to October. Addison was Steele's main contributor, with over fifty essays to his credit. P wrote at least seven: Ault raised this tally to fourteen, but not all his ascriptions have been accepted (*Prose*, vol. i, pp. lvi–lxxii). See also the edition of the *Guardian* by J. C. Stephens (1982), 25–6, the most comprehensive treatment of the journal. The best-known item by P is no. 40, on the pastoral, later reprinted in the appendix to *The Dunciad* (see pp. 559–65).

For P's lifelong obsession with gardening, see P. E. Martin, *Pursuing*

Innocent Pleasures: The Gardening World of Alexander Pope (1983).

Virgil. Georgics, iv. 122: 'The late narcissus, and the winding trail / of bear's foot, myrtles green, and ivy pale' (trans. Dryden, 1697, ll. 184–5).

Martial. Epigrams, ii. 58, ll. 1–5: 'The Baian villa of our friend Faustinus, Bassus, is not devoted to empty tracts of useless myrtles, or planes bereft of mates, or shaven box-trees, but it delights in true rustic expanses.'

nicer. More refined or sophisticated.

63 *Virgil's account.* In *Georgics*, iv. 127–46, trans. by Dryden (1697) and Addison (1694).

Homer's. In *Odyssey*, vii. 78–132. This version by P was reprinted in the *Works* (1717) and used in the full *Odyssey* translation.

64 *Sir William Temple.* In his essay 'Upon the Gardens of Epicurus' (1690).

jaculantia citria Vallos. Source unknown; possibly written by P himself. For a translation which appeared in later editions of *The Guardian*, see Stephens, 749.

65 *giants.* Statues of Gog and Magog, which were set up in the Guildhall in London.

round thy table. P's own version of Ps. 128: 3.

the Great Storm. The famous tempest which ravaged southern Britain on the night of 26/27 November 1703.

66 *The Wife of Bath from Chaucer.* Composed ?1704–5, probably revised *c.*1713 after performance of a comedy by P's new friend John Gay, *The Wife of Bath* (a two-night run in May). Published 29 December 1713 in Tonson's *Miscellanies.* P was building on the work of Dryden who had modernized Chaucer in his *Fables* (1700). At the age of 13 in 1701, P had been given a copy of a 1598 edition of Chaucer, which remained in his library till his death.

P reduces the Wife's prologue from 828 lines to 439. He telescopes, bridges, and combines passages; for fuller details, see notes in *TE*, ii. 57–8. For a general assessment of P's relation to Chaucer, see *TE*, ii. 3–12. One of the clearest comparisons is between Chaucer, ll. 9–29, and P, ll. 9–18.

l. 7. *since fifteen.* Raised from Chaucer's 12 (l. 4).

l. 9. *the scripture.* John 2: 1–11.

l. 14. *the Samaritan.* Luke 10: 30–7.

l. 17. *Increase and multiply.* Gen. 1: 22 and elsewhere: 'be fruitful' for 'increase' in Authorized Version (as often, Pope may be making his own translation of the Vulgate, or using the Common Prayer Book version).

ll. 19–20. *This too ... cleave.* Gen. 2: 24.

l. 21. *Solomon were tried*. According to 1 Kgs. 11: 3, Solomon had 700 wives and 300 concubines.

67 l. 22. *belied*. Has been misrepresented or even libelled.

l. 23. *merry fit*. Taken over bodily from Chaucer (l. 42).

ll. 28–9. *Paul . . . burn*. 1 Cor. 7: 9.

ll. 42–3. *Not every . . . poor*. Paraphrasing gospel texts, e.g. Matt. 19: 21.

l. 51. *talent it has given*. P gives a sexual meaning to the parable of the talents, in Matt. 25: 14–30. (Chaucer is less oblique, with the word 'instrument', l. 149.) Milton's sonnet on his blindness may underlie the couplet.

l. 54. *mine*. 1 Cor. 7: 4: 'Likewise the husband hath not power over his own body, but the wife'.

68 l. 64. *gold*. Zeus visited Danaë in a shower of gold.

l. 89. *vapours*. Fits of hypochondria.

ll. 98–9. *There swims . . . mate*. This may have been already proverbial when used by Chaucer (ll. 269–70): see Tilley G362.

l. 101. *ring*. Test by tapping or knocking.

69 l. 125. *mine*. By the terms of the marriage service.

l. 128. *eyes*. A proverbial formula (Tilley S764).

70 l. 157. *bedight*. An archaic form, following Chaucer's *dighte* (l. 398), with the meaning 'lay with'.

l. 161. *cully*. Cheat.

l. 164. *still*. Always.

l. 165. *curtain-lectures*. 'A reproof given by a wife to her husband in bed' (Johnson): Tilley C925.

l. 172. *tassels*. Tercels, that is male falcons.

71 l. 186. *preach*. Tilley J59. The couplet bends another proverb, Tilley P537a.

l. 210. *pye*. Magpie.

l. 212. *Philomel*. The nightingale. The quail-pipe is a whistle imitating the call of a quail, to lure birds into a trap.

l. 214. *nut-brown bowl*. Parodies Milton, *L'Allegro*, l. 100, 'spicy nut-brown ale'.

72 l. 244. *gossips*. Close women friends.

l. 245. *rood*. Cross.

ll. 248–9. *Than that . . . Darius lay*. The famous Mausoleum at Halicarnassus, built by Artemisia, widow of the ruler of Caria in Asia Minor, Mausolus (d. 377 BC). Darius I of Persia built a tomb to himself in his own lifetime.

l. 255. *hearty*. Chaucer had said rather 'daungerous' (l. 514), that is stand-offish.

73 l. 285. *stations*. Station days, that is regular fasts.

l. 288. *array*. A near-blasphemous recollection of biblical texts such as Luke 12: 33.

l. 298. *One poor hole*. The proverb normally ran, 'The mouse that has but one hole is quickly taken' (Tilley M1236). *TE*, ii. 71, glosses 'soul' as 'intellectual or spiritual power', but there seems to be a sense of spirit or resourcefulness.

74 l. 344. *Gracchus' mother*. Cornelia, mother of the Gracchi, daughter of Scipio Africanus, in Rome of the second century BC.   *Duilius' wife*. Bilia. Both celebrated by St Jerome.

l. 347. *sands*. Matt. 7: 26–7, and thence proverbial (Tilley S88).

75 ll. 359–61. *Valerius ... loves*. The references are to Valerius Maximus, compiler of Roman anecdotes; the Church Fathers Jerome (340–420) and Tertullian (*c.* AD 160–220), and incongruously lodged between them the Stoic Chrysippus (*c.*280–204 BC); the humorous and plain-spoken *Art of Love* by Ovid; the biblical Proverbs; and the story of Eloisa and Abelard, later to be treated by P (p. 620 below).

l. 365. *man*. Alluding to the fable by Aesop, no. 219, of the lion and the man; retold by Steele in *Spectator*, no. 11 (13 March 1711).

ll. 381–2. *How Samson fell ... set on fire*. Alluding to Samson and Delila, in Judg. 16: 4–21, and Hercules and Dejanira, his wife, who sent him the poisoned shirt of Nessus.

ll. 383–4. *How cursed ... laid*. Eriphyle, the treacherous wife of Amphiarus, and Clytemnestra, who murdered her husband Agamemnon.

l. 385. *Cretan dame*. Pasiphae, wife of King Minos of Crete, fell in love with a bull and gave birth to the minotaur.

l. 388. *Xantippe*. The reputedly shrewish wife of Socrates.

76 l. 392. *rain follows thunder*. Proverbial, from this story (Tilley T275).

l. 393. *Arius*. An ancient story, quoted in its simplest form by Cicero *De Oratore*, and subsequently best known in the medieval *Gesta Romanorum*, where the tale is told of Paletinus and Arrius.

THE RAPE OF THE LOCK

77 The earlier two-canto version of this poem was probably written around August or September 1711. P's friend John Caryll had been staying with Lord Petre at Ingatestone, Essex, the assumed setting of the 'rape'. It was Caryll who brought the family quarrel to the attention of P, remarking that the Petres and the Fermors had lived 'long in great friendship before'. Caryll suggested that Pope should 'write a poem to make a jest of it, and

laugh them together again' (Spence, i. 44). P certainly performed the first of these functions with relish; how far he was committed or successful in respect of the latter function is open to more question. On 21 September 1711 P sent Caryll 'a little poetical present ... which I dare not trust by the post ... for I am a little apprehensive of putting it into Lewis's hands, who is too much a bookseller to be trusted with rhyme or reputation' (*Corr.* i. 133; M. Mack, *Collected in Himself* (1982), 461). This was most likely the first version of the poem, published by Lintot in a miscellany on 20 May 1712; P was paid £7 for the *Rape*, along with larger sums for other items.

Though P claimed that the poem 'was well received and had its effect in the two families' (Spence, i. 44), there is evidence that the equivocal handling of the amorous affair had caused as much embarrassment as reconciliation, something which can hardly have surprised P. Nor was the miscellany a best seller, although Addison gave the *Rape* a generous commendation in *Spectator*, no. 523 (30 October 1712), as a welcome sign of 'rising genius among my countrymen'. P accordingly set about revising and expanding the poem, ostensibly to safeguard Arabella's honour, in reality to fill out the literary resonances of his mock-epic. He worked on the revision for the next year and was able to report to both Swift and Caryll in December 1713 that the new version was complete (*Corr.* i. 203). In its full form it appeared on 2 March 1714; Lintot this time paid P the sum of £15. P told Caryll a few days later that the sale had reached 3,000 in four days, a prodigious success for the time (*Corr.* i. 214). This edition was garnished with six plates by Louis Du Guernier. An important part of the afterlife of the poem has been its history of illustration: see Robert Halsband, *The Rape of the Lock and its Illustrators 1714–1896* (Oxford, 1980).

The version in two cantos ran to no more than 334 lines, whereas the expanded poem contains 794 lines. Major additions include the entire machinery of sylphs and gnomes, starting from Belinda's dream at the outset. Also new are the description of the toilet in Canto I; the scene on the Thames in Canto II; the game of ombre in Canto III; the Cave of Spleen in Canto IV: and (from 1717) Clarissa's speech in Canto V, which was otherwise less disturbed. Addison had tried to deter P from meddling with a 'delicious little thing'; with justice P considered this as astonishing at best, and ill-willed at worst. But others including Samuel Garth approved of the wider imaginative scope made possible by the machinery.

The most immediate models for Pope's venture into mock-heroic were Boileau's *Le Lutrin* (1674–83), a satire in six cantos on ecclesiastical politics; and Samuel Garth's *Dispensary* (1699). Garth's poem went through several revisions and the 1706 edition was in P's library; it also influenced the translation of *Le Lutrin* made in 1708, another work hovering behind P's text. Garth (*c.*1661–1719) was a leading physician, knighted in 1714 by George I for his Whig loyalties, and an important translator. He was one of those who had read and approved P's *Pastorals*; P may have met him at Will's coffee-house, where Garth had been a member of Dryden's circle.

Mock-heroic is a mode of satire by means at once of belittlement and aggrandizement. Epic action is scaled down, but trivial doings are accorded the dignity of inflated language. The *Rape* contains the plot of a full-dress epic in a comically reduced compass; equally it reduces a world of epic adventures to a domestic frame. Instead of the plains of Ilium, a young lady's boudoir; instead of the wine-dark Aegean stretching to the horizon, a short stretch of urban waterway (which is yet given the lyrical cognomen of 'the silver Thames'). Moreover, specific elements of the standard epic are parodied: the arming of the hero feminized into a make-up session (i. 121–48); the epic voyage as a boat-trip on the Thames (ii. 1–52); heroic sports transformed downwards into a fashionable card-game (iii. 25–100); gargantuan feasts into an English tea-table (iii. 105–20); mortal combats into a domestic tiff (v. 75–112). Along with the appropriate changes in stylistic register, these inversions of epic expectation serve to achieve the main literary effect of the poem, that is to realize in narrative terms the proverbial idea of a storm in a teacup, hinted at in the two opening lines.

A brief identification suffices for the 'real' hero and heroine, since they were little more than the occasion for the poem. Belinda is based on Arabella Fermor (*c*.1689–1738), daughter of a well-established Catholic family settled in Oxfordshire. The Baron derives from Robert, seventh Baron Petre (1690–1713), member of one of the main English families of the Catholic faith, with a seat at Ingatestone, Essex. He married a different woman in 1712. Sir Plume is a caricature of Sir George Browne (d. 1730), a relative of the Fermors. For fuller details, see *TE*, ii. 371–8. The episode underlying the poem took place probably in 1711, quite likely at Ingatestone; Pope's informant was his friend John Caryll (*c*.1666–1736), a wealthy Catholic squire, who was a relative of the Petres and had been staying at Ingatestone that summer. For Caryll and his family, see Howard Erskine-Hill, *The Social Milieu of Alexander Pope* (1975), 42–102. Arabella married a Berkshire gentleman in 1714 or 1715 and lived an uneventful life thereafter. It will be seen that the separate marriage of both parties and the Baron's death took place before the poem was a year old. The pair were saved from total obscurity only by *The Rape of the Lock*.

The poem is one of the most fecund ever written in terms of literary allusion. As well as the parody of ancient epic (Homer and Virgil above all), there are numerous hints of Milton, Spenser, and many other English poets; Boileau and Garth are frequently enlisted, and incidental passages recall less obviously relevant poets such as Ovid and Dryden. Few of these can be recorded in the notes here, but their presence should not be forgotten. Excellent documentation will be found in Tillotson's apparatus in *TE*, ii. 81–212; this includes a reprint of the two-canto version. A valuable collection of materials which P drew on is supplied by William Kinsley (ed.), *Contexts 2: The Rape of the Lock* (Hamden, Conn., 1979).

Mrs Arabella Fermor. Added with the expanded version in 1714. P wrote to Caryll in December 1713 that he intended to dedicate the new poem to Arabella, suggesting somewhat dubiously that to remove her anonymity would undo the harm to her reputation done by gossip which the first version of the poem had provoked. In January 1714 he asserted, 'As to the *Rape of the Lock*, I believe I have managed the dedication so nicely that it can neither hurt the lady, nor the author' (*Corr.* i. 203–7). Arabella was said to have 'approved' of the step, which suggests she was not altogether a good judge of the likely consequences. The dedication, though not openly insulting, is much less flattering than it appears.

machinery. The technical term in epic for the gods and supernatural forces influencing the action, developed by critics such as René Le Bossu.

78 *Rosicrucians.* A kind of philosophy which grew up in the seventeenth and flourished in the eighteenth century, and which had been used as the basis of a light and erotic fantasy by the Abbé de Villars, *Le Comte de Gabalis* (1670). The enterprising bookseller Edmund Curll rushed into print with a translation by John Ozell in response to the success of the *Rape*. For the philosophy in general, see Frances Yates, *The Rosicrucian Enlightenment* (1975). For its possible use by P, see note to *Windsor Forest*, l. 387.

four elements. For P's adaptations of the elementals in *Gabalis*, see *TE*, ii. 378–83. The spirits belong respectively to the four substances once thought to constitute the universe, that is air, earth, water, and fire. A whole series of correspondences in Renaissance lore went with the different elements: thus there is a connection with times of day and with stages in life. Here, Canto I is dominated by the sylphs, by air, by morning, and by youth. Canto IV is pervaded by the gnomes, by earth, by evening, and by age and experience. Canto I is sanguine; Canto IV melancholy. The pattern of correspondences is not maintained consistently, but can be traced at numerous junctures (the watery Canto II at noon, with nymphs on the verge of adulthood; the fiery contests and choleric outbursts of teatime in Canto III, etc.).

Canto I

Martial. Book II, Epigram 86 (dropped by P in 1714 but restored in 1717): 'It is not for me, Belinda, to lay violent hands upon your hair, but it delights me to pay you the tribute you have entreated.' In 1751 Warburton wrote a long note, which he attributes to P, claiming that the motto shows Arabella had requested the poem to be published. The evidence is not convincing. P's own footnote concerning the date of composition is a little misleading, see headnote.

79 l. 3. *I sing.* One of the marks of the epic proposition, which invoked the muses' assistance to the poet, was inversion of word-order and esp. putting the object at the head of the statement (*arma virumque cano*).

l. 9. *unexplored.* Undiscovered.

l. 10. *belle.* A recent importation from the French, underlying the name 'Belinda'.

l. 11. *little men.* 'Pope is stating the mock-heroic discrepancy; he is also referring to Lord Petre's short stature' (*TE*, ii. 145). He is also remembering his own puny size, as often, and slyly asking a question on the side about his own potential attractions as a lover. For P's constant awareness of this issue in his poetry, see M. Mack, *Collected in Himself*, 372–92: and Mack, *Life, passim.*

l. 18. *sound.* The recently introduced 'repeater' watch, one of many expensive toys belonging to the consumerist Belinda, sounded a chime when the pendant was pressed in.

ll. 21–6. *'Twas he . . . to say.* In epic, gods often gave signals to mortals through apparitions during sleep.

l. 23. *birth-night beau.* A fashionable young man in the splendid court dress worn on royal birthdays.

l. 35. *know.* Suggesting the Annunciation: Luke 1: 26–38. 'Thy own importance know' is blasphemously close to 'Hail, thou that art highly favoured.'

80 ll. 37–8. *Some secret . . . revealed.* Cf. Matt. 11: 25.

l. 44. *the Ring.* A small circular course in Hyde Park, used to parade fashionable coaches, and more honestly 'for gentlemen and ladies to have a view of each other' (*The Foreigner's Guide*, quoted by Clarence Tracy (ed.), *The Rape Observ'd* (1974), 8).

l. 45. *equipage.* 'A carriage and horses, with attendant footmen' (*OED*).

l. 46. *chair.* Sedan chair.

l. 55. *chariots.* At once epic diction and a normal contemporary usage for coaches.

l. 56. *ombre.* See Canto III, l. 27.

l. 58. *elements.* The doctrine of the four elements underlies not just this passage but also much of the poem. It was a physical and psychological way of distinguishing between character types.

l. 59. *termagants.* A termagant was 'a bawling turbulent woman' (Johnson).

l. 60. *salamander.* For a salamander as 'a kind of heroine in chastity', naturally resistant to male assaults, see *Spectator*, no. 198 (17 October 1711), as well as *Gabalis*, in Kinsley (ed.), *Contexts*, 192.

l. 62. *tea.* A good rhyme as the word was pronounced 'tay'.

ll. 69–70. *For spirits . . . please.* A parody of *Paradise Lost*, i. 423–4.

81 l. 73. *spark.* 'A lively, showy, gay man' (Johnson).

l. 89. *blush.* By means of using rouge.

l. 94. *impertinence.* 'Trifle: thing of no value' (Johnson).

l. 100. *moving toyshop*. The adjective means unstable or fickle; the noun refers to a shop where gewgaws and baubles were sold; there were still few playthings specifically designed for children. The nearest equivalent today might be 'gift shop'. See also *Guardian*, no. 106 (13 July 1713), possibly written by P, and repr. in Kinsley (ed.), *Contexts*, 282-3.

l. 101. *sword-knots*. Ribbons tied round the hilt of a sword.

82 l. 115. *Shock*. A shough was a shaggy-coated lapdog. It is apt that such a hairy breed should be Belinda's choice. Arabella's own dog was called Fidele (Rumbold, *Women's Place*, 73). P's deep affection for dogs is discussed by Ault, 337-50.

l. 121. *toilet*. Dressing-table. As well as the arming of an epic hero, the passage recalls Juno's dressing herself in *Iliad*, Book XIV.

l. 130. *appear*. P took the hint for this line from Addison, *Spectator*, no. 69 (19 May 1711).

l. 138. *bibles*. It has been suggested that the reason the bibles were there is that the pages were torn out to provide curl-paper for Belinda's hair; but more likely they were pretty bijou editions to add tone to the knick-knacks.

l. 144. *eyes*. By the use of eye-drops to enlarge the pupils.

83 l. 148. *Betty*. A stock name for a maidservant.

Canto II

l. 4. *silver Thames*. In sober reality, as pointed out in *TE*, ii. 139, the shores of the river were encrusted with coal-dust. In addition, the sewers of the city flowed directly into the Thames; it is to be hoped that Belinda embarked upstream from the Fleet Ditch.

l. 7. *sparkling cross*. Arabella was actually depicted with such a cross in a portrait painted *c*.1714; the confusion of piety and vanity is reinforced by our awareness that she had been educated at a convent in Paris from 1693 to 1704.

l. 20. *locks*. The emphasis throughout on Belinda's hair may be a sly allusion to the fact that 'it was the fashion some years ago [written 1721] for virgins to go bare-headed': these words were designed as a gloss on the proverb, 'All are not maidens that wear bare hair' (Tilley A115). If so, the very mode by which Belinda proclaims her chastity makes that attribute more vulnerable.

84 l. 45. *prayer*. *Aeneid*, xi. 794-5.

l. 64. *dew*. Gossamer was popularly thought to be made by spiders from dried dew (see *EC*, ii. 155).

85 l. 99. *invention*. Creative skill.

l. 100. *furbelow*. 'A piece of stuff plaited and puckered together . . . on the petticoats or gowns of women. This ... is the child of mere caprice' (Johnson).

l. 105. *Diana's law.* Chastity.

86 l. 113. *drops.* Pendant ear-rings.

l. 118. *petticoat.* Not then an undergarment so much as a skirt, made visible by the pinning back of the gown; the whalebone hoops (l. 120) went beneath the petticoat. See Tracy (ed.), *Rape Observ'd*, 29, for an illustration. Here the petticoat takes the place of the shield in epic contexts.

l. 131. *styptics.* Styptic or astringent preparations (used to help dry sores, etc.) were commonly made of alum, a compound of potassium and aluminium, which was mined in Britain.

l. 132. *rivelled.* To rivel was to 'contract into wrinkles and corrugations' (Johnson).

l. 133. *Ixion.* For his temerity in trying to win the love of Hera, Zeus punished Ixion by having him bound on a wheel which turned everlastingly in the underworld.

l. 134. *whirling mill.* Tracy illustrates a contemporary coffee-mill, 'a kind of swizzle-stick' which was fitted through the lid of the chocolate-pot (*Rape Observ'd*, 134).

Canto III

86 l. 4. *Hampton.* Hampton Court, standing on the banks of the Thames some twenty miles by river from Westminster, was Queen Anne's favourite amongst the royal palaces.

l. 7. *three realms.* England, Ireland, and Scotland.

87 l. 14. *Indian screen.* Usually a copy of oriental designs rather than an imported item: the main purpose was to shield ladies' complexions from the fire.

l. 17. *snuff.* A recent craze among the fashionable.

l. 23. *th' Exchange.* Italicized in the original text, indicating not a general reference but a specific allusion to the Royal Exchange, the principal place for transacting business in the City of London.

l. 27. *ombre.* A three-handed card-game in which nine cards are dealt to each player; it was the aim of each player to win a majority of the nine tricks. Belinda is the 'ombre' who has the option of declaring the trump suit. The course of the game is briefly as follows: Belinda calls spades as trumps, since she has a strong hand with the three matadors or highest-ranking cards, as well as the king of spades. She wins the first four tricks (ll. 47–64), but then mistakenly leads the king of clubs, which the Baron trumps with his queen of spades. He goes on to win the next three tricks with a strong hand of diamonds (ll. 65–92). The ninth trick will be decisive, and fortunately for Belinda her king of hearts defeats the ace led by the Baron. For the course of the game, see *TE*, ii. 383–92, and W. K. Wimsatt, 'Belinda Ludens', *New Literary History*, 4 (1973), 357–74.

l. 30. *sacred nine*. The nine Muses.

l. 32. *important*. More like 'significant' in modern usage.

l. 33. *matadore*. The highest-ranking cards in ombre (mentioned individually in ll. 49–53).

l. 41. *succinct*. A comically elevated word for 'short'; the knaves in a contemporary pack illustrated by Tracy (*Rape Observ'd*, 41) have short coats.

l. 46. *they were*. A blasphemous rephrasal of Gen. 1: 3, which had become the stock example of sublimity in expression.

88 l. 49. *Spadillio*. The ace of spades, the pre-eminent matadore.

l. 51. *Manillio*. The two of spades, another matadore.

l. 52. *verdant field*. The green cloth of the card-table seen as the site of battle and as a heraldic display.

l. 53. *Basto*. The ace of clubs, also a matadore card.

l. 61. *Pam*. The knave of clubs in the game of loo (l. 62).

ll. 69–74. *The club's . . . globe*. The details concerning the king of clubs match the card illustrated in Tracy (*Rape Observ'd*, 37). The king of diamonds is depicted in profile (see l. 76).

89 l. 92. *codille*. Defeat of the ombre, which would mean that Belinda must pay the entire stakes of the hand.

l. 94. *trick*. Punning on the term in cards and the sense of stratagem.

l. 106. *mill turns round*. P remarked in a letter to Arbuthnot that Swift roasted the grains when making coffee 'with his own hands in an engine for the purpose' (*Corr*. i. 234).

l. 107. *shining altars of Japan*. Japanned or lacquered tables, often designed in a mock-oriental style.

l. 117. *coffee*. Coffee-houses were centres of political gossip and news-mongering.

ll. 122–4. *Fear . . . injured hair*. Ovid tells the story of a princess of Megara named Scylla, obsessed by her love for the invader Minos. She pulled out a single purple hair from the head of her father, King Nisus, which was thought to ensure the safety of the realm, and presented it to the besieger Minos. She was spurned by Minos and transformed into a bird.

l. 128. *two-edged weapon*. Scissors here, in mock-heroic diction, but P may be recalling the 'two-edged sword' of Heb. 4: 12, 'piercing even the dividing asunder of soul and spirit'.

90 l. 152. *unites again*. The reference in *Paradise Lost*, vi. 330–53, is to angels.

l. 164. *coach and six*. A splendid carriage drawn by three pairs of horses.

l. 165. *Atalantis.* P refers with heavy irony to *The New Atalantis*, by Delarivière Manley (1709), a popular *chronique scandaleuse* which concealed the identity of well-known figures behind fanciful names. It was a work in a genre which P would not have expected to endure though in fact such books contributed to the rise of the novel.

91 l. 174. *Troy.* According to legend, the walls of Troy had been built by Apollo and Neptune.

Canto IV

l. 1. *oppressed.* Parodies (as P's note explains) a passage in Book IV of the *Aeneid.* 'Anxious cares' is taken straight from the opening line of Dryden's translation.

l. 8. *manteau.* A loose outer garment which could be pinned back so as to reveal the petticoat beneath. Cynthia might be a name from a romance, but more strongly suggests the virgin goddess Diana, who would have had better things to think about. The comic idea called up is of the huntress pinning up her skirts while ranging the forest.

ll. 11-88. An extended parody of the journey to the underworld which was a stock motif in epic, and in particular the shades visited by Aeneas in *Aeneid*, Book VI. The gnomes are the tutelary spirits of this dark underside of fashionable life, and the controlling idea is that of sexual repression.

l. 16. *Spleen.* A word whose meaning extends from melancholy and depression to bad temper or peevishness through to neurosis. It was particularly seen as a disease incident to the upper classes, and in particular to those with too much time on their hands, like Belinda. In the old humours psychology, the organ was the seat of melancholia, since an excess of black bile (produced in this organ) would cause depressive tendencies. But in this passage P seems to be using the organ as a cover for the womb, presumed seat of hysteria (see ll. 57-64). There is also parody of Virgil's underworld, as translated by Dryden (*Aeneid*, vi. 384-403).

l. 18. *vapour.* Punning on 'the vapours', a popular expression for depression.

l. 20. *east.* Like a moist climate (l. 18), a wind from the east was supposed to induce fits of melancholia.

l. 24. *side.* On the left, where the spleen is located.   *megrim.* 'A disorder of the head' (Johnson).

92 l. 25. *wait.* Wait on.

l. 33. *aside.* In *Tatler*, no. 77 (6 October 1709), Steele writes on affectation, instancing 'a race of lispers' and noting that 'Alexander the Great had a wry neck, which made it the fashion in his court to carry their heads on one side' (from Plutarch, *Lives*, 'Alexander', 4).

l. 34. *with pride.* The same *Tatler* paper describes 'the valetudinarians':

'Lady Dainty is convinced, that it is necessary for a Gentlewoman to be out of order.'

l. 41. *haunted shades*. Cf. Pope to Lady Mary Wortley Montagu: 'Methinks I am imitating, in my ravings, the dreams of splenetic enthusiasts and solitaries, who fall in love with saints' (letter of 3 February 1717, *Corr.* i. 389–90).

ll. 43–6. *Now glaring fiends . . . machines*. Effects drawn from the elaborate staging devices used in the popular theatre, esp. the 'pantomimes' which were currently all the rage. Machines also puns on epic machinery.

l. 43. *spires*. Spirals or coils.

l. 51. *pipkin*. Small pot made of earthenware. The line alludes to Homer's description of the Halls of Vulcan in *Iliad*, Book XVIII.

l. 56. *spleenwort in his hand*. 'Like Aeneas, who carried a golden bough with him as a safeguard on his visit to Hades, Umbriel carries with him a sprig of an herb thought to be a specific in cases of spleen' (Tracy, *Rape Observ'd*, 53). Spleenwort is a genus of ferns.

l. 58. *from fifteen*. Perhaps recalling *Tatler*, no. 61 (30 August 1709), on 'How far, and to what age, women ought to make their beauty their chief concern', where Steele remarks, 'There is no necessity for fifty to be fifteen'; but P is obviously using the span of years to cover sexual maturity in a woman.

93 l. 69. *citron-waters*. Brandy distilled with lemon-peel.

l. 71. *horns*. Those of the cuckold.

l. 77. *chagrin*. Another word which historically had implied 'melancholy' but was now coming to suggest merely vexation or bad temper.

l. 78. *half the world*. Men.

l. 82. *Ulysses*. In *Odyssey*, Book X.

l. 89. *Thalestris*. Queen of the Amazons. Perhaps based in the *poème à clef* on the sister of Sir George Browne (see iv. 121).

l. 97. *Was it for this*. An epic formula.

l. 99. *paper durance*. Referring to curl-papers for the hair, held in place by thin strips of lead.

94 l. 109. *toast*. 'A celebrated woman whose health is often drunk' (Johnson).

l. 117. *Hyde Park Circus*. Same as the Ring (i. 44 above).

l. 118. *sound of Bow*. The mercantile city popularly identified with the region in earshot of St Mary le Bow, as opposed to the fashionable districts of Westminster.

l. 121. *Sir Plume*. Based on Sir George Browne (see headnote) but also a type-figure of the foppish man about town.

l. 124. *clouded cane*. 'A walking stick having an amber head with streaks of a darker colour' (Tracy, *Rape Observ'd*, 59). Alastair Fowler suggests that this is also a magic staff, like the cloud-controlling magic rod of Mercury.

ll. 126–30. *He first . . . rapped his box.* Cf. the profanity and the play with a snuff-box in a foolish lover described in *Tatler*, no. 110 (22 December 1709).

95 ll. 147–76. The basis for this speech is the lament by Achilles for his friend Patroclus in *Iliad*, Book XVIII.

l. 156. *bohea.* A superior variety of tea, very black in colour.

l. 161. *omens.* Another epic property.

l. 162. *patch-box.* A decorative container in which women kept the patches they wore on their face.

Canto V

96 ll. 1–6. *She said . . . in vain.* Parodying the story of Dido and Aeneas in *Aeneid*, Book IV. The opening directly recalls Dryden's translation: 'His hardened heart nor prayers nor threatening move, / Fate, and the God, had stopped his ears' (ll. 636–7). Anna, Dido's sister, had been sent to Aeneas to beg him to stay in Carthage.

l. 7. *Clarissa.* P's footnote refers to an episode in the *Iliad*, Book XII, which he had translated in 1709, and again in his full version of the epic (the relevant volume appeared also in 1717). P also drew on Denham's version of the speech (1668), repr. in Kinsley (ed.), *Contexts*, 64–5.

l. 20. *smallpox.* Lord Petre had died of this ever-present scourge in 1713, even before the five-canto edition had made its first appearance.

97 l. 37. *virago.* 'A female warrior, a woman with the qualities of a man' (Johnson).

l. 47. *Latona.* Daughter of the Titans, and mother of Apollo and Diana.

l. 53. *sconce.* 'A pensile candlestick' (Johnson). See illustration in Tracy, *Rape Observ'd*, 68.

l. 53 note. In *Odyssey*, Book XXII.

ll. 53–6 note. i.e. in order to keep the machinery active and visible in the poem.

ll. 62–3. *Dapperwit . . . Sir Fopling.* Names of fashionable society characters in plays by Wycherley and Etherege.

l. 64 note. An opera by Buononcini (1706), popular for some years.

98 l. 65 note. In Ovid, *Heroides*, vii. 1–2. The Meander was a river with a serpentine course flowing into the Aegean from Phrygia. The line alludes to the poetic conceit that swans sang at the approach of death.

l. 78. *to die.* Punning on the sexual sense.

l. 88. *bodkin.* 'A bodkin, which to Hamlet had been a stiletto, was more and more degenerating into an ornament for the head and a dressmaker's tool' (Tracy, *Rape Observ'd*, 66). The mock-heroic effect is the greater here because a bodkin *had* once been a serious weapon, the absurd epic aggrandizement here applied to a domestic trinket.

99 l. 114 note. In *Orlando Furioso*, Canto XXXIV, Astolfo journeys to the moon, where he finds the hero's missing wits. See Kinsley (ed.), *Contexts*, 222–5.

l. 126. *Proculus*. Romulus was transported to heaven under the cover of a cloud; he was never seen again on earth, apart from a brief apparition before Julius Proculus. See Livy, Book I, repr. in Kinsley (ed.), *Contexts*, 210.

l. 127. *liquid*. Lat. *liquidus*, pure or transparent. A sudden star appearing unexpectedly, in this case a comet, itself a pun on Gk. *komitis*, long-haired.

l. 129. *Berenice*. Wife of Ptolemy III of Egypt; she dedicated a lock of her hair to the gods when her husband embarked on war to ensure his safe return. It subsequently disappeared and the court astronomer devised a story that it had been transformed into a constellation to be known as *Coma Berenices*. The myth is told in a Greek poem by Callimachus, translated into Latin by Catullus. An English version of the poem by Catullus was published in 1707 (repr. in Kinsley (ed.), *Contexts*, 207–9).

l. 133. *the Mall*. A fashionable walk in St James's Park, not yet a major thoroughfare.

100 l. 136. *Rosamonda's lake*. An ornamental pond in St James's Park, which was a noted trysting place for lovers. This and the Mall are illustrated in Tracy, *Rape Observ'd*, 75.

l. 138. *Galileo's eyes*. Galileo had made large improvements in the telescope and enabled astronomy to take great strides.

l. 140. *Louis*. Louis XIV. The end of the long-running War of Spanish Succession, pitting Britain against France, had occurred between the appearance of the two-canto version and the five-canto text of the poem.

l. 142. *sphere*. Pronounced 'sphare', as regularly in P.

To Belinda, on 'The Rape of the Lock'. Probably written in 1713 or early 1714, as the revised version of *The Rape of the Lock* was made ready for the press. It has been speculated (*TE*, vi. 108–9) that this poem was an alternative 'preface' to the five-canto *Rape*, submitted to Arabella Fermor as a substitute for the dedication actually used. But this is conjecture. See P to Caryll, 9 January 1714 (*Corr.* i. 207). First published anonymously in a miscellany (1717), now known to have been edited by P—this is the basis for the text here.

ll. 7–8. *Thus Helen's rape . . . great Homer's song*. Convincing evidence that the translation of the *Iliad* was uppermost in P's mind, though not yet started.

l. 9. *golden fleece*. Sought by Jason and the Argonauts, an adventure described by Pindar, Apollonius Rhodius, and Valerius Flaccus amongst others.

101 l. 22. *example.* Warning, object-lesson.

l. 28. *Jervas. Epistle to Mr Jervas*, l. 78. For Jervas, see also p. 613.

ll. 29–30. *who censure most . . . muse.* Cf. *Rape of the Lock*, iv. 175–6.

Letter to Martha Blount. Text based on *Corr.* i. 268–9, which also supplies the date.

Coronation. That of George I, which took place on 20 October 1714; see *To Miss Blount, on her leaving the Town after the Coronation.* Martha Blount was suffering from smallpox and unable to be present at the ceremony.

102 *your sister.* Teresa Blount.

Mr Caryll. John Caryll, jun., P's close Catholic friend: see Biographical Index.

Mrs Patty. Martha herself.

Mrs Fermor. Arabella Fermor, the original of Belinda in *The Rape of the Lock*, who had married Francis Gorham shortly before this.

Radcliffe. Dr John Radcliffe, the prominent and wealthy physician, had died on 1 November; he left most of his estate to Oxford University, including the sum which went to the creation of the Radcliffe Library.

Parnell. Thomas Parnell, a fellow member of the Scriblerus Club, who had returned to Ireland.

103 *Gay's poem. A Letter to a Lady.*

The Temple of Fame. The work is a free adaptation of Chaucer's *House of Fame* (?1370), an allegorical poem in three books left unfinished after some 2,150 lines. P draws most of his material from the third book, omitting Chaucer's opening vision of the temple of Venus. The relation between the two poems is best described by Geoffrey Tillotson in *TE*, ii. 222:

> The *Temple of Fame* is everywhere cleared of the engaging 'Chaucerian' element of pother and hotchpotch. The comedian naivete of the narrator, his grumblings and gapings, the icy affability of the eagle—all this is shed completely. . . . For Chaucer's cinematographic speed and lightness there is Pope's Handelian tempo and harmony, for Chaucer's narrative, Pope's scene.

P claimed that the poem was 'written in the year 1711', but this may not be quite accurate. A version was sent to Steele in 1712 (see *Spectator*, no. 532 and *Corr.* i. 152), but the poem was not published until 1 February 1715. The bookseller Lintot paid £32. 5s. [£32.25] to P for the rights. This version was revised in 1717 for the collected works; a few further changes were made by the time of Warburton's edition of 1751, which is the basis for the text here.

'Fame' here retains some of the ancient sense of rumour, still strong in Chaucer, which derived from the Latin *fama*. By P's time the modern sense of reputation had become the predominant one.

l. 1. P substitutes spring for Chaucer's midwinter setting (l. 111).

l. 1 note. Pope's footnote replaces a longer defence of allegory placed at the head of the poem in early editions. *The Flower and the Leaf*, which had been modernized by Dryden, is a fifteenth-century allegorical poem generally attributed to Chaucer until Thomas Tyrwhitt cast doubt on the ascription in the 1770s.

l. 4. *relenting*. Becoming more mild after a frozen spell.

l. 10. *intellectual*. 'Ideal; perceived by the intellect, not the senses' (Johnson).

104 l. 29. *Parian*. White marble from the Greek island of Paros, much used for statues, hence symbolic of immortal renown.

105 l. 62. *not reared by mortal hands*. Recalling 2 Cor. 5: 1.

l. 65. *dome*. Less specific than today; an impressive building of any shape.

l. 75. *frontispiece*. Main front of a building.

l. 81. *Alcides*. Hercules. In the footnote 'position' means attitude. The marble statue of a giant figure, preserved in the Farnese palace at Rome, was one of the most highly regarded of all works of art surviving from antiquity.

l. 82. *th' Hesperian spoil*. The eleventh labour of Hercules was to gather the golden apples of the Hesperides.

106 l. 87. *Cythæron*. A mountain range between Attica and Boeotia.

l. 104. *sigils*. 'An occult sign . . . supposed to have magical powers' (*OED*).

l. 105. *planetary hour*. When the planets exercised special influence because of their conjunction.

107 ll. 119–36. A key passage in the history of taste, setting out the supposed attributes of Gothic culture, and defining the 'northern' qualities of barbaric simplicity, as opposed to the civilized virtues of Mediterranean culture.

l. 136. *romantic*. Suggesting 'fabulous' or 'imaginative'; the nearest modern word might be 'mythopoeic', but with a hint of unreliability about the legends spread by fame.

108 l. 148. *His scythe reversed*. The heraldic scene involves a 'reversed' emblem, which is a sign of disgrace.

l. 154. *belied*. Falsely simulated or counterfeited on a coin.

109 l. 179. *Six pompous columns*. The heroes now shift from soldiers, statesmen, and philosophers to the highest pantheon. For the choice of heroes in this

poem, see *TE*, ii. 229–34. Pope's nomination of Homer, Virgil, Pindar, Horace, Aristotle, and Cicero as the six great literary figures of antiquity was fairly conventional, though Joseph Warton noted the omission of 'the lofty grave tragedians' of Greece (*Essay on . . . Pope* (1806), i. 360–1).

110 l. 222. *Ausonian.* Poetic for Italian.

l. 227. *outlasting monumental brass.* Paraphrasing the famous opening of Horace, *Odes*, iii. 30. There are other submerged references to Horace's poetry in this passage.

l. 233. *Stragyrite.* Aristotle.

l. 238. *Tully.* Cicero.

111 l. 259. *cubit.* An ancient measure equal to the length of the human forearm.

l. 270. *the tuneful Nine.* The Muses.

l. 276. *Around these wonders.* The passage starting here anticipates in close detail the summoning of the dunces in *Dunciad*, iv. 71 ff., a satiric reworking of the call of Fame.

112 l. 284. *tempt.* Brave.

l. 291. *narrative.* Pròsy.

113 l. 340. *purple.* Vivid, resplendent. In l. 347 the sense is more like 'crimson with blood'.

114 l. 376. *spirit.* A breath of wind.

l. 401. *people's fable.* Byword for absurdity.

116 l. 453. *stars with blazing hair.* i.e. comets.

l. 463. *projectors.* The devisers of wild schemes ('projects', l. 455), either by way of financial swindles or political deceptions.

117 l. 508. *fine.* A payment made by a tenant on starting to rent a property.

l. 514. *She comes . . . if she comes at all.* It is evident that P was recalling *1 Henry IV*, v. iii. 64, from a letter to Wycherley on 20 May 1709: 'As for gaining any [fame], I am as indifferent in the matter as Falstaff was, and may say of fame as he did of honour, "If it comes, it comes unlooked for; and there's an end on it" ' (*Corr.* i. 60).

118 *A Farewell to London in the Year 1715.* As the title indicates, written in 1715, but never acknowledged by P and not published until 1775. The text here is based on the first appearance in P's collected works, which occurred in 1776. Charles Jervas wrote to P on 12 June 1715 that '[John] Gay had a copy of the *Farewell*, with your injunctions. No other extant' (*Corr.* i. 295). This gives a terminal date and the death of Lord Halifax (see l. 26) supplies the earliest possible date. P had been in London throughout the earlier part of the year, preparing for the publication of the first volume of his Homer on 4 June. Just before that date he was

relieved to be able to return to the quieter world of Binfield. In addition to the business surrounding his Homer, he was concerned at the approaching impeachment of his friends Oxford and Bolingbroke. A proclamation in July was to forbid Catholics to come within ten miles of London—a symptom of fears of a Jacobite rising, which in fact took place six months later. P probably ignored the proclamation but the poem makes sport of what could have become an unpleasant necessity.

The figures named are friends and acquaintances of Pope in London. His closest allies among them are the painter Jervas (at whose house he had been living); his fellow members of the Scriblerus Club, Arbuthnot and Gay; the poet Garth; and the grandee-patron Burlington. Lintot and Tonson were publishers, the former issuing P's Homer. Nicholas Rowe, the dramatist, was currently Poet Laureate: for his relations with P, see Ault, 128–55. Younger and Bicknell were sisters and minor actresses: see Gay's *Welcome to Mr Pope* (1720), which is the poem closest in feeling to the present item and celebrates P's escape from captivity at the other end of his Homeric undertaking.

l. 4. *Ye harlots . . . ease.* Part of P's unconvincing self-presentation as a rake.

l. 5. *Bethel . . . Craggs.* The politician James Craggs is certainly indicated, but the suggestion of Hugh Bethel, later a very close friend of Pope, is tentative.

119 l. 26. *Halifax's urn.* Charles Montagu, Earl of Halifax (1661–1715), a prominent politician of the Whig junto, and literary patron, who had died on 19 May. He had been appointed first lord of the Treasury on the accession of George I in 1714, but had not been able to take a decisive hold on power. See Biographical Index.

ll. 33–4. *Why make I . . . no favour seek?* An excessive claim, though it is fair to note that the Homer translation was dedicated to William Congreve, a professional writer, rather than to a powerful aristocrat—this was a dramatic break with tradition.

ll. 47–8. *And Burlington's . . . tarts, and pease.* Burlington's mansion in Piccadilly was famous amongst other things for splendid entertainment, enjoyed by Handel and Gay as well as P. See *Corr.* i. 338. At one time P lived with Burlington at his Chiswick villa; for further details on this 'Apollo of the Arts', see *Epistle to Burlington*, headnote, p. 637 below, and Biographical Index.

120 *Epistle to Mr Jervas.* Written probably in the summer or autumn of 1715: a draft is reprinted in Ault, 72–3. First published in an edition of Dryden's translation of Dufresnoy on 20 March 1716. P's footnote was added in later years and involves a small lapse of memory. The text here is based on the 1751 works. An early draft version has been edited by M. Mack (*L&GA*, 91–6).

Dryden's translation had first appeared in 1695 with an important preface. *De arte graphica* by Charles-Alphonse Dufresnoy (1611–65) was a highly influential verse treatise, translated later by William Mason with copious notes by Joshua Reynolds (1783).

Charles Jervas (1673?–1739), a successful portrait painter, was one of P's closest allies in the earlier part of his career. Pope had lived at his London home for most of 1713 and took lessons in painting: see 'Mr Alexander Pope: Painter' in Ault, 68–100. Jervas's own depictions of P are described in W. K. Wimsatt, *The Portraits of Alexander Pope* (1965), 7–26. The fullest discussion of P's relations to the visual arts will be found in Morris R. Brownell, *Alexander Pope and the Arts of Georgian England* (Oxford, 1978): see also James Sambrook, 'Pope and the Visual Arts', in Peter Dixon (ed.), *Writers and their Background: Alexander Pope* (1972), 143–71. All these provide insights into the present poem.

l. 12. *rage.* Poetic ardour.

l. 13. *sister-arts.* A key term and slogan, stressing the common goals and methods of poetry and painting: deriving from classical sources, but turned into an artistic commonplace in the seventeenth and eighteenth centuries, until opposed by theorists such as Lessing. See Jean H. Hagstrum, *The Sister Arts* (Chicago, 1958).

l. 14. *And met congenial.* P probably met Jervas soon after a famous tribute to the painter by Steele in *Tatler*, no. 4 (18 April 1709): Jervas's house in Cleveland Court, St James, became a mecca for collectors and connoisseurs, but also for literary men. Jervas painted Addison, Swift, Martha Blount, Arbuthnot, and Isaac Newton as well as many members of aristocratic society.

l. 28. *Maro.* Virgil.

l. 29. *Tully.* Cicero.

121 ll. 36–8. *Raphael's grace . . . Titian's warmth.* A litany made up of many of the most highly admired painters in this period, including artists of the Roman, Bolognese, and Venetian schools. In particular Guido Reni (1575–1642), Annibale Carracci (1560–1609), and Antonio Correggio (*c*.1489–1534) enjoyed an immense prestige throughout the eighteenth century, in comparison with their modern reputation. 'Paulo' is Paolo Veronese (*c*.1528–88). The terms of praise derive from Dufresnoy but had become conventional.

l. 46. *Bridgewater.* Elizabeth, Countess of Bridgewater (1688–1714), a daughter of the great Duke of Marlborough, who had been much admired by Jervas before her untimely death from smallpox. 'He fell, or affected to fall, in love with her' (*DNB*).

l. 59. *Churchill's race.* The four beautiful daughters of the Duke and Duchess of Marlborough, who included the Countess of Godolphin, the Countess of Sunderland, and the Duchess of Montagu. These Kit Cat toasts represented a Whig establishment from which P would be increasingly alienated.

l. 60. *Worsley*. P originally had Lady Mary Wortley Montagu in mind, but after their quarrel he changed the name somewhat awkwardly to that of Lady Worsley, the wife of a baronet, and someone with far less personal meaning for P.

l. 61. *Each pleasing Blount*. The sisters Teresa and Mary Blount, P's long-time close friends: see Biographical Index.

l. 62. *Belinda*. Arabella Fermor of *The Rape of the Lock*.

l. 66. *Soft . . . gay*. A characteristic use of chiasmus.

122   l. 75. *Zeuxis*. Greek painter of the fifth century BC.

l. 76. *Granville's Myra*. P's early patron George Granville, Lord Lansdowne (1667–1735), had addressed his poetic mistress as Myra.

Epistle to Miss Blount, on her leaving the Town after the Coronation. Written probably in 1714; first published in *Works* (1717). The text here is based on Warburton's 1751 edition.

The coronation of George I took place on 20 October 1714. The recipient is the elder of the Blount sisters, Teresa; for her relationship to P, and background to the poem, see Valerie Rumbold, *Women's Place in Pope's Poetry* (1989). The Blounts had to leave town immediately after the coronation; Martha had caught smallpox and missed the actual ceremony. The poem sports with a standard town–country contrast, in which rustication is felt to be a form of penance by young ladies especially: see P. Rogers, 'Wholesome Country Air', in G. S. Rousseau and P. Rogers (eds.), *The Enduring Monument: Alexander Pope Tercentenary Essays* (Cambridge, 1988), 187–98.

l. 1. *fond*. Tender-hearted, all too ready for emotional engagements.

l. 3. *roll a melting eye*. Language appropriate to romantic heroines.

l. 4. *spark*. 'A lively, showy, splendid, gay man' (Johnson).

l. 7. *Zephalinda*. Suggesting the extravagant world of the seventeenth-century French romance *de longue haleine*; Teresa had actually used the name in her letters.

l. 11. *plain-work*. 'Needlework as distinguished from embroidery; the common practice of sewing or making linen garments' (Johnson).

l. 15. *bohea*. 'A species of tea, of higher colour, and more astringent taste, than green tea' (Johnson). The rhyme is *bohay/tay*.

l. 17. *Or o'er cold coffee . . . spoon*. A deliberately cacophonous line to emphasize boredom and routine.

l. 18. *dine exact at noon*. Unduly early hours for a fashionable lady: cf. *Rape of the Lock*, i. 16.

123 l. 23. *rack*. Get the better of, torment.

l. 24. *whisk*. Whist (not the most fashionable game). *a toast in sack*. The squire's idea of a delicate compliment is to drink the lady's health with a glass of strong Spanish wine, redolent of Falstaff rather than a Hanoverian beau.

l. 26. *buss*. Kiss.

l. 32. *triumphs*. Punning on coronation ceremonies and conquests in love.

l. 38. *flirt*. 'A quick elastic motion' but also calling up the newer sense of 'a pert young hussey' (Johnson).

l. 46. *Parthenia*. This may refer to Martha Blount, who had adopted the fanciful name 'Parthenissa' in some of her letters. The root sense is that of virginity.

l. 47. *Gay*. John Gay.

l. 48. *chairs*. Sedan-chairs.

l. 50. For sixteen lines in continuation (though possibly belonging to a different poem), see *TE*, vi. 232–3.

124 *A Full and True Account of a Horrid and Barbarous Revenge*. Publication must have followed very quickly on composition, and can be narrowed down to the period 29 March 1716 (the supposed date of the narrative) to 2 April: see the account below. The text here is based on the first edition; there were a few small changes in the text of the pamphlet when it was reprinted in P's *Miscellanies* from 1732.

P's quarrel with the bookseller Edmund Curll (see Biographical Index) lasted from 1714 to his death; indeed, Curll got in another blow with an unfriendly biography of P in 1745, the year after the poet died. He had first offended Swift with piratical publications in 1711, so that P would have been alerted to Curll's habits by the time the bookseller began to assault him personally; this took the form of attacks on P which Curll published from about April 1714, and more seriously reprinting anonymous works by P of an indelicate kind with the author's name proclaimed. Matters came to a head in early 1716 when the aftermath of the Jacobite rebellion coincided with the appearance of the second volume of P's Homer. As P became more famous, and his work impinged more directly on matters of national concern, it was Curll who cast him into the full blaze of publicity—not without some connivance on P's part.

The sequence of key events leading up to the first major exchange with Curll, documented in the present pamphlet, can be summarized as follows: (1) The second volume of the *Iliad* was published on 24 March. (2) On 26 March Curll issued *Court Poems*, works attributed to P, Gay, and Lady Mary Wortley Montagu (actually hers is the main responsibility). Curll had obtained these through the agency of the Whig writer John Oldmixon, another longtime adversary of P. (3) According to the pamphlet, the emetic was administered on 28 March and the narrative written the following day: publication must have followed shortly. (4) On 3 April Oldmixon issued a denial in the press that he had been the 'publisher' (editor) of the *Court Poems*. P described this 'most ridiculous quarrel with a bookseller' in a letter to Caryll on 20 April (*Corr.* i. 339).

This was, however, no more than the opening salvo in a prolonged battle. By 7 April Curll was beginning his series of ripostes, advertising 'The Second Part of Mr Pope's Popish Translation of Homer', by which was meant not a pirated version of the *Iliad*, but the trade edition published by Bernard Lintot, sold in the ordinary way at Curll's retail outlet. He also promised a 'detection' of P's blunders in his translation, a threat he held over the poet for many years but which was never realized. At the start of May, Curll produced another item embarrassing to P, called *The Worms*, which he reprinted in a collection shortly afterwards. At the end of the same month he was involved in two strong attacks on P, one by Oldmixon called *The Catholic Poet*, and one by John Dennis called *A True Character of Mr Pope*. By this time matters were taking shape for the appearance of P's second pamphlet: see headnote to the following item. The events summarized here can be followed in G. Sherburn, *The Early Career of Alexander Pope* (Oxford, 1934), 162-80; *Prose*, vol. i, pp. xciv-xcviii; and R. Straus, *The Unspeakable Curll* (1928), 50-64.

Lady of Quality. Lady Mary Wortley Montagu, then on good terms with P.

Wiquefort's Ambassador. This was *The Embassador and his Functions, written by Monsieur [Abraham] de Wicquefort*, trans. by Mr [Kenelm] Digby, which was published by Lintot around 17 April (*London Gazette*). It was a large folio with an impressive title-page; Oldmixon had compiled the index. It is likely that P got this advance news of trade matters from Lintot himself; perhaps the letter to Burlington, describing a prolonged conversation that had already occurred.

125 *wrote the Preface.* Curll witnessed the denial of this fact by Oldmixon (see headnote), but long after, in 1735 he admitted Oldmixon's share in the proceedings, stating that 'my neighbour Mr Pemberton and myself had each of us a share in the said pamphlet. For this you were pleased to treat me, with half a pint of canary, antimonially prepared' (quoted by Sherburn, 171). This is one of the indications that the episode described in this pamphlet really did take place.

Jane Wenham. The last person to be condemned for witchcraft in England, in 1712; she was eventually pardoned and lived until 1730.

Mr Pemberton. John Pemberton, sen. (d. 1739), bookseller at the sign of the Buck and Sun in Fleet Street, close to Curll's shop. He published a pamphlet on Jane Wenham in 1712 and issued many of Oldmixon's books over thirty years.

Tonson. Jacob Tonson, sen., the greatest publisher of the age, who had issued several of P's works: see Biographical Index.

126 *Ormond.* James Butler, second Duke of Ormonde (1665–1745), soldier and politician set up by the High Church party against the Whig champion Marlborough; attainted as a Jacobite, 1715.

copy money. Payment by the bookseller to the author for the right to publish; there were no royalties.

Conduct of the Earl of Nottingham. Another sign of how well informed P was on Curll's current and future activities. The Earl of Nottingham had got wind of a plan by Curll to bring out a life of the Earl by Oldmixon; after negotiations, the book was suppressed, and copies printed were called in—none survives. The surprising feature is that these events were going on well into the summer of 1717, a year and more after P's reference. See Pat Rogers, 'The *Conduct* of the Earl of Nottingham', *RES* 21 (1970), 175–81.

Mr Prior. In 1716 Matthew Prior advertised in the press that a 'second collection' of his poems published by Curll was spurious, containing items that were 'not genuine, others imperfect and incorrect, and the whole not published with my knowledge or approbation'.

French Cato. John Ozell's translation of Deschamps's play on Cato of Utica was published in May 1716; the version with 'parallel between this piece and the tragedy of *Cato*, written by Mr Addison', was issued under the name of John Morphew (a rival bookseller who did occasionally work with Curll) in April. Anne Dacier (c.1654–1732), the leading French critic and translator, whose work P consulted in making his own version of the *Iliad*.

Mr Rowe. Curll had published the poetical works of Nicholas Rowe in 1715, including his translation of Quillet's *Callipedia*.

127 *Mr Gildon's Rehearsal.* Charles Gildon's critique of Rowe's plays was published in April 1714, and reissued on 14 May 1715 with opprobrious reference to P deleted.

Trials of Sodomy. A regular item in Curll's list.

Sir Richard Blackmore's Essays. The first volume of two, published by Curll and Pemberton in March 1716.

Madam Mascranny. Unexplained.

Rochester's bawdy poems. Another staple item on Curll's list: see Straus, *Curll*, 205.

The Case of Impotence. Curll had produced a bestseller, *The Case of Impotency Debated*, in June 1714.

Mr Maynwaring's Life. Curll had been behind Oldmixon's *Life and Works* of Arthur Maynwaring (1668–1712), the leading Whig polemicist, which was published in August 1715. Anne Oldfield, the actress, had been Maynwaring's mistress.

Lord Halifax. Curll and Pemberton had published the *Works and Life* of the politician and patron Halifax in September 1715; the author was probably William Pittis.

Mr Oldmixon. For the historian, pamphleteer, and miscellaneous writer, John Oldmixon, see Biographical Index. He and P tangled over a period of almost thirty years.

taking title-pages. 'He was like Curll, who had a number of fine title-pages, if anyone could have written books to answer them' (James Northcote, reported by William Hazlitt in *Conversations with Northcote* (1830)).

128 *Mrs Centlivre.* The dramatist Susannah Centlivre: see Biographical Index.

A Further Account of the Condition of Edmund Curll. Published in 1716, but the exact date is uncertain. Earlier authorities conjectured a date soon after *A Full Account*; Ault, in *Prose*, vol. i, pp. xcviii–ci, argues for a date as late as November on internal evidence. But his contention that 'it is . . . hardly credible that Pope should have been aware, in the early part of this year, of this wholly unknown young man's contact with Curll' (i.e. Thomas Purney), does not stand up in view of P's astonishingly close knowledge of what Curll was up to, displayed in the present pamphlet and in its predecessor. A more likely date may be August or September 1716.

Since *A Full and True Account* appeared, Curll had kept up his war against P. On 30 June the *Flying Post* advertised that 'the Pope-ish controversy continues', with the appearance of a blasphemous 'Roman Catholic version' of the First Psalm, which P had unwisely let slip from his hands. He inserted a disclaimer in the press at the end of July, but Curll went on printing it as his in miscellanies, and few accepted P's protestations. P needed something to carry the battle against his adversary, and this occurred early in August when the scholars of Westminster School organized a second humiliation of Curll, by tossing him in a blanket in the school yard. See Sherburn, 171–84, and Straus, *Curll*, 65–76. P's final riposte of this year may have been a squib attributed to 'E. Parker, Philomath', published on 10 December, promising further punishment in store for Curll.

There is a third prose attack on Curll, not included in this edition, *A Strange but True Relation*; this is dated by Ault April 1720, though it does not appear to have entered print until the *Miscellanies* of 1732 (see *Prose*, vol. i, pp. cvii–cix). This item describes Curll's conversion to the Jewish religion and his circumcision (an operation which predictably goes wrong, and to the removal of more than was intended). Equally predictable is Curll's vigorous response in the press. However, it was several years before the controversy came to life again over the publication of P's letters and *The Dunciad*. Thereafter the two men were always at odds, and finally in 1741 P actually took action against Curll in Chancery for piracy of his letters.

129 *Blackmore.* Quoted from the *Essays* which Curll had recently published (see *A Full and True Account*).

130 *Instructions.* The detailed identifications of the persons meant, and the topography of the passage, are discussed in Pat Rogers, *Grub Street* (1972), 76–83.

Mr Summers. There was a real thief-taker named Somers in Lewkners Lane (*Applebee's Weekly Journal*, 8 September 1716—a story P had probably just caught in the press, and which gives a dating clue). Lewkner Lane, now Macklin Street, runs eastwards of Drury Lane. The writer located here was Charles Gildon (see *A Full and True Account*).

Tooting. Here Tothill Fields, a large open area in the vicinity of modern Vauxhall Bridge Road.

131 *cook's wife.* Susannah Centlivre, the dramatist, who was married to a 'yeoman of the mouth' to Queen Anne in 1707; from 1713 they lived in Buckingham Court, near the Admiralty Office at the top of Whitehall. See also Biographical Index.

Gradus ad Parnassum. Ladder, but punning on the sense of a primer in grammar and composition.

disturbances of this kingdom. The first Jacobite rising, which had begun in August 1715 and had subsided in February 1716.

132 *Mr Barnivelt.* 'Esdras Barnivelt, Apoth' was a pseudonym of the Scriblerus group, used by P for his *Key to the Lock* (1715).

Mr C——y. Possibly Henry Carey (*c.*1687–1743), author of *Sally in our Alley* and, according to some sources, *God Save the King*. More likely the better-heeled Walter Carey (1685–1757), a courtier and MP who was a friend of Edward Young and moved in Addison's circle (see Spence, i. 78).

133 *a ballad. The Catholic Poet*, published on 31 May 1716. Curll later made it clear that it was written by Oldmixon unaided.

134 *rags ye were.* Parodying Gen. 3: 19.

passage-house. Privy.

Letter to Lord Burlington. Text based on *Corr.* i. 371–5, which also supplies the date.

Lintot. Bernard Lintot, who had published much of P's work to date, including the ongoing Homer translation, but who occupied a less lofty position in the trade than the great Jacob Tonson: see Biographical Index for both publishers.

publisher. Here distributor or wholesaler.

135 *Mr Oldmixon.* John Oldmixon, a hero of the *Dunciad*; see Biographical Index.

Speaker. Sir Spencer Compton (*c.*1674–1743), of Compton Place, East-bourne.

Oldisworth. William Oldisworth, author of *A Dialogue between Timothy and Philatheus* (1709–11). See Biographical Index.

136 *Dr King.* William King (1663–1712), miscellaneous author.

Sir Richard. Blackmore: see Biographical Index.

Sewell. George Sewell (*c.*1690–1726), miscellaneous writer. His version of Lucretius does not seem to have appeared; it would have had great difficulty in supplanting the translation by Thomas Creech (1683), which long remained standard.

137 *Lord Carleton.* Henry Boyle, Baron Carleton, Whig politician, an uncle of Burlington: see Biographical Index.

Eloisa to Abelard. P wrote to Martha Blount *c.* March 1716, 'The Epistle of Eloise grows warm, and begins to have some breathings of the heart in it, which may make posterity think I was in love. I can scarce find in my heart to leave out the conclusion I once intended for it . . .' (*Corr.* i. 338). This is the only clue as to the date of composition. *TE*, ii. 312 suggests the letter is rather from March 1717 but the evidence is not conclusive. First published in the *Works* (1717). There are no really important changes between this and the 1751 edition, which is the basis of the text here.

P is imitating Ovid's *Heroides* or 'letters from heroines', twenty-one poems in elegiac verse, which had been popular in England since the Renaissance and had spawned native versions such as Drayton's *England's Heroical Epistles* (1597–9). The original letters of Abelard and Eloisa had appeared in Latin in 1616, but the immediate source for P was a version by John Hughes in 1713. This was in fact a translation into English prose of a French adaptation. Underlying this influential form was the wider popularity of the figure of the abandoned woman in literature: for this topic, see Lawrence Lipking, *Abandoned Women and Poetic Tradition* (Chicago, 1988).

P's treatment is affected by his own Roman Catholic faith, his interest in landscape and in 'Gothick' (very broadly, romantic) properties, and by his own amatory experience. As well as the hint to Martha Blount just quoted, there is reference in a letter to Lady Mary Wortley Montagu in June 1717 suggesting a personal application: see note to ll. 361–2 below.

Peter Abelard (1079–1142), French theologian, fell in love with his pupil Heloise, who bore him a son, and was privately married to him. After this was discovered, Abelard was castrated and entered monastic life whilst Heloise took the veil. Abelard's retreat became the abbey of the Paraclete (a name for the Holy Spirit), near Troyes. This was a favourite pilgrimage for English travellers, esp. Catholics.

Argument. The liaison began in 1117, when Abelard was 38 and Heloise 17.

138 l. 16. *dictates.* Stress on first syllable, as always in P.

l. 20. *shagged with horrid thorn.* Adapting *Comus*, l. 429, one of several Miltonic references in the poem. 'Horrid' means 'bristling'.

139 l. 56. *excuse.* Do away with the need for.

l. 63. *attempering.* Moderating, soothing.

140 l. 104. *common.* Shared.

141 l. 126. *partial.* Fond.

l. 133. *these hallowed walls.* The Paraclete, where Heloise had become sister after Abelard had moved to the Abbey of St Gildas in Brittany.

l. 142. *domes.* Structures, edifices.

143 l. 192. *love th'offender . . . offence.* Playing on the proverbial 'hate the sin but love the sinner', deriving ultimately from St Augustine.

l. 212. *'Obedient slumbers . . . weep'.* Crashaw, 'Description of a Religious House', l. 16.

l. 219. *spouse prepares the bridal ring.* Nuns as the bride of Christ wear his ring.

144 l. 229. *all-conscious night.* Night when Heloise is made aware of all her feelings and exposed to a sense of guilt.

145 l. 282. *dispute.* Bring contrary arguments to my attention. Abelard was a famous dialectician.

l. 284. *idea of the skies.* Image or sentiment provoked by or connected with the heavens.

l. 288. *fiends.* Agents of evil, diabolic spirits.

146 l. 343 note. The statement is true, but in 1817 both were reburied in a single tomb at Père Lachaise in Paris.

147 l. 351. *mutual pity.* Pity for both of them.

l. 354. *dreadful sacrifice.* 'The technical term for the celebration of the Eucharist' (*TE*, ii. 348).

l. 355. *relenting.* Warming.

ll. 361–2. *Condemned . . . no more.* In June 1717 P sent Lady Mary Wortley Montagu, then in Constantinople, a copy of his *Works* which contained the first printing of this poem, adding 'in [*Eloisa*] you will find one passage, that I can't tell whether to wish you to understand, or not?' (*Corr.* i. 407). Almost certainly P has these lines in mind.

Elegy to the Memory of an Unfortunate Lady. First published (as *Verses to the Memory . . .*) in the *Works* (1717), and generally assumed to be written around the same year, though there are no references to the work prior to its publication. The first separate appearance was in 1720. However, there were no significant revisions before it was reprinted in the *Works* of 1751, the basis for the text here.

P's friend John Caryll wrote to him in July and August 1717, asking for details of the lady at the centre of the poem, for 'I think that you once gave me her history' (*Corr.* i. 416–17). This set off a long debate on the supposed identity of a 'real' lady, which is summarized in *EC*, ii. 199– 205. The most popular choice has been Mrs Elizabeth Weston (d. 1724), but modern scholarship inclines to the view that no single individual is meant. Certain details, e.g. at l. 70, indicate that P might have been contemplating the death of Lady Mary Wortley Montagu amid the perils of the Orient: see Geoffrey Tillotson in *RES* 12 (1936), 401–12. But this is some way from applicability in terms of suicide.

P has several models, mostly Roman: Ovid's epistles and the elegies of Tibullus helped to provide him with the 'plan' he considered necessary in such poems (Spence, i. 266). The style is deliberately heightened, as in *Eloisa to Abelard*, with long tirades of rhetoric used to create an intense fervour.

Title note. Warburton's note is misleading because the vague page reference cannot be certainly placed; but *TE*, ii. 355 suggests that it refers to letters elsewhere in the 1751 edition, in which P, Congreve, and the Duke of Buckingham address Lady Mary in fulsome terms.

l. 8. *a Roman's part.* Follow the acceptable Roman practice of suicide.

l. 9. *reversion.* A right of succession (esp. in property).

148 l. 14. *glorious fault.* The rebel angels, as in *Paradise Lost*, and the Titans who waged war on Zeus, before they were flung into Hell—the fate held out in P's time to suicides.

l. 35. *ball.* The earth as orb or emblem of justice.

l. 41. *Furies.* The three avenging goddesses or Erinyes.

149 l. 64. *green turf . . . breast.* Paraphrasing the familiar roman inscription on gravestones, *sit tibi terra levis.*

l. 68. *ground . . . made.* 'Her remains have "made sacred" the common earth in which she was buried' (*EC*, ii. 214).

150 *Letter to Teresa and Martha Blount.* Text based on *Corr.* i. 429–31, which also supplies the dating. Stonor Park near Henley-on-Thames was the home of an old recusant family, then headed by P's friend Thomas Stonor.

151 *Bolton Street.* Off Piccadilly in London, where the Blount sisters had recently settled.

Lord Harcourt. Simon, first Viscount Harcourt (*c.*1661–1727), a friend of P and Swift.

Lady Jane Hyde. The beautiful sister of the Duchess of Queensberry, a daughter of the Earl of Clarendon, subsequently married to the Earl of Essex. The Hyde family were close allies of P.

Letter to Lady Mary Wortley Montagu. Text based on *Corr.* i. 505–8, where it is suggested that the letter dates from September 1718. P was then in the throes of an apparently unrequited love affair with Lady Mary, prior to their violent quarrel in later years. She was just on the point of arriving home from her sojourn at the court of Constantinople, which was to produce the famous Turkish letters. P's letter describes his period at Stanton Harcourt near Oxford, where he had spent much of the summer, working in seclusion on the *Iliad* translation. Shortly before, he had sent Lady Mary an account of two lovers killed by lightning in the village; he sent some tender verses on the subject, and she responded with a more cynical poem (*Corr.* i. 493–6, 522–4).

152 *genuine ancient country seat.* Stanton Harcourt was the seat of P's friend Lord Harcourt (see letter to Teresa and Martha Blount, September 1717). The manor-house was built around 1499, three hundred years after the Harcourts first settled in the district. The feature known as Pope's Tower dates from 1470. For a full description of the house, tower, and adjoining church, see *Stanton Harcourt: A Short History* (n.p., 1962).

Amphion's time. Amphion was the legendary ruler of Thebes, whose harp-playing was so melodious that the stones danced their way into their place in the walls of the city.

153 *Arachne.* In legend she pitted her skill as a spinner against Athene, who destroyed her web. Arachne hanged herself, but was transformed by Athene into a spider.

154 *Lady Frances.* For a slightly different legend, involving the ghost of Lady Alice Harcourt, see *Stanton Harcourt,* 7.

Mr Wortley. Edward Wortley Montagu, Lady Mary's husband. See *Epistle to Bathurst,* l. 62.

155 *The Iliad: Book XVIII.* P had loved Homer from early boyhood, first through John Ogilby's translation (1660, 1669), and then in the original. As a very young man he made verse renderings of Homer, notably the episode of Sarpedon from Book XVI of the *Iliad.* It was not until 1713 that he undertook to translate the entire *Iliad.* The work eventually appeared in six volumes (four books per volume), in more or less annual instalments between 1715 and 1720. There were two modes of publication, a special subscription series heavily patronized by the nation's élite (though P had to use persistence and energy to recruit this audience), and a trade edition mainly for the profit of the publisher Bernard Lintot. P managed to obtain good terms from Lintot and achieved an unprecedented degree of financial independence by the success of this venture. After this P moved on to

translate the *Odyssey*, published in a similar manner in 1725-6, but his creative energies had been drained, and he was forced to seek the help of two minor poets, William Broome and Elijah Fenton, who translated half the *Odyssey* between them. Broome also provided the main part of the commentary in this case.

P was not a profound Greek scholar, but he knew enough of the language to know what he was about poetically. He consulted all the leading authorities, ancient and modern, available to him; and he had the help of his friend Thomas Parnell, who contributed the essay on Homer at the head of the *Iliad* version. P himself was responsible for an important preface, which unfortunately has had to be squeezed out of this selection, and for comprehensive notes on points of historical, doctrinal, and poetic interest. For a full assessment of P's aims, and the success he enjoyed in different parts of his undertaking, see the introductory material in *TE*, vol. vii.

Book XVIII of the *Iliad*, reprinted here, describes the grief of Achilles at the death of Patroclus, and later the new armour forged for the hero by Vulcan. P placed at the end of the book extensive 'observations' on the shield of Achilles, reconstructing its design and allegorical meaning in considerable detail. For reasons of space this addendum has had to be omitted, along with the comprehensive notes P appended to the translation.

The text here is based on the first edition (folio), published in vol. vi (1720).

l. 4. *Nestor's son.* Antilochus.

156 l. 14. *Myrmidonian band.* The tribe of Thessalian warriors of which Achilles was the chief.

l. 16. *Patroclus.* The dearest friend of Achilles, who had been slain by the Trojan champion Hector.

l. 29. *Purple.* Vividly coloured (poetic).

l. 45. *Nereids.* Sea-maidens, daughter of the benevolent 'old man of the sea', Nereus.

158 l. 100. *Thunderer.* Jove.

ll. 107-12. Achilles was the son of the mortal Peleus (hence his name 'Pelides') and the sea-goddess Thetis. In l. 112 'equal' is transferred to the bed from its occupant.

159 l. 148. *Alcides.* Hercules, poisoned by the shirt of Nessus.

l. 163. *Caerulean.* Of the sea (from Lat. *caeruleus*, blue).

160 l. 204. *messenger.* Iris, goddess of the rainbow.

161 l. 230. *Telamonian.* As borne by Ajax, son of Telamon, king of Salamis.

l. 233. *Menoetius' son.* Patroclus.

162 l. 286. *Achaean band.* Used for the Greeks as a body.

l. 289. *sudden.* Immediate.

163 l. 313. *Ilion.* Troy.

164 l. 342. *Maeonia.* Lydia, in Asia Minor (Homer's supposed birthplace).

166 l. 435. *lame architect.* Vulcan, god of fire and whose forge produced armour
for the immortals, as well as the thunderbolts of Jove.

l. 449. *Charis.* One of the *Charites* or Graces, daughters of Jove.

167 l. 463. *my proud mother.* Hera (or Juno), who is said to have thrown Vulcan
(or Hephaestus) out of heaven on finding his body so ugly.

168 l. 522. *his friend.* Patroclus.

169 l. 561. *Hyades.* Nymphs who were turned into a heavenly constellation
and whose appearance portended rain, as did in other circumstances the
Pleiades (originally the seven daughters of Atlas).

170 l. 619. *confessed.* Made manifest.

171 l. 662. *Linus.* A hero 'whose untimely death (in circumstances that are
variously told) was celebrated in a dirge, sung annually from Homeric
times at harvest time' (Sir Paul Harvey, *Oxford Companion to Classical
Literature*).

172 l. 683. *Daedalean art.* Daedalus, the Athenian craftsman, was banished to
Crete, where he constructed the elaborate labyrinth; Gnossos is Cnossos,
and the Cretan queen is Ariadne.

173 *To Mr Gay, Congratulating Pope on finishing his house and gardens.* The lines
must have been written around 1722: Lady Mary Wortley Montagu quotes
them in a letter to her sister *c.* April of that year (*Complete Letters of Lady
Mary Wortley Montagu*, ed. R. Halsband (Oxford, 1965–7), ii. 15–16).
Lines 7–14 were published in 1737, attached to the end of a poem by
another hand. The poem as a whole first appeared in Lady Mary's letters
in 1830. P would not have wished to give it further currency as he had
fallen out with Lady Mary soon after the date of the poem, and they had
been fiercely at odds for the remainder of his life. Gay's letter has not
been traced.

l. 11. *struck deer.* Recalls the 'stricken deer' in *Hamlet*, III. ii. 282, a phrase
which was later to be taken over by Cowper, *The Task*, iii. 108.

174 *To Mr Addison, Occasioned by his Dialogue on Medals.* First published in
1720, under a slightly different title; subsequently removed to become
the fifth of the *Moral Essays*, but here restored to its more appropriate
independent status. P's statement that it was written in 1715 may or
may not be accurate; if it was, then we cannot be sure that Addison was
the intended recipient from the start. Addison had died in 1719, after
some years of strained relations with P; the poem appeared in a possibly

unauthorized collection of P's works prior to its official debut in the sumptu-
ous set of Addison's *Works* (1721), edited by Thomas Tickell. By this time
James Craggs, who like Addison had been a Secretary of State in recent
Whig administrations, had also died. For fuller discussion of these points,
see Ault, 119–24.

The fullest literary estimate of the poem is Howard Erskine-Hill, 'The
Medal against Time: A Study of Pope's Epistle to Mr Addison', *Journal
of the Warburg and Courtauld Institutes*, 28 (1965), 274–98.

medals. Coins.

ll. 7–8. *theatres . . . her floods*. 'Woods unpeopled of wild beasts to provide
for the Roman spectacles, and a countryside drained of water for the
mimic naval combats, in amphitheatre or naumachia' (see *EC*, iii. 203).

l. 9. *fanes*. Temples.

l. 18. *give to Titus old Vespasian's due*. The emperors Titus (reigned AD
79–81) and Vespasian (reigned AD 70–79) bore the same full name, and
so an inscription on a coin might be applied to the wrong man.

l. 21. *moles*. Piers.

l. 24. *triumphs*. Triumphal ceremonies.

ll. 26–30. Motifs on coins of various emperors.   *Prostrate* (l. 28)
refers to heraldic figures of the river gods in a recumbent posi-
tion.   *Eagles* (l. 30) refers to the Roman emblem, borne as a battle
standard.

175 l. 35. *sharpened*. By the use of a magnifying glass.

l. 37. *varnish*. 'The differently coloured patina on bronze coins' (*TE*, vi.
207).

l. 39. *Pescennius*. 'Coins of the pretender Pescennius Niger [d. AD 194]
are the rarest any ordinary collector hopes to possess' (T. O. Mabbott,
quoted in *TE*, vi. 207).   '

l. 40. *Cecrops*. A legendary ancestor of the Athenian kings, whose non-
existent coins might be imposed on a credulous collector.

ll. 41–2. *Vadius*. A cipher for the antiquarian Dr John Woodward, who
was a regular butt of the Scriblerian group: see Joseph M. Levine, *Dr
Woodward's Shield* (Berkeley, Calif., 1977).

l. 44. *Otho*. 'Coins of Otho are the rarest in the popular series of the twelve
Caesars' (Mabbott, quoted in *TE*, vi. 207). Not surprisingly, since Otho
took his life after a reign of only three months.

l. 50. *rage*. Inspiration.

l. 55. *living*. Coins of the present day, but also animated with the great
deeds depicted on them.

l. 57. *rising bold*. Etched in relief on the surface of the coin.

l. 60. *Plato's . . . looks*. A fashion for honouring the eminent dead by medallic likenesses grew up in the period.

l. 64. *Pollio*. G. Asinius Pollio (76 BC–AD 5), author and patron of Virgil.

176 ll. 67–72. The lines on Craggs were used as the basis of the inscription to his monument in Westminster Abbey (*TE*, vi. 281–2).

Epistle to Robert Earl of Oxford and Earl Mortimer. P's friend Thomas Parnell had died in 1718; shortly afterwards Swift suggested that P should write a tribute 'especially if it is intended . . . that some of Parnell's scattered things are to be published together' (Swift, *Correspondence*, ed. H. Williams (Oxford, 1963–5), ii. 311). The poem, dated 25 September 1721, was sent in a draft form to Robert Harley on 21 October; Harley replied gratefully on 6 November, giving P permission to use the poem as a dedication at the head of Parnell's works (*Corr*. ii. 90–1). This posthumous collection, edited by P, appeared on 7 December.

Thomas Parnell was an Irish clergyman and member of the Scriblerus Club. For further information, see his *Poems*, ed. C. Rawson and F. P. Lock (Oxford, 1989), and Biographical Index. Robert Harley was a statesman who formed a Tory Government in 1710, with Swift and Defoe, largely unknown to each other, directing the propaganda campaign on behalf of the ministry. In 1711 Harley was made Earl of Oxford and Lord Treasurer. After his fall in 1714 he was imprisoned in the Tower of London and faced impeachment, but he was released in 1717 and retired to the family estate. A prominent collector, he was along with P, Swift, Gay, Arbuthnot, and Parnell one of the Scriblerus Club, whose activities formed the basis of some of the greatest Augustan satire. See further Biographical Index.

For a full reading of the poem, see Geoffrey Tillotson, 'Pope's *Epistle to Harley*', *Augustan Studies* (1961), 162–83.

l. 1. *poet*. Parnell.

l. 5. *science*. Branch of knowledge.

l. 11. *dexterous*. Disyllabic; usually spelt (as in the original text here) 'dextrous'. The meaning is 'adroit'.

l. 13. *Absent or dead*. Swift is absent in Ireland, Parnell dead.

177 ll. 27–8. *In vain . . . thy silent shade*. Alluding to Harley's retreat in Herefordshire: 'shade' was used as a conventional term for retirement or deliberate obscurity (*OED*).

l. 33. *scaffold*. Not unduly melodramatic, as some of the Whigs in power would have liked to send Harley to the executioner's block. He was one of the first deposed Lord Treasurers to escape without heavy penalties.

l. 40. *Mortimer*. Harley's secondary title, with many 'connotations of heroic grandeur' (Tillotson, *Augustan Studies*, 179).

Pope to Swift, August 1723. Text and dating from *Corr.* ii. 183–6. P was replying to a letter from Swift now lost; indeed no letter between the two men survives since an open letter which Swift dated 10 January 1721—an unusually long gap in this correspondence.

178 *Lord Oxford.* The former Robert Harley, father of Lord Harley mentioned later in the sentence. For both, see Biographical Index, s.v. 'Oxford'.

Lord Bolingbroke. He had been given a limited pardon for his Jacobite activities and was allowed to return to England in June 1723, although not to resume his seat in the House of Lords.

Bishop of Rochester. Francis Atterbury.

Lord Peterborough. On his promotion to General of the Marines in 1722, the Earl had faced criticism. Swift assumed when he replied to this letter on 20 September that Peterborough had been accused of complicity in the Atterbury plot, which had recently led to the bishop's sentence of exile; but this was not the case. See *Corr.* ii. 189, 198.

179 *Horace. Epistles,* I. xvii. 35.

his hand. That of Bolingbroke, whose accompanying letter to Swift is found in *Corr.* ii. 186–9.

Letter to Martha Blount. Text based on *Corr.* ii. 236–40; P's visit to Sherborne in Dorset used to be placed in 1722, but the dating in *Corr.* seems more plausible. The friendship between P and the fifth Baron Digby (1662–1752) seemed to have been made through the intermediary of the peer's son Robert (1691/2–1726): see H. Erskine-Hill, *The Social Milieu of Alexander Pope* (New Haven, Conn., 1975), 132–65. For P's taste in landscape gardening, as evidenced in this letter, see M. R. Brownell, *Alexander Pope and the Arts of Georgian England* (Oxford, 1978), 113–17.

Ralegh. He acquired the twelfth-century castle and park in 1592, originally on a ninety-nine year lease. He settled there after his marriage and built a new mansion nearby. A branch of the Digby family acquired the estate when it was confiscated from Ralegh after his attainder in 1604: the family have occupied the house continuously since 1617.

180 *first Earl of Bristol.* John Digby (1580–1653), diplomat. He was ambassador to Madrid between 1610–22.

contrast. A newly introduced technical term in art for 'the deliberate juxtaposition of varied forms, colours, etc.' (*OED*), which had not yet entered everyday usage.

183 *any lady. Corr.* ii. 240, indicates that Mrs Howard and Marble Hill are meant. P was designing her garden.

Wilton. The seat of the Earl of Pembroke, famous both for the architecture by Inigo Jones and the splendid collection of paintings. See also *Epistle to a Lady*, l. 7.

Preface to the Works of Shakespeare. P's edition of Shakespeare appeared in six volumes in March 1724 (a seventh volume containing the poems was added by George Sewell at the same time). The preface was sent round in proof to various noble patrons, and returned to P by Jacob Tonson, jun. on 23 December 1724 (*Corr.* ii. 279–80). This suggests composition can be allocated to that year. He had evidently finished it by 31 October (*Corr.* ii. 270). The edition, unlike the Homer, was for the benefit of the publisher rather than for P's; he took less trouble over getting subscribers, who were far less numerous, and found only moderate satisfaction in what near the end of the *Preface* he significantly calls 'the dull duty of an editor'. However, the *Preface* itself remained an outstanding example of his critical skill.

P came in second in a long line of Shakespearian editors in the eighteenth century, which included Rowe, Johnson, Capell, and Malone. P's edition was an advance on Rowe's (1709), in particular in its attempt to collate the quarto readings. But its habits of signalizing choice passages with marginal marks and stars has not won the favour of posterity, whilst its relegation of lines 'which are excessively bad' to footnotes has excited outright derision. More seriously, P's limitations as a scholar of Elizabethan history and drama were manifest, despite his hiring two gentlemen at Oxford to ease him 'of part of the drudgery of Shakespeare' (*Corr.* ii. 81). These failings were mercilessly exposed by Lewis Theobald in *Shakespeare Restored* (1726): see Peter Seary, *Lewis Theobald and the Editing of Shakespeare* (Oxford, 1990), 48–101. The immediate result was that Theobald was enthroned as king of the dunces in the original *Dunciad* (1728), and P had some splendid fun in the notes with accurate parodies of Theobald's manner. But in his heart he knew that Theobald was a far more able performer in the mechanical parts of scholarship, and he was glad to put behind him the phase when his fate was 'ten years to comment and translate' (*Dunciad*, iii. 332).

The text here is based on the first edition of 1725, modernized in the same way as the poems. For a thorough recent edition of the *Preface*, see *Prose*, ii. 1–40.

184 *Egyptian strainers and channels.* 'It was generally held that Homer had travelled in Egypt, the first home of the arts and sciences, and drawn there much of his knowledge (both Mme Dacier and Parnell make a strong point of this)' (*Prose*, ii. 27).

185 *may be born.* Playing with the Latin tag, *poeta nascitur, non fit.*

mechanics. Manual labourers.

clowns. Peasants.

186 *Grex.* Company of actors.

novel. Tale, romance.

187 *Ben Jonson.* See *Timber, or Discoveries* (1640). Jonson is recalling what John Heminge and Henry Condell had written in the preface to the first folio of Shakespeare (1623).

his want of learning. The extent of Shakespeare's learning was the prime obsession of eighteenth-century critics, an argument still vigorously waged in the time of Johnson and Malone. P here errs by treating alternative versions (some pirated) as 'revisions' by Shakespeare.

superfetations. Excrescences.

188 *translations from Ovid.* i.e. *Venus and Adonis* and *The Rape of the Lock*.

one of his plays. *The Comedy of Errors*.

another. That is, *Troilus and Cressida*. Dares Phrygius, a priest in the *Iliad*, was supposed to have written a poem on the siege of Troy; it did not survive, but a spurious Latin 'translation' was known and plundered by writers on the Trojan legend.

novels. Novellas such as those of Boccaccio or Cinzio.

189 *Tacitus. Agricola*, 41: 'the worst kind of enemies, those who praise you.'

Virgil. Eclogues, vii. 27-8: 'if he should praise me excessively, put a wreath of foxglove round my brow, in case he should harm my poetic powers.'

Mr Dryden. Dryden in his *Discourse on Satire* (1693) had termed Jonson's commendation 'an insolent, sparing, and invidious panegyric'.

190 *Enter three Witches solus.* Apparently an invention on P's part, as it does not figure in the early editions of *Macbeth*.

blunders of Hector. In *Troilus and Cressida*, II. ii. 166-7.

eleven. Actually fifteen. P's vagueness is not culpable in view of the limited scholarship of his time.

191 *Hamlet. Hamlet*, II. ii. 44, in modern texts.

their very names. P added a note specifying *Much Ado About Nothing*, in the first and second folios, with cast members listed instead of *dramatis personae*.

192 *Pericles.* First included in the canon in the third folio of 1664, but still a contentious item. P added to the list of dubia in subsequent printings 'a thing called *The Double Falsehood*', that is the play which Theobald had brought out in 1717 and attributed to Shakespeare. Its exact status remains unclear.

193 *Ben Jonson.* 'Some mouldy tale, / Like *Pericles*': 'Ode', *The New Inn* (1629).

194 *glaring.* Brilliant, resplendent.

195 *Peri Bathous: or, Martinus Scriblerus, his Treatise of the Art of Sinking in Poetry.* Published on 8 March 1728 in the third volume of Pope–Swift

Miscellanies. This place had originally been allocated to *The Dunciad*, which in the event appeared separately two months later. Later reprinted in various of the *Miscellanies*, entering P's *Works* in 1741. The text here is based on the first edition; the contents, which always appeared at the end, have been moved to the beginning for the present edition.

The genesis of the work goes back to the collaborative projects of the Scriblerus Club around 1712–14, when P, Swift, Arbuthnot, Gay, and Parnell planned satires on the 'works of the unlearned' and on the misapplication of knowledge generally. The first precise hint we can pick up occurs in a letter from Arbuthnot to Swift on 26 June 1714: 'Pope has been collecting high flights of poetry, which are very good, they are to be solemn nonsense' (*Correspondence of Swift*, ed. H. Williams (Oxford, 1963–5), ii. 43). After Swift left for Ireland, Arbuthnot was P's principal coadjutor, but it seems that in the final stages he was no longer taking an active part: 'The third volume of the *Miscellanies* is coming out post now, in which I have inserted the treatise *Peri Bathous*. I have entirely methodized and in a manner written it all, the Dr [Arbuthnot] grew quite indolent in it' (*Corr.* ii. 468). Like *Gulliver's Travels* and *The Dunciad*, the work has its roots in earlier Scriblerian schemes but ultimately deals with the topical concerns of the 1720s. Along with the *Memoirs of Martinus Scriblerus*, published in 1714, it is the most direct literary outcome of the whole Scriblerian enterprise.

The treatise is a subversion of the *ars* or manual on poetics. It specifically parodies the influential *Peri Hypsous*, a guide to the high style attributed to the third-century Greek critic Longinus, who had achieved immense currency after the translation into French by Boileau (1674): see S. H. Monk, *The Sublime* (New York, 1935). There are a large number of direct correspondences between Longinus and P's parody. The regular trick is to convert praise of the sublime into mock-praise of the 'profound'. Like Latin *altus*, the Greek *bathus* can mean either 'deep' or 'high' (so also with the noun *altitudo* and *bathos*); P exploits this ambiguity to such effect that his use of 'bathos' to mean 'ludicrous descent from the elevated to the commonplace in writing or in speech' (*OED*), first seen in this work, has remained current in English ever since.

It followed that this ironic treatise constituted an inverted statement of P's views on style. He himself told Spence in 1736, '*The Profound*, though written in so ludicrous a way, may be well worth reading seriously as an art of rhetoric' (Spence, i. 57). In particular the emphasis on affectation, pertness, needless complexity, confusion, and obfuscation can be seen as expressing P's own quest for simplicity, directness, and point. It is a matter of debate whether Longinus himself suffers oblique criticism, although the evidence seems to be that P had a much less full-hearted admiration for the sublime than did contemporaries such as John Dennis.

Dennis comes in for his share of criticism, but the main butt is the epic poet Sir Richard Blackmore. There is a wide measure of overlap with the nearly contemporaneous *Dunciad*; in Chap. VI, the sets of different initials cover twenty-five individuals, out of whom fifteen appeared in *The Dunciad*.

Thirteen authors other than Blackmore are identified by P in the illustrative quotations; eight of these were contemporaries of P. The most prominent of these cited in examples are Addison, Aphra Behn, Cleveland, Dennis, Eusden, Nathaniel Lee, Ambrose Philips, Quarles, Steele, Theobald, and Tickell. For fuller identifications, see *EC*, x. 344–409; the edition by E. L. Steeves (New York, 1952), pp. xlvii–li; and *Prose*, ii. 238–76. Steeves supplies the fullest information on the literary background, on the degree of collaboration in the work's authorship, and on other matters discussed in this headnote. Except in cases of special interest, identifications are not discussed in the notes to the present edition: see Biographical Index for individuals mentioned in the text.

Martinus Scriblerus. Scriblerus, whose career is described in the *Memoirs* (1741), is the type of a foolish pedant, given to word-chopping, ingenious antiquarian fantasies, and pretentious theorizing.

196 *Master of Alexander.* Aristotle.

Secretary of the renowned Zenobia. Longinus. 'Institute' here means a set of principles, such as those of the great rhetorician Quintilian.

198 *gusto.* A fashionable variant for taste, but used here with a pejorative sense of 'particular liking, fondness or relish' (*OED*).

Et prodesse . . . Poetae. Horace, *Ars poetica*, l. 333, with *et* substituted for *aut.* P makes *prodesse* suggest 'profit or gain' financially, rather than benefit morally.

199 *Nascimur Poetae.* Adapting a tag (see *Preface to Shakespeare*, p. 185 n.).

Pruritus. itching.

Horace. Alluding to *Ars poetica*, ll. 372–3: 'For poets to be no more than mediocre, neither the gods nor men nor the booksellers will concede.'

golden mean. An ancient Greek watchword, taken up by Horace (*Odes*, II. x. 5), and thence proverbial in English (Tilley M792).

English author. Falstaff in *Merry Wives of Windsor*, III. v. 12.

200 *small beer.* Beer of a weak or inferior quality, but also matters of no consequence, from *Othello*, II. i. 161, and then proverbial (Tilley T195), used by Swift in *Polite Conversation*.

201 *gout de travers.* Perverse or wrong-headed taste.

Serpentes avibus . . . agni. Horace, *Ars poetica*, l. 13: 'Serpents couple with birds, lambs with tigers.'

jack-pudding. Clown.

selling bargains. Engaging in sexually loaded *badinage*.

perspective glass. Telescope.

lutestring. A glossy silk fabric.

204 *Fuller.* One who shrinks and beats cloth to make it stronger.

cerulean. Sky-blue.

205 *great author*. Blackmore, who specialized in the 'greater poetry' (epic).

Germanicus. Nero Claudius Germanicus (15 BC–AD 19), adopted son of Emperor Tiberius, author and general.

what authors. The best-established identifications in the list which follows are: George Sewell, Aaron Hill, Charles Gildon, Lewis Theobald, Daniel Defoe (D.F.), Laurence Eusden, William Broome, Colley Cibber, Leonard Welsted, Sir William Yonge, John Dennis, John Oldmixon, Edward Ward, James Moore [Smythe], Thomas Durfey, and Ambrose Philips: see Biographical Index. Other initials are less certainly attributed: see *Prose*, ii. 248–55.

206 *Didapper*. A small diving water-fowl; a dabchick.

207 *approves*. Recommends himself as worthy of approval.

triticalness. Triteness (a word seemingly invented by the Scriblerians).

208 *Smithfield*. Home of Bartholomew Fair; see *Dunciad*, i. 2.

209 *Job*. See Job 29: 6.

211 *pursy*. Asthmatic.

212 *Withers*. George Wither, John Ogilby, and John Taylor the Water Poet, long consecrated examples of the bad poet. For Tate, Ward, and Eusden, see Biographical Index.

Ennius. Latin author (239–169 BC), the greatest of early Roman poets.

Aeneid. iii. 571–7.

213 *Horace*. See *Odes*, I. i. 36.

play. Nicholas Rowe's *Lady Jane Grey* (1715), V. i. 36.

points. Witty turns of phrase.

214 *refer*. Reproduce.

exquisite. Accomplished, excellent.

215 *British spectator*. Another attack on the popularity of John Rich's harlequinades on the current London stage, a theme of *The Dunciad*.

smart toupee. These lines are possibly from a youthful poem by P himself. He later added a note explaining the allusions to stays, a tweezer-case, a watch, and a fan respectively, in the first three lines.

Tom-Turd-man. One who emptied cesspools at night.

White Staff. Holder of a high post (esp. Lord Treasurer) who carried this symbol of office.

218 *St-. on Q. Mary*. From *The Profession* (1695), an early poem by P's former friend Richard Steele.

Vet. Aut. Old author (unidentified).

220 *cabinet*. 'A room devoted to . . . the display of works of art and objects of vertu' (*OED*).

223 *Camp.* That is Addison's famous poem *The Campaign* (1705). See also Spence, i. 76: 'Tautology, a frequent fault of Addison: much more faults in his *Campaign* than anyone would easily imagine.'

224 *Thetis.* The mother of Achilles.

honest citizen. Monsieur Jourdain, in Molière's *Le Bourgeois Gentilhomme* (1670).

225 *same hand.* Actually by Addison, not Tickell, suggesting that P accepted the story that Addison was the true author of the rival translation of the *Iliad* (1715).

227 *Spies and Trips.* Ned Ward had written *The London Spy* and various works entitled *A Trip to* ——.

Josephus. Roger L'Estrange had translated the historian Josephus in 1702. The *British Gazetteer* was a Whig weekly newspaper.

Asgill. John Asgill (1659–1738), theological and controversial author, noted for his short-winded, abrupt way of writing.

snipsnap. Sharp repartee: see *Dunciad*, ii. 240.

228 *Sesostris.* The Greek name of a legendary Egyptian king, supposed to have made large conquests in Asia.

Κιββερισμος *and* Ολφιελδισμος. Kibberism and Oldfieldism. For Anne Oldfield the actress, see Biographical Index.

231 *economy.* Systematic arrangement.

Aristotle. In *Rhetoric*, III. xi. 16.

green hastings. Early ripening fruit.

sentences. Rhetorical topics.

places. Rhetorical topics.

232 *economical.* Domestic.

233 *blue, green and red.* Colours respectively of the ribbons of the Orders of the Garter, the Thistle, and the Bath; the leading orders of chivalry and symbolic of the topmost echelon of nobility and power.

facility. Courtesy, affability.

Chap. XV. First published in *Guardian*, no. 78 (10 June 1713), slightly revised.

Receipt. Recipe.

234 *Molière.* In *L'Avare* (1668), III. i.

Don Belianis. A Spanish chivalric romance of the sixteenth century.

235 *Horace.* From *Ars poetica*, ll. 191–2: 'And let no god intervene, unless a problem should arise worthy of such a denouement.'

236 *advise with your bookseller.* Consult the publisher.

Wilks. For the theatrical managers Barton Booth and Robert Wilks, see Biographical Index.

out-doings. Cibber became notorious for this absurd phrase, used in the preface to his recently performed play *The Provoked Husband* (1728).

Royal Academy of Music. A private organization set up in 1719 to promote opera in London.

Figg. The prizefighter James Figg.

Violante. A well-known rope-dancer.

237 *frank*. Free.

Somerset House. In a state of neglect and dilapidation prior to the erection of the imposing new buildings by Sir William Chambers in 1776–96.

Projectors. Entrepreneurs.

eunuchs. Operatic castrati.

238 *place of privilege*. For immunity from arrest for debt.

239 *Vale & Fruere*. Farewell and enjoy yourself.

Pope to Jonathan Swift, November 28, 1729. Text based on *Corr*. iii. 79.

Rhapsody. A medley or string of diverse topics.

as a wit. With a deliberate aim at ingenuity, grace, or pointed effect.

fall into his hands. Curll had published many letters of P obtained surreptitiously, although not without P's own contrivance.

subito ingenio. 'With a start of genius' (later note).

another. P's mother.

Cur . . . aevo. Horace, *Odes*, II. xvi. 17: 'Why these extended cares, and strife, / And trouble, for so short a life?' (Creech).

240 *wholly disinterested*. The disgraced South Sea cashier, Robert Knight, had offered a bribe to Queen Caroline. The present from Swift was perhaps a gift of Irish poplin, which Swift had made as a reminder of Irish manufactures, inhibited by English measures.

poor woman. In fact P's mother survived until 1733.

imbecility. Feebleness.

noble friend. Presumably the second Earl of Oxford. P's correspondence appeared in Wycherley's *Posthumous Works*, vol. ii (published 4 November 1729), a riposte to a volume edited by Theobald in the previous year. P conceals his own responsibility.

241 *our friend*. Dr Arbuthnot's brother Robert had sent Swift some wine, which proved to be sour on arrival.

Mr Dodington. George Bubb Dodington (see Biographical Index).

certain Lord. Lord Carteret.

Mr Craggs. James Craggs, jun. (see Biographical Index).

Dean Berkeley. The philosopher George Berkeley, Dean of Derry.

Mr Hutchinson. John Hutchinson (1674-1737), religious writer.

Lord B. Bolingbroke, who had sent P his own letter of 19 November, to be completed and sent on to Swift; for the text, see *Corr.* iii. 70-2.

system of ethics. An early hint of the *Essay on Man.*

242 *Epitaph, Intended for Sir Isaac Newton.* Newton died at the age of 84 on 20 March 1727. P's epitaph was first published in June 1730, entering the *Works* in 1735; it was probably written not long before its first publication. The Latin portion may be rendered, 'Isaac Newton, whom time, nature, and heaven declare to be immortal, while this stone acknowledges his mortal being.' The transformation of Gen. 1: 3 may have precluded the use of this epitaph in an ecclesiastical setting. It was perhaps unfortunate for the dignity of the lines that P had previously burlesqued the same scriptural verse in *Rape of the Lock*, iii. 46. A different Latin inscription was in fact added to Newton's tomb at Westminster Abbey in 1731.

An Epistle to Richard Boyle, Earl of Burlington. Published on 13 December 1731; composed 1730-1, since the bones of the poem were present in the account of P's work in progress which he gave to Joseph Spence in May 1730 (Spence, i. 158). The subtitle varies in early editions, sometimes incorporating the phrase 'Of Taste' or 'Of False Taste'.

The poem was the first to appear of the four which were to comprise the *Epistles to Several Persons* or *Moral Essays.* The present poem was placed fourth in the sequence, also comprising the epistles to Cobham, to a lady, and Bathurst, when this grouping was first established in the *Works* (1735). However, it is clear that the sequence had not been properly defined when P published this first epistle in 1731. For the relation to P's wider poetic scheme at this date, see Miriam Leranbaum, *Alexander Pope's 'Opus Magnum' 1729-1744* (Oxford, 1977). For other issues involved, see Note on the Text, pp. xxvii-xxix above. A single leaf of manuscript draft survives, corresponding roughly to ll. 1-98; it has been edited by M. Mack (*L&GA*, 156-67), together with a transcript of the entire poem preserved at Chatsworth.

In this edition the text is based on the 1744 'deathbed' edition, which differs in only small particulars from the *Works* (1735).

When the poem came out, all other responses were drowned by a highly public controversy over the character of Timon (ll. 99-168). The rumour had spread (possibly fomented by P's enemies) that this was an attack on the Duke of Chandos, a wealthy politician, patron, and grandee. P repeatedly denied this charge, and most modern authorities have accepted this disclaimer (see esp. *TE*, iii/2, 164–8). If Timon's seat is not meant as Canons, the palatial home of Chandos, then it is probably a generalized portrait of a stately mansion, with details taken from Walpole's Houghton as well as Blenheim and Chatsworth.

For the Earl of Burlington, see Biographical Index, as well as James Lees-Milne, *Earls of Creation* (1962), 103–69.

Argument. P attached to the third edition of the poem at this point an open letter to Chandos, reiterating his answers to those who had claimed that Timon was a caricature of the Duke. Another more satirical defence in prose of the *Epistle*, entitled *A Master Key to Popery*, was written but suppressed; this was first published in 1949, and reprinted in *TE*, iii/2, 170–82 and *Prose*, ii. 410–30.

243 l. 6. *artists*. Acting in the capacity of connoisseurs and consultants on matters of *virtu*.

l. 7. *Topham*. A prominent antiquarian and collector (d. 1753).

l. 8. *Pembroke*. For the Earl of Pembroke, see Biographical Index and Lees-Milne, *Earls of Creation*, 59–100.

l. 9. *Hearne*. Thomas Hearne, the great medieval scholar: see Biographical Index.

l. 10. *Mead*. Dr Richard Mead.   *Sloane*. Sir Hans Sloane. Both notable as physicians and as collectors: see Biographical Index.

l. 15. *Sir Visto*. Suggesting one given to the fine contrived views treasured by landscape gardeners; it is possible P had Walpole in mind.

l. 18. *Ripley*. Thomas Ripley worked for Walpole at Houghton: see Biographical Index.

l. 20. *Bubo*. Latin for an owl, suggesting stupidity; P may intend George Bubb Dodington (see Biographical Index), who had raised an expensive but short-lived pile in Dorset.

244 l. 32. *dog-hole*. 'a mean habitation' (Johnson).

l. 34. *rustic*. Rusticated stone, i.e. left with an irregular surface.

l. 36 note. A window with an arch at the top and two narrower panes at the sides.

l. 46. *Le Nôtre*. Andre Le Nôtre (1613–1700) designed the gardens at Versailles for Louis XIV.

245 l. 57. *genius of the place*. Anglicizing *genius loci*, the presiding spirit guarding a favoured place. For the concept in gardening, see J. D. Hunt and P. Willis (eds.), *The Genius of the Place* (1975).

l. 63. *intending*. Directing the gaze of the eyes (from Lat. *intendere oculos*).

l. 70. *Stowe*. For P's connections with Stowe, see also *Epistle to Cobham*, headnote. He had first visited the house in 1724, after Bridgeman and Vanbrugh had completed the first phase of its elaborately planned garden.

In 1731 P wrote to a friend, 'If anything under paradise could set me beyond all earthly cogitations, Stowe might do it' (*Corr.* iii. 217). See further M. R. Brownell, *Alexander Pope and the Arts of Georgian England* (Oxford, 1978), 195-207.

l. 72. *Nero's terraces*. Referring to Nero's Golden House: see Suetonius, *Nero*, 31.

l. 73. *parterres*. Ornamental flower-beds laid out in a regular pattern.

l. 78. *hermitage*. Alluding to the installation of busts, including that of the theologian Samuel Clarke (see Biographical Index) in the mock-rustic garden feature at Richmond Park which was known as the Hermitage; it was the private shrine of Queen Caroline. P added this couplet to the 1744 text, after the Queen was safely dead.

l. 80. *espaliers*. A framework of stakes along which ornamental fruit-trees are trained.

246 l. 99. *Timon's villa*. See headnote for the intense controversy which grew up around allegations that P was aiming at the Duke of Chandos and his house at Canons, near Edgware (now destroyed). Modern discussions are listed in *Prose*, ii. 408.

247 l. 123. *Amphitrite*. Sea-goddess, the wife of Neptune.

l. 124 note. Two of the most famous statues from the ancient world.

l. 126. *Nilus*. The Nile, as commemorated in the standard way by an urn representing the river-god.

l. 136. *Aldus*. Aldo Manutio (1450-1515), Venetian printer famous for Aldine classics.   *Du Suëil*. Augustin Deseuil (1673-1746), French cleric and bookbinder.

248 l. 146. *Verrio*. Antonio Verrio (1630-1707), Italian decorative painter, who came to England in 1671 and worked mainly on royal commissions.   *Laguerre*. Louis Laguerre (1663-1721), French decorative artist, came to England c.1684.

l. 149. *soft dean*. Probably Knightly Chetwood (1650-1720), Dean of Gloucester, a friend of Dryden.

l. 155. *genial*. Punning on various senses of the word listed in *OED*: 'pertaining to a feast; festive'; 'cheering, enlivening'; 'pleasantly warm, mild'; 'natural'.

l. 160. *Sancho's dread doctor*. From *Don Quixote*, ii. 47, where a doctor whisks away dishes set before Sancho Panza without giving him a chance to eat.

249 l. 174. *slope*. An artificially constructed bank in landscape-gardening.

l. 176. *Ceres*. Goddess of agriculture.

l. 178. *Bathurst*. See Biographical Index.   *Boyle*. Burlington's family name.

l. 190. *country*. 'A tract or district . . . owned by the same lord or proprietor' (*OED*).

l. 193. *Palladio*. Burlington had published designs by Palladio in 1730 and by Inigo Jones in 1727, both with the assistance of William Kent (see P's note to l. 23).

l. 195 note. P refers to the problems with some of the new 'Queen Anne' churches in London, damaged by subsidence and faulty workmanship; to the ineffective measures to remedy a breach of the Thames at Dagenham in 1707; and to the political wranglings over the proposed second London bridge at Westminster, not completed until after P's death.

250 l. 200. *mole*. Breakwater.

An Epistle to Allen Lord Bathurst. First published on 15 January 1733. The process of composition probably goes back to 1730, when P gave Joseph Spence an outline of his planned *opus magnum*, with several details which look forward to the content of this poem (Spence, i. 132). There were some revisions when the item appeared in the *Works* (1735), now placed third in the series which formed what was later called the *Epistles to Several Persons* (or *Moral Essays*). Other changes were made in the 'deathbed' edition P prepared with the help of Warburton in 1744 (published posthumously in 1748), and Warburton's own edition of 1751 introduced yet further innovations. For reasons discussed in the Note on the Text above, pp. xxvii–xxix, the text here is based on the 1744 version, though F. W. Bateson has argued powerfully for retaining the earlier ordering of the lines, which was considerably altered in 1744 (see *TE*, iii/2, 74–7). P told Spence that '*The Use of Riches* was as much laboured as any one of my works' (Spence, i. 139), and there is evidence that he continued to tinker with the poem up to his death.

Two substantial working drafts survive and have been edited by E. R. Wasserman (Baltimore, 1960). For the involved relation of this *Epistle* to P's planned masterwork, see Miriam Leranbaum, *Alexander Pope's 'Opus Magnum' 1729–1744* (Oxford, 1977), 82–106.

For P's long-time friend, Allen Lord Bathurst, see Biographical Index, as well as James Lees-Milne, *Earls of Creation* (1962), 21–56.

251 l. 1. *doctors*. The learned.

l. 3. *Momus*. The god of satire and derision.

l. 20. *Ward . . . Chartres*. In addition to P's note on Ward, Peter Wa[l]ter, and Chart[eris], see Biographical Index and Howard Erskine-Hill, *The Social Milieu of Alexander Pope* (New Haven, Conn. 1975), 103–31. This book provides an essential context for reading the *Epistles*.

253 l. 34. *saps*. Undermines.

l. 39. *supply*. Recourse.

l. 41. *imped*. From a word used in falconry, meaning 'to strengthen or improve the flight' of a bird (*OED*).

l. 45. *sibyls*. The Roman sibyls inscribed their prophecies on leaves, left outside their cave. P's note refers to the *Aeneid*, Book VI, involving the Cumaean sibyl.

254 l. 51. *Rome*. Home of the Pretender's court.

l. 53. *confound*. 'Confuse . . . the brain with liquor' (*OED*).

l. 54. *water all the quorum*. Bribe the justices of the peace.

l. 62. *Worldly*. Edward Wortley Montagu (1681–1761), the mean and self-contained husband (by now estranged) of Lady Mary Wortley Montagu.

l. 65. *Colepepper*. A nonentity (1668–1740), only remembered for P's mention.

l. 67. *White's*. The gaming club in St James's Street, London.

l. 73. *Adonis*. A type of the fop, but P may be thinking of his regular adversary Lord Hervey (see Biographical Index), esp. as the manuscript suggests 'Uxorio' in l. 59 may refer to Hervey's father, the Earl of Bristol.

l. 76. *quadrille*. The most fashionable card-game.

255 l. 82. *Turner*. Richard 'Plum' Turner, a Turkey merchant (d. 1733), otherwise almost entirely lost to history.

l. 84. *Wharton*. See *Epistle to Cobham*, l. 179.

l. 85. *Hopkins*. John Hopkins (*c*.1663–1732), a notoriously grasping financier.

l. 86. *vigour*. Sexual prowess.   *Japhet*. Japhet Crook (1662–1734); the events described in P's note took place in 1731.

l. 87. *Hippia*. One with the 'hips' or neurotic depression.

l. 91. *Harpax*. Robber (Greek).

256 l. 96. *cat*. P's note indicates the Duchess of Richmond (1647–1702), who allegedly made a bequest to her cats.

l. 100. *Bond*. For Denis Bond, see Biographical Index: according to a parliamentary inquiry, he had said to his fellow directors of the Charitable Corporation, 'Damn the poor, let us go into the City where we may get money.' He had already been expelled from the House of Commons (R. Sedgwick, *The House of Commons 1715–1754* (1970), i. 470–1).

l. 101. *Sir Gilbert*. See Biographical Index for Heathcote, a leading City magnate famous for his meanness.

l. 103. *Blunt*. See l. 133 for Sir John Blunt.

l. 107. *pelf*. Riches.

l. 117. *South-Sea Year*. 1720, when the South Sea Bubble burst and thousands of investors and annuitants were ruined. The directors of the company were prosecuted for their corrupt management.

ll. 119–20. *Phryne . . . excise*. The name Phryne is taken from that of a Greek courtesan; it is probably applied here to Walpole's mistress Molly Skerret, who would have had advance notice of the Prime Minister's unpopular Excise scheme of 1733: see Paul Langford, *The Excise Crisis* (Oxford, 1975).

257 l. 122. *plum*. Slang for £100,000; one who had assets of this size would be equivalent to the later millionaire.

l. 123. *Peter*. Peter Walter (see l. 20).

l. 127. *crown of Poland*. This was elective and had several times been offered to the highest bidder; it had become vacant in 1733 when Augustus II died.

l. 128. *Gage*. For Joseph Gage, see Biographical Index. He had attempted to buy the Polish crown in 1719 on the profits he had made from the Mississippi scheme. He gained a monopoly right to work the gold mines in Austria from the King of Spain. His supposed wife, Lady Mary Herbert, had previously sought a royal consort: her mother, the Marchioness of Powis, was allegedly the illegitimate daughter of James II.

l. 133. *Blunt*. See Biographical Index, and esp. Erskine-Hill, *Social Milieu*, 166–203. Blunt was seen, with some justice, as the very linchpin of the South Sea swindle.

l. 139. *statesman and patriot*. Government and Opposition.

258 l. 140. *box*. In the theatre.

l. 141. *job*. Use their office corruptly.　　　　　*bite*. Cheat.

l. 142. *pack*. Shuffle fraudulently.

l. 144. Referring to the historic victories in the reign of Edward III, notably Crécy, and of Anne, notably Blenheim.

l. 145. *scrivener*. Blunt had been apprenticed to a scrivener, or moneylender, in Holborn; the scrivener was also 'simultaneously the solicitor, the estate agent and the business agency of that enterprising age' (quoted by Erskine-Hill, *Social Milieu*, 170).

ll. 161–2. Quoted from *Essay on Man*, ii. 165–6 (adapted), ii. 205–6 (adapted).

l. 167. *change*. The Royal Exchange, centre of financial dealing.

259 l. 183. *pulse*. Peas and beans.

l. 187. *Chartreux*. The Carthusian monastery, used as an emblem of austere living.

l. 196. *eat*. Pronounced 'ate'.

l. 203. *hecatombs*. Large public sacrifices of animals (literally one hundred oxen).

l. 208. *that great house*. That of the Hanoverians.

l. 210. *sylvans groan . . . for the fleet*. The meaning may be either, 'The inhabitants of the forest lament the despoliation of their landscape and livelihood', or else 'the trees screech as they are cut down to provide timber for shipbuilding.'

l. 214. *train-bands*. A form of civic militia.   *burns a Pope*. Ritual burning of the Pope in effigy was a standard feature of anti-Catholic protest in P's youth.

260 l. 235. *ambergris*. A secretion of the sperm-whale, used in making perfume.

l. 243. *Oxford*. P's note identifies his friend the second Earl; see Biographical Index, and Lees-Milne, *Earls of Creation*, 173–218.

l. 250. *Man of Ross*. For John Kyrle, see Erskine-Hill, *Social Milieu*, 15–41.

l. 251. *Vaga*. The River Wye.

261 l. 267. *portioned*. With a marriage portion bestowed on them.

l. 282. *stars*. The insignia of the chivalric orders, specifically those of knighthood.

262 l. 296. *buckle*. 'The state of the hair crisped and curled by being kept long in the same state' (Johnson).   *Parian stone*. Stone from the island of Paros, a white marble famed for its long-lasting qualities.

l. 301. *flock-bed*. One stuffed with scraps of cloth rather than the feathers used in superior circles.

l. 303. *George and garter*. Insignia of the Order of the Garter, including an emblem of St George.

l. 305 note. George Villiers, Duke of Buckingham (1628–87), playwright and politician. The account of his death here is fanciful.

l. 308 note. The event took place in 1668.

l. 310. *king*. i.e. Charles II.

l. 315. *Cutler*. Sir John Cutler (*c*.1608–93), a parsimonious City grandee who may also be the basis of Old Cotta above (l. 178).

263 l. 342. *Balaam*. The name is biblical (Num. 22: 21–35 tells the story of Balaam and his ass), but otherwise there is no direct link.

264 l. 358. *chirping*. *OED* quotes a slang expression, '*chirping-merry*, very pleasant over a glass of good liquor'.

l. 362. *factor*. A junior official of the East India Company.   *gem*. Thomas Pitt, ancestor of the great Pitt dynasty, bought the famous Pitt diamond while governor of Madras.

l. 364. *bit*. Cheated.

l. 378. *lucky hit*. A stock phrase, almost proverbial, for a stroke of any kind, here a financial coup; often used by Swift.

l. 384. *catched*. Just beginning to be an informal past tense, if not yet quite a vulgarism.

l. 388. *St James's air*. The salubrious atmosphere of the West End, as opposed to the busy city of London.

265 l. 394. *St Stephen*. A metonym for Parliament.

l. 397. *Coningsby*. See Biographical Index: he had taken a leading part in the impeachment of Robert Harley, but he is in effect used as a stock figure of the hypocritical Whig and Hanoverian.

The First Satire of the Second Book of Horace Imitated. First published on 15 February 1733. Written with unusual speed during a spell of ill-health in the previous month, when P was confined to his room at Lord Oxford's house for several days. Then, as P told Spence in 1744, 'Lord Bolingbroke came to see me, happened to take up a Horace that lay on the table, and in turning it over dipped on the First Satire of the Second Book. He observed how well that would hit my case, if I were to imitate it in English. After he was gone, I read it over, translated it in a morning or two, and sent it to the press in a week or fortnight after. And this was the occasion of my imitating some other of the Satires and Epistles afterwards' (Spence, i. 143). A manuscript, partly in the hand of an amanuensis, survives in the New York Public Library; it has been edited by M. Mack (*L&GA*, 168–87).

The poem was reprinted in the *Works* (1735) and since that time has regularly stood at the head of the assembled *Imitations of Horace*. However, as the remarks to Spence show, the series was not planned when the first poem appeared, and in this edition the various imitations are printed separately in the order of their first appearance. See further Note on the Text, pp. xxvii–xxix above. Here the text is based on Warburton's 1751 edition.

The satires particularly 'hit [P's] case', as Bolingbroke put it, because of the opportunities for political comment, but also because Horace himself confronts the public role of the satirist in terms of which P could exploit. For the nature of the undertaking, see Frank Stack, *Pope and Horace: Studies in Imitation* (Cambridge, 1985). In early editions the Latin text was printed opposite the English version, so that well-equipped readers (always a minority) could compare the respective wordings.

Fortescue. William Fortescue was almost P's only close friend in government circles; he had served as Walpole's secretary, and he later became a senior judge. P consulted Fortescue for advice in his capacity as a private lawyer; they had known each other for some twenty years. See also Biographical Index.

l. 3. *complaisant.* Polite, courteous.

ll. 3–4. *Peter . . . Chartres.* P states in the Advertisement which he appended to the collected *Imitations of Horace* in 1735 that 'the occasion of publishing these imitations was the clamour raised on some of my *Epistles*'. He refers in these lines to Peter Walter and Francis Charteris, whom he had named in the *Epistle to Bathurst.*

l. 6. *Lord Fanny.* Lord Hervey (see Biographical Index).

266 l. 8. *counsel.* William Fortescue, who was a barrister.

l. 18. *lettuce.* Believed to act as a bromide.

l. 19. *Celsus*. Aulus Cornelius Celsus, who wrote eight influential works on medicine in the first century AD.

l. 20. *hartshorn*. Sal volatile or ammonium carbonate, used not as smelling-salts to revive a patient but as a sedative.

l. 21. *Caesar*. George II.

l. 22. *bays*. The post of laureate.

l. 23. *Sir Richard*. Blackmore (see Biographical Index).

l. 24. *Brunswick*. The house of Brunswick: George I's mother was the heiress of the Dukes of Brunswick-Luneburg. P's reference makes the political point that the Hanoverian line were foreigners.

l. 27. *Budgell*. Eustace Budgell (see Biographical Index) had written a poem, celebrating the King's exploits at the battle of Oudenarde in 1708, when he led a cavalry charge and had his horse shot from under him.

l. 30. *Carolina*. Perhaps not the Queen but her somewhat unattractive daughter Caroline.

l. 31. *Amelia*. Another daughter of the King and Queen.   *the nine.* The Muses.

l. 34. *twice a year*. The Poet Laureate had to produce official odes at the New Year and on the King's birthday.

l. 38. *quadrille*. Referring back to *Epistle to Bathurst*, l. 38; the joke is that blasphemy should be reserved for such trivial pursuits.

l. 40. *Peter*. Peter Walter.

l. 42. *Timon*. See *Epistle to Burlington*, l. 99.   *Balaam.* See *Epistle to Bathurst*, l. 342.

267 l. 44. *Bond*. See *Epistle to Bathurst*, l. 100.   *Harpax.* See *Epistle to Bathurst*, l. 92.

l. 46. *Scarsdale*. The fourth Earl (1682–1736). A minor politician.   *Darty.* Charles Dartiquenave (1664–1737), an epicure and friend of the Scriblerus group.

l. 47. *Ridotta*. A woman addicted to socializing.

l. 49. *Fox*. The brothers Stephen and Henry Fox; the latter, at this time a rake, was to become a prominent politician. Stephen was a close friend of Lord Hervey.   *Hockley Hole.* A bear-garden in north London.

l. 52. *Shippen*. See Biographical Index.

l. 71. *Hectors*. Rowdies and street-brawlers.

l. 72. *supercargoes*. Cargo-superintendents, reputed to gain corrupt wealth.   *directors.* South Sea Managers.

l. 75. *Fleury*. The leading minister of France, Cardinal Fleury (1653–1743).

l. 80. *burden*. Refrain.

l. 82. *Page*. The notorious judge: see Biographical Index.

l. 83. *Sappho*. Lady Mary Wortley Montagu. (*P–xed* also refers to her campaign for smallpox inoculation.)

268 l. 89. *Walter*. Peter Walter.

l. 100. *Lee*. The dramatist Nathaniel Lee (1653–92), who had been lodged in Bethlehem Hospital ('Bedlam') from 1684 to 1689.   *Budgell*. He was believed to have taken his own life by drowning after the accusation of embezzlement.

l. 103. *plums*. In effect, millionaires.

l. 104. *testers*. Sixpences ('club' means collect together).

l. 108. *star*. That of knighthood.

l. 112. *Louis*. Louis XIV, Boileau's patron.

l. 113. *pimp and friar*. Dryden, whilst Poet Laureate to Charles II (as he was to James II), had created the character of an immoral priest in *The Spanish Friar* (1680).

269 l. 127. *St John*. Lord Bolingbroke.

l. 129. *Iberian lines*. The Earl of Peterborough (see Biographical Index), P's close friend, who had become famous in the Peninsular campaign.

l. 130. *quincunx*. Four trees planted at the corners of a square, with a fifth at the middle point. There were quincunxes in P's own garden (Mack, *Life*, 361).

l. 145. *Richard*. P refers to the case of a poet named Collingbourne during the reign of Richard III. He was a Wiltshire gentleman, hanged at Tower Hill in 1484 for a rhyme satirizing the King and his counsellors.

ll. 147–8. *quart. . . . quint. Eliz.* Early acts against libel and sedition, including 3/4 Edward VI, c. 15; 1 Elizabeth I, c. 6; and 5 Elizabeth I, c. 15.

l. 153. *Sir Robert*. Walpole.

270 *An Essay on Man*. The four epistles were published separately at intervals between 20 February 1733 and 24 January 1734. We do not know the exact date of composition; the first hints of the work appear in P's correspondence in 1730. By 2 August 1731 Bolingbroke was able to report to Swift that P had completed the first three epistles and was at work on the fourth (*Corr.* iii. 213–14). The fourth seems to have caused the most trouble in the writing.

As the subtitle suggests, the *Essay* was intended to form the prelude to a much larger survey of human experience. In its original plan, this master-work would have comprised four considerable sections, with the *Essay* as the opening book. The scale of the undertaking was later cut back, and the only existing poems which would probably have gone directly into the scheme are the four *Moral Essays*—perhaps in a slightly different version. For a full account, see M. Leranbaum, *Alexander Pope's 'Opus Magnum' 1729–1744* (Oxford, 1977).

The epistles were all issued anonymously—a deliberate ploy by P, who was able to enjoy the spectacle of widespread obeisance to the author of this noble poem—often expressed most fervently by his long-time enemies, in their ignorance of the real circumstances. P did not reveal himself until the poem went into a major collection of the *Works*, vol. ii (1735). But by then the facts were an open secret, and Voltaire, a great admirer of the poem, was early on apprised of the truth.

The *Essay* achieved great success in England and abroad. There were soon two French translations (the first of many into all the major languages during the following century), and it was the animadversions of a Swiss cleric named Crousaz which set off a debate over much of Europe as to the orthodoxy of P's moral and theological position. For this debate, through which William Warburton first came into prominence as a champion of P, see *TE*, vol. iii/1, pp. xviii–xxii; and A. D. Nuttall, *Pope's 'Essay on Man'* (1984), a useful general survey of the work.

An equally fierce and latterly more vigorous controversy surrounds the degree of P's debt to the thought of his mentor Bolingbroke. For an account relegating Bolingbroke's role in the formation of the poem, see M. Mack's introduction to *TE*, vol. iii/1; for a more positive assessment, see B. S. Hammond, *Pope and Bolingbroke* (Columbia, Mo., 1984). Mack provides the fullest review of the thought of the poem in relation to classical and Renaissance forebears.

A manuscript of the poem survives in the Pierpont Morgan Library, New York, and has been edited by Mack (Oxford, 1962).

EPISTLE I

272 l. 1. *St John*. Bolingbroke (see Biographical Index). P originally used the cover name 'Laelius', taken from a Roman patron celebrated by Horace.

l. 5. *expatiate*. Speak at length.

l. 6. *but not*. The original reading was 'of walks without a plan', but P altered the wording when the line was interpreted to mean not just that human beings could not discern the order in the universe but that there actually was no such order.

ll. 9–10. *beat . . . open . . . covert*. A metaphor from hunting.

l. 15. *candid*. Indulgent, uncritical.

273 l. 33. *chain*. The great chain of being (see l. 207 below).

l. 42. *satellites*. A Latin form, pronounced 'sat-ell-i-tes'.

l. 60. *a part we see, and not a whole*. Recalling 1 Cor. 13: 12.

274 l. 64. *Egypt's god*. The bull of Memphis, Apis, regarded as sacred.

l. 77. *book of fate*. Taken from *Henry IV*, III. i. 45.

l. 81. *riot*. Wild revelling, debauchery.

l. 88. *sparrow fall*. Recalling Matt. 10: 29.

l. 98. *expatiates*. Roams freely.

275 l. 99. *Indian*. i.e. American Indian, in the northern or southern continent.

l. 110. *seraph's fire*. Seraphs traditionally were associated with the attribute of fire.

l. 111. *equal*. Here, benign.

l. 117. *gust*. Taste.

l. 121. *balance*. The scales of justice.

l. 133. *genial*. Generative.

276 l. 142. *burning suns . . . livid deaths descend*. It was thought that plagues were caused by the heat of the sun.

l. 156. *Borgia*. P probably has chiefly in mind Cesare Borgia (1476–1507), the archetypal Renaissance prince.   *Catiline*. L. Sergius Catiline (*c*.108–62 BC), Roman conspirator.

l. 160. *Ammon*. Alexander the Great.

277 l. 174. *little less than angel*. Taken from Ps. 8: 5.

l. 181. *compensated*. Stress on second syllable.

278 l. 213. *headlong lioness*. As P's note indicates, the lion was thought to have a poor sense of smell and so to rely on sudden surprise attacks on its prey.

l. 214. *sagacious*. 'Acute in perception, esp. by the sense of smell' (*OED*).   *tainted*. 'Imbued with the scent of . . . a hunted animal' (*OED*).

l. 219. *nice*. Delicately skilful.

l. 223. *barrier*. Accented on last syllable.

279 l. 240. *glass*. Telescope or microscope.

l. 243. *leave a void*. Recalling the old maxim, 'nature abhors a vacuum' (Tilley N42).

l. 248. *amazing*. Stronger than today; wondrous, overpowering.

280 l. 278. *rapt seraph that . . . burns*. *TE*, iii/1, 278, quotes Aquinas, *Summa contra gentiles*, iii. 80: 'These are called Seraphim, i.e. fiery . . . because fire is used to designate intensity of love or desire' (here, of course, spiritual love).

l. 280. *equals all*. Makes all equal.

l. 283. *Kind*. Appropriate.

l. 285. *sphere*. Pronounced 'sphare'.

l. 294. '*Whatever is, is* RIGHT'. P used the same phrase in a letter to Swift around the same date, 2 April 1733 (*Corr*. iii. 465).

EPISTLE II

281 l. 1. *scan*. Criticize, judge with improper minuteness.

l. 23. *th'empyreal sphere*. The highest region of the heavens, where Plato's ideas had their being.

282 l. 44. *equipage*. Equipment, appurtenances.

l. 59. *acts*. Sets into action.

l. 63. *peculiar*. Particular.

283 l. 89. *that*. Self-love (as opposed to 'this', reason, in l. 90).

l. 91. *or . . . or*. Either (i) wrongly; or (ii) rightly, understood.

l. 99. *those, that imparted*. The passions, when imbued with reason.

284 l. 108. *card*. A mariner's compass.

ll. 111–12. *Passions . . . unite*. Alluding to the blend of the four contrary elements and the corresponding 'humours', which was necessary for a healthy personality and a balanced outlook.

l. 132. *Aaron's serpent*. Aaron's rod which was transformed into a serpent (Exod. 7: 10–12).

285 l. 144. *peccant*. Morbid (because of an excess of one humour).

ll. 159–60. *small humours . . . driven them out*. It was believed that the onset of 'gout' (then a vaguely defined condition) drove out other sickness latent in the body; here the humours are seen as concentrating in the extremities and thus freeing the rest of the body of the morbid excess which provoked illness.

l. 161. *preferred*. Pronounced 'prefarred'.

l. 177. *mercury of Man*. All metals were supposed to be based on a primal constituent of mercury; the word 'mercury' also carries the sense of elusiveness, capriciousness. In combination with the word 'virtue' in the next line, however, there is a clear additional reference to alchemy; this would provide the sense, 'thus, by the alchemy of Providence, a mysterious harmony is achieved in the life of the passions.'

286 l. 181. *ungrateful*. Unresponsive.

ll. 186–94. *spleen . . . shame*. P adapts the traditional seven deadly sins, omitting gluttony but adding shame.

l. 197. *bias*. As in bowling.

l. 198. *Titus*. T. Flavius Vespasianus (AD 39–81), Emperor of Rome AD 79–81, regarded as one of the most benevolent of the early emperors.

l. 200. *Decius*. Publius Decius, a Roman consul who sacrificed himself in battle in 337 BC.   *Curtius*. Marcus Curtius, who leapt fully armed into a chasm to preserve the Roman forum. Both stories are drawn from Livy.

ll. 203–4. *light and darkness . . . the mind*. Recalling Gen. 1: 4.

287 l. 223. *Orcades*. The Orkney Islands.

l. 224. *Zembla*. Novaya Zemlya, off the arctic coast of Russia.

l. 237. *several.* Separate.

288   l. 261. *pelf.* Riches.

l. 269. *chemist.* Alchemist, in search of the elixir to turn base metals into gold.

l. 279. *scarves.* The sashes worn by doctors of divinity.   *garters.* The insignia of the Order of the Garter.

l. 280. *beads.* The rosary.

l. 282. *life's poor play is o'er.* Recalling Macbeth's speech in the last scene of the tragedy (v. v. 19–28).

l. 288. *bubble.* Literally and in the sense of a deception or duping appearance.

EPISTLE III

289   l. 9. *plastic nature.* 'The informing and forming power of God, as manifested in the creativity of nature: cf. the *natura naturans* of the Schools' (*TE*, iii/1, 93).

290   l. 38. *vindicate.* Lay claim to (Lat. *vindicare*).

291   l. 53. *stooping.* Swooping.

l. 56. *Philomela.* The nightingale.

l. 64. *savage.* Wild beast.

292   l. 84. *Council.* 'The Roman Catholic council, which claims to be infallible' (*EC*, ii. 406).

l. 86. *pressed.* Impressed, as for military service.

ll. 101–2. *Prescient . . . beneath the sand.* Alluding to the halcyon, which was fabled to nest on the wave, and the kingfisher (the likely basis of the mythical halcyon), which nests in the banks of rivers.

l. 104. *De Moivre.* Abraham de Moivre (1667–1754), French mathematician, who settled in England: FRS, 1697.

l. 118. *genial.* Generative.

293   l. 146. *kind.* The family line.

294   l. 184. *ant's republic . . . bees.* Ants were thought to organize their colonies in what might be termed a 'democratic' fashion; bees lived under the 'realm' of a queen.

295   ll. 219–22. *from the wondering furrow . . . the ground.* Describing the conquest of the four elements.

296   l. 232. *saw that all was right.* Recalling Gen. 1: 31.

l. 242. *enormous.* Irregular, deviant (Lat. *enormis*).

l. 265. *flamen.* Priest.

297   l. 286. *moral.* Morality.

l. 292. *touching.* The usual word for striking the keys or strings of a musical instrument, which is the standard metaphor employed here for achieving harmony in the state.

298 l. 311. *generous*. Fertile.

l. 315. *act*. Actuate.

299 l. 10. *diamonds in the flaming mine*. Alluding to the pervasive belief that minerals were ripened in the earth by the influence of the sun.

l. 15. *sincere*. Unadulterated (Lat. *sincerus*).

301 ll. 73–6. *sons of earth . . . heaps they raise*. Alluding to the Titans, who were buried beneath the mountains they had raised in their rebellion against Jupiter and Saturn.

l. 80. *competence*. As in 'a competence', that is adequate means to live on.

302 l. 99. *Falkland*. The heroic figure of Civil War legend, Lucius Cary, Viscount Falkland (1610–43), killed at the battle of Newbury.

l. 100. *Turenne*. Henri d'Auvergne, vicomte de Turenne (1611–75), French general, killed during a German campaign.

l. 101. *Sidney*. Sir Philip Sidney (1554–86), killed at the siege of Zutphen in the Netherlands. All these paragons were killed in relatively unimportant or indecisive contests, rather than major battles.

l. 104. *Digby*. Hon. Robert Digby, who had died in 1726 at the age of 40; he was a close friend of P. The father, William, fifth Lord Digby, survived his son by many years. See Howard Erskine-Hill, *The Social Milieu of Alexander Pope* (New Haven, Conn. 1975), 132–65.

l. 107. *bishop*. The Bishop of Marseilles, Belsunce (1671–1775) had lived through the plague epidemic in the city in 1720, despite constant ministrations to the sick. This was the last major outbreak of plague in northern Europe. The plague was thought to be transmitted by miasma passing through the air.

l. 110. *parent*. P's mother had died on 7 June 1733, at the age of 91.

l. 118. *Abel*. See Gen. 4: 1–15.

l. 120. *disease*. Syphilis.

l. 123. *sage*. Empedocles (*c.*500–430 BC), who was said to have perished on Mount Etna, either by self-immolation or by accident.

l. 126. *Bethel*. Hugh Bethel: see Biographical Index.

l. 130. *Charters*. Francis Charteris: see Biographical Index.

303 ll. 145–6. *This world . . . made for Caesar*. A commonplace utilized in Addison's *Cato*, IV. iv. 23–4, and picked up in P's letter to Swift of 23 March 1728 (*Corr.* ii. 480).

l. 171. *gown*. A preacher's or a doctor's gown.

304 l. 201. *monarch*. Probably Philip V of Spain, who had retired to a monastery.

l. 204. *Leather or prunella.* That is, dress; 'leather' for the cobbler's apron; 'prunella', a worsted twill, for the parson's gown.

l. 205. *strings.* The ribbons of honours awarded to persons of consequence.

l. 216. *Howards.* The great line of the Howard family, long prominent in English life: esp. in the premier dukedom, that of Norfolk. P may instance this family out of loyalty to their Catholic heritage.

305   l. 220. *Macedonia's madman.* Alexander the Great.   *Swede.* Charles XII of Sweden, often identified with Alexander for his daring, rashness, and ambition.

l. 235. *Aurelius.* Marcus Aurelius (AD 121–80), Roman emperor and philosopher.

l. 240. *Tully.* Cicero.

l. 244. *Eugene.* Prince Eugene of Savoy (1663–1736), commander of the Imperial Forces, in alliance with Marlborough at Blenheim and other battles during the War of the Spanish Succession.

l. 247. *A wit's a feather, and a chief a rod. TE*, iii/1, 151, quotes Mark Pattison: 'Alluding to the pen with which the wit writes, and the baton . . . of the general.'

l. 250. *justice tears his body from the grave.* It was not uncommon for bodies of those who had fallen into disfavour to be exhumed and subjected to scorn and revilement. The most famous case was Oliver Cromwell, whose remains were gibbeted at Tyburn after the Restoration.

l. 257. *Marcellus.* M. Claudius Marcellus (d. 46 BC), exiled after the defeat of Pompey at Pharsalus.

306   l. 277. *ribbons.* The trappings of office or nobility.

l. 280. *Gripus.* Indicating a miser.

ll. 291–308. Later transferred by P to the Duke of Marlborough in a separate epigram, reprinted in *TE*, vi. 358–9.

307   l. 307. *enormous.* See iii. 242, above.

308   l. 373. *genius.* Tutelary spirit.

309   l. 378. *temper.* Composure.

l. 389. *pretend.* Proclaim (Lat. *praetendere*).

Pope to Jonathan Swift, 20 April 1733. Text based on *Corr.* iii. 365–7. John Gay had died suddenly on 4 December 1732. Since then P and Swift had exchanged letters concerning his works, his monument in Westminster Abbey, and other matters. Originally printed under the date '2 April', but since it refers to items in Swift's letter of 30–31 March, received in London on 16 April, *Corr.* iii. 365, proposes 20 April for the present letter.

310   *whatever Is, is Right.* See *Essay on Man*, i. 294.

epitaph. P had sent Swift a draft of his inscription for Gay's tomb, and Swift had suggested a number of small alterations (*Corr*. iii. 360–1), some adopted by P. The monument was finally unveiled in the Abbey on 28 April 1737, erected at the expense of the Duke and Duchess of Queensberry. For the text of the poem, see *TE*, vi. 349–50.

performance. The *Verses* in reply to P's first imitation of Horace, addressed to Fortescue, which Lady Mary Wortley Montagu and Lady Hervey had published on 9 March.

collection. P had apparently got wind of a project germinating in Swift's mind, which was to eventuate in his *Works*, published by Faulkner in 1735.

another of my Epistles. This possibly means the third part of the *Essay on Man*, published a few days after this letter.

311 *another of Horace's*. That is, the *Second Satire of the Second Book*, published in 1734. Swift is given a small speaking role in ll. 161–4.

our poor lady. Henrietta Howard, now Countess of Suffolk. She was no longer in the King's favour, but remained at court until after the death of her husband on 28 September following. Swift never made his planned visit to England.

The Fourth Satire of Dr John Donne Versified. First anonymously published on 5 November 1733, as *The Impertinent; or a Visit to the Court*. Included in the *Works* (1735) under the present title, with Donne's text alongside. A few revisions were made by the time it appeared in Warburton's edition of 1751, which is the basis for the text here. The poem may incorporate early attempts to modernize Donne, but the likeliest time for composition is the summer of 1733, with the poem possibly completed during a three-week visit to Lord Peterborough in September (see Mack, *Life*, 603).

Donne's *Satyre IV* (*c*.1597) is itself modelled on the ninth satire in the first book of Horace, so that P is once again imitating Horace, although at one remove. For a full discussion of this triangular relationship, see H. Erskine-Hill, *The Augustan Idea in English Literature* (1983), 74–98. The contact between P and Donne is explored in Ian Jack, 'Pope and the Weighty Bullion of Dr Donne's Satires', *PLMA* 66 (1951), 1009–22. For P's various statements on the poetry of Donne, see Spence, i. 187–8, including the comment, 'Donne had no imagination, but as much wit, I think, as any writer can possibly have.' (See p. 574.)

l. 17. *fine*. Legislation dating back to the reign of Elizabeth I imposed fines and imprisonment on Catholics who attended mass.

312 l. 30. *Sloane or Woodward's wondrous shelves*. Two of the largest collections of curiosities and specimens (of geology, natural history, etc.), belonging to Sir Hans Sloane and Dr John Woodward, a pioneer archaeologist and antiquarian. See Biographical Index, and *Dunciad*, iv. 347–96.

l. 34. *make*. Invent (as, P implies, had happened in the case of the most famous 'plot' of 1678). See J. P. Kenyon, *The Popish Plot* (1972) for analysis of fact and fiction.

l. 41. *in the youth of good Queen Bess*. There is an underlying proverbial usage behind the line, as in Swift, *Cadenus and Vanessa*, ll. 398–9: 'They rallied next Vanessa's dress, / "That gown was made for old Queen Bess",' and in his *Polite Conversation*.

l. 42. *tuftaffeta*. 'A kind of taffeta with a pile or nap arranged in tufts' (*OED*).

l. 45. *rash*. Smooth silk.

ll. 50–1. *Motteux . . . Henley . . . Budgell*. For these writers, see Biographical Index.

l. 52. *wormwood style*. Harsh and bitter, like the plant of this name; the doctor may well be Bentley.

l. 53. *Gonson*. The Westminster magistrate, Sir John Gonson, well known for his eloquent charges to the jury.

l. 58. *scores*. Debts owing for goods obtained on credit.

l. 59. *cozen*. Cheat.

313   l. 61. *Oldmixon . . . Burnet*. For these historians, see Biographical Index.

l. 68. *King's*. Turning the cliché 'the King's English' towards a jibe at George II's German accent.

l. 71. *Onslow*. Arthur Onslow (1691–1768), the long-serving Speaker of the House of Commons.

l. 72. *closer*. More taut and compressed.

l. 73. *Hoadly*. Bishop Benjamin Hoadly: see Biographical Index.

l. 75. *Panurge*. In Rabelais's *Pantagruel and Gargantua*, ii. 9, the cunning rogue Panurge launches into a variety of languages.

l. 77. *gift of tongues*. As on the day of Pentecost (Acts 2: 1–4).

l. 83. *druggerman*. Or dragoman, an Arabic word for interpreter. For the Tower of Babel, see Gen. 11: 1–9.

l. 91. *Tully*. Cicero, *De officiis*, III. i. ('never less alone').

l. 95. *Aretine*. Pietro Aretino (1492–1557), generally regarded then as the type of a lascivious writer.

314   l. 102. *tombs*. The memorials in Westminster Abbey were among the major sights of London.

l. 108. *mechanic*. Manual worker.

l. 113. *paduasoy*. A corded silk fabric then widely used for clothes.

l. 125. *eunuchs, harlequins, and operas*. Again P jibes at contemporary stage spectacles, including opera with its castrati singers and the pantomimes of John Rich. See also *Dunciad*, iii. 249–64.

l. 130. *birth-nights*. The celebrations surrounding royal birthdays.

l. 131. *Holinsheds, or Halls, or Stows.* Alluding to three leading chroniclers of English history: Ralph Holinshed, Edward Hall, and John Stow.

l. 132. *Queen.* Donne had meant Queen Elizabeth; P suggests that Queen Caroline is the real power behind the throne (and through her Walpole).

l. 134. *rug.* Safe.

315 l. 142. *trust or charity.* Another allusion to the scandal of the Charitable Corporation; see *Epistle to Bathurst,* l. 102.

l. 144. *clown.* Peasant.

l. 146. *chuck.* Play at chuck-farthing, a game in which coins were tossed at a target.   *vole.* Win all the tricks, esp. at ombre.

l. 147. *excising.* A further reference to the Excise Crisis of 1733, the hot topic of the moment.

l. 151. *whited wall.* The 'whited sepulchres' of Matt. 23: 27.

l. 152. *Woodward's patients.* Dr John Woodward (l. 30) was often satirized because of his inclination to prescribe emetics. 'The great wisdom and happiness of man', he had written in 1718, 'consists in a due care of the stomach and digestion.'

l. 154. *Europe's balance.* The death of the king of Poland (an elective office) in 1733 had provoked a complex European diplomatic struggle.

l. 155. *Gazettes and Post Boys.* Perhaps newspapers in general, but suggesting the *London Gazette* (started 1665, a dull official record), and the *Post Boy*, later *Daily Post Boy* (started 1695), a Tory journal which had by this time lost its peak of popularity and influence.

l. 157. *cast.* Vomit.

l. 159. *great man.* Walpole.

l. 162. *price.* It was Opposition tactics to foment the charge that Walpole used bribery on an unprecedented scale (not true), and that he believed 'every man has his price' (another canard).

l. 165. *Spain robs on.* See *First Epistle of the Second Book,* l. 2. *Dunkirk.* There were allegations in Parliament that Dunkirk, whose fortifications were destroyed according to the Treaty of Utrecht in 1713, was being repaired —so that it could again provide a base for French privateers to attack English shipping.

l. 166. *Circe's guests.* See *Odyssey,* Book X.

l. 174. *nice.* Delicate.

l. 175. *atilt.* Just poised ready.

l. 178. *Fannius.* Lord Hervey.

316 l. 183. *actions.* Legal suits.

l. 206 note. Such a waxworks was on display in London in 1731.

l. 213. *Figg's.* James Figg (d. 1734) ran his boxing establishment near

Tyburn in Marylebone.   *White's*. See *Second Satire of Donne*, l. 88.

317 l. 222. *courtiers' clothes*. The 'birthday suits' worn in the royal reception will be passed on to the playhouse: see *First Epistle of the Second Book*, ll. 332–3.

l. 233. *Sir Fopling*. The hero of Etherege's comedy *The Man of Mode* (1676), a role in which Cibber had starred.

l. 236. *Heraclitus*. The ancient Greek thinker (*fl.* 500 BC), whose melancholy ideas brought him the name of the 'weeping philosopher'.

l. 238. *presence*. The royal presence-chamber at court, where the sovereign received guests.

l. 239. *Mahound*. Mahommed.   *pagod*. An idol, set in its temple.

l. 240. *Dürer's rules*. Referring to Dürer's *Four Books on Human Proportion* (published posthumously, 1528).

l. 251. *band*. Neckband.

l. 252. *Sharon*. Song of Solomon 2: 1.

l. 255. *protest*. Make protestations of their faith.

318 l. 263. *buff*. Leather.

l. 267. *hangdogs*. Those who crucified Christ.   *tapestry*. Flemish tapestries of the sixteenth century, which hung at Hampton Court.

l. 277. *Temple Bar and Charing Cross*. Temple Bar still occupied its historic site where Fleet Street adjoined the Strand; Charing Cross was destroyed in 1647 as a relic of popish superstition. P's failure to delete Charing Cross (still standing when Donne wrote) indicates a deliberate strategy, since he did add Temple Bar of his own accord.

319 *An Epistle to Sir Richard Temple, Lord Cobham*. First published on 16 January 1734, eight days before the last epistle of the *Essay on Man*. This was the third to appear of the poems which would be grouped together in the *Works* (1735) and later given by P the collective title *Epistles to Several Persons*. In this grouping the poem to Cobham always took first place in the sequence. The date of composition is not known precisely: a conversation which P had with Joseph Spence in May 1730 shows that the guiding ideas of the poem were already in P's mind (Spence, i. 142).

The work had an assigned position in P's plan for his *opus magnum*, the overarching philosophical compendium in verse which P was projecting in the early 1730s (see headnote to *Essay on Man*, p. 645 above). In fact, as F. W. Bateson has suggested, the epistle to Cobham is the 'only one of the four Epistles that was written *primarily* to fit into the expanded . . . scheme' on which P had embarked (*TE*, vol. iii/2, pp. xxxiv).

As with the *Epistle to Bathurst*, the text was rearranged in the so-called 'deathbed' edition which P prepared for his friends in 1744 (not published until 1748). Essentially this was a matter of reordering lines without changing their content. Bateson argues that Warburton was responsible for this process and P merely acquiescent (*TE*, iii/2, 6); for the decision to base the text here on the 1744 version, that is with the revised line-sequence, see Note on the Text, pp. xxvii–xxix above. See p. 636 for the abandonment of the grouping of collected 'Epistles' in this edition.

For Cobham, see Biographical Index. P had come to know him around 1724, in the wake of the Berkshire Blacks affair involving P's brother-in-law, arrested for game-stealing, and Cobham, who was Governor of Windsor Castle. See E. P. Thompson, *Whigs and Hunters*, rev. edn. (Harmondsworth, 1977). P visited Cobham at Stowe many times on his later rambles, and a bust of the poet was to be set in the Temple of British Worthies in the gardens at Stowe.

320   l. 7. *passenger*. Passer-by.

321   l. 46. *sense*. Consciousness.

l. 54. *Chandos*. The princely Duke: see Biographical Index. P was trying to undo the harm caused by the popular identification of the tasteless Timon with Chandos: see *Epistle to Burlington*, l. 99.

l. 55. *Shylock*. Generically a grasping usurer, but possibly alluding to a real individual, the Earl of Selkirk (MS note by P, now lost, cited by *EC*, iii. 58).

l. 56. *at squat*. In a squatting position.

l. 57. *generous*. Frank, liberal-minded.   *Manly*. Type name for an open-hearted character, derived from the hero of Wycherley's *Plain Dealer* (1676).

l. 59. *Umbra*. A type name for a flatterer or intriguer.

l. 62. *spleen*. Misanthropy.

l. 73. *hazard*. Gaming.

l. 76. *Hackney ... Whitehall*. Middlesex candidates were nominated at Hackney, in north London; 'Whitehall' refers to the seat of power for those who successfully arrived in Parliament.

l. 77. *Catius*. An epicure (from 'cates', delicacies).

322   l. 86. *Newmarket*. Already famous as a centre of horse-racing.

l. 87. *Charron*. Pierre Charron (1531–1603), author of *De la sagesse* (1601), a work of stoic philosophy.

l. 88. *Otho*. M. Salvius Otho (AD 32–69), Emperor of Rome for just three months, who committed suicide after defeat by Vitellius.

l. 93. *a woman, child, or dotard rule?*. The probable references are to the Czarina Anna of Russia, Louis XV of France, and Pope Clement XII.

l. 104. *shave their crowns*. Become monks.

l. 107. *adust*. Dry, indicating a disposition towards hot temper and disputativeness.

l. 108. *Charles ... Philip to the field*. Charles V (1500–58), Holy Roman

Emperor, who abdicated in 1555 and retired to a monastery; Philip II of Spain (1527–98), son of the last-named.

323 l. 131. *punk*. Prostitute (i.e. Cleopatra).

l. 134. *conduct*. Distinguished leadership.

l. 136. *crape*. As worn by lower clergy.   *lawn*. As worn by bishops.

l. 141. *gems*. Precious stones were supposed to be ripened in the ground by the influence of the sun.

324 l. 154. *scrivener*. Here, money-lender.

l. 158. *Scoto*. Generic for a Scotsman, but also probably indicating James Johnston (1655–1737), a politician and a neighbour of P's.

l. 167. *take place*. Take first place.

l. 172. *humours*. Temperaments.

l. 178. *clue*. Thread (the original meaning).

l. 179. *Wharton*. Philip, Duke of Wharton: see Biographical Index. The Duke's recent death had brought to an end a short but highly varied career; as a Catholic convert, a Jacobite intriguer and a poet he had crossed P's path more than once.

325 l. 212. *Catiline*. The type of a conspirator, from the Roman original L. Sergius Catalina (*c*.108–62 BC).

l. 213. *noble dame*. Servilia, sister of Cato the younger, mother of Marcus Brutus, and mistress of Julius Caesar.

l. 216. *Scipio*. Scipio Africanus (*c*.237–183 BC), who defeated Carthage.

l. 218. *Lucullus*. L. Lucullus (*c*.114–57 BC), Roman general celebrated for his luxurious way of life.

l. 220. *toil*. Pronounced *tile*.

l. 225. *sand*. From an hour-glass.

326 l. 231. *Lanesborough*. James Lane, second Viscount Lanesborough (1650–1724), known in Ireland as a 'dancing peer'.

l. 238. *Helluo*. Glutton.

l. 246. *odious*. An example of 'feminine' speech as then perceived.

l. 247. *Narcissa*. The actress mentioned in the note by P is Anne Oldfield (1683–1730), who had often played Narcissa in Colley Cibber's *Love's Last Shift*. By Act of Parliament it was illegal to be buried in any other material than wool (a measure to protect British industry against imported silks and linen).

l. 251. *Betty*. Generic name for a lady's maid.

327 *The Second Satire of the Second Book of Horace Imitated*. First published on 4 July 1734; in the following year reprinted in the *Works*, vol. ii, following the

satire addressed to Fortescue and preceding the version of Donne's fourth satire. From 1739 there was a regular grouping of imitations of Horace. Text here based on the 1751 edition. For composition, see letter to Swift, 20 April 1733, p. 309 above.

Warburton in 1751 was the first to add the subtitle, but that Bethel was the person addressed is apparent from l. 9 as well as P's letter to him on 6 August 1734, a month after publication (*Corr.* iii. 427). For Bethel, the representative here of sturdy country values and independence, see Biographical Index.

l. 8. *mantling*. Foaming.

l. 9. *schools*. Scholastic philosophy.

l. 17. *curious*. Fussy.

l. 19. *hens of Guinea*. Guinea fowl.

328 l. 25. *Oldfield*. Warburton glosses him as 'an eminent glutton'.

l. 26 note. *barbecued*. As P's note may suggest, the word was a recent importation.

l. 31. *treat*. Feast.

ll. 37-8. *Robin-redbreast . . . a martin's nest*. Superstitions had protected robins and the swallow family from being killed for the table.

l. 39. *beccaficos*. Small migratory birds, regarded in Italy esp. as a delicacy.

l. 42 note. The Bedford Head, in Covent Garden, was frequented by theatrical and literary people.

l. 49. *Avidien*. Probably Edward Wortley Montagu, notorious for his mean habits, and his soon-to-be estranged wife Lady Mary. 'Presented' (l. 51) refers to gifts made to the couple.

l. 56. *their son*. The eccentric and profligate Edward Wortley Montagu, jun. (1713-76), who travelled extensively in the East.

329 l. 84. *coming*. Forthcoming, ready.

l. 89. *cordial drop*. A medicine which invigorates the heart and stimulates circulation.

l. 98. *coxcomb-pies*. Not clear, but 'presumably pies filled with crests or combs of cocks' (Aubrey Williams), i.e. fancy modern cooking.

l. 101. *Lord Fanny*. Hervey.

330 l. 105. *pelf*. Riches.

l. 119. *new-built churches*. The 'Queen Anne churches' in London: see *Windsor Forest*, l. 378.

l. 120. *bridges*. Proposals had been made for some time to add to the medieval London Bridge another crossing of the Thames; this need was not met until Westminster Bridge opened in 1750.   *Whitehall*. The ancient palace, largely destroyed by fire in 1696, was never rebuilt.

l. 127. *preventing*. Precautioning.

l. 131. *equal*. Calm, judicious.

l. 134. *excised*. Referring to Walpole's unpopular Excise scheme of 1733, eventually abandoned in the face of strong opposition.

l. 135. *forest*. Windsor Forest, where P's father had retired from London.

l. 136. *five acres*. P rented his house at Twickenham in 1718.

l. 137. *piddle*. Trifle, toy.

l. 139. *out of play*. Out of office.

331　l. 143. *Hounslow Heath . . . Banstead Down*. Referring to what were then agricultural districts providing food for London.

l. 152. *double taxed*. By 1 George I, 2 (1715), Catholics were subject to particularly severe taxation.

l. 154. *standing armies*. Regarded by the Tories and Country interest as a threat to national liberty.

l. 159. *Homer's rule*. 'Welcome the coming, speed the parting guest' (*Odyssey*, xv. 83–4, trans. P).

l. 166. *Vernon*. Thomas Vernon (d. 1726), from whom P had leased his house.

l. 170. *jointure*. An estate settled on a wife for life to take effect on the death of her husband.

l. 171. *equity*. The specialized body of law practised in the Court of Chancery, famed for its slow and cumbrous workings.

l. 175. *shades*. Francis Bacon's family home near St Albans had passed to Viscount Grimston, a favourite butt of the satirists on account of his literary aspirations.

l. 177. *proud Buckingham's delight*. Helmsley, the Yorkshire estate of George Villiers, Duke of Buckingham, was sold after his death to a London banker, Sir Charles Duncombe.

332　*The Second Satire of the First Book of Horace*. First published in December 1734 as *Sober Advice from Horace*, entered the *Works* in 1738 with the title used here, as 'imitated in the manner of Mr Pope'. The text here is based on the 1738 version; editors from Warburton to *EC* omitted this item as indecent.

　　Composition belongs to 1734 also; on 6 July Bolingbroke told Swift that P had begun to imitate this satire of Horace, 'and has chosen rather to weaken the images than to hurt chaste ears overmuch. He has sent it to me, but I shall keep his secret, as he desires, and shall not I think return him the copy, for the rogue has fixed a ridicule upon me' (*Corr.* iii. 413–14). Despite what Bolingbroke said, the matter of the poem was too strong to allow P to acknowledge it initially, and he engaged in what he elsewhere called 'genteel equivocation' after publication, following threats from Richard Bentley's son, who was irritated by notes (later removed) which P had attributed to the great scholar in the manner of *The Dunciad* apparatus. 'Here is a piece of poetry from Horace come out', P wrote to Caryll on 31 December 1734, 'which I warn you not to take for mine, though some people are very willing to fix it on me. In truth I should think it a very indecent sermon, after the *Essays on Man*' (*Corr.* iii. 447; see also iii. 446, 451). Though the poem went into the works it retained the prevaricatory formula, 'imitated in the manner of Mr Pope'. P also included in the original printing a mock dedication 'To Alexander Pope, Esq.', with further sneers at Bentley's edition of Milton; this was omitted from later editions.

l. 2. *Lord Fanny's, Lady Mary's*. Lord Hervey and Lady Mary Wortley Montagu.

l. 4. *Oldfield*. Anne Oldfield, the actress, who had enjoyed a varied life: see Biographical Index.

l. 11. *Con. Phillips*. Constantia Philips (1709–65), the best-known court-esan of her time, whose ghosted autobiography created wide interest in 1748.

l. 16. *Sir Herbert*. Not identified.

l. 18. *Fufidia*. Usually identified as Lady Mary Wortley Montagu.

l. 21. *job*. A corrupt deal, possibly relating here to Lady Mary's manœuvres connecting her sister Lady Mar, wife of the Jacobite leader, who was declared insane and consigned to her sister's care. See Robert Halsband, *The Life of Lady Mary Wortley Montagu* (Oxford, 1956), 133–52, both for Lady Mary's family difficulties and for her treatment by P.

l. 22. *fob*. A small pocket sewn into the waistband of breeches, used for carry-ing valuables.

l. 25. *self-tormentor*. P's original note identifies the play by Terence, *Heauton Timorumenos*, which Bentley had recently edited. The reference is to the Athenian father, Menedemus, who drives his son Clinia out of the country because of his love for a poor woman.

333 l. 29. *Rufa*. See *Epistle to a Lady*, l. 23.   *shore*. Sewer.

l. 30. *civet-cat*. An African mammal bred in England for an anal secretion used in perfumery.   *boar*. Tom-cat.

l. 34. *Spreads her fore-buttocks to the navel bare*. 'A line taken from Mr P' (P's original note, pointing to the first version of *The Dunciad*, ii. 141: the line was dropped from the later version).

l. 39. *London*. The Bishop of London, Edmund Gibson (see Biographical Index).

l. 40. *Dean*. Probably the notorious Thomas Sawbridge, Dean of Ferns, the subject of Swift's poem *The True English Dean to be Hanged for a Rape* (1730).

l. 44. *my Lord of York.* i.e. the Archbishop of York, Lancelot Blackburne (see Biographical Index).

l. 45. *Jefferies.* An obscure figure who was accused by Viscount Hillsborough of criminal conversation with his wife.

l. 53. *Monsieur.* Almost certainly pointing at Nicolas-François Rémond, an adventurer with whom Lady Mary had become involved: see Halsband, 94–112.

l. 60. *Budgell.* Eustace Budgell: see Biographical Index.

l. 63. *Sallust.* A name from the Roman historian, apparently indicating Bolingbroke. See Bolingbroke's letter, quoted in the headnote, and Spence, i. 128.

334   l. 71. *Palmer.* Perhaps Sir Thomas Palmer (1682–1723), an extravagant man of pleasure.

l. 81. *Ellis.* The politician John Ellis, one of the lovers of the Duchess of Cleveland, a mistress of Charles II. Ellis was succeeded by Jacob Hall (l. 86), a rope-dancer.

l. 88. *Sir Robert.* Walpole.   *Sir Paul.* Methuen (see Biographical Index).

335   l. 118. *chaps.* Chapmen, 'punters'.

l. 121. *Tyrawley.* The second Baron Tyrawley, an ambassador noted for his amatory feats; see Biographical Index.

l. 129. *cousins.* Punning on the name of a staymaker (see l. 131), named Cozens.

l. 133. *Needham.* Mother Needham, the madam of a fashionable brothel: see Biographical Index.

l. 138. *scut.* A hare's tail.

l. 139. *Suckling.* The poet Sir John Suckling, though the quotation seems to be invented by P.

336   l. 150. *Bedford Head.* See *Second Satire of the Second Book*, l. 42.

l. 158. *Bathurst.* Lord Bathurst: see Biographical Index.

l. 173. *posts.* Whipping posts.   *pumps.* Used to administer rough punishment by drenching the victim.

l. 176. *Mistress Heysham . . . Lady Buck.* Mrs Heysham and Lady Buck had witnessed the alleged indiscretions of Lady Hillsborough (see l. 45).

l. 178. *Liddel.* Richard Liddel, accused of criminal conversation by Lord Abergavenny.   *Jefferies.* See l. 45 above.   *Onslow.* A member of the Onslow family, who provided several MPs in the period.

Epistle to Dr Arbuthnot. First published on 2 January 1735; incorporated into the *Works*, vol. ii, later that year. P acknowledged that the poem had been spliced together from existing fragments, some written many years before: the clearest example is the Atticus section, where ll. 193–214 had appeared in earlier versions (see Ault, 101–27). However, the act of assemblage and the forging of a coherent poem took place in 1734.

On 17 July 1734 P's long-time friend, the former royal physician John Arbuthnot, wrote to P disclosing that his own illness was terminal. P replied on 2 August, expressing his famous opinion that 'general satire in times of general vice has no force, and is no punishment', and hinting at a new satiric onslaught. On 25 August the plan had become firmer, for P told Arbuthnot that he intended to address to his friend 'one of my epistles, written by piece-meal many years, and which I have now made haste to put together'. By 3 September P was able to assure Arbuthnot that the poem was completed and would serve as 'the best memorial I can leave, both of my friendship to you, and of my character' (*Corr.* iii. 416–17, 423, 428, 431). Arbuthnot died on 27 February 1735.

It is now clear from extant manuscript drafts that the poem as we have it evolved from one planned around 1732 and addressed to William Cleland (see Biographical Index). The manuscripts have been edited by M. Mack (*L&GA*, 419–54).

The text here is based mainly on the Warburton edition of 1751. However, I have departed from Warburton in a few places, and in particular have deleted the subtitle, 'the Prologue to the Satires', which Warburton added. The poem had not previously been set at the head of the *Imitations of Horace*, and since it is removed from that place in the present edition, the subtitle becomes obsolete once more. See also Note on the Text, pp. xxvii–xxix above.

337 *rank and fortune.* P refers to Lady Mary Wortley Montagu and Lord Hervey; for a detailed description of Lady Mary's *Verses* (published in March 1733), and Hervey's *Epistle* (published in November 1733), see J. V. Guerinot, *Pamphlet Attacks on Alexander Pope 1711–1744* (1969), 224–6, 239–41.

l. 1. *John.* P's servant and gardener, John Serle.

l. 3. *dog-star.* Sirius, which appears in the sky in northern latitudes in August; this was always the time of year when poetry recitations were held in Rome.

l. 8. *grot.* P's famous grotto at Twickenham, with a view towards the nearby Thames.

338 l. 12. *sabbath day.* Debtors were immune from arrest on Sundays, as they were in the Mint (l. 13), a sanctuary in Southwark.

l. 15. *parson.* Revd Laurence Eusden, the previous Poet Laureate (see Biographical Index); P's phrase 'bemused in beer' is more than a pun and a rhyme, since Eusden was notoriously bibulous.

l. 18. *engross.* Copy out legal documents.

l. 23. *Arthur.* The corrupt politician Arthur Moore (1666–1730), an adventurer and company promoter; his son was the dunce James Moore Smythe (see Biographical Index).

l. 25. *Cornus*. From *cornu*, (Lat.) a horn; that is, cuckolded.

l. 29. *drop*. Patent medicine.

l. 40. *nine years*. Taken from Horace, *Ars poetica*, ll. 388–9.

l. 41. *high*. Up in a garret.   *Drury Lane*. Then a street with some dubious associations, including squalid courts where criminals and prostitutes flourished.

l. 43. *term*. The legal and publishing season.

339 l. 53. *Curll*. One of P's most regular adversaries, the bookseller Edmund Curll; see Biographical Index.

l. 62. *Lintot*. Another bookseller, Bernard Lintot: see Biographical Index.

l. 66. *go snacks*. Share: proverbial (Tilley S578).

l. 72 note. The most famous source for the story of Midas is Ovid, *Metamorphoses*, Book XI, which is explicitly named by Chaucer.

340 l. 85. *Codrus*. The type of a bad poet, from references by Virgil and Juvenal.

l. 97. *Colley*. Cibber.

l. 98. *Henley*. John 'Orator' Henley, who had delivered a sermon on butchers in 1729: see Biographical Index.   *Freemasons*. Moore Smythe was a freemason, according to Warburton.

l. 99. *Bavius*. A bad poet, derived from one who is mentioned by Horace and Virgil.

l. 100. *one bishop*. Ambrose Philips (see Biographical Index) had acted as secretary to Hugh Boulter, Archbishop of Armagh.

l. 106. *slaver*. Saliva.

l. 113. *Letters*. By a complicated subterfuge P had arranged it so that Curll published an 'unauthorized' edition of his letters in 1726.

l. 117. *Ammon's great son*. Alexander the Great; P is alluding to his own deformity.

341 l. 122. *Maro*. Virgil, from his cognomen.

l. 135. *Granville*. George Granville, Baron Lansdowne: see Biographical Index.

l. 136. *Walsh*. William Walsh: see *Pastorals*, headnote, and Biographical Index.

l. 137. *Garth*. The poet and physician Sir Samuel Garth: see Biographical Index.

l. 139. *Talbot, Somers, Sheffield*. Literary patrons: the Duke of Shrewsbury, John, Baron Somers, and P's friend the Duke of Buckingham (see Biographical Index).

l. 140. *Rochester*. Francis Atterbury, Bishop of Rochester.

l. 141. *St John*. Bolingbroke.

l. 146. *Burnets, Oldmixons, and Cookes.* For these miscellaneous writers, all mentioned in *The Dunciad*, see Biographical Index.

l. 149. *Fanny.* Pointing to Lord Hervey; the name derived from Fannius, a poetaster mentioned by Horace as *ineptus* (vapid).

342   l. 151. *Gildon.* Charles Gildon: see Biographical Index.

l. 153. *Dennis.* The critic John Dennis, one of P's sturdiest opponents.

l. 158. *kissed the rod.* Proverbial (Tilley R156).

l. 163. *ribalds.* Abusive and scurrilous louts.

l. 164. *Bentley . . . piddling Tibbalds.* Linking the classical scholar Richard Bentley and the Shakespearian editor Lewis Theobald, hero of the first version of *The Dunciad*: see Biographical Index.

l. 179. *pilfered pastorals.* P alleged that Philips's pastorals were a tissue of plagiarisms: see *Guardian*, no. 40, p. 559 above.

343   l. 190. *Tate.* Nahum Tate, best known for his improved *King Lear;* see Biographical Index.

l. 193. *one.* Atticus is a portrait of Addison, built up from a number of earlier versions; see headnote.

l. 209. *Cato.* Cato the younger (95–46 BC), famous for his austere patriotism and his high-principled suicide at Utica, which forms the subject of Addison's successful tragedy *Cato* (1713).

l. 211. *templars.* Young law students, noted for their desire to shine as literary pundits.

l. 214. *Atticus.* The name is taken from Cicero's friend and correspondent T. Pomponius Atticus (109–32 BC), a patron and promoter of literature.

l. 215. *rubric.* With red lettering on the title-page, which was displayed by booksellers as there were then no dust-jackets or cover designs.

l. 216. *claps.* Posters.

l. 222. *birthday song.* The Poet Laureate's chief duty was to compose a birthday ode for the monarch every year.

344   l. 230. *Bufo.* A toad in Latin, here suggesting a patron who enjoys the flattery of toadying authors; it may point to George Bubb Dodington or else to Lord Halifax (see Biographical Index).   *Castalian.* Relating to the spring sacred to the Muses on Mount Parnassus.

l. 260. *Queensberry.* The Duke and Duchess of Queensberry were Gay's most loyal supporters, esp. after the banning of his follow-up to *The Beggar's Opera*, entitled *Polly*, 1728.

345   l. 280. *Sir Will.* Possibly Sir William Yonge, a loquacious supporter of Walpole.   *Bubo.* Probably Bubb Dodington.

l. 282. *style.* P told Spence in 1735, 'there is nothing more foolish than to pretend to be sure of knowing a great writer by his style' (Spence, i. 171).

346   l. 305. *Sporus*. Derived from the catamite of the emperor Nero (Suetonius, *Nero*, 28). The character attacks Lord Hervey.

l. 306. *ass's milk*. Given to invalids and convalescents; taken by Hervey but also by P himself (*Corr.* i. 414).

l. 309. *bug*. Bedbug.

l. 310. *painted child*. Hervey used cosmetics to disguise his extreme pallor.

l. 318. *prompter*. Walpole.   *puppet*. Hervey himself.

l. 319. *Eve*. Queen Caroline.

l. 324. *now master up, now miss*. Hervey was probably bisexual.

l. 330. *rabbins*. Rabbis.

347   l. 341. *stooped*. Swooped, like a falcon.

l. 343. *stood*. Withstood.

l. 353. *pictured shape*. P was often depicted in attacks as an ape or some kind of deformed monster.

l. 355. *friend in exile*. Atterbury.

l. 363. *Japhet*. Japhet Crook: see *Epistle to Bathurst*, l. 86.

l. 365. *knight of the post*. One who made a living by giving false evidence. A knight of the shire was the MP for a county.

348   l. 371. *his distress*. When Dennis fell on hard times at the end of his life, P gave him assistance, including a prologue written for a benefit performance (see *TE*, vi. 355–6).

l. 375. *Welsted*. The writer Leonard Welsted, also featured in *The Dunciad*: see Biographical Index.

l. 378. *Budgell*. Eustace Budgell was convicted of forging a will: see Biographical Index.

l. 380. *two Curlls*. The real Curll and Hervey.

l. 381 note. P is wrong in several particulars, including the age of his father at his death (71). See Mack, *Life*, for the real facts.

l. 383. *sin to call our neighbour fool*. Recalling the Sermon on the Mount (Matt. 5: 22).

349   l. 391. *Bestia*. Possibly indicating Marlborough; the name is taken from a corrupt Roman consul in the late second century BC.

l. 397. *oath*. By early Hanoverian legislation, Catholics were required to take oaths of loyalty; if they refused, they were excluded from public office.

l. 405. *Who sprung from kings shall know less joy than I*. Paraphrasing the last line of Horace, *Sat.* I. iii.

l. 410. *lenient*. Gentle, caring. *OED* quotes Arbuthnot's own *Rules of Diet* (1732): 'One should begin with the gentlest [remedies] first, as the lenient'.

350   l. 417. *Queen*. Arbuthnot had been physician to Queen Anne 1705–14.

An Epistle to a Lady. First published in February 1735; two months later included in the *Works* as part of the so-called 'Ethic Epistles'. Here it stood in second place, a position it has ever since occupied in the four *Epistles to Several Persons* (alternatively *Moral Essays*), although it was the last to be published. Composition seems to date from about 1732. An oblique reference in a letter from P to Caryll in January 1733 seems to indicate that the poem already existed in some form (*Corr.* iii. 340).

On its original appearance the text omitted the characters of Philomede (ll. 69–86 as the poem now stands), Atossa (ll. 115–50), and Cloe (ll. 157–98). The reasons underlying these omissions are discussed in the notes at the relevant point. The passages were first included in the suppressed 'deathbed' edition of 1744 which P sent to his friends but was not published until 1748. The text here is based on the 1744 version. The design of the poem is intricate, which further complicated the bibliographical issues. The fullest survey is Frank Brady, 'The History and Structure of Pope's *To a Lady*', *Studies in English Literature 1500–1800*, 9 (1969), 439–62.

The lady of the title is undoubtedly Martha Blount, P's closest woman friend. See V. Rumbold, *Women's Place in Pope's World* (Cambridge, 1989), 251–94.

l. 7. *Arcadia's Countess.* A great lady such as the Countess of Pembroke who was frequently painted in different guises: P may have in mind one of the wives of the eighth Earl, his contemporary. The allusion is to Philip Sidney's *Arcadia* (1590), linked in its full title to Sidney's sister Mary, Countess of Pembroke. P had visited Wilton, the family seat and home of many notable portraits, in 1724.

l. 8. *Pastora.* Suggests the lady is depicted as a shepherdess (there is an example at Wilton).

l. 9. *Fannia.* Based on a notorious Roman adulteress.

l. 12. *Magdalen.* Mary Magdalene, who wiped the feet of Jesus with her hair (John 11: 2), a common subject in historical paintings.

351   l. 16. *romantic.* Excessive, hyperbolic.

l. 18. *trick her off.* Sketch roughly.

l. 20. *Cynthia.* The moon-goddess, symbolizing instability.

l. 21. *Rufa.* Red-haired (Lat.), then associated with sexual promiscuity.

ll. 24–6. *Sappho's diamonds . . . an evening mask.* Sappho is probably P's code-word for his familiar target Lady Mary Wortley Montagu (see Biographical Index), who was known as a poet, for her social and sexual freedom, and for her slovenly ways—though our principal informants, P and Horace Walpole, are not necessarily reliable.

l. 31. *nice.* Genteel, refined.

l. 37. *Papillia.* Taken from the Latin for butterfly.

l. 38. *charming.* Like 'odious' (l. 40), a 'feminine' expression.

l. 45. *Calypso*. Goddess of the *Odyssey*, who at the start of the poem has detained the hero on her island for seven years.

352 l. 54. *wash*. A lotion or cleansing cosmetic.

l. 57. *trim*. Get-up, pose.

l. 63. *Taylor*. The great devotional writer, Bishop Jeremy Taylor, famous for the much-reprinted handbooks on *Holy Living* (1650) and *Holy Dying* (1651).   *Book of Martyrs*. John Foxe's martyrology, first published in 1563.

l. 64. *citron*. Brandy flavoured with lemon-peel.   *Chartres*. The notorious rake and rogue Francis Charteris: see Biographical Index.

l. 70. *punk*. Prostitute.

l. 73. *fault*. Pronounced 'fawt'.

l. 78. *Tallboy*. A booby squire.   *Charles*. A footman.

l. 79. *Helluo*. A glutton.

l. 80. *hautgout*. Applied to food 'with a strong relish or strong scent' (Johnson).

l. 83. *Philomedé*. The character of Philomedé is possibly based on Henrietta, daughter and heiress of the Duke and Duchess of Marlborough; the name has been seen as suggesting 'a lover of the Medes', i.e. one with exotic tastes. This passage was suppressed until the 'deathbed' edition, indicating that P had a real person in mind.

353 l. 92. *Rosamonda's bowl*. Referring to 'fair Rosamond' Clifford (d. ?1176), mistress of Henry II. Legend recounts that Queen Eleanor of Aquitaine forced her to drink from a poisoned bowl. Her link with Woodstock suggests that P may have had Blenheim and the Marlborough family in mind again.

l. 101. *Simo*. A simian character.

l. 110. *ratafie*. Cherry-brandy.

l. 115. *Atossa*. Taken from the Persian queen, daughter of Cyrus. This passage was not printed until the 1744 version; it has been seen as a satire on the Duchess of Buckingham, and less plausibly on the great Duchess of Marlborough. For a full discussion, see *TE*, iii/2, 155–64.

354 l. 142. *cheat*. As often in P's time, to be pronounced 'chate'.

l. 155. *do the knack*. Bring off the effect. The word 'equal' means uniform.

l. 157. *Cloe*. This passage was also omitted until 1744, although it had appeared separately in 1738 and may not have formed part of the original poem. The name suggests the Greek *khloi*, a tender shoot or green foliage. The character has generally been seen as based on P's friend the Countess of Suffolk (see Biographical Index, s.v. Howard). However, see Ault, 266–75, for a different view. There would have been no particular reason to suppress the passage in 1735, or to insert it in 1744 (when the Countess was still alive), if the traditional attribution were correct.

355   l. 182. *Queen*. Queen Caroline.

l. 184. *ball*. The orb of royalty.

l. 193. *Queensberry*. The beautiful and eccentric Duchess of Queensberry: see Biographical Index.

l. 198. *Parson Hale*. P's neighbour, the pioneer physiologist Revd Stephen Hales: see Biographical Index.

356   l. 239. *hags*. Witches.

357   l. 241. *round and round*. As in the carriage-ride at the Ring (l. 251) in Hyde Park.

l. 249. *friend*. P addressed Martha Blount directly.

l. 257. *temper*. Equanimity.

l. 266. *tickets*. Lottery tickets.   *codille*. The losing hand at ombre.

l. 267. *smallpox*. Martha had herself suffered from the disease in her youth.

358   l. 283. *year*. Martha was about 49 when the poem first appeared. P borrows the manner of Swift's poems to Stella.

l. 285. *ascendant*. In the sky and so astrologically dominant.

l. 289. *wit and gold refines*. The sun-god Apollo presided over poetry and also 'ripened' gold in the ground.

Second Satire of Dr John Donne Versified. First published in the *Works* (1735); it was there grouped with the imitation of Donne's fourth satire, published two years earlier. The text here is based on Warburton's edition (1751), which has only small departures from the earliest printing. P had first prepared a version of Donne's satires 'at the desire of the Earl of Oxford while he was Lord Treasurer' (*TE*, iv. 3); a manuscript copy, possibly dating from about 1713, survives in the British Library. This differs very considerably from the version published in 1735; P added many biting topical and personal touches to his later imitation. For the earlier text, see *TE*, iv. 132–8.

P added an epigraph from Horace, *Satires*, i. x. 56–9, when the two Donne poems were collected: 'What prevents us either from asking, as we read the writings of Lucilius, whether it was the nature of his own qualities, or those of his harsh themes which precluded more polished and gentle verses.'

l. 8. *Excise*. Alluding to the Excise Crisis of 1733: see *Second Satire of the Second Book*, l. 134.   *Army*. Debates surrounded a standing army, often opposed by independent 'country' politicians.

l. 12. *poor and disarmed*. Catholics were taxed at a higher rate and, in the wake of the 1715 Rebellion, otherwise limited in their personal freedoms: see *Second Satire of the Second Book*, ll. 58–67.

ll. 15–16. *thief . . . who cannot read*. By benefit of clergy, the ability to read a given text (usually from Psalm 51, the 'neck-verse') exempted a first offender from the sentence passed.

359   l. 22. *no rat is rhymed*. Incantations were used in efforts to destroy rats.

l. 24. *the flesh, the devil*. Prayer-book formula from the Creed, thence proverbial.

l. 35. *confessors*. 'One who avows his religion in the face of danger' (*OED*). Stress on first syllable.

l. 36. *Sutton*. Most likely Richard Sutton, MP (1674–1737), 'an atheistical, debauched man'. For Francis Charteris, a familiar victim, see Biographical Index.

l. 37. *old Esdras*. A voluminous moralist, like the Old Testament prophet.

l. 40. *Prisca*. From *priscus* (Lat.), ancient, former, or old-fashioned.   *Confessor*. Here a priest taking confession.

l. 43. *canonist*. Expert on ecclesiastical law.

l. 47. *clap*. Gonorrhea.   *pox*. Syphilis.

l. 58. *lime-twigs*. Branches covered with birdlime, to catch birds.

360   l. 60. *Pleas and Bench*. The high courts of Common Pleas and the King's Bench.

l. 61. *Boreas . . . Auster*. The north and south winds.

l. 64. *Drury Lane*. See *Epistle to Arbuthnot*, l. 41.

l. 66. *Peter*. Peter Walter.

l. 70. *suretyship*. Legal responsibility taken on behalf of another.

l. 76. *affects*. Professes, takes upon himself.

l. 77. *And lies to every lord in everything*. This line is taken over bodily from the original poem, but it was 'a very Popian line of Donne' (H. Erskine-Hill, *The Social Milieu of Alexander Pope* (New Haven, Conn., 1975), 247).

l. 80. *to godly* **. The blank probably hides the name 'Paul', though one might then have expected an antithesis such as 'From wicked Peter.' The exact individual has not been identified.

l. 88. *duke*. The third Duke of Bedford, who lost almost £4,000 to Sir Henry Janssen in a single day in 1731.   *White's*. Gaming club in St James's Street, originally a coffee-house; depicted in pl. iv of Hogarth's *Rake's Progress* (1735). White's Club as such dates from 1736.

l. 93. *fencing*. Metaphorically, protecting; but the concrete sense is also of enclosing and rendering estates private with high walls.

361   l. 102. *place*. A locus in the text.

l. 106. *beads*. The rosary.

l. 108. *'power and glory' clause.* The conclusion of the Lord's Prayer, omitted in Catholic versions; inserted by Luther into the Reformed version of the scriptures (1521).

l. 118. *Carthusian.* Strict and austere, like the rule of Carthusian monks.

l. 123. *wardrobes.* 'It were to be wished people would now and then look upon good works, as they do upon old wardrobes, merely in case any of them should come into use again' (P to Caryll, 28 December 1717, *Corr.* i. 457).

Pope to Jonathan Swift, 25 March 1736. Text based on *Corr.* iv. 5-6.

addressed to you. Never written.

four epistles. A version of the planned masterwork, which was not carried through: see Spence, i. 132-3, and M. Leranbaum, *Alexander Pope's 'Opus Magnum' 1729-1744* (Oxford, 1977).

362 *non sum qualis eram.* Horace, *Odes,* IV. i. 3.

Mr Cheselden. William Cheselden (1668-1752), a prominent surgeon, esp. noted for 'cutting the [gall] stone', and a friend as well as medical advisor to P.

Lord B. Bolingbroke had retreated to France almost a year before, for reasons of political frustration together with financial embarrassment.

patriots. The opposition to Walpole, and here specifically the group of 'Boy Patriots' from the Cobham circle, including William Pitt (later Earl of Cobham), George Grenville, and P's friend George Lyttelton.

kind . . . housewife. Presumably P's mother: the agreeable neighbour may be Mrs Howard, who since her second marriage in 1735 spent more time abroad, and passed the summer of 1736 in France.

363 *Tully.* Not traced in Cicero in this form.

Tales Animae Concordes. [May there be] such souls in harmony.

The Second Epistle of the Second Book of Horace Imitated. First published on 28 April 1737 by Dodsley; included in the *Works* (1738) and also separately in a volume of *Epistles of Horace Imitated.* It appears among the Horatian group in vol. iv of Warburton's edition (1751) and the text here is based on this.

Composition seems to belong to the later part of 1736. Swift quoted a snatch of Horace's epistle to P in a letter dated 2 December 1736 (this corresponds to ll. 71-9 in P's imitation). P probably sent his version of these lines, if not the whole poem, along with his letter to Swift on 30 December. Swift acknowledged receipt on 9 February 1737 (*Corr.* iv. 44, 56). At this time the correspondence of Swift and P was dwelling on the loss of friends, which Horace treated in this part of his poem.

Horace. This is l. 124 of the Latin text: 'he will give the impression of being at play, and yet be suffering on the rack.'

l. 1. *Colonel.* The addressee is not known for certain. The likeliest candidate is P's friend James Dormer, who was colonel of a regiment though he held the rank of lieutenant-general by this time. Another possibility is Colonel Arthur Browne (d. 1742), who was tenant of Abscourt (l. 232) and was known to P. See also Mack, *Life*, 680. For Cobham, see *Epistle to Cobham*, headnote, and Biographical Index.

l. 4. *Blois.* Many English people studied at Blois, in Touraine, partly because of the standard French which could be acquired there; Addison spent a year at Blois in 1699–1700 for this purpose.

l. 10. *upholsterer.* Decorator, interior designer.

364 l. 24 note. In fact the painter Sir Godfrey Kneller (see Biographical Index), who was reputed to have dealt quixotically with an alleged thief.

l. 33. *Anna's wars.* Those of Queen Anne, i.e. the War of Spanish Succession (1702–13).

l. 36. *to a doit.* To the last farthing: a small Dutch coin, here pronounced 'dite', used proverbially for 'a jot' (Tilley D430).

365 l. 51. *groat.* A coin worth fourpence which circulated in England until 1662: for the proverbial 'not worth a groat', see Tilley G458.

l. 53. *Peleus' son.* Achilles: P early acquired a love of the *Iliad*.

l. 57. *Maudlin.* Magdalen College, Oxford, where some of P's friends, including Robert Digby, studied. P was debarred from attending the university by his Catholicism.

ll. 58–67. Referring to the penal measures against Catholics under William III and in the first years of the Hanoverian regime. See Mack, *Life*, 39–40, 285, for various measures; see also *TE*, iv. 168–9.

l. 67. *convict.* Convicted (stress on first syllable).

l. 68. *Homer.* That is, the financial success of the Homer translations.

l. 70. *Munro.* James Munro (1680–1752), physician to Bethlehem Hospital, 1728–52.

ll. 72–9. See headnote for Swift and P in correspondence over this passage. P also recalled Montaigne's use of the lines (see F. Stack, *Pope and Horace* (Cambridge, 1985), 127). Line 76 recalls Milton's sonnet, 'How soon hath Time, the subtle thief of youth'.

l. 87. *Oldfield.* See *Second Satire of the Second Book*, l. 25.   *Dartineuf.* Charles Dartinquenave: see *First Satire of the Second Book*, l. 46.

366 ll. 94–7. '*Palace Yard . . . exact at one*'. A rapid peregrination of central London: Palace Yard lies outside the Palace of Westminster, including the House of Lords, whilst Bloomsbury Square was part of the growth of

the city northwards, and rehearsals would be held in the vicinity of Drury Lane or Covent Garden.

l. 102. *pig*. Ingot.

l. 104. *Guildhall's narrow pass*. A narrow alley to the side of the Guildhall, widening eastwards into Basinghall Street.

l. 107. *s-r-v-nce*. Sir reverence (excrement).   *car*. Chariot.

l. 110. *grottoes*. A characteristic self-implicatory joke by P.

l. 116. *Isis' calm retreat*. Oxford. It took seven years (l. 117) to proceed to a master's degree.

l. 124. *duns*. Debt-collectors or bailiffs.

l. 127. *serjeants*. Members of the higher branch of the barrister's profession, centred on the Inns of Court such as the Temple; a class abolished in 1880.

367 l. 130. *th' Exchequer . . . the Rolls*. Two of the High Courts; the Rolls here means Chancery, from the Rolls Building in Chancery Lane (later the Public Record Office).

l. 132. *Murray*. William Murray; see *Sixth Epistle of the First Book*, headnote, and Biographical Index.

l. 134. *Cowper*. Lord Cowper.   *Talbot*. Lord Talbot. Both became Lord Chancellor; see Biographical Index.

l. 137. *Tibbald*. Lewis Theobald; see Biographical Index and *The Dunciad*, headnote.   *the nine*. The Muses.

l. 139. *Merlin's Cave*. See *First Epistle of the Second Book*, l. 355.

l. 140. *Stephen*. Stephen Duck, the keeper of the cave: see Biographical Index.

l. 143. *Tibullus*. Albius Tibullus (*c*.60–19 BC), Roman elegiac poet.

368 ll. 178–9. *'But ease in writing . . . learned to dance'*. Adapted from *Essay on Criticism*, ll. 362–3.

l. 193. *cupped*. Bled, using a cupping-glass.

l. 196. *patriot*. A high-toned independent politician, inclined towards opposition to the ministry.

l. 201. *e'en*. Probably in the sense of 'right away'.

l. 208. *Hyde Park Corner*. i.e. leaving what was then the outer limit of London on his way to Twickenham.

369 l. 218. *evil*. The king's evil, or scrofula, which the monarch was supposed to cure by touch; gold coins, known as angels, were presented to the patient. Queen Anne was the last monarch to touch, and Samuel Johnson one of the last sufferers to be touched.

l. 229. *Devonshire*. The third Duke of Devonshire (1698–1755), a supporter of Walpole.

l. 232. *Abscourt*. An estate a few miles up-river from Twickenham, near Walton on Thames. Colonel Browne was the tenant (see l. 1).

l. 234. *Worldly*. Edward Wortley Montagu.

l. 240. *Heathcote*. Sir Gilbert Heathcote: see *Epistle to Bathurst*, l. 101, and Biographical Dictionary.

l. 241. *fat Evesham ... Lincoln fen*. Rich agricultural districts; Heathcote owned large estates in Lincolnshire.

l. 245. *devil o'erlooks from Lincoln town*. Adapting the proverb, 'He looks as the devil over Lincoln' (Tilley D277), used by Swift in *Polite Conversation*.

l. 247. *perpetuity*. 'Of an estate: the quality ... of being inalienable perpetually, or beyond certain limits fixed ... by the general law' (*OED*).

370 ll. 253-6. *Heir urges heir ... what will they avail?* P is especially close to the standard translation by Thomas Creech here: 'So since perpetual use to none's allowed, / But heir crowd heir, as in a rolling flood / Wave urges wave, ah what doth it avail, / To join large groves to grove, and vale to vale.' For Creech's version, see *Sixth Epistle of the First Book*, l. 4.

l. 257. *Sapperton*. A few miles west of Bathurst's seat at Cirencester, where P was acting as his adviser in laying out the estate. P envisaged the joining of the Thames and the Severn in a letter of 1722 (*Corr*. ii. 116), and later in the century the Sapperton Tunnel actually linked the rivers.

l. 273. *Townshend*. The second Viscount ('Turnip') Townshend (1674-1738), formerly coadjutor of Walpole, who had retired to his Norfolk estate and agricultural pursuits.   *Grosvenor*. The rich family who became the Dukes of Westminster in 1874; the current representative was Sir Robert Grosvenor (1695-1755). They owned a large number of Welsh lead-mines, the foundation of their wealth.

l. 274. *Bubb*. George Bubb Dodington: see Biographical Index.

l. 277. *Oglethorpe*. The colonial pioneer James Oglethorpe, mentioned here mainly for his work on behalf of those in gaol. See Biographical Index.

l. 284. *heap*. Another word borrowed from Creech.

371 l. 300. *strut*. Stretch out (to one's full size; P alludes to his own diminutive stature).

l. 323. *eat*. A normal form of the past participle until the nineteenth century, pronounced 'ate'.

372 *The First Epistle of the Second Book of Horace Imitated*. First published on 25 May 1737. Incorporated into the *Works* in 1738; the text here is based on Warburton's edition of 1751, which contains a few revisions of detail.
     Composition goes back to 1736. On 22 May George II left England for Hanover and the 'arms' of his new mistress, Madam von Walmoden (see l. 3). P soon afterwards left for Peterborough's house near Southampton

and began the poem. On 21 September he reported to Fortescue, 'there [at Bevis Mount] . . . [I] began an Imitation of the finest [epistle] in Horace this spring; which I propose to finish there this autumn' (*Corr.* iv. 33). By the end of the year P was able to send Swift at least that portion of the poem which compliments his friend (ll. 221–8). On 9 February 1737 Swift responded with gratitude for the lines, which 'are to do me the greatest honour I shall ever receive from posterity, will outweigh the malignity of ten thousand enemies' (*Corr.* iv. 56). This passage caused official displeasure, and indeed the Privy Council are said to have 'toyed with the idea of taking Pope into custody for his blunt tribute to Swift . . . as Ireland's saviour from Wood's halfpence' (Mack, *Life*, 683). But a face-saving formula was found to the effect that Swift's activities had taken place 'in the late King's reign', and nothing was done. Swift reported on the poem's reception in Ireland, when he wrote to P on 31 May: 'The curious are looking out, some for flattery, some for ironies in it; the sour folks think they have found out some' (*Corr.* iv. 72).

The principal irony of the poem is indicated by its subtitle: 'Augustus' was George II's second name, and P daringly transmutes Horace's praise of the emperor to satire on the British monarch. It is true that some people in 'Augustan' England held a low opinion of the Emperor Augustus, and that he could be seen as a parallel rather than an antitype to George. But Horace seems to have shared these doubts only to a limited extent, and that is the crucial fact for P's purposes. For the issues at stake, see esp. H. Weinbrot, *Augustus Caesar in 'Augustan' England* (Princeton, NJ, 1978), and H. Erskine-Hill, *The Augustan Idea in English Literature* (1983). As well as the political theme, the poem contains one of the first sustained appraisals of English literary history, esp. in relation to France.

P originally placed as an epigraph l. 267 (shortened) of the Latin text: 'ne rubeam pingui donatus munere' (lest I have to blush at receiving a foolish gift).

Admonebat Praetores. From Suetonius, *Lives of the Caesars*, 'Augustus', 89. 'He instructed the praetors not to allow his name to be abused.'

373 l. 2. *main.* Suggests the Spanish Main, where British shipping was being harassed by Spanish privateers; the Opposition claimed that Walpole was turning a blind eye to these losses, and finally in 1739 public opinion forced England into the War of Jenkins's Ear on a trumped-up occasion.

l. 3. *arms. Armis* is literal in Horace, but P puns on the sense of the arms of the royal mistress, Amelie von Walmoden (see headnote).

ll. 5–6. *How shall the muse . . . the public weal?* The irony is that George II devoted no time to literature, with little interest in any of the arts except music.

ll. 7–8. *Edward and Henry . . . Alfred.* Edward III, Henry V, and Alfred the Great, regularly used by the Opposition as heroes of patriotic zeal and liberty; the King by contrast is seen as supine and addicted to selfish pleasures, uncommitted to his adopted country, and unaware of threats from abroad.

l. 17. *Alcides*. Hercules. The last labour of the hero, involving the capture of Cerberus in Hades, was allegorized to mean the conquest of death itself.

l. 24. *mature the praise*. The Horatian text has *maturos . . . honores*, suggesting 'timely' praises; P manages to intimate (i) that the commendations have been a long time appearing, and (ii) that the king is now past whatever peak he had.

374 l. 38 note. 'Skelton's works were reprinted in 1736 for the first time since 1568' (*TE*, iv. 196). For P's low opinion of Skelton, common enough in his age, see Spence, i. 180.

l. 40 note. The ballad has been attributed to James I and James V; it was reprinted by Allan Ramsay.

l. 42 note. The Devil and St Dunstan tavern in Fleet Street.

l. 57. *compound*. Settle for a lesser amount.

l. 62. *courtesy of England*. 'A tenure by which a husband, after his wife's death, holds certain kinds of property which she has inherited' (*OED*); by extension here, through a customary legal fiction.

375 l. 66. *Stow*. John Stow (1525–1605), chronicler and historian.

l. 75. *Cowley*. He was one of the most widely read poets in the language until new Augustan standards of clarity and correctness brought about a loss of popularity in the eighteenth century, which led ultimately to the unsympathetic view of his work in Johnson's *Lives of the Poets* (1779).

ll. 85–6. *Shadwell . . . Wycherley . . . Southerne . . . Rowe*. Representative figures respectively of comedy and tragedy in the Restoration; P knew all personally except Shadwell, who died in 1692.

l. 88. *Heywood*. John Heywood (*c.*1497–*c.*1580), who wrote early Tudor drama of a kind regarded in P's day as primitive and rough-hewn.

l. 91 note. *Gammer Gurton's Needle* (1556), written in long rhymed doggerel lines, again regarded as primitive at this date.

l. 92. *The Careless Husband*. One of Cibber's most successful plays (1704).

376 l. 97. *Spenser himself affects the obsolete*. Echoing Ben Jonson's remark in *Discoveries* (1640): 'Spenser, in affecting the ancients, writ no language.'

l. 98. *on Roman feet*. Sidney included poems in classical metres in *Arcadia*.

l. 104. *hook*. Bentley had enclosed in brackets what he regarded as 'spurious' words in the text of *Paradise Lost* (which he edited in 1732).

l. 109. *Sprat, Carew, Sedley*. Thomas Sprat (1635–1713), Thomas Carew (*c.*1594–1640), and Sir Charles Sedley (*c.*1639–1701), all instanced as witty but limited writers. For P's views of this phase in poetry, and further remarks on these figures, see Spence, i. 188–200.

l. 120. *weed*. For P's views of the 'defects' of Shakespeare, and the matter interpolated by others which needed to be weeded out by a modern editor, see his *Preface to Shakespeare*, pp. 191–4 above.

l. 122. *Betterton*. The actor Thomas Betterton: see Biographical Index. 'Booth' in l. 123 is Barton Booth, Betterton's successor as the leading tragic actor of his day.

377 l. 132. *Merlin's prophecy*. Found in Geoffrey of Monmouth, whose work had been translated by Aaron Thompson (1718) with the active support of P. There is also a dig at Merlin's Cave, the Queen's retreat at Richmond; and reference to sons and sires (l. 134) hints at the difficulties between the King and the Prince of Wales.

l. 142 note. See *Windsor Forest*, headnote.

l. 144. *Newmarket*. The rise of Newmarket as a centre of horse-racing can be dated to the time of Charles II.

l. 149. *Lely*. Sir Peter Lely (1618–80), Dutch-born portrait painter who settled in England *c*.1643.

l. 153 note. This was actually a heroic play 'with the story sung in recitative music', composed by Coleman and Hudson.

l. 154. *eunuch's throat*. Italian castrati, popular on the operatic stage in England, esp. during the 1720s and 1730s.

l. 160. *noble cause*. The effects of liberty.

378 l. 176. *Not —'s self*. A deliberately teasing blank, but Cibber or (more likely) Walpole would fit metrically.

l. 182 note. For Joshua Ward, see Biographical Index.

l. 183. *Radcliffe*. For Dr John Radcliffe, see Biographical Index, and P's letter to Martha Blount, November 1714 (p. 102 above).

l. 186. *Ripley*. The architect Thomas Ripley: cf. *Epistle to Burlington*, l. 18, and Biographical Index.

l. 195. *flight of cashiers*. The cashier of the South Sea Company, Robert Knight, had fled to France after the Bubble burst, in order to escape arrest.

l. 197. *Peter*. Peter Walter. Ward may be either a proper noun or a common noun, depending on the unknown depredation Walter had practised.

l. 200. *diet*. Course of life.

379 l. 206. *foreigner*. Such as George II, P insinuates. The King is said to have spoken English 'loudly and fluently, with much gesticulation and an atrocious accent' (C. Chenevix Trench, *George II* (1973), 40–1).

l. 212. *unbelieving*. Hinting at the reputed free-thinking of the Queen.

l. 214. *Roscommon*. See *Essay on Criticism*, l. 725.

ll. 221–8. See headnote for Swift's reaction to these lines, as well as ministerial displeasure.

l. 222. *supplied*. Came to the aid of, augmented.

l. 226 note. Swift had already announced his intention of bequeathing money for the foundation of a hospital for the insane (what was to become St Patrick's Hospital in Dublin, opened in 1757). 'He gave the little wealth he had / To build a house for fools and mad' (*Verses on the Death of Dr Swift*, ll. 483–4).

l. 230. *Hopkins and Sternhold*. The most famous metrical version of the Psalms, used in the Book of Common Prayer from 1562; its authors were Thomas Sternhold (d. 1549) and John Hopkins (d. 1570).

l. 231. *charity*. An oblique allusion to the scandal of the Charitable Corporation, a recent case of the poor defrauded by the powerful, as well as to the growing number of charity schools set up to provide basic education for the needy.

380 l. 236. *Pope and Turk*. A favourite joke of P's, drawing on a line in the metrical Psalm, 'from Pope and Turk defend us, Lord', which P exploited as a mock-litany directed against himself and his fellow Catholics.

l. 259. *nice*. Fastidious.

ll. 267–9. *Waller . . . divine*. The triplet is a tribute to Dryden, who particularly favoured this device at moments of heightened emphasis. 'Energy' (l. 269) was a key critical term of the age, indicating not just force and vigour in style, but also loosely the sense of Gk. *enargeia*, i.e. pictorial vividness.

381 l. 277. *Otway*. The tragic dramatist Thomas Otway (1652–85).

l. 279. *Shakespeare scarce effaced a line*. Alluding to Ben Jonson's comment, based on Heminge and Condell, that Shakespeare never blotted a line: see *Preface to Shakespeare*, p. 186 above.

l. 288. *Farquhar*. George Farquhar (1677–1707), comic dramatist.

l. 289. *Van*. Sir John Vanbrugh (1664–1726), dramatist and architect.

l. 290. *Astraea*. For Aphra Behn, see Biographical Index.

l. 293. *Pinky*. In a play by Cibber performed in 1700, the comic actor William Penkethman had made a theatrical coup by rapidly swallowing two chickens.

382 l. 309. *bear*. A dancing bear.   '*Black Joke*'. A popular tune to which numerous indecent lyrics were set. The original words were, 'Her black joke and belly so white', where 'figuratively the black signifies the monosyllable' (Francis Grose, *Classical Dictionary of the Vulgar Tongue*); see Smollett, *Roderick Random*, chap. 53.

l. 315. *scenes*. Movable painted scenery.

l. 317. *ermine, gold and lawn*. Ermine was worn by peers at official ceremonies, gold by the state heralds and officers of chivalric orders, lawn by the peers; the passage refers to a coronation ceremony, as portrayed on the stage (see l. 319).

l. 318. *Champion*. The King's Champion, who traditionally presented himself at the coronation on horseback, challenging any potential adversary of the new monarch.

l. 319 note. After the coronation of George II in October 1727, Drury Lane theatre scored a great success with its elaborately staged coronation scene in *Henry VIII*. P had used some details in the first version of *The Dunciad*: see Pat Rogers, 'Ermine, Gold and Lawn: *The Dunciad* and the Coronation of George II', in *Literature and Popular Culture in Eighteenth-Century England* (Brighton, 1985), 120–50.

l. 331. *Quin*. The actor James Quin (1693–1776), who took many of the heroic roles which were then dressed in a high-plumed hat.

l. 332. *birthday suit*. Grand new clothes worn on the royal birthday.

l. 337. *Cato*. Booth had taken the part of Cato in Addison's celebrated tragedy (1713).

l. 338. *rally*. Make sport or raillery.

383   l. 347. *To Thebes, to Athens*. Adapted by Johnson in his later refutation of dramatic unities (*Preface to Shakespeare*), where he instances a shift of scene from Thebes to Persepolis, and from Athens to Sicily.

l. 353. *their mountain*. Parnassus.   *their spring*. Castalia.

l. 355 note. The thresher poet Stephen Duck was appointed 'cave and library keeper' in 1735, which excited the derision of P and his friends. The iconography of P's own garden was partly designed as a counterblast to the Queen's shrine at Richmond. It was Capability Brown who 'levelled' the cave and its surroundings in 1771.

l. 372. *historians*. Under Charles II, Poets Laureate had also been his historiographers royal. Equally Racine and Boileau had held this post under Louis XIV.

l. 378. *minister*. Walpole, who had overseen the appointment of Cibber as Poet Laureate in 1730.

384   l. 381. *Bernini*. The bust of Charles I (1636–7) by Gianlorenzo Bernini (1598–1680).

l. 382. *Kneller*. The equestrian portrait of William III (Nassau) by Godfrey Kneller (see Biographical Index), painted in 1701.

l. 387. *Blackmore*. Knighted by William III in 1697, as court physician (see Biographical Index).   *Quarles*. Francis Quarles (1592–1644), a type of the bad poet.

l. 394. *Maeonian wing*. Homeric (derived from the supposed birthplace of the poet).

l. 397. *your country's peace.* Another attack on what the Opposition derided as Walpole's pacific foreign policy.

l. 404. *your Majesty disdains.* The Emperor Augustus was said to have disdained praise unless it came from distinguished writers (Suetonius, *Augustus*, 89). P suggests that George II, on the contrary, spurns the best poet, while Walpole employs only hack journalists to promote his cause.

l. 417. *Eusden, Philips, Settle.* See Biographical Index for these well-patronized authors, all of whom figure in *The Dunciad*, while the first two are severely treated in *Peri Bathous*.

l. 419. *Bedlam and Soho.* Alluding to traditional demeaning functions for unread works of literature. Pamphlets were displayed by being hung in rows in Moorfields (near Bethlehem Hospital). Soho seems to be mentioned as a mixed area on the fringes of the fashionable West End, at once a little seedy and raffish.

385 *The Sixth Epistle of the First Book of Horace Imitated.* First published separately on 23 January 1738; included in the *Works* later in the same year. The text in this edition is based on Warburton (1751). There is no clue to the exact date of composition but all natural assumptions would place it not long before publication. Lines 83–4 seem to refer to events in 1737.

It was only in 1751 that the subtitle 'To Mr Murray' was added, but it can be taken as reliable. P had known the future Solicitor-General, Attorney-General, and (as Lord Mansfield) Lord Chief Justice for perhaps two or three years; Murray was also to become P's executor. See Biographical Index for other details.

l. 1. *Not to admire.* Rendering Horace's opening, a well-known tag, *nil admirari* ('admire' has the sense of gawp or wonder at in a foolish manner). For P's comments on the phrase, see Spence, i. 147, where the editor points out that Bolingbroke's coat of arms bore the phrase as a motto.

l. 3. *Murray.* See headnote.

l. 4. *Creech.* Thomas Creech (1659–1700), whose translation of Horace (first published in 1684) remained widely known. P's note slightly exaggerated the debt to Creech, whose first three lines in the current 1720 edition read, 'To admire nothing (as most are wont to do) / Is the only method that I know, / To make men happy, and to keep 'em so.'

l. 14. *stars and strings.* Insignia and ribbons of knighthood.

386 l. 31. *Parian.* See *Epistle to Bathurst*, l. 296.

l. 32. *Tyrian dye.* See *Windsor Forest*, l. 142.

l. 33. *birthday . . . livery.* See *First Epistle of the Second Book*, l. 332.

l. 36. *senate.* Parliament. *Second Book*, l. 130). high courts sat.   *Rolls.* Chancery (see *Second Epistle of the Hall.* Westminster Hall, where the other

ll. 38–43. For what can be discovered about Murray's search for a high-born wife, see Spence, ii. 634.

l. 45. *Craggs*. P's friend James Craggs, jun. (see *Epistle to James Craggs* and Biographical Index) became Secretary of State; his father, from 'very low beginnings', reached the position of Postmaster-General.

l. 50. *another*. Westminster Abbey, where Murray was ultimately buried in 1793.

l. 53. *Hyde*. Edward Hyde, Earl of Clarendon (1608–74), statesman and historian.

l. 56. *Ward*. Joshua Ward: see Biographical Index; P had already used his name in the *Second Epistle of the First Book*, l. 172.

l. 57. *Dover*. Thomas Dover, a physician whose status bordered on that of a quack: see Biographical Index.

l. 61. *Cornbury*. P's friend Lord Cornbury (1710–53), a great-grandson of Lord Clarendon, and Opposition MP. For his ostentatious rejection of political patronage, see Spence, i. 145.

l. 64. *Tindal*. The deist Matthew Tindal: see Biographical Index.

387   l. 72. *prevent*. Outstrip.

l. 82. *Anstis*. As Garter King of Arms, John Anstis was the chief heraldic officer and controlled the granting of titles. See Biographical Index.

ll. 83–4. *German prince . . . poor of purse*. Alluding to the limited allowance made to the Prince of Wales, an issue raised in Parliament by the Opposition as an example of the King's parsimony. William Pulteney proposed doubling the Prince's allowance to £100,000, but Walpole just achieved a majority to defeat the proposal. This was in February 1737, which supplies a dating clue for the poem (see headnote).

l. 86. *groat*. See *Second Epistle of the Second Book*, l. 51.

l. 88. *poet's day*. The third performance, when proceeds were devoted to the benefit of the dramatist.

l. 98. *joy*. Using the fashionable pronunciation, 'jie'.

l. 104. *Cornwall*. The parliamentary representation of Cornwall was out of proportion to the size of the county. Apart from the two knights of the shire, there were two members returned by each of twenty-one boroughs. Many of these were small constituencies under Treasury control. Walpole's fall four years later was hastened by the reverses which the ministry suffered in the 1741 election around their Cornish stronghold: ten seats were lost, mostly to the Prince of Wales's interest. Berkshire may be there for the rhyme, but the county stood at the other extreme. The shire constituency was a large and open one, with Tory landowners usually gaining election. P may have known some of the individuals involved in the politics of his home county, as at the small and fiercely contested borough of Windsor; in March 1738 (six weeks after the poem appeared) a by-election resulted in a tie of 133 each for the two candidates (one supported by the dowager Duchess of Marlborough).

l. 105. *near the chair*. This may mean 'will soon be in line for the office of Lord Mayor', or 'is close to the Speaker'. The couplet alludes to the head-counting which went on in both Government and Opposition circles at the time of elections and crucial votes, a process chronicled fully in the work of Sir Lewis Namier.

388 l. 107. *protest*. Profess loyalty.

l. 115. *Russell*. Various identifications have been suggested by Horace Walpole and others, but none is very cogent.

l. 119. *bagnios*. Brothels.

l. 120. *Chartres*. P's favourite target, Francis Charteris.

l. 121. *Kinnoul*. The Earl of Kinnoul.   *Tyrawley*. Lord Tyrawley. Both were ambassadors abroad with a reputation for dissolute living.

l. 122. *Latian*. Italian.   *Circean*. Worthy of the beguiling sorceress Circe. Young noblemen on the Grand Tour were esp. vulnerable to the temptations P describes; a minor industry existed in France and Italy to lure them into dissipation and expense.

l. 124. *punk*. Prostitute.

l. 126. *Wilmot*. John Wilmot, Earl of Rochester, the poet. Line 127 alludes to his *Letter from Artemisa, in the Town*, ll. 44–5.

l. 128. *Vive la bagatelle*. Cited by Swift as his maxim in a letter to Gay in July 1732: see *Corr.* iii. 298.

389 *The First Epistle of the First Book of Horace Imitated*. Publication as a separate poem on 7 March 1738: then into the *Works* in May 1739. Here the basis of the text is Warburton's edition of 1751, which incorporates a few revisions. Line 3, if accurate, suggests that composition took place in 1737.

l. 1. *St John*. Bolingbroke. It was he who had originally started P off on his imitations of Horace (see *First Satire of the Second Book*, headnote); this was the last of the main series to appear, followed only by the two-part epilogue and the fragmentary addendum *1740*, published by Joseph Warton in 1797.

l. 3. *sabbath*. Punning on the senses of 'day of rest', i.e. a well-earned period of retirement, and a multiplication of seven times seven, since Pope had his forty-ninth birthday on 21 May 1737. The ages of man were most commonly divided into periods of seven years, leading up to the grand climacteric (63) and the natural term (70).

l. 10. *Brunswick's cause*. In the Hanoverian interest, nominally that of England but (P suggests) often that of the King's original German electorate.

l. 16 note. The idiom of *The Dunciad*, where Blackmore also figures. The physician lived in Cheapside and was supported by his neighbours in the business community.

l. 19. *What right . . . we justly call.* Recalling Phil. 4: 8.

390   l. 23. *doctors.* The learned, in general.

l. 26. *Montaigne . . . Locke.* P may have had in mind his friend Prior's dialogue of the dead between the two men, published in 1718.

l. 27. *patriot.* Independent-minded politician, usually associated with the opposition to Walpole.

l. 29. *Lyttelton.* P's friend the poet and politician Lyttelton who had come to the fore in the campaign against Walpole: see also Biographical Index.

l. 31. *Aristippus.* P's note cites Horace, *Epistles*, I. xvii. 23, 'Every form and state and object of life became Aristippus' (the pupil of Socrates and pre-Epicurean hedonistic philosopher).   *St Paul.* Most obviously I Cor. 9: 22, 'I am become all things to all men'; I Cor. 10: 33, 'I also please all men in all things'; Phil. 4: 5, 'Let your forbearance be known to all men.'

l. 32. *candour.* Kindly disposition.

l. 50. *lynx.* Regarded as the keenest-sighted animal. P suffered from short sight at least as early as 1709 (*Corr.* i. 66).

l. 51. *Mead.* Dr Richard Mead.   *Cheselden.* William Cheselden. For these two eminent medical men, see Biographical Index. Cheselden was famous for his ophthalmological work, particularly on cataracts; for his relations with P, see M. H. Nicolson and G. S. Rousseau, *This Long Disease, My Life* (Princeton, NJ, 1968), 58–62; for Mead, 62–4.

l. 57. *control.* Overpower, master.

391   l. 63. *Switz . . . Low Dutch bear.* Stereotyped Swiss, German, or Dutch 'boors', or uncouth foreigners (such as, for example, the Hanoverian line).

l. 69. *either India.* The West or East Indies.

l. 82. *low St James's.* St James's, Piccadilly, had been associated with the latitudinarian wing of the Church since Samuel Clarke was appointed rector in 1709. See also *Dunciad*, iv. 608.   *high St Paul.* St Paul's Cathedral, traditionally High Church in this area. But in addition St James's is a squat, low building, as against the towering cathedral.

l. 84. *notches sticks.* Referring to the ancient tallies which were then still used in Exchequer accounting.

l. 85. *Barnard.* The Opposition MP and City figure Sir John Barnard; see Biographical Index.

l. 87. *harness.* The Garter, as representing knightly accoutrements.

l. 88. *Bug.* Usually identified as Duke of Kent (1671–1740).

Dorimant. A fashionable beau, from the character in Etherege's *Man of Mode*.

l. 89. *cit*. Citizen (contemptuous).

l. 90. *D*l*. Not certainly identified.

l. 95. *Screen . . . brass*. Both nicknames for Walpole.

392 l. 100. *Cressy and Poitiers*. Victories over France at Crécy and Poitiers in the Hundred Years War were used by the Opposition as examples of the ancient glory of England under the patriot hero Edward III.

l. 105. *eunuchs*. Operatic castrati. George II was a prominent supporter of opera.

l. 110. *St James's air*. In the vicinity of fashionable St James's, esp. in the Park and the Palace (l. 113).

l. 112. *Schutz*. Augustus Schutz (d. 1757), an official in George II's court.

ll. 114-19. From the fable of the fox and the lion. The 'royal cave' is probably another dig at Merlin's Cave at Richmond.

l. 128. *farm*. In effect, steal from.

l. 131. *chine and brawn*. Cuts of meat but also their own bodily attributes.

l. 138. *Sir Job*. One who engages in jobbery or financial manipulation of public assets; no original has been convincingly proposed for this role.

393 l. 147. *snug's the word*. It is best to stay safe and quiet (proverbial).

l. 148. *stocking*. 'An old custom according to which on the wedding night the bride's stocking was thrown amongst the guests; it was supposed that the person hit by it would be the first of the company to be married' (*OED*).

l. 156. *japanner*. Bootblack.

l. 157. *discharge*. Quit, renounce.

l. 158. *chaise and one*. A carriage drawn by a single horse.

l. 159. *sculler*. Thames waterman.

l. 162. *band*. Neckband.

l. 164. *Lady Mary*. Again alluding to the slovenly habits P attributes to Lady Mary Wortley Montagu.

l. 169. *I plant . . . confound*. Recalling Jer. 1: 10.

l. 173. *Hales*. Dr Richard Hale (1670-1728), former physician to Bedlam.

l. 177. *my guide, philosopher, and friend*. Quoting *Essay on Man*, iv. 390.

394 l. 181. *without title*. Following his Jacobite intrigues and exile, Bolingbroke had his honours of nobility stripped from him.

l. 182. *plundered*. By the act of attainder which confiscated his estates in 1715.

l. 184. *in the Tower*. Bolingbroke escaped this, unlike his colleague Oxford.

Epilogue to the Satires: Dialogue I. Published separately on 16 May 1738 (five days before P's 50th birthday), under the title *One Thousand Seven Hundred and Thirty Eight: A Dialogue Something like Horace.* It was grouped with the second dialogue (published two months later) in the *Works* (1739) under the title *Epilogue to the Satires. Written in 1738.* The text here is based on Warburton's edition of 1751, where a few revisions are incorporated. The process of composition cannot be traced in detail, but the work is clearly a response to hostile criticism of the earlier versions of Horace, and was probably completed only shortly before publication. (See for instance the letter to Ralph Allen, note to l. 135 below.)

According to Joseph Warton, the Epilogue was 'more diligently laboured, and more frequently corrected than any of our author's compositions'. Robert Dodsley made a clean copy, and then 'every line was written twice over; and when he afterwards sent it to Mr Dodsley to be printed, he found every line had been written twice over a second time' (quoted in *TE*, vol. iv, p. xxxix). No manuscript is now known to survive.

While the *Epilogue* is not a direct imitation, only 'something like Horace', it has been pointed out that it is a poem 'of self-assertion and self-questioning, modelled on Horace's *Satires*, ii. iii and vii' (F. Stack, *Pope and Horace* (Cambridge, 1985), 276). *Fr* is 'friend'.

l. 1 note. The source is Horace, *Satires*, ii. iii. 1–4.

l. 8. '*Tories . . . a Tory*'. Adapted from *Second Satire of the First Book*, l. 68.

l. 10. '*To laugh at fools . . . trust in Peter*'. Adapted from *Second Satire of the First Book*, l. 40. Peter Walter, once more.

l. 11. *nice.* Discreet.

l. 12 note. Any owlish commentator, but perhaps George Bubb Dodington in particular.

395 l. 13. *Sir Billy.* Sir William Yonge: see Biographical Index.

l. 14. *Blunt.* See *Epistle to Bathurst*, l. 133.   *Huggins.* See Biographical Index.

l. 15. *Sappho.* Lady Mary Wortley Montagu.

l. 18 note. A facetious reference to one of the most contentious political issues of the day, which actually brought about the War of Jenkins' Ear in 1739 (see *Second Epistle of the First Book*, l. 2).

l. 22 note. *Persius. Satires*, i. 116.   *Screen.* A nickname for Walpole, also known as Screenmaster-General. He was thought to have allowed the ministerial agents of the South Sea affair to escape, and to have shielded allies from parliamentary inquiry. Caricatures often involved the use of a screen as an emblem: see e.g. *The Prevailing Candidate* (1722), reproduced in P. Langford, *Walpole and the Robinocracy* (Cambridge, 1986), 5.

l. 26 note. Walpole. For the depiction of Walpole as a symbol of power, represented by physical grossness, see H. M. Atherton, *Political Prints in the Age of Hogarth* (Oxford, 1974), 191–208.

l. 34. *what he thinks mankind.* Walpole was widely identified with the maxim, 'Every man has his price', but this was a distortion of the view he actually expressed.

396 l. 39 note. See Biographical Index for Sir Joseph Jekyll, who opposed the Government in a crucial division in 1735.   *Old Whig.* One of the ancient breed of 'honest' Revolution Whigs, contrasted with the new men who had come to power under Walpole.

l. 40. *wig.* Full-bottomed wigs had gone out of fashion in favour of the shorter tie-wigs, but Jekyll, aptly perhaps for a senior judge, clung on to the older style.

l. 42. *Lord Chamberlains.* By the theatrical Licensing Act of 1737, all new plays had to be submitted to the Lord Chamberlain for censorship, a practice which survived until 1968.

l. 47 note. Lyttelton, one of P's closest allies now and a leader of the opposition centred on the Prince of Wales: see Biographical Index.

l. 50. *Lord Fanny.* Hervey.

l. 51 note. *Sejanus, Wolsey.* 'Walpole's enemies found an odious parallel in Wolsey's rise from humble beginnings and in his engrossment of power, wealth and honours' (Atherton, *Political Prints*, 192). See also an item in *The Craftsman* (1729), linking Sejanus and Wolsey (quoted by Atherton, ibid. 193).   *Fleury.* André de Fleury (1653–1743), cardinal and chief minister of France; Opposition satire depicted Walpole as unduly conciliatory towards Fleury (Langford, *Walpole*, 23).

397 l. 66. *Henley . . . Osborne.* John 'Orator' Henley and James Pitt ('Mother Osborne'): see Biographical Index.

l. 69 note. Referring to a speech of condolence on the death of the Queen in 1737, addressed to the King by Henry Fox, but perhaps written by Hervey, who used it in a Latin epitaph on the Queen.

l. 75. *Middleton and Bland.* Conyers Middleton, author of a life of Cicero, and Henry Bland, headmaster of Eton, who are suggested as the true authors of the Latin epitaph (there is no evidence to support this).

l. 82. *All parts performed . . . children blessed.* 'Contemporary gossip reported that the Queen had died without taking the last sacrament and without being reconciled to the Prince of Wales' (*TE*, iv. 304, where supporting evidence is cited).

l. 84. *gazetteer.* Official Government spokesman in the press, or merely a hack journalist paid to put the party line.

l. 92. *Selkirk . . . De la Ware.* The Earl of Selkirk and Earl De La Warr: see Dialogue II, l. 61 and Biographical Index.

398 l. 98. *nepenthe.* A herb that dulls sorrow and induces oblivion.

l. 102. *All tears . . . all eyes*. Alluding to Isa. 25: 8.

l. 104. *lose a question*. Suffer defeat in Parliament.   *job*. A corruptly organized deal.

l. 108. *gracious Prince*. A coded message, expressing Opposition hopes of a glorious future under the Prince of Wales, who was in fact to predecease his father.

l. 115. *Cibber's son*. The actor Theophilus Cibber: see Biographical Index.

l. 116. *Rich*. John Rich. See Biographical Index.

l. 119. *Ward*. John Ward, the MP expelled for forgery: see *Epistle to Bathurst*, l. 20.

l. 120. *Japhet*. Japhet Crook, also a forger: see *Epistle to Bathurst*, l. 86.   *his Grace*. The Archbishop of Canterbury, William Wake, who had helped to suppress a will left by George I.

l. 121. *Bond*. Denis Bond: see *Epistle to Bathurst*, l. 100.   *Peter*. Peter Walter.

l. 123. *Blount*. Charles Blount (1654–93), deistical writer, who committed suicide in unclear circumstances.

l. 124. *Passeran*. The Count of Passerano (1698–1737), Italian free-thinker, was arrested in 1732 for publishing his book in favour of the right to suicide. He was also reviled as a homosexual. 'Passeran was actually blamed for a number of suicides in 1732–3, on the grounds that his doctrine had encouraged them, and one Englishman left a note stating that he had been reading Passeran at the time he slit his wrists' (G. S. Rousseau, *Sexual Underworlds of the Enlightenment*, ed. Rousseau and R. Porter (Chapel Hill, NC, 1988), 104).

l. 125 note. The individual has been identified as Richard Smith, who hanged himself along with his wife in 1732; see *TE*, iv. 307.

399   l. 130 note. The first Gin Act of 1736 attempted to put a stop to the gin trade by prohibitive duties, but it proved unenforceable. The Opposition contested its passage through Parliament.

l. 131. *Foster*. James Foster (1697–1753), an anabaptist preacher.

l. 133. *Quaker's wife*. In fact Mary Drummond (d. 1777) was the sister of the Edinburgh Quaker, George Drummond; she became famous for preaching to large congregations in London in 1735.

l. 134 note. Llandaff was one of the poorest seats for a bishop to occupy, worth barely £200 at the start of the century. Its current incumbent was John Harris (1680–1738), thought to have been the author of a pamphlet attack on P and Swift.

l. 135. *Allen*. P's great friend, the Bath philanthropist Ralph Allen. On 28 April 1738 P had written to Allen, 'Pray tell me if you have any objection to my putting your name into a poem of mine . . . provided I say something of you which most people would take ill, for example, that you are no man of high birth or quality?' (*Corr.* iv. 93). Perhaps Allen did object; at all events, P wrote to him on 2 November 1738, describing a change in the text from 'low-born', as it stood in the first edition, to 'humble' (*Corr.* iv. 144–5). For P's relations with Allen, see B. Boyce, *The Benevolent Man* (Cambridge, Mass., 1967), 56–162.

l. 138. *Virtue.* Implies the political probity of the Opposition, against the corruption ('Vice') of the Government.

l. 149. *scarlet head.* Suggesting the Whore of Babylon: Rev. 17, 18. Parallels have also been discovered with the prostitute Theodora who married the Emperor Justinian, and with Walpole's mistress Molly Skerrett. See J. M. Osborn, 'Pope, the Byzantine Empress, and Walpole's Whore', *RES* 6 (1955), 372–82, for a full discussion.

l. 150. *carted.* Prostitutes were drawn through the streets on a cart as part of their punishment.

l. 154. *flag inverted.* A sign of dishonour.

l. 157. *pagod.* Idol.

400 *Epilogue to the Satires: Dialogue II.* First published 18 July 1738, two months after the first dialogue, under the title *One Thousand Seven Hundred Thirty Eight, Dialogue II.* Then joined to its predecessor in the *Works* under the present title. A few more revisions were made before Warburton printed it in his edition of 1751, the basis for the text here.

Swift wrote to P on 8 August, mentioning the poem: 'I take your second Dialogue that you lately sent me, to equal almost anything you ever writ', though he claimed to be unable to understand many of the allusions to life in London and esp. at court (*Corr.* iv. 115). P himself felt that he had exhausted his Horatian vein, for on 17 May 1739 he wrote to Swift, 'You compliment me in vain on retaining my poetical spirit. I am sinking fast into prose ... since my *protest* (as I call the Dialogue of *1738*) I have written but ten lines' (*Corr.* iv. 178). In fact he published very little for the next four years, and apart from the revised *Dunciad* with its new fourth book he was to produce no more major poetry.

l. 1. *Paxton.* Nicholas Paxton, the Treasury Solicitor, who oversaw the regulation of the press and conducted government prosecutions: see Biographical Index.

l. 6. *amain.* At full speed.

l. 7. *Invention.* Imagination.

l. 11 note. James Guthrie succeeded the poet Thomas Purney as Ordinary, or chaplain, of Newgate Prison. It was part of his role to publish penitent deathbed confessions by the condemned criminals. See L. B. Faller, *Turned to Account* (Cambridge, 1987) for these twopenny *Accounts*, dating back to at least 1679.

l. 15. *souze.* Swoop like a hawk.

l. 17. *Hall.* Westminster Hall, symbolic of justice.

401 l. 20. See *Dialogue I*, l. 112.

l. 22. *the poisoning dame.* Probably referring to *First Satire of the Second Book*, l. 81.

l. 29. *royal harts.* A hart royal was a stag 'that has been chased by a royal personage' (*OED*); it might then be 'proclaimed', i.e. an order issued that none should pursue it any more.

l. 39. *Wild.* The thief-taker Jonathan Wild (1683–1725), the great criminal boss of London. Defoe, Gay, and Fielding wrote works centred on this notorious figure.

l. 41. *drench.* Duck at a pump in the street.

l. 49. *directors.* Still a word with baneful South Sea overtones; indicates leaders of the large city institutions such as the East India Company.   *plums.* £100,000.

402 l. 57. *Peter.* Peter Walter.

l. 61. *Selkirk.* Charles Douglas, Earl of Selkirk (1663–1739) a Scottish peer.

l. 65. *Scarborough.* When this note was written, Scarborough was dead, having committed suicide in 1740.

l. 67. *Kent.* The architect William Kent, who laid out the gardens at Esher.   *Pelham.* Henry Pelham (1694–1754), Prime Minister from 1746 to his death. P may have been trying to drive a wedge between Walpole and the Pelhams, but the brothers remained loyal to Walpole until his fall.

ll. 71–2. *Secker ... Rundle ... Benson.* For the prelates Secker, Rundle, and Benson, see Biographical Index. It has been suspected that the epithet 'decent' is ironic, but this is implausible (see Spence, i. 143).

l. 73. *Berkeley.* The philosopher George Berkeley, a friend of Swift. See Biographical Index.

l. 77. *Somers ... Halifax.* Somers and Halifax were the leading patrons of their time, and both took an interest in the young P's work; see P's opening note to 'Spring' in the *Pastorals*.

403 ll. 79–80. *Shrewsbury ... Carleton ... Stanhope.* For Shrewsbury, Henry Boyle (Lord Carleton) and James Stanhope, see Biographical Index.

ll. 82–9. *Atterbury's softer hour ... and his own.* Atterbury had been imprisoned in the Tower of London before his exile. He had died in 1732; the remaining names form a roll-call of Opposition heroes and a pantheon of P's private heroes among statesmen. For individuals, see Biographical Index.

l. 99. *Man of Ross.* John Kyrle: see *Epistle to Bathurst*, l. 250. For John Barnard, Lord Mayor, see Biographical Index.

404 l. 110. *stoop.* Swoop.

l. 111. *number*. Lat. *numerus*, the (undistinguished) many.

l. 116. *Louis*. Louis XIV and his father's powerful minister, Cardinal Richelieu.

l. 117. *young Ammon*. Alexander the Great.

l. 120. *one honest line*. *Aeneid*, viii. 670 ('Secretos pios, his dantem iura Catonem'), which P originally read as a tribute to the republican hero Cato the younger: see Spence, i. 230.

l. 129. *Arnall*. The Government hack William Arnall: see Biographical Index.

l. 130. *Cobham*. See *Epistle to Cobham*, headnote.   *Polwarth.* Henry Hume, Lord Polwarth (1708–94); as Lord Marchmont, he had a distinguished career in national politics and was one of P's executors.

l. 137. *Verres*. See *Dialogue I*, l. 51. Verres, from the corrupt governor of Sicily attacked by Cicero, had become another Opposition nickname for Walpole.

405   l. 142. *pretend*. Take upon himself, presume.

l. 150. *Turenne*. Vicomte de Turenne (1611–75), Marshal of France.

l. 159. *Page*. The brutal Judge Page: see Biographical Index.

l. 160. *bard*. P's note refers to a poem by George Bubb Dodington, addressed to Walpole in 1726.

l. 166. *florid youth*. Not, as formerly believed, Henry Fox but his brother Stephen (see Carolyn Williams, *British Journal for Eighteenth-Century Studies*, 9 (1986), 23).

l. 172. *Westphaly*. Westphalia, the German region noted for producing ham.

406   l. 183. *civet-cats*. See *Second Satire of the First Book*, l. 30.

ll. 185–6. *Japhet . . . Chartres*. Japhet Crook, the forger, and Colonel Francis Charteris.

l. 187. *Pindus*. A mountain in Thessaly, home of the Muses.

l. 191. *gin*. Referring again to the agitation over the Gin Act: see *Dialogue I*, l. 130.

l. 192. *in*. In office.

l. 194. *on his brows*. The horns of the cuckold.

l. 204. *who feel for all mankind*. Recalling Terence's famous line from *Heauton Timorumenos*, l. 77 ('I am a man, and consider nothing human alien to me').

407   l. 218. *tardy Hall*. Westminster Hall, centre of the obstructive system of justice.

l. 227. *Gazette*. The *London Gazette*, the official record of government.   *address*. Official address from the Lords or Commons to the monarch.

l. 230. *Waller's wreath.* Waller had mourned the death of Cromwell in a poem published in 1659.

l. 231. *feather to a star.* Boileau's *Ode* had made a star of the French King's hat-plume, as a comet portending disaster to his enemies.

l. 237 note. For Anstis, see Biographical Index.

l. 238. *other stars than * and **.* The stars may indicate George and Frederick, the King and Prince of Wales.

l. 239. *Mordington.* A particularly anonymous Earl.   *Stair.* John Dalrymple, second Earl, soldier and diplomat.

408   l. 241. *Digby.* Lord Digby (1662–1752), father of P's friend Robert Digby. See H. Erskine-Hill, *The Social Milieu of Alexander Pope* (New Haven, Conn., 1975), 133–65.

l. 252. *that cause.* Liberty.

Epigram Engraved on the Collar of a Dog. Written around 1736 or 1737; first published in the *Works*, vol. ii (1738). The dog in question was apparently one of the puppies of P's own bitch, Bounce, and was presented to Frederick, Prince of Wales (the focus of opposition to the court) in 1736: see a letter from Lyttelton to P on 22 December 1736 (*Corr.* iv. 48). For Bounce and P's other much-loved dogs, see Ault, 337–50. The year 1737 was the year of the irrevocable break between the Prince and his father, King George II. The Prince had lived at Kew House since 1732.

   For an elaborate teasing out of possible meanings to be derived from this lapidary couplet, see Harold Beaver, *British Journal for Eighteenth-Century Studies*, 3 (1980), 208–15.

409   *Epitaph, for one who would not be buried in Westminster-Abbey.* Published in P's *Works* in 1738; the date of composition is unknown. Warburton later took the lines as self-referential and appended them to a monument he erected to the memory of P in Twickenham church. This was going beyond P's expressed intentions, but there can be no doubt that P had his own ostentatious independence in mind when he wrote the lines.

Pope to Hugh Bethel, 19 March 1744. Text based on *Corr.* iv. 508–9. Written ten weeks before P's death, it gives some indication of the state of his health towards the end. Hugh Bethel, like P, suffered from asthma, but had been able to spend over a year in Italy, which prolonged his life. For a 'medical case-history' of this period, see M. H. Nicolson and G. S. Rousseau, *This Long Disease, My Life* (Princeton, NJ, 1968), 70–81.

Dr Burton. Simon Burton (1690–1744), an eminent physician who practised in Savile Row.

asses' milk. See *Epistle to Arbuthnot*, l. 306.

garlic. Clove of garlic esp. was used as a herbal remedy.

horehound. An aromatic herb used mainly for respiratory complaints.

alkalized mercury. Quicksilver taken in an amalgam to reduce the corrosive power of the metal. Bethel commented on 25 March, 'Ass's milk is good if it does not increase phlegm. Alkalized mercury is only crude quicksilver with crab's eyes' (*Corr.* iv. 512).

cheap one. A house in Berkeley Street, next to Berkeley Square, of which P was buying the lease. Martha Blount completed the purchase and lived there for the remainder of her life. She is 'the friend' mentioned in the next sentence.

your brother. Slingsby Bethel (1695–1758), a city merchant and MP.

410 *Mr Kent.* The architect and designer William Kent. The picture was never painted (W. K. Wimsatt, *The Portraits of Alexander Pope* (New Haven, Conn., 1965), 114).

see you in my bedchamber. Bethel had sent his portrait in February (*Corr.* iv. 500). It was painted in Rome and was the only portrait listed in the inventory as hung in P's own room when he died.

Mr Moyser. James Moyser (*c.*1693–1753), a Yorkshire country gentleman and amateur architect. He was a neighbour of Bethel, who seems not to have travelled south in time to see P before the latter's death.

THE DUNCIAD

411 The history of *The Dunciad* is exceedingly complicated, as regards both composition and publication. For purposes of clarity, four stages may be identified: (1) The original work in three books, published on 18 May 1728. It had been P's first plan to include the poem in the third volume of *Miscellanies*, issued two months earlier, but this scheme was jettisoned (see *Peri Bathous*, headnote). (2) The poem garnished with an extensive prose apparatus and many blanks filled in with real names: this was known as *The Dunciad Variorum*, and published on 10 April 1729. (3) A fourth book, added on 20 March 1742, entitled *The New Dunciad*. (4) The complete four-book version, published on 29 October 1743. In this, the king of the dunces became Colley Cibber, in place of Lewis Theobald. There are many intermediate stages between (2) and (3). P was responding to an immense body of criticism and riposte (esp. from the dunces themselves): for a summary of this material, see J. V. Guerinot, *Pamphlet Attacks on Alexander Pope 1711–1744* (1969), 110–326. P told Spence in 1735, '*The Dunciad* cost me as much pains as anything I ever wrote' (Spence, i. 147), and the elaborate working up of the text can be indicated only briefly here: for a full collation of successive changes, see *TE*, vol. v, where the three-book version is printed separately.

The text here is based on the 1743 version. However, some of the voluminous preliminaries and appendices have been omitted, as follows: (1) An

'Advertisement to the Reader', attributed to Warburton but probably P's own. (2) 'Testimonies of Authors', a satirical conspectus of the views of his victims and adversaries. (3) Various appendices, including a list of attacks on P prior to the appearance of *The Dunciad*; an advertisement (preface) to the new fourth book in 1742; a short notice in the press from 1730; a 'Parallel of the Characters of Mr Dryden and Mr Pope', drawn from contemporary sources; a 'Declaration' by the author of the authenticity of the poem, in mock-legal form; and an index to the 'matters' of the poem. Most of these items are of some interest but they require extensive annotation to make their point today, and do not contribute to the central thrust of the work. I have however retained the satire on Bentley, probably written by Warburton, as it supports a main section of the poem in its parody of misapplied scholarship.

No original manuscripts of the poem survive, but some of the draft readings which P rejected in compiling the 1728 and 1729 versions can be assembled from a list of variants made by his friend Jonathan Richardson. These are recorded in M. Mack, *L&GA*, 97–155.

P had been amassing materials to discountenance his enemies for many years, but *The Dunciad* itself took shape only in the later 1720s: one of the first clear hints of his intent occurs in a letter to Swift on 15 October 1725 (*Corr.* ii. 332). During Swift's visit to England in 1726, the project seems to have gained momentum; Swift was later to claim that he 'had reason to put Mr Pope on writing the poem called *The Dunciad*' (*Correspondence*, ed. Williams, iv. 53). One spur to action had been the appearance of *Shakespeare Restored* by Lewis Theobald in 1726, a work whose assault on P's credentials as an editor led to the enthronement of Theobald as the original king of the dunces. However, it was only in 1727 that the poem really took shape: and it was as late as March 1728 that P informed Swift that the work formerly known as 'The Progress of Dulness' was now to be called *The Dunciad* (*Corr.* ii. 480). The correspondence of both P and Swift is the best place to study the genesis of the poem. It should be noted that the coronation of George II gave P new opportunities and may have influenced the choice of a Lord Mayor's installation as the setting (see P. Rogers, *Literature and Popular Culture in Eighteenth-Century England* (Brighton, 1985), 120–50). The fourth book was mostly composed whilst P was staying with Ralph Allen at Bath in the winter of 1741/2: see *Corr.* iv. 387. The intermediate stages of the poem can be traced in a variety of places, as can the complicated publishing manœuvres and legal battles surrounding the poem: see *TE*, vol. v, pp. ix–xxix. P described the piece to Swift as his 'chef d'œuvre' (*Corr.* ii. 468); it was certainly the item which engaged most of his time and nervous energy.

The fullest reading of the poem, including its epic background, its use of Lord Mayor's Day pageantry, its use of the migrations of cultures (here from the east, i.e. the City of London, to the polite west, i.e. St James's) and its inversions of Christian theology, remains A. Williams, *Pope's 'Dunciad'* (1955). For the use of mock-heroic techniques, see Ian Jack, *Augustan Satire* (Oxford, 1952), 115–34, where the relation of the poem to Dryden's *Mac Flecknoe*, Boileau's *Le Lutrin*, and Garth's *Dispensary* is discussed. Douglas

Brooks-Davies, *Pope's 'Dunciad' and the Queen of the Night* (Manchester, 1985) supplies alchemical and hermetic background to suggest a core of 'emotional Jacobitism' in the poem. Roger D. Lund has indicated a pervasive debt to Thomas Newcomb's *Bibliotheca* (1712); see *British Journal for Eighteenth-Century Studies*, 14 (1991), 171–89.

The annotation in this edition has had to be strictly limited in order to avoid swamping the volume. Specifically, it should be noted that (1) individuals mentioned in the text will normally be found in the Biographical Index, other than those who have left so minuscule a footprint in the sands of time that they cannot be properly identified. Except in special cases, no such references to persons is glossed in the notes. (2) P's own notes are in general not annotated, unless there is some crucial point at stake for understanding the text. (3) Only sustained and significant literary allusions are glossed, most notably those to P's epic predecessors.

Ovid. From *Metamorphoses*, xi. 58–60: 'But Phoebus is at hand to freeze the monster as it reappears to bite, and fixes its mouth in a rictus with gaping jaws.'

Preliminaries

412 *Tibbald.* P's own name for Theobald, not apparently the pronunciation actually in use (just as he perverted to 'Kibber' the name of the new king of the dunces, who seems to have been known as 'Sibber').

ƆC. Ch. Charles (Fitzroy, Duke of Grafton, Lord) Chamberlain. It was he who had been granted the power to pre-censor plays under the theatrical Licensing Act of 1737. But the ƆC monogram also suggests Colley Cibber.

414 *A Letter to the Publisher.* Attributed on its first appearance to P's friend William Cleland (father of the novelist John), but certainly written by P himself.

415 *not the least mention.* Untrue, as shown by the pamphlets against Curll and, just before *The Dunciad* was published, *Peri Bathous.*

416 *gentleman.* Perhaps Richard Savage, who was P's informant on the byways of Grub Street living.

apothecary. Romeo and Juliet, v. i. 68–76.

417 *subsisting.* Existent, carrying on their independent life.

418 *Codrus.* An impoverished poet described in Juvenal, *Satires*, iii. 203–11. See also *Dunciad*, ii. 144.

Damon. The poet in Boileau's *Satire* i.

his translators. P added a note, omitted here, on the French translations of his poems.

Perrault. Charles Perrault (1628–1703), French author, now best known for his fairy tales, but celebrated in his time as principal champion of the moderns in the great *Querelle*, as Boileau was of the ancients. P refers to the *Lettre à M. Perrault* (1700).

Quinault. Philippe Quinault (1635–88), dramatist, ridiculed by Boileau for his high-flown tragedy.

419 *Mr Wycherley*. For William Wycherley and others named here, see Biographical Index.

GRATIAM. Pliny, *Natural History*, preface; 'to give novelty to the old, elegance to the shabby, resplendence to the dark, favour to the despised.'

420 *piece by Homer*. *Margites*, a lost satirical epic of Greek antiquity, often supposed to be by Homer.

Eustathius. Twelfth-century Archbishop of Thessalonica, famous for his commentary on Homer.

Brute. Brutus, mythical descendant of Aeneas, supposed to have founded the race of Britons; subject of a fragmentary epic (in a serious vein) which P began towards the end of his life.

Godfrey. Godfrey de Bouillon (*c.*1060–1100), led the capture of Jerusalem in the First Crusade, the subject of Tasso's epic *Gerusalemme liberata* (1575). Charlemagne is instanced for his role in Ariosto's *Orlando furioso* (1532).

Flecknoe. Richard Flecknoe (d. *c.*1678), poet and dramatist, established as the aboriginal dunce in Dryden's *Mac Flecknoe* (1682).

422 *He finds it to be* ——. Cibber, in this version.

fable. Plot, main narrative.

proposition. Opening statement of the theme.

episodes. Incidental narratives, digressions.

More. James Moore Smythe: see Biographical Index.

Eliza. Eliza Haywood: see Biographical Index.

neoterics. Moderns.

423 *forty*. *The Dunciad* was published three days before P's fortieth birthday.

Rymer. Thomas Rymer (1641–1713), historian and critic, regarded as the dogmatic literary oracle.

twenty. A slight understatement of P's age: see *Essay on Criticism*, headnote.

Of the Hero of the Poem. Added in 1743: written by Warburton (who was thanked by P on 28 December 1742, *Corr.* iv. 434), but thoroughly Popian in its satire of Bentley's brand of scholarship.

424 *Monsieur Bossu*. René Le Bossu (1631–80). 'A Gallic critic' simulates Bentley's condescension towards the most influential modern authority on epic, notably in his *Traité du poème épique* (1675).

putid. Foul, rotten (an authentic Bentleyism).

undertakers. Contractors, developers. P has in mind the new breed of speculative builders in London, such as Nicolas Barbon (*c.*1640–98).

descendit. Identified in *TE*, v. 255, as the work of the third-century writer Lactantius.

little epic. Apparently here not the epyllion, but formal satire, regarded as a natural descendant of epic.

Euripides. P refers to his satiric drama *Cyclops*.

426 *Mezentius.* A cruel tyrant who opposed the Trojan forces in the *Aeneid*, and was killed by the hero in Book X.

summer-teeming lust. Macbeth, IV. iii. 86: Warburton's emendation of the standard reading, 'summer-seeming'.

certain strainers. See *Essay on Man*, ii. 189.

fourscore. In fact Cibber was no more than 72.

427 *processerat.* Horace, *Ars poetica*, ll. 126–7: 'let it be kept until the last, in the form it originally appeared.'

late king of Sweden. Charles XII.

428 *Durandarte.* Legendary Spanish hero: see *Don Quixote*, II. xxiii, for his story told by the hero of the novel. He uses the proverbial 'pacencia y barajar' (let us wait and see): compare Tilley P105.

429 *Omar.* Omar Caliph of Islam, conquered Syria in the seventh century.

John of Leiden. Jan Beuckelzoon (1509–36), Dutch anabaptist and revolutionary.

Roman historian. Sallust.

Machiavel. It has not been possible to identify the source of this quotation in Machiavelli.

a statuary. Cibber's father, Caius Gabriel Cibber (1630–1700), sculptor.

430 *Solon.* See Herodotus, i. 32.

Epopoeian. Epic.

Book I

431 *hastes into the midst of things.* Horace, *Ars poetica*, l. 148.

432 l. 1. *Mighty Mother.* Magna mater, sometimes confused with other maternal deities: see Williams, *Pope's 'Dunciad'*, 26–9.

434 l. 2. *Smithfield muses.* P suggests that the low entertainments of the fairground, traditionally held like Bartholomew Fair in the less salubrious environs of the City, have now invaded the West End.

l. 6. *Dunce the first.* Unmistakably pointing to the succession of George II to his father in 1727.

l. 10. *Thunderer.* Jove (epic diction).

435 l. 20. *Dean.* Swift is celebrated as Dean of St Patrick's, and author of the *Drapier's Letters* and the *Bickerstaff Papers*, as well as *Gulliver's Travels*. P had sent the first draft of these lines to Swift in advance of the original *Dunciad*, in January 1728 (*Corr.* ii. 468–9).

l. 25. *Boeotia*. The district north of Athens which became, unfairly, proverbial for the stupidity of its inhabitants.

ll. 29–30. *Close to those walls . . . Monro would take her down*. Bedlam, or Bethlehem Hospital, stood in London Wall, about two hundred yards east of Grub Street, on the northern fringe of the historic City. James Monroe was physician to the hospital.

437 l. 39. *miscellanies*. Poetic anthologies (stress on first syllable).

l. 42. *journals, medleys, merc'ries, magazines*. Titles used by journals: the first 'magazine' in the modern sense dates from 1731.

l. 44. *Grub Street*. A real location near Bedlam and Moorfields which had become synonymous with indigent hack writers.

438 l. 46. *virtues*. The four traditionally recognized cardinal virtues.

l. 50. *who thirst for scribbling sake*. Recalling Matt. 5: 6 (righteousness, rather than scribbling).

l. 57. *Jacob*. Jacob Tonson.   *third day*. The benefit night for dramatists.

439 l. 74. *Zembla*. The Arctic land Novaya Zemlya.   *Barca*. In the desert region of Libya (modern El Marj).

440 l. 85. *when ** rich and grave*. In the original version of the poem, the name of Sir George Thorold, Lord Mayor in 1719, had been spelt out.

l. 91. *shrieves*. Sheriffs.

l. 101. *Bruin*. Bears were supposed to lick their young into shape (the origin of this expression).

443 l. 108. *Bays*. Cibber, who was adorned with laurel by virtue of his office; also suggests a line of descent from the foolish playwright in Buckingham's *Rehearsal* (1672).

444 l. 126. *sooterkins*. Small animals which according to folklore were born to Dutchwomen huddled over their stoves. By extension, abortive literary productions.

445 l. 144. *jakes*. Privy.

446 l. 145. *Gothic*. Of the dark ages, medieval (pejorative).   *Rome*. Pronounced 'room'.

447 l. 168. *butt and bays*. The Poet Laureate was entitled to a cask of wine annually, along with his imaginary laurels. But the phrase wonderfully suggests a low tavern.

449 l. 202. *box*. Dice-box.

l. 203. *White's*. The gaming club in St James's Street.

l. 209. *Curtius*. See *Essay on Man*, ii. 200.

l. 211. *Rome's ancient geese*. The Romans were warned by geese of the approach of the enemy when the Gauls attacked the Capitol in 390 BC, allowing Manlius Capitolinus to resist the assault.

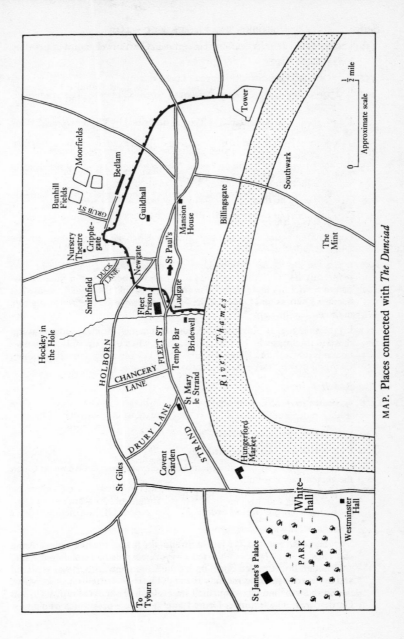

MAP. Places connected with *The Dunciad*

450 l. 222. *Hockley Hole*. A bear-baiting centre in Clerkenwell, north of London.

l. 224. *fiddle*. Jester.

451 l. 234. *mundungus*. Strong tobacco of poor quality.

452 ll. 250–3. *the Cid . . . dear Nonjuror claims*. Cibber's plays and play-doctorings.

l. 256. *Ilion*. The destruction of Troy as described by Virgil in *Aeneid*, Book II.

454 l. 281. *'scape*. By benefit of clergy: see *The Second Satire of Donne*, l. 16.

455 ll. 289–91. *her bird . . . on his crown*. A blasphemous parody of the descent of the dove after Christ's baptism (Matt. 3: 16).

l. 298. *fool of quality*. Perhaps Lord Hervey, who may also be the 'aide de camp' in l. 305.

l. 306. *points*. Sharp turns of wit.

l. 307. *Billingsgate*. Coarse and abusive language, appropriate to the Thames-side fish-market.

456 l. 312. *nursing-mother*. Brooks-Davies ('*Dunciad*' *and the Queen of Night*, 100) points out that a relevant verse in Isa. 49: 23 had been used in Stuart coronation services. The same scholar argues (p. 8) that the dead Caroline has become Dulness and Queen of the Night, inverting the true nurturing role of the monarch.

457 l. 330. *King Log*. In Aesop's fable, Jove first sends a useless lump of wood down to the frogs who had asked for a king; when they are still dissatisfied, he sends down a stork which devours them. The meaning is that the wooden George I may be succeeded by a rapacious George II.

Book II

458 *by Aeneas*. In *Aeneid*, Book V.

fustian. Bombastic, inflated.

459 l. 4. *showers*. Of eggs and rotten fruit.

460 l. 14. *scarlet hats*. Those of cardinals.

l. 16. *seven hills*. The Septimontium, seven elevated parts of Rome on which the ancient city was built.

l. 21. *bags*. Bag-wigs, with the back-hair of the wig in a pouch.

l. 22. *crapes*. Of the clerical order.   *garters*. Of the knightly order.

l. 24. *hacks*. Hackney carriages.

l. 27. *that area*. Around St Mary le Strand, the first of the new Queen Anne churches, built by James Gibbs 1714–17. A maypole had stood on the site, and though it was pulled down under the Commonwealth, it was replaced and the last one set up as recently as 1713. The church stood on a spot where the Strand was then joined by small streets leading out of the raffish Covent Garden area. The 'saints of Drury Lane' (l. 30) are prostitutes who populated the district. 'The exact geography of the games seems partly determined by the fact that the Strand and Drury Lane were the actual sites of many printing-houses and theatres, and so could mark the encroachment of literary dulness on Westminster' (Williams, *Pope's 'Dunciad'*, 36). Jacob Tonson's shop stood opposite Catherine Street, about a hundred yards west of the church.

l. 31. *stationers*. The book trade in general.

461 l. 37. *adust*. Dark and gloomy.

462 l. 50. *More*. James Moore Smythe.

463 l. 63. *dabchick*. Same as the didapper of *Peri Bathous*, chap. vi.

464 l. 72. *cates*. Provisions, dainties.

465 l. 78. *vaticide*. Murderer of poets (by mangling their works, etc.).

l. 82. *the Bible . . . the Pope's Arms*. See P's note. Curll's shop had been opposite Catherine Street (see l. 27), but he later moved to Covent Garden and the Pope's Head in nearby Rose Street. Lintot's shop was near Temple Bar, some two hundred yards further east along the Strand.

l. 92. *Ichor*. The fluid supposed to flow in the veins of the gods.

l. 98. *black grottos*. Coal wharves which lay at the foot of Milford Lane, which ran south from the Strand between St Mary's and the western end of the Temple (see contemporary illustration in H. Phillips, *The Thames about 1750* (1951), 94).

l. 100. *link-boys*. Boys who carried torches in the streets to light the way.

466 l. 103. *sympathetic*. Acting by an occult affinity.

l. 107. *vindicates*. Lays claim to (as victor).

467 l. 128. *empty Joseph*. 'The ambiguity of the word Joseph, which likewise signifies a loose upper-coat, gives much pleasantry to the idea' (Warburton).

l. 135. *hapless Monsieur*. Nicolas-François Rémond: see *Second Satire of Second Book of Horace*, l. 53, for his relations with Lady Mary Wortley Montagu.

470 l. 146. *confessors*. Those who proclaim the faith (stress on first syllable).

l. 147. *Defoe*. He was put in the pillory in 1703 on account of the ill-managed irony of *The Shortest Way with the Dissenters*. He did not actually lose his ears.

471 l. 155. *labours*. Travail.

472 l. 171. *lettered post*. A post used as a billboard to advertise books.

473 l. 181. *horns*. Associated with river-gods (like that of Eridanus, sometimes identified with the Po, but also the river into which Phaethon was cast by Jove's thunderbolt), and with cuckolds.

l. 184. *burn*. P's note suggests that Curll's 'condition' was venereal infection.

476 l. 218. *only tender part*. Paris shot Achilles in his vulnerable heel and killed him.

l. 226 note. The anecdote is the basis of the expression 'to steal someone's thunder', though this did not pass into general usage until the twentieth century.

477 l. 238. *Norton.* Defoe's son Benjamin Norton Defoe. *brangling.* wrangling.

l. 240. *snipsnap.* Sharp repartee.

l. 242. *major, minor, and conclusion quick.* Referring to the term of a syllogism in formal logic.

l. 251. *Sir Gilbert.* Heathcote.

l. 255. *enthusiast.* Here, a canting, fanatical preacher belonging to a radical religious sect.

478 ll. 261–8. For the topographic limits of this bray, see Williams, *Pope's 'Dunciad'*, 36–8. Rufus's hall is Westminster Hall, which went back to the time of William II (Rufus). Hungerford Market lay on the river side of the Strand at its western end, on the site now occupied by Charing Cross station. See Phillips, *Thames about 1750*, 212.

479 l. 269. *Bridewell.* The house of correction for vagrant women and prostitutes, located near the junction of the Thames and Fleet Ditch.

l. 271. *disemboguing.* Discharging, into a larger current.

480 l. 281. *pig.* Ingot.

481 l. 287. *lighter.* Thames barge.

482 l. 295. *.* Probably Aaron Hill, a dramatist and poet who attempted to form a friendship with P despite various clashes. He was a member of Samuel Richardson's circle.

l. 311. *Niobe.* According to myth, her seven sons and seven daughters were killed by Apollo and Diana; Niobe wept for them until she was turned into stone.

l. 312. *Mother Osborne.* In reality James Pitt.

484 ll. 333–4. *Lutetia . . . Nigrina . . . Merdamante.* Names suggesting dirt and dung: Lutetia was the Latin name for Paris, from its muddy location.

l. 336. *Hylas.* The page of Hercules, drawn down into a spring by waternymphs enamoured of his beauty.

485 l. 341. *Alpheus.* A Greek river which rose in Greece, near the Grecian town Posa, flowed through the sea and came up in the fountain of Arethusa in Sicily.

l. 346. *from Paul's to Aldgate.* i.e. from St Paul's cathedral to the eastern gate of the city at Aldgate.

l. 350. *surcingle.* A girdle round a priest's cassock.

l. 353. *confess.* Make confession to.

l. 354. *flamen.* Priest.

l. 358. *Heaven's Swiss*. Mercenaries, as in the proverbial phrase, 'Law, logic and the Switzers fight for anybody' (Tilley L108).

486 l. 359. *Lud's famed gates*. Ludgate, where Fleet Street enters the ancient walled city: Lud was a legendary British king.

l. 374. *Ulysses' ear . . . Argus' eye*. Ulysses filled the ears of his men with wax to ensure that they resisted the call of the Sirens; Argus was a herdsman with eyes all over his body, which rendered him perpetually awake.

l. 379. *sophs*. Sophomores, students.   *templars*. Students of law at the Temple.

487 l. 385. *mum*. A beer of German origin.

l. 398. *Arthur*. Blackmore had written epics on *Prince Arthur* and *King Arthur*.

l. 400. *Christ's no kingdom*. Bishop Benjamin Hoadley had set off the so-called Bangorian controversy with a sermon in 1717, denying the secular authority of the Church and opposing High Church ideas of ecclesiastical politics.

488 l. 409. *nutation*. Nodding.

489 l. 416. *front*. Forehead, but also impudence.

l. 420. *bulks*. Framework projecting from the shopfront, supposed to be the appropriate sleeping-place for a destitute poet.

l. 424. *round-house*. Gaol.

l. 425. *sink*. Sewer.

l. 427. *neighbouring Fleet*. The Fleet Prison stood by the Ditch, just north of Ludgate; needy writers did in reality find themselves incarcerated there, including Defoe.

Book III

490 *virtue*. Supernatural power.

491 l. 4. *Cimmerian*. Cimmeria was a fabulous land on the outermost edge of the world, shrouded in perpetual mists.

l. 6. *refined from reason*. (1) Ostensibly, minds made specially acute by the power of reason; (2) ironically, minds too 'fine' to be penetrated by an idea.

l. 11. *chemist's flame*. In the alchemical still.

ll. 13–14. *on fancy's easy wing . . . th'Elysian shade*. A descent into the under-world, modelled particularly on *Aeneid*, Book VI; compare *Rape of the Lock*, iv. 11–88.

l. 18. *Castalia's streams*. The spring sacred to the Muses on Parnassus, but the whole line suggests the unwashed woman devotee of the Muses found elsewhere in P.

492 l. 26. *proof.* Invulnerability (as of armour).

494 l. 37. *band.* Collar.

l. 51. *thrid.* Thread.

495 l. 54. *owl's ivy.* The ivy of poetic honour inappropriately linked to the solemn fatuity of the owl.

l. 70. *burning line.* The Equator.

l. 74. *science.* Knowledge.

496 l. 85. *Hyperborean.* Belonging to the extreme north.

l. 87. *Maeotis.* The Sea of Azov adjoining the Crimea. The Tanais or Don enters the sea on its northern shore.

l. 91. *Alaric.* King of the Visigoths, who sacked Rome in AD 410.

l. 92. *Genseric.* King of the Vandals who pillaged Rome in AD 455.
Attila. King of the Huns (*c.* AD 410–453), known as 'scourge of God'.

l. 93. *Ostrogoths.* Eastern Goths.   *Latium.* Italy.

l. 94. *Visigoths.* Western Goths.

497 l. 105. *Livy.* Born at Patuvium (Padua).

l. 106. *Vigilius.* St Virgilius, the Irish-born Bishop of Salzburg (*c.* AD 700–784), condemned for asserting the existence of antipodean lands.

l. 107. *cirque.* The Colosseum.

l. 112. *Phidias . . . Apelles.* The greatest sculptor and painter, respectively, of antiquity.

l. 115. *linsey-wolsey.* Confused, indeterminate.

498 l. 131. *Berecynthia.* The *magna mater,* Cybele, a goddess of nature (see i. 1).

499 l. 142. *new Cibber.* The son of Colley, Theophilus Cibber.

l. 147. *gillhouse.* Tavern, drinking-house.

500 l. 160. *jacks.* Referring to the creaking of the turnspit used in cooking.

l. 162. *break Priscian's head.* Break the rules of grammar (proverbial: Tilley P595), from the fifth-century Latin grammarian.

l. 163. *larum.* 'Rush down with loud cries' (*OED*).

502 l. 179. *yon pair.* Probably Thomas Burnet and George Duckett.

503 l. 187. *myster wight.* Seemingly 'uncouth man'; P misunderstood an archaism he found in Spenser.

504 l. 195. *type.* Symbol.

l. 196. *pot.* Tankard.

506 l. 233. *sorcerer.* The passage refers to theatrical spectacles which became popular in the 1720s, esp. with John Thurmond's *Harlequin Dr Faustus* (1723) and John Rich's rival *Necromancer* in the same year. Theobald had

also contributed with a play called *The Rape of Proserpine* (1727), but Rich was the acknowledged master of the stage effects described here.

l. 243. *Cynthia*. Symbolizing the moon.

507   l. 254. *sarsenet*. A fine soft silk used for dresses.

l. 264. *Rides in the whirlwind, and directs the storm*. As P's note indicates, this is a parody of the famous line in Addison's *Campaign* (1705), l. 292.

508   l. 276. *foreseen*. By Settle as City Poet, when he had been in charge of the pageantry for the Lord Mayor's Day show. As Williams (*Pope's 'Dunciad'*, 40) points out, he was the last City Poet to carry out this role. See also P. Rogers, 'Pope, Settle, and the Fall of Troy', in *Literature and Popular Culture in Eighteenth-Century England* (Brighton, 1985), 87–101.

l. 278. *Bow's stupendous bells*. Bow bells, i.e. those of St Mary le Bow in Cheapside, traditionally defining the true 'city' by the range within which they could be heard.

509   l. 291. *carted*. Dragged through the street in a cart as a form of punishment.

l. 299. *booths*. The primitive theatrical stalls at a fair.

l. 301. *opera*. Italian opera had become highly fashionable in the 1720s: see Rogers, *Literature and Popular Culture*, 102–19.

510   l. 315. *Semele*. Semele was consumed by lightning when Jove made love to her, but her unborn child was rescued: this was Dionysus. Congreve had written the text for an opera on the subject in 1707; Handel's version of the same text was to follow in 1744, incorporating some lines from P's *Pastorals*.

l. 324. *Midas*. King Midas of Phrygia showed his folly by judging Pan superior to Apollo in a contest of flute-playing.

511   l. 327. *new Whitehall*. Whitehall Palace in fact was never rebuilt after being destroyed by fire in 1698. Cf. *Windsor Forest*, l. 380.

l. 328. *Boyle*. The Earl of Burlington.

512   l. 331. *Hibernian politics*. Swift had been preoccupied by Irish affairs since the time of the *Drapier's Letters* in 1724.

l. 336. *Westminster*. The school.

l. 337. *Isis' elders*. Oxford dons.

l. 340. *ivory gate*. According to Homer (*Odyssey*, Book XIX), there were two gates of dreams, one ivory (the source of false dreams) and one of horn (the source of true dreams). The passage from Virgil in the note renders the same idea.

513   *Book IV*

514   l. 3. *darkness visible*. See *Paradise Lost*, i. 63.

515   l. 9. *dog-star*. See *Epistle to Arbuthnot*, l. 3.

516   l. 18 note. The 'old adage' is often quoted as 'The higher the ape goes, the more he shows his tail' (Tilley A271).

l. 21. *science*. Learning.

l. 22. *wit*. Imagination, creativity.

517 l. 28. *Chicane in furs, and casuistry in lawn*. i.e. legal manœuvring by the ermine-clad judges, and sophistical reasoning by the lawn-clad bishops.

l. 31. *Mathesis*. Mathematics.

518 l. 41. *Thalia*. Muse of comedy.

519 l. 66. *Briareus*. One of the Hekatoncheires, sons of Uranus and Gaia, giants with a hundred hands.

521 l. 93. *bow the knee to Baal*. Proverbial from Rom. 11: 4, for worshipping false gods.

l. 96. *head*. A bust.

l. 103. *Narcissus*. Probably P's favourite target Lord Hervey, with his pallor and the fulsome praise he received from Dr Conyers Middleton.

l. 105. *Montalto*. Sir Thomas Hanmer, a high-bred politician who became Speaker of the Commons and then attempted a showy edition of Shakespeare in 1743–4. P knew in advance of the projected publication of this edition at Oxford, and ll. 115–18 seem to refer to the reception which it will be given by the obsequious university.

522 l. 121. *Medea*. She restored Jason's father Aeson to Youth by boiling him in a cauldron with magic herbs.

523 l. 139. *spectre*. That of the famous Dr Richard Busby (1605–95), the strict and long-serving Master of Westminster School.

l. 141. *beavered brow*. Wearing a hat of beaver fur.

l. 144. *Winton*. Winchester College.

525 l. 180. *Council*. Privy Council.

526 l. 187. *Cam and Isis*. Cambridge and Oxford universities.

527 l. 198. *Crousaz*. Jean-Pierre de Crousaz, Swiss philosopher who had attacked the *Essay on Man*.   *Burgersdyck*. Francis Burgersdyck, professor of philosophy at Leiden.

l. 200. *Margaret and Clare Hall*. i.e. St John's and Clare Colleges at Cambridge.

l. 206. *Walker*. Dr Richard Walker, Vice-Master to Bentley at Trinity.

528 l. 217. *like Saul*. 1 Sam. 9: 2: 'from his shoulders and upward [Saul] was higher than any of his people'.

l. 222. *to C or K*. There is a hidden joke here because P has converted Cibber's name from a soft c to a hard c.

529 l. 226. *Manilius*. Bentley had edited the minor Latin writer in 1739.   *Solinus*. Obscure Latin compiler of the third century.

l. 237. *Kuster*. Ludolph Kuster (1670–1716), whom Bentley had assisted in an edition of the compiler Suidas.   *Burman*. Pieter Burmann (1668–1741), Dutch scholar who published some of Bentley's emendations.   *Wasse*. Joseph Wasse (1672–1738), classical scholar, who also helped Kuster in his edition of Suidas.

l. 243. *head of many a house*. i.e. college principal in the universities.

532 l. 272. *governor*. Tutor on the Grand Tour. In P's own estimation, 'I think the travelling governor's speech one of the best things in my new addition to the *Dunciad*' (Spence, i. 150).

l. 278. *opening*. Beginning to cry.

l. 283. *sacred*. Protected.

533 l. 298. *Bourbon*. The King of France.

534 l. 322. *turned air*. Turned into nothing more than operatic arias.

l. 328. *not undone*. Not arrested, because once elected for a borough he would be immune from arrest for debt.

535 l. 347. *Annius*. Possibly based on the ninth Earl of Pembroke, known as the architect earl.

536 l. 364. *Mahomet*. Mohammed was fabled to have caused a pigeon to take grains from his ear, under the pretence that he was receiving messages from God.

l. 366. *Lares*. Domestic possessions.

l. 367. *Phoebe*. A goddess sometimes associated with Diana, and thus with chastity.

l. 369. *Otho*. See *Epistle to Mr Addison*, l. 44.

l. 370. *Niger*. Another Roman emperor who reigned only for a year, with consequently few coins from his reign surviving.

537 l. 374. *sistrum*. An ancient Egyptian musical instrument, used in the rituals of the Egyptian Club, whose doings P evidently followed. 'Mummius' may be a leading figure in the Society, such as the fourth Earl of Sandwich; alternatively he may be Dr John Woodward, the prominent antiquarian and collector.

l. 380. *Sallee rovers*. The notorious Moorish pirates who swept the waters of the Mediterranean and North Atlantic.

538 l. 398. *tribe*. Antiquarians and virtuosi who formed cabinets of curiosities (not unlike the contents of P's own grotto).

539 l. 421. *th'enamelled race*. Butterflies.

540 l. 452. *Wilkins' wings*. Dr John Wilkins (1614–72), the prominent Royal Society figure, whose projects included a voyage to the moon.

l. 459. *clerk*. Clergyman.

l. 460. *mystery*. Revelation.

541 l. 463. *implicit faith*. 'Faith in spiritual matters, not independently arrived at by the individual, but involved in or subordinate to the general belief of the Church' (*OED*).

542 l. 479. *local*. Special, peculiar, not universal.

l. 484. *as Lucretius drew*. i.e. a god with no concern for or relevance to human beings, as expressed in the poem *De rerum natura*.

543 l. 488. *Theocles*. P refers to Shaftesbury's *Characteristics* (1711), including a 'rhapsody' entitled *The Moralists* uttered by one Theocles.

544 l. 511. *Kent, so Berkeley*. Apparently suggesting that the courtiers the Duke of Kent and the Earl of Berkeley owed their posts to corruption involving a royal mistress.

l. 516. *Magus*. Oriental magician or sorcerer.

545 l. 520. *star*. Of knighthood.

l. 521. *feather*. Worn by Knights of the Garter in their headdress.

546 l. 549. *succinct in amice white*. Girdled in white linen resembling clerical garb. The passage parodies the transubstantiation of the host during the Eucharist.

547 l. 561. *crowds undone*. By the South Sea Bubble, which Knight helped to bring about as cashier of the Company.

549 l. 585. *cap and switch*. Belonging to a jockey ('switch' is a whip).

l. 586. *staff and pumps*. Belonging to running footmen.

l. 592. *cricket*. Prominent peers involved in the game at this time were Lord Sandwich, the Duke of Dorset, and the Duke of Bedford.

l. 593. *Bishop*. Based on William Talbot, Bishop of Durham.

l. 602. *first ministers*. Prime Ministers, and esp. Walpole.

l. 603. *three estates*. Lords spiritual, lords temporal, and Commons.

550 l. 609. *Hall*. Westminster Hall, centre of the judicial system.

l. 610. *Convocation*. The assembly of clergy which had been prorogued in 1717 and did not meet for another century.

l. 614. *Palinurus*. The helmsman of Aeneas, who fell into the ocean after dropping asleep (*Aeneid*, Books V–VI). Here representing Walpole as a leader not alert to the threat posed by foreign powers.

552 l. 635. *Medea*. As a priestess of Hecate she had supernatural powers and was able to bring down the constellations from the sky.

l. 637. *Argus' eyes by Hermes' wand oppressed*. Hermes slew Argus, the monster with a hundred eyes, with the help of his caduceus.

553 l. 656. *buries all*. The reading had been 'covers all' in the first version of the poem, where the conclusion of Book III had contained a passage

(ll. 329–56), largely corresponding to iv. 626–56 in the revised version. This is the only portion of the new book which had existed in the earlier state of the poem from 1728 onwards.

554 *Appendices*

Preface

1727. The year 1727 in the heading is a mistake for 1728.

555 *Orcades.* Orkneys.

557 *Lusiad.* P originally included Voltaire's recent epic of French history, the *Henriade* (1728), but omitted this when reprinting the preface.

Mr T., Mr E., Sir R.B. Theobald, Eusden, and Blackmore.

Advertisement

558 *Boileau.* In his *Satires* and *Epîtres* in imitation of Horace.

Vida. Marco Girolamo Vida (1480–1566), neo-Latin poet (see *Essay on Criticism*, l. 705), whose works included a mock-heroic on chess, *Scacchia ludus* (1527), translated into English 1736, as well as the *Art of Poetry* mentioned by P.

Fracastorius. Girolamo Fracastoro (1478–1553), Italian humanist and poet, author of the poem *Syphilis* (1530), originating this term, and utilizing many Virgilian allusions.

559 *The Guardian*

P chose to reprint here the most famous of his *Guardian* pieces (see also p. 594 above). Thomas Tickell, an acolyte of Addison, had written five papers in the *Guardian* containing fulsome praise of the limp pastorals of Ambrose Philips. He paid no attention to P's *Pastorals*, published together with those of Philips in 1709. P's response, which appeared anonymously, carries Tickell's praise to further absurdity.

nobis. Virgil, *Eclogues*, vii. 2, 70: 'Corydon and Thyrsis had driven their flocks together into one group. . . . From that time it is "Corydon, Corydon" with us.'

author. That is, P.

Heinsius. Daniel Heinsius (1580–1655), a major Dutch classical scholar.

Salmasius. Claudius Salmasius or Claude de Saumaise (1588–1653), eminent French Huguenot scholar.

Rapin. René Rapin (1621–87), one of the most important critics of the age.

560 *Ennius.* Quintus Ennius (239–169 BC), the early Roman poet.

Doric. From the Greek region of Doris, here meaning broad and uncouth in dialect.

Strada. Famianus Strada (1572–1649), Italian poet.

sensitive life. i.e. that of creatures capable of perceiving impressions.

wolves in England. Wolves had disappeared from England at least two hundred years earlier.

562 *feet and eyes.* See *Pastorals*, 'Spring', ll. 53–60.

in beauteous order lie. See *Pastorals*, 'Spring', ll. 35–40.

564 *one of his pastorals.* Spenser, *Shepheardes Calendar*, 'September', ll. 1–4.

565 *Moschus and Bion.* Greek pastoral poets of the second century BC, the former possibly the pupil and elegist of the latter.

Of the Poet Laureate

P draws on the *Elogia doctorum virorum* (1557) by Paulus Jovius.

566 *Leo X.* Pope 1513–21, patron of the arts and inspiration behind the decoration of the Sistine Chapel.

567 *rural genius.* Stephen Duck.

568 *cabbage.* Pieces of cloth cut out by tailors and kept for their own use, a form of licensed pilfering.

Anstis. The herald John Anstis.

Caesar in Egypt. 'For his *Caesar in Egypt* (1724) the stage carpenter had made pasteboard swans to swim on an imaginary Nile. When drawn across the stage, they occasioned some ridicule among the audience' (*TE*, v. 416).

569 *our society.* The corporation of Grub Street, celebrated in the poem and in *Peri Bathous*.

572 *Epitaph on Bounce.* One of P's last poems, if not the very last. He wrote to Lord Orrery on 10 April 1744, enquiring about the death of Bounce, who had been consigned to the care of Orrery at Marston, Somerset, in 1742. The letter proceeded: 'I doubt not how much Bounce was lamented. They might say as the Athenians did to Arcite, in Chaucer, "Ah, Arcite! gentle knight! why wouldst thou die, / When thou hadst gold enough, and Emily?" [*Knight's Tale*, ll. 1977–8, misquoted]' (*Corr.* iv. 517), followed by the epigram printed here. For P's successive dogs named Bounce, see Ault, 337–50. P died seven weeks after the date of this letter.

573 *Conversations with Joseph Spence.* Extracts from the record of P's conversation, taken by his friend Revd Joseph Spence (1699–1768). Spence came to the notice of the poet after publishing *An Essay on Pope's Odyssey* (1726), and was elected Professor of Poetry at Oxford in 1728 with P's help. The main series of conversations took place between 1728 and P's death; Spence spent much time with the poet in his last days. The extracts here are drawn from the edition of Spence's *Observations, Anecdotes and Characters of Books*

and Men by J. M. Osborn (1966), abbreviated in other references as 'Spence'.

Extract (l) refers to an occasion just two weeks before P's death, when he was visited by George Lyttelton (see Biographical Index). His doctor had told P that he was breathing well and that his pulse was good, together with 'several other encouraging things'. 'Dying of a hundred good symptoms' picks up a proverbial usage found in Swift's *Conduct of the Allies*.

FURTHER READING

REFERENCE

R. H. Griffith, *Alexander Pope: A Bibliography* (2 vols.; Austin, Tex., 1922–7).
J. V. Guerinot, *Pamphlet Attacks on Alexander Pope, 1711–1744: A Descriptive Bibliography* (London, 1969).

EDITIONS

J. Butt *et al.* (eds.), *The Twickenham Edition of the Poems of Alexander Pope* (11 vols.; London, 1939–69).
W. Elwin and W. J. Courthope (eds.), *The Works of Alexander Pope* (10 vols.; London, 1871–89).
B. A. Goldgar (ed.), *The Literary Criticism of Alexander Pope* (Lincoln, Nebr., 1965).
P. Hammond (ed.), *Selected Prose* (Cambridge, 1987).
C. Kerby-Miller (ed.), *Memoirs of the Life of Martinus Scriblerus* (New Haven, Conn., 1950; repr. Oxford, 1989).
The Prose Works of Alexander Pope, vol. i, ed. N. Ault (Oxford, 1936); vol. ii, ed. R. Cowler (Oxford, 1986).
G. Sherburn (ed.), *The Correspondence of Alexander Pope* (5 vols.; Oxford, 1956).
H. Erskine-Hill (ed.), *Selected Letters* (Oxford, 2000).

Editions of individual poems include: *The Rape Observ'd*, ed. C. Tracy (Toronto, 1974), a text of *The Rape of the Lock* with many contemporary illustrations; *The Iliad*, ed. S. Shankman (London, 1996); and *The Dunciad in Four Books*, ed. V. Rumbold (Harlow, 1999).

BIOGRAPHY

N. Ault, *New Light on Pope* (London, 1949).
M. Mack, *Alexander Pope: A Life* (London, 1985).
M. H. Nicolson and G. S. Rousseau, *This Long Disease, My Life* (Princeton, NJ, 1968).
G. Sherburn, *The Early Career of Alexander Pope* (Oxford, 1934).
J. Spence, *Observations, Anecdotes, and Characters of Books and Men*, ed. J. M. Osborn (2 vols.; Oxford, 1966).

CRITICISM

Aids to Study

P. Baines, *The Complete Critical Guide to Alexander Pope* (London, 2000).

J. Barnard (ed.), *Pope: The Critical Heritage* (London, 1973).

F. W. Bateson and N. A. Joukovsky (eds.), *Pope: A Critical Anthology* (Harmondsworth, 1971).

R. Berry, *A Pope Chronology* (Basingstoke, 1988).

P. Dixon (ed.), *Writers and their Background: Alexander Pope* (London, 1972).

M. Mack (ed.), *Essential Articles for the Study of Alexander Pope* (Hamden, Conn., 1968).

—— (ed.), *The Last and Greatest Art: Some Unpublished Poetical Manuscripts of Alexander Pope* (Newark, Del., 1984).

—— and J. A. Winn (eds.), *Pope: Recent Essays* (Hamden, Conn., 1980).

P. Rogers, *The Alexander Pope Encyclopedia* (Westport, Conn., 2004).

General Criticism

R. A. Brower, *Alexander Pope: The Poetry of Allusion* (Oxford, 1959).

L. Damrosch, *The Imaginative World of Alexander Pope* (Berkeley and Los Angeles, 1987).

H. Deutsch, *Resemblance and Disgrace: Alexander Pope and the Deformation of Culture* (Cambridge, Mass., 1996).

H. Erskine-Hill, *The Social Milieu of Alexander Pope* (London, 1985).

—— and A. Smith (eds.), *The Art of Alexander Pope* (London, 1979).

—— (ed.), *Pope: World and Word* (Oxford, 1998).

D. Fairer, *Pope's Imagination* (Manchester, 1984).

D. Griffin, *Alexander Pope: The Poet in the Poems* (Princeton, NJ, 1978).

B. Hammond (ed.), *Pope* (Harlow, 1996).

M. Mack, *The Garden and the City* (Toronto, 1969).

—— *Collected in Himself: Essays Critical, Biographical and Bibliographical on Pope and some of his Contemporaries* (London, 1982).

D. Morris, *Alexander Pope: The Genius of Sense* (Cambridge, Mass., 1984).

C. Nicholson (ed.), *Alexander Pope: Essays for the Tercentenary* (Aberdeen, 1988).

J. Noggle, *The Skeptical Sublime: Aesthetic Ideology in Pope and the Tory Satirists* (Oxford, 2001).

P. Rogers, *Essays on Pope* (Cambridge, 1994).

G. S. Rousseau and P. Rogers (eds.), *The Enduring Monument: Alexander Pope Tercentenary Essays* (Cambridge, 1988).

H. Weinbrot, *Alexander Pope and the Traditions of Formal Verse Satire* (Princeton, NJ, 1982).

Style

J. A. Jones, *Pope's Couplet Art* (Athens, Oh., 1969).

P. M. Spacks, *An Argument of Images: The Poetry of Alexander Pope* (Cambridge, Mass., 1971).

G. Tillotson, *On the Poetry of Pope*, 2nd edn. (Oxford, 1950).

Feminist Approaches

C. Fabricant, 'Binding and Dressing Nature's Loose Tresses', *Studies in Eighteenth-Century Culture*, 8 (1979), 109–35.

C. Knellwolf, *A Contradiction Still: Representations of Women in the Poetry of Alexander Pope* (Manchester, 1998).

E. Pollak, *The Poetics of Sexual Myth: Gender and Ideology in the Poetry of Swift and Pope* (Chicago, 1985).

V. Rumbold, *Women's Place in Pope's World* (Cambridge, 1989).

Special Topics

M. Batey, *Alexander Pope: The Poet and the Landscape* (London, 1999).

M. R. Brownell, *Alexander Pope and the Arts of Georgian England* (Oxford, 1978).

D. Foxon, *Pope and the Early Eighteenth-Century Book Trade*, ed. J. McLaverty (Oxford, 1991).

J. McLaverty, *Pope, Print, and Meaning* (Oxford, 2001).

P. Martin, *Pursuing Innocent Pleasures: The Gardening World of Alexander Pope* (Hamden, Conn., 1983).

W. K. Wimsatt, *The Portraits of Alexander Pope* (New Haven, Conn., 1965).

Criticism of Particular Works

J. S. Cunningham, *Pope: The Rape of the Lock* (London, 1961).

R. Halsband, *The Rape of the Lock and its Illustrations, 1714–1896* (Oxford, 1980).

W. Kinsley (ed.), *Contexts 2: The Rape of the Lock* (Hamden, Conn., 1979).

P. Rogers, *Pope and the Destiny of the Stuarts: History, Politics, and Mythology in the Age of Queen Anne* (Oxford, 2005).

—— *The Symbolic Design of Windsor-Forest: Iconography, Pageant, and Prophecy in Pope's Early Work* (Newark, Del., 2004).

D. Brooks-Davies, *Pope's 'Dunciad' and the Queen of the Night* (Manchester, 1985).

H. Erskine-Hill, *Pope: The Dunciad* (London, 1977).

E. Jones, 'Pope and Dullness', *Proceedings of the British Academy*, 54 (1969), 232–63.

J. E. Sitter, *The Poetry of Pope's 'Dunciad'* (Minneapolis, 1971).

A. Williams, *Pope's 'Dunciad': A Study of its Meaning* (London, 1955).

B. S. Hammond, *Pope and Bolingbroke* (Columbia, Mo., 1984).

M. Leranbaum, *Alexander Pope's 'Opus Magnum' 1729–1744* (Oxford, 1977), esp. for the *Essay on Man*.

A. D. Nuttall, *Pope's 'Essay on Man'* (London, 1984).

E. R. Wasserman, *Pope's 'Epistle to Bathurst': A Critical Reading* (Baltimore, 1960).

J. M. Aden, *Something like Horace* (Nashville, Tenn., 1969).

P. Dixon, *The World of Pope's Satires* (London, 1968).

M. Goldstein, *Pope and the Augustan Stage* (Stanford, Calif., 1958).

S. Shankman, *Pope's 'Iliad': Homer in the Age of Reason* (Princeton, NJ, 1983).

F. Stack, *Pope and Horace* (Cambridge, 1985).

J. A. Winn, *A Window in the Bosom: The Letters of Alexander Pope* (Hamden, Conn., 1977).

BACKGROUND

P. Baines and P. Rogers, *Edmund Curll, Bookseller* (Oxford, 2006).

H. Erskine-Hill, *The Poetry of Opposition and Revolution: Dryden to Wordsworth* (Oxford, 1996).

C. Gerrard, *The Patriot Opposition to Walpole: Politics, Poetry, and National Myth, 1725–1742* (Oxford, 1994).

B. Hammond, *Professional Imaginative Writing in England, 1670–1740: 'Hackney for Bread'* (Oxford, 1997).

A. R. Humphreys, *The Augustan World* (London, 1954).

A. Ingram, *Intricate Laughter in the Satire of Swift and Pope* (Basingstoke, 1986).

C. Ingrassia, *Authorship, Commerce, and Gender in Early Eighteenth-Century England: A Culture of Paper Credit* (Cambridge, 1998).

I. Kramnick, *Bolingbroke and his Circle: The Politics of Nostalgia* (Cambridge, Mass., 1968).

C. Nicholson, *Writing and the Rise of Finance: Capital Satires of the Early Eighteenth Century* (Cambridge, 1994).

C. Rawson, *Order from Confusion Sprung* (London, 1985).

P. Rogers, *Grub Street: Studies in a Subculture* (London, 1972).

—— *Literature and Popular Culture in Eighteenth-Century England* (Brighton, 1985).

E. P. Thompson, *Whigs and Hunters* (London, 1975).

D. Todd, *Imagining Monsters: Miscreations of the Self in Eighteenth-Century England* (Chicago, 1995).

H. D. Weinbrot, *The Formal Strain: Studies in Augustan Imitation and Satire* (Chicago, 1969).

BIOGRAPHICAL INDEX

ADDISON, JOSEPH (1672–1719) Essayist, dramatist, and politician. On good terms with P during the period of the *Spectator*, but later their relationship cooled as Addison supported a rival translation of Homer. Depicted as Atticus in the *Epistle to Arbuthnot*.

ALLEN, RALPH (1693–1764) Philanthropist, postal reformer, and one of the creators of Bath. Patron of Fielding. P became a close friend and spent much time in his later years at Allen's home, Prior Park.

ANNE, QUEEN (1665–1714) The last Stuart monarch (1702–14), daughter of James II; a strong supporter of the Church and esp. High Church interests.

ANSTIS, JOHN (1669–1744) Herald; Garter King of Arms 1718. An MP with Jacobite leanings, he was also connected with P's patron George Granville (q.v.).

ARBUTHNOT, JOHN (1667–1735) Doctor and writer, a friend of Swift and member of the Scriblerus group. Physician to Queen Anne. His works range from the political satire *John Bull* to studies in the history of science. One of P's closest friends and literary collaborators.

ARGYLL, JOHN CAMPBELL, Duke of (1678–1743). Former soldier and Hanoverian politician, who took a prominent part in suppressing the Jacobite rising of 1715. In 1738 he turned decisively against Walpole and threw his considerable patronage and power behind the Opposition.

ARNALL, WILLIAM (*c.*1700–36) Journalist. A protégé of Sir William Yonge, he wrote regularly for Walpole and was the most highly paid member of the Government's propagandists.

ATTERBURY, FRANCIS (1662–1732) Churchman. Dean of Christ Church, Oxford, and then in 1713 Bishop of Rochester and Dean of Westminster. A strong Tory, he was at the centre of the alleged Jacobite plot in 1723, which led to his arrest, his trial before the House of Lords (P appearing as a witness), and banishment to France. Regarded by P as a symbol of the old values suppressed under Walpole.

BARNARD, Sir JOHN (1685–1764) Merchant, MP for the City of London, alderman, and Lord Mayor. An independent member who opposed Walpole on financial measures, including the Excise Bill, and led the attack on the Charitable Corporation frauds. A High Churchman, although a Whig in politics.

BATHURST, ALLEN, Lord (1684–1775) One of the twelve peers created in 1712 to secure a Tory majority. His park at Cirencester was landscaped with the advice of P. Created an earl in 1772; his son became Lord Chancellor.

BEHN, APHRA (1640–89) Dramatist and miscellaneous writer; author of important early works of fiction, including the celebrated *Oroonoko* (1688).

Some of her plays, especially *The Rover* (1677), retained popularity into the eighteenth century, while her wide corpus of poetry would have been known to P. She died too soon for any personal contact to be possible, and P probably relied on vague folk-memory for any view he had of her.

BENSON, MARTIN (1689–1752) Churchman. Bishop of Gloucester, 1735. A respected and learned man, he was promoted by Lord Chancellor Talbot (q.v.) and befriended the latter's daughter Catherine, a prominent member of the bluestocking group.

BENSON, WILLIAM (1682–1754) Politician. He succeeded Wren as Surveyor-General, but revealed his incompetence by his blunder over the state of the House of Lords (see *Dunciad*, iii. 325). A champion of Milton, his ventures into amateur architecture included Wilbury House, he excited derision in more than one sphere; but his strong Whig sentiments account for some of the hostility expressed by P and his friends.

BENTLEY, RICHARD (1662–1742) Classical scholar. Master of Trinity College, Cambridge, 1700. He had led the assault on the Ancients in the Battle of the Books and incurred Swift's dislike from that moment. He produced an important edition of Horace which P consulted, but his edition of Milton (1732), suggesting numerous corruptions in the standard text, placed him firmly among the pedantic wordchoppers attacked in *The Dunciad*.

BERKELEY, GEORGE (*c*.1685–1753) Philosopher; Bishop of Cloyne 1734. A friend of Swift who met P around 1713 and maintained cordial, if not esp. close, relations thereafter.

BETHEL, HUGH (1689–1747) MP and country gentleman, among the closest of P's friends, a member of the extended Burlington circle in Yorkshire.

BETTERTON, THOMAS (*c*.1635–1710) Actor. The greatest tragedian of the Restoration stage; well known to P as a boy, and painted by the younger man.

BLACKBURNE, LANCELOT (1658–1743) Churchman. Archbishop of York, 1724. His reputation was that of a man of pleasure and as a womanizer.

BLACKMORE, Sir RICHARD (1654–1729) Poet and physician, and royal physician to both William III and Anne. Published a succession of wordy epics and became a target for the wits before P began to single out his work for special ridicule in *Peri Bathous*.

BLOUNT, MARTHA (1690–1763) and TERESA (1688–1759) The Blount sisters were Catholic neighbours of P, who came to know them as a boy. He originally seems to have felt some attraction towards Teresa, but he grew disturbed by her casual ways, and for the last twenty-five years of his life it was Martha who was his closest woman friend and main legatee.

BLUNT, Sir JOHN (1667–1733) Director of the South Sea Company and projector, considered by many the leading architect of the South Sea disaster. Most of his large financial estate was confiscated after a parliamentary inquiry into the operations of the company.

BOLINGBROKE, HENRY ST JOHN, Viscount (1678–1751) Politician, philosopher, and writer. P came to know him when he was Secretary of State in the Tory administration of 1710–14. He was attainted after the Hanoverian accession and fled to the Pretender's court. Given a limited pardon in 1723, he returned to England and led the opposition to Walpole, but retired again in disappointment in 1735. His role in forming P's mind, esp. as this affects the *Essay on Man*, is a matter of dispute, but he certainly enjoyed immense respect from P.

BOND, DENIS (1676–1747) Lawyer, landowner, and MP, expelled from the House in 1732 for corruption, and soon in trouble again as a director of the fraudulent Charitable Corporation. A representative figure for P, rather than an immediate object of personal dislike.

BOOTH, BARTON (1681–1733) Actor. His great success came with the title role in Addison's *Cato* (1713); later joint manager of Drury Lane with Cibber and Wilks (q.v.).

BOYER, ABEL (1667–1729) Journalist, lexicographer, and historian. A French *émigré* and a strong Whig: 'the mild reference to him in the *Dunciad* hardly suggests that Pope had any personal grievance' (*TE*, v. 430).

BOYLE, HENRY, Lord CARLETON (*c.*1672–1725) Whig politician who held high office between 1699 and 1710, and remained a loyal if moderate party man under George I. P had no strong personal links, though Carleton subscribed to the *Iliad* and the *Odyssey*.

BREVAL, JOHN DURANT (*c.*1680–1738) Minor poet and dramatist who earned his niche in *The Dunciad* by severe satires on P and the other Scriblerians.

BROOME, WILLIAM (1689–1745) Clergyman, poet, and translator. Helped P on the version of the *Iliad* and then took part in the collaborative translation of the *Odyssey*. After this the relations of the two men cooled, and Broome found himself in *Peri Bathous* and the original *Dunciad*.

BROWN, THOMAS (1663–1704) Prolific poet and satirist who joined in the battle of the wits against Blackmore, and was one of the most highly visible figures in popular literature in P's youth.

BUCKINGHAM, JOHN SHEFFIELD, Duke of (1648–1721) Politician and poet whose works were edited by P in 1723. One of the last surviving links with Restoration culture and the world of Dryden.

BUDGELL, EUSTACE (1686–1737) Writer and functionary in Ireland, who had contributed essays to the *Spectator*. Became embroiled in a controversy surrounding the will of Tindal (q.v.) and 'his later life was one long litigation' (*TE*, v. 432). Committed suicide by throwing himself into the Thames.

BURLINGTON, RICHARD BOYLE, Earl of (1695–1753) Architect and patron, the 'Apollo of the Arts'. Promoter of the Palladian movement, connoisseur, supporter of artists like Handel and Gay, and a lukewarm Whig politician. P became friendly with the Earl and Countess in the second half of his life.

BURNET, THOMAS (1694–1753) Lawyer (later judge) and pamphleteer. A son of the great Bishop Burnet. A Whig who emerged from the Addison circle to launch a number of attacks on P, sometimes in collaboration with George Duckett (q.v.). Grew respectable with middle age.

CAROLINE, QUEEN (1683–1737) Daughter of the Margrave of Anspach; married Prince of Hanover (later George II), 1705, and succeeded with him to English throne, 1727. A patron of free-thinking philosophers and Low-Church theologians, as well as the hapless thresher poet Duck (q.v.). Like Swift, P seems to have found her more interesting, if not more intellectually acceptable, than her husband.

CARYLL, JOHN (1667–1736) Country gentleman from an old Catholic family, a lifelong friend of P and one of his most regular correspondents. Like most of his family, held Jacobite sympathies, but less ready than others in expressing these actively.

CENTLIVRE, SUSANNAH (c.1670–1723) Dramatist, with a string of successful plays in the first years of the century. A Whig who frequented a circle of writers mostly hostile to P, she produced perhaps one or two satires on P (though perhaps none at all) and earned a brief retort from the poet.

CHANDOS, JAMES BRYDGES, Duke of (1673–1744) Grandee, artistic patron and entrepreneur. He amassed his money as Paymaster of the Forces under Anne, and spent it on a variety of projects, including his sumptuous mansion, Canons, near Edgware, where he employed Handel. Popularly supposed to be the 'Timon' of the *Epistle to Burlington*; though this was strongly denied by P. Their relations were never cordial from this time. Chandos lived in a princely style and, in fairness, bestowed considerable largesse on the world of arts.

CHARTERIS, FRANCIS (1675–1732) Rake, profligate, convicted rapist, gambler, adventurer, usurer, pimp, and (if contemporary attacks are to be believed) much else. The attacks of P, Arbuthnot, Swift, Fielding, and others depict him as a heartless rogue, but his connection with Walpole (he tried unsuccessfully to gain a seat in Parliament) may have contributed. His escape from punishment for rape led to the suspicion that the ministry had screened him.

CHESELDEN, WILLIAM (1688–1752) Surgeon. He became surgeon to the Queen in 1727, and was famous both for his dexterity in cutting for the stone and for his skill in operations for cataracts. A friend and professional advisor to P in the poet's last tears.

CHESTERFIELD, PHILIP DORMER STANHOPE, Earl of (1694–1773) The famous letter-writer, known in his own day as a diplomat and politician. In P's later years he was a leading figure in the Opposition to Walpole; after P's death he entered the Pelham ministry and became secretary of state.

CIBBER, COLLEY (1671–1757) Dramatist and actor. A specialist in comic roles, esp. as the fop, Cibber achieved fame as a playwright with *Love's Last Shift* (1696) and *The Careless Husband* (1704), as well as a much-performed adaptation of Shakespeare's *Richard III*. Hostilities with P began around 1717, but Cibber has only a minor presence in *Peri Bathous* and the first *Dunciad*. It was Cibber's elevation to the post of Poet Laureate in 1730, despite the lack of any poetic talent, and his gossipy *Apology* for his own life (1740), which fitted him for the role of king of the dunces in the later *Dunciad*. For the first time Cibber was provoked by P's onslaughts, and their combat was at its most fierce in the last two years of P's life.

CIBBER, THEOPHILUS (1703–58) Actor and dramatist. The son of Colley, he was 'an unattractive replica of his father' (*TE*, v. 434), though possessed of less ability as actor, playwright, or manager. He would probably have escaped the attentions of P but for his parentage, though his share in a notorious criminal conversation suit concerning his wife, the singer Susanna Arne, would have provided the poet with good copy if he had chosen to use it.

CLARKE, SAMUEL. (1675–1729) Theologian. He came to fame with his Boyle lectures in 1705–6 and then stood at the head of latitudinarian thought. Corresponded with Leibniz. Rector of St James's, Piccadilly, 1709. P enlisted him chiefly as a protégé of Queen Caroline.

CLELAND, WILLIAM (*c.*1674–1714) An obscure figure, who had been a soldier and then a commissioner for the land tax. The origins of his friendship with P are hard to piece together. P addressed to him a fragmentary poem which eventually turned into the *Epistle to Arbuthnot*. He was perhaps chosen as a front-man for *The Dunciad* precisely because P's enemies could not assail this anonymous figure with any confidence. Father of the novelist John Cleland.

COBHAM, RICHARD TEMPLE, Viscount (1675–1749) Soldier and politician. In the mid 1730s he became leader of the most important group of the Opposition to Walpole, including William Pitt and George Lyttelton (q.v.). His house at Stowe became a centre for Opposition feeling, and its gardens a shrine of 'Patriot' virtue, containing tributes to classical heroes and British worthies. P played a small part in the making of this famous landscape garden, to which Bridgeman, Vanbrugh, Kent, Gibbs, and eventually Capability Brown contributed. The setting was celebrated by Thomson and other poets.

CONCANEN, MATTHEW (1704–49) Miscellaneous writer, who came from Ireland to join the circle of Theobald. One of P's open critics, he also incurred the dislike of Swift. Appointed Attorney-General of Jamaica in 1732. P's note, stating that he was 'surprisingly promoted to administer justice and law', implies that he had been enjoying ministerial support all along.

CONGREVE, WILLIAM (1670–1729) Dramatist. His plays had all been written by the time that P, as a young man, met him and received a compliment on the *Pastorals*. P ostentatiously dedicated the *Iliad* to Congreve in 1720, where it would have been usual to select a powerful nobleman. Others such as Voltaire may have seen Congreve as worldly and idle; P respected him much more, not least for the direct link with Dryden.

CONINGSBY, THOMAS, Earl (1656–1729) Whig politician, with a particular family grudge against the Harleys; he was one of the managers of the impeachment of the Earl of Oxford. Hotheaded, litigious, and unbalanced, he was removed from the Privy Council in 1724 after wild acts of revenge against his enemies in Herefordshire.

COOKE, THOMAS (1703–56) Poet and translator. Published several attacks on P, the best known among them being *The Battle of the Poets* (revised 1729). A friend of Theobald, Moore Smythe, and Concanen, though more talented than the two latter: his version of Hesiod (1728) was standard for many years.

COWPER, WILLIAM, Earl (*c.*1664–1723) Lawyer and statesman. Lord Keeper and then Lord Chancellor under Anne; presided at the trial of Dr Sacheverell, 1710. Originally a strong Whig who opposed Bolingbroke and again served as Lord Chancellor after the accession of George I, he was suspected of Jacobite intrigues at the end of his life.

CRAGGS, JAMES, jun. (1686–1721) Politician. Secretary of State, 1718. Seriously implicated in the South Sea scandal (he had given shares in the company to P); his father, even more deeply embroiled, committed suicide a month after the sudden death of Craggs, jun. from smallpox. Much of the Craggs wealth survived the heavy confiscations imposed on other guilty men by Parliament in the aftermath of the Bubble. P remained loyal to the memory of one who, differently viewed, could be seen as a prime case of opportunistic political manœuvring.

CURLL, EDMUND (1683–1747) Bookseller. The most notorious publisher of his day, he specialized in scandalous memoirs, instant biographies of the famous dead, pirated and purloined editions of major writers, obscene and *risqué* items, and other disreputable productions (although he did publish some serious works of antiquarian and legal interest). A pioneer of creative advertising and publicity. His battles with P began in 1714 and extended even beyond the poet's death, with an unpleasant biography (1745) by 'William Ayre', who might well have been Curll himself. P needed Curll as a gadfly, satiric catalyst, and convenient enemy; but his masterpiece of literary strategy was to inveigle Curll into publishing his letters (1735), thus providing the opportunity for an 'authorized' version by P himself.

DEFOE, DANIEL (1660–1731) Novelist and writer on almost every topic. P gave Spence a famous verdict: 'Defoe wrote a vast many things; and none bad, though none excellent. There's something good in all he has writ' (Spence, i. 213). This was perceptive, since the extent of Defoe's writing was hard to establish (almost all was anonymous), and the qualities which would lift him above duncehood in the eyes of posterity were not apparent to most contemporaries.

DELAWARE or DE LA WARR, JOHN WEST, Earl of (1693–1766) Politician. Held a number of positions at court under Walpole. For P, simply a copy-book Whig, a servile administrator, and a possessor of 'the white staff and red ribbon' of the Garter, with no other claim to attention.

DENNIS, JOHN (1657–1734) Critic and dramatist. First provoked by P as a result of the *Essay on Criticism*, and thereafter engaged in regular bouts with the poet. P's feelings softened a little, despite references in *Peri Bathous* and

The Dunciad, and he was prepared to write a prologue for a benefit performance on behalf of Dennis, who had fallen on hard times. Dennis can be seen as the first true professional critic, and despite his vagaries he was one of the dunces who made substantive responses to the content of P's writing.

DODINGTON, GEORGE BUBB (1691–1762) Politician and patron of literature. Allied in turn to the Walpole ministry and to the faction of the Opposition centred on the Prince of Wales (to disregard the allegiances he formed after P's death). Dodington's comic potential started with his name and his portly appearance, but it extended to his quest for influence and his cultivation of the role of Maecenas, the aspect which attracted P's notice.

DOVER, THOMAS (1660–1742) Physician, or some would have it quack. Known as the 'Quicksilver doctor' for his reliance on mercury as a specific. His treatment by sweating (an opium-based drug known as Dover's powder) was long in use for feverish illness. He embarked on a privateering expedition in 1708 and was one of those who rescued Alexander Selkirk from Juan Fernandez.

DUCK, STEPHEN (1705–56) The thresher poet. An agricultural labourer in Wiltshire, he was discovered and brought to London; his life written by P's friend Joseph Spence. Appointed keeper of Merlin's Cave at Richmond by Queen Caroline, 1735. Ordained in 1746; finally drowned himself in a bout of depression. P seems to have thought him personally worthy but poetically untalented.

DUCKETT, GEORGE (1684–1732) A minor politician who made his faint impress on history chiefly by attacking P in some light-hearted squibs in collaboration with his friend Thomas Burnet (q.v.).

DUNTON, JOHN (1659–1733) Eccentric author and bookseller, who had helped to pioneer the developing field of popular journalism with the *Athenian Mercury* (to which Swift contributed in the 1690s). As time went on he became totally unhinged, and his attacks on P incorporated the beams of a larger lunacy.

DURFEY, THOMAS (1653–1723) Poet and songwriter, whose ditties were amongst the most popular of their time. As observed in *TE*, v. 439, 'Durfey had been a recognized butt of the wits from Dryden's day, and was no doubt introduced into the *Dunciad* for that reason alone.'

EUSDEN, LAURENCE (1688–1730) Clergyman and poet, whose elevation to the post of Poet Laureate in 1718 caused outrage and incredulity. A confirmed drinker, he otherwise offered fewer handles to P than his successor Colley Cibber.

FORTESCUE, WILLIAM (1687–1749) Lawyer and politician. He had been private secretary to Walpole and remained loyal to the ministry, despite the blandishments of P, to emerge with important legal posts culminating in the high office of Master of the Rolls in 1741. Fortescue advised P on legal matters and their friendship easily withstood Fortescue's rise to eminence in the very world which P assaulted in his satire.

FREDERICK, Prince of Wales (1707–51) Followed the approved Hanoverian pattern by quarrelling bitterly with his father, George II. His reversionary prospects attracted many Opposition politicians, though he was ultimately to die several years before his father. He sought out P at the time of his leadership of the Patriot group, but P never became an active Opposition campaigner outside the text of his poetry.

GAGE, JOSEPH (*c.*1677–1753) Adventurer, labelled in *DNB* 'grandee of Spain'. He came from a Catholic family and became a commander of the Spanish army, after fleeing from losses in the Mississippi scheme. His bizarre attempts to buy foreign crowns and his marriage to a member of the noble Herbert family are noted in the *Epistle to Bathurst*, l. 130.

GARTH, Sir SAMUEL (1661–1719) Physician and poet. He came to prominence with his satire on a medical dispute, *The Dispensary* (1699), a major influence on *The Rape of the Lock*. Supported P's early work on the *Pastorals*. A Whig, member of the Kit Cat Club, and later physician to George I, his good nature and literary talent endeared him to P, who contributed to the translation of Ovid's *Metamorphoses* which Garth edited in 1717.

GAY, JOHN (1685–1732) Poet and dramatist. Soon after P met Gay around 1711, they were fellow members of the Scriblerus Club, and ever afterwards firm friends. They collaborated in satiric drama and co-authored Scriblerian squibs. Gay's huge success with his *Fables* (1727, 1738) and *The Beggar's Opera* came too late to rescue him from dependence, esp. as a sequel to the opera, entitled *Polly*, was banned by the court. P wrote a famous epitaph for his friend.

GEORGE II (1683–1760) King of England from 1727. Regarded by P as an uncultivated interloper, preoccupied by his Hanoverian domain, and easily manipulated by his wife and Walpole. Assailed in *The Dunciad* as 'Dunce the second' succeeding Dunce the first; Opposition hostility reflects in part disappointment that the hopes which had grown up during the reign of George I for a total change of men and measures were not to be realized.

GIBSON, EDMUND (1669–1748) Churchman who became Bishop of London in 1723 and managed ecclesiastical affairs for Walpole. He was a distinguished scholar who had edited Camden's *Britannia* (1695) and produced an important collection of canon law (hence his nickname Codex). P could not deny him ability or diligence in his office.

GILBERT, JOHN (1693–1761) Bishop of Llandaff, 1740, and of Salisbury, 1749; Archbishop of Canterbury, 1757. Gilbert earns admission to *The Dunciad* chiefly on account of a fulsome sermon he preached for Queen Caroline in 1737.

GILDON, CHARLES (1665–1724) Dramatist, critic, and miscellaneous writer. One of the most persistent, if less malicious, critics of P, who treats Gildon with good-natured contempt in *Peri Bathous* and *The Dunciad*. His works include a reply to *Robinson Crusoe*, a life of Wycherley, an art of poetry, a version of Apuleius and other translations, and many plays including a popular adaptation of *Measure for Measure*. All round he was among the most able of the dunces.

GOODE, BARNHAM (1674–*c.*1750) Journalist. A master at Eton who had been a schoolfellow of Walpole, he wrote for Curll and was a friend of Theobald —guilt by association may account for P's notice of him.

GRANVILLE, GEORGE, Baron LANSDOWNE (1667–1735) Politician and poet. Secretary at War in the Harley administration, and one of the twelve new peers created to ensure the passage of the peace treaty in 1712. Imprisoned in the Tower on suspicion of Jacobite activity, 1715–17. He had encouraged P's early work and was used as an emblem of Tory peacemaking in *Windsor Forest*.

HALES, STEPHEN (1677–1761) Clergyman and plant physiologist. A major scientist (FRS 1718), whose *Vegetable Statics* (1727) made an important contribution to botany. He was a neighbour of P as perpetual curate of Teddington, and they remained good friends in spite of P's dislike of Hales's activity in vivisection experiments, esp. those on dogs (Spence, i. 118).

HALIFAX, CHARLES MONTAGU, Earl of (1661–1715) Statesman and literary patron. A leading figure in national affairs under William III, he was a member of the Whig Junto and was involved in the foundation of the Bank of England. Appointed First Lord of the Treasury on the Hanoverian accession but too ill to exercise much power. He had been a patron of Matthew Prior and supported P's *Iliad*, but his reputation was that of a distant and condescending patron despite an impressive barrage of tributes from aspiring authors.

HANDEL, GEORGE FRIDERIC (1685–1759) Composer. P had little fondness for opera, the main sphere of Handel's activity for the greater part of P's life. However, he recognized the composer's merit and provided the book for *Esther* (1720). Royal patronage for Handel's rival Buononcini meant that he became something of an Opposition hero in the 1730s.

HARE, FRANCIS (1671–1740) Churchman. A strong Whig, he was closely linked to Walpole and became Bishop of Chichester (as well as Dean of St Paul's). P saw him as an ecclesiastical careerist.

HAYWOOD, ELIZA (1693–1756) Novelist, dramatist, and journalist. Apart from practising the disreputable form of *chronique scandaleuse*, she committed the offences of attacking Martha Blount and of contracting a friendship with Theobald. Her greatest success, *Betsy Thoughtless*, came out seven years after P's death, but perhaps she had already been guilty of a further indiscretion in becoming a prominent woman writer.

HEARNE, THOMAS (1678–1735) Antiquarian and medievalist, one of the most distinguished students of the Middle Ages England had yet produced. P shared the common view of his time that Hearne's editions of old 'monkish' writers represented freaks of pedantry. Hearne's high Tory sentiments do not seem to have come into the matter; he was the Oxford scholar as Dryasdust, blinded by historical and linguistic issues to what P considered the true literary concerns of a genuine scholar.

HEATHCOTE, Sir GILBERT (1652–1733) City financier. A governor of the Bank of England, a government contractor, and an MP, he was among the richest men of the day. He bought large estates in Lincolnshire and Rutland. His reputation for avarice is what P principally trades on in satirizing Heathcote.

HENLEY, JOHN (1692–1756) Preacher. Famed for his eccentric addresses and lessons in elocution, as well as the Whiggish journal *The Hyp Doctor*. His public renown as 'Orator' Henley left P with very little work to do in converting him into a figure of fun.

HERVEY, JOHN, Baron (1696–1743) Courtier. A son of the Earl of Bristol, he married P's friend Mary Lepel, and may also have maintained homosexual relations with Stephen Fox and others. A loyal supporter of Walpole and a confidant of the Prince of Wales, it was his growing alliance with Lady Mary Wortley Montagu which set off the war of words between P and himself. His famous *Memoirs* were not published until 1848. Hervey was colourful, individual, and talented enough to be worthy of P's prolonged attention, unlike most of Walpole's acolytes.

HILL, AARON (1683–1750) Poet, dramatist, and projector. His fluctuating relations with P are summarized in *TE*, v. 444–5. Educated at Westminster school, he had led a varied life involving much travel and commercial endeavour. He was also a pioneer drama critic, a close friend of Samuel Richardson, and an operatic librettist.

HOADLY, BENJAMIN (1676–1721) Churchman. Held four increasingly valuable bishoprics in turn, ending up with Winchester in 1734. He had achieved this eminence chiefly by his famous sermon in 1717, which set out an extreme Erastian position and provoked High Church responses in number (the so-called Bangorian controversy). The antithesis in spiritual and political matters of P's friend Atterbury, whom Hoadly had attacked, and who traced a descending curve as Hoadly moved ever upwards.

HORNECK, PHILIP (d. 1728) Solicitor to the Treasury. A government functionary involved in prosecuting writers and booksellers. This was his main offence for P, though his Whiggish journalism and occasional attacks on the Scriblerians compounded this.

HOWARD, HENRIETTA, Countess of Suffolk (c.1687–1767) Courtier. She was *maitresse en titre* to George II, whilst married to an inconsequential gentleman (later Earl of Suffolk). She retired from court in 1735 and later made a second marriage to the Hon. George Berkeley. Her home at Marble Hill lay close to P's house, and she was a close friend of P, Swift, Gay, and Peterborough.

HUGGINS, JOHN (d. 1745) Warden of the Fleet Prison. He was accused by the House of Commons in 1729 of cruelty and extortion towards prisoners for debt and was even accused of murder (though subsequently acquitted). A type of the corrupt gaol management exposed by Oglethorpe (q.v.).

JACOB, GILES (1686–1744) Compiler. He specialized in manuals on law, but also wrote collective biographies of English poets and dramatists. P figured in *The Poetical Register* (1719–20), a work which may have given him ideas and materials for *The Dunciad*. Jacob became a more vehement critic of P after his inclusion in the first version of that poem.

JEKYLL, Sir JOSEPH (1663–1738) Judge; Master of the Rolls, 1717. A strong Whig of traditional Revolution principles, he was active in the impeachment of the first Earl of Oxford (q.v.).

JERVAS, CHARLES (c.1675–1739) Portrait-painter of Irish origin (pronounced 'Jarvis'). Studied under Kneller; later taught P painting. He also translated *Don Quixote* (published posthumously, 1742). Principal painter to George I and George II. P lived for some time at his London house and for many years he was among the poet's closest friends.

KING, PETER, Baron (1669–1734) Judge. Chief Justice of Common Pleas, 1714; Lord Chancellor, 1725. Another Whiggish lawyer who had been involved in the prosecution of Sacheverell.

KNELLER, Sir GODFREY (1646–1723) Portrait painter, born in Lubeck. Came to England, 1675; patronized by Charles II, William III, Anne, and George I. A neighbour of P's. The two men had dealings over a number of years without great intimacy; the epitaph which P supplied for Kneller's tomb in Westminster Abbey was the result of a deathbed request by the artist: 'I think 'tis the worst thing I ever wrote in my life' (Spence, i. 49).

KNIGHT, ROBERT (1675–1744) Cashier of the South Sea Company. One of the main rogues of the episode, he fled to France in 1721; he was eventually pardoned in 1742.

LINTOT, BARNABY BERNARD (1675–1736) Bookseller. Published many of P's early works, including *The Rape of the Lock, Windsor Forest*, and the Homer translations. Less manipulable than most of his colleagues in the trade, he resisted P's plans and lost the poet's business.

LYTTELTON, GEORGE, Baron (1709–73) Politician and poet. A key Opposition figure in the 1730s, with links both to the Prince of Wales and to the Cobham connection. A patron of Thomson and dedicatee of *Tom Jones*. Both his political career (though he was a Lord of the Treasury and Chancellor of the Exchequer in later years) and his poetical reputation traced a descending curve —Johnson angered his remaining friends by scornful reference in *The Lives of the Poets*. Nevertheless, he enjoyed contemporary success with his *Letters from a Persian in England* (1735), and a *History of Henry II* (1767–71). P greatly admired him, and indeed his role in P's later career is much underestimated today.

MARLBOROUGH, JOHN CHURCHILL, Duke of (1650–1722) and SARAH CHURCHILL, Duchess of (1660–1744) P accepted the common view of Tory critics (probably taken over from Swift) that the Duke was avaricious and self-seeking, having prolonged the war against France unduly to preserve his own perquisites. Late in her life the Duchess contracted a surprising friendship with P, though behind her back he was not always reverential towards her.

MAYNWARING, ARTHUR (1668–1712) Politician and writer. He was a leading Kit Cat member, a friend of Addison and Steele, and a controller of Whig publicity in opposition to Swift's campaigns on behalf of the Harley administration. His *Medley* (1710–11), written with Oldmixon, combated Swift's *Examiner* papers.

MEAD, RICHARD (1673–1754) Medical man and virtuoso. He was physician to George II and Caroline, and had a fashionable private practice. He owned a large collection of books and *objets d'art*. A generous patron of literature. Fought a duel with John Woodward (q.v.), 1719, over the treatment of smallpox. Mead attended P in his last struggles against illness.

METHUEN, Sir PAUL (1672–1757) Diplomat and politician. Ambassador to Portugal, who helped to arrange the famous treaty of 1703, which had been engineered by his father. Secretary of State, 1716. A moderate and self-important Whig.

MILBOURNE, LUKE (1649–1720) Poet and clergyman. Educated at Cambridge. A High Churchman who was accused of loose living. He attacked Dryden's translation of Virgil in an essay published in 1698: Dryden retaliated in the preface to his *Fables* (1700) that whilst Milbourne lived he should not 'be thought the worst poet of the age'. Milbourne's metrical psalms (1698) according to the *DNB* 'deservedly attracted no attention'.

MIST, NATHANIEL (d. 1737) Bookseller who edited and published the most aggressive high Tory organ, *Mist's Weekly Journal*. Mist regularly incurred ministerial disapproval and ended up in court even more frequently than Curll. In 1728 he fled to Boulogne but the paper carried on.

MONTAGU, Lady MARY WORTLEY (1689–1762) Daughter of the Duke of Kingston, she married the Whig politician Edward Wortley Montagu in 1712, and went with him to Constantinople (1716–18). She brought back the first successful smallpox inoculation technique. Wrote in a variety of forms, including her famous letters and some short satirical poems, at first in concert with P and later satirizing him. They were friends since about 1715, and P seems to have fallen in love with her; but in the 1720s, when they were neighbours in Twickenham, they quarrelled bitterly. Thereafter P could seldom resist a scornful reference to Lady Mary as dirty, slovenly, pretentious, and sexually loose, whilst she replied with allusions to his malice and sexual inadequacy. Her intimacy with Lord Hervey gave her a coadjutor in these battles but also another reason for P's dislike.

MOORE SMYTHE, JAMES (1702–34) Author and man about town, son of the venal politician Arthur Moore. His quarrel with P started obscurely over some lines in his play *The Rival Modes* (1727); after this, it was pursued with energy on both sides, though P may simply have found the vocable 'Moore' a convenient one in verses about the community of dunces—he was not a serious threat in the same way as Theobald, Cibber, or Dennis.

MORRICE, BEZALEEL (*c.*1675–1749) An energetic producer of verses, whose life is otherwise almost totally lost to view. He brushed against P several times, perhaps by inadvertence.

MOTTEUX, PETER ANTHONY (1663–1718) Dramatist and translator; a French immigrant (originally Pierre-Antoine) who edited an early literary magazine and produced a free translation of *Don Quixote* (1700–3), which held a brief currency.

MURRAY, WILLIAM, Earl of MANSFIELD (1705–93) Judge. The great legal figure became known to P whilst still an ambitious young barrister; it was only just before P died that he became an MP and Solicitor-General, the first steps to his ultimate renown as Lord Chief Justice for over thirty years. Murray gave occasional legal advice in the later 1730s and early 1740s.

NEEDHAM, ELIZABETH (d. 1731) Procuress; employed by Charteris (q.v.), and both figure in Hogarth's series *The Harlot's Progress* (1732), pl. i. Known as Mother Needham, she was sent to the pillory for keeping a disorderly house and was so badly pelted by the mob that she died a few days later. Fielding used the character of Mother Needham in his afterpiece *The Covent Garden Tragedy* (1731).

OGLETHORPE, JAMES (1696–1785) Philanthropist and colonial pioneer. He chaired the parliamentary inquiry into the conditions in debtors' prisons in 1729, and took the leading part in devising the settlement of the new colony of Georgia to help rehabilitate poor people living in sordid surroundings. He acted in effect as the first governor. Meanwhile he continued to serve as an MP in England (many were 'uncertain whether he was a Whig or a Jacobite') and as a soldier—he performed without distinction in the 1745 rebellion and his regiment was disbanded. He survived to become familiar with Johnson and Boswell, bridging the ages of Walpole and Lord North.

OLDFIELD, ANNE (1683–1730) Actress. Successful in leading roles in both comedy and tragedy. Mistress of Arthur Maynwaring (q.v.). Admired by Cibber and others; no personal link with P established.

OLDISWORTH, WILLIAM (1680–1734) Writer, journalist, and translator. He edited the Tory *Examiner* after it was relinquished by Swift. Died in a debtor's gaol.

OLDMIXON, JOHN (c.1673–1742) Historian, critic, and miscellaneous writer. Turned his hand to almost every known species of authorship, generally in the Whig cause. Repeatedly brushed with P from around 1714, by reprinting works without permission, parodying and attacking other works, and generally affronting the literary standards P proclaimed. His *Essay On Criticism* (1728) set out an aesthetic in which P held a low place, whilst his later histories put a slender value on the Harley administration (including the contribution of Swift). He had a long association with Curll, Lintot, and Tonson, and indeed most leading members of the book trade.

OXFORD, ROBERT HARLEY, first Earl of (1661–1724) Politician. In turn Speaker of the Commons, Secretary of State and then (1711) Lord Treasurer; led the last Tory ministry for half a century, 1710–14. Impeached and sent to the Tower after the Hanoverian accession, but released without further punishment. A close friend of Swift and P, he took part in the Scriblerus Club's activities.

OXFORD, EDWARD HARLEY, second Earl of (1689–1741) Mainly known as a book collector (supplementing his father's collection of manuscripts) and as a patron, who supported Prior as well as P and Swift.

OZELL, JOHN (d. 1743) Translator, the most prolific and versatile active in P's time. Worked regularly for Curll. Reacted angrily on finding himself in *The Dunciad*, a prominence he had not formerly attained in the literary world.

PAGE, Sir FRANCIS (*c*.1661–1741) Judge. On the bench in all three of the common law high courts. Notorious for the severity of his judgments and the roughness of his tongue. Conducted the trial of Richard Savage for murder; sentenced some of the Berkshire Blacks, with whom P's own brother-in-law was involved.

PARNELL, THOMAS (1679–1718) Poet. Irish clergyman and scholar who became known to Swift and was a member of the Scriblerus Club. Helped P in assembling notes for the *Iliad*, and wrote introductory life of Homer. Heavy drinking may have contributed to his early death.

PAXTON, NICHOLAS (d. 1744) Solicitor to the Treasury. He was in day-to-day charge of government prosecutions against writers and booksellers, and had also been involved in prosecuting the Blacks in 1723. Accused of corruption after the fall of Walpole but remained silent, and was sent to Newgate.

PEMBROKE, THOMAS HERBERT, Earl of (1656–1733) Politician and collector. Held a number of offices of state under William and Anne. Noted for his collections of pictures, statues, and coins. His son, the ninth Earl (1693–1751), was the well-known 'architect Earl'.

PETERBOROUGH, CHARLES MORDAUNT, Earl of (1658–1735) Soldier and ambassador. Came to prominence in the Peninsular campaign in the reign of Anne. A Tory hero who lost official favour after the Hanoverian accession. Shared P's interest in landscape gardening, and often entertained the poet at his house near Southampton. Also friendly with Mrs Howard, Swift, Gay, and Arbuthnot.

PHILIPS, AMBROSE (1674–1749) Poet. His pastorals were published along with P's in Tonson's *Miscellanies* of 1709, leading to P's ironic *Guardian* in 1713 (see p. 559). Philips had links with the Addison circle, and later held official posts in Ireland, neither circumstance being likely to encourage P's approval. His verses addressed to children prompted the invention by Henry Carey (1726) of the term 'nambypamby'.

PITT, JAMES (1679–1763) Journalist who wrote for Walpole in the press, sometimes under the name 'Francis Osborne'. The Opposition journal the *Craftsman* nicknamed him Mother Osborne. A former schoolmaster who was given a customs post as a reward for his work on behalf of the ministry.

POPPLE, WILLIAM (1701–64) Dramatist. Collaborated with Aaron Hill in the journal the *Prompter*, where some attacks on P appeared. Later Governor of the Bermudas, 1745.

PRIOR, MATTHEW (1664–1721) Poet and diplomat. Helped to negotiate the Peace of Utrecht on behalf of the Tory ministry; imprisoned after the accession of George I, but later released. A versatile, skilful, and witty poet, who wrote distinguished verse in a serious vein such as *Solomon* and also high-spirited comic works such as *Alma*. He was patronized by the second Earl of Oxford (q.v.). Though never an intimate of P, the two men shared many political and literary alliances.

PULTENEY, WILLIAM, Earl of BATH (1684–1764) Politician. He was one of the main props of the Opposition to Walpole throughout the 1720s and 1730s. After the fall of Walpole he took a seat in the Lords and never regained his former influence, devoting himself to literary pursuits in his retirement. Closer to Gay than to P, but until the late 1730s P continued to regard him as one of the chief hopes of a political restoration after the years of Walpole.

QUEENSBERRY, CHARLES DOUGLAS, Duke of (1698–1778) Together with his beautiful and eccentric wife Catherine (c.1700–77) he supported Gay, esp. at the time of the banning of *Polly* in 1728. The couple also gave patronage to Thomson, Congreve, Prior, and others.

RADCLIFFE, JOHN (1653–1714) Physician who enjoyed royal patronage and amassed a large fortune. His bequest to Oxford University led to the endowment of an infirmary, a library, and an observatory. A clinical practitioner rather than a medical scholar, he attended both P and Martha Blount.

RALPH, JAMES (c.1705–62) American-born author and journalist. Came to England with Benjamin Franklin, 1724. A friend and coadjutor in journalism with Fielding. Attacked P in *Sawney* (1728) and never altogether lived down P's reply, though he worked in a number of forms including dramatic and architectural criticism. A client of George Bubb Dodington (q.v.).

RAYMOND, Sir ROBERT (1673–1733) Lord Chief Justice, 1725. A Tory lawyer and MP who served as Solicitor-General and (after accommodating his views to those of the Whig establishment) Attorney-General. Nothing much is known of the son to whom P alludes in *The Dunciad*.

RICH, JOHN (1692–1761) Theatrical manager. A grotesque performer on 'the stage as "Lun" ', he developed a highly popular form of spectacle allied to the harlequinade, then known as pantomime. It was he who produced *The Beggar's Opera* at Lincoln's Inn Fields in 1728. The epitome of the new popular entertainment beloved of fashionable London, which is attacked in *The Dunciad*.

RIDPATH, GEORGE (d. 1726) Journalist, who conducted the strongly Whig newspaper the *Flying Post* around the time of the Harley ministry. Fled to Holland in order to escape prosecution for libel. Returned to England after the change of ministry and became a leading opponent of the high-flying paper of Mist (q.v.). Involved in the scandal of the Harburg lottery in 1723.

RIPLEY, THOMAS (c.1683–1758) Architect. Patronized by Walpole, for whom he supervised the building of Houghton Hall (designed by Colen Campbell and William Kent). Main architect of the Admiralty in London. Submitted plans for Fulham Bridge, 1728, but a design by the surgeon William Cheselden (q.v.) was preferred. He was also unsuccessful with plans for Westminster Bridge in 1738. Held many official positions including Comptroller of the Works.

ROLLI, PAOLO (1687–1767) Poet and librettist. Came from Florence to London c.1718 and acted as Secretary of the operatic company known as the

Royal Academy of Music. Took a leading part in the world of Italian opera, as well as translating English works into Italian. Enjoyed the favour of royalty and the aristocracy, serving as language master to the daughters of George II and Caroline. His letters home provide the fullest picture of the opera scene in London during the heyday of Handel.

ROWE, NICHOLAS (1674–1718) Dramatist and poet. He was the most successful writer of tragedy between the Restoration and the nineteenth century, with a number of popular plays chiefly based on the theme of distressed women. The first to make a full edition of Shakespeare (1709). Poet Laureate, 1715. Admired and liked by P. Published a widely read translation of Lucan, 1718.

RUNDLE, THOMAS (c.1688–1743) Churchman. Bishop of Derry, 1743, having been refused the expected see of Gloucester in 1730 by Bishop Gibson (q.v.), apparently because of his allegedly Arian views. Much admired by P.

SECKER, THOMAS (1693–1768) Churchman. Successively Bishop of Bristol and of Oxford, Dean of St Paul's, and then Archbishop of Canterbury, 1758. A moderate in ecclesiastical politics who had good links at court, and who managed the church successfully and reconciled divergent strands in the Anglican community.

SELKIRK, CHARLES DOUGLAS, Earl of (1663–1739). A Scottish peer who supported the Whig revolution and the Union of the two kingdoms. It is not very clear what he did to offend P, although he probably stands merely for the time-serving politician who clung on to his limited power over several reigns.

SETTLE, ELKANAH (1648–1724) Poet and dramatist. The last City Poet, 1691, charged with mounting the pageants at the Lord Mayor's Day show. His great speciality was complimentary poems and funeral tributes to the eminent dead, but P singles out his work as a fairground dramatist, producing drolls for Bartholomew Fair. Since Dryden's day often treated as a figure of fun, on account of his obsequious hunt for patrons and his extreme bitterness against Catholics.

SEWELL, GEORGE (1687–1726) Miscellaneous writer, who originally practised as a doctor. Wrote poems, plays, translations, and pamphlets, many of them for Curll. Edited an additional volume of poems to go with P's Shakespeare (1725). Took part in a number of other collective works and all round was one of the abler hack writers mentioned in Peri Bathous.

SHIPPEN, WILLIAM (1673–1743) Politician. An MP for over thirty years, and the most outspoken Jacobite in the House. A fierce critic of the South Sea affair and unrelenting opponent of Walpole. Increasingly isolated in his last years, he remained uncompromising, highly principled, and austere to the end.

SHERLOCK, THOMAS (1678–1761) Churchman. Bishop of Bangor, Salisbury, and then London (1748). A famous preacher, his unremitting support for Walpole in the Lords occasioned the dislike of the Opposition.

SHREWSBURY, CHARLES TALBOT, Duke of (1660–1718) Politician and courtier, who served as Lord Chamberlain under William, Anne, and George I. A moderate Tory who had been lined up to succeed Harley in 1714, a short-lived position owing to the death of the Queen. Admired by Swift and P, who submitted early work to him for approval.

SLOANE, Sir HANS (1660–1753) Doctor and virtuoso. He was royal physician to Anne and George II, and President of the Royal College of Physicians, as well as Secretary of the Royal Society (President, 1727). Founded botanic gardens in Chelsea. His collection of scientific and artistic materials formed the basis of the British Museum on its formation in 1754.

SMEDLEY, JONATHAN (1671–1729) Clergyman and author. Dean of Killala, 1718, and of Clogher, 1724. A virulent Irish critic of Swift who later started to pursue P as well. He eventually left for India but died on the voyage.

SOMERS, JOHN, Baron (1651–1716) Lawyer and politician. A key figure in the Whig party after the Revolution, he served in turn as Lord Keeper and Lord Chancellor. Ill-health in later years reduced his influence, though scarcely his reputation. A member of the Kit Cat Club, he patronized Dryden, Swift (in the early part of his career), Addison, Steele, and Congreve as well as P. He worked with Locke and Newton in the reform of the currency in the 1690s, and by some contemporaries would have been set on a par with these men.

STANHOPE, JAMES, Earl (1673–1721) Soldier and statesman. After a successful campaign in Spain during the Marlborough wars, he became Secretary of State after the accession of George I. In the Whig schism (1717), he and the Earl of Sunderland were ranged against Walpole and Townshend; the former emerged victorious, but their position was weakened by the South Sea episode and Stanhope died suddenly at the height of the affair. His dealings with P were probably slight.

STEELE, Sir RICHARD (1672–1729) Author and Whig politician. At the time of the *Tatler*, *Spectator*, and *Guardian* (1709–13), Steele was on good terms with P, but they were severed by the 'curse of party' as Steele took an increasingly active share in the Opposition to Harley. Knighted 1715. As manager of Drury Lane theatre, he came into conflict with the Lord Chamberlain, who transferred the patent to Cibber and his group. Steele also broke with Addison before the latter's death. Increasingly oppressed by debts and ill-health, he spent his last years obscurely in Wales.

SWIFT, JONATHAN (1667–1745) Became associated with P after he came to London and directed the Harley ministry's propaganda campaign, 1710–14; they were both involved in the Scriblerus Club. After he moved to Dublin as Dean of St Patrick's in 1714, Swift saw little of P, but they corresponded and supported each other's work, with P usually taking the lead and controlling the release of material for publication; e.g. in their joint *Miscellanies* (1727–35). P's closest literary ally, whose work he parodied in Horatian imitations (not included in this selection).

TALBOT, WILLIAM (*c.*1659–1730) Churchman. Bishop successively of Oxford, Salisbury, and Durham. A successful and ambitious ecclesiastical politician. His son, CHARLES TALBOT (1685–1737), became Lord Chancellor in 1733, whilst his granddaughter was the author Catherine Talbot.

TATE, NAHUM (1652–1715) Dramatist and poet. Poet Laureate, 1692. Known for his version of *King Lear* (1681) with a happy ending, and a metrical version of the Psalms with Nicholas Brady (1696). Added a second part to Dryden's *Absalom and Achitophel* (1682).

THEOBALD, LEWIS (1688–1744) Editor and dramatist. He had written in a number of forms, often for Curll, before he incurred P's displeasure by a response to the edition of Shakespeare entitled *Shakespeare Restored* (1726), followed by his own edition of the plays in 1734. He also produced a new play, *The Double Falsehood* (1728), allegedly based on a Shakespearian original. He provided pantomimes for the London theatres at the height of the rage for these spectacles. These combined to equip him for the role of king of the dunces in the first *Dunciad* in 1728, but events conspired to fit Cibber better for the role in 1743.

TICKELL, THOMAS (1686–1740) Poet. Professor of Poetry at Oxford, 1711. A disciple of Addison, who was thought to have promoted his translation of the first book of the *Iliad* (1715) in opposition to P's. This underlay the worsening relations of Addison and P. Tickell edited Addison's works in 1721 (P subscribed). On good terms with Swift during his spell in Ireland as secretary to the Lord Justices.

TINDAL, MATTHEW (1657–1733) Deist. His most famous work was *Christianity as Old as the Creation* (1730), a statement of natural religious doctrine, but he had long angered Swift and other orthodox believers with his rationalist approach to Christianity. Second only to Toland as a figure of menace to traditional churchmen.

TOLAND, JOHN (1670–1722) Writer and deist. Achieved notoriety by *Christianity not Mysterious* (1696), one of the key documents of deist thought; also wrote on a variety of topics including Celtic antiquities, Druidism, classical literature, and hermetic subjects.

TONSON, JACOB (1656–1737) Publisher. The major bookseller of his age, with a large stake in Milton and Shakespeare, and enjoyed a long association with Dryden. Secretary of the Kit Cat Club and familiar with all the prominent Whig leaders. Published work by Addison, Steele, Tickell, as well as the Shakespeare editions of Rowe and P. Issued some of P's earlier poems.

TRUMBULL, Sir WILLIAM (1639–1716) Ambassador and statesman. Held several high offices including Secretary of State, 1695. Retired to Windsor Forest in 1698, where he became the boy P's mentor. Supported Dryden's translation of Virgil. Chiefly remembered as instigating P's Homer, and celebrated in P's *Windsor Forest*.

TUTCHIN, JOHN (1661–1707) Journalist. Conducted the Whig newspaper the *Observator* from 1702. Died after an attack by street ruffians, probably politically motivated.

TYRAWLEY, JAMES O'HARA, Baron (1690–1773) Soldier and diplomat; ambassador to Portugal, 1728–41, 1752–63. High-spirited, rough, and licentious in his personal life.

WALPOLE, Sir ROBERT (1676–1745) The first 'prime minister' of Britain, *eo nomine*. P apparently met Walpole after he had come to power in the aftermath of the South Sea Bubble, and they maintained reasonably friendly relations at a personal level despite P's unrelenting criticism and support of Opposition goals in the 1730s. P attempted, 'when mentioning [Walpole's] name, to distinguish between the politician and the man' (*TE*, iv. 389). This may have been because of a favour Walpole had done to the poet, or (as E. P. Thompson has suggested) because the Prime Minister held over P the threat of punishment for his delinquent brother-in-law.

WALSH, WILLIAM (1663–1708) Poet and critic. A Whig who knew Dryden and Vanbrugh; member of the Kit Cat Club. Minor writer chiefly remembered for his support for the young P when he first embarked on his career.

WALTER, PETER (*c.*1664–1746) The archetypal villain of Augustan satire: a money-lender, estate manager, marriage-broker, steward, attorney, and land-owner in Dorset. It was P who first gave Walter his bad name; Swift inherited this dislike at a distance, whilst Fielding's satire of 'Peter Pounce' in *Joseph Andrews* can be explained by the novelist's experience of Walter's depredations locally, near Shaftesbury.

WARD, EDWARD 'NED' (1667–1731) Poet and miscellaneous writer. Best known for his *London Spy* in monthly parts (1698–1700), but also wrote many varied works on city life and assorted travels. No real contact with P until he was included in *Peri Bathous* and *The Dunciad*; retorted with *Durgen* (1729). Used by P as a representative writer of popular literature.

WARD, JOHN (d. 1755) MP, 'a wealthy and unscrupulous businessman' from Hackney. Expelled from the Commons for fraud, and subsequently convicted of forgery and sentenced to stand in the pillory in Palace Yard (1727).

WARD, JOSHUA (1685–1761) Quack doctor. Became famous for his universal remedy, the 'drop', which was in fact largely composed of antimony. Gained a large fortune from this source.

WELSTED, LEONARD (1688–1747) Gentleman poet, and translator of Longinus. A client of the Duke of Newcastle. Began attacking the Scriblerians in 1717 and kept up the attack for many years, including a scathing reply to P's supposed attack on the Duke of Chandos in the *Epistle to Burlington*. One of P's most savage opponents among the dunces.

WHARTON, PHILIP, Duke of (1698–1731) Poet, man of pleasure, and crypto-Jacobite; a son of the Whig magnate Thomas, Earl of Wharton, he blazed across the early Hanoverian sky and burnt himself out by the age of 33; the object of cautionary tales as a member of supposed Hell Fire Clubs.

WHITEFIELD, GEORGE (1714–60) The most prominent member of the Calvinist wing of the Methodists. A famous itinerant preacher who carried out missionary work in the emerging colony of Georgia, and later in the northern colonies; died in Massachusetts.

WILKS, ROBERT (*c.*1665–1732) Actor. Achieved success in both tragic and comic roles. Joint manager of Drury Lane theatre with Cibber and Booth from around 1710 (with intervals).

WOODWARD, JOHN (1665–1728) Physician, geologist, and antiquarian. Famous alike for his impressive collection of scientific curiosities and his some-times bizarre theories about the early history of the earth. Satirized in the Scriblerian farce *Three Hours after Marriage* (1717) and, probably, in *The Dunciad*. A figure of fun to many, he nevertheless made important contributions to science and to the developing study of archaeology.

WYCHERLEY, WILLIAM (1641–1716) Dramatist. His great comedies *The Country Wife* (1675) and *The Plain Dealer* (1676) were long in the past when he befriended the young P and offered advice, not all of it taken. His *Posthumous Works* appeared in 1728–9, one volume edited by Theobald and the other by P (this containing correspondence between P and Wycherley).

WYNDHAM, Sir WILLIAM (1687–1740) Politician. Leader of the Tories in opposition to Walpole; sent to the Tower for rather half-hearted participation in the Jacobite rebellion of 1715, but soon released. An ally of Bolingbroke. Admired by P but not a personal friend.

YONGE, Sir WILLIAM (1693–1755) Politician. A loyal supporter of Walpole who helped to steer the Government's business through the Commons. Regarded by the Opposition as the acme of a lickspittle politician.

INDEX OF TITLES

INDEX OF FIRST LINES

INDEX OF CORRESPONDENTS